THE SEASONS

The earth revolves around the sun once a year in an anti-clockwise direction. The earth is tilted at an angle of 66½ degrees to the plane of its orbit and always points into space in the same direction. In June the northern hemisphere is tilted towards the sun and it is the northern summer – days are longer and it is generally warmer. The southern hemisphere is pointing away from the sun. It is cooler and the days are shorter – the southern winter. In December the reverse is the case.

...the year ...gth, owing ...ator.

...year, ...when ...ics ...ghest ...of 23½° North or

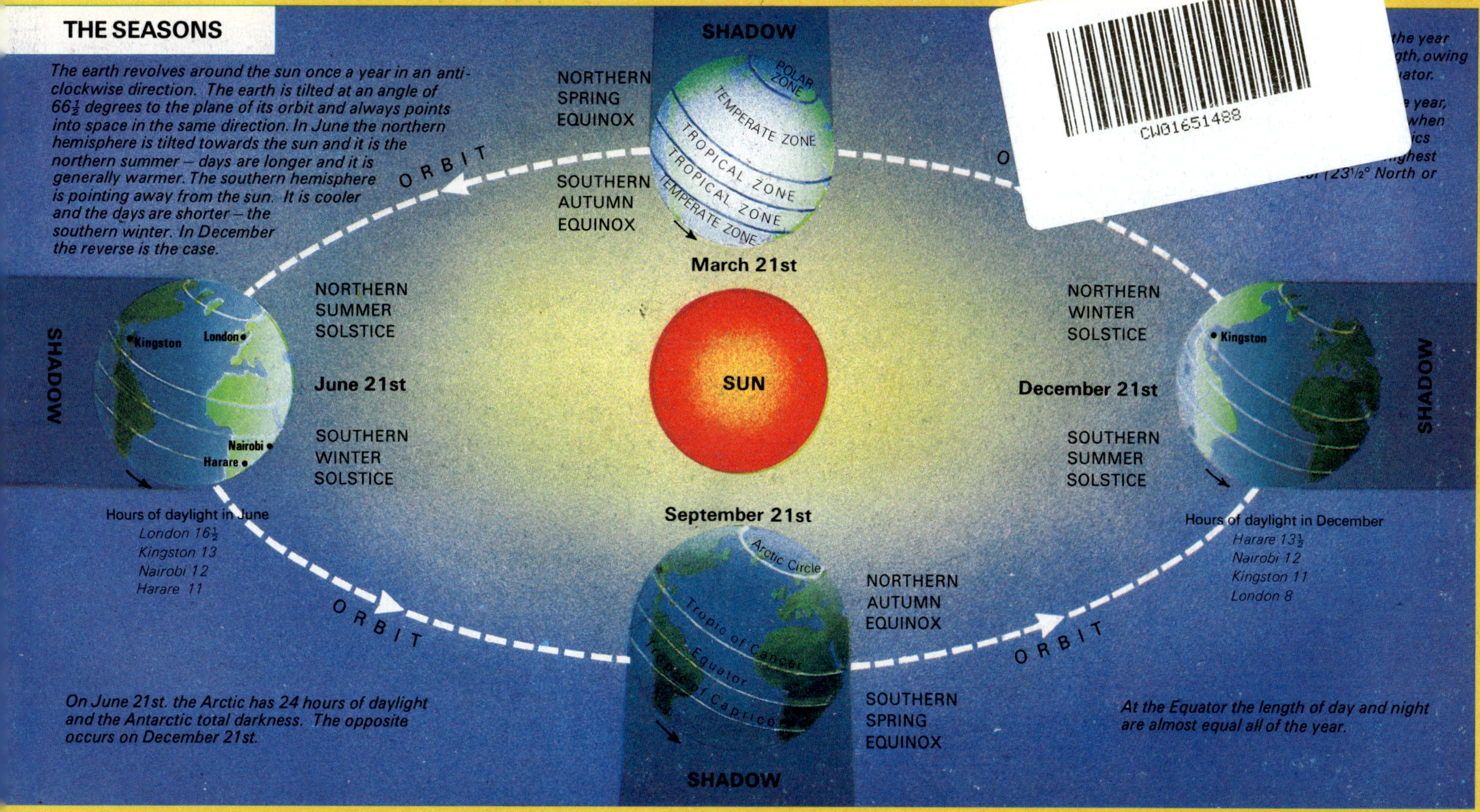

On June 21st. the Arctic has 24 hours of daylight and the Antarctic total darkness. The opposite occurs on December 21st.

At the Equator the length of day and night are almost equal all of the year.

LENGTH OF DAY AND NIGHT ON THE EARTH

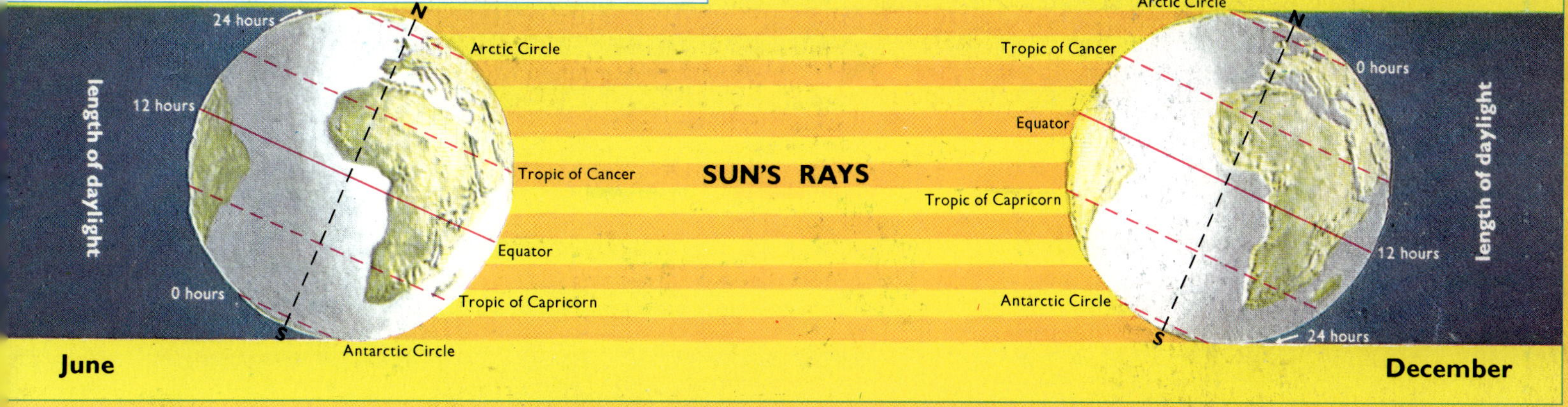

TIME

The Year *– the time taken by the Earth to revolve around the Sun, or 365¼ days.*

The Month *– the approximate time taken by the Moon to revolve around the Earth. The twelve months of the year in fact vary from 28 (29 in a Leap Year) to 31 days.*

The Week *– an artificial period of 7 days, not based on astronomical time.*

The Day *– the time taken by the Earth to complete one rotation on its axis.*

The Hour *– 24 hours make one day. Usually the day is divided into hours A.M. (ante meridiem or before noon) and P.M. (post meridiem or after noon), although most timetables now use the 24-hour system, from midnight to midnight, for example, 1p.m. = 13.00 hours.*

SUNRISE AND SUNSET

From the diagrams below it is possible to find out the time of sunrise or sunset on a given date and for latitudes between 60°N and 60°S.

SUNRISE

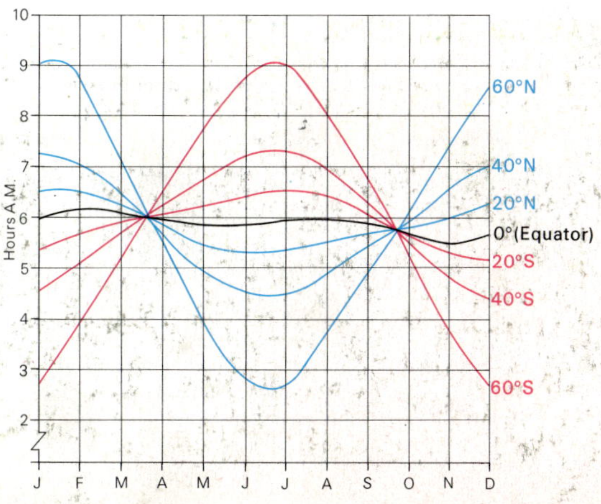

SUNSET

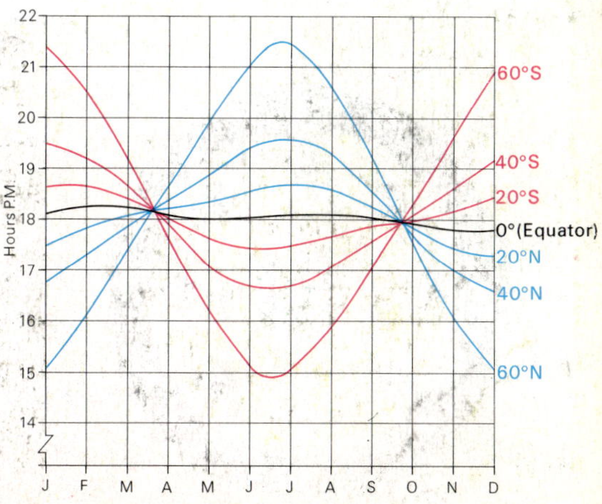

Emma Lockley
Alleynes high school
9WAJ 95.

~~Emma Lockley~~ 2Y
~~Tel. 817891~~

PHILIPS' MODERN SCHOOL ATLAS

Contents

Front Endpaper: Astronomical Geography

British Isles

4 Physical ~ 1:4M
Geology ~ 1:16M
5 Administrative ~ 1:4M
6 Climate
7 Transport
8 Population
9 Agriculture
10 Energy and Industry
11 Employment, Leisure and Trade
12-13 Climate Graphs
14-15 South and South-East England ~ 1:1M
16 South-West England ~ 1:1M
17 Wales ~ 1:1M
18-19 Northern England ~ 1:1M
20-21 Scotland: South ~ 1:1M
22-23 Scotland: North ~ 1:1M
24-25 Ireland ~ 1:1,25M

Europe

26 Physical ~ 1:20M
27 Political ~ 1:20M
28 Climate and Natural Vegetation ~ 1:40M
29 Economic ~ 1:20M
30-31 Themes
32-33 Statistics
34-35 France and Western Europe ~ 1:4M
36 Low Countries and Lower Rhine ~ 1:2M
37 Spain and Portugal ~ 1:5M
38-39 Mediterranean Lands ~ 1:10M
40-41 Italy and the Balkan States ~ 1:5M
42-43 Central Europe ~ 1:5M
44-45 Scandinavia and the Baltic Lands ~ 1:6M
46-47 European Russia and Turkey ~ 1:10M
48-49 Union of Soviet Socialist Republics ~ 1:20M

Asia

50 Physical ~ 1:50M
51 Political ~ 1:50M
52 Climate and Natural Vegetation ~ 1:100M
53 Economic ~ 1:50M
54-55 Statistics (*including Oceania*)
56-57 South-West Asia ~ 1:15M
The Holy Land ~ 1:1,5M
58-59 South Asia ~ 1:10M
60-61 China and Korea ~ 1:15M
62 Japan ~ 1:7,5M
63 South-East Asia ~ 1:15M
64-65 Pacific Ocean ~ 1:54M

Australia and New Zealand

66-67 Australia ~ 1:12M
Political ~ 1:80M
68 Climate and Natural Vegetation ~ 1:60M
69 Economic ~ 1:20M
70 South-East Australia ~ 1:4,5M
71 New Zealand ~ 1:6M
Samoa, Fiji and Tonga Islands ~ 1:12M

Africa

72 Physical ~ 1:40M
73 Political ~ 1:40M
74 Climate and Natural Vegetation ~ 1:80M
75 Economic ~ 1:40M
76-77 Statistics
78-79 Northern Africa ~ 1:15M
80-81 Central and Southern Africa ~ 1:15M

Edited By

B.M. Willett, *Cartographic Editor*
D. Gaylard, *Assistant Cartographic Editor*
and L. Prince-Smith, J. Russell, R. Smith and A. Wells
George Philip and Son Ltd., London.

Maps prepared by

George Philip Cartographic Services Ltd., London under the direction of A.G. Poynter, *Director of Cartography*.

Eighty-third Edition

ISBN 0 540 05528 X (Educational Edition)
0 540 05529 8

Printed in Great Britain by Redwood Offset, Trowbridge

Contents

North America

82 Physical ~ 1:35M
83 Political ~ 1:35M
84 Climate and Natural Vegetation ~ 1:70M
85 Economic ~ 1:32M
86-87 Statistics (*including South America*)
88-89 Canada ~ 1:15M
Alaska ~ 1:30M
90-91 United States ~ 1:12M
Hawaiian Islands ~ 1:10M
92-93 Basin of the St Lawrence and North-East United States ~ 1:6M
94-95 Mexico, Central America and the West Indies ~ 1:15M
Panama Canal ~ 1:1M
Jamaica, Trinidad and Tobago, Leeward and Windward Islands ~ 1:5M

South America

96 Physical ~ 1:30M
97 Political ~ 1:30M
98 Climate and Natural Vegetation ~ 1:70M
99 Economic ~ 1:30M
100-101 South America: North ~ 1:16M
102 South America: South ~ 1:16M

The World

103 Polar Regions ~ 1:50M
104-105 Physical ~ 1:80M
106-107 Structure, Volcanoes and Earthquakes
108-109 Climatic Regions, Soils and Vegetation
110-113 Climate Statistics
114 Temperature and Ocean Currents
115 Pressure, Winds and Annual Precipitation
116-117 Density of Population
118-119 Population of Cities
120 Languages and Religions
121 International Organisations
122-123 Population Trends
124-125 Quality of Life
126-127 Economic Facts of Life
128-129 Political ~ 1:80M
130-131 Time and Distance

Index

Back Endpaper: Map Projections

General Reference

SETTLEMENTS

Settlement symbols in order of size

LONDON · Osaka · Venice · Andropov · *Toledo* · *Cromer* · *Interlaken*

Settlement symbols and type styles vary according to the scale of each map and indicate the importance of towns on the map rather than specific population figures.

ADMINISTRATION

- International Boundaries
- International Boundaries (*Undemarcated or undefined*)
- Internal Boundaries

International boundaries show the 'de facto' situation where there are rival claims to territory.

COMMUNICATIONS

- Motorways in UK
- Principal Roads
- Tracks and Seasonal Roads
- Road Tunnels
- Principal Railways
- Railways under construction
- Railway Tunnels
- Passes
- Principal Canals
- Principal Oil Pipelines
- Principal Airports

PHYSICAL FEATURES

- Perennial Streams
- Seasonal Streams
- Seasonal Lakes and Salt Flats
- Swamps and Marshes
- Permanent Ice and Glaciers
- Wells in Desert
- ▲ 8848 Elevations in metres
- ▼ 8050 Sea Depths in metres
- *1134* Height of Lakes

BRITISH ISLES : Physical

1:4 000 000

Projection: Conical with two standard parallels

1:4 000 000

50 0 50 100 150 km

1:12 000 000

January Temperature

Actual surface temperature

°C: 7, 6, 5, 4, 3, 2, 1, 0

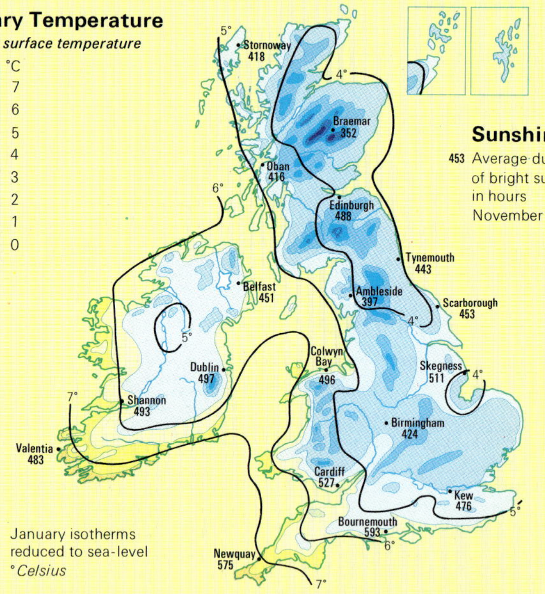

Sunshine

453 Average duration of bright sunshine in hours November - April

— January isotherms reduced to sea-level *°Celsius*

July Temperature

Actual surface temperature

°C: 17, 16, 15, 14, 13, 12, 11, 10

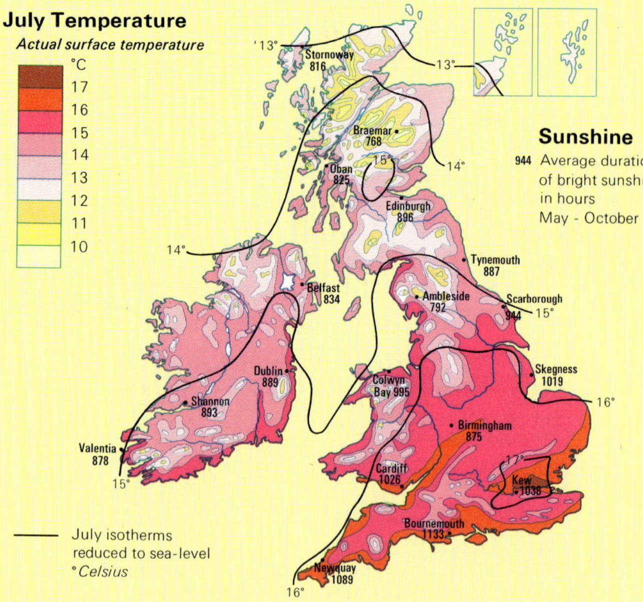

Sunshine

944 Average duration of bright sunshine in hours May - October

— July isotherms reduced to sea-level *°Celsius*

Annual Rainfall

mm: 2500, 2000, 1500, 1000, 750, 625

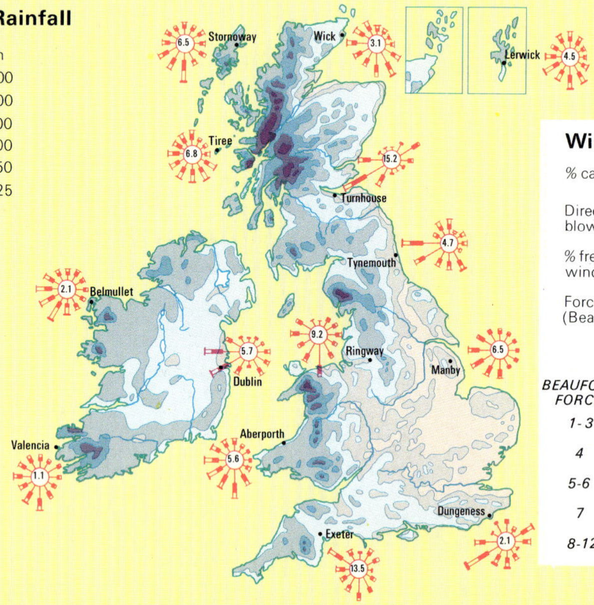

Wind

% calms in a year (3.4)

Direction the wind blows from (N, E, S, W)

% frequency of wind from a direction (20 10)

Force of wind (Beaufort scale) (7+, 5-6, 4, 1-3)

BEAUFORT FORCE	SPEED (K.P.H.)	CATEGORY
1-3	1-20	Light breeze
4	21-29	Moderate breeze
5-6	30-50	Fresh to strong wind
7	51-61	Moderate gale
8-12	over 62	Gale, storm or hurricane

Snow

Average number of mornings with snow cover per year

- more than 50
- 20-50
- 15-20
- 10-15
- 5-10
- less than 5

(after Manley, 1970)

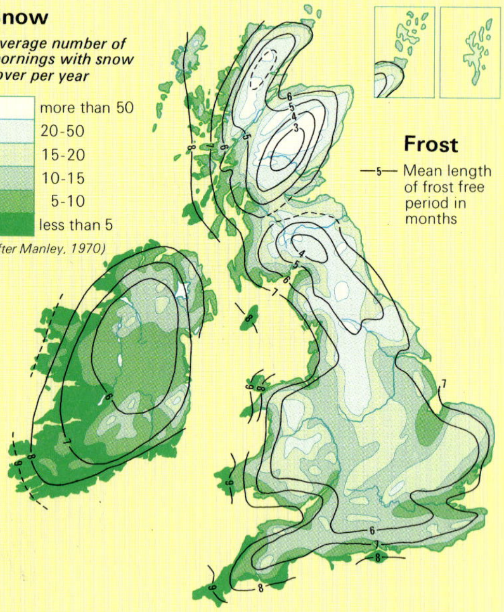

Frost

—5— Mean length of frost free period in months

Variability of Rain

The percentage frequency with which rainfall varies from the normal rainfall regime in an area: the higher the percentage figure, the more variable the rainfall.

- over 20%
- 18-20%
- 16-18%
- 14-16%
- 12-14%
- 10-12%
- under 10%

(after Gregory, 1955)

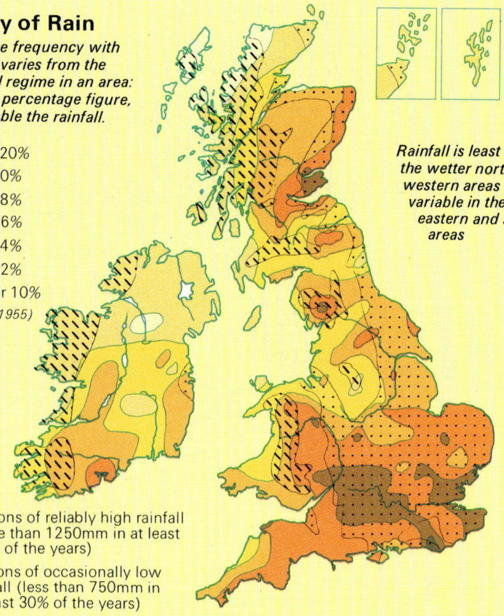

Rainfall is least variable in the wetter northern and western areas and most variable in the drier eastern and southern areas

Regions of reliably high rainfall (more than 1250mm in at least 70% of the years)

Regions of occasionally low rainfall (less than 750mm in at least 30% of the years)

Synoptic Chart for a Typical Winter Depression

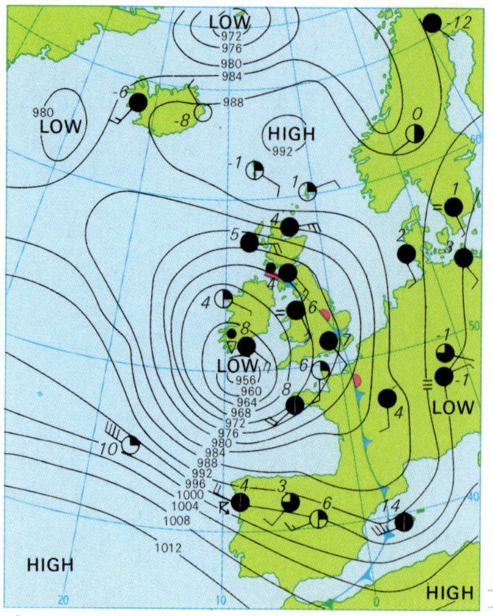

Based upon the Meteorological Office Weather Charts, with the sanction of the Controller of H.M. Stationery Office

HOUR OF OBSERVATION
06h00 GREENWICH MEAN TIME

PRESSURE

Isobars are drawn at intervals of 4 mb.

WIND

Arrows fly with the wind. A full length feather represents 18 k.p.h. and a short feather 9 k.p.h. A solid pennant represents 90 k.p.h. Calm is indicated by a circle outside the weather symbol

TEMPERATURE

Given in °C and is shown on the charts by a figure alongside the station circle.

CLOUD SYMBOLS

- Clear sky
- Sky ⅛ covered
- Sky ¼ covered
- Sky ⅜ covered
- Sky ½ covered
- Sky ⅝ covered
- Sky ¾ covered
- Sky ⅞ covered
- Sky covered
- Sky obscured

WEATHER SYMBOLS

- Rain
- Drizzle
- Snow
- Rain and Snow
- Hail
- Shower
- Thunderstorm
- Fog
- Mist

FRONTS

- Warm front on the surface
- Cold front on the surface
- Occluded front

Roads and Ferry Routes

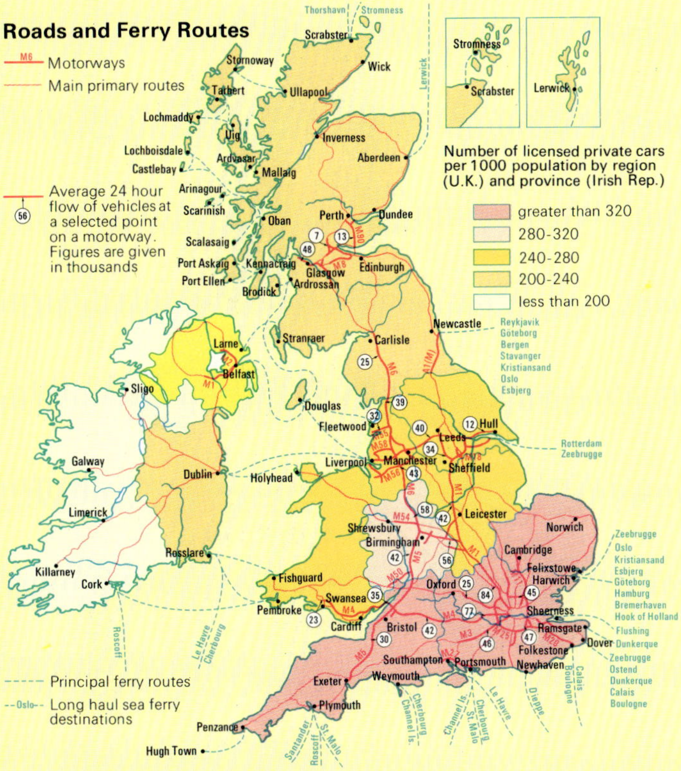

Railways

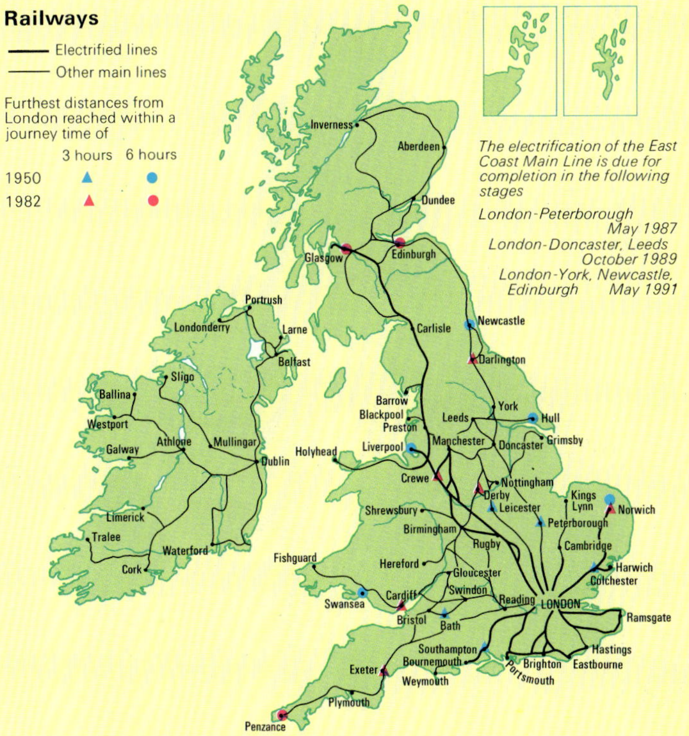

Means of Transportation Within the U.K.

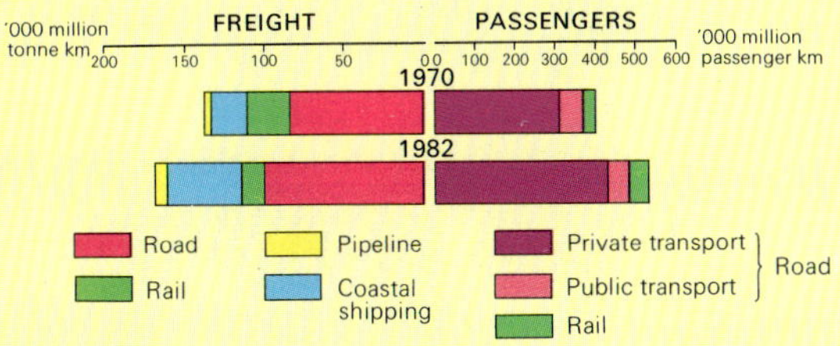

(Air transport accounted for only 2000 million passenger km in 1970 and 3000 million in 1982)

Regional Freight Movement

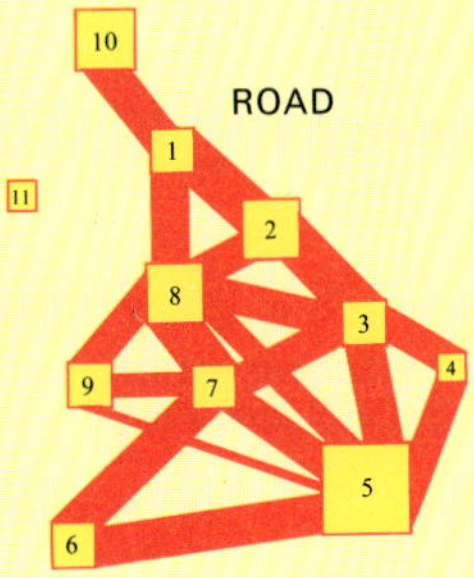

Within regions (million tonnes): 200-250, 100-150, 0-50, 50-100, 150-200

Between regions (million tonnes): less than 2·5, 2·5-5, 5-7·5, 7·5-10, 10-20, 20-30, 30-40

1. North
2. Yorkshire & Humberside
3. East Midlands
4. East Anglia
5. South East
6. South West
7. West Midlands
8. North West
9. Wales
10. Scotland
11. Northern Ireland

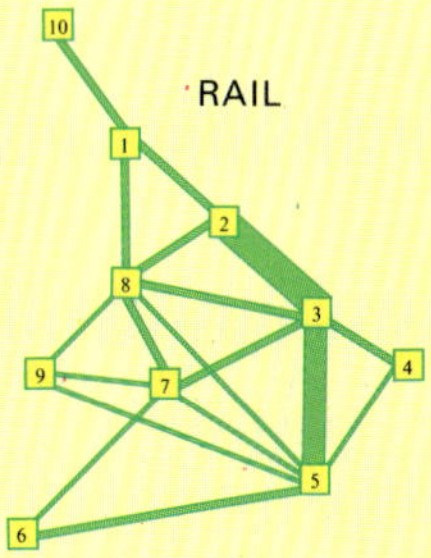

Rail freight movement is negligible within Northern Ireland

Ports

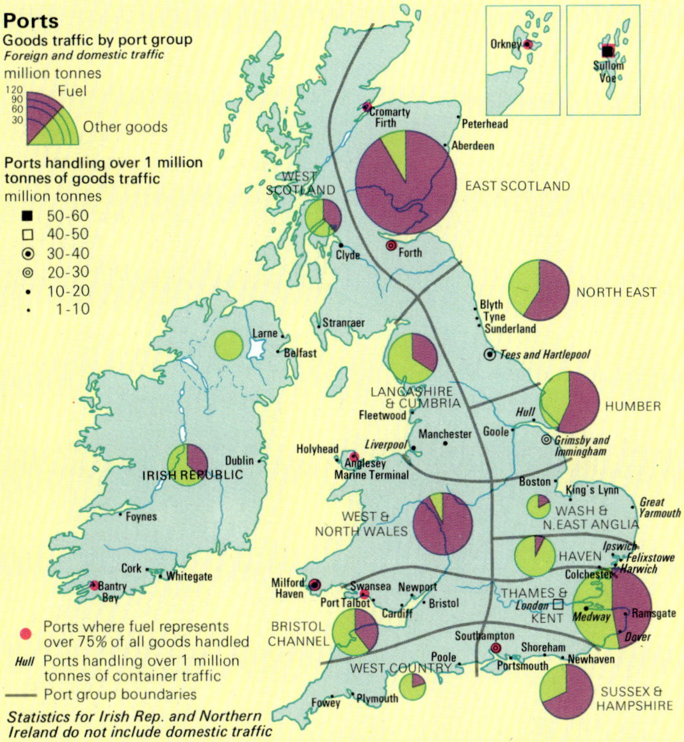

Statistics for Irish Rep. and Northern Ireland do not include domestic traffic

Airports

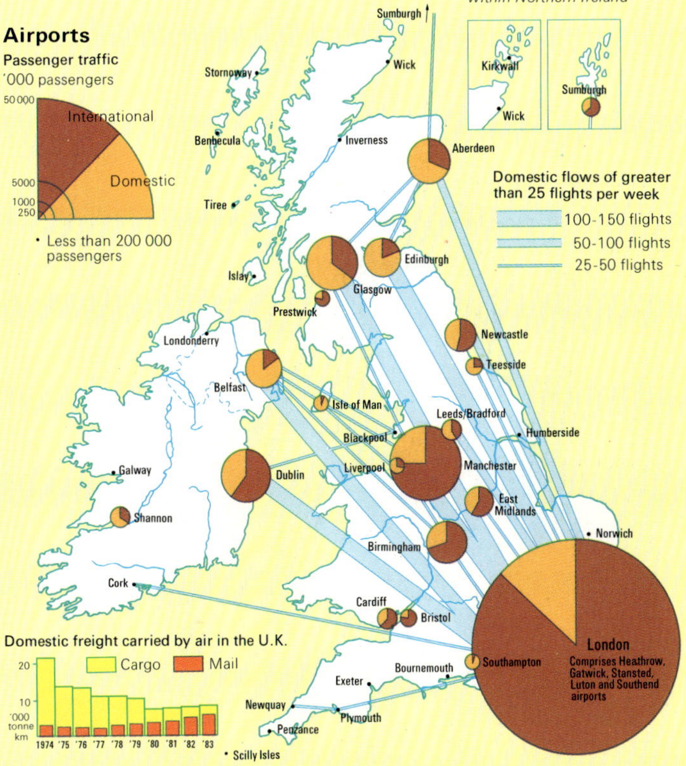

Population Density and Principal Towns

1:8 500 000

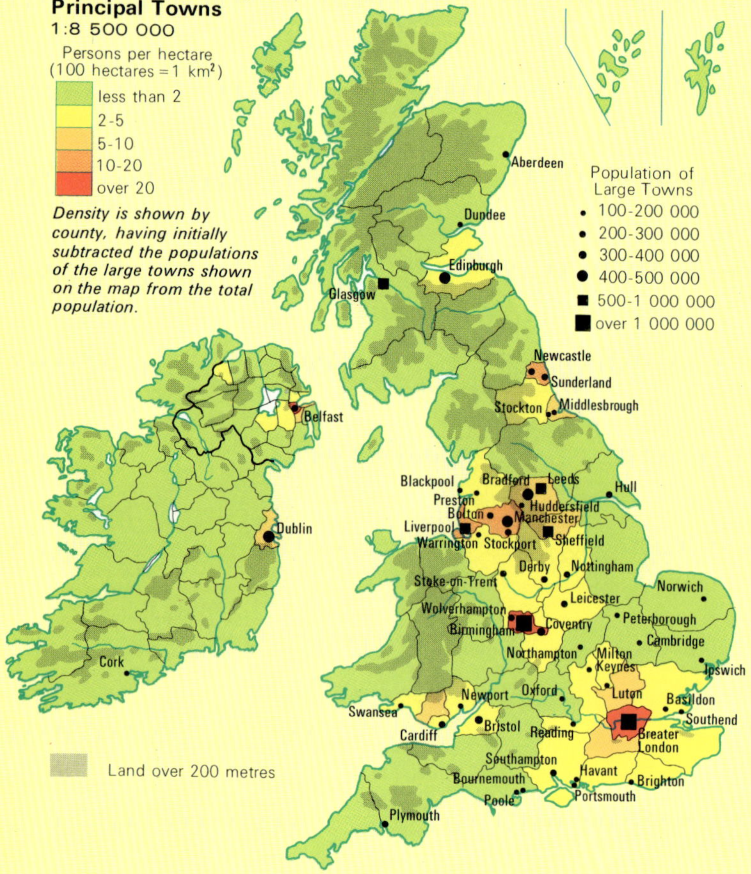

Population Change 1961-1981

1:8 500 000

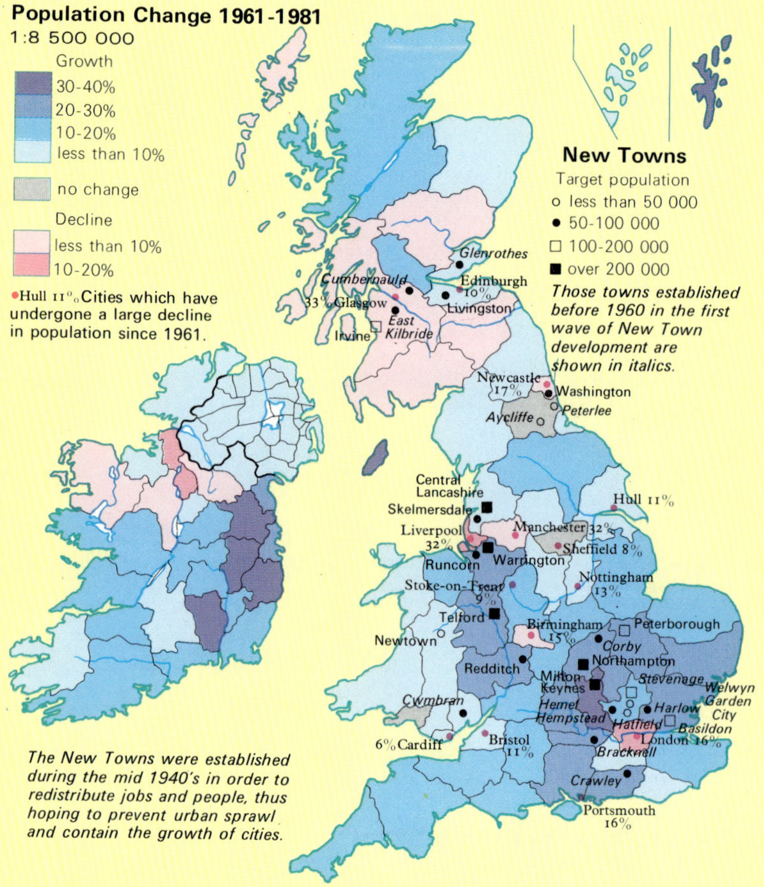

Dependency Ratio

1:10 000 000

The dependency ratio is the number of people aged under 15 years plus those of retiring age (60 and over for females, 65 and over for males) per 100 people of working age.

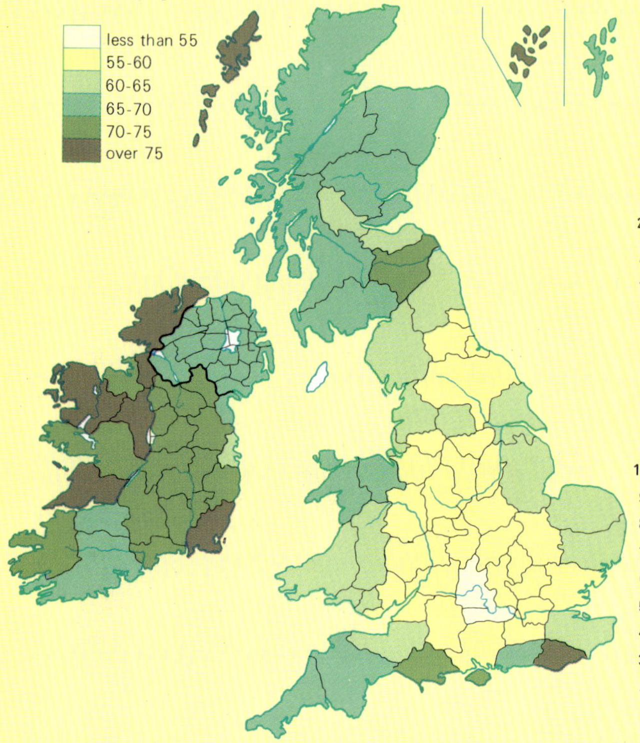

Age Structure of the U.K. in 1901, 1983 and Projected to 2051.

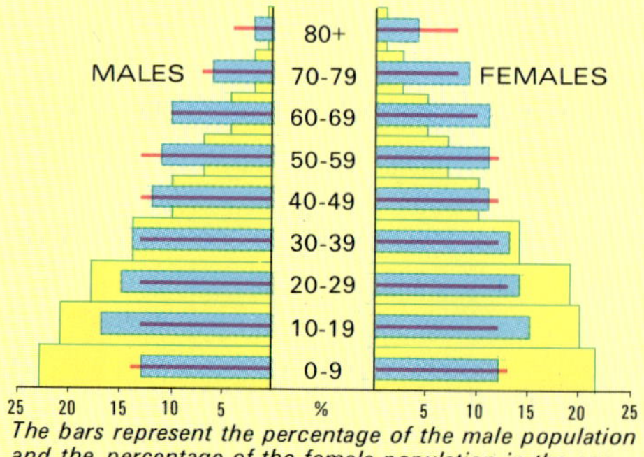

The bars represent the percentage of the male population and the percentage of the female population in the age group shown. 1901 1983 2051

Age Group Distribution Within the Population of the U.K.

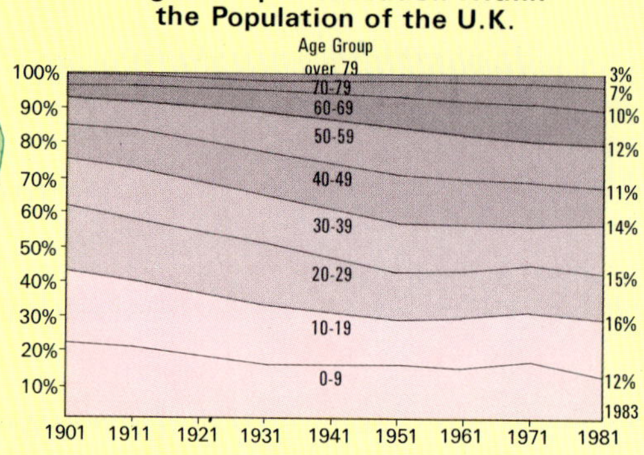

U.K. Vital Statistics, 1900-2000

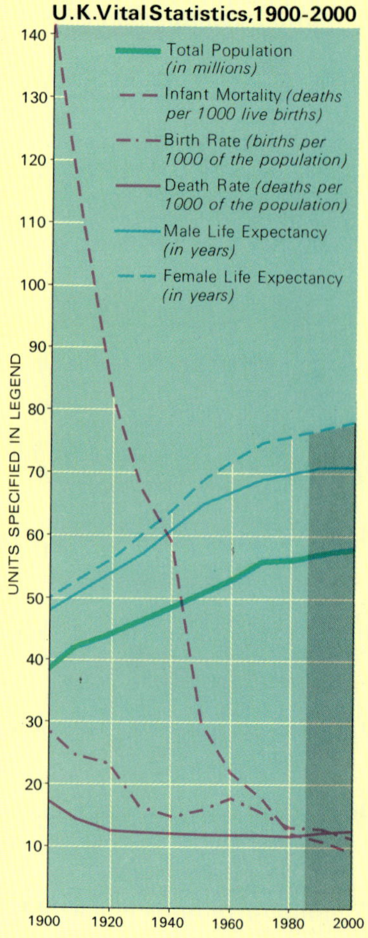

Agricultural Land Use Capability
1:10 000 000

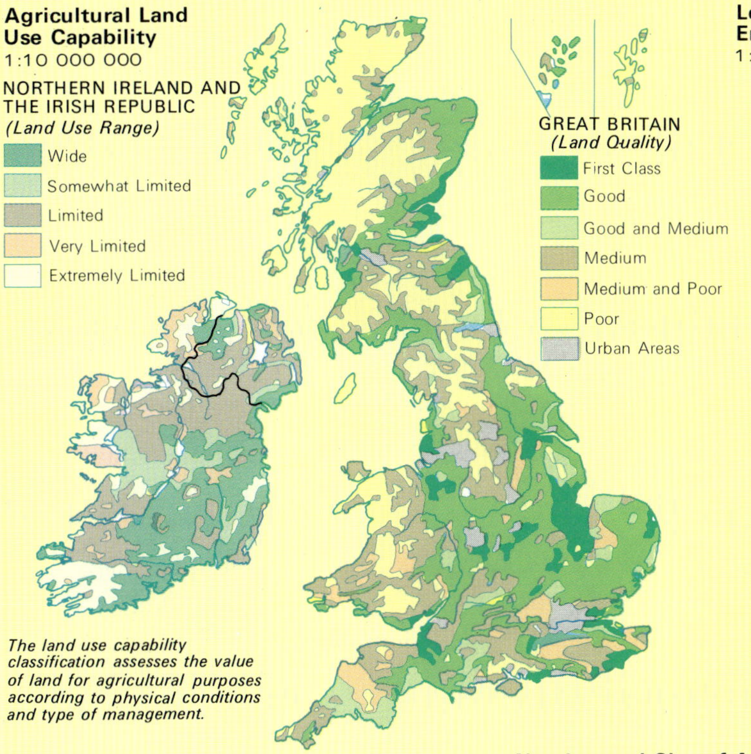

The land use capability classification assesses the value of land for agricultural purposes according to physical conditions and type of management.

Leading Agricultural Enterprises
1:10 000 000

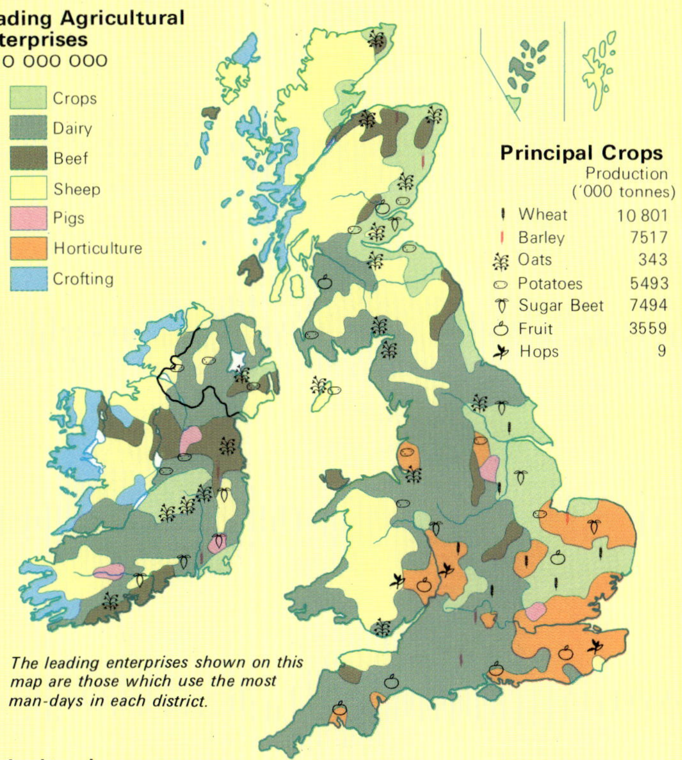

The leading enterprises shown on this map are those which use the most man-days in each district.

Yield of Selected Crops in the U.K.

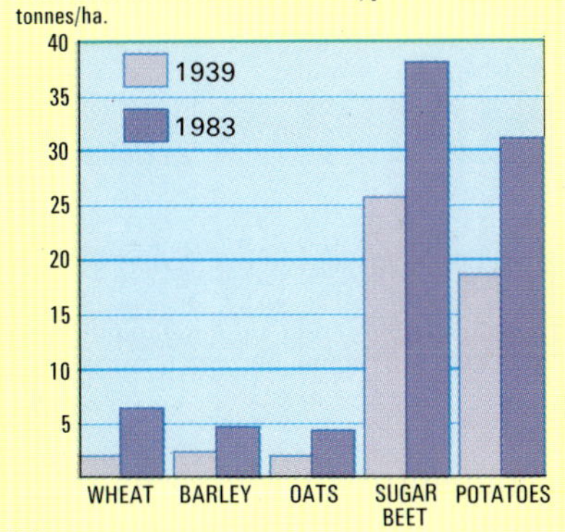

Number and Size of Agricultural Holdings in the U.K.

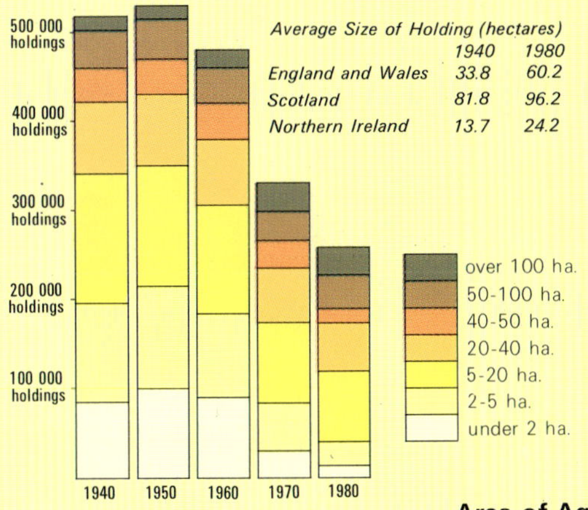

Average Size of Holding (hectares)

	1940	1980
England and Wales	33.8	60.2
Scotland	81.8	96.2
Northern Ireland	13.7	24.2

Self-Sufficiency of the U.K. in Agricultural Production
(home production given as a percentage of total consumption)

PRODUCT	1969	1977	1982
Wheat	42%	61%	96%
Barley	90%	121%	130%
Potatoes	91%	95%	96%
Sugar	33%	40%	49%
Cheese	45%	67%	71%
Butter	12%	40%	49%
Beef	77%	72%	83%
Pork	101%	62%	67%
Poultry	100%	100%	99%

Fishing
1:10 000 000

Quantity of fish landed by domestic vessels at major ports, (port districts in Scotland.)

Forestry

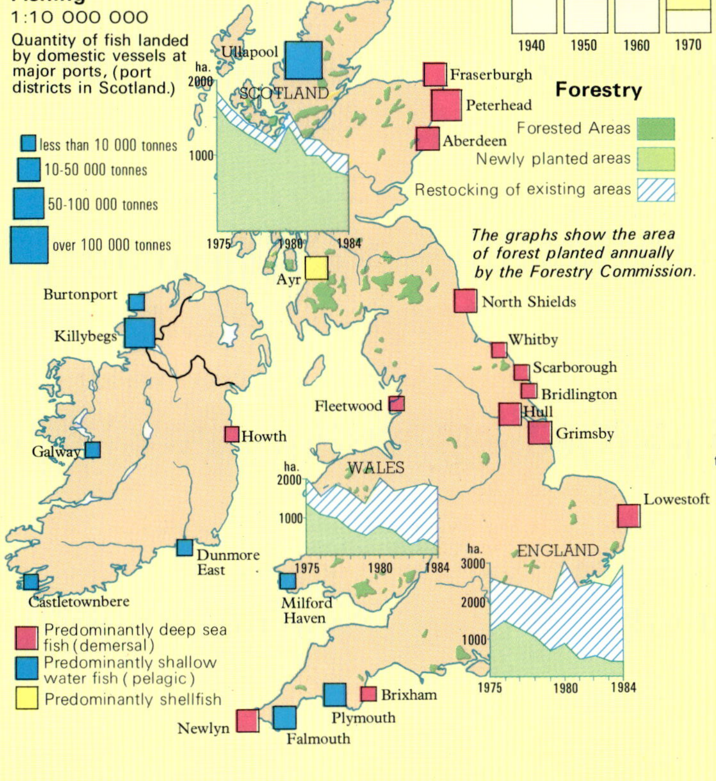

The graphs show the area of forest planted annually by the Forestry Commission.

Area of Agricultural Land Under Selected Enterprises

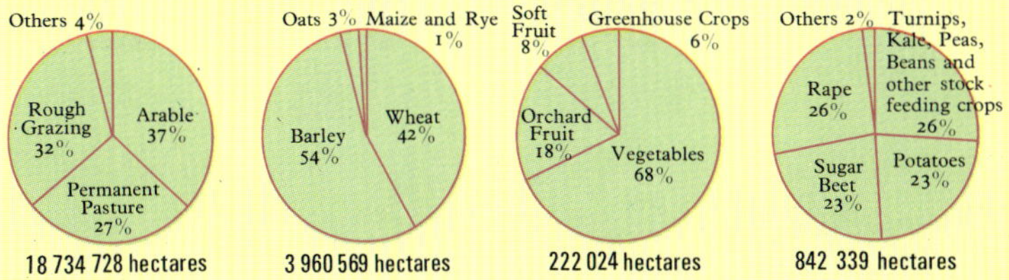

Quantity of Fish Landed by British Vessels in all Fishing Areas

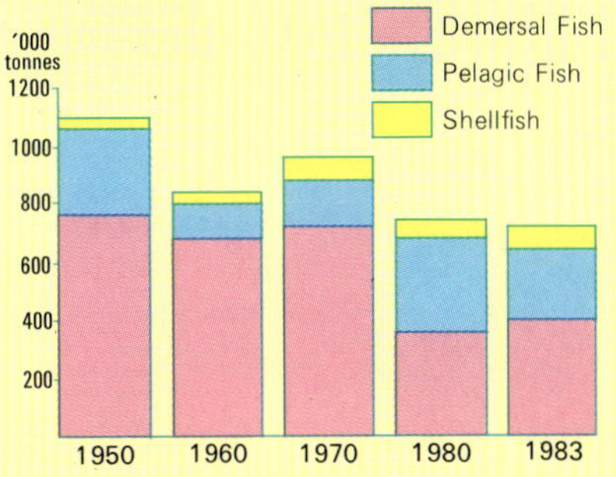

Number and Size of Livestock Holdings in the U.K.

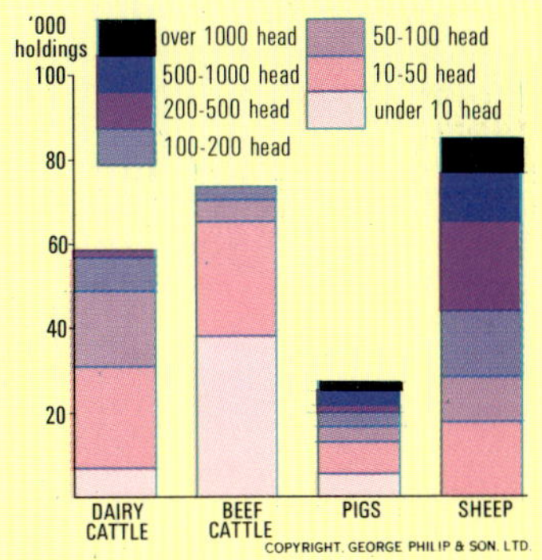

Coal and Power 1:8 500 000

Coalfields	Saleable Output (million tonnes)	Output per Manshift (tonnes)
1 Scottish	5.3	1.95
2 North East	10.9	2.23
3 Western	9.1	2.44
4 South Wales	6.6	1.57
5 North Yorkshire	7.7	3.11
6 Doncaster	5.8	2.31
7 Barnsley	6.3	2.36
8 South Yorkshire	6.6	2.47
9 North Derbyshire	6.3	2.90
10 North Nottinghamshire	11.6	3.35
11 South Nottinghamshire	6.9	2.55
12 South Midlands	6.6	2.41
13 Kent	0.7	1.4

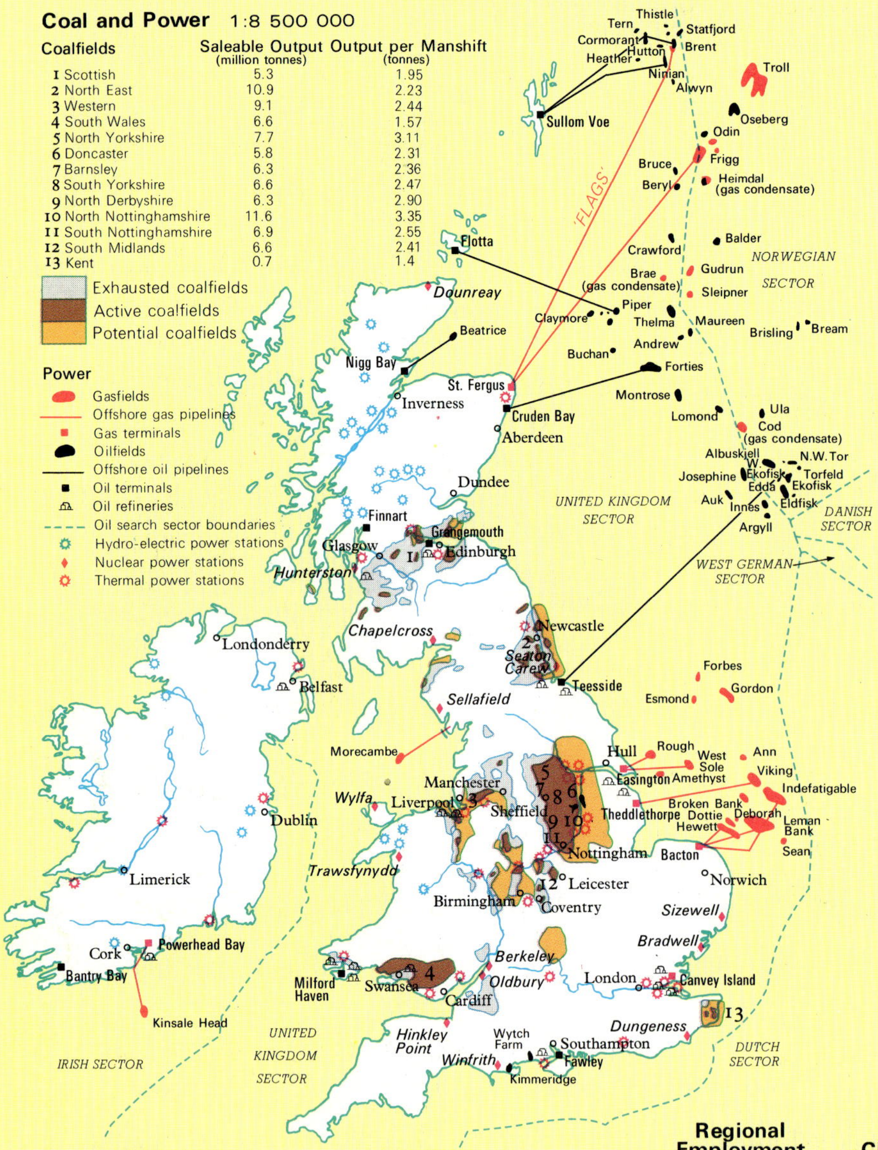

Production of Primary Fuels in the U.K.

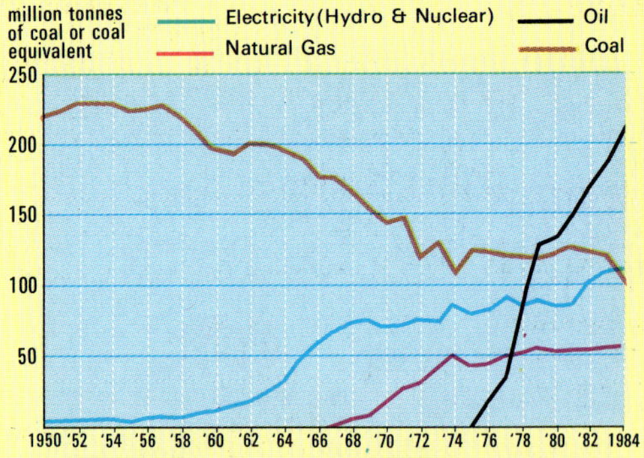

Consumption of Primary Fuels in the U.K.

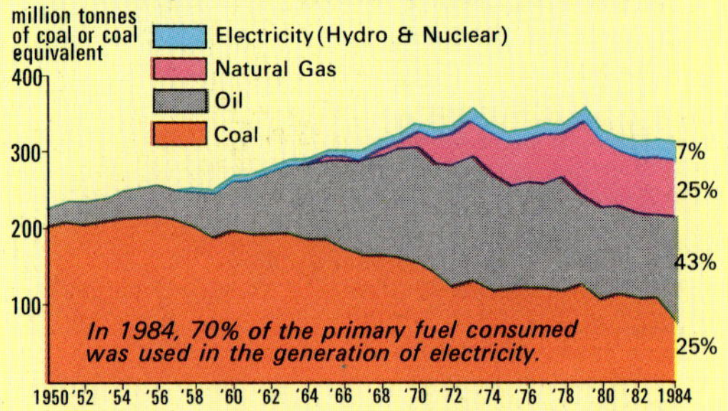

Coal Consumption in the U.K.

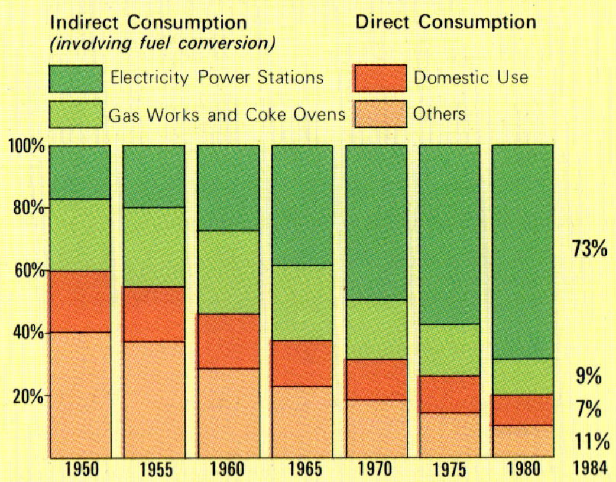

Minerals 1:10 000 000

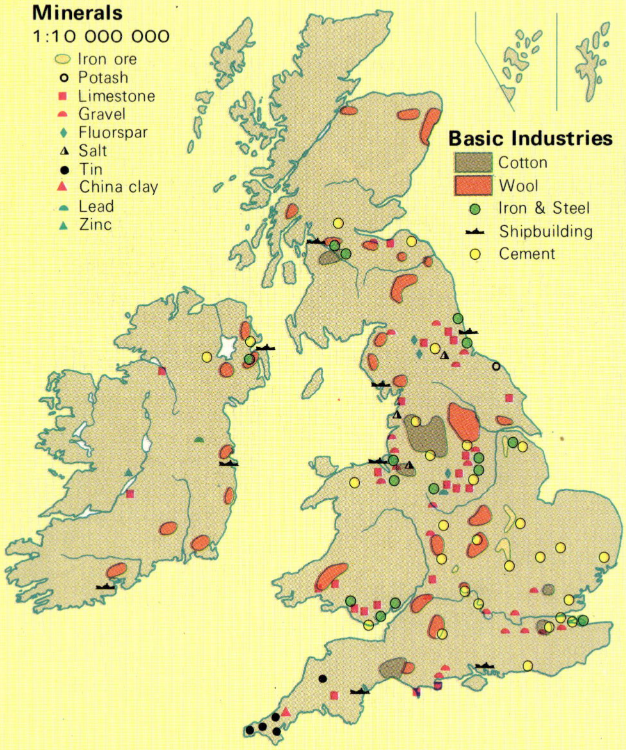

Regional Employment by Industry

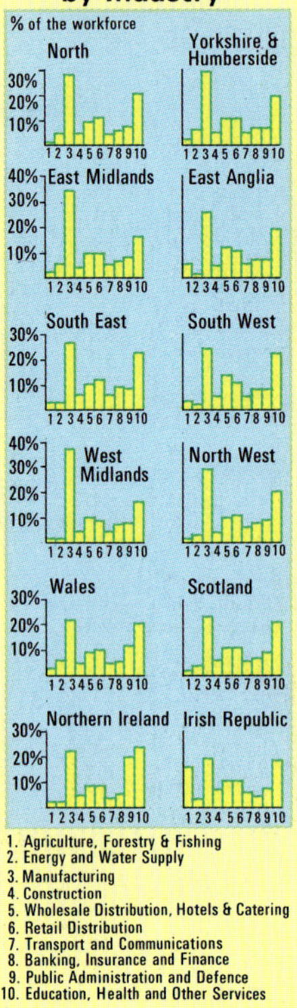

1. Agriculture, Forestry & Fishing
2. Energy and Water Supply
3. Manufacturing
4. Construction
5. Wholesale Distribution, Hotels & Catering
6. Retail Distribution
7. Transport and Communications
8. Banking, Insurance and Finance
9. Public Administration and Defence
10. Education, Health and Other Services

Change in Manufacturing Employment by County 1961-1981

1:10 000 000

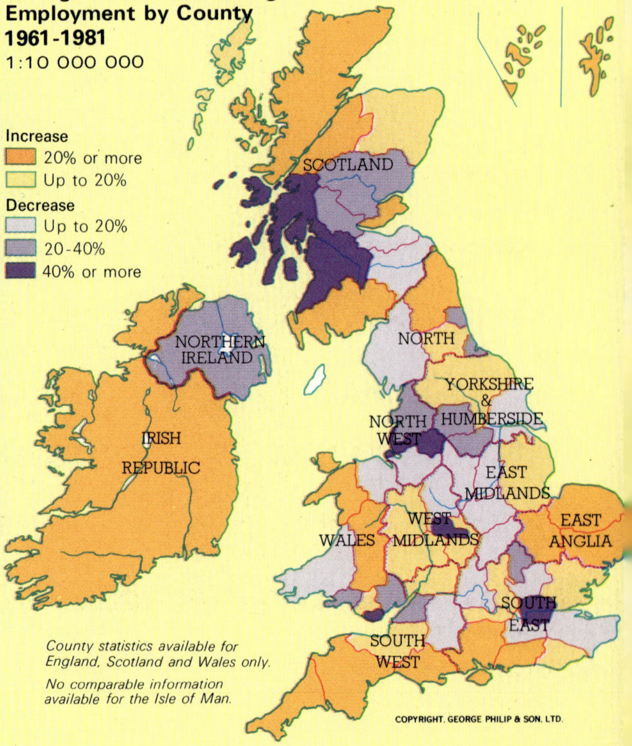

County statistics available for England, Scotland and Wales only.

No comparable information available for the Isle of Man.

Employment in the U.K. by Industry

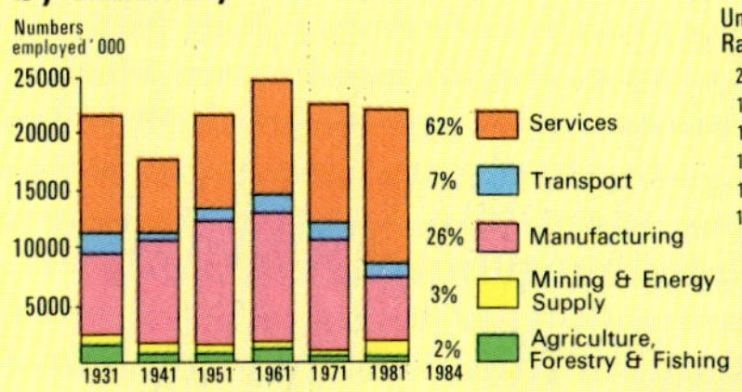

Unemployment Rates for Selected Regions

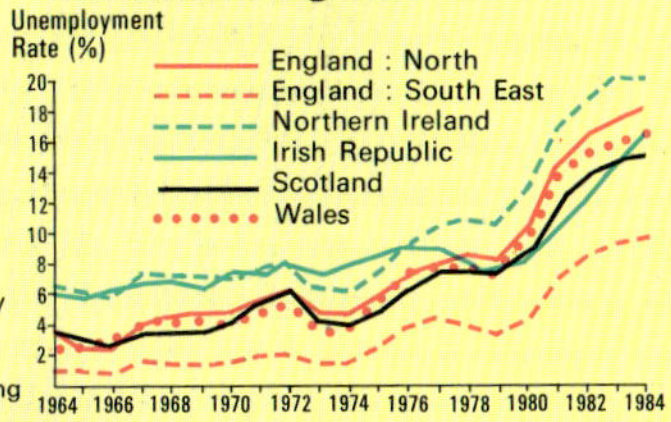

Leisure

1:8 500 000

Forest Parks in Northern Ireland & the Irish Republic

1. Ards	11. Lough Key
2. Glenariff	12. Killykeen
3. Gortin Glen	13. Dun a Ri
4. Davagh	14. Portumna
5. Drum Manor	15. Avondale
6. Gosford	16. Curraghchase
7. Castlewellan	17. Doneraile
8. Florence Court	18. Farran
9. Rossmore	19. Gougane Barra
10. Tollymore	

Unemployment

1:10 000 000

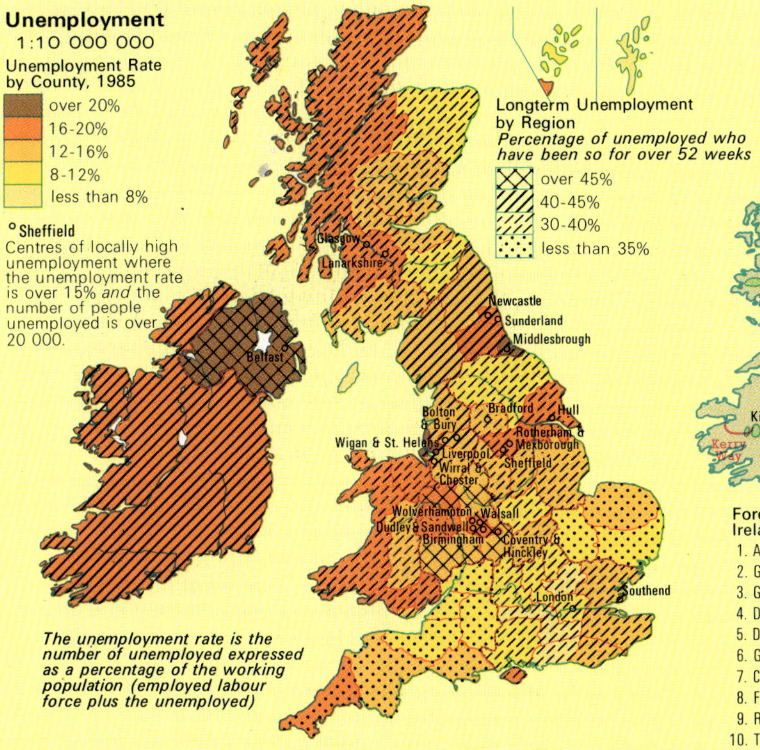

The unemployment rate is the number of unemployed expressed as a percentage of the working population (employed labour force plus the unemployed)

Top Ten Trading Partners with the U.K. by Value of Goods

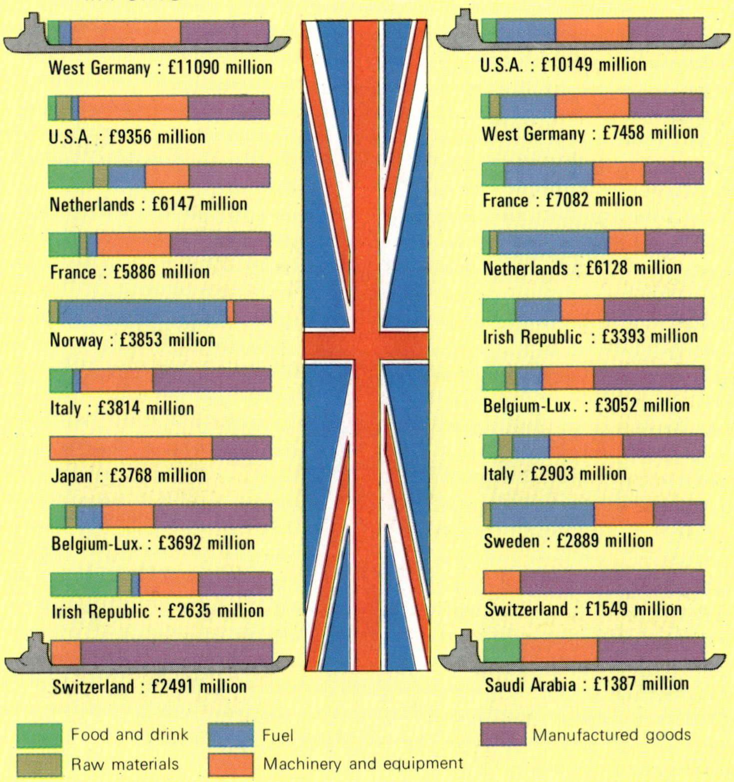

U.K. Trade by Country Group and Commodity Type

(percentages are given by value of trade)

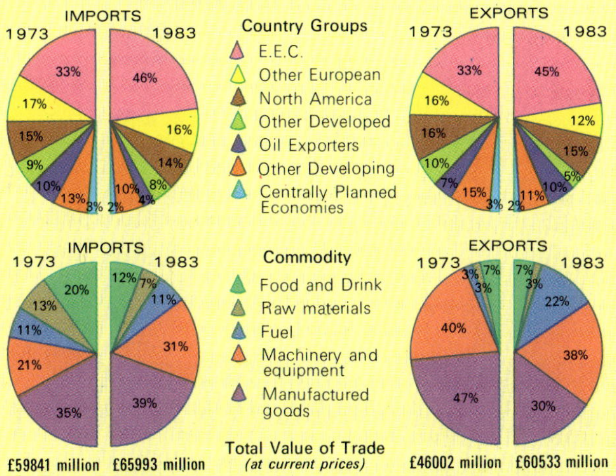

Balance of Payments (£ million)

		1963	1973	1983
CREDITS	Visibles *(Exports)*	4331	11937	60625
	Invisibles	2515	8506	34975
	Total	6846	20443	95600
DEBITS	Visibles *(Imports)*	4450	14523	61341
	Invisibles	2271	6899	31343
	Total	6721	21422	92684
BALANCE		+125	−979	+2916

Visible trade involves transactions of goods while invisible trade involves transactions of money and services.

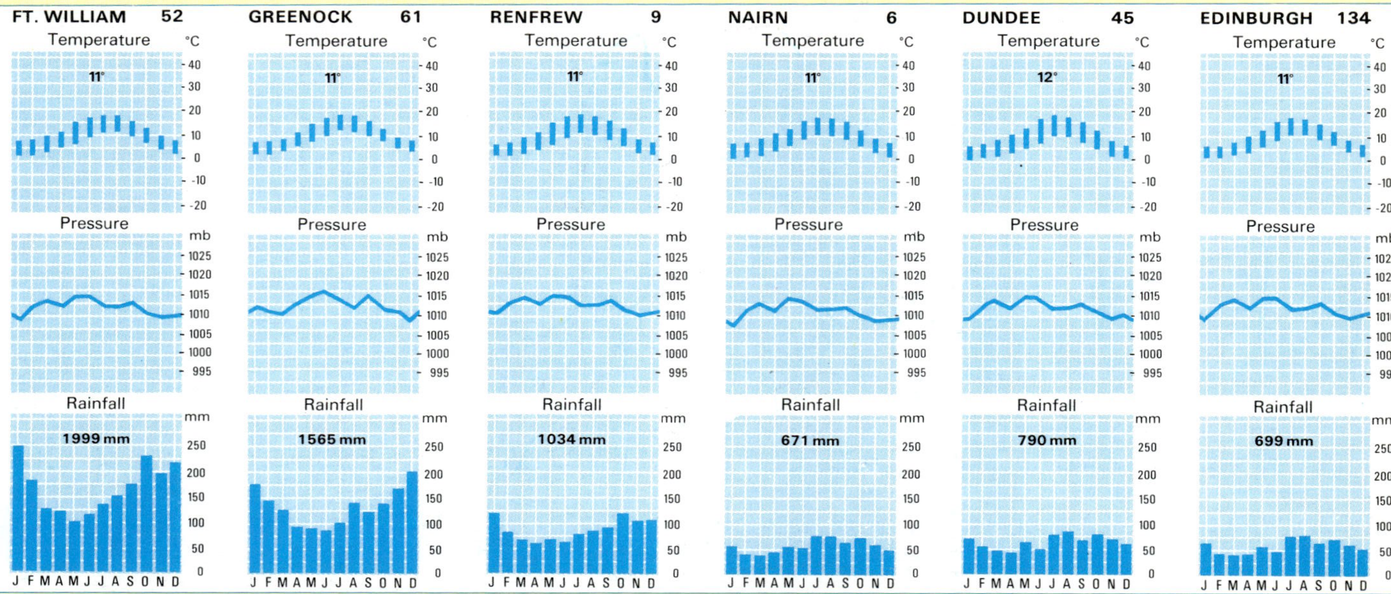

The climate graphs should be used in conjunction with the maps illustrating the climate of the British Isles on page 6. The stations have been selected to show climatic variations throughout the British Isles. On each graph the name of the station is followed by its height in metres above sea level, so that comparisons between stations can be made allowing for elevation. Temperature is shown by a bar, the top of the bar representing the mean monthly maximum and the bottom of the bar the mean monthly minimum temperature. A mid point between these is the mean monthly temperature; the mean annual range of temperature (in degrees Celsius) is given above the graph. The line on the pressure graphs shows the mean monthly pressure (in millibars and reduced to sea level). The rainfall graphs show the average monthly rainfall and above them is given the average total annual rainfall (in millimetres).

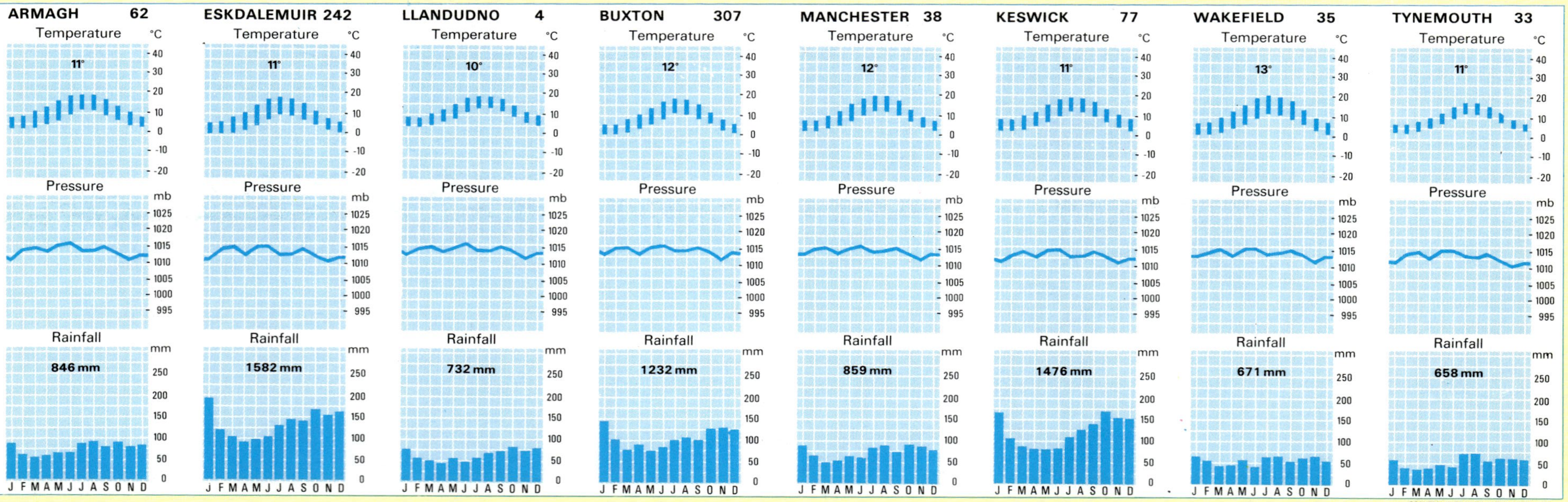

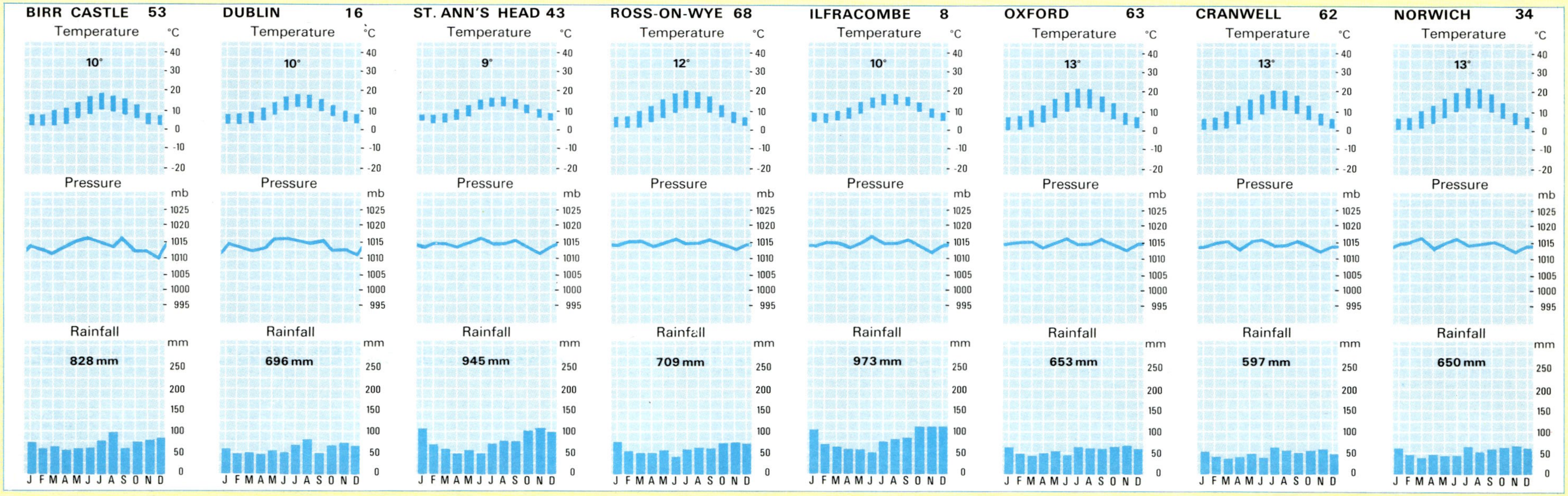
BIRR CASTLE 53
Temperature °C
10°
Pressure mb
Rainfall mm
828 mm
DUBLIN 16
Temperature °C
10°
Pressure mb
Rainfall mm
696 mm
ST. ANN'S HEAD 43
Temperature °C
9°
Pressure mb
Rainfall mm
945 mm
ROSS-ON-WYE 68
Temperature °C
12°
Pressure mb
Rainfall mm
709 mm
ILFRACOMBE 8
Temperature °C
10°
Pressure mb
Rainfall mm
973 mm
OXFORD 63
Temperature °C
13°
Pressure mb
Rainfall mm
653 mm
CRANWELL 62
Temperature °C
13°
Pressure mb
Rainfall mm
597 mm
NORWICH 34
Temperature °C
13°
Pressure mb
Rainfall mm
650 mm
40 30 20 10 0 -10 -20
1025 1020 1015 1010 1005 1000 995
250 200 150 100 50 0
J F M A M J J A S O N D

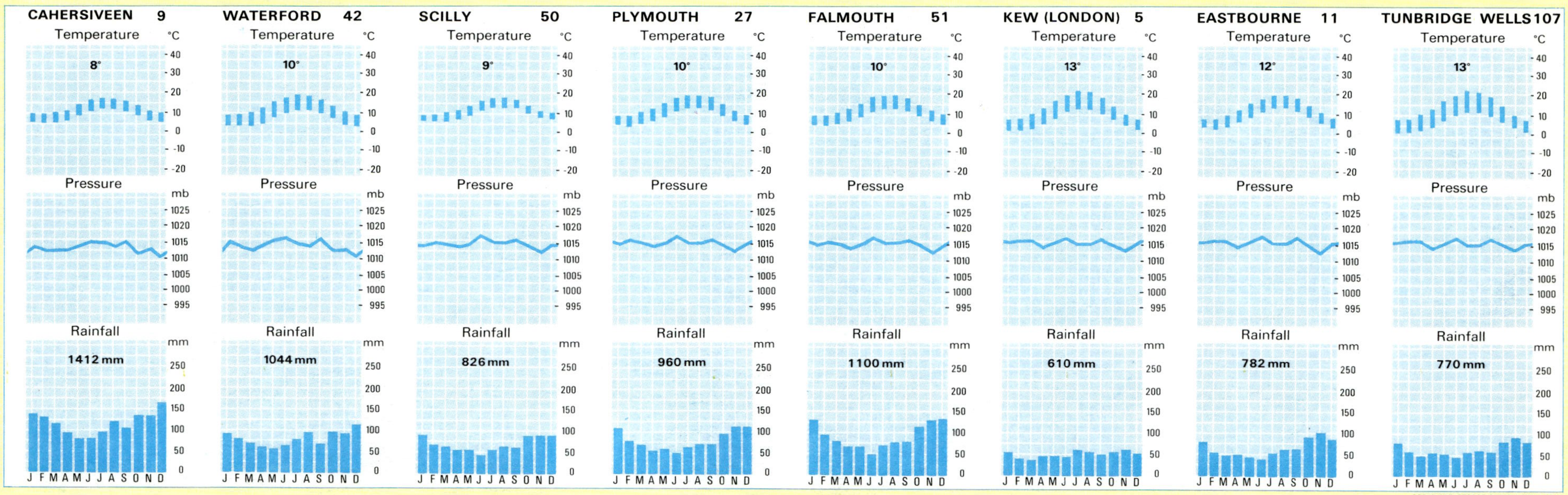
CAHERSIVEEN 9
Temperature °C
8°
Pressure mb
Rainfall mm
1412 mm
WATERFORD 42
Temperature °C
10°
Pressure mb
Rainfall mm
1044 mm
SCILLY 50
Temperature °C
9°
Pressure mb
Rainfall mm
826 mm
PLYMOUTH 27
Temperature °C
10°
Pressure mb
Rainfall mm
960 mm
FALMOUTH 51
Temperature °C
10°
Pressure mb
Rainfall mm
1100 mm
KEW (LONDON) 5
Temperature °C
13°
Pressure mb
Rainfall mm
610 mm
EASTBOURNE 11
Temperature °C
12°
Pressure mb
Rainfall mm
782 mm
TUNBRIDGE WELLS 107
Temperature °C
13°
Pressure mb
Rainfall mm
770 mm
40 30 20 10 0 -10 -20
1025 1020 1015 1010 1005 1000 995
250 200 150 100 50 0
J F M A M J J A S O N D

GWYNEDD
Dolgellau
Machynlleth
Oswestry
Shrewsbury
Welshpool
Newtown
Stafford
STAFFORDSHIRE
Burton upon Trent
Telford
Wellington
Cannock
Lichfield
Tamworth
WOLVERHAMPTON
Walsall
Sutton Coldfield
Dudley
West Bromwich
BIRMINGHAM
Solihull
WEST MIDLANDS
COVENTRY
Nuneaton
Hinckley
Rugby
Long Eaton
Loughborough
Coalville
SHROPSHIRE
Long Mynd
Wenlock Edge
Bridgnorth
Kidderminster
Stourport-on-Severn
Bromsgrove
Redditch
Royal Leamington Spa
Warwick
Kenilworth
WARWICKSHIRE
Stratford-upon-Avon
Ludlow
Leominster
Worcester
Droitwich
HEREFORD AND WORCESTER
Great Malvern
Hereford
Evesham
Pershore
Tewkesbury
Banbury
POWYS
Llandrindod Wells
Builth Wells
Brecon
Black Mountains
DYFED
Mynydd Eppynt
Mynydd Du (Black Mt.)
Ross-on-Wye
Monmouth
Abergavenny
Cheltenham
Gloucester
GLOUCESTERSHIRE
Stroud
Cirencester
Oxford
Witney
Abingdon
Didcot
Wallingford
Merthyr Tydfil
Ebbw Vale
Pontypool
Cwmbran
GWENT
Newport
Chepstow
MID GLAMORGAN
WEST GLAMORGAN
Swansea
Neath
Port Talbot
Bridgend
Caerphilly
Pontypridd
SOUTH GLAMORGAN
CARDIFF
Barry
Bristol Channel
Weston-super-Mare
Clevedon
BRISTOL
AVON
Bath
Swindon
Chippenham
Marlborough
Newbury
Devizes
WILTSHIRE
Trowbridge
Salisbury Plain
Salisbury
Basingstoke
Andover
Winchester
HAMPSHIRE
SOUTHAMPTON
Portsmouth
Gosport
Fareham
Eastleigh
Minehead
Exmoor
Bridgwater
Burnham-on-Sea
Mendip Hills
Wells
Glastonbury
SOMERSET
Taunton
Yeovil
Frome
Shaftesbury
DEVON
Tiverton
Exeter
Exmouth
Sidmouth
Dorchester
Weymouth
I. of Portland
DORSET
Bridport
Poole
Bournemouth
Christchurch
Wareham
Swanage
ISLE OF WIGHT
Newport
Ryde
Shanklin
Ventnor
The Solent
Projection: Conical with two standard parallels

Based upon the Ordnance Survey Map with the permission of the Controller of Her Majesty's Stationery Office. Crown Copyright Reserved.

1:1 000 000

10 0 10 20 30 40 km

Based upon the Ordnance Survey Map with the permission of the Controller of Her Majesty's Stationery Office. Crown Copyright Reserved.

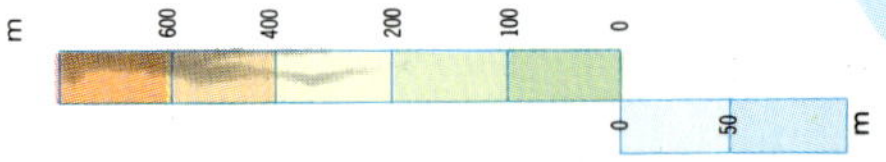

1:1 000 000

10 0 10 20 30 40 km

Projection: Conical with two standard parallels

m
1000
800
600
400
200
100
0
50
100
m

Projection: Conical with two standard parallels

1:1 000 000

10 0 10 20 30 40 km

Based upon the Ordnance Survey Map with the permission of the Controller of Her Majesty's Stationery Office. Crown Copyright Reserved.

ATLANTIC
OCEAN
NORTH CHANNEL
NORTHERN IRELAND
ULSTER
LONDONDERRY
ANTRIM
TYRONE
Coll
Tiree
Mull
Islay
Jura
Colonsay
Oronsay
Arran
Kintyre
Knapdale
Morvern
Ardnamurchan
Sunart
Breadalbane
Cowal
Argyll
Carrick
Galloway
Kyle
Cunninghame
Rannoch Moor
Glen Coe
Glen Etive
Glen Orchy
Glen Lyon
Firth of Lorn
Firth of Clyde
Sd. of Mull
Sound of Jura
Sound of Islay
Sd. of Bute
Kilbrannan Sound
Loch Fyne
Loch Linnhe
Loch Etive
Loch Awe
Loch Lomond
L. Katrine
L. Tulla
L. Leven
L. Laidon
L. Rannoch
L. Earn
L. Voil
L. Sunart
L. Frisa
L. Tuath
L. na Keal
L. Scridain
L. Spelve
L. Buie
L. Avich
L. Melfort
L. Craignish
L. Tarbert
L. Caolisport
L. Indaal
L. Eck
L. Goil
L. Long
L. Striven
Gare L.
Kyles of Bute
Lough Foyle
Lough Neagh
Larne Lough
Belfast Lough
L. Ryan
Luce Bay
Wigtown Bay
Passage of Tiree
Passage of Oronsay
G. of Corryvreckan
Crinan Can.
Mull of Kintyre
Mull of Oa
Mull of Galloway
Sperrin Mts.
Mountains of Antrim
The Rhins
The Machars
Oban
Tobermory
Campbeltown
Lochgilphead
Inveraray
Dunoon
Rothesay
Greenock
Gourock
Helensburgh
Dumbarton
Clydebank
GLASGOW
Paisley
Renfrew
Rutherglen
Johnstone
Kilmarnock
Irvine
Troon
Prestwick
Ayr
Girvan
Stranraer
Newton Stewart
Wigtown
DUMFRIES
Alexandria
Milngavie
Bearsden
Largs
Saltcoats
Ardrossan
Stevenston
Kilwinning
Stewarton
Dalry
Kilbirnie
Barrhead
Tarbert
Brodick
Lamlash
Lochranza
Holy I.
Pladda
Sanda I.
Ailsa Craig
Gigha I.
Cumbrae Is.
Bute
Kerrera
Lismore
Seil
Luing
Scarba
Garvellachs
Iona
Staffa
Ulva
Gometra
Treshnish Isles
Torran Rocks
Dubh Artach
Rathlin
Inishtrahull
Londonderry
Coleraine
Portrush
Portstewart
Ballymoney
Ballymena
Ballycastle
Bushmills
Limavady
Larne
Antrim
Ballyclare
Carrickfergus
Newtownabbey
BELFAST
Holywood
Bangor
Newtownards
Donaghadee
Cookstown
Dungannon
Omagh
Moneymore
Magherafelt
Moville
Inishowen
Giants Causeway
Fair Hd.
Benbane Hd.
Malin Pen.
Copeland I.
Projection: Conical with two standard parallels
West from Greenwich

1:1 000 000

10 0 10 20 30 40 km

Projection: Conical with two standard parallels

10 0 10 20 30 40 km
ORKNEY ISLANDS
on same scale
Papa Westray
Westray
Mull Hd.
N. Ronaldsay
N. Ronaldsay Firth
Dennis Hd.
Hollandstoun
Start Pt.
The North Sound
Noup Hd.
Pierowall
Papa Sd.
Sanday
Overbister
Berst Ness
Rapness
Westray Firth
Eday
Eday Sd.
Sacquoy Hd.
Wasbister
Rousay
Brinyan
Egilsay
Eynhallow Sd.
Sanday Sound
Papa Stronsay
Whitehall
Aith
Stronsay
Lamb Hd.
Brough Hd.
Twatt
Redland
Dounby
Wyre
Gairsay
Balfour
Stronsay
Shapinsay
Y Firth
Auskerry
L. of Harray
ORKNEY
Wide Firth
Finstown
Shapinsay Sd.
L. of Stenness
Voy
Stromness
Kirkwall
Mainland
Deer Sd.
Mull Hd.
Deerness
Graemsay
Sd.
Hoy
Gritley
Pt. of Ayre
Copinsay
Old Man of Hoy
477
Ward Hill
Orphir
St. Mary's
Rora Hd.
Rackwick
Scapa Flow
Burray
Rose Ness
Hoy
Lyness
Flotta
St. Margaret's Hope
South Ronaldsay
Hurliness
Tor Ness
S. Walls
Swona
Cleat
Pentland Firth
Pentland Skerries
Dunnet Hd.
Stroma
John o' Groats
Duncansby Hd.
Mey
Canisbay
Pentland Firth
Stroma
Dunnet Hd.
Dunnet B.
Holborn Hd.
Scrabster
Thurso
Mey
John o' Groats
Duncansby Hd.
Dunnet
Canisbay
Duncansby
Freswick
Castletown
Nybster
Keiss
Sortat
Sordale
Hastigrow
Sinclair's B.
Halkirk
Reiss
Noss Head
Staxigoe
Wick
Olgrinmore
Watten
Mybster
Thrumster
Ulbster
Achavanich
Lybster
Latheron
Dunbeath
Braemore
705 Morven
Berriedale
Ousdale
Ord of Caithness
Helmsdale
Kildonan
Strath of Kildonan
Kinbrace
628 B. Dhorain
Brora
L. Brora
Golspie
L. Fleet
Embo
Dornoch
Dornoch Firth
Tarbat Ness
Portmahomack
Tain
Edderton
Fearn
Balintore
Faraid Hd.
Whiten Hd.
Durness
Strathy Pt.
Kyle of Tongue
Portskerra
Strathy
Melvich
Dounreay
Reay
Strath Halladale
Bettyhill
Craigtown
Dalhalvaig
Forsinain
Forsinard
Tongue
Borgie
L. Eriboll
Heilam
Loch Hope
927 Ben Hope
763 B. Loyal
Loch Loyal
Strath Naver
Naver
Strathmore
B. Hee
L. Naver
Altnaharra
B. Klibreck
961
L. nan Clar
Kinloch
Loch Shin
Ben More Assynt
998
Lairg
Fleet
Torroboll
Shin
Culrain
Rosehall
Auchness
Oykel
Oykel Br.
Invercassley
Bonarbridge
Clashmore
Kincardine
Carron
Freevater Forest
Easter Ross
B. Tharsuinn
692
Alness
Kilmuir
Alness
Invergordon
Nigg
Nigg B.
Balnapaling
Cromarty Firth
Cromarty
Evanton
Balblair
B. Wyvis
1045
Ross
Strathpeffer
Black Isle
Rosemarkie
Fortrose
Dingwall
L. Luichart
Contin
Conon Bridge
Avoch
Nth. Kessock
Glen Orrin
Muir of Ord
Beauly F.
Beauly
Inverness
Caledonian Canal
The Aird
Strath Glass
Affric
Moray Firth
Burghead
Burghead B.
Hopeman
Branderburgh
Lossiemouth
Spey B.
Findochty
Portknockie
Cullen
Portsoy
Buckie
Spey Bay
Garmouth
Portgordon
Fordyce
Banff
Macduff
Troup Hd.
Rosehearty
Kinnairds Hd.
Fraserburgh
Gardenstown
Inverallochy
New Aberdour
St. Combs
Rathen
Rattray Hd.
Strichen
Crimond
Findhorn
Kinloss
Elgin
Lhanbryde
Fochabers
Witchyburn
Forres
Nairn
Campbelltown
Auldearn
Kellas
Dallas
Rothes
Craigellachie
Newmill
Keith
Aberchirder
Deveron
Turriff
Newbyth
New Pitsligo
Cuminestown
Buchan
Mintlaw
St. Fergus
Peterhead
Boddam
Buchan Ness
Longside
Old Deer
Maud
New Deer
Fortrie
Cawdor
Littlemill
Culloden Moor
Balloch
Ferness
Archiestown
Charlestown of Aberlour
Dufftown
840
Huntly
Strathbogie
Badenscoth
Fyvie
Methlick
Ythan
Hatton
Cruden Bay
Tarves
Ellon
Rothienorman
Formartine
Oldmeldrum
Newburgh
Craggie
Findhorn
Moy
Farr
Dores
L. Duntelchaig
Carn Glas-choire 659
Tomatin
Lettoch
Spey
Delehirach
Laggan
Deveron
Colpy
Insch
Grantown-on-Spey
Dulnain Bridge
Hills of Cromdale
Strath Avon
Tomnavoulin
Ardwell
Rhynie
Cabrach
722 The Buck
Lumsden
Grampian
Inverurie
Newmachar
Don
Dyce
Bankhead
Balmedie
Bridge of Don
Aberdeen
Girdle Ness
Cove Bay
Milton
Lewiston
Mealfuarvonie 696
Torness
Loch Ness
Glen Moriston
Invermoriston
Foyers
Errogie
Carn na Saobhaidhe 810
Strath Dearn
Highland
Carrbridge
Nethy Bridge
Tomintoul
803
Ladder Hills
Carn Mor
Strathdon
Alford
Kemnay
Monymusk
Kintore
Ordhead
Westhill
Bucksburn
Cults
White Bridge
Monadhliath Mts.
Boat of Garten
Aviemore
Alvie
Strathspey
Avon
Don
Mar
Fort Augustus
Glen
Carn Ban 941
Cairn Gorm 1245
B. Avon 1171
Morven 872
Tarland
Lumphanan
Torphins
Echt
Peterculter
Dee
Kincraig
Kingussie
Newtonmore
Ruthven
Spey
Invergarry
Cairngorm Mts.
Braeriach 1295
1311 B. Macdhui
Braemar
Crathie
Balmoral Castle
Ordie
Aboyne
Dee
Ballater
Banchory
Cammachmore
Newtonhill
Muchalls
Stonehaven
Strachan
Loggan
Lochlaggan Hotel
Creag Meagaidh 1128
L. Lochy
L. Laggan
Dalwhinnie
Badenoch
Dee
Balmoral Forest
1154 Lochnagar
Mt. Keen 938
Glen Esk
North Esk
Auchenblae
Howe of the Mearns
Laurencekirk
Inverbervie
Gourdon
Johnshaven
Roybridge
Glen Spean
B. Alder 1148
B. Dearg 1008
Mountains
Glas Maol 1067
Braes of Angus
Clova
Forest of Atholl
Beinn a' Ghlo 1121
Fettercairn
Edzell
Marykirk
St. Cyrus
L. Treig
L. Ericht
Grampian
Glen Garry
Garry
Tilt
Blair Atholl
Scotland
Glen Shee
South Esk
Rottal
Brechin
Montrose
NORTH SEA
Blackwater Res.
Errochty
Kinloch Rannoch
Rannoch Sta.
Tummel
L. Tummel
Schiehallion 1081
Pass of Killiecrankie
Kirkmichael
Pitlochry
Isla
Dykehead
Kirriemuir
Forfar
Lunan B.
Inverkeilor
L. Laidon
Rannoch Moor
L. Rannoch
Tay
Strath Tay
Ballinluig
Tayside
Alyth
Strathmore
Friockheim
Carmyllie
Marywell
Arbroath
Clach Leathad 1098
Glen Lyon
B. Lawers 1214
Fearnan
Lawers
Aberfeldy
Dalguise
Kenmore
Blairgowrie
Rattray
Dunkeld
Coupar Angus
Sidlaw Hills
455
Muirdrum
Carnoustie
Barry
Buddon Ness
Monifieth
Broughty Ferry
Dundee
Burrelton
Bankfoot
L. Tulla
1078
B. Dorain 1074
Breadalbane
Loch Tay
West from Greenwich
58
57
59

DISTRICTS IN NORTHERN IRELAND
1 Londonderry
2 Limavady
3 Coleraine
4 Ballymoney
5 Moyle
6 Larne
7 Ballymena
8 Magherafelt
9 Cookstown
10 Strabane
11 Omagh
12 Fermanagh
13 Dungannon
14 Craigavon
15 Armagh
16 Newry and Mourne
17 Banbridge
18 Down
19 Lisburn
20 Antrim
21 Newtownabbey
22 Carrickfergus
23 North Down
24 Ards
25 Castlereagh
26 Belfast
NORTHERN IRELAND
ULSTER
CONNACHT
LEINSTER
DONEGAL
LONDONDERRY
ANTRIM
TYRONE
FERMANAGH
ARMAGH
DOWN
MONAGHAN
CAVAN
LOUTH
MEATH
SLIGO
LEITRIM
ROSCOMMON
LONGFORD
WESTMEATH
MAYO
DUBLIN
Donegal Bay
Sligo Bay
Lough Neagh
Lough Foyle
Lough Swilly
Dundalk Bay
Clew Bay
Achill I.
Belfast
Londonderry (Derry)
Dundalk
Drogheda
Sligo
Donegal

ATLANTIC
OCEAN
LEINSTER
MUNSTER
CONNACHT
KILDARE
WICKLOW
WEXFORD
CARLOW
KILKENNY
LAOIS
OFFALY
TIPPERARY
WATERFORD
CORK
KERRY
LIMERICK
CLARE
Dublin (Baile Átha Cliath)
Dún Laoghaire (Dunleary)
Galway Bay
Aran Is. (Galway)
Limerick
Cork
Waterford
Wexford
Kilkenny
Tralee
Killarney
Shannon
Wicklow Mts.
Galty Mts.
Knockmealdown Mts.
Comeragh Mts.
Macgillycuddy's Reeks
Bantry Bay
Dingle Bay
Cork Harbour
Youghal Bay
Waterford Harbour
Wexford Harbour
Fastnet Rock
West from Greenwich
Projection: Conical with two standard parallels
m
1000
800
600
400
200
100
0
50
100
m

1:20 000 000

200 0 200 400 600 800 km

1:20 000 000

200 0 200 400 600 800 km

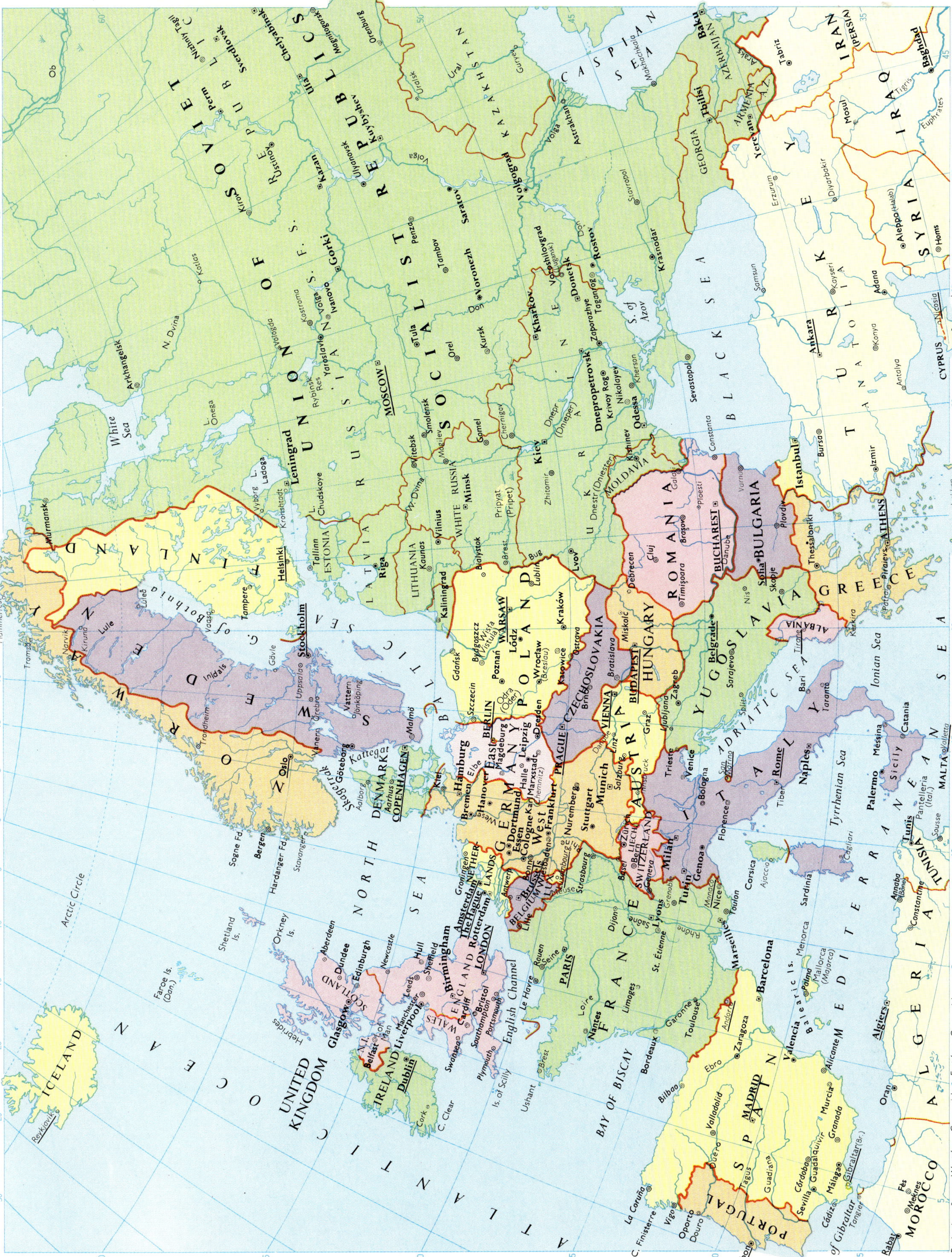

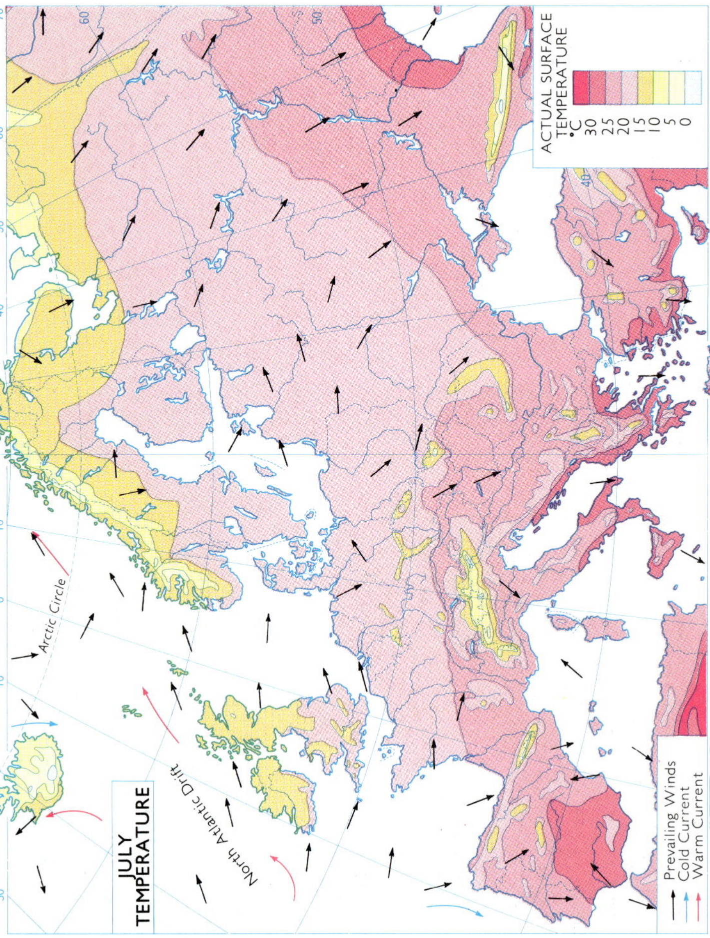
JULY TEMPERATURE
ACTUAL SURFACE TEMPERATURE °C
30
25
20
15
10
5
0
Prevailing Winds
Cold Current
Warm Current
North Atlantic Drift
Arctic Circle

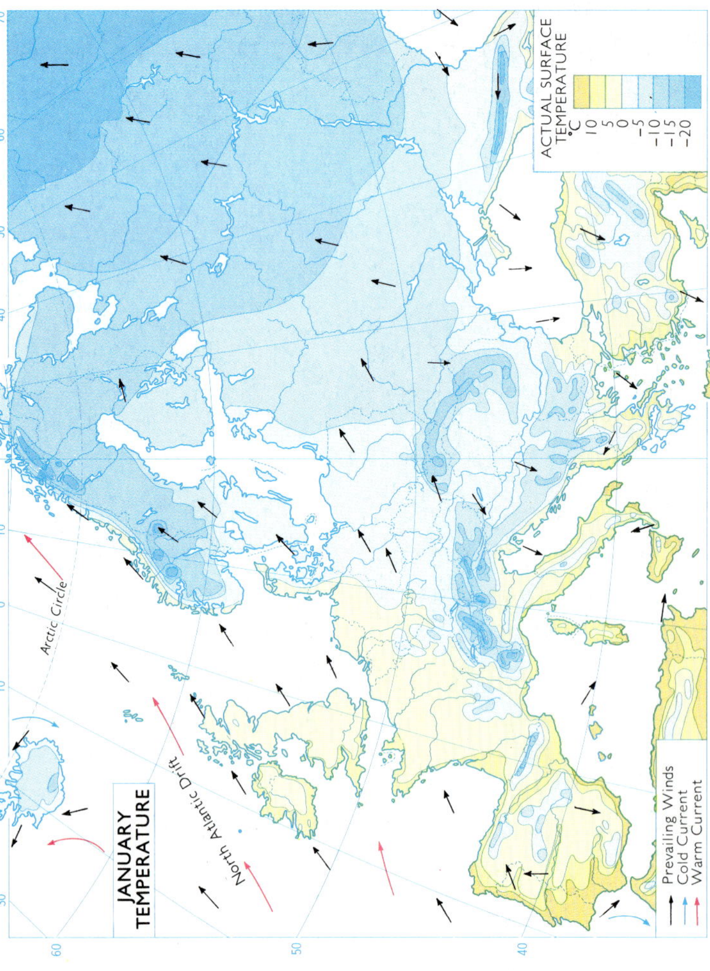
JANUARY TEMPERATURE
ACTUAL SURFACE TEMPERATURE °C
10
5
0
−5
−10
−15
−20
Prevailing Winds
Cold Current
Warm Current
North Atlantic Drift
Arctic Circle

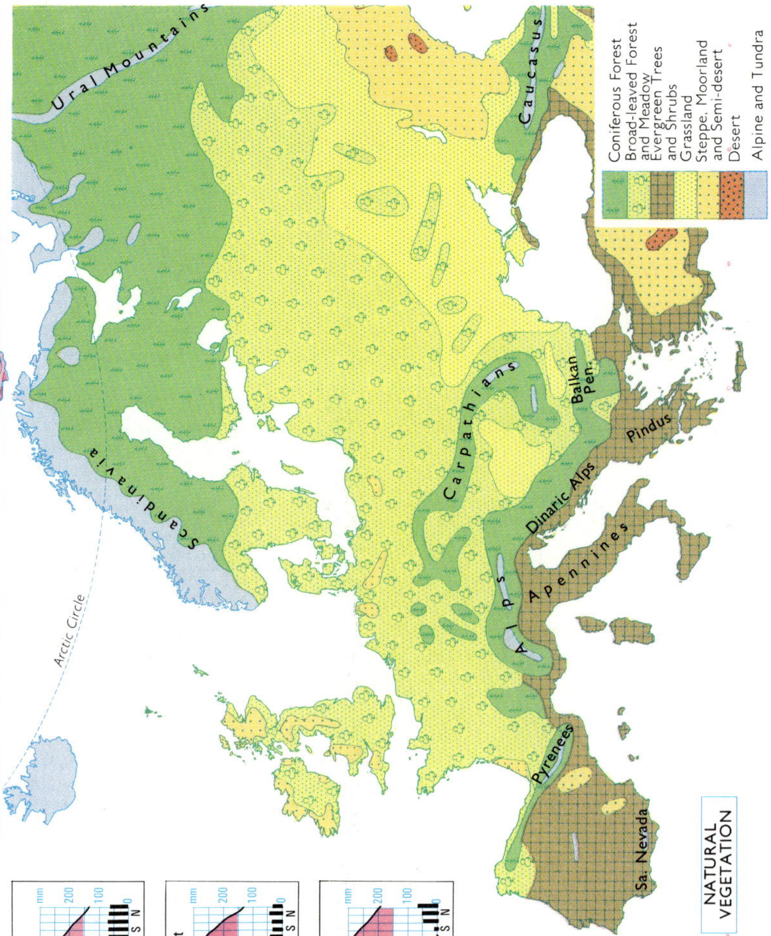
NATURAL VEGETATION
Coniferous Forest
Broad-leaved Forest and Meadow
Evergreen Trees and Shrubs
Grassland
Steppe, Moorland and Semi-desert
Desert
Alpine and Tundra
Ural Mountains
Caucasus
Scandinavia
Carpathians
Balkan Pen.
Pindus
Dinaric Alps
Apennines
Alps
Pyrenees
Sa. Nevada
Arctic Circle

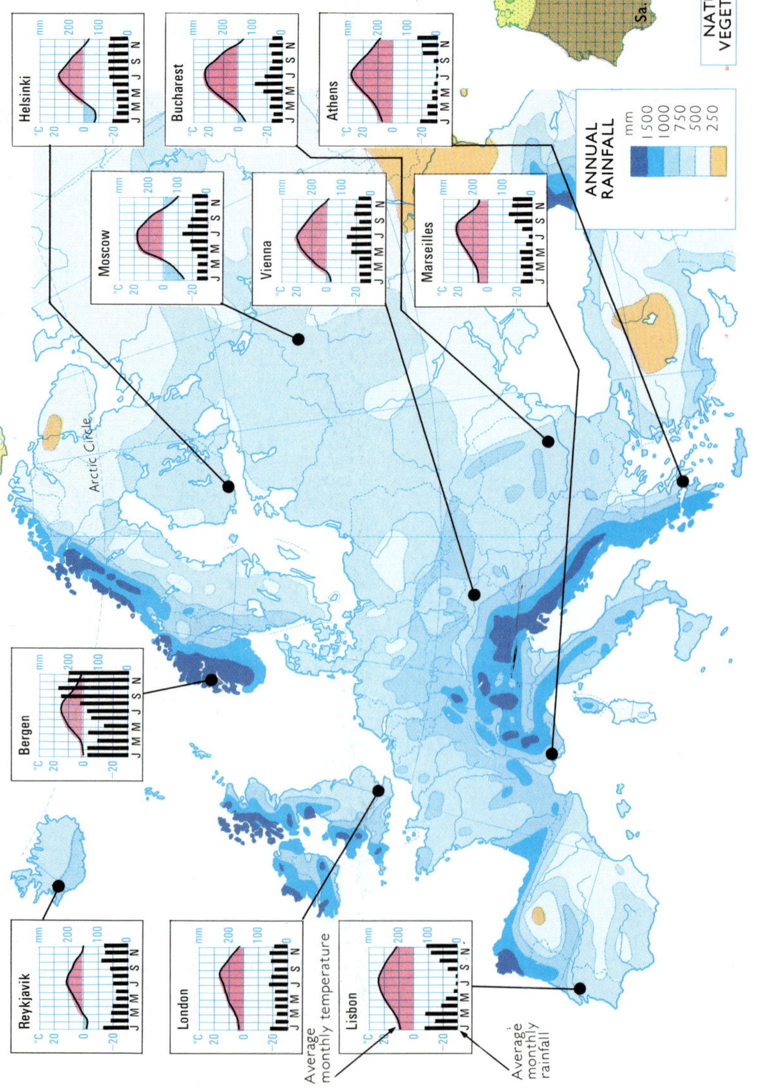
ANNUAL RAINFALL
mm
1500
1000
750
500
250
Arctic Circle
Helsinki
Bucharest
Athens
Moscow
Vienna
Marseilles
Bergen
Reykjavik
London
Lisbon
Average monthly temperature
Average monthly rainfall
°C
mm
J M M J S N

1:20 000 000

200 0 200 400 600 800 km

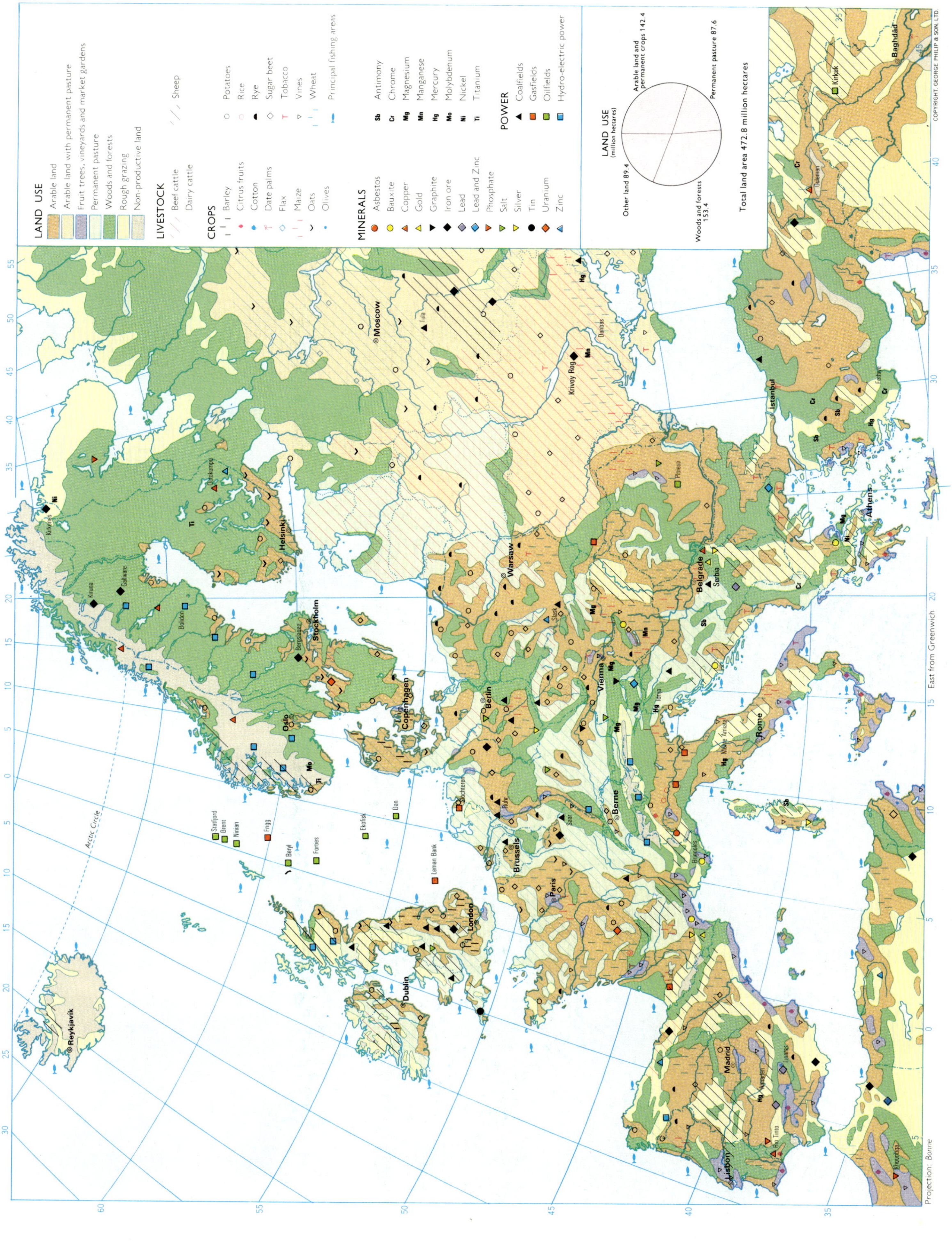

DENSITY OF POPULATION

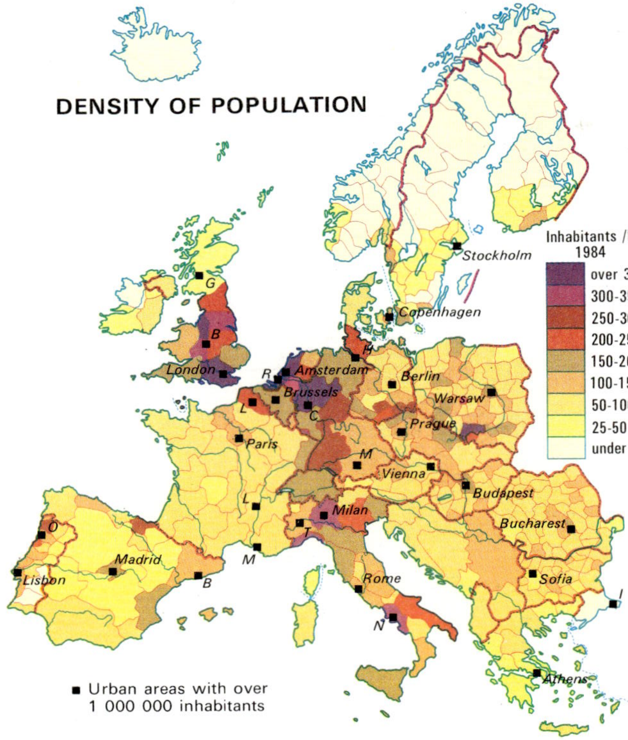

■ Urban areas with over 1 000 000 inhabitants

POPULATION CHANGE

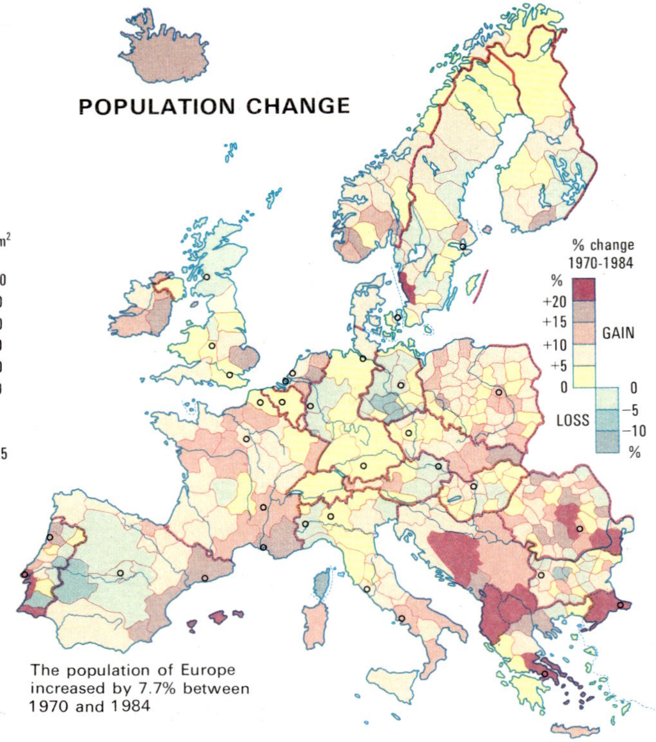

The population of Europe increased by 7.7% between 1970 and 1984

HEALTH

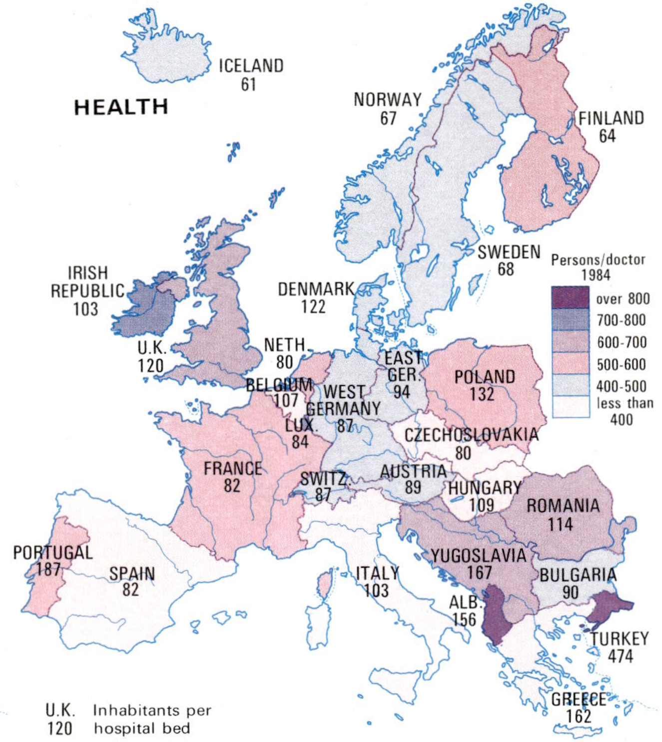

U.K. 120 Inhabitants per hospital bed

UNEMPLOYMENT

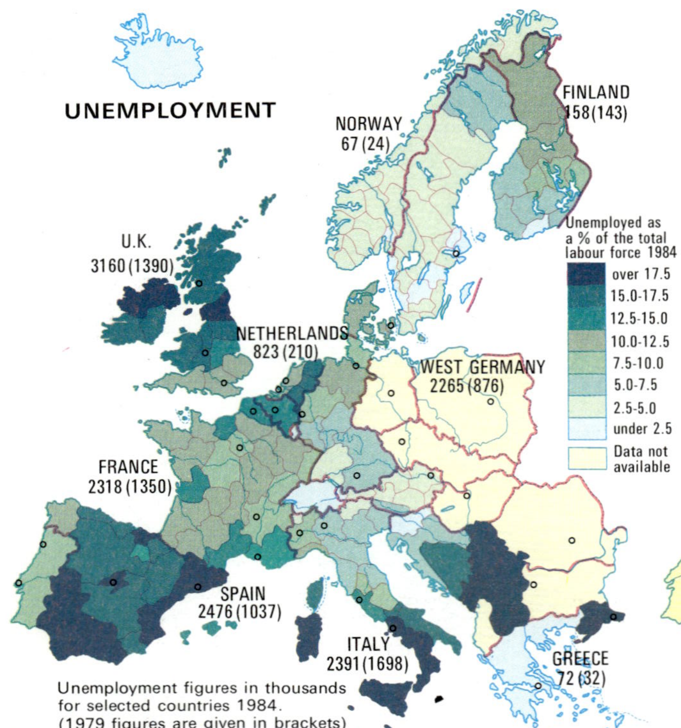

Unemployment figures in thousands for selected countries 1984. (1979 figures are given in brackets)

EMPLOYMENT BY ECONOMIC ACTIVITY

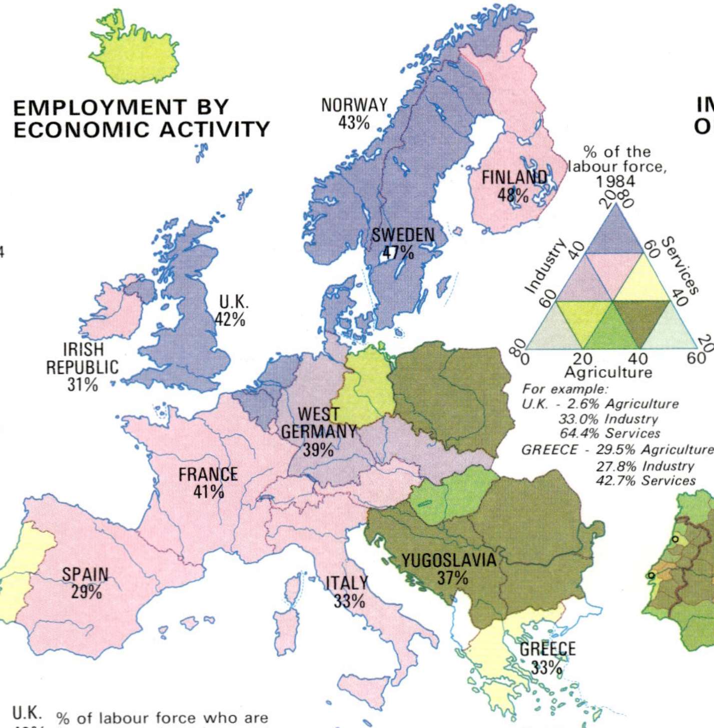

U.K. 42% % of labour force who are female for selected countries

IMPORTANCE OF AGRICULTURE

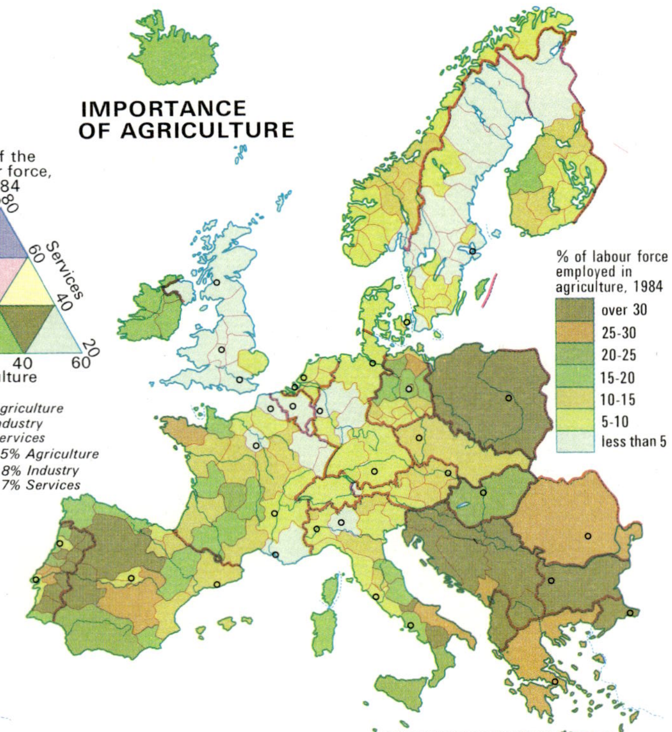

STANDARDS OF LIVING

Gross Domestic Product (GDP) is a measure of a country's total production of goods and services.

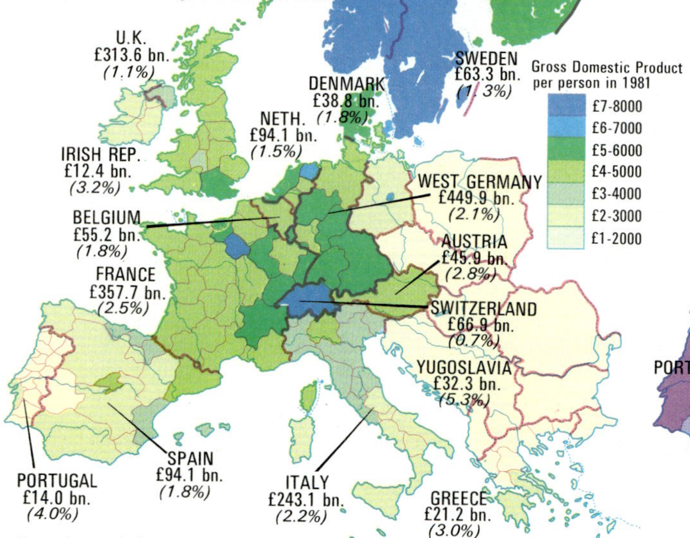

Gross Domestic Product in 1983 in £ billions
(% annual average growth 1973-83 is given in brackets)

INFLATION

The rate of inflation shows the increase in the price of a broad selection of household goods and services in each country.

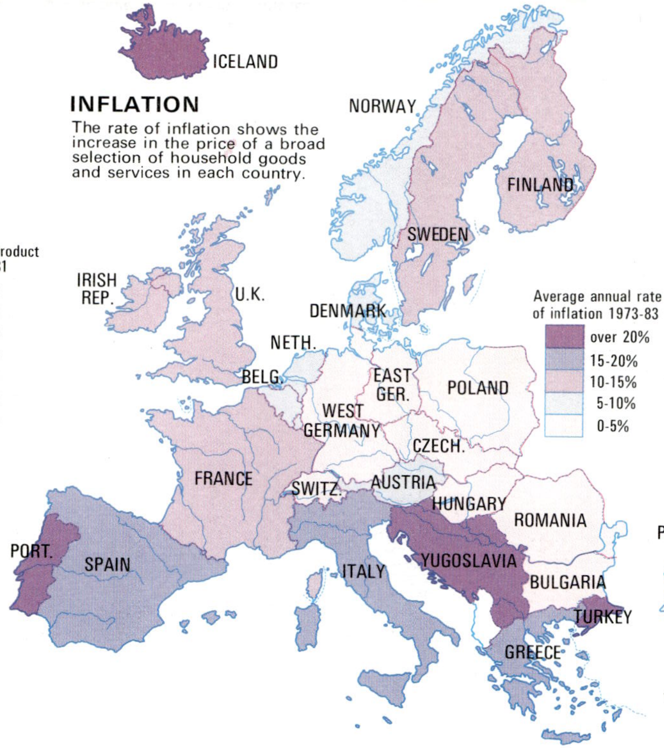

ENERGY CONSUMPTION

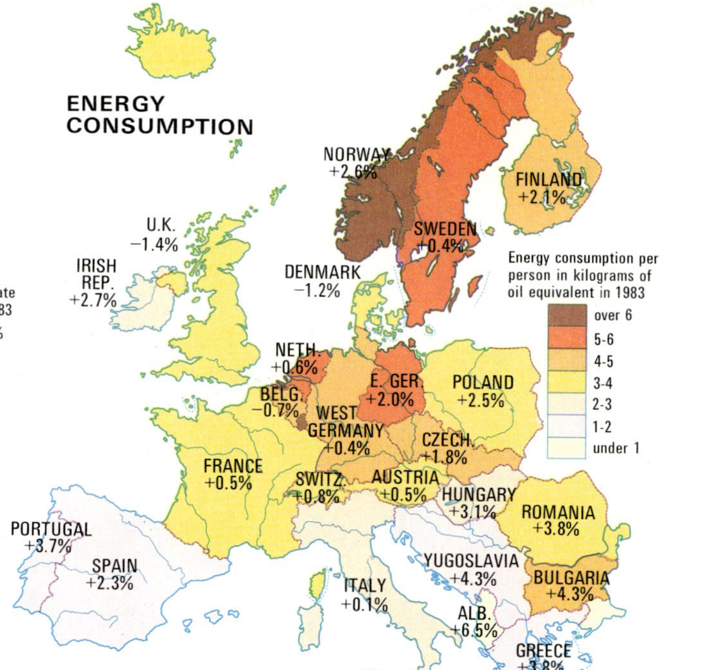

TRADE ORGANISATIONS

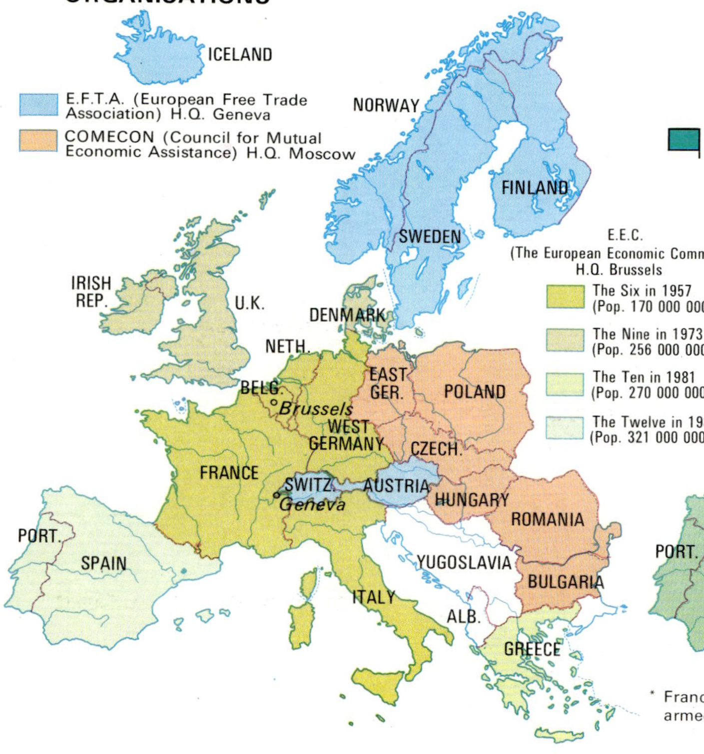

DEFENCE ORGANISATIONS

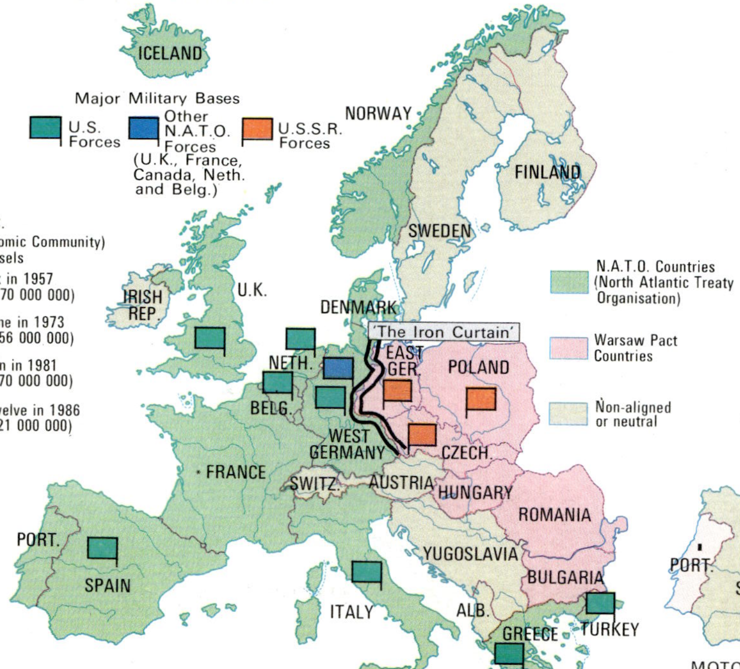

* France is a member of N.A.T.O. but its armed forces are not formally committed.

TRANSPORT

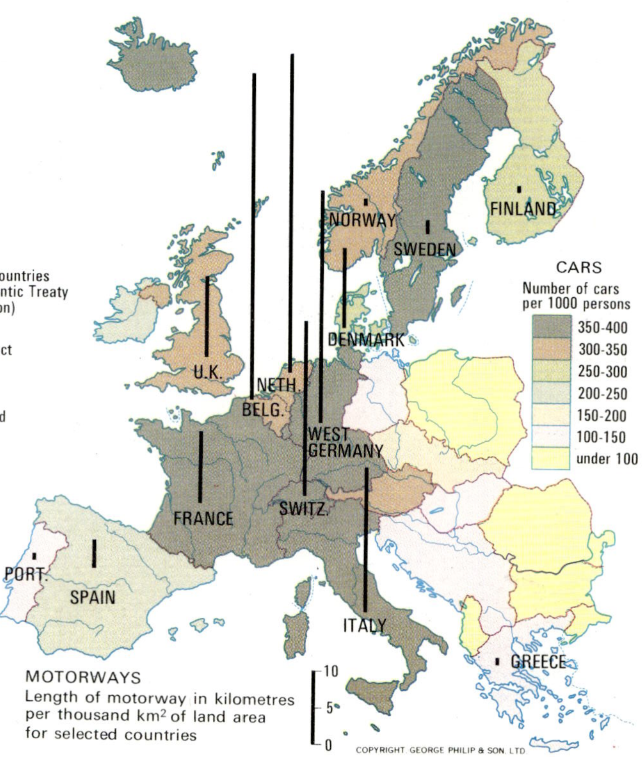

MOTORWAYS
Length of motorway in kilometres per thousand km^2 of land area for selected countries

	Population								Land			Agriculture		
	Total	Density	Birth Rate	Death Rate	Life Expectancy	Growth 1965-73	Growth 1973-83	Urban	Area	Arable	Forest	Agricultural Population	Index of Production	Food intake
	th.	persons per km²	per th. popn.	per th. popn.	yrs.	av. % per annum	av. % per annum	%	th. km²	th. km²	th. km²	% of total popn.	1974-76 = 100	calories per day
Albania	2 901	107	26	6	71	2.6	2.1	38	27	7	12	58	130	3 063
Austria	7 552	91	12	12	73	0.4	0.2	56	83	16	33	7.9	113	3 426
Belgium*	9 877	329	12	11	73	0.4	0.1	89	30	8.3	7.0	2.7	104	3 774
Bulgaria	8 961	81	14	11	70	0.6	0.1	67	111	42	39	30	118	3 622
Czechoslovakia	15 459	124	15	12	70	0.3	0.6	65	125	52	46	8.8	117	3 395
Denmark	5 112	122	10	11	74	0.7	0.2	85	42	27	4.9	6.1	120	3 548
Finland	4 882	16	14	9	73	0.2	0.4	60	305	24	233	11	115	3 079
France	54 947	101	14	10	75	0.8	0.4	80	546	186	146	7.5	115	3 530
Germany,East	16 671	157	14	13	71	0.5	0.1	76	106	50	30	8.7	102	3 689
Germany,West	61 181	251	10	11	75	0.7	0.1	86	244	75	73	3.3	113	3 351
Greece	9 896	76	14	9	75	0.5	1.1	64	131	39	26	35	105	3 668
Hungary	10 665	116	12	14	70	0.3	0.3	55	92	53	16	14	126	3 484
Iceland	239	2.3	18	7	77	1.6	0.8	89	100	0.1	1.2	10	108	3 274
Ireland	3 535	51	19	9	73	0.8	1.3	56	69	9.7	3.3	19	106	3 699
Italy	56 983	194	11	10	76	0.6	0.3	71	294	124	64	9.5	113	3 688
Luxembourg*	363	140	12	11	69	0.9	0.2	78	2.6					
Malta	380	1 267	15	8	71	0.1	1.8	85	0.3	0.1		4.5	152	2 843
Netherlands	14 420	424	12	8	76	1.1	0.7	52	34	8.6	2.9	4.7	123	3 618
Norway	4 140	13	12	10	77	0.8	0.4	55	308	8.4	83	6.7	117	3 392
Poland	36 914	121	19	10	71	0.7	0.9	59	305	148	87	28	97	3 479
Portugal	10 164	110	14	9	71	0.2	1.1	30	92	36	36	24	84	3 205
Romania	22 897	100	15	10	71	1.2	0.8	51	230	105	63	45	117	3 346
Spain	38 717	76	13	7	75	1.0	1.0	76	499	205	156	15	108	3 296
Sweden	8 337	20	11	11	78	0.7	0.2	85	412	30	264	4.3	102	3 146
Switzerland	6 442	161	11	9	79	1.2	0.2	59	40	4.1	11	4.6	116	3 455
U.K.	55 624	230	13	12	74	0.4	0.1	91	242	70	21	1.8	120	3 249
Yugoslavia	22 963	90	17	10	69	0.9	0.8	45	255	78	93	34	116	3 550
U.S.S.R.	275 000	12	20	10	69	0.9	0.9	65	22 272	2 323	9 200	15	108	3 360

*Many figures for Luxembourg included in Belgium.

Population. This is the United Nations' estimate for the mid-year 1984 (thousands).

Population density. This is the quoted population total divided by the quoted land area (persons per square kilometre).

Birth Rates and Death Rates. These are the registered or United Nations' estimated rates per thousand population.

Life Expectancy. This figure indicates the number of years that a child born today can expect to live if the levels of death of today last throughout its life. The figure is an average of that for men and women. The figure for women is usually higher than that for men (U.K. male 70, female 76 years).

Population Growth. This shows the average annual percentage change in population for two periods 1965-1973 and 1973-1983.

Urbanization. This is the percentage of the total population living in urban areas. The definition of urban is that of the individual nation and usually includes quite small towns.

Land Area. This is the total area of the country minus the area covered by major lakes and rivers (thousand square kilometres).

Arable Land and Permanent Crops. This excludes fallow land but includes temporary pasture (thousand square kilometres).

Forest and Woodland. This includes natural and planted woodland and land recently cleared of timber which will be replanted (thousand square kilometres).

Agricultural Population. This is the percentage of the economically active population working in agriculture. It includes those people working also in forestry, hunting and fishing.

Index of Agricultural Production. The base period for this index is 1974-1976 and it shows the level of production in each country in 1983 in comparision with that of the earlier period. Only edible crops and meat are included.

Food Supply. The figures are the average intake per person in calories per day in the period 1979-1981.

Trade		Education		Health	Energy	Consumer Price Index	G.N.P		G.D.P. Part formed by		Loans & Debt		
Imports	Exports	Primary	Secondary	Popn. per doctor	Consumption in kgs of oil equiv. per capita	1970 = 100	US$ per capita	Growth per capita % per yr. 1973-82	Agric.	Indust.	end 1983 US$ millions	as % of GNP	
US$ per capita		% of age group							%				
		100	66		982								Albania
2 598	2 083	99	74	400	3 083	234	9 210	2.7	4	31	181	0.3	Austria
5 395	5 049	98	94	400	4 401	286	9 160	1.6	2	28	410	0.6	Belgium*
1 414	1 432	100	82	410	4 390		3 800		19	48			Bulgaria
1 105	1 112	89	46	360	4 691	123	5 000		7	61			Czechoslovakia
3 322	3 196	98	100	480	3 061	376	11 490	1.2	5	18	449	0.9	Denmark
2 549	2 768	98	98	530	4 649	443	10 440	2.2	8	29	178	0.4	Finland
1 888	1 698	100	87	580	3 429	398	10 390	2.2	4	28	3 790	0.8	France
1 376	1 490	94	88	520	5 370		6 800		9	73			Germany,East
2 489	2 758	100	94	450	4 156	199	11 420	2.3	2	36	2 767	0.5	Germany,West
960	486	100	81	430	1 790	959	3 970	2.4	16	21			Greece
760	803	100	73	400	2 968	216	2 150	5.6	15	37			Hungary
3 417	3 033	100		488	3 364	9 898	10 270	1.7					Iceland
2 730	2 720	100	95	780	2 354	640	4 810	1.3	11	35			Ireland
1 414	1 292	100	74	340	2 458	708	6 350	2.0	6	35	1 105	0.3	Italy
		100		495	9 000	266	12 190	2.3	2	33			Luxembourg*
1 887	1 037	100		383	1 180	99	3 710	9.1	3	37			Malta
4 309	4 569	98	98	540	5 397	249	9 910	0.9	4	26	1 268	1.0	Netherlands
3 355	4 568	99	95	520	8 087	346	13 820	3.2	4	35	526	1.0	Norway
269	304	100	75	570	3 133	383	3 700		30	42			Poland
767	510	100	50	540	1 194	637	2 190	1.9	8	32			Portugal
435	578	100	71	680	3 305		2 500		16	57			Romania
744	608	100	88	450	1 858	732	4 800	0.8	7	27			Spain
3 159	3 518	99	85	490	5 821	373	12 400	0.8	3	24	737	0.8	Sweden
4 577	4 016	100		410	3 794	200	16 390	0.8			286	0.3	Switzerland
1 775	1 628	100	83	650	3 461	515	9 050	1.0	2	29	1 432	0.3	U.K.
522	447	100	83	550	1 903	3 368	2 570	4.3	14	42			Yugoslavia
293	333	100	97	270	4 505		5 300		15	51			U.S.S.R.

Andorra, Land 0.5/Popn. 34; Faeroe Is. 1.4/45; Gibraltar 0.01/28; Liechtenstein 0.2/27; Monaco 0.0015/27; San Marino 0.06/22; Svalbard 62/3.

Trade. The trade figures are normally for the year 1983 or 1984. The total trade figures have been divided by the population and are a measure of the country's external trade (U.S. $ per capita).

Education. The ages of primary school are taken to be 6-11 years and secondary school 12-17 years. The percentage of the total school age group in this type of education is shown.

Energy. All forms of energy have been converted to their equivalent in oil. Firewood and other traditional forms used in developing countries are not included and so the energy consumption in those countries is understated (kilograms of oil equivalent per capita).

Consumer Price Index. The base year is 1970 which is 100 and the level of consumer prices in 1984 or 1985 are shown in relation to the base year. It is a measure of inflation.

G.N.P. (Gross National Product) This figure is an estimate of the average production per person measured in U.S. dollars and for 1983. The G.N.P. measures the value of goods and services produced in a country, plus the balance, positive or negative, of income from abroad, for example investments, interest on capital, money returned from foreign labour, etc. The rate of change is the average annual percentage change during the period 1973-1982 in the G.D.P. The G.D.P. (Gross Domestic Product) is the G.N.P. minus the foreign balances. The adjoining two columns show the percentage contribution to the G.D.P. made by the agricultural and mining and manufacturing sectors.

Loans and Debt. This figure in millions of U.S. dollars shows the external public debt at the end of 1983. This is then shown as a percentage of the annual G.N.P. The figures in red show official development assistance made by the developed countries and also as a percentage of the donor country's G.N.P.

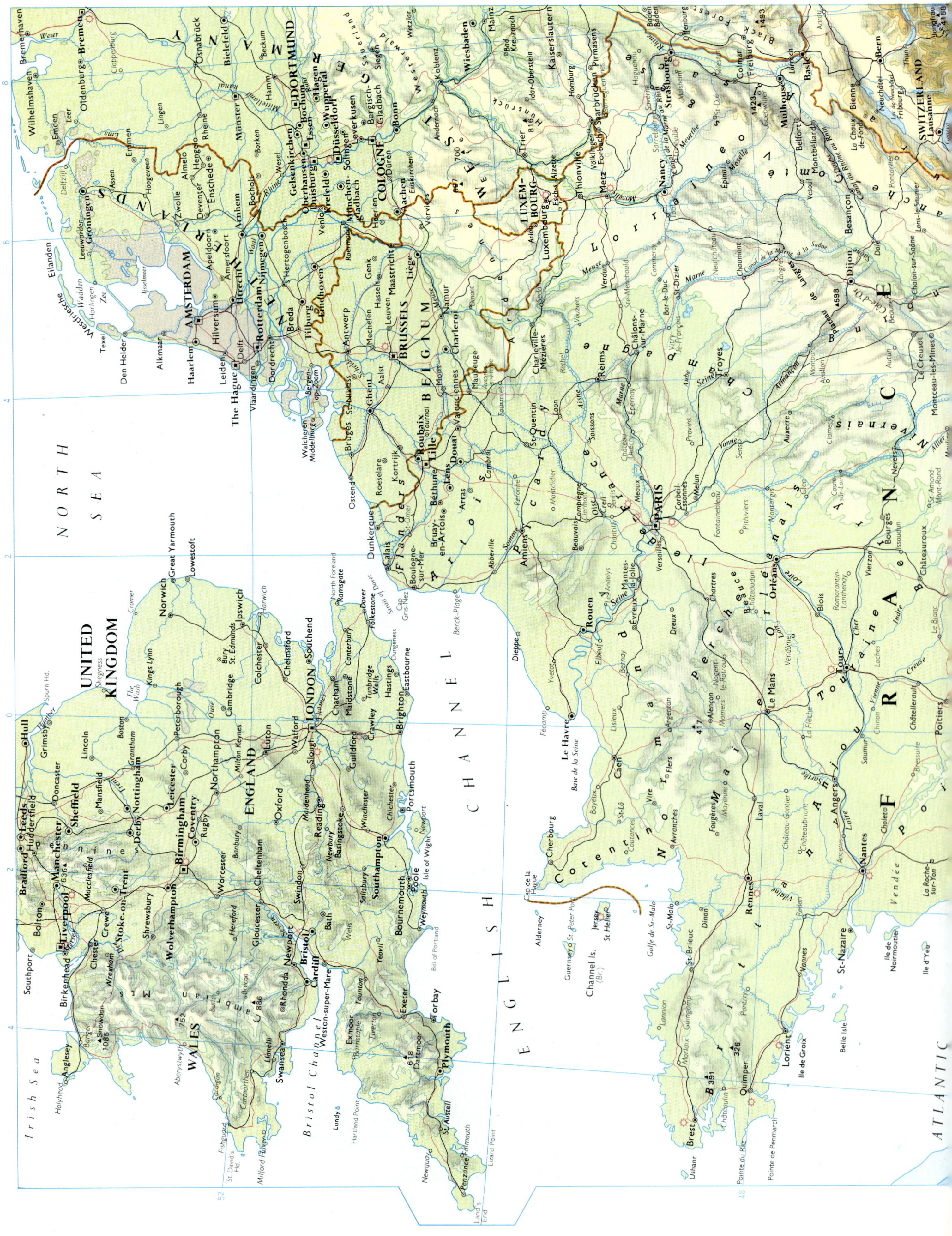
NORTH SEA
ENGLISH CHANNEL
UNITED KINGDOM
ENGLAND
WALES
Irish Sea
Bristol Channel
LONDON
PARIS
BRUSSELS
AMSTERDAM
COLOGNE
DORTMUND
LUXEMBOURG
SWITZERLAND
BELGIUM
FRANCE
ATLANTIC
Channel Is. (Br.)

1:4 000 000

20 0 20 40 60 80 100 120 km

LOW COUNTRIES AND LOWER RHINE

1:2 000 000

Projection: Conical with two standard parallels

East from Greenwich

1:5 000 000

50 0 50 100 150 200 km

LONDON
Bristol
Southampton
Plymouth
Portsmouth
Brighton
English Channel
Bay of Biscay
The Hague
Amsterdam
Rotterdam
NETH.
BELGIUM
Brussels
Antwerp
Ghent
Lille
Cologne
Düsseldorf
Essen
Dortmund
GERMANY
Frankfurt
Wiesbaden
Koblenz
Bonn
Aachen
Liège
LUX.
Mainz
Mannheim
Heidelberg
Karlsruhe
Stuttgart
Nürnberg
Würzburg
Regensburg
Augsburg
Munich
Hanover
Brunswick
Magdeburg
Münster
Halle
Leipzig
Dresden
Erfurt
Karl Marx Stadt
Prague
Plzen
BERLIN
Potsdam
Linz
Salzburg
Innsbruck
Klagenfurt
PARIS
Versailles
Rouen
Le Havre
Caen
Cherbourg
Brest
Rennes
Le Mans
Angers
Nantes
Tours
Orleans
Reims
Amiens
Nancy
Strasbourg
Troyes
Dijon
FRANCE
Limoges
Bordeaux
Clermont Ferrand
St. Étienne
Lyons
Grenoble
Avignon
Nîmes
Montpellier
Beziers
Toulouse
Perpignan
Marseilles
Toulon
Cannes
Nice
Basle
Zürich
Bern
Geneva
SWITZERLAND
Lausanne
Freiburg
Turin
Milan
Novara
Como
Bergamo
Brescia
Verona
Vicenza
Padua
Venice
Trieste
Rijeka
Ljubljana
Udine
Bolzano
Genoa
Alessandria
Parma
Reggio
Modena
Bologna
Ferrara
Ravenna
Forlì
Rimini
San Marino
La Spezia
Pisa
Leghorn
Florence
Ancona
Perugia
ROME
Pescara
Naples
Salerno
Corsica
Ajaccio
Bastia
Sardinia
Sassari
Cagliari
Ligurian Sea
Tyrrhenian Sea
ADRIATIC
APENNINES
Palermo
Messina
Catania
Sicily
Lipari Is.
MALTA
Gozo
Valletta
MADRID
SPAIN
PORTUGAL
Lisbon
Oporto
Coimbra
La Coruña
Ferrol
Santiago
Vigo
Orense
Oviedo
Gijón
Santander
Bilbao
San Sebastián
León
Cantabrian Mts.
Burgos
Vitoria
Pamplona
Pyrenees
Valladolid
Salamanca
Zaragoza
Lérida
Barcelona
Tarragona
Castellón
Valencia
Albacete
Alicante
Murcia
Cartagena
Lorca
Almería
Granada
Jaén
Málaga
Córdoba
Linares
Sierra Morena
Seville
Huelva
Cádiz
Jerez
Badajoz
Cáceres
Gibraltar (Br.)
Tangier
Ceuta (Sp.)
Balearic Is.
Mallorca (Majorca)
Menorca (Minorca)
Ibiza
Palma
Formentera
MEDITERRANEAN
Algiers
Oran
Bejaia
Skikda
Annaba
Constantine
Tunis
Sousse
Sfax
Djerba
Gabès
Kairouan
Tlemcen
Sidi-Bel-Abbès
Oujda
Fès
Meknès
Rabat
MOROCCO
Great Atlas
ALGERIA
TUNISIA
Saharan Atlas
Biskra
Touggourt
Ghardaïa
Ouargla
Hassi Messaoud
Béchar
Tripoli
Misratah
Tripolitania
Pantelleria (It.)
Lampedusa (It.)
Projection: Conical with two standard parallels.
West from Greenwich
East from Greenwich

1:10 000 000

100 0 100 200 300 400 km

--- Division between Greeks and Turks in Cyprus; Turks to the North.

Projection: Conical with two standard parallels

1:5 000 000

50 0 50 100 150 200 km

Projection: Conical with two standard parallels

East from Greenwich

1:5 000 000

50 0 50 100 150 200 km

BARENTS SEA
NORWEGIAN SEA
U.S.S.R.
FINNMARK
TROMS
NORDLAND
NORRBOTTEN
VÄSTERBOTTEN
LAPPI
OULU
KUOPIO
KESKI-SUOMI
MIKKELI
POHJOIS-KARJALA
VAASA
JÄMTLAND
VÄSTERNORRLAND
NORD-TRØNDELAG
SØR-TRØNDELAG
MØRE OG ROMSDAL
SOGN OG FJORDANE
HEDMARK
GULF OF BOTHNIA
Arctic Circle
Murmansk
Kandalaksha
Kandalaksha Gulf
Nikel
Kirkenes
Vadsø
Varanger Fjord
Tana Fjord
Lakse Fjord
Porsangen
North Cape
Hammerfest
Sørøya
Seiland
Lopphavet
Kvænangen
Tromsø
Senja
Vesterålen
Lofoten
Langøy
Vest Fjorden
Narvik
Kiruna
Gällivare
Malmberget
Torneträsk
Kebnekaise
Stora Lulevatten
Sarektjåkkå
Jokkmokk
Boden
Luleå
Piteå
Skellefteå
Umeå
Lycksele
Storuman
Vilhelmina
Strömsund
Östersund
Storsjön
Sundsvall
Hudiksvall
Härnösand
Kramfors
Örnsköldsvik
Kvarken
Vaasa
Kokkola (Gamlakarleby)
Pietarsaari
Oulu
Kemi
Tornio
Haparanda
Rovaniemi
Kemijärvi
Inari
Inarijärvi
Porttipahta Res.
Lokka Res.
Kajaani
Iisalmi
Kuopio
Varkaus
Savonlinna
Joensuu
Nurmes
Jyväskylä
Mikkeli
Kuusamo
Bodø
Fauske
Mosjøen
Mo i Rana
Svartisen
Vefsna
Vega
Namsos
Steinkjer
Levanger
Trondheim
Frohavet
Hitra
Kristiansund
Molde
Ålesund
Florø
Femund
Sylarna
Orkla
Gaula
Dombås
Snøhetta
Jotunheimen
Galdhøpiggen
Sognefjorden
Stadlandet
ICELAND
At the same scale as main map
Reykjavík
Keflavík
Hafnarfjörður
Akranes
Akureyri
Húsavík
Ísafjörður
Siglufjörður
Sauðárkrókur
Vestmannaeyjar
Surtsey
Vatnajökull
Hofsjökull
Langjökull
Mýrdalsjökull
Snæfellsjökull
Hvannadalshnúkur
Hekla
Faxaflói
Breiðafjörður
Húnaflói
Skagafjörður
Eyjafjörður
Vopnafjörður
Seyðisfjörður
Grímsey
Arctic Circle
West from Greenwich

1: 6 000 000

50 0 50 100 150 200 250 km

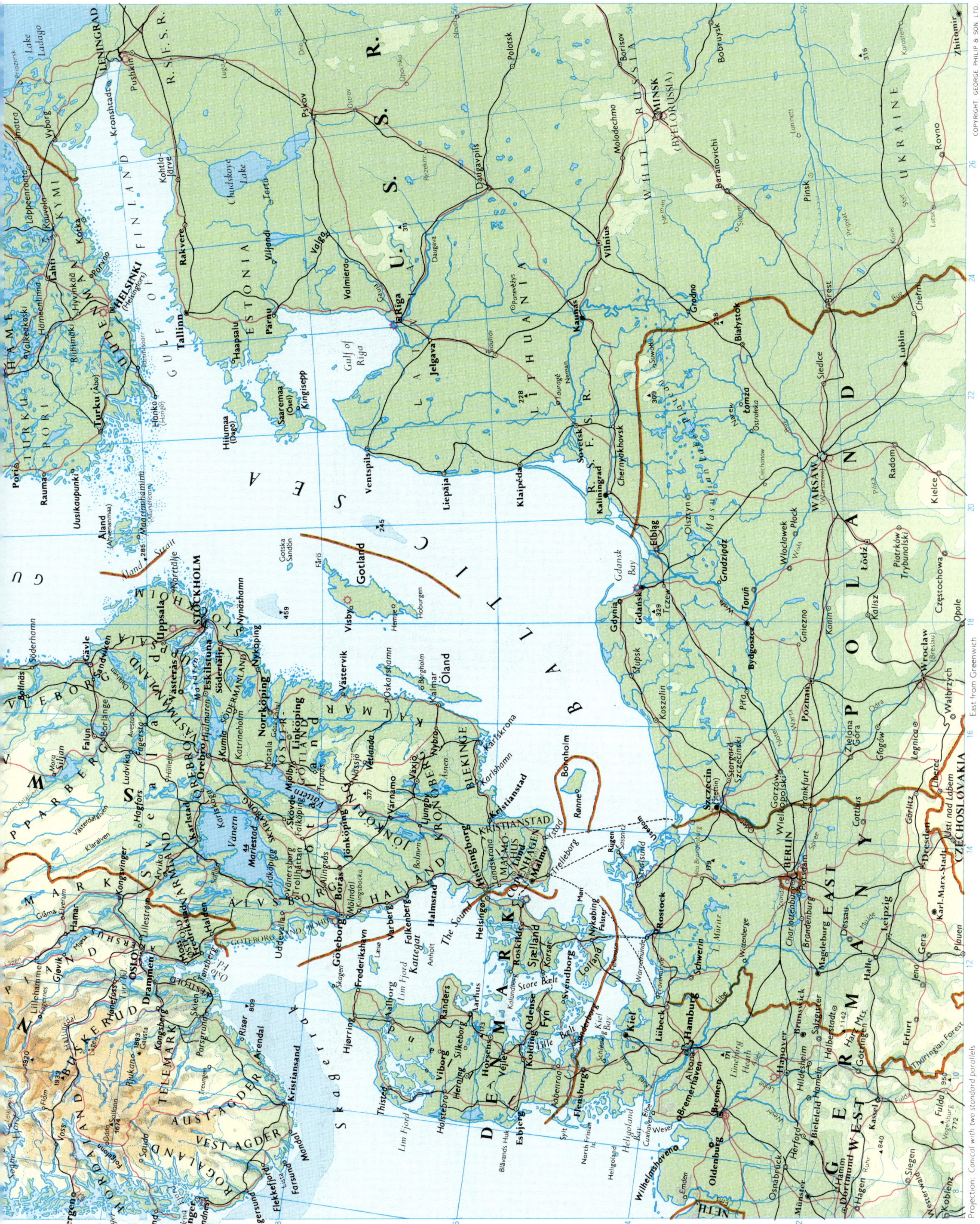

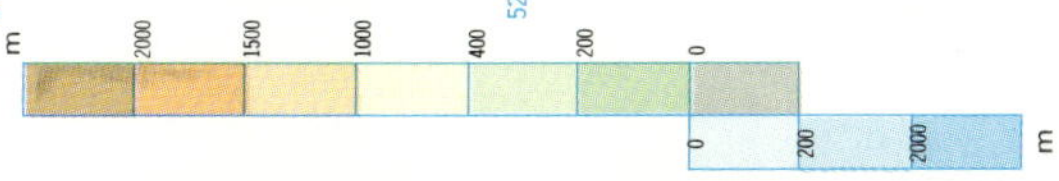

Vorkuta
Salekhard
Nizhniy Tagil
SVERDLOVSK
Zlatoust
Miass
Magnitogorsk
Beloretsk
Orsk
Novotroitsk
UFA
Orenburg
Perm
Solikamsk
Berezniki
Serov
Krasnoturinsk
Kolguyev
Kanin Pen.
Chesha B.
Timan Ridge
Pechora
Ust Tsilma
Naryan-Mar
Bolshezemelsk Tundra
Malozemelsk Tundra
Ukhta
Syktyvkar
Kotlas
Kirov
Glazov
Ustinov (Izhevsk)
Votkinsk
Sarapul
Brezhnev
KAZAN
Cheboksary
Yoshkar Ola
Ulyanovsk
Syzran
Tolyatti
KUYBYSHEV
Novokuybyshevsk
Saratov
Engels
Penza
Saransk
Arkhangelsk (Archangel)
Severodvinsk (Molotovsk)
Mezen
White Sea
Kola Pen.
Murmansk
Rybachi Pen.
Kandalaksha
Monchegorsk
Kirovsk
Kem
Belomorsk
Petrozavodsk
L. Onega
L. Ladoga
Vologda
Cherepovets
Rybinsk Reservoir
Andropov (Rybinsk)
Yaroslavl
Kostroma
Ivanovo
GORKI
Dzerzhinsk
Vladimir
Ryazan
Tambov
Lipetsk
Voronezh
Tula
Kaluga
Orel
Kursk
Bryansk
MOSCOW
Kalinin
Smolensk
Vitebsk
Mogilev
Gomel
MINSK
Brest
Vilnius
Kaunas
Riga
Tallinn
ESTONIA
LATVIA
LITHUANIA
Pskov
Novgorod
LENINGRAD
Vyborg
Helsinki
Turku
Tampere
FINLAND
Oulu
Gulf of Bothnia
G. of Finland
G. of Riga
Stockholm
Hiiumaa
Saaremaa
Åland Is. (Ahvenanmaa)
Klaipeda (Memel)
Liepaja
Kaliningrad (Königsberg)
WARSAW (Warszawa)
POLAND
Bialystok
Lublin
SWEDEN
NORWAY
Luleå
Kiruna
Gällivare
L. Inari
U r a l M o u n t a i n s
R U S S I A N S O V I E T F E D E R A T I V E S O C I A L I S T R E P U B L I C
WHITE RUSSIA (BYELORUSSIA)
Pripyat Marshes
Valdai Hills
Arctic Circle

1:10 000 000

100 0 100 200 300 400 km

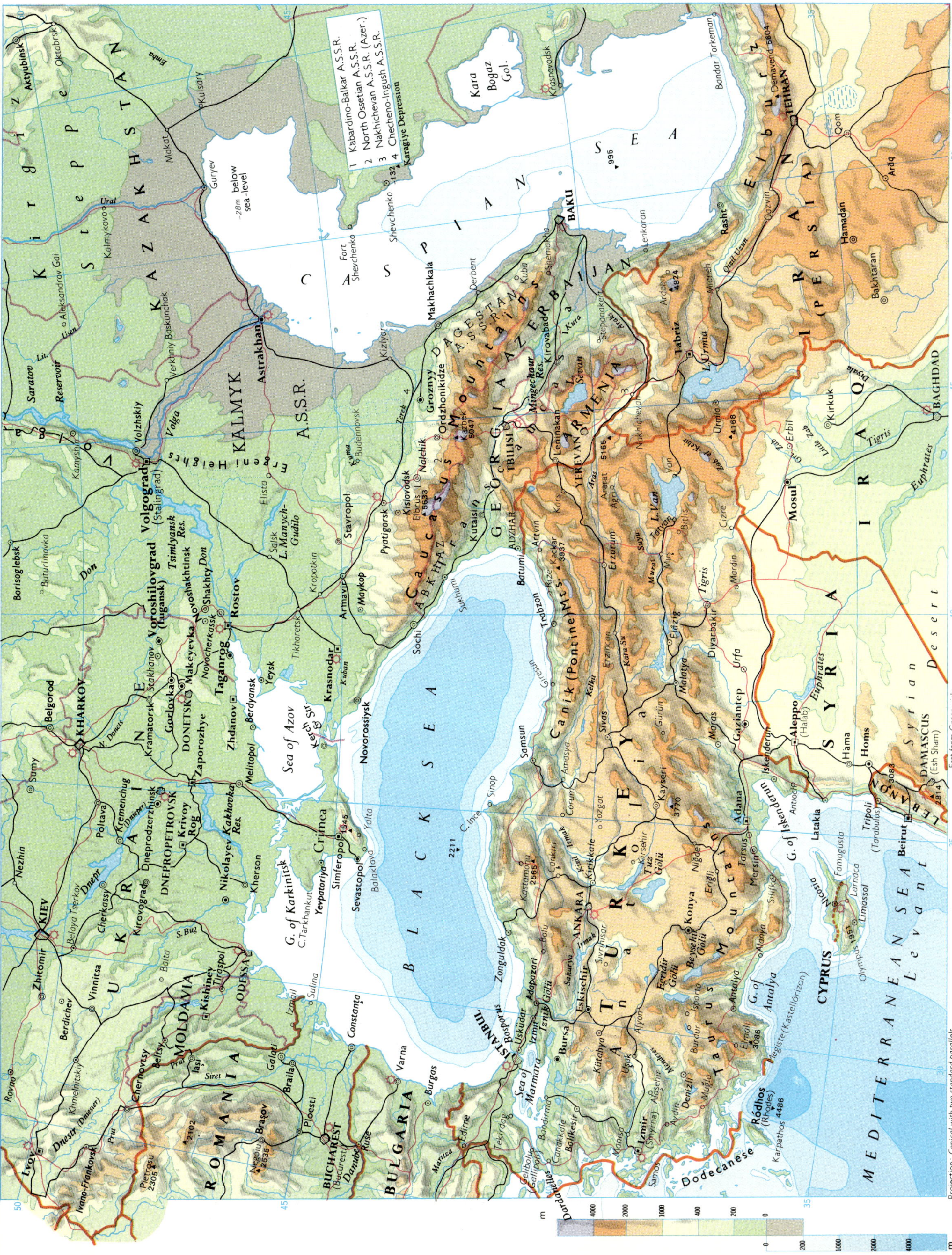

East from Greenwich

Projection: Conical with two standard parallels

Division between Greeks and Turks in Cyprus, Turks to the North

Projection: Conical Orthomorphic with two standard parallels

1:20 000 000

200 0 200 400 600 800 km

1:50 000 000

500 0 500 1000 1500 2000 km

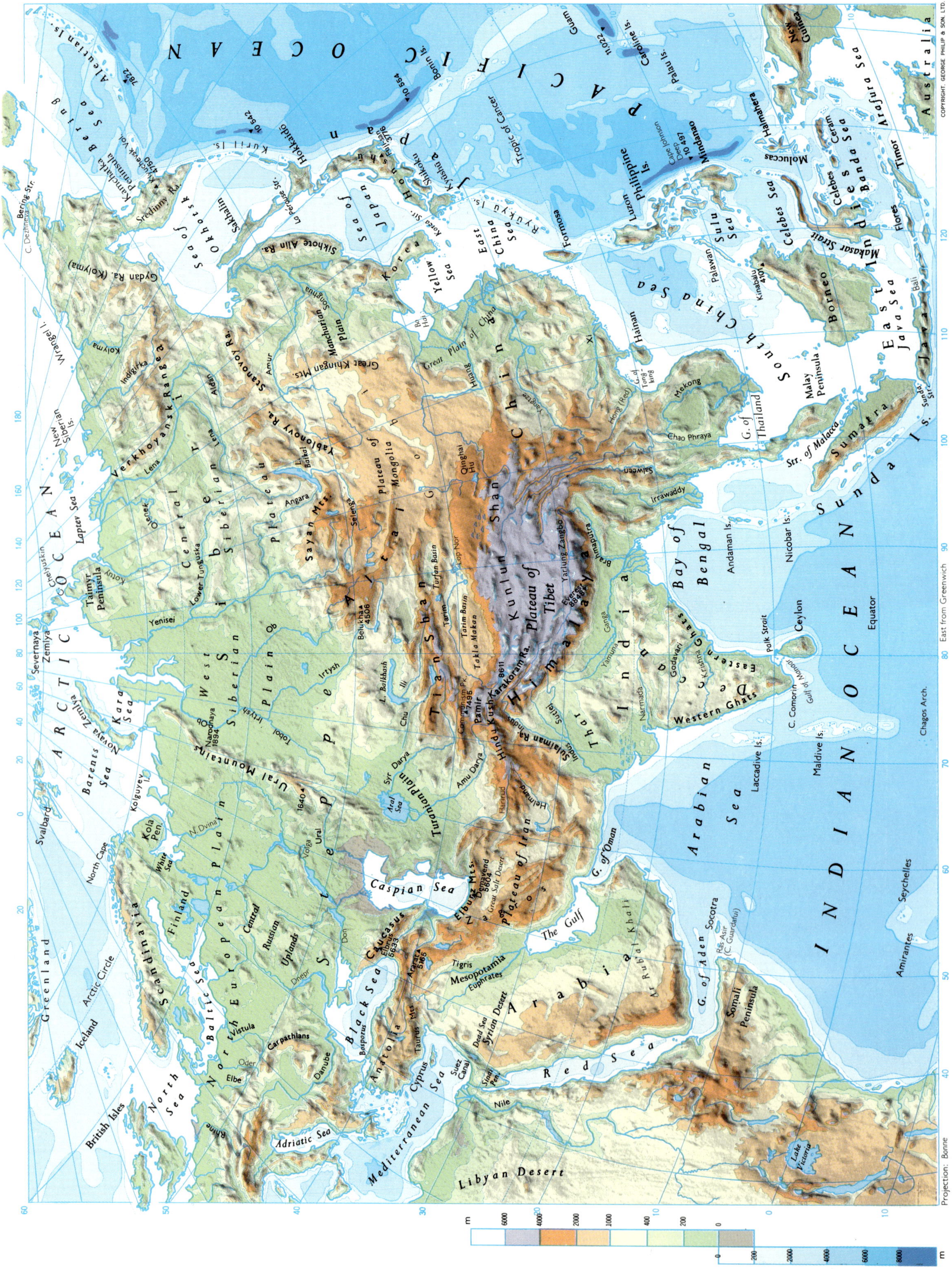

1:50 000 000

500 0 500 1000 1500 2000 km

Peking Capital Cities

Projection: Bonne

East from Greenwich

1:100 000 000

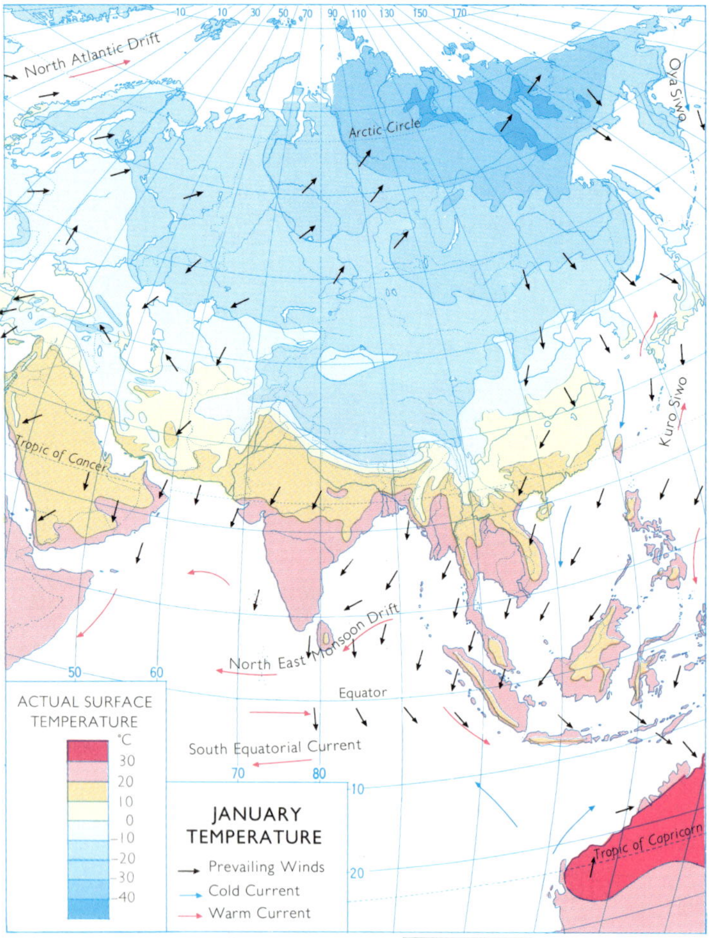

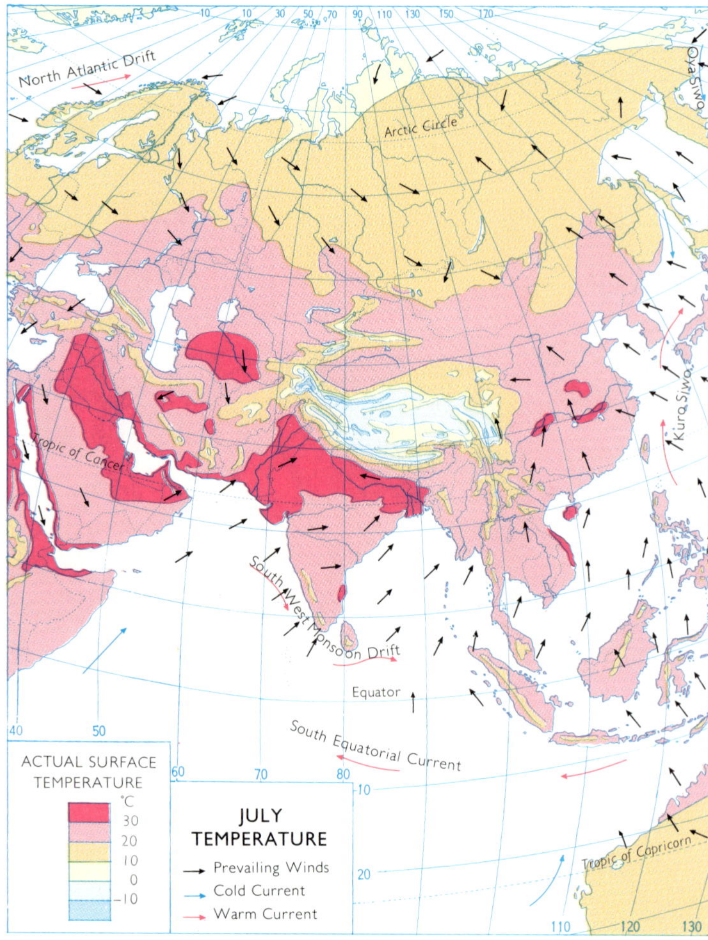

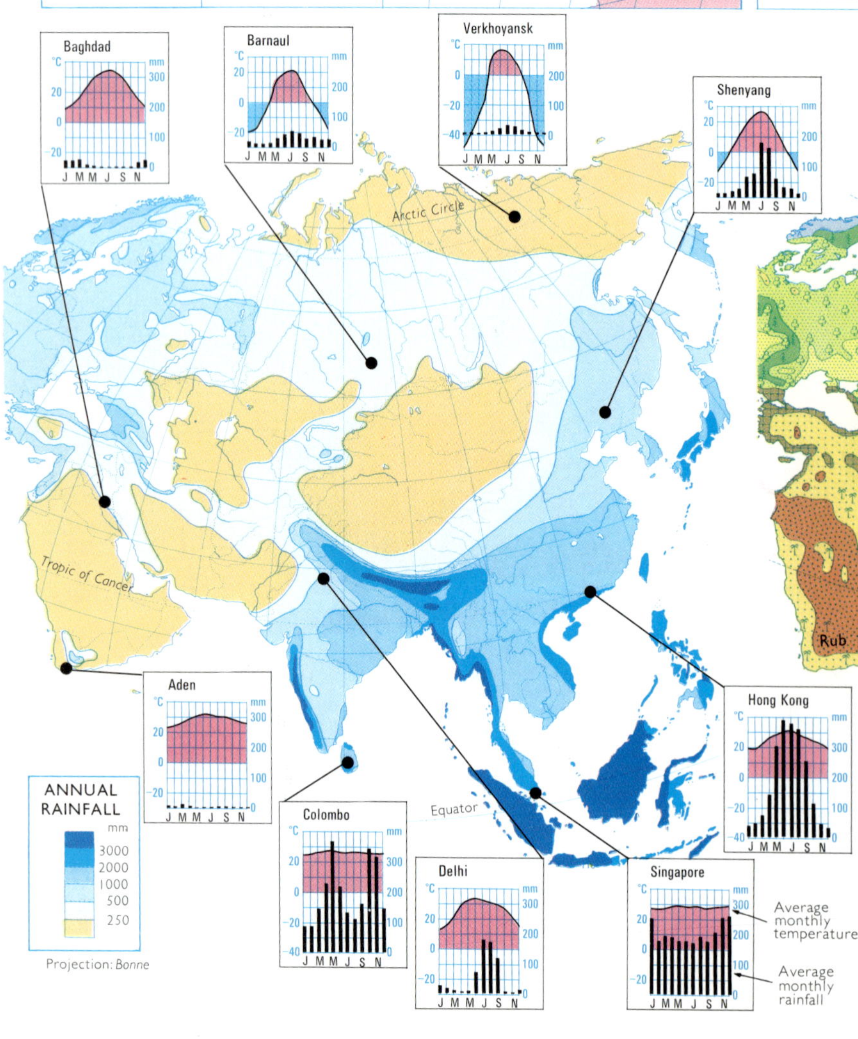

Projection: *Bonne*

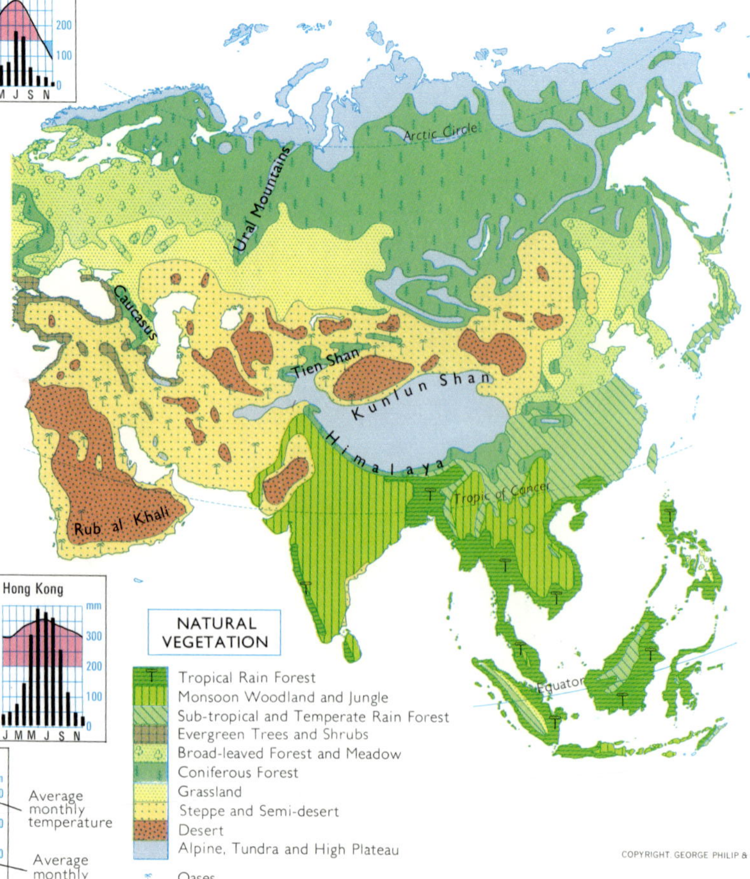

1:50 000 000

500 0 500 1000 1500 2000 km

Projection: Bonne

	Population								Land			Agriculture		
	Total	Density	Birth Rate	Death Rate	Life Expectancy	Growth 1965-73	Growth 1973-83	Urban	Area	Arable	Forest	Agricultural Population	Index of Production	Food intake
Asia	th.	persons per km²	per th. popn.		yrs.	av. % per annum		%	th. km²	th. km²	th. km²	% of total popn.	1974-76 = 100	calories per day
Afghanistan	17 672	27	48	22	36	2.3	2.6	17	648	81	19	77	115	2 055
Bangladesh	96 730	722	47	19	50	2.6	2.4	17	134	91	21	83	125	1 837
Burma	37 614	57	39	14	55	2.3	2.0	29	658	101	322	50	150	2 420
Cambodia	7 149	40	30	40	31	1.8			177	30	134	72	104	1 922
China	1 051 551	113	22	8	67	2.7	1.5	21	9 326	1 009	1 282	57	145	2 426
Cyprus	657	73	20	9	74		0.6		9	4.3	1.7	33	113	3 378
Hong Kong	5 364	5 364	14	5	76	2.0	2.5	92	1	0.1	0.1	2.1	67	2 771
India	746 742	251	34	12	55	2.3	2.3	24	2 973	1 695	675	61	132	2 056
Indonesia	159 895	88	36	15	54	2.1	2.3	24	1 812	196	1 218	57	140	2 373
Iran	43 414	27	43	12	60	3.3	3.1	53	1 636	137	180	36	116	2 834
Iraq	15 158	35	47	13	59	3.3	3.6	69	434	55	15	38	136	2 789
Israel	4 194	210	24	7	74	3.1	2.3	90	20	4.2	1.2	6.2	121	3 062
Japan	120 018	323	13	6	77	1.2	0.9	76	371	48	252	9.2	99	2 852
Jordan	3 375	35	48	10	64	3.0	2.7	72	97	4.1	0.4	24	136	2 498
Korea, North	19 630	164	33	8	65	2.8	2.5	62	120	23	90	43	138	2 995
Korea, South	40 578	414	23	6	67	2.2	1.6	62	98	22	66	35	122	3 056
Laos	4 315	19	43	17	44	1.4	2.2	15	231	8.9	128	72	150	1 927
Lebanon	2 644	264	30	9	65	2.6	0.3	78	10	2.9	0.7	7.9	123	2 995
Malaysia	15 204	46	31	7	67	2.6	2.4	31	329	43	219	45	127	2 518
Mongolia	1 820	1.1	37	8	63	3.1	2.8	54	1 565	13	152	45	111	2 757
Nepal	16 107	118	45	21	46	2.0	2.6	7	137	23	45	92	117	1 933
Pakistan	93 286	120	42	10	50	3.1	3.0	29	779	203	29	52	132	2 180
Philippines	53 351	179	34	8	64	2.9	2.7	39	298	118	122	44	133	2 405
Saudi Arabia	10 824	5	46	14	56	4.0	4.7	71	2 150	11	16	58	36	2 947
Singapore	2 529	4 215	16	5	73	1.8	1.3	100	0.6	0.007	0.003	1.9	75	3 165
Sri Lanka	15 606	240	26	6	69	2.0	1.7	26	65	22	24	52	124	2 255
Syria	9 934	54	46	9	67	3.4	3.3	48	184	58	4.9	46	166	3 010
Taiwan	19 012	528	20	5	72				36	8.9	1.9	22	121	2 811
Thailand	50 396	98	31	8	63	2.9	2.3	18	512	190	158	74	134	2 330
Turkey	48 265	63	35	10	63	2.5	2.2	45	771	273	202	50	121	3 002
Vietnam	58 307	179	39	12	64	3.1	2.7	20	325	61	102	69	136	2 034
Yemen, North	6 386	33	49	24	44	2.6	2.9	18	195	28	16	74	79	2 478
Yemen, South	2 225	6.6	48	21	46	2.1	2.2	37	333	2	24	57	101	2 276
U.S.S.R.†														
Oceania														
Australia	15 544	2	16	7	76	2.1	1.3	86	7 618	465	1 060	5.2	122	3 055
New Zealand	3 233	12	16	8	74	1.4	0.6	83	269	4.7	100	8.6	117	3 572
Papua New Guinea	3 601	8	43	16	54	2.5	2.1	14	452	3.7	322	81	122	2 074

† See in Europe

Population. This is the United Nations' estimate for the mid-year 1984 (thousands).

Population density. This is the quoted population total divided by the quoted land area (persons per square kilometre).

Birth Rates and Death Rates. These are the registered or United Nations' estimated rates per thousand population.

Life Expectancy. This figure indicates the number of years that a child born today can expect to live if the levels of death of today last throughout its life. The figure is an average of that for men and women. The figure for women is usually higher than that for men (U.K. male 70, female 76 years).

Population Growth. This shows the average annual percentage change in population for two periods 1965-1973 and 1973-1983.

Urbanization. This is the percentage of the total population living in urban areas. The definition of urban is that of the individual nation and usually includes quite small towns.

Land Area. This is the total area of the country minus the area covered by major lakes and rivers (thousand square kilometres).

Arable Land and Permanent Crops. This excludes fallow land but includes temporary pasture (thousand square kilometres).

Forest and Woodland. This includes natural and planted woodland and land recently cleared of timber which will be replanted (thousand square kilometres).

Agricultural Population. This is the percentage of the economically active population working in agriculture. It includes those people working also in forestry, hunting and fishing.

Index of Agricultural Production. The base period for this index is 1974-1976 and it shows the level of production in each country in 1983 in comparision with that of the earlier period. Only edible crops and meat are included.

Food Supply. The figures are the average intake per person in calories per day in the period 1979-1981.

Trade		Education		Health	Energy	Consumer Price Index	G.N.P.		G.D.P. Part formed by		Loans & Debt		
Imports	Exports	Primary	Secondary					Growth per capita	Agric.	Indust.			
US$ per capita		% of age group		Popn. per doctor	Consumption in kgs of oil equiv. per capita	1970 = 100	US$ per capita	% per yr. 1973-82	%		end 1983 US$ millions	as % of GNP	**Asia**
41	42	35	12	16 730	46				63	20			Afghanistan
21	10	60	15	7 810	36	642	130	3.2	48	8	4 185	38	Bangladesh
6	8	84	20	4 680	65	327	180	3.6	47	11	2 226	36	Burma
				20 000	2 093								Cambodia
19	21	100	35	1 740	455		290	4.5	42	43			China
2 067	871	84		1 060	2 000	182	3 720		9	20			Cyprus
5 329	5 283	100	67	1 210	1 647	350	6 000	6.8	1	27	224	0.8	Hong Kong
18	11	79	30	3 690	182	323	260	1.8	32	19	21 277	11	India
87	137	100	33	11 530	204	159	560	4.6	24	36	21 685	29	Indonesia
283	476	97	40	6 090	976	699			17	22			Iran
	668	109	59	1 800	763				7	53			Iraq
2 036	1 190	95	74	370	1 932	683th	5 630	0.2	6	29	15 149	70	Israel
1 137	1 148	100	92	780	2 929	271	10 100	3.3	3	34	4 319	0.4	Japan
824	222	100	77	900	790	130	1 710	7.8	6	18	1 940	48	Jordan
		100		430	2 093								Korea, North
755	721	100	89	1 440	1 168	634	2 010	5.6	17	32	21 472		Korea, South
31	81	97	18	20 000	76								Laos
1 364	334	100	58	540	610				9	18	182		Lebanon
963	958	92	49	4 000	702	126	1 870	4.9	25	28	10 665	39	Malaysia
388	258	106	89	450	1 137		1 500		15	29			Mongolia
27	6	73	21	30 060	13	210	170	0.3	63	4	346	14	Nepal
63	35	44	14	3 480	197	184	390	2.9	27	18	9 755	31	Pakistan
153	96	100	64	7 970	252	351	760	2.9	23	29	10 385	30	Philippines
3 763	4 505	67	32	1 670	3 536	370	12 180	6.2	1	67			Saudi Arabia
11 394	9 567	100	66	1 150	4 757	220	6 620	6.5	1	32	1 244	7.6	Singapore
118	93	100	54	7 170	143	411	330	3.2	27	19	2 205	44	Sri Lanka
414	187	100	51	2 240	847	507	1 680	4.9	18	24	2 305	14	Syria
1 163	1 613	100	95	1 242		331	2 570						Taiwan
203	147	96	29	7100	269	320	810	4.0	24	23	7 060	18	Thailand
224	147	100	39	1 630	599	269	1 230	1.4	21	28	15 396	30	Turkey
		100	48	4 190	90		170						Vietnam
250	6	59	7	11 670	116		510	3.5	28	8	1 574	38	Yemen, North
332	212	64	18	7 120	934		510	6.4	10	13	1 263	119	Yemen, South
													U.S.S.R.†
													Oceania
1 507	1 529	100	90	560	4 811	387	10 780	0.9	6	30	773	0.5	Australia
1 860	1 659	100	81	640	3 808	568	7 410	0.3	11	27	59	0.3	New Zealand
305	247	65	13	13 590	223	299	790	0.7	36	19	911	40	Papua New Guinea

† See in Europe

Bahrain Land 0.6/Popn. 400; Bhutan 47/1 338; Brunei 5.3/269/Kuwait 17.8/1 787;Macau 0.02/343; Maldives 0.3/173; Oman 212.5/1 181; Qatar 11/291; U.A.E. 83.6/1 255. American Samoa 0.2/34; Cocos Is.0.01/0.5; Cook Is 0.2/19; Fiji 18.3/686; Fr. Polynesia 3.7/160; Guam 0.6/112; Johnston I. 0.001/1; Kiribati 0.7/62; Midway I. 0.005/2; Nauru 0.02/8; New Caledonia 18.8/152; Niue I. 0.26/3; Norfolk I. 0.036/2; Pacific Is. 1.8/149; Samoa 2.9/159; Solomon Is.27.5/269; Tokelau 0.01/1.6; Tonga 0.7/107; Tuvalu 0.2/8; Vanuatu 14.8/128; Wake Is.0.008/2; Wallis & Futuna 0.2/10

Trade. The trade figures are normally for the year 1983 or 1984. The total trade figures have been divided by the population and are a measure of the country's external trade (U.S. $ per capita).

Education. The ages of primary school are taken to be 6-11 years and secondary school 12-17 years. The percentage of the total school age group in this type of education is shown.

Energy. All forms of energy have been converted to their equivalent in oil. Firewood and other traditional forms used in developing countries are not included and so the energy consumption in those countries is understated (kilograms of oil equivalent per capita).

Consumer Price Index. The base year is 1970 which is 100 and the level of consumer prices in 1984 or 1985 are shown in relation to the base year. It is a measure of inflation.

G.N.P. (Gross National Product) This figure is an estimate of the average production per person measured in U.S. dollars and for 1983. The G.N.P. measures the value of goods and services produced in a country, plus the balance, positive or negative, of income from abroad, for example investments, interest on capital, money returned from foreign labour, etc. The rate of change is the average annual percentage change during the period 1973-1982 in the G.D.P. The G.D.P. (Gross Domestic Product) is the G.N.P. minus the foreign balances. The adjoining two columns show the percentage contribution to the G.D.P. made by the agricultural and mining and manufacturing sectors.

Loans and Debt. This figure in millions of U.S. dollars shows the external public debt at the end of 1983. This is then shown as a percentage of the annual G.N.P. The figures in red show official development assistance made by the developed countries and also as a percentage of the donor country's G.N.P.

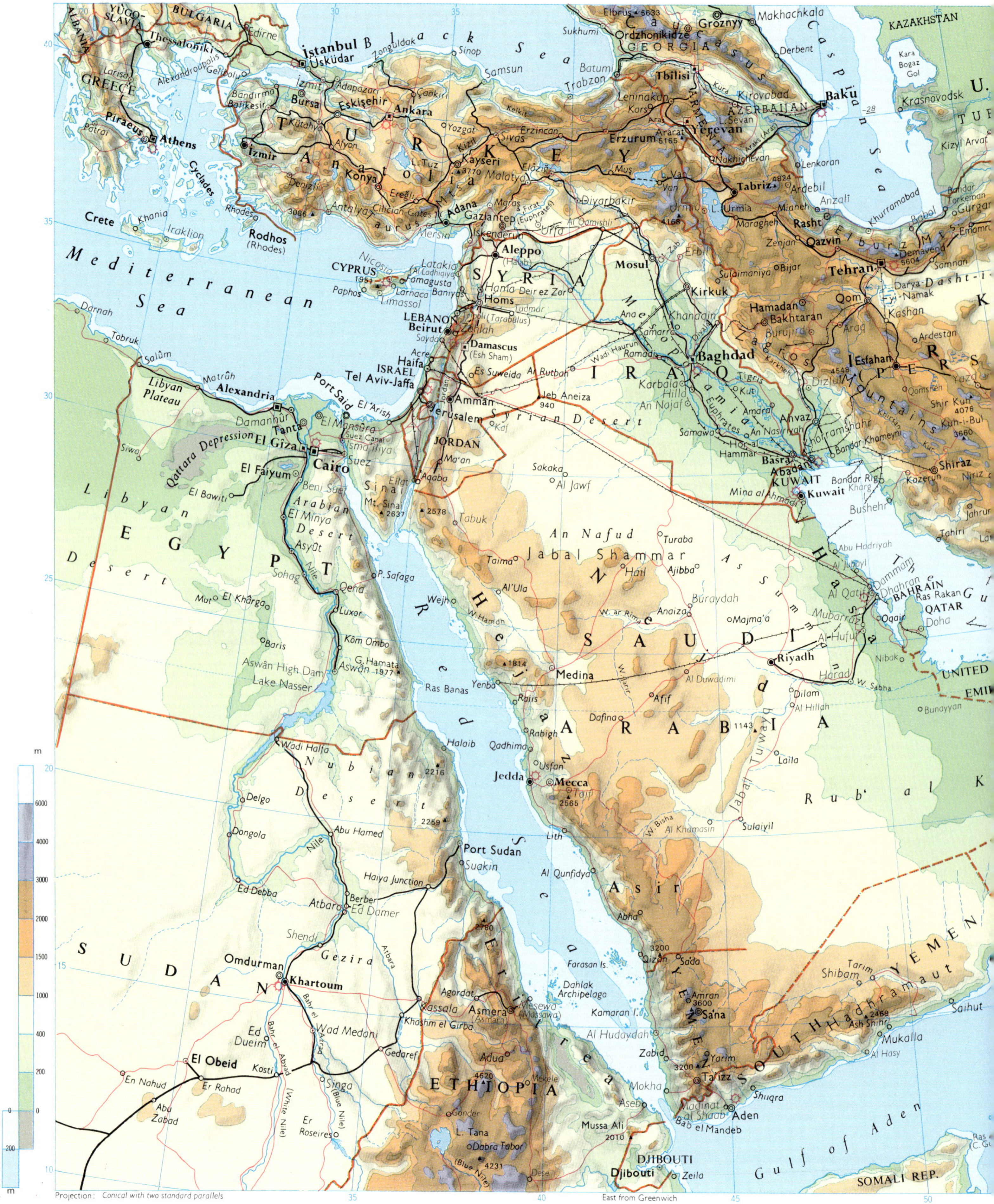

Projection: Conical with two standard parallels

East from Greenwich

1:15 000 000

100 0 100 200 300 400 500 600 km

THE HOLY LAND

Armistice boundaries between Arab States and Israel, 1949-1974

1:1 500 000

10 0 10 20 30 40 50 km

East from Greenwich

ARABIAN SEA
Continuation Southwards on same scale
Projection: Conical with two standard parallels

1:10 000 000

100 0 100 200 300 400 km

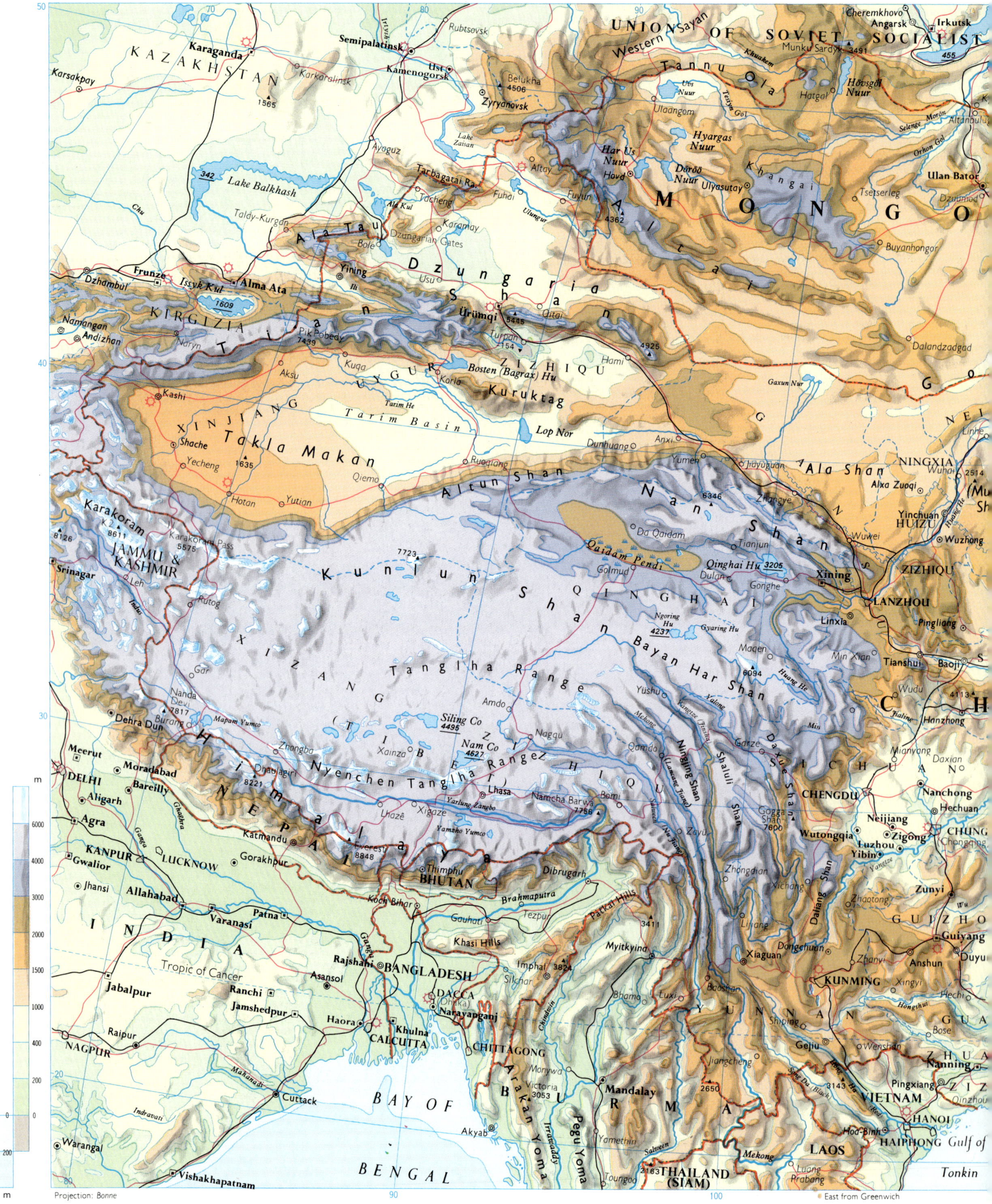
UNION OF SOVIET SOCIALIST
KAZAKHSTAN
Karaganda
Karsakpay
Semipalatinsk
Rubtsovsk
Ust Kamenogorsk
Karkaralinsk
Belukha 4506
Zyryanovsk
Cheremkhovo
Angarsk
Irkutsk
Western Sayan
Munku Sardyk 3491
Tannu Ola
Hövsgöl Nuur
Hatgal
Uvs Nuur
Ulaangom
Hyargas Nuur
Har Us Nuur
Hovd
Dörgön Nuur
Ulyasutay
Khangai
MONGO
Ulan Bator
Tsetserleg
Selenge Mörön
Orhon Gol
Altai
4362
Buyanhongor
Lake Balkhash
342
Taldy-Kurgan
Ayaguz
Lake Zaisan
Tarbagatai Ra.
Ala Kul
Tacheng
Altay
Fuhai
Fuyun
Ulungur
Karamay
Dzungarian Gates
Chu
Ala Tau
Bole
Dzungaria
Frunze
Dzhambul
Issyk Kul
1609
Alma Ata
Yining
Ili
Usu
Shan
Ürümqi
5445
Qitai
KIRGIZIA
Namangan
Andizhan
Naryn
Tian
Pik Pobedy 7439
Turpan
154
4925
Dalandzadgad
Hami
Aksu
Kuqa
UYGUR
ZIZHIQU
Korla
Bosten (Bagrax) Hu
Kuruktag
Gaxun Nur
Kashi
XINJIANG
Tarim He
Tarim Basin
Lop Nor
Shache
Takla Makan
Yecheng
1635
Qiemo
Ruoqiang
Dunhuang
Anxi
Yumen
Jiayuguan
Ala Shan
NINGXIA
Alxa Zuoqi
Yinchuan
HUIZU
Hotan
Yutian
Altun Shan
Nan Shan
6346
Zhangye
Wuwei
Wuzhong
Karakoram
K2 8611
8126
Karakoram Pass
5575
JAMMU & KASHMIR
Srinagar
Leh
Indus
7723
Kunlun Shan
Da Qaidam
Qaidam Pendi
Golmud
Tianjun
Qinghai Hu
3205
Dulan
Gonghe
Xining
ZIZHIQU
LANZHOU
Linxia
Pingliang
Rutog
QINGHAI
Ngoring Hu
4237
Gyaring Hu
Maqen
Min Xian
Tianshui
Baoji
XIZANG
Gar
Tanglha Range
Bayan Har Shan
6094
Huang He
Wudu
Nanda Devi 7817
Burang
Mapam Yumco
Amdo
Yushu
Hanzhong
Siling Co 4495
Nam Co 4627
Nagqu
Dehra Dun
Himalaya
Zhongba
Dhaulagiri 8221
Xainza
TIBET
Nyenchen Tanglha Range
Lhasa
Namcha Barwa 7756
Qamdo
Garze
Mianyang
Meerut
DELHI
Moradabad
Bareilly
Aligarh
Agra
Ghaghra
Lhazê
Xigazê
Yarlung Zangbo
Yamzho Yumco
Bomi
Nujiang
Salween
Daxue Shan
Gongga Shan 7600
CHENGDU
Nanchong
Hechuan
NEPAL
Katmandu
Everest 8848
Thimphu
BHUTAN
Dibrugarh
Neijiang
Zigong
Wutongqia
Luzhou
Yibin
Yangtze
CHUNG
Chongqing
KANPUR
Gwalior
LUCKNOW
Gorakhpur
Jhansi
Allahabad
Varanasi
Patna
Koch Bihar
Brahmaputra
Tezpur
Gauhati
Patkai Hills
3411
Zhongdian
Xichang
Daliang Shan
Zhaotong
Zunyi
INDIA
Ganga
Khasi Hills
Myitkyina
Lijiang
Dongchuan
Guiyang
Anshun
Duyun
Tropic of Cancer
Rajshahi
BANGLADESH
Imphal
3826
Silchar
Xiaguan
KUNMING
Zhanyi
Xingyi
Jabalpur
Ranchi
Asansol
DACCA (Dhaka)
Narayanganj
Bhamo
Lu Xi
Baoshan
YUNNAN
Jamshedpur
Haora
Khulna
CALCUTTA
Chindwin
Hongshui
Raipur
NAGPUR
CHITTAGONG
Monywa
Victoria 3053
Shiping
Gejiu
Bose
Wenshan
Mahanadi
Cuttack
BAY OF BENGAL
Arakan Yoma
Mandalay
BURMA
Jiangcheng
2650
3143
Pingxiang
Nanning
VIETNAM
HANOI
HAIPHONG
Gulf of Tonkin
Indravati
Akyab
Irrawaddy
Pegu Yoma
Yamethin
Mekong
LAOS
Hoa Binh
Warangal
Vishakhapatnam
Toungoo
2183
THAILAND (SIAM)
Luang Prabang
50
40
30
20
70
80
90
100
m
6000
4000
3000
2000
1500
1000
400
200
0
200
Projection: Bonne
East from Greenwich

1:15 000 000

100 0 100 200 300 400 500 600 km

1:7 500 000

50 0 50 100 150 200 250 300 km

Projection: Bonne

East from Greenwich

1:15 000 000

100 0 100 200 300 400 500 600 km

Leningrad
E U R O P E
Moskva
Sverdlovsk
U. S. S. R.
Tomsk
Novosibirsk
Irkutsk
Ozero Baykal
Chita
Semipalatinsk
Okhotsk
Sea of Okhotsk
Kamchatka
Komandorskie Is. (U.S.S.R.)
Bering Sea
Petropavlovsk
Sakhalin
G. of Sakhalin
Blagoveshchensk
Amur
Khabarovsk
Aleutian Is.
Andreanov Is.
7822
Aleutian Trench
L. Balkhash
Aral Sea
Alma Ata
Urumqi
Altai
MONGOLIA
Ulan Bator
Manchuria
Harbin
Changchun
Shenyang
A S I A
La Pérouse Strait
Kuril Is.
10,542
Kuril Trench
Vladivostok
Hakodate
7168
Emperor Seamount Chain
Tashkent
Peking
Tientsin
Taiyuan
Dalian
KOREA
Seoul
Sea of Japan
JAPAN
Sendai
Kyōto
TŌKYŌ
8412
Yokohama
Nagoya
Ōsaka
Shikoku
Kyūshū
Fuji-san 3776
Japan Trench
10,554
AFGHANISTAN
Kabul
Indus
Srinagar
Himalaya
Kunlun
TIBET
Lanzhou
Huang
Xian
Qingdao
Kitakyūshū
CHINA
Nanking
Yellow Sea
SHANGHAI
Lahore
PAKISTAN
Delhi
Mt. Everest 8848
Lhasa
NEPAL
Chungking
Wuhan
Yangtze
Brahmaputra
Changsha
Kanpur
Ganges
BANGLA-DESH
Calcutta
Dacca
Irrawaddy
Salween
Kunming
Fuzhou
East China Sea
Taipei
Ryukyu Is.
South Honshu Ridge
Bonin Is.
Volcano Is.
6603
Midway Is.
Hawaii
Lisianski I.
Canton
MACAU (Port.)
HONG KONG
Taiwan (Formosa)
Marcus I.
Marcus Necker Ridge
INDIA
BURMA
Mandalay
Hanoi
Chiengmai
Hainan
Hyderabad
Bay of Bengal
Rangoon
THAILAND
VIETNAM
Mekong
Bangkok
CAMBODIA
C. Engano
Manila
Northern Marianas
Wake I. (U.S.)
P A
Madras
Andaman Is.
Mindoro
PHILIPPINES
Mariana Trench
Guam (U.S.)
U.S. TRUST TERR. OF THE PACIFIC ISLANDS
Bikini Atoll
Marshall Is.
11,022
Micronesia
Gulf of Thailand
Phnom Penh
Ho Chi Minh City
South China Sea
Palawan
Samar
10,497
Sulu Sea
Mindanao Trench
Enewetak Atoll
Yap
SRI LANKA
Colombo
Nicobar Is.
Belau
Fed. States of Micronesia
Truk
Mindanao
4101
SABAH
BRUNEI
Pohnpei
Caroline Islands
Jaluit
International Date Line
Kuala Lumpur
PEN. MALAYSIA
MALAYSIA
SARAWAK
SINGAPORE
Celebes Sea
Butaritari
Sumatra
Melanesia
Gilbert Is.
Baker I. (U.S.)
O
Moluccas
Halmahera
Borneo
Celebes
NAURU
Banaba
Admiralty Is.
INDONESIA
Buru
Ceram
Irian Jaya
New Guinea
PAPUA NEW GUINEA
Bismarck Arch.
New Ireland
Abariringa
Palembang
Java Sea
Ujung Pandang
5029
Banda Sea
7440
Rabaul
New Britain
9103
K I R
Jakarta
Flores Sea
Sunda Strait
Surabaya
SOLOMON IS.
TUVALU (Ellice Is.)
Tokelau Is.
Java
Bali
Flores
Timor
Arafura Sea
Torres Strait
Fly
Port Moresby
Honiara
Guadalcanal
Christmas I. (Austral.)
Java Trench
7450
Sumbawa
Sumba
Sunda Islands
C. Arnhem
C. York
Sta. Cruz I.
9165
Rotuma
Wallis & Futuna (Fr.)
WESTERN SAMOA
Apia
Cocos (Keeling) Is. (Austral.)
Darwin
G. of Carpentaria
Louisiade Arch. (Austral.)
INDIAN OCEAN
Cairns
Coral Sea
VANUATU
FIJI
Vanua Levu
Viti Levu
Suva
Tonga Trench
NORTHERN TERRITORY
Townsville
Chesterfield Is.
7570
Loyalty Is.
N.W. Cape
Mt. Isa
Great Divide
New Caledonia (Fr.)
TONGA
Friendly Is.
AUSTRALIA
Rockhampton
Nouméa
10,882
Alice Springs
QUEENSLAND
WESTERN AUSTRALIA
Lord Howe Ridge
Brisbane
L. Eyre
SOUTH AUSTRALIA
Norfolk I. (Aust.)
Kermadec Is. (N.Z.)
Darling
Kermadec Trench
NEW SOUTH WALES
Lord Howe I. (Aust.)
10,047
Perth
Sydney
Great Australian Bight
Adelaide
Tasman Sea
Murray
Canberra
VICTORIA
Mt. Kosciusko 2230
Auckland
NEW ZEALAND
Amsterdam I. (Fr.)
St. Paul I. (Fr.)
Melbourne
Cook Strait
Wellington
Mid-Indian Ridge
Bass Strait
TASMANIA
Hobart
Mt. Cook 3764
Christchurch
Chatham Is. (N.Z.)
Crozet Is. (Fr.)
Dunedin
Invercargill
Kerguelen (Fr.)
Bounty Is. (N.Z.)
Antipodes Is. (N.Z.)
Auckland Is. (N.Z.)
Heard Is. (Aust.)
Macquarie Is. (Austral.)
Campbell I. (N.Z.)
m
10
6000
4000
2000
1000
200
0
200
2000
4000
6000
8000
m
Projection: Mollweide's Homolographic
East from Greenwich
20
40
60
80
100
120
140
160
180
10
20
30
40
50
60

ALASKA
Bristol Bay
Gulf of Alaska
Juneau
6050
Prince of Wales I.
Prince Rupert
Kitimat
Queen Charlotte Is.
Hudson Bay
GREENLAND
C. Farewell
CANADA
Edmonton
L. Winnipeg
Labrador
NORTH AMERICA
NORTH
Newfoundland
Rocky Mountains
Calgary
Vancouver
Vancouver I.
Victoria
Regina
Winnipeg
St. Lawrence
Quebec
Pr. Edward I.
Montréal
Saint John
Seattle
L. Superior
Missouri
Ottawa
L. Huron
Portland
Minneapolis
Toronto
L. Ontario
Boston
C. Sable
Michigan
Boise
Snake
Buffalo
L. Erie
Pittsburgh
NEW YORK
CHICAGO
Detroit
Philadelphia
C. Mendocino
Salt Lake City
Denver
Kansas
Cincinnati
Baltimore
Washington
ATLANTIC
Colorado
St. Louis
San Francisco
4418
UNITED STATES
Appalachian Mts.
Memphis
Oklahoma
Mississippi
C. Hatteras
Atlanta
6741
Los Angeles
San Diego
Dallas
Jacksonville
Bermuda (U.K.)
Ciudad Juarez
New Orleans
Houston
San Antonio
6225
MEXICO
Sierra Madre
Gulf of California
OCEAN
Gulf of Mexico
Miami
Florida Strait
BAHAMAS
Monterrey
Laysan I.
Hawaiian Ridge
Tropic of Cancer
Havana
CUBA
Hawaiian Is. (U.S.A.)
Oahu
Honolulu
Hawaii
Yucatan Channel
Mérida
West Indies
Hispaniola
9200
Revilla Gigedo Is. (Mexico)
Guadalajara
México
Puebla
5700
DOM. REP.
HAITI
7680
JAMAICA
Kingston
PUERTO RICO
Leeward Is.
Johnston I. (U.S.)
Acapulco
BELIZE
PACIFIC
Caribbean Sea
HONDURAS
GUATEMALA
Guatemala
6662
BARBADOS
N.W. Christmas Island Ridge
Salvador
EL SALVADOR
NICARAGUA
Managua
Windward Is.
TRINIDAD & TOBAGO
CENTRAL AMERICA
Clipperton I. (Fr.)
Barranquilla
Maracaibo
San José
COSTA RICA
Colón
Panama
PANAMA
Canal
Caracas
Orinoco
VENEZUELA
Palmyra Is. (U.S.)
Teraina
Tabuaeran
Cocos I.
Medellín
Bogota
Kiritimati
Cali
COLOMBIA
OCEAN
Equator
Jarvis I. (U.S.)
Galápagos (Ecuador)
Quito
ECUADOR
Guayaquil
Canterbury I.
Phoenix Is.
Malden I.
Iquitos
Manaus
Amazon
KIRIBATI
Starbuck I.
C. Pariñas
BRAZIL
Marquesas Is.
Line Is.
Tongareva
Penrhyn Is.
Caroline I.
East Pacific Ridge
Trujillo
SOUTH
Vostok I.
Flint I.
Manihiki
Pukapuka
Suwarrow Is.
PERU
Lima
6369
AMERICA
Tutuila
AMER. SAMOA
Leeward Is.
Cuzco
Cook Islands
Society Is.
Tuamotu Archipelago
Titicaca
Illampu & Ancohuma
6550
Arequipa
La Paz
BOLIVIA
Windward Is.
Tahiti
FRENCH POLYNESIA
6866
Peru-
Manuae
Niue (N.Z.)
Austral Seamount Chain
Tuamotu Ridge
Iquique
Chile
Rarotonga
Pitcairn I. (U.K.)
Ducie I.
Tropic of Capricorn
8050
Antofagasta
Trench
PARAGUAY
Tubuai Is. (Austral Is.)
Asunción
Sala-y-Gomez (Chile)
San Félix (Chile)
Easter Is. (Chile)
San Ambrosio (Chile)
Tucumán
Rapa Iti
Pto. Alegre
Córdoba
6960
Arch. de Juan Fernández (Chile)
Valparaíso
Rosario
URUGUAY
Santiago
Buenos Aires
Montevideo
Pacific-Antarctic Ridge
Chile Rise
Concepción
ARGENTINA
Río de la Plata
Andes
Patagonia
SOUTH ATLANTIC OCEAN
Chonos Arch.
G. of Penas
6212
Falkland Is. (U.K.)
Punta Arenas
Str. of Magellan
Tierra del Fuego
South Georgia
C. Horn
West from Greenwich

Java Trench
6389
TIMOR SEA
Ashmore Reef
Scott Reef
Bonaparte Archipelago
Rowley Shoals
INDIAN OCEAN
Croker I.
Cobourg Pen.
Melville I.
Bathurst I.
Van Diemen Gulf
Clarence Str.
P. Darwin
Darwin
Crocodile Is.
Arnhem B.
Arnhem Land
Rum Jungle
Anson B.
Batchelor
Daly
Katherine
Roper
Limmen
Mataranka
Birdum
Daly
McArthur
C. Londonderry
C. Bougainville
Admiralty G.
Cambridge G.
Joseph Bonaparte Gulf
Drysdale
Wyndham
Kununurra
Victoria
Mt. Hann
776
Kimberley
L. Argyle
Ord
Collier B.
King Sd.
C. Levêque
Lacepede Is.
King Leopold Ras.
Mt. Ord
1007
Durack Range
Derby
Hall's Creek
Wave Hill
Newcastle Waters
L. Woods
Barkly
Roebuck B.
Broome
Fitzroy
Fitzroy Crossing
Gordon Downs
Tanami Desert
Tennant Creek
Sturt
Eighty Mile Beach
NORTHERN TERRITORY
Gregory Lake
Hordern Hills
Murchison Ra.
Davenport Ra.
Dampier Archipelago
P. Hedland
Mount Goldsworthy
De Grey
Great Sandy Desert
Mt. Singleton
808
Sandover
Barrow I.
C. Dampier
Karratha
Roebourne
Pilbara
Marble Bar
Throssell Ra.
L. Dora
L. Mackay
Reynolds Ra.
998
Fortescue
Nullagine
Mt. Ziel
1510
N.W. Cape
Exmouth G.
Exmouth
Learmonth
Onslow
Hamersley Ra.
Mt. Bruce
1235
Tom Price
Ophthalmia Ra.
L. Macdonald
Macdonnell Ras.
Alice Springs
Robertson Ra.
L. Disappointment
James Ras.
Hugh
Ashburton
Paraburdoo
Mount Whaleback
Newman
Gibson Desert
Palmer
Finke
WESTERN AUSTRALIA
Rawlinson Ra.
L. Amadeus
Mt. Olga
1069
Ayers Rock
868
Simpson Desert
L. McLeod
Lyons
Mt. Augustus
1105
Blackstone Ra.
Musgrave Ranges
1549
Mt. Woodroffe
Geographe Chan.
Carnarvon
Gascoyne
Wooramel
Robinson Ra.
Peak Hill
L. Carnegie
L. Wells
661
Hamilton
Alberga
Everard Ras.
Oodnadatta
Shark B.
Denham
Dirk Hartog I.
Murchison
Meekatharra
Wiluna
Warrina
L. Yeo
L. Austin
Sandstone
Tallering Peak
453
Mt. Magnet
Laverton
Great Victoria Desert
Coober Pedy
Stuart Ra.
Houtman Abrolhos
Northampton
Mullewa
Geraldton
L. Monger
L. Barlee
Leonora
L. Carey
L. Minigwal
SOUTH AUSTRALIA
L. Ballard
Menzies
Ooldea
Tarcoola
Dongara
L. Moore
Kanowna
Kalgoorlie-Boulder
Rawlinna
Deakin
Nullarbor Plain
Bonnie Rock
Darling Range
Bencubbin
Coolgardie
L. Lefroy
Hampton Tableland
L. Everard
L. Gairdner
Penong
Ceduna
Nukey Bluff
472
Head of Bight
C. Adieu
Eyre
Southern Cross
L. Cowan
Swan
Northam
Kellerberrin
The Johnston Lakes
Norseman
L. Dundas
Perth
Fremantle
Kwinana
York
Nuyts Archipelago
Streaky B.
Kimba
Anxious B.
Eyre Penin.
Great Australian Bight
Narrogin
Pinjarra
Bunbury
Collie
Wagin
Esperance
Geographe B.
Katanning
C. Pasley
Archipelago of the Recherche
Coffin B. Penin.
Port Lincoln
Busselton
Bridgetown
Stirling Ra.
Manjimup
Mt Barker
Albany
C. Knob
Augusta
C. Leeuwin
Flinders B.
Invest
m
2000
1500
1000
400
200
0
0
200
2000
4000
6000
m
115
120
125
130
135
15
20
25
30
35
Projection: Bonne
East from Greenwich

1:12 000 000

100 0 100 200 300 400 500 km

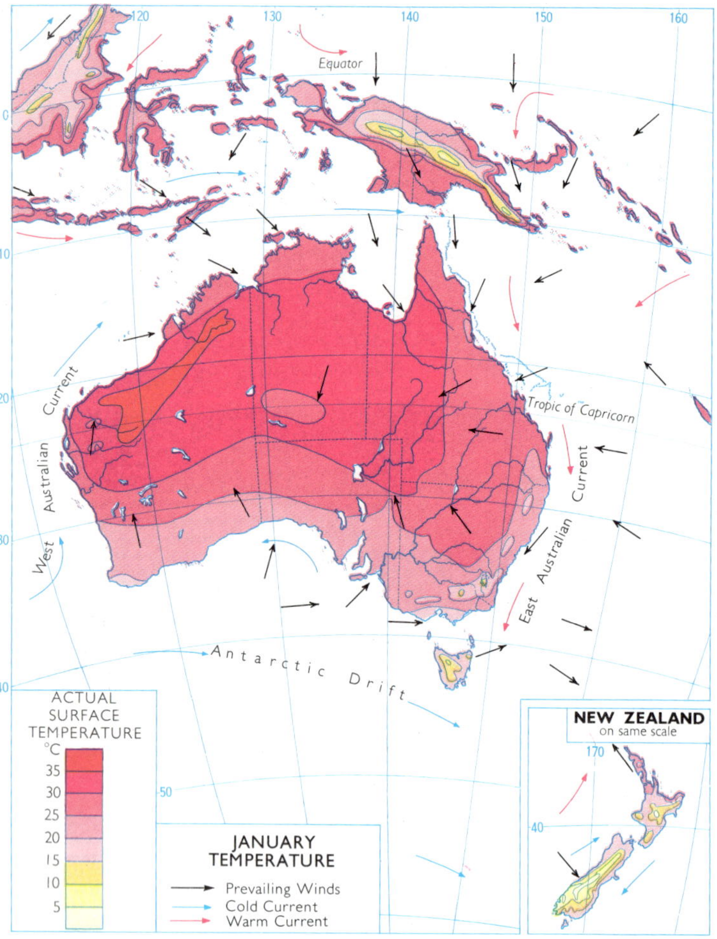
Equator
West
Australian
Current
East
Australian
Current
Tropic of Capricorn
Antarctic Drift
ACTUAL SURFACE TEMPERATURE
°C
35
30
25
20
15
10
5
NEW ZEALAND
on same scale
JANUARY TEMPERATURE
Prevailing Winds
Cold Current
Warm Current

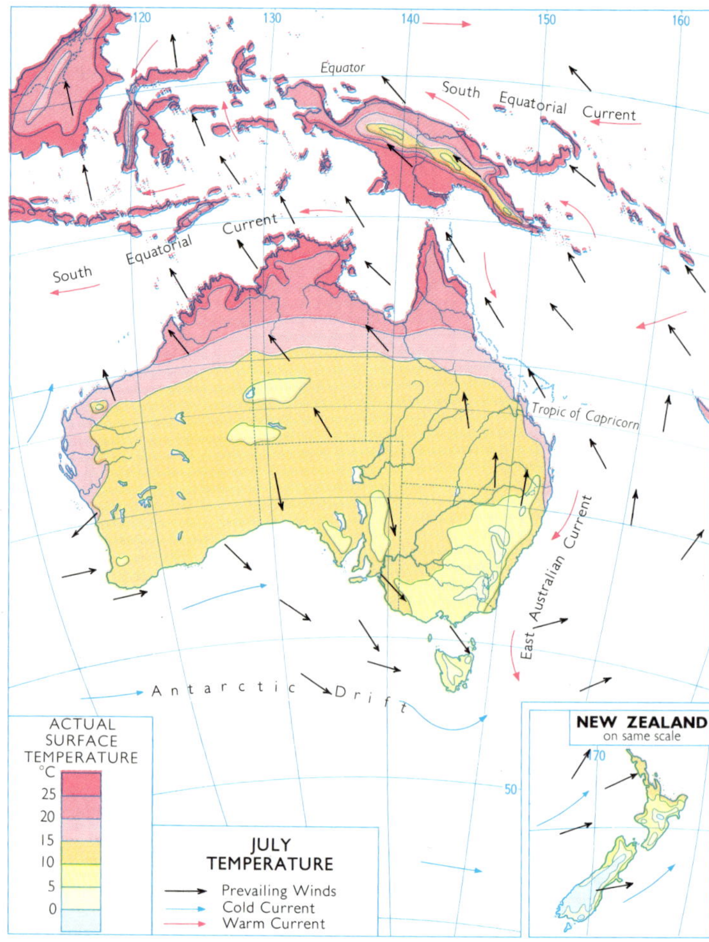
Equator
South Equatorial Current
South Equatorial Current
Tropic of Capricorn
East Australian Current
Antarctic Drift
ACTUAL SURFACE TEMPERATURE
°C
25
20
15
10
5
0
NEW ZEALAND
on same scale
JULY TEMPERATURE
Prevailing Winds
Cold Current
Warm Current

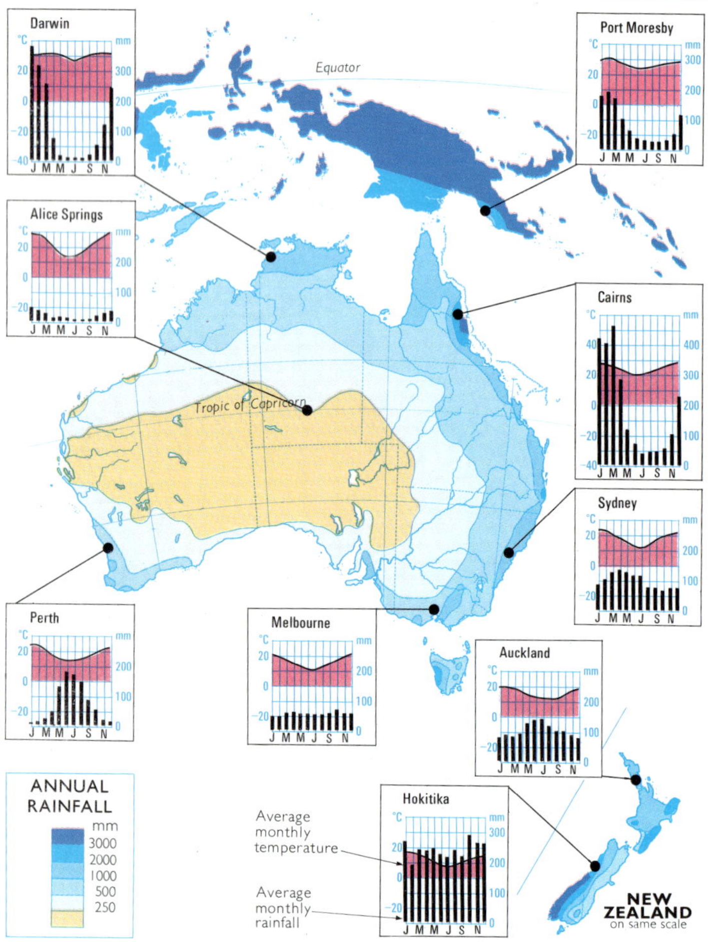
Equator
Tropic of Capricorn
Darwin
Port Moresby
Alice Springs
Cairns
Sydney
Perth
Melbourne
Auckland
Hokitika
J M M J S N
°C
mm
ANNUAL RAINFALL
mm
3000
2000
1000
500
250
Average monthly temperature
Average monthly rainfall
NEW ZEALAND
on same scale

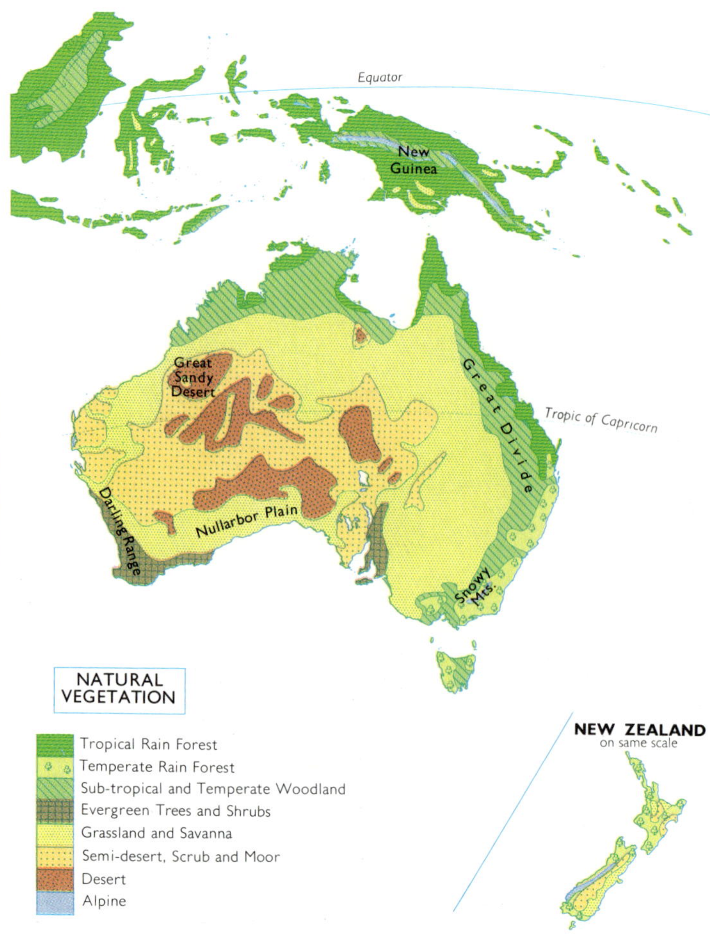
Equator
New Guinea
Great Sandy Desert
Great Divide
Tropic of Capricorn
Darling Range
Nullarbor Plain
Snowy Mts.
NATURAL VEGETATION
Tropical Rain Forest
Temperate Rain Forest
Sub-tropical and Temperate Woodland
Evergreen Trees and Shrubs
Grassland and Savanna
Semi-desert, Scrub and Moor
Desert
Alpine
NEW ZEALAND
on same scale

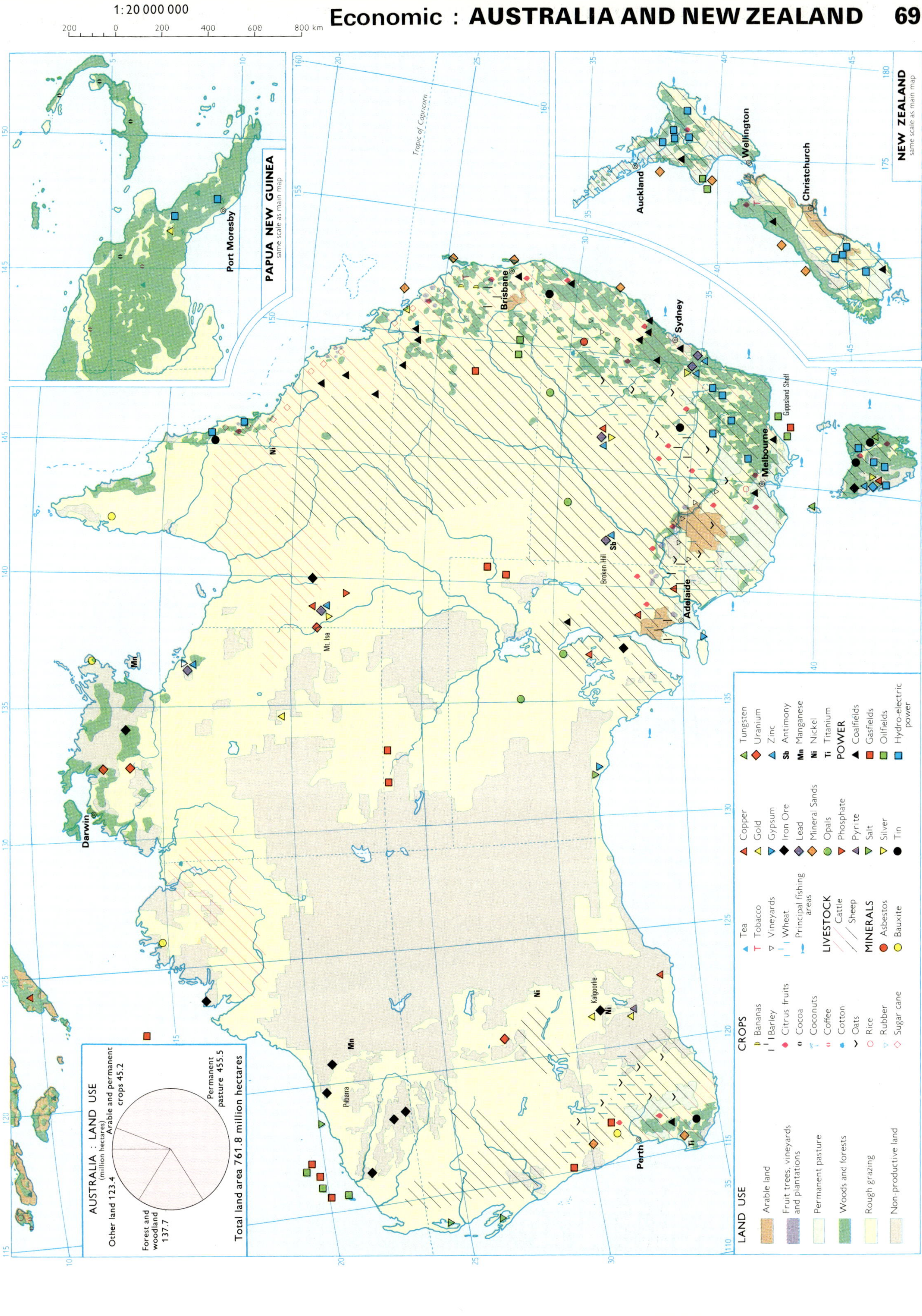
1:20 000 000
200 0 200 400 600 800 km
PAPUA NEW GUINEA
same scale as main map
Port Moresby
NEW ZEALAND
same scale as main map
Auckland
Wellington
Christchurch
COPYRIGHT GEORGE PHILIP & SON LTD
Tropic of Capricorn
Darwin
Mt. Isa
Brisbane
Sydney
Gippsland Shelf
Melbourne
Adelaide
Broken Hill
Pilbarra
Kalgoorlie
Perth
East from Greenwich 145
AUSTRALIA : LAND USE
(million hectares)
Arable and permanent crops 45.2
Permanent pasture 455.5
Forest and woodland 137.7
Other land 123.4
Total land area 761.8 million hectares
LAND USE
Arable land
Fruit trees, vineyards and plantations
Permanent pasture
Woods and forests
Rough grazing
Non-productive land
CROPS
Bananas
Barley
Citrus fruits
Cocoa
Coconuts
Coffee
Cotton
Oats
Rice
Rubber
Sugar cane
Tea
Tobacco
Vineyards
Wheat
Principal fishing areas
LIVESTOCK
Cattle
Sheep
MINERALS
Asbestos
Bauxite
Copper
Gold
Gypsum
Iron Ore
Lead
Mineral Sands
Opals
Phosphate
Pyrite
Salt
Silver
Tin
Tungsten
Uranium
Zinc
Sb Antimony
Mn Manganese
Ni Nickel
Ti Titanium
POWER
Coalfields
Gasfields
Oilfields
Hydro-electric power
Projection: Bonne

1:4 500 000

25 0 25 50 75 100 125 150 175 200 km

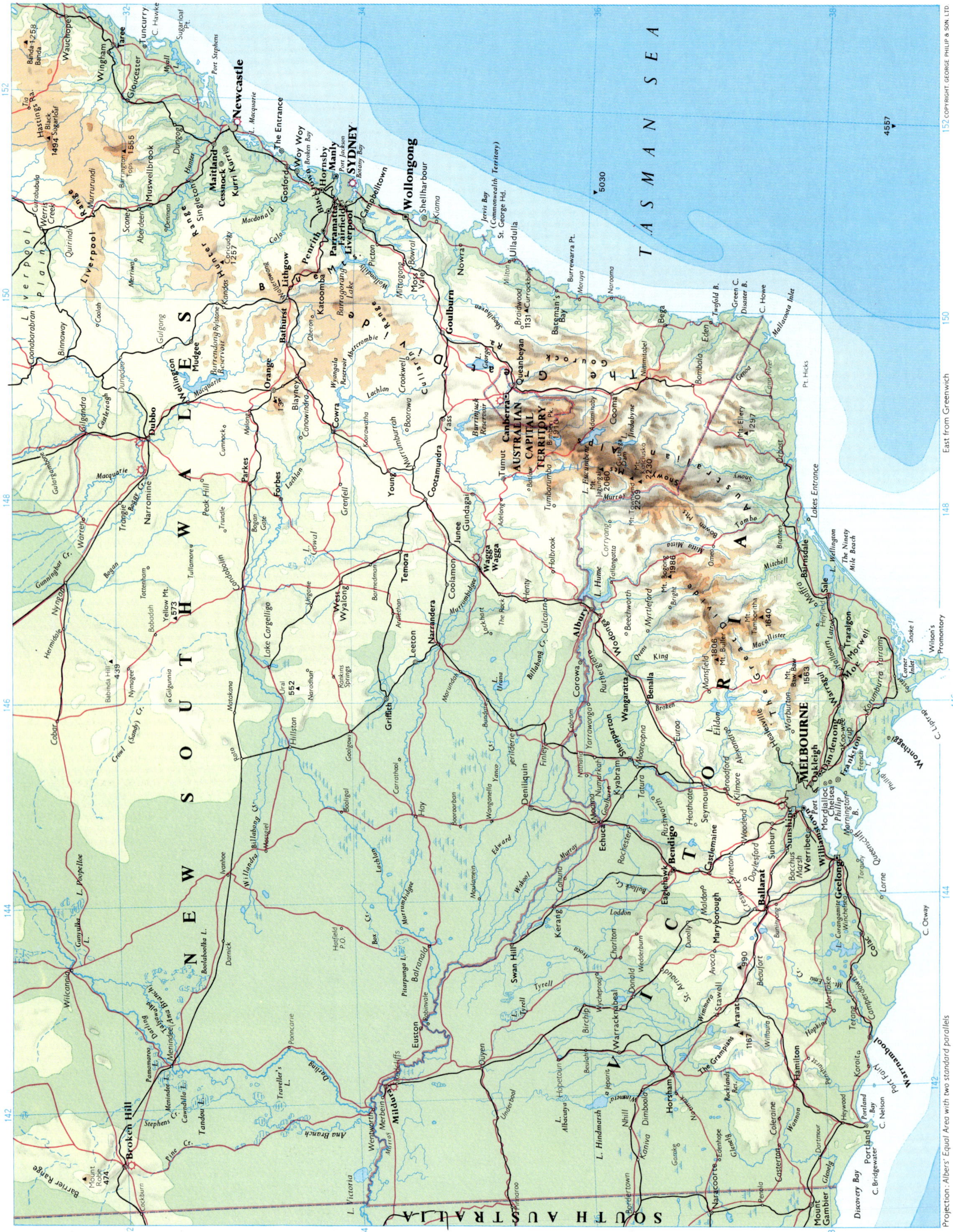

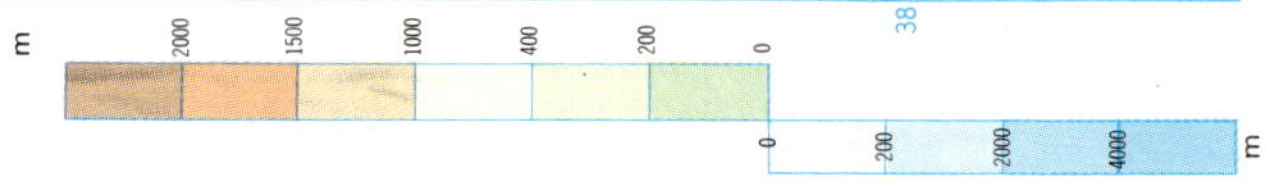

1:6 000 000

50 0 50 100 150 200 250 km

Projection: Conical with two standard parallels

1: 40 000 000

Projection: *Zenithal Equidistant.* 10 West from Greenwich 0 East from Greenwich 10 20 30 40 50

1:40 000 000

400 0 400 800 1200 1600 km

Projection: Zenithal Equidistant. West from Greenwich 0 East from Greenwich

1:80 000 000

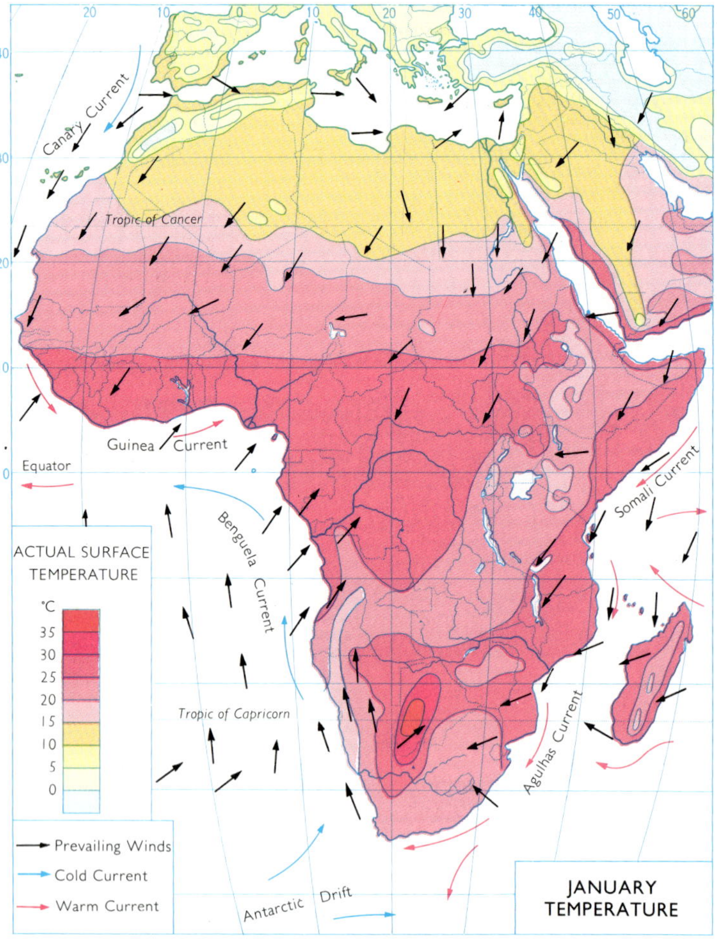

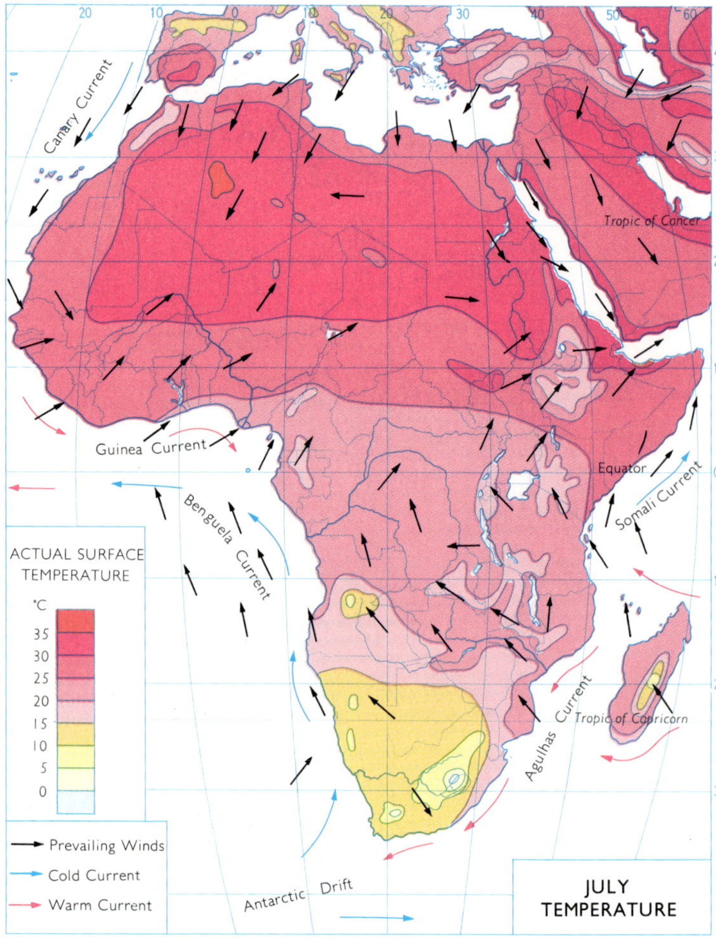

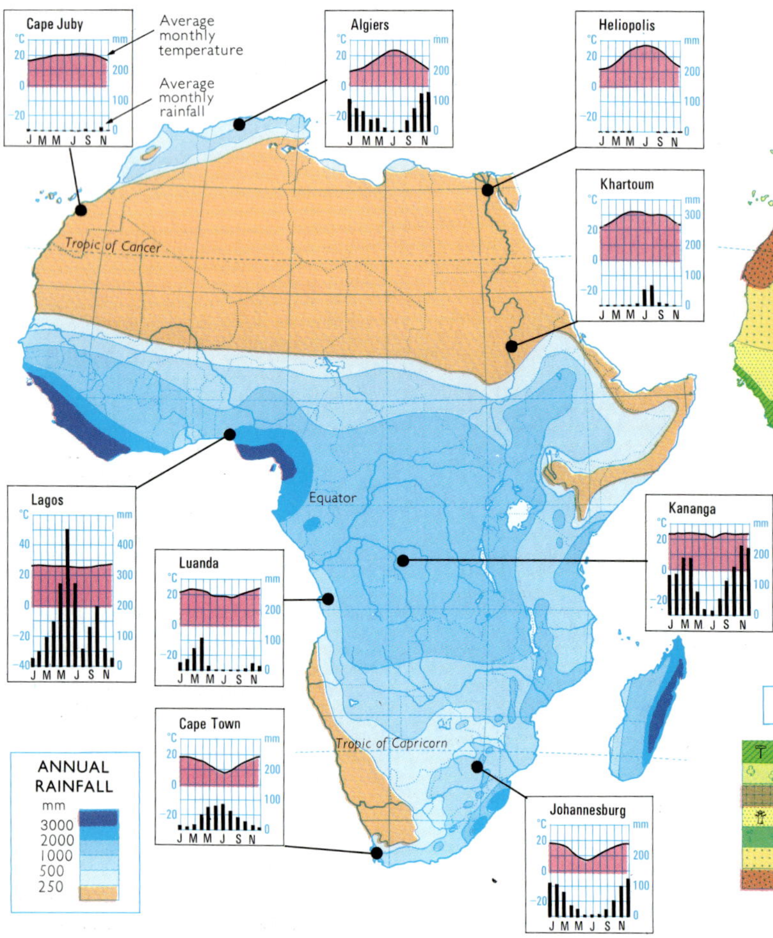

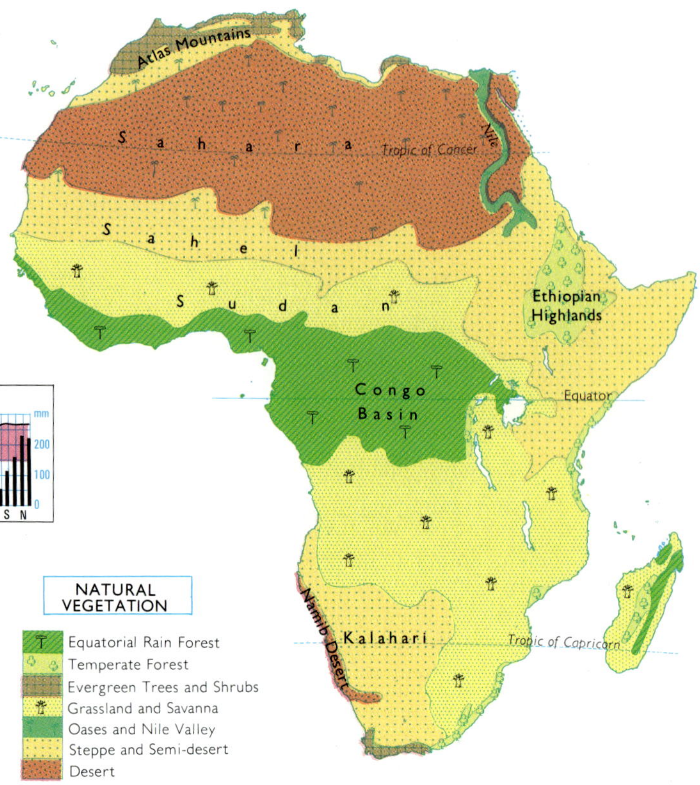

Projection: *Sanson-Flamsteed's Sinusoidal*

1:40 000 000

400 0 400 800 1200 1600 km

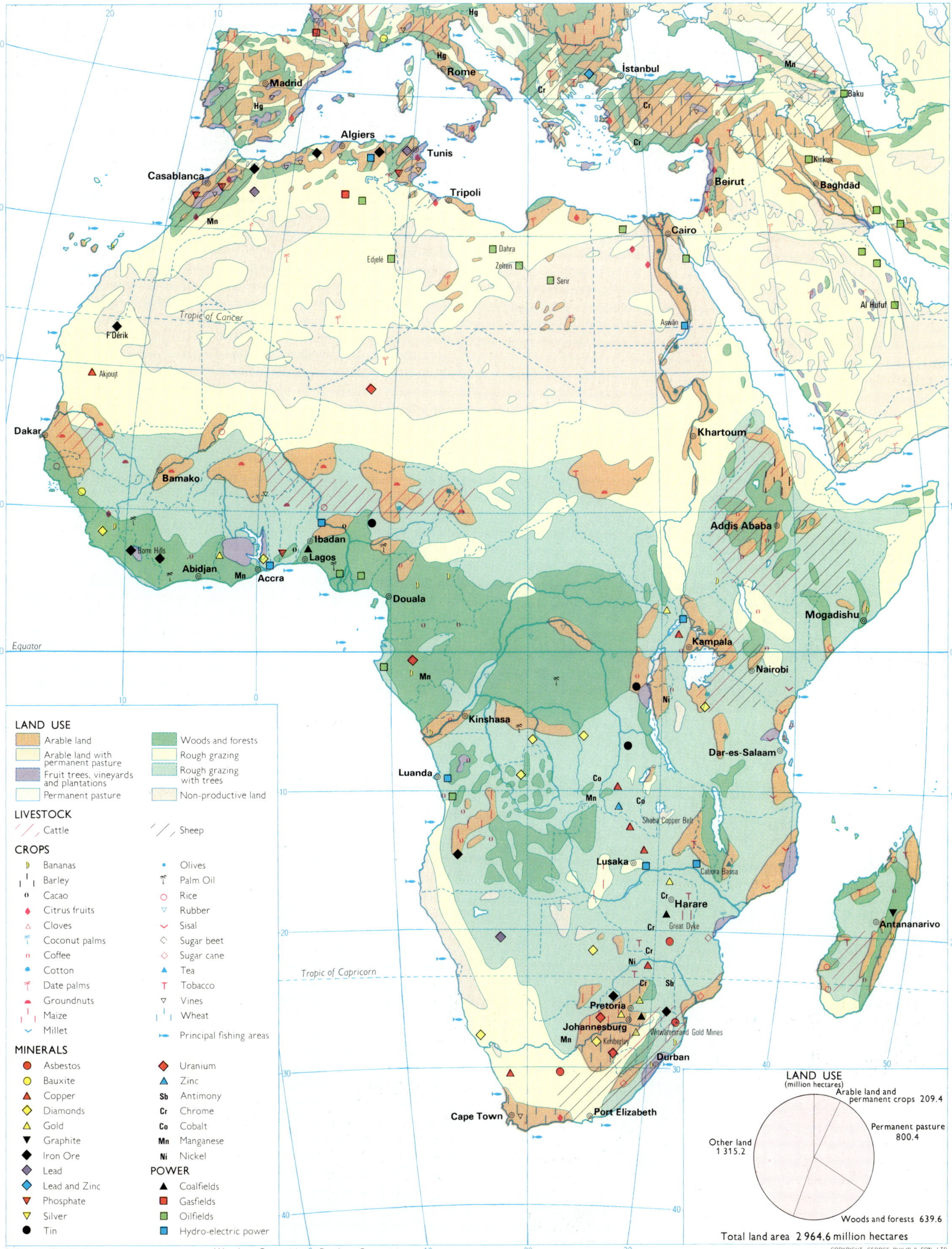

Projection: *Zenithal Equidistant*

West from Greenwich 0 East from Greenwich

	Population								Land			Agriculture		
	Total	Density	Birth Rate	Death Rate	Life Expectancy	Growth 1965-73	Growth 1973-83	Urban	Area	Arable	Forest	Agricultural Population	Index of Production	Food intake
	th.	persons per km²	per th. popn.	per th. popn.	yrs.	av. % per annum	av. % per annum	%	th. km²	th. km²	th. km²	% of total popn.	1974-76 = 100	calories per day
Algeria	21 272	8.9	47	13	57	2.9	3.1	46	2 382	75	44	47	98	2 586
Angola	8 540	6.8	48	24	43	2.2	2.6	23	1 247	35	536	56	83	2 353
Benin	3 825	34	51	25	48	2.6	2.8	16	111	18	39	45	119	2 174
Botswana	1 051	1.8	51	14	53		4.6	16	585	14	10	78	97	2 352
Burkina Faso	6 582	24	48	24	44	2.0	1.9	11	274	26	71	79	114	2 009
Burundi	4 537	175	42	20	47	1.4	2.2	2	26	13	0.6	82	118	2 353
Cameroon	9 467	20	43	19	54	2.4	3.1	39	469	70	254	79	100	2 295
Central Africa	2 508	4.0	45	24	48	1.6	2.3	44	623	20	397	86	107	2 117
Chad	4 901	3.9	44	24	43	1.8	2.1	20	1 259	32	203	81	114	1 823
Congo	1 695	5.0	45	20	63	2.6	3.1	55	342	6.7	213	32	113	2 433
Egypt	45 657	46	37	10	58	2.3	2.5	45	995	25	0	49	119	3 183
Ethiopia	35 420	32	49	23	43	2.6	2.7	15	1 101	140	265	77	128	2 149
Gabon	1 146	4.4	33	19	40		1.4		258	4.5	200	75	113	2 763
Gambia	630	63	48	30	34		3.7	18	10	1.6	2.0	77	73	2 251
Ghana	13 044	57	47	16	59	2.2	3.1	38	230	28	86	48	76	1 769
Guinea	5 301	22	47	25	37	1.8	2.0	26	246	16	105	79	107	1 880
Guinea-Bissau	875	31	41	22	41		4.6		28	2.9	11	80	92	2 176
Ivory Coast	9 474	30	46	20	52	4.6	4.6	44	318	40	89	78	137	2 613
Kenya	19 536	34	56	16	57	3.7	4.0	17	569	24	25	76	124	2 011
Lesotho	1 481	49	37	15	53	2.1	2.5	13	30	3.0	0	81	95	2 424
Liberia	2 109	22	50	21	49	2.8	3.3	38	96	3.7	38	68	111	2 276
Libya	3 624	2.1	38	13	56	4.1	4.3	61	1 760	21	6.2	12	112	3 812
Madagascar	9 731	17	45	18	49	2.4	2.6	20	582	30	132	81	110	2 491
Malawi	6 839	73	49	25	44	2.9	3.0	11	94	23	43	82	137	2 208
Mali	7 719	6.3	43	18	45	2.6	2.5	19	1 220	206	87	85	117	1 894
Mauritania	1 832	1.8	50	23	46	2.3	2.2	25	1 030	2.1	151	81	119	2 072
Morocco	22 848	51	45	14	52	2.4	2.6	43	446	84	52	49	113	2 607
Mozambique	13 693	17	45	17	46	2.3	2.6	17	784	31	152	61	77	1 881
Namibia	1 507	1.8	45	19	47		2.7		823	6.6	104	46	109	2 197
Niger	5 940	4.7	51	25	45	2.6	3.0	14	1 267	37	28	86	147	2 440
Nigeria	92 037	101	51	19	49	2.5	2.7	22	911	304	143	51	119	2 378
Rwanda	5 903	236	51	22	47	3.1	3.4	5	25	10	2.6	88	138	2 274
Senegal	6 352	33	55	23	46	2.4	2.8	34	192	52	53	73	75	2 346
Sierra Leone	3 536	49	48	32	38	1.7	2.1	23	72	18	21	63	120	1 938
Somalia	5 423	5.9	46	21	45	3.5	2.8	33	927	11	88	78	113	1 986
South Africa	31 586	26	38	15	64	2.6	2.4	35	1 221	136	46	28	91	2 862
Sudan	20 945	8.8	47	19	48	2.6	3.2	20	2 376	124	483	75	113	2 314
Swaziland	649	38	47	19	46		3.5	20	17	1.3	1.0	70	147	2 553
Tanzania	21 062	24	51	17	51	3.1	3.3	14	886	52	419	79	118	1 955
Togo	2 838	53	46	19	49	2.8	2.6	22	54	14	16	66	120	2 126
Tunisia	7 042	45	33	11	62	2.0	2.5	54	155	50	5.6	38	104	2 763
Uganda	15 150	76	50	16	49	3.5	2.8	7	200	58	60	79	119	1 784
Zaire	32 084	14	46	17	51	2.1	2.5	38	2 268	64	1 769	73	115	2 130
Zambia	6 445	8.7	48	17	51	3.0	3.2	47	741	52	206	65	93	2 146
Zimbabwe	7 980	21	47	14	56	3.4	3.2	24	387	28	238	57	90	2 108

For explanations see pages 54-55 or 86-87.

Trade		Education		Health	Energy	Consumer Price Index	G.N.P.		G.D.P. Part formed by		Loans & Debt		
Imports	Exports	Primary	Secondary					Growth per capita	Agric.	Indust.			
US$ per capita		% of age group		Popn. per doctor	Consumption in kgs of oil equiv. per capita	1970 = 100	US$ per capita	% per yr. 1973-82	%		end 1983 US$ millions	as % of GNP	
484	602	93	36	2 630	982	265	2 400	2.4	6	41	12 942	28	Algeria
74	238				226								Angola
97	18	65	21	16 980	39		290	2.7	44	7	615	59	Benin
				7 378		245	920	5.0	12	34			Botswana
45	9	28	3	48 510	22		180	1.6	37	12	398	38	Burkina Faso
41	22	33	3	45 020	17	382	240		51	9	284	26	Burundi
117	93	100	19	13 990	128	448	800	4.6	29	19	1 883	27	Cameroon
53	45	70	14	26 750	35		280	1.3	31	18	215	33	Central Africa
23	12		3	47 640	30	145	80	7.7	41	17	129	44	Chad
488	646		69	5 510	216	383	1 230	3.6	8	46	1 487	76	Congo
224	70	78	54	970	532	459	700	6.6	22	28	15 229	49	Egypt
27	12	46	12	69 390	19	363	140	0.7	45	10	1 223	26	Ethiopia
755	1 748			2 560	941	440	4 250	4.7	5	50			Gabon
156	75			11 632	230	474	290	0.8					Gambia
200	160	76	34	7 160	111	24 648	320	3.8	61	10	1 095	28	Ghana
		33	16	17 110	54		300	0.5			1 216	69	Guinea
59	14			7 306	50		180	2.1					Guinea-Bissau
194	222	76	17	15 234	186	407	720	1.1	27	13	4 824	79	Ivory Coast
73	52	100	20	7 890	109	467	340	1.0	28	13	2 384	43	Kenya
		100	20	18 640		447	470	4.0	24	13	145	23	Lesotho
288	298	66	20	8 550	357	260	470	0.9	17	18	699	72	Liberia
2 155	4 189		67	660	2 769	167	7 500	0.3	2	56	85	0.4	Libya
41	43	100	14	10 220	59	594	290	2.5	33	19	1 490	52	Madagascar
47	33	62	4	41 460	45	182	210	1.1	38	15	719	55	Malawi
46	22	27	9	22 130	22	567	150	2.1	46	11	881	89	Mali
106	161	33	10	14 500	130	150	440	0.7	22	19	1 171	158	Mauritania
169	92	80	28	10 750	258	270	750	2.1	14	23	9 445	70	Morocco
65	18	100	6	39 140	95								Mozambique
							1 760	1.8					Namibia
79	59	23	5	38 790	43	352	240	2.8	50	14	631	49	Niger
151	127	98	16	12 550	150	466	760	0.7	20	32	11 757	18	Nigeria
48	14	70	2	31 340	35	265	270	2.3	46	17	220	14	Rwanda
164	86	48	12	13 780	151	461	440	0.7	18	28	1 496	61	Senegal
47	42	40	12	17 520	102	1 776	380	0.3	31	17	359	35	Sierra Leone
65	39	30	11	15 630	84	217	250	1.9	50	11	1 149	62	Somalia
472	314			1 906	2 278	482	2 450	0.5	7	44			South Africa
67	31	52	18	8 930	66	1 498	400	3.5	34	10	5 726	78	Sudan
				7 000		544	890	0	20	21			Swaziland
40	18	98	3	17 740	38	760	240	0.1	43	8	2 584	59	Tanzania
103	59	100	27	18 100	88	354	280	0.4	27	17	805	114	Togo
452	269	100	32	3 690	473	190	1 290	4.1	14	26	3 427	43	Tunisia
22	26	60	8	26 810	23	730	220	5.6	73	7	623	18	Uganda
16	36	90	23	13 940	77	1 813	160	4.2	26	16	4 022	92	Zaire
88	100	96	16	7 670	432	640	580	2.5	17	27	2 638	84	Zambia
120	136	100	23	5 900	491	192	740	3.3	16	31	1 497	28	Zimbabwe

British Indian Oc. Terr. Land 0.08/Popn. 2; Cape Verde 4.0/317; Comoros 2.2/443; Djibouti 22/354; Eq. Guinea 28/383; Mauritius 1.9/1 011; Reunion 2.5/555; St.Helena 0.3/6; Sao Tome 0.9/94; Seychelles 0.3/65; Western Sahara 266/151

NORTH ATLANTIC
OCEAN
Madeira (Port.)
Funchal
Canary Is. (Span.)
Lanzarote
Fuerteventura
Palma
Tenerife
Sta. Cruz
Gomera
Hierro
Gran Canaria
Las Palmas
SPAIN
Málaga
Cádiz
Gibraltar (Br.)
Str. of Gibraltar
Tangier
Ceuta (Sp.)
Tétouan
Melilla (Sp.)
Ksar er Kebir
Kenitra
Salé
Rabat
Fes
Meknès
CASABLANCA
El Jadida
Settat
Khouribga
Safi
Essaouira
Marrakesh
Agadir
Ifni
Tarfaya (Villa Bens)
El Aaiun
C. Bojador
WESTERN SAHARA
Dakhla
Nouadhibou (Port Etienne)
MOROCCO
Middle Atlas
High Atlas
Anti Atlas
Ar Rachidiya
Bechar
Oujda
Tlemcen
Oran
Sidi Bel Abbes
Mostaganem
Mascara
Ech Cheliff
ALGIERS (Alger)
Blida
Medea
Tizi-Ouzou
Bejaia
Skikda
Annaba (Bône)
Bizerte
Tunis
Constantine
Sétif
Batna
Tébessa
Kairouan
Gafsa
Gabès
Biskra
Djelfa
Laghouat
Tiaret
Saida
Touggourt
Ouargla
Ghardaia
El Goléa
Hassi Inifel
Ghadames
Beni Abbès
Abadla
Tindouf
Timimoun
Adrar
Plateau du Tademait
In Salah
Bordj Omar Driss
Zaouiet Reggane
Bj. Fly Ste. Marie
ALGERIA
Chech
Erg
Arak
Ideles
Tahat 2918
Tamanrasset
Ahaggar (Hoggar)
Djanet
Illizi
Tanezrouft
Poste Maurice Cortier (Bidon 5)
TRANS SAHARAN MOTOR ROUTE
Tessalit
Adrar
Mabrouk
Araouane
Kidal
Aïr (Azbine)
Iférouane
Tamgak Mts.
Agadès
MAURITANIA
Bir Mogrein (Ft. Trinquet)
Zouérate
El Djouf
Atar
Chinguetti
Akjoujt
Nouakchott
Tidjikdja
Moudjeria
Boutilimit
Kiffa
Néma
Rosso
St. Louis
Louga
Thiès
Diourbel
DAKAR
Kaolack
SENEGAL
GAMBIA
Banjul
Tambacounda
Ziguinchor
GUINEA-BISSAU
Bissau
Bissagos Is.
Fouta Djalon
Labe
Kayes
MALI
Tombouctou (Timbuktu)
Goundam
Bamba
Bourem
Gao
Ansongo
Ménaka
Mopti
Ségou
Bamako
Koulikoro
Kita
Sikasso
Nioro
Nara
NIGER
Tahoua
Niamey
Dosso
Filingué
Maradi
Zinder
Tanout
BURKINA FASO
Ouagadougou
Ouahigouya
Koudougou
Bobo-Dioulasso
Fada N'Gourma
Tenkodogo
GUINEA
Kankan
Kindia
Conakry
SIERRA LEONE
Freetown
Sherbro I.
LIBERIA
Monrovia
Buchanan
Greenville
C. Palmas
IVORY COAST
Korhogo
Bouake
Man
Daloa
Gagnoa
Abidjan
Grand Bassam
San Pedro
GHANA
Bolgatanga
Wa
Tamale
Lake Volta
Kumasi
Koforidua
Accra
Tema
Takoradi
Sekondi-Takoradi
Cape Coast
TOGO
Lomé
BENIN
Natitingou
Cotonou
Porto Novo
Bight of Benin
NIGERIA
Sokoto
Katsina
Kano
Zaria
Kaduna
Jos
Bauchi
Minna
Abuja
Bida
Ilorin
Ogbomosho
Oshogbo
Ibadan
Abeokuta
LAGOS
Benin City
Onitsha
Enugu
Aba
Port Harcourt
Calabar
Makurdi
Niger Delta
CAMEROON
Bamenda
Douala
Yaoundé
Rey Malabo
Bioko
Projection: Sanson Flamsteed's Sinusoidal
West from Greenwich
East from Greenwich
EQUATORIAL GUINEA

1:15 000 000

100 0 100 200 300 400 500 600 km

ETHIOPIA
ADDIS ABABA
SUDAN
KHARTOUM
Khartoum
Omdurman
Kassala
Wad Medani
Gedaref
El Obeid
Kosti
NORTHERN KORDOFAN
SOUTHERN KORDOFAN
NORTHERN DARFUR
SOUTHERN DARFUR
BAHR EL GHAZAL
UPPER NILE
JONGLEI
EASTERN EQUATORIA
WESTERN EQUATORIA
CHAD
Ndjamena
L. Chad
NIGER
Zinder
NIGERIA
Kano
CAMEROON
Yaoundé
Douala
CENTRAL AFRICAN REPUBLIC
Bangui
EQUATORIAL GUINEA
GABON
Libreville
CONGO
Brazzaville
KINSHASA
ZAÏRE
Kisangani
Mbandaka
Kananga
CABINDA
Luanda
UGANDA
Kampala
Entebbe
KENYA
Nairobi
Mombasa
RWANDA
Kigali
BURUNDI
Bujumbura
TANZANIA
Dar-es-Salaam
Dodoma
Zanzibar
L. Victoria
L. Tanganyika
L. Turkana (L. Rudolf)
Kilimanjaro 5895
Mt. Kenya 5199
Sudd

1:15 000 000

100 0 100 200 300 400 500 600 km

1:35 000 000

400 0 400 800 1200 km
Asia
ARCTIC OCEAN
3800
Beaufort Sea
Bering Sea
Bering Strait
St. Lawrence I.
Nunivak I.
Wrangel I.
Brooks Range
Alaska
Alaska Range
Mt. McKinley 6194
Alaska Pen.
Kodiak I.
Gulf of Alaska
Yukon
Porcupine
Mackenzie Mts.
Mackenzie
Mt. St. Elias 5489
Mt. Logan 6050
Alexander Archipelago
Queen Charlotte Islands
Queen Charlotte Sound
Vancouver I.
Vancouver
Juan de Fuca Strait
C. Flattery
Coast Mountains
Mt. Waddington 4042
Rocky Mountains
Mt. Robson 3954
Yellowhead Pass
Edmonton
Calgary
Kicking Horse Pass
Crowsnest Pass
Great Bear L.
Great Slave L.
Arctic Circle
Back
Peace
Athabasca
L. Athabasca
Reindeer L.
Churchill
Nelson
N. Saskatchewan
S. Saskatchewan
Regina
Winnipeg
Lake Winnipeg
Great Plains
Greenland
Queen Elizabeth Islands
Axel Heiberg Land
Sverdrup Is.
Ellesmere I.
Nares Str.
Kane Basin
Thule
Parry Is.
Melville I.
Melville Sound
McClure Strait
Banks I.
Devon I.
Lancaster Sound
Prince of Wales I.
Victoria I.
C. Bathurst
Boothia Pen.
Gulf of Boothia
Melville Pen.
Foxe Basin
Foxe Channel
Southampton I.
Chesterfield Inlet
Baffin Bay
Baffin Island
Davis Strait
Disko I.
Cumberland Sound
Frobisher Bay
Resolution I.
Hudson Strait
Ungava Peninsula
Labrador
Hamilton Inlet
Belle Isle Strait
C. Charles
Newfoundland
St. John's
C. Race
Gulf of St. Lawrence
Anticosti I.
Pr. Edward I.
C. Breton
Nova Scotia
Halifax
Sable I.
C. Sable
Bay of Fundy
Saint John
Hudson Bay
Belcher Is.
James Bay
Eastmain
Laurentian Plateau
Godthåb
Julianehåb
C. Farewell
Denmark Strait
Iceland
2119
Petermann Peak 2940
Gunnbjørns Fjeld 3700
Mt. Forel 3360
2591
1676
Québec
Montreal
Ottawa
Toronto
Hamilton
Niagara Falls
Detroit
L. Superior
L. Huron
L. Michigan
L. Ontario
L. Erie
Minneapolis
Mississippi
Missouri
Chicago
St. Louis
Kansas City
Ozark Plateau
Memphis
Cumberland Plateau
Appalachian Mts.
Allegheny Mts.
Blue Ridge
2037
Mt. Washington 1917
Hudson
Long I.
Nantucket I.
C. Cod
New York
Philadelphia
Washington
Chesapeake Bay
C. Hatteras
Bermuda
Atlanta
Florida
New Orleans
Houston
Dallas
Red
Arkansas
Llano Estacado
Denver
Mt. Elbert 4399
4378 Blanca Pk.
N. Platte
S. Platte
Wasatch Mountains
Great Basin
Great Salt Lake
Colorado Plateau
Colorado
Grand Canyon
Gila
Snake
Columbia
Seattle
Mt. Rainier 4392
Portland
Cascade Range
Mt. Shasta 4317
C. Blanco
C. Mendocino
Coast Range
Sacramento
San Francisco
San Joaquin
Sierra Nevada
Mt. Whitney 4418
Los Angeles
Mendocino Seascarp
Murray Seascarp
PACIFIC OCEAN
6225
Tropic of Cancer
Lower California
Gulf of California
C. San Lucas
Western Sierra Madre
Mexican Plateau
Eastern Sierra Madre
Monterrey
Rio Grande
C. Corrientes
Guadalajara
Mexico
Puebla
Popocatepetl 5452
Citlaltepetl 5700
Balsas
Isthmus of Tehuantepec
G. of Tehuantepec
Guatemala Trench
6662
Guatemala
Clarion Fracture Zone
Revilla Gigedo Is.
Gulf of Mexico
Mississippi Delta
Gulf of Campeche
Yucatán Peninsula
C. Catoche
Yucatán Strait
Yucatán Basin
Gulf of Honduras
Coco
C. Gracias a Dios
L. Nicaragua
3837
Panama Canal
G. of Panama
G. of Darien
Cuba
Havana
Florida Strait
Bahama Islands
Greater Antilles
Jamaica
Cayman Trough
7680
Hispaniola
Port-au-Prince
Puerto Rico
Milwaukee Deep 9200
Caribbean Sea
Colombian Basin
Venezuelan Basin
G. of Venezuela
Maracaibo
Sa. Nevada de Sta. Marta 5800
Sierra de Mérida
Andes
Magdalena
ATLANTIC OCEAN
6399
m
4000
2000
1000
400
200
0
200
2000
4000
6000
8000
m
Projection: Bonne
West from Greenwich

1:35 000 000

400 0 400 800 1200 km

Projection: Bonne

120 110 100 West from Greenwich 90 80

1:70 000 000

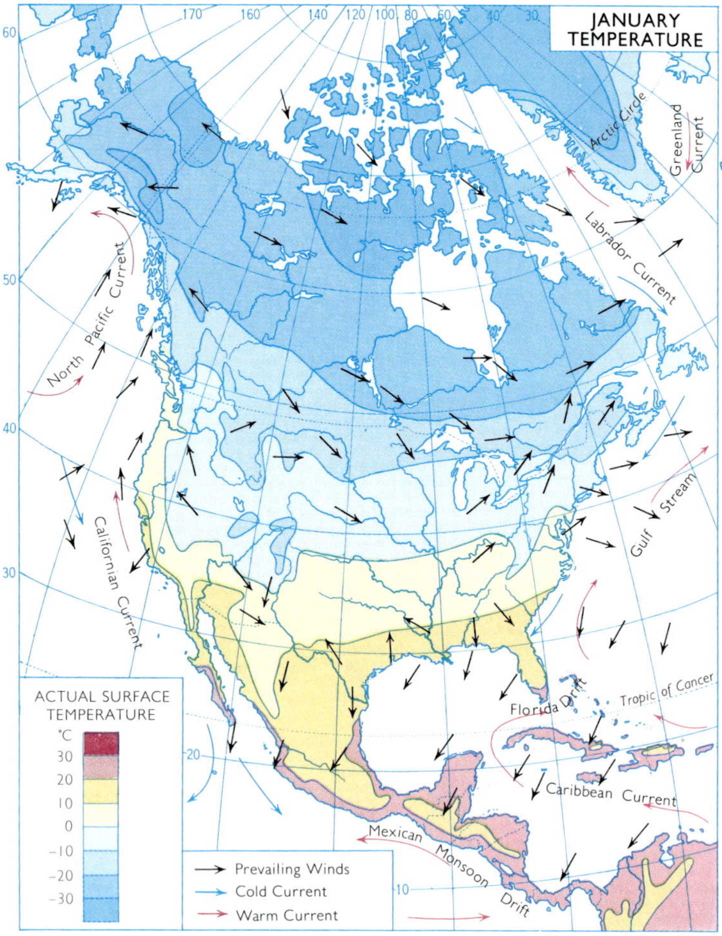

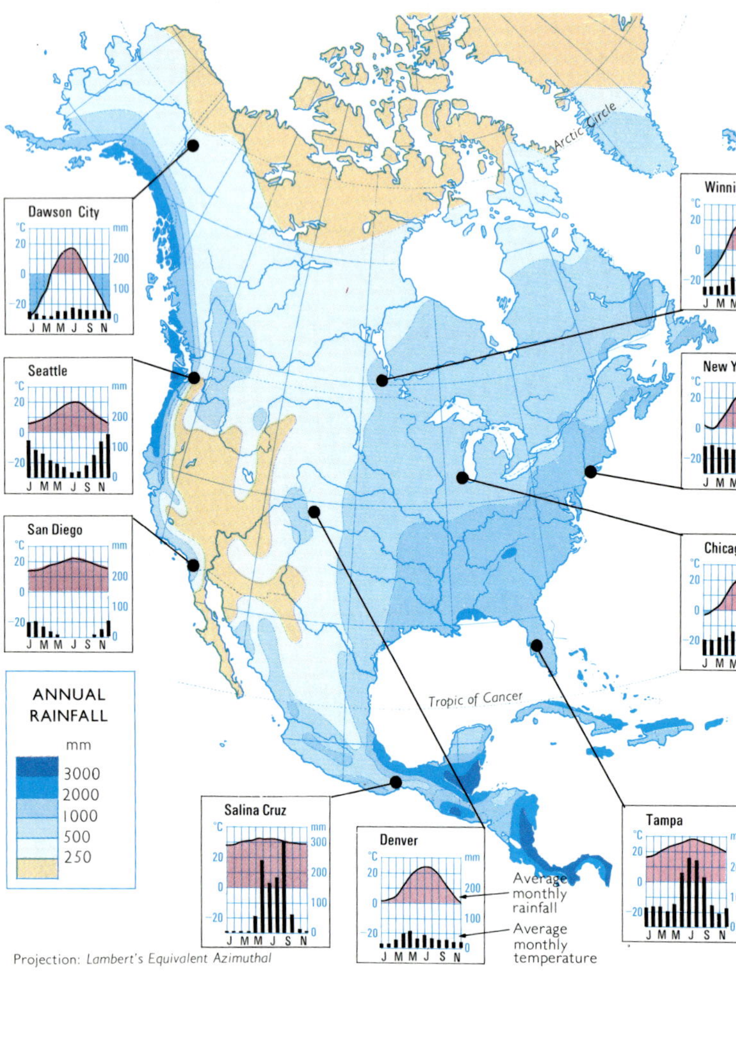

Projection: *Lambert's Equivalent Azimuthal*

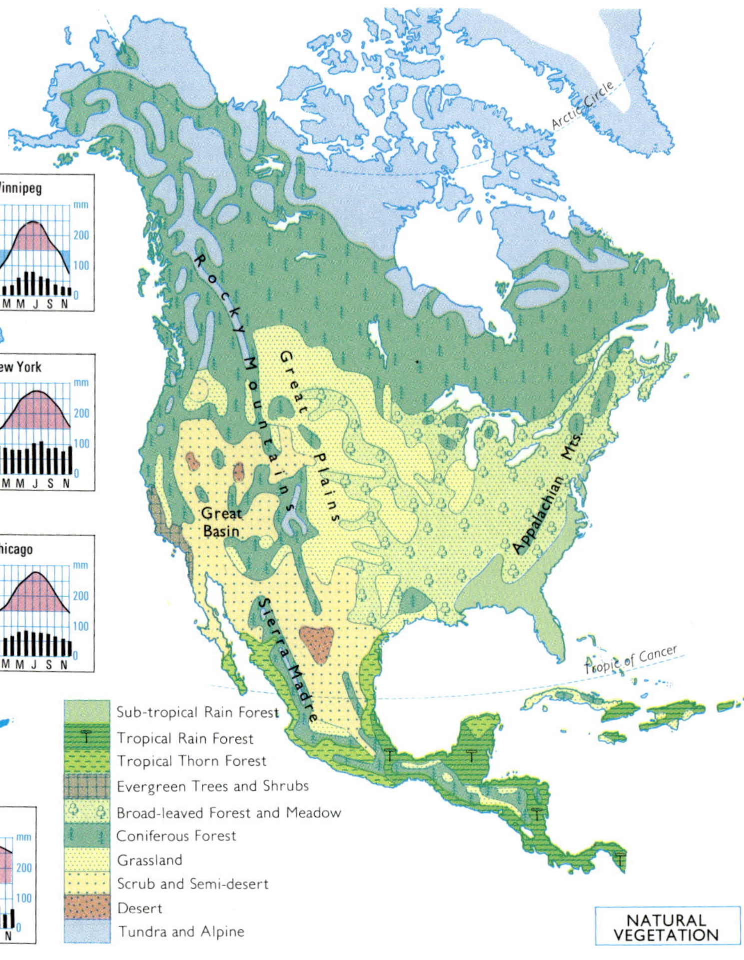

1:32 000 000

Projection: Polyconic

	Population								Land			Agriculture		
	Total	Density	Birth Rate	Death Rate	Life Expectancy	Growth 1965-73	Growth 1973-83	Urban	Area	Arable	Forest	Agricultural Population	Index of Production	Food intake
	th.	persons per km²	per th. popn.		yrs.	av. % per annum		%	th. km²	th. km²	th. km²	% of total popn.	1974-76 = 100	calories per day
Bahamas	226	23	24	5	67		1.3		10	0	3.2	8		2 200
Barbados	252	630	17	8	67		0.4		0.4	0.3	0	16	116	3 020
Canada	25 150	2.7	15	7	76	1.4	1.2	75	9 221	462	3 261	4	130	3 346
Costa Rica	2 534	50	30	4	74	3.0	2.4	45	51	6.3	16	33	118	2 653
Cuba	9 992	87	17	6	72	1.8	0.8	70	115	32	19	21	128	2 795
Dominican Rep.	6 102	127	35	9	63	2.9	2.4	54	48	15	6.3	55	115	2 131
El Salvador	5 388	257	28	6	64	3.4	3.0	42	21	7.3	1.3	49	103	2 155
Guadeloupe	331	184	20	7	71		0.4		1.8	0.4	0.7	14	90	2 491
Guatemala	7 740	72	39	7	60	3.0	3.1	40	108	18	44	53	115	2 138
Haiti	5 185	185	42	16	54	1.5	1.8	27	28	8.9	1.0	64	106	1 904
Honduras	4 232	38	47	12	60	2.9	3.5	38	112	18	39	61	141	2 135
Jamaica	2 290	208	28	6	70	1.5	1.3	52	11	2.7	3.0	19	101	2 542
Martinique	327	297	17	7			0.6		1.1	0.2	0.3	13	82	2 673
Mexico	76 792	40	38	6	66	3.3	2.9	69	1 923	235	474	34	131	2 890
Nicaragua	3 162	27	46	12	58	2.9	3.9	55	119	13	43	40	98	2 188
Panama	2 134	28	20	7	71	2.7	2.3	50	76	5.8	41	33	122	2 338
Puerto Rico	3 404	382	20	7	73		0.8		8.9	1.3	1.8	2.4	94	
Trinidad & Tobago	1 105	217	25	7	68	0.9	0.6	22	5.1	1.6	2.3	15	71	2 837
U.S.A.	236 681	26	16	9	75	1.1	1.0	74	9 127	1 906	2 845	1.9	98	3 641
Argentina	30 097	11	24	8	70	1.5	1.6	84	2 737	358	600	12	119	3 380
Bolivia	6 253	5.7	47	18	51	2.4	2.6	43	1 084	34	561	48	82	2 082
Brazil	132 580	16	32	9	64	2.5	2.3	71	8 456	746	5 701	36	133	2 580
Chile	11 878	16	23	6	70	1.9	1.7	82	749	55	155	17	112	2 759
Colombia	28 217	27	32	8	64	2.6	1.9	66	1 039	57	516	25	125	2 494
Ecuador	9 115	33	42	10	63	2.7	2.6	46	277	26	144	43	109	2 114
Guyana	936	4.8	28	7			0.8		197	4.9	164	20	102	2 359
Paraguay	3 278	8.3	37	8	65	2.7	2.5	41	397	19	205	48	143	2 839
Peru	19 198	15	38	12	58	2.8	2.4	67	1 280	35	704	35	100	2 195
Surinam	352	2.2	28	8					161	0.6	155	16	139	2 524
Uruguay	2 990	17	18	9	73	0.6	0.5	85	174	14	6.3	11	113	2 886
Venezuela	16 851	19	37	6	68	3.6	3.5	85	882	38	344	16	116	2 649

Population. This is the United Nations' estimate for the mid-year 1984 (thousands).

Population density. This is the quoted population total divided by the quoted land area (persons per square kilometre).

Birth Rates and Death Rates. These are the registered or United Nations' estimated rates per thousand population.

Life Expectancy. This figure indicates the number of years that a child born today can expect to live if the levels of death of today last throughout its life. The figure is an average of that for men and women. The figure for women is usually higher than that for men (U.K. male 70, female 76 years).

Population Growth. This shows the average annual percentage change in population for two periods 1965-1973 and 1973-1983.

Urbanization. This is the percentage of the total population living in urban areas. The definition of urban is that of the individual nation and usually includes quite small towns.

Land Area. This is the total area of the country minus the area covered by major lakes and rivers (thousand square kilometres).

Arable Land and Permanent Crops. This excludes fallow land but includes temporary pasture (thousand square kilometres).

Forest and Woodland. This includes natural and planted woodland and land recently cleared of timber which will be replanted (thousand square kilometres).

Agricultural Population. This is the percentage of the economically active population working in agriculture. It includes those people working also in forestry, hunting and fishing.

Index of Agricultural Production. The base period for this index is 1974-1976 and it shows the level of production in each country in 1983 in comparision with that of the earlier period. Only edible crops and meat are included.

Food Supply. The figures are the average intake per person in calories per day in the period 1979-1981.

Trade: Imports	Trade: Exports	Education: Primary	Education: Secondary	Health: Popn. per doctor	Energy: Consumption in kgs of oil equiv. per capita	Consumer Price Index: 1970 = 100	G.N.P: US$ per capita	G.N.P: Growth per capita, % per yr. 1973-82	G.D.P.: Part formed by Agric. %	G.D.P.: Part formed by Indust. %	Loans & Debt: end 1983 US$ millions	Loans & Debt: as % of GNP	
US$ per capita		% of age group											
13 152	10 361	99		1 200	5 400	243	4 060	0.5	4	12			Bahamas
2 636	1 564	100		1 300	1 060	544	3 930	2.9	7	13			Barbados
2 942	3 455	100	95	550	8 847	310	12 000	1.1	4	26	1 535	0.5	Canada
443	372	100	48	1 460	609	1 220	1 020	0.4	23	22	3 315	126	Costa Rica
815	618	100	72	720	1 042		1 400		4	43			Cuba
215	132	100	41	2 410	407	226	1 380	1.5	18	20	1 065	29	Dominican Rep
171	141	61	20	3 220	190	214	710	2.3	23	17			El Salvador
1 855	261			1 000	860	426	4 330	4.7	7	7			Guadeloupe
151	154	73	16	8 610	178	116	1 120	1.4	25	18	1 405	16	Guatemala
61	36	69	13	8 200	55	142	320	1.9	38	18	433	27	Haiti
188	169	99	32	3 120	204	300	670	0.7	25	18	1 570	56	Honduras
513	339	99	58	2 830	980	996	1 300	4.0	8	31	1 950	65	Jamaica
1 960	318			900	900	460	4 270	3.3	11	5			Martinique
146	306	100	54	2 000	1 332	4 092	2 240	3.2	8	30	66 732	49	Mexico
256	124	100	41	1 800	262		900	5.3	25	23	3 417	133	Nicaragua
668	120	100	63	980	2 082	231	2 070	2.5	10	14	2 986	74	Panama
		82		4 000	2 500	232	2 890	0.8	2	41			Puerto Rico
2 245	2 046	99	61	1 360	5 191	615	6 900	5.2	2	44	887	12	Trinidad & Tobago
1 376	921	100	97	520	7 030	278	14 090	1.5	3	29	8 698	0.2	U.S.A.
151	269	100	59	430	1 460	157th	2 030	1.1	9	29	24 593	32	Argentina
101	124	86	34	2000	292	4.8 mill	510	1.1	16	25	2 969	78	Bolivia
115	204	96	32	1 600	745	58 763	1 890	2.8	11	24	58 068	29	Brazil
269	308	100	59	1 930	755	265	1 870	1.4	7	29	6 827	39	Chile
181	112	125	46	1 710	786	1 888	1 470	2.7	19	27	6 899	18	Colombia
188	282	100	56	760	675	286	1 430	3.0	12	30	6 239	63	Ecuador
639	97	95		9 000	700	449	520	1.3	19	19			Guyana
146	82	100	36	1 310	187	407	1 140	6.8	28	19	1 161	29	Paraguay
97	163	100	59	1 390	550	37th	1 040	0.4	9	38	7 932	48	Peru
1 274	686	100		1 700	3 160	287	3 520	5.1	9	25			Surinam
265	352	100	63	540	776	74th	2 490	2.9	7	23	2 523	48	Uruguay
407	915	100	40	990	2 295	373	4 100	0	6	40	12 911	20	Venezuela

Antigua & Barbuda Land 0.4/Popn. 79; Belize 23/156; Bermuda 0.05/56; Br. Virgin Is. 0.2/13; Cayman Is. 0.3/19; Dominica 0.8/77; Greenland 342/53; Grenada 0.3/112; Montserrat 0.1/13; Netherlands Antilles 1/260; St. Christopher-Nevis 0.4/51; St Lucia 0.6/134; St Pierre & M. 0.2/6; St Vincent 0.3/104; Turks and Caicos Is. 0.4/8; U.S. Virgin Is. 0.3/103. Falkland Is. 12/2; Fr.Guiana 89/72.

Trade. The trade figures are normally for the year 1983 or 1984. The total trade figures have been divided by the population and are a measure of the country's external trade (U.S. $ per capita).

Education. The ages of primary school are taken to be 6-11 years and secondary school 12-17 years. The percentage of the total school age group in this type of education is shown.

Energy. All forms of energy have been converted to their equivalent in oil. Firewood and other traditional forms used in developing countries are not included and so the energy consumption in those countries is understated (kilograms of oil equivalent per capita).

Consumer Price Index. The base year is 1970 which is 100 and the level of consumer prices in 1984 or 1985 are shown in relation to the base year. It is a measure of inflation.

G.N.P. (Gross National Product) This figure is an estimate of the average production per person measured in U.S. dollars and for 1983. The G.N.P. measures the value of goods and services produced in a country, plus the balance, positive or negative, of income from abroad, for example investments, interest on capital, money returned from foreign labour, etc. The rate of change is the average annual percentage change during the period 1973-1982 in the G.D.P. The G.D.P. (Gross Domestic Product) is the G.N.P. minus the foreign balances. The adjoining two columns show the percentage contribution to the G.D.P. made by the agricultural and mining and manufacturing sectors.

Loans and Debt. This figure in millions of U.S. dollars shows the external public debt at the end of 1983. This is then shown as a percentage of the annual G.N.P. The figures in red show official development assistance made by the developed countries and also as a percentage of the donor country's G.N.P.

PACIFIC OCEAN
ALASKA
YUKON TERRITORY
NORTHWEST TERRITORIES
BRITISH COLUMBIA
ALBERTA
SASKATCHEWAN
MANITOBA
CANADA
UNITED STATES
WASHINGTON
MONTANA
NORTH DAKOTA
SOUTH DAKOTA
MINNESOTA
NEBRASKA
WYOMING
IOWA
INUVIK
KITIKMEOT
FORT SMITH
KEEWATIN
Anchorage
Fairbanks
Whitehorse
Dawson
Juneau
Skagway
Sitka
Inuvik
Yellowknife
Great Slave L.
Gt. Bear Lake
Lake Athabasca
Victoria Island
Banks Island
Prince of Wales Island
Amundsen Gulf
Coronation Gulf
Queen Maud Gulf
Boothia Peninsula
M'Clintock Channel
Viscount Melville Sound
Mackenzie Mountains
Rocky Mountains
Coast Mountains
Cassiar Mountains
Columbia Mountains
Selkirk Mts.
ALASKA HIGHWAY
Queen Charlotte Is.
Vancouver I.
Prince Rupert
Prince George
Edmonton
Calgary
VANCOUVER
Victoria
SEATTLE
Tacoma
Spokane
Kamloops
Kelowna
Lethbridge
Medicine Hat
Red Deer
Saskatoon
Regina
Moose Jaw
Prince Albert
Lake Winnipeg
L. Manitoba
Winnipeg
L. of the Woods
Brandon
Minot
Bismarck
Fargo
Grand Forks
Duluth
Minneapolis
St. Paul
Pierre
Rapid City
Sioux Falls
Sioux City
Omaha
Des Moines
Cedar Rapids
Waterloo
Mt. Logan 6050
Mt. Robson 3954
Mt. Waddington 3994
Projection: Bonne
ALASKA
1:30 000 000
0 200 400 600 km
BERING SEA
GULF OF ALASKA
Aleutian Is.
Brooks Range
Alaska Range
Seward Pen.
Nome
Kodiak I.
Alaska Peninsula
Bristol Bay
Kuskokwim Bay
Nunivak I.
St. Lawrence I.
Bering Strait
Chukot Sea
U.S.S.R.
Gulf of Anadyr
Alexander Archipelago
PACIFIC OCEAN
West from Greenwich
m
3000
2000
1500
1000
400
200
0
200
2000
m

1:15 000 000

100 0 100 200 300 400 500 600 km

Projection: Albers' Equal Area with two standard parallels

1:12 000 000

100 0 100 200 300 400 500 km

Projection: Albers' Equal Area with two standard parallels

1:6 000 000

50 0 50 100 150 200 250 km

UNITED STATES
MEXICO
GULF OF MEXICO
PACIFIC OCEAN
Gulf of California
Lower California
Sierra Madre
Gulf of Campeche
Yucatan
Isthmus of Tehuantepec
G. of Tehuantepec
Tropic of Cancer
San Diego
Tijuana
Mexicali
Phoenix
Tucson
Ciudad Juárez
El Paso
Hermosillo
Chihuahua
Monterrey
Saltillo
Torreón
Durango
Culiacán
Mazatlán
Zacatecas
San Luis Potosí
Aguascalientes
Guadalajara
León
Querétaro
Morelia
MEXICO
Toluca
Puebla
Veracruz
Tampico
Acapulco
Oaxaca
Mérida
Campeche
San Antonio
Houston
New Orleans
Dallas
Fort Worth
Corpus Christi
Birmingham
Jackson
Baton Rouge
Mobile
Shreveport
Austin
BELIZE
Belmopan
GUATEMALA
Guatemala
HONDURAS
Tegucigalpa
S. Pedro Sula
EL SALVADOR
San Salvador
NICARAGUA
Managua
PANAMA CANAL
1:1 000 000
Colón
Gatun
Balboa
PANAMA
Pedro Miguel Locks
Miraflores Locks
JAMAICA
1:5 000 000
KINGSTON
Montego Bay
Spanish Town
TRINIDAD AND TOBAGO
1:5 000 000
Port of Spain
San Fernando
Scarborough
Tobago
TRINIDAD
Gulf of Paria
LEEWARD ISLANDS
1:5 000 000
Anguilla (Br.)
St. Martin (Fr.)
St. Maarten (Neth.)
ST. CHRISTOPHER-NEVIS
Basseterre
Barbuda
ANTIGUA & BARBUDA
St. John's
Antigua
Montserrat
Plymouth
GUADELOUPE (Fr.)
Basse Terre
Pointe-à-Pitre
Marie-Galante (Fr.)
DOMINICA (Windward Is.)
Roseau
WINDWARD ISLANDS
1:5 000 000
MARTINIQUE (Fr.)
Fort de France
ST. LUCIA
Castries
ST. VINCENT
Kingstown
BARBADOS
Bridgetown
THE GRENADINES
GRENADA
St. George's
Projection: Bonne

1:15 000 000

100 0 100 200 300 400 500 600 km

West from Greenwich

1: 30 000 000

200 0 200 400 600 800 1000 km

Projection: *Lambert's Equivalent Azimuthal*

West from Greenwich

1:30 000 000

200 0 200 400 600 800 1000 km

Projection: Lambert's Equivalent Azimuthal

West from Greenwich

BUENOS AIRES Capital Cities

1:70 000 000

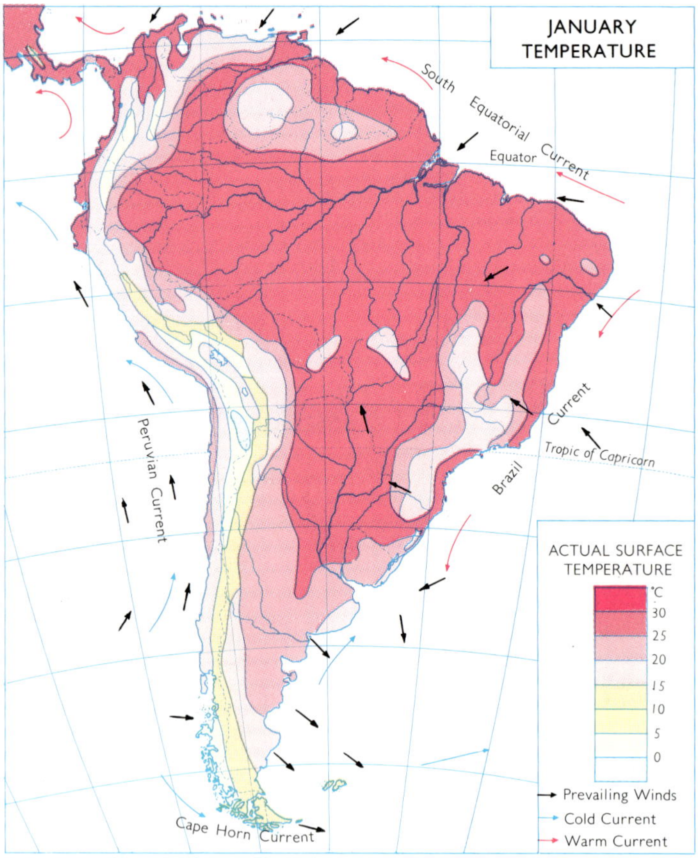

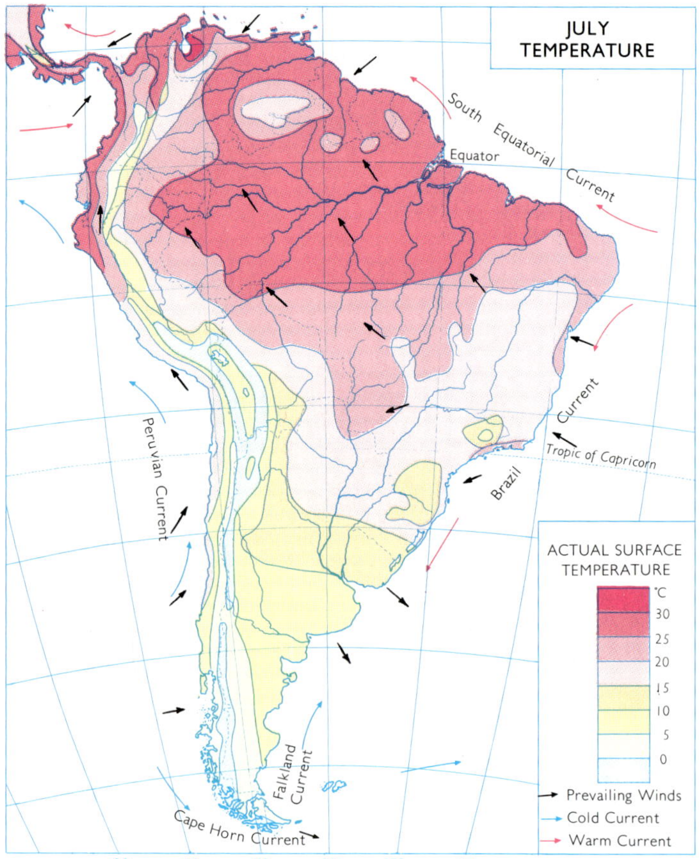

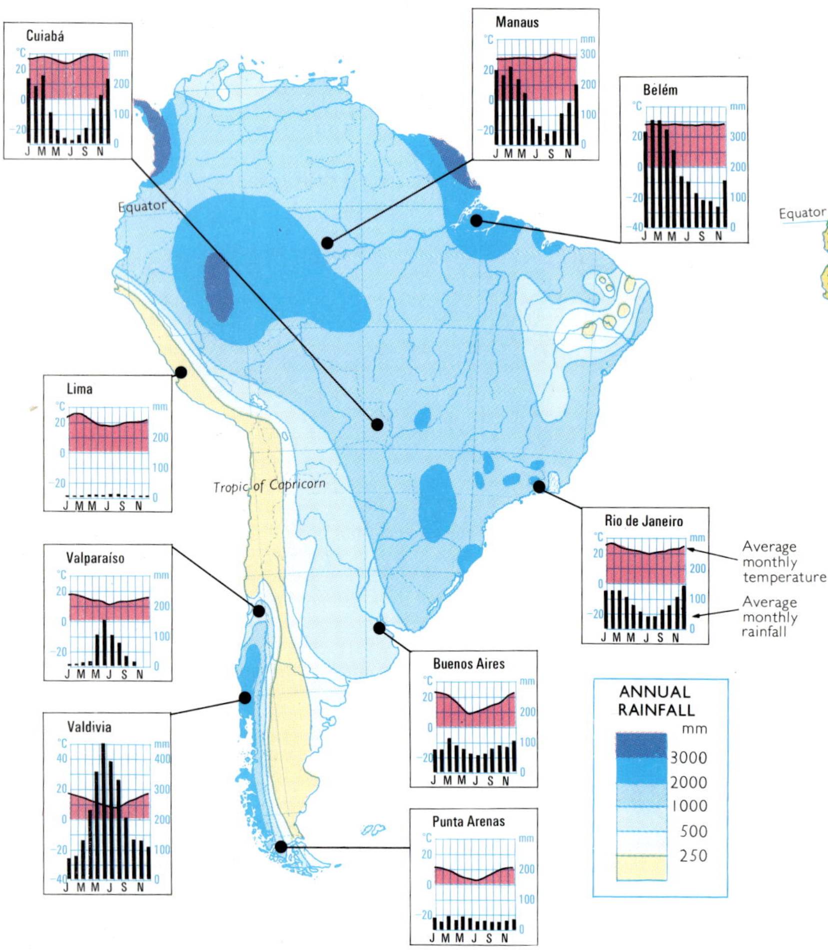

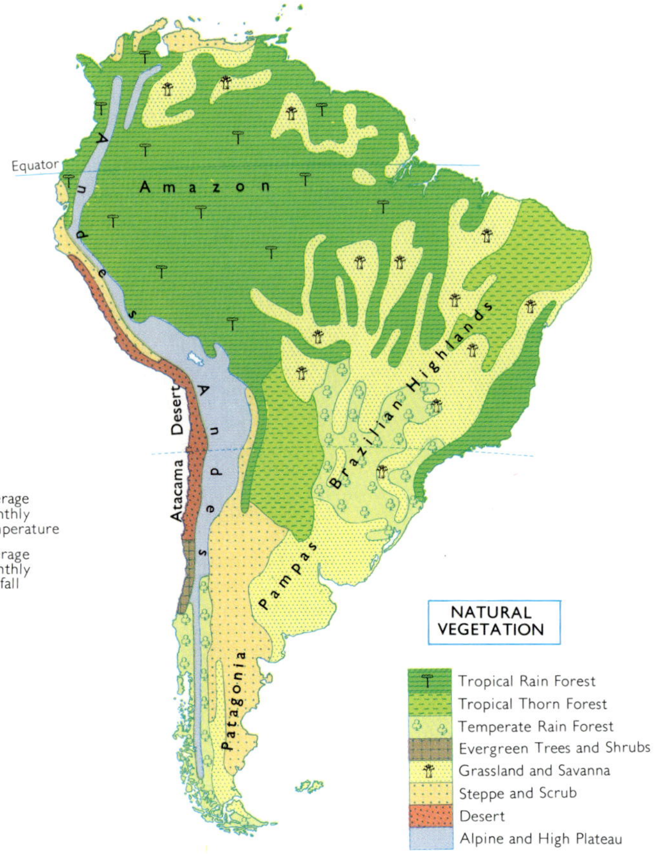

Projection: *Lambert's Equivalent Azimuthal*

1:30 000 000

200 0 200 400 600 800 1000 km

Projection: *Lambert's Equivalent Azimuthal*

Projection: Sanson-Flamsteed's Sinusoidal

West from

1:16 000 000

200 100 0 200 400 600 km

1:16 000 000

200 100 0 200 400 600 km

Projection: Sanson-Flamsteed's Sinusoidal — West from Greenwich

1:50 000 000

500 0 500 1000 1500 2000 km

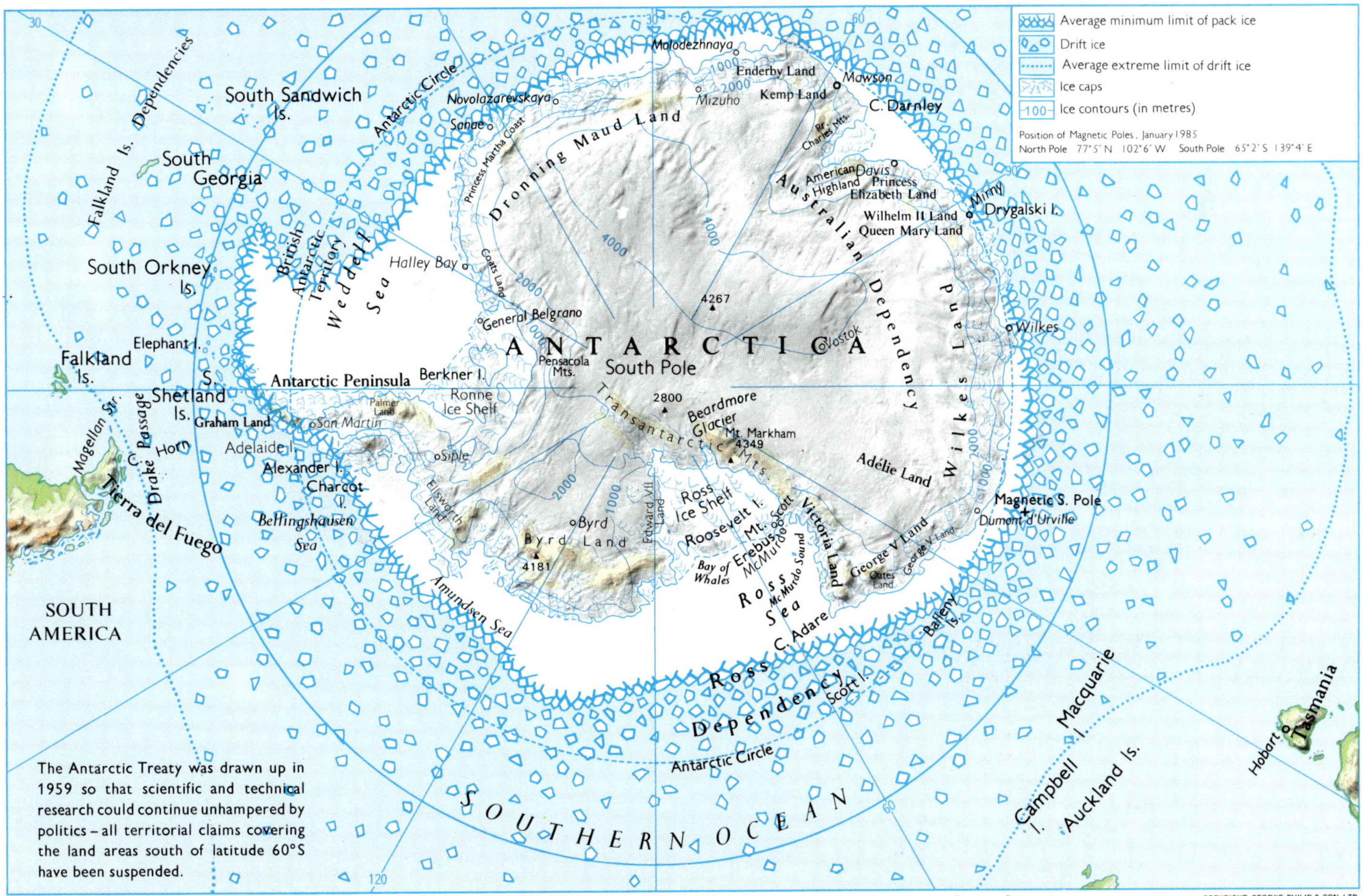

Average minimum limit of pack ice
Drift ice
Average extreme limit of drift ice
Ice caps
Ice contours (in metres)

Position of Magnetic Poles, January 1985
North Pole 77°5' N 102°6' W South Pole 65°2' S 139°4' E

The Antarctic Treaty was drawn up in 1959 so that scientific and technical research could continue unhampered by politics – all territorial claims covering the land areas south of latitude 60°S have been suspended.

m: 4000, 2000, 1000, 400, 200, 0

Projection: *Zenithal Equidistant*

Queen Elizabeth Is.
Ellesmere I.
North Magnetic Pole
Victoria I.
Greenland
Baffin Island
Davis Str.
Bering Str.
Yukon
Mt. McKinley 6199
Mackenzie
Gt. Bear L.
Gt. Slave L.
Bering Sea
Aleutian Is.
Hudson Str.
Hudson Bay
Arctic Circle
Iceland
C. Farewell
British Isles
Labrador
Coast Ra.
Rocky Mountains
Vancouver I.
L. Winnipeg
Great Plains
Great Lakes
St. Lawrence
Newfoundland
C. Race
Cascade Ra.
Sa. Nevada
Missouri
Arkansas
Ohio
Appalachian Mts.
Mt. Whitney 4418
Colorado
Mississippi
C. Hatteras
Iberian Pen.
Azores
Str. of Gibraltar
Bermuda
Lower California
Rio Grande
Sierra Madre
Gulf of Mexico
Florida Str.
Bahama Islands
ATLANTIC
Canary Is.
Atlas Mts.
Tropic of Cancer
Hawaiian Is.
Mauna Kea 4202
Cuba
Popocatepetl 5452
Citlaltepetl 5700
Yucatan
Greater Antilles
Hispaniola
Jamaica
Caribbean Sea
Lesser Antilles
C. Verde Is.
C. Verde
Palmyra Is.
PACIFIC
Tabuaeran
Kiritimati
Isthmus of Panama
Llanos
Orinoco
Guiana Highlands
Roraima 2772
OCEAN
C. Palmas
G. of
Negro
Equator
Galapagos Is.
Chimborazo 6267
Amazon
Andes
Selvas
C. de São Roque
Phoenix Is.
Madeira
Tocantins
Ascension
Tokelau Is.
Marquesas Is.
OCEAN
Samoa Is.
Mato Grosso
Society Is.
Tuamotu Archipelago
L. Titicaca
St. Helena
Tahiti
Cook Is.
Brazilian Highlands
Tonga Is.
Tubuai Is.
Gran Chaco
Paraguay
C. Frio
Tropic of Capricorn
Atacama Desert
Pitcairn I.
Easter I.
Ojos del Salado 6863
Parana
Kermadec Is.
Aconcagua 6960
Pampas
R. de la Plata
Tristan da Cunha
Negro
Patagonia
Chatham Is.
Falkland Is.
Tierra del Fuego
S. Georgia
Magellan's Str.
C. Horn
Drake Passage
Graham Land
Antarctic Peninsula
Antarctic Circle
Weddell Sea
Palmer Land
Ellsworth Land
Caird Coast
Coats Land
Byrd Land
Ross Sea
West from Greenwich

HEIGHT OF LAND
in metres
Above 6 000
4 000–6 000
2 000–4 000
1000–2 000
200–1000
0–200
Below Sea-Level
DEPTH OF SEA
in metres
0–200
200–4000
4000–8000
Below 8000
ARCTIC OCEAN
Svalbard
Novaya Zemlya
Severnaya Zemlya
New Siberian Is.
N. Cape
Scandinavia
Baltic Sea
L. Ladoga
North Sea
North European Plain
Ural Mts.
West Siberian Plain
Siberia
Yenisey
Ob
Lr. Tunguska
Lena
Aldan
Angara
Irtysh
Stanovoy Ra.
Sea of Okhotsk
L. Baikal
Sakhalin
Amur
Sayan Mts.
Altai
Rhine
Carpathians
Volga
Don
Mt. Blanc 4810
Alps
Danube
Apennines
Balkan Pen.
Black Sea
Elbrus 5633
Caucasus
Caspian Sea
Aral Sea
L. Balkhash
Syr Darya
Amu Darya
Tian Shan
Gobi
Huang
Hokkaido
Sea of Japan
Honshu
Mt. Fuji 3776
Mediterranean Sea
Anatolia
Elburz Mts.
Tigris
Euphrates
Pamirs
Hindu Kush
Karakoram
Kunlun
Nan Shan
Plateau of Tibet
Himalaya
Mt. Everest 8848
Sulaiman Ra.
Indus
Thar Desert
Ganges
Yangtze
North China Plain
Yellow Sea
East China Sea
PACIFIC OCEAN
Taiwan
Xi
Libyan Desert
Nile
Red Sea
The Gulf
Hoggar
Tibesti
Sahara
Arabia
Rub 'al Khali
Arabian Sea
Deccan
W. Ghats
E. Ghats
Bay of Bengal
Salween
Mekong
Hainan
South China Sea
Philippine Is.
Mariana Is.
Wake I.
Guam
Marshall Is.
Niger
L. Chad
Blue Nile
White Nile
Socotra
C. Guardafui
Ethiopian Highlands
C. Comorin
Ceylon
Str. of Malacca
Kinabalu 4101
Caroline Islands
Gilbert Is.
Guinea
Cameroon Pk. 4070
Uele
(Congo)
L. Turkana
Mt. Kenya 5199
L. Victoria
Kilimanjaro 5895
Zaire
INDIAN OCEAN
Sumatra
Sunda Is.
Celebes Sea
Borneo
Moluccas
Celebes
Nauru
Bismarck Arch.
New Guinea
Solomon Is.
Ellice Is.
Seychelles
L. Tanganyika
Kasai
Java Sea
Java
Banda Sea
Timor
Torres Str.
C. York
L. Malawi
Zambezi
Comoro Is.
Mozambique Chan.
Madagascar
Cocos or Keeling Is.
Coral Sea
Gt. Barrier Reef
New Hebrides
Fiji Is.
Cubango
Kalahari Desert
Mauritius
Réunion
Hamersley Ra.
Macdonnell Ra.
Great Dividing Range
New Caledonia
Orange
Drakensberg
Great Victoria Desert
C. of Good Hope
C. Leeuwin
Great Australian Bight
Darling
Murray
Australian Alps
Mt. Kosciusko 2230
North I.
Bass Str.
New Zealand
Tasmania
Mt. Cook 3764
South I.
Crozet Is.
Kerguelen Is.
SOUTHERN OCEAN
Queen Maud Land
Enderby Land
Queen Mary Coast
Wilkes Land
Adélie Land
South Magnetic Pole
Victoria Land
East from Greenwich

STRUCTURE

1: 95 000 000

Structural Regions of the Land

- Pre-Cambrian shields
- Sedimentary cover on Pre-Cambrian shields
- Palæozoic (Caledonian and Hercynian) folding
- Sedimentary cover on Palæozoic folding
- Mesozoic folding
- Sedimentary cover on Mesozoic folding
- Cainozoic folding
- Sedimentary cover on Cainozoic folding
- Intensive Mesozoic and Cainozoic vulcanism
- Oceanic-type crust raised above sea level

Structural Regions of the Oceans

- Regions of continental-type crust
- Limit of continental shelf
- Oceanic marginal troughs
- Mid-oceanic volcanic ridges
- Rift valleys in mid-oceanic ridges
- Principal faults
- Frontal line of overthrust folds

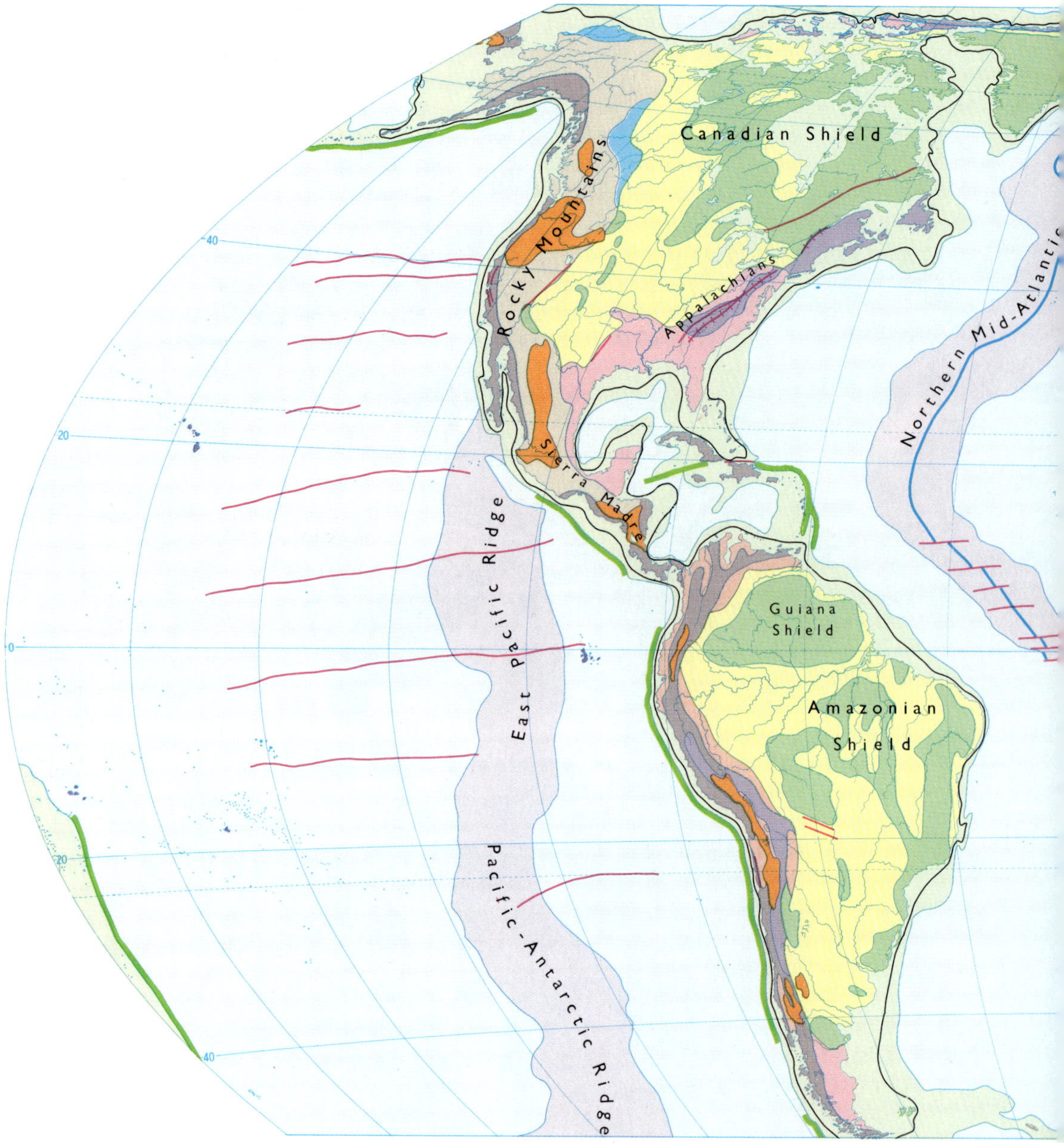

GEOLOGICAL TIME SCALE

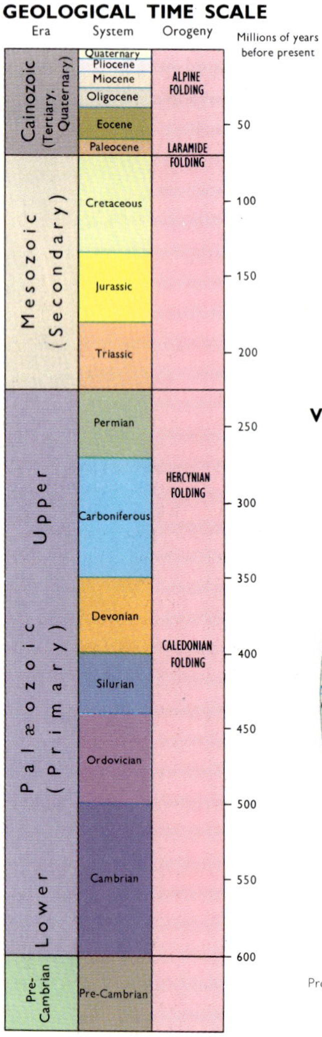

VOLCANOES

Equatorial Scale 1: 280 000 000

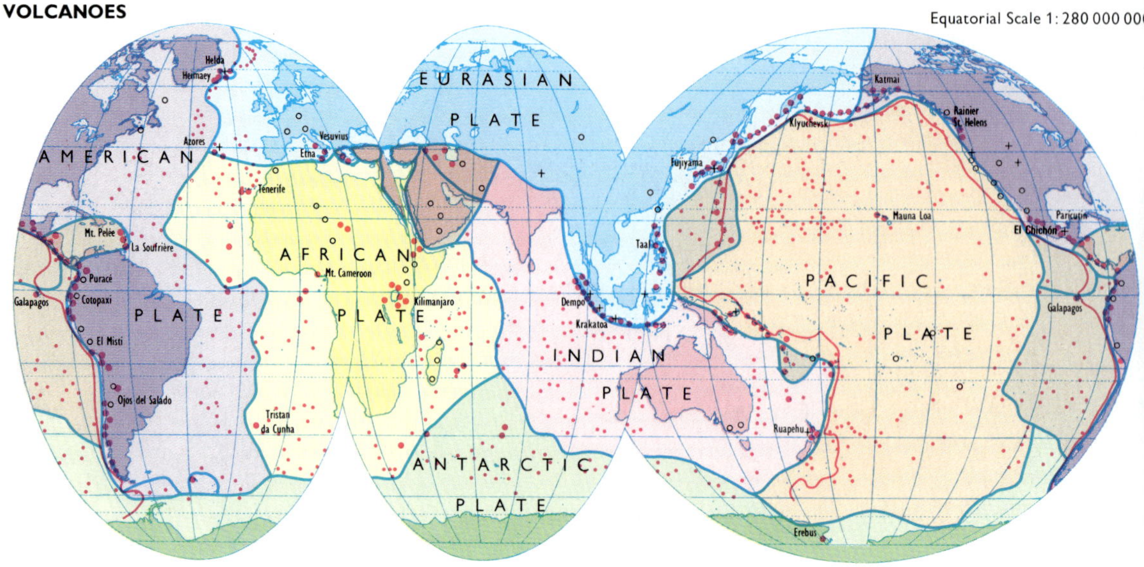

Projection: *Interrupted Mollweide's Homolographic*

- Land volcanoes active since 1700
- Land volcanoes inactive since 1700
- Submarine volcanoes
- Geysers
- Plate boundaries
- Andesite line (boundary between sial continental crust and sima oceanic crust in the Pacific)

1: 95 000 000

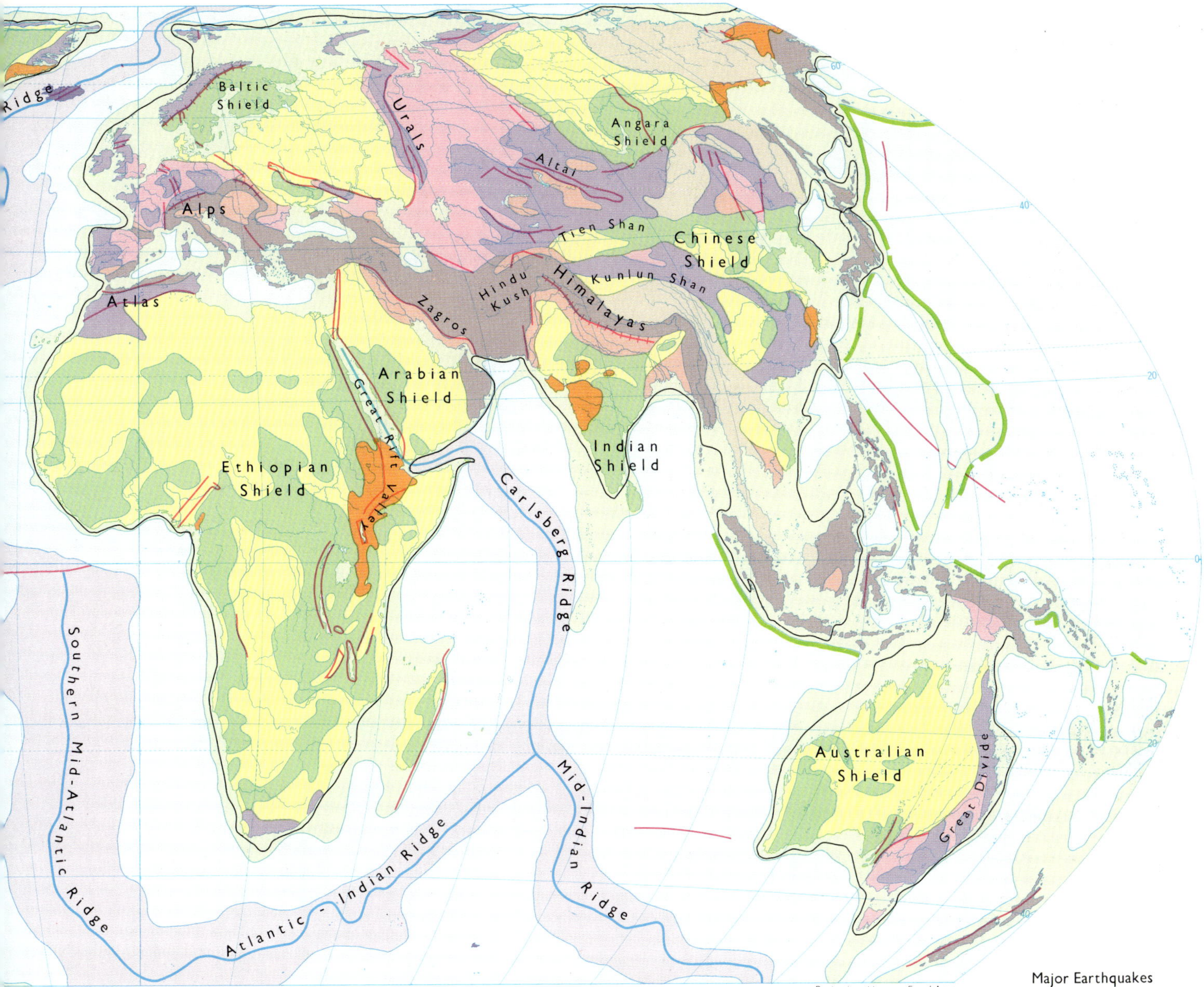

Projection: *Hammer Equal Area*

EARTHQUAKES

Equatorial Scale 1: 280 000 000

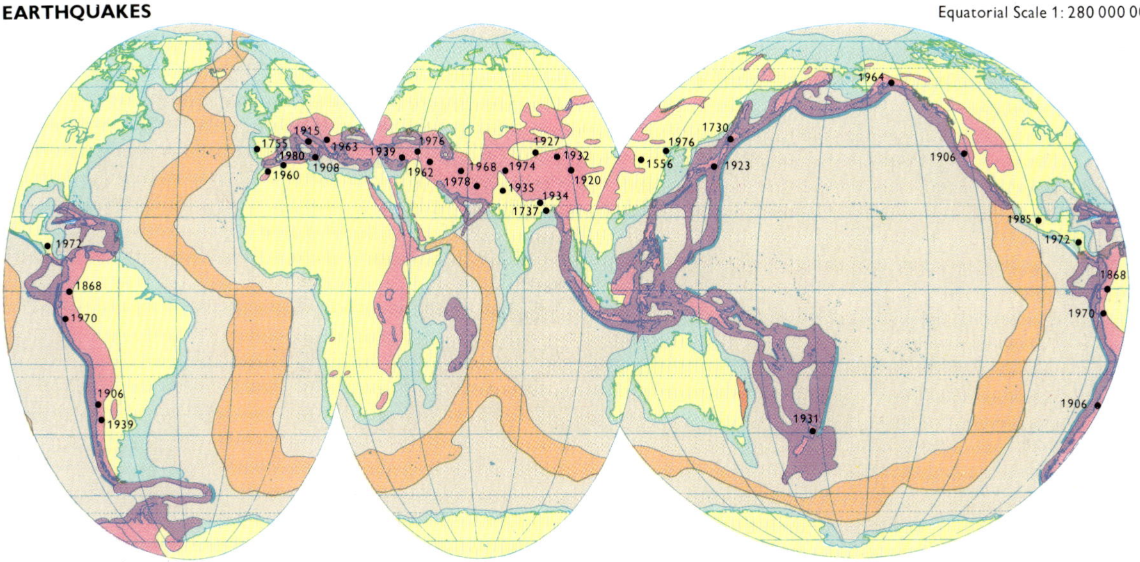

• 1906 Principal earthquakes and their dates

Oceanic marginal troughs

Mobile land areas

Submarine zones of mobile land areas

Stable land platforms

Submarine extensions of stable land platforms

Mid-oceanic volcanic ridges

Oceanic platforms

Major Earthquakes

		Nos. killed
1556	Shaanxi, China	830 000
1730	Hokkaido, Japan	137 000
1737	Calcutta, India	300 000
1755	Lisbon, Portugal	60 000
1868	Ecuador and N. Peru	40 000
1906	Valparaiso, Chile	22 000
1906	San Francisco, U.S.A.	450
1908	Messina, Italy	77 000
1915	Avezzano, Italy	30 000
1920	Gansu, China	180 000
1923	Yokohama, Japan	143 000
1927	Nan Shan, China	200 000
1931	Napier, N. Zealand	250
1932	Gansu, China	70 000
1934	Nepal	11 700
1935	Quetta, Pakistan	30 000
1939	Erzincan, Turkey	30 000
1960	Agadir, Morocco	12 000
1962	Khorasan, Iran	10 000
1963	Skopje, Yugoslavia	1000
1964	Anchorage, Alaska	100
1968	N.E. Iran	12 000
1970	N. Peru	67 000
1972	Managua, Nicaragua	7 000
1974	N. Pakistan	10 000
1976	Tangshan, China	650 000
1978	Tabas, Iran	11 000
1980	El Asnam, Algeria	20 000
1985	Mexico	20 000

CLIMATES

after Köppen

Climatic group		Climate	Temperature		Rainfall
A TROPICAL RAINY CLIMATES	Af	RAIN-FOREST CLIMATE	All mean monthly temperatures above 18°C		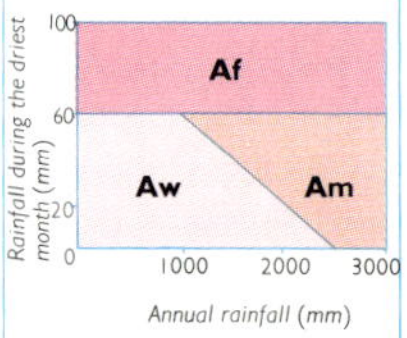
	Am	MONSOON CLIMATE			
	Aw	SAVANNA CLIMATE			
B DRY CLIMATES	BS	STEPPE CLIMATE	Mean annual temperature **h** = above 18°C **k** = below 18°C		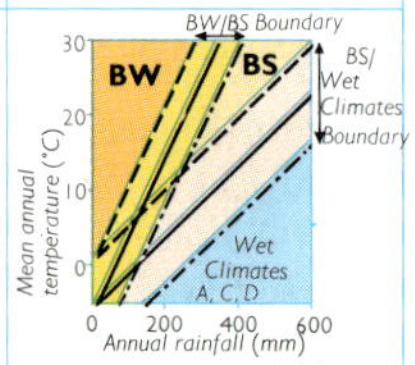 summer rainfall (dashed line) winter rainfall (solid line) rainfall evenly distributed (dash-dot line)
	BW	DESERT CLIMATE			
C WARM TEMPERATE RAINY CLIMATES	Cw	DRY WINTER CLIMATE	Mean temperature of the coldest month between −3°C to 18°C	**a** Mean temperature of hottest month above 22°C, and with more than 4 months of over 10°C	**w** dry winter Rainfall of the driest month of the cold season is one-tenth or less of the rainfall of the wettest month of the hot season
	Cs	DRY SUMMER CLIMATE (Mediterranean)		**b** Mean temperature of hottest month below 22°C and with more than 4 months of over 10°C	
	Cf	CLIMATE WITH NO DRY SEASON			**s** dry summer Rainfall of the driest month of the hot season is less than one-third of the rainfall of the wettest month of the cold season and less than 40mm.
D COLD TEMPERATE RAINY CLIMATES	Dw	DRY WINTER CLIMATE	Mean temperature of the coldest month below −3°C	**c** Mean temperature of hottest month below 22°C, but with less than 4 months of over 10°C	**f** with no dry season Rainfall does not correspond to w or s climates
	Df	CLIMATE WITH NO DRY SEASON		**d** Mean temperature of hottest month below 22°C, and of the coldest month below −38°C	
E POLAR CLIMATES	ET	TUNDRA CLIMATE	Mean temperature of the hottest month below 10°C	Mean temperature of the hottest month between 0°C and 10°C	**H** More than 1500m above sea level
	EF	PERPETUAL FROST		Mean temperature of the hottest month between 0°C and 10°C	

SOIL REGIONS

1:240 000 000

after Glinka, Stremme, Marbut, and others

- Tundra Soil
- Podzols
- Brown Forest Soil
- Lightly leached Dry Forest Soil
- Red and yellow Sub-tropical Forest Soil
- Reddish Savanna Soil and Tropical Red Earths
- Laterites
- Chernozem
- Degraded Chernozem
- Black Savanna Soil
- Chestnut Steppe Soil
- Grey, light brown and red brown Desert Steppe Soils
- Alluvium
- Mountain and High Plateau Soils
- Oases Soil
- Tropical and Mangrove Swamp

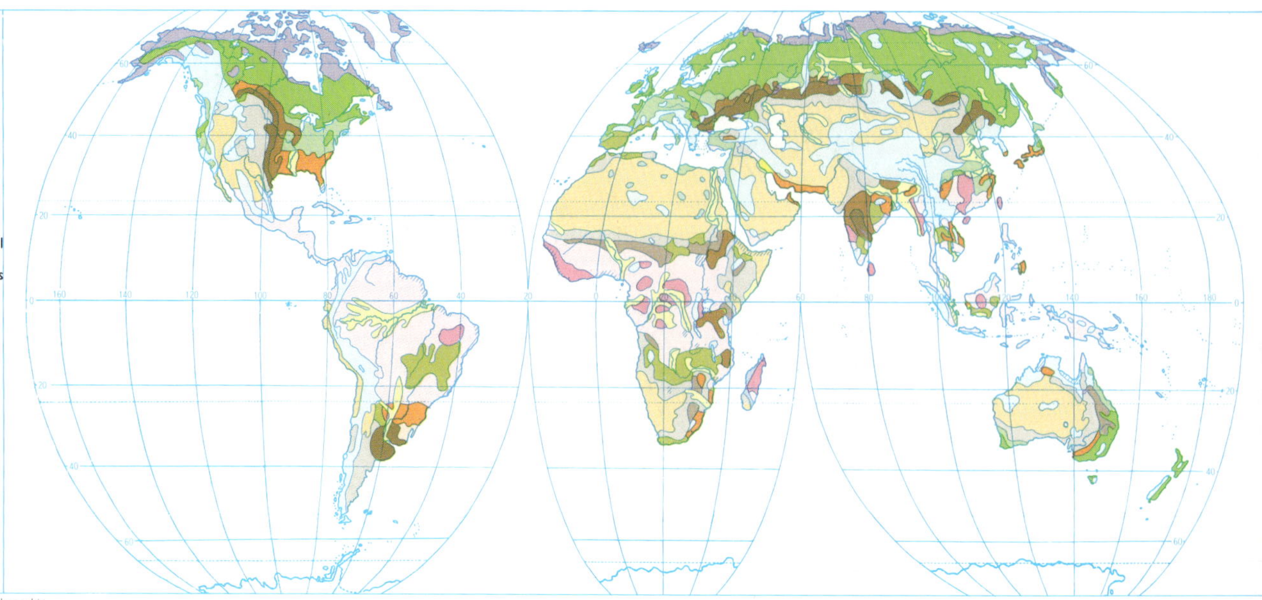

Projection: *Interrupted Mollweide's Homolographic*

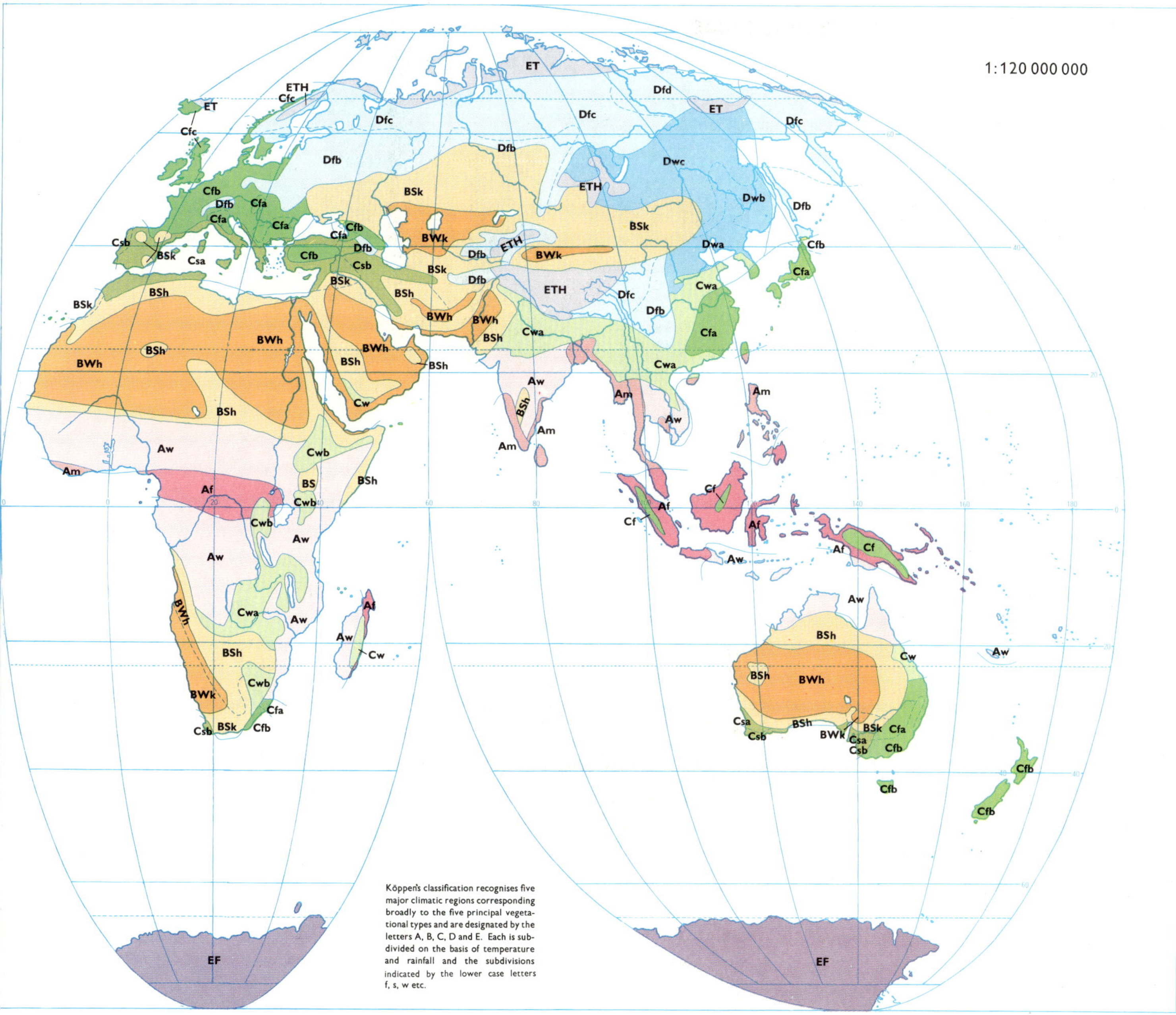

Köppen's classification recognises five major climatic regions corresponding broadly to the five principal vegetational types and are designated by the letters A, B, C, D and E. Each is subdivided on the basis of temperature and rainfall and the subdivisions indicated by the lower case letters f, s, w etc.

NATURAL VEGETATION

1:240 000 000

- Coniferous Forest
- Broad-leaved Forest and Meadow
- Evergreen Trees and Shrubs
- Temperate Rain Forest
- Monsoon Forest
- Tropical Rain Forest
- Thorn Forest
- Grassland
- Scrub, Steppe and Semi-desert
- Desert
- Alpine Tundra and Ice Desert

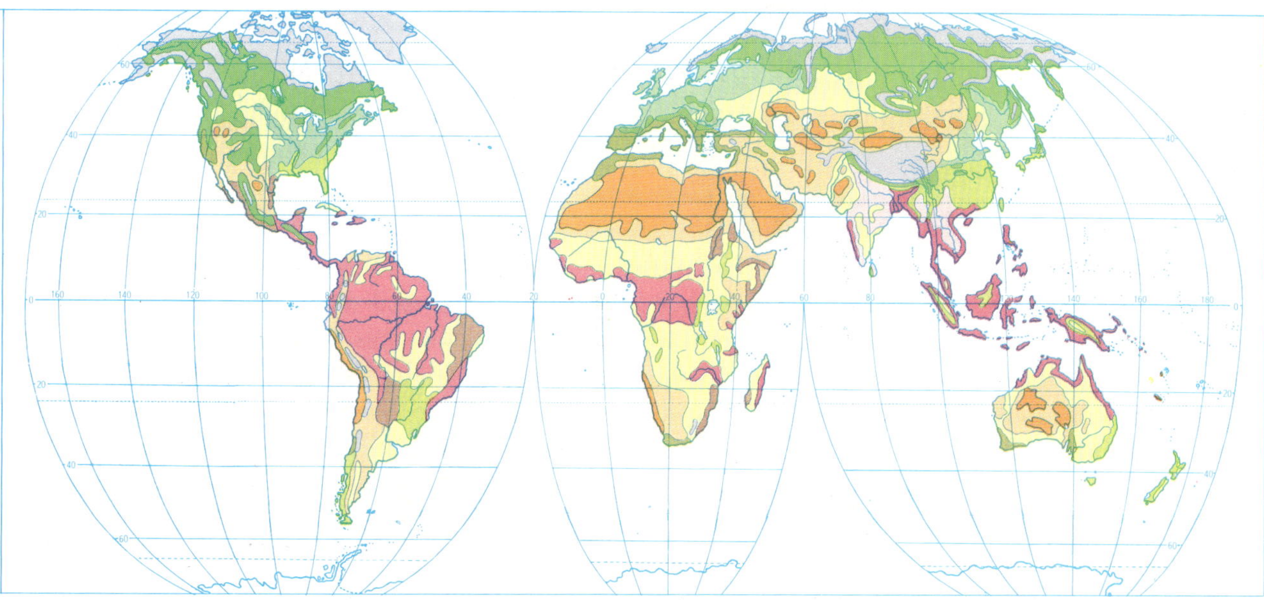

These four pages give temperature and precipitation statistics for over 80 stations, which are arranged by listing the continents and the places within each continent in alphabetical order. The elevation of each station, in metres above mean sea level, is stated beneath its name. The average monthly temperature, in degrees Celsius, and the average monthly precipitation, in millimetres, are given. To the right, the average yearly rainfall, the average yearly temperature, and the annual range of temperature (the difference between the warmest and the coldest months) are also stated.

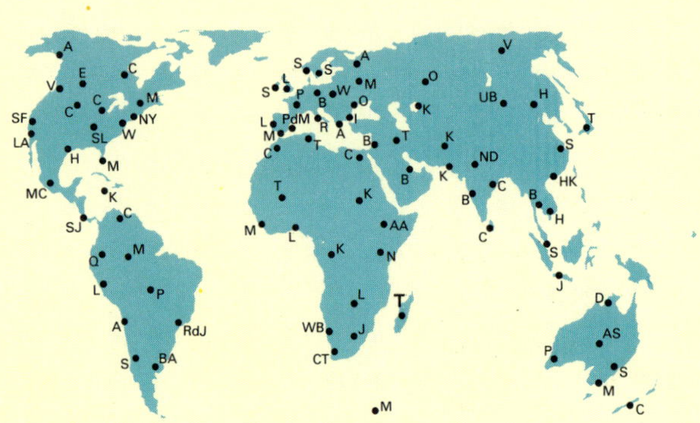

AFRICA

		Jan.	Feb.	Mar.	Apr.	May	June	July	Aug.	Sept.	Oct.	Nov.	Dec.	Year	Annual Range
Addis Ababa, Ethiopia															
	Precipitation	201	206	239	102	28	< 3	0	< 3	3	25	135	213	1 151	
2 450 m	*Temperature*	19	20	20	20	19	18	18	19	21	22	21	20	20	4
Cairo, Egypt															
	Precipitation	5	5	5	3	3	< 3	0	0	< 3	< 3	3	5	28	
116 m	*Temperature*	13	15	18	21	25	28	28	28	26	24	20	15	22	15
Cape Town, South Africa															
	Precipitation	15	8	18	48	79	84	89	66	43	31	18	10	508	
17 m	*Temperature*	21	21	20	17	14	13	12	13	14	16	18	19	17	9
Casablanca, Morocco															
	Precipitation	53	48	56	36	23	5	0	< 3	8	38	66	71	404	
50 m	*Temperature*	13	13	14	16	18	20	22	23	22	19	16	13	18	10
Johannesburg, South Africa															
	Precipitation	114	109	89	38	25	8	8	8	23	56	107	125	709	
1 665 m	*Temperature*	20	20	18	16	13	10	11	13	16	18	19	20	16	10
Khartoum, Sudan															
	Precipitation	< 3	< 3	< 3	< 3	3	8	53	71	18	5	< 3	0	158	
390 m	*Temperature*	24	25	28	31	33	34	32	31	32	32	28	25	29	9
Kinshasa, Zaïre															
	Precipitation	135	145	196	196	158	8	3	3	31	119	221	142	1 354	
325 m	*Temperature*	26	26	27	27	26	24	23	24	25	26	26	26	25	4
Lagos, Nigeria															
	Precipitation	28	46	102	150	269	460	279	64	140	206	69	25	1 836	
3 m	*Temperature*	27	28	29	28	28	26	26	25	26	26	28	28	27	4
Lusaka, Zambia															
	Precipitation	231	191	142	18	3	< 3	< 3	0	< 3	10	91	150	836	
1 277 m	*Temperature*	21	22	21	21	19	16	16	18	22	24	23	22	21	8
Monrovia, Liberia															
	Precipitation	31	56	97	216	516	973	996	373	744	772	236	130	5 138	
23 m	*Temperature*	26	26	27	27	26	25	24	25	25	25	26	26	26	3
Nairobi, Kenya															
	Precipitation	38	64	125	211	158	46	15	23	31	53	109	86	958	
1 820 m	*Temperature*	19	19	19	19	18	16	16	16	18	19	18	18	18	3
Tananarive, Madagascar															
	Precipitation	300	279	178	53	18	8	8	10	18	61	135	287	1 356	
1 372 m	*Temperature*	21	21	21	19	18	15	14	15	17	19	21	21	19	7
Timbuktu, Mali															
	Precipitation	< 3	< 3	3	< 3	5	23	79	81	38	3	< 3	< 3	231	
301 m	*Temperature*	22	24	28	32	34	35	32	30	32	31	28	23	29	13
Tunis, Tunisia															
	Precipitation	64	51	41	36	18	8	3	8	33	51	48	61	419	
66 m	*Temperature*	10	11	13	16	19	23	26	27	25	20	16	11	18	17
Walvis Bay, South Africa															
	Precipitation	< 3	5	8	3	3	< 3	< 3	3	< 3	< 3	< 3	< 3	23	
7 m	*Temperature*	19	19	19	18	17	16	15	14	14	15	17	18	18	5

AMERICA, NORTH

		Jan.	Feb.	Mar.	Apr.	May	June	July	Aug.	Sept.	Oct.	Nov.	Dec.	Year	Annual Range
Anchorage, Alaska, U.S.A.															
	Precipitation	20	18	15	10	13	18	41	66	66	56	25	23	371	
40 m	*Temperature*	–11	–8	–5	2	7	12	14	13	9	2	–5	–11	2	25
Cheyenne, Wyo., U.S.A.															
	Precipitation	10	15	25	48	61	41	53	41	31	25	13	13	376	
1 871 m	*Temperature*	–4	–3	1	5	10	16	19	19	14	7	1	–2	7	23
Chicago, Ill., U.S.A.															
	Precipitation	51	51	66	71	86	89	84	81	79	66	61	51	836	
251 m	*Temperature*	–4	–3	2	9	14	20	23	22	19	12	5	–1	10	27
Churchill, Man., Canada															
	Precipitation	15	13	18	23	32	44	46	58	51	43	39	21	402	
13 m	*Temperature*	– 28	– 26	– 20	– 10	– 2	6	12	11	5	– 2	– 12	– 22	– 7	40

		Jan.	Feb.	Mar.	Apr.	May	June	July	Aug.	Sept.	Oct.	Nov.	Dec.	Year	Annual range
Edmonton, Alta., Canada															
	Precipitation	25	19	19	22	43	77	89	78	39	17	16	25	466	
676 m	*Temperature*	– 15	– 10	– 5	4	11	15	17	16	11	6	– 4	– 10	3	32
Honolulu, Hawaii, U.S.A.															
	Precipitation	104	66	79	48	25	18	23	28	36	48	64	104	643	
12 m	*Temperature*	23	18	19	20	22	24	25	26	26	24	22	19	22	8
Houston, Tex., U.S.A.															
	Precipitation	89	76	84	91	119	117	99	99	104	94	89	109	1 171	
12 m	*Temperature*	12	13	17	21	24	27	28	29	26	22	16	12	21	17
Kingston, Jamaica															
	Precipitation	23	15	23	31	102	89	38	91	99	180	74	36	800	
34 m	*Temperature*	25	25	25	26	26	28	28	28	27	27	26	26	26	3
Los Angeles, Calif., U.S.A.															
	Precipitation	79	76	71	25	10	3	< 3	< 3	5	15	31	66	381	
95 m	*Temperature*	13	14	14	16	17	19	21	22	21	18	16	14	17	9
Mexico City, Mexico															
	Precipitation	13	5	10	20	53	119	170	152	130	51	18	8	747	
2 309 m	*Temperature*	12	13	16	18	19	19	17	18	18	16	14	13	16	7
Miami, Fla., U.S.A.															
	Precipitation	71	53	64	81	173	178	155	160	203	234	71	51	1 516	
8 m	*Temperature*	20	20	22	23	25	27	28	28	27	25	22	21	24	8
Montreal, Que., Canada															
	Precipitation	72	65	74	74	66	82	90	92	88	76	81	87	946	
57 m	*Temperature*	– 10	– 9	– 3	– 6	13	18	21	20	15	9	2	– 7	6	31
New York, N.Y., U.S.A.															
	Precipitation	94	97	91	81	81	84	107	109	86	89	76	91	1 092	
96 m	*Temperature*	–1	–1	3	10	16	20	23	23	21	15	7	2	8	24
St. Louis, Mo., U.S.A.															
	Precipitation	58	64	89	97	114	114	89	86	81	74	71	64	1 001	
173 m	*Temperature*	0	1	7	13	19	24	26	26	22	15	8	2	14	26
San Francisco, Calif., U.S.A.															
	Precipitation	119	97	79	38	18	3	< 3	< 3	8	25	64	112	561	
16 m	*Temperature*	10	12	13	13	14	15	15	15	17	16	14	11	14	7
San José, Costa Rica															
	Precipitation	15	5	20	46	229	241	211	241	305	300	145	41	1 798	
1 146 m	*Temperature*	19	19	21	21	22	21	21	21	21	20	20	19	20	2
Vancouver, B.C., Canada															
	Precipitation	154	115	101	60	52	45	32	41	67	114	150	182	1113	
14 m	*Temperature*	3	5	6	9	12	15	17	17	14	10	6	4	10	14
Washington, D.C., U.S.A.															
	Precipitation	86	76	91	84	94	99	112	109	94	74	66	79	1 064	
22 m	*Temperature*	1	2	7	12	18	23	25	24	20	14	8	3	13	24

AMERICA, SOUTH

		Jan.	Feb.	Mar.	Apr.	May	June	July	Aug.	Sept.	Oct.	Nov.	Dec.	Year	Annual range
Antofagasta, Chile															
	Precipitation	0	0	0	< 3	< 3	3	5	3	< 3	3	< 3	0	13	
94 m	*Temperature*	21	21	20	18	16	15	14	14	15	16	18	19	17	7
Buenos Aires, Argentina															
	Precipitation	79	71	109	89	76	61	56	61	79	86	84	99	950	
27 m	*Temperature*	23	23	21	17	13	9	10	11	13	15	19	22	16	14
Caracas, Venezuela															
	Precipitation	23	10	15	33	79	102	109	109	107	109	94	46	836	
1 042 m	*Temperature*	19	19	20	21	22	21	21	21	21	21	20	20	21	3
Lima, Peru															
	Precipitation	3	< 3	< 3	< 3	5	5	8	8	8	3	3	< 3	41	
120 m	*Temperature*	23	24	24	22	19	17	17	16	17	18	19	21	20	8
Manaus, Brazil															
	Precipitation	249	231	262	221	170	84	58	38	46	107	142	203	1 811	
44 m	*Temperature*	28	28	28	27	28	28	28	28	29	29	29	28	28	2
Paraná, Brazil															
	Precipitation	287	236	239	102	13	< 3	3	5	28	127	231	310	1 582	
260 m	*Temperature*	23	23	23	23	23	21	21	22	24	24	24	23	23	3
Quito, Ecuador															
	Precipitation	99	112	142	175	137	43	20	31	69	112	97	79	1 115	
2 879 m	*Temperature*	15	15	15	15	15	14	14	15	15	15	15	15	15	1
Rio de Janeiro, Brazil															
	Precipitation	125	122	130	107	79	53	41	43	66	79	104	137	1 082	
61 m	*Temperature*	26	26	25	24	22	21	21	21	21	22	23	25	23	5
Santiago, Chile															
	Precipitation	3	3	5	13	64	84	76	56	31	15	8	5	358	
520 m	*Temperature*	21	20	18	15	12	9	9	10	12	15	17	19	15	12

ASIA

		Jan.	Feb.	Mar.	Apr.	May	June	July	Aug.	Sept.	Oct.	Nov.	Dec.	Year	Annual range
Bahrain															
	Precipitation	8	18	13	8	<3	0	0	0	0	0	18	18	81	
5 m	*Temperature*	17	18	21	25	29	32	33	34	31	28	24	19	26	16
Bangkok, Thailand															
	Precipitation	8	20	36	58	198	160	160	175	305	206	66	5	1 397	
2 m	*Temperature*	26	28	29	30	29	29	28	28	28	28	26	25	28	5
Beirut, Lebanon															
	Precipitation	191	158	94	53	18	3	<3	<3	5	51	132	185	892	
34 m	*Temperature*	14	14	16	18	22	24	27	28	26	24	19	16	21	14
Bombay, India															
	Precipitation	3	3	3	<3	18	485	617	340	264	64	13	3	1 809	
11 m	*Temperature*	24	24	26	28	30	29	27	27	27	28	27	26	27	6
Calcutta, India															
	Precipitation	10	31	36	43	140	297	325	328	252	114	20	5	1 600	
6 m	*Temperature*	20	22	27	30	30	30	29	29	29	28	23	19	26	11
Colombo, Sri Lanka															
	Precipitation	89	69	147	231	371	224	135	109	160	348	315	147	2 365	
7 m	*Temperature*	26	26	27	28	28	27	27	27	27	27	26	26	27	2
Harbin, China															
	Precipitation	5	5	10	23	43	94	112	104	46	33	8	5	488	
160 m	*Temperature*	–18	–15	–5	6	13	19	22	21	14	4	–6	–16	3	40
Ho Chi Minh City, Vietnam															
	Precipitation	15	3	13	43	221	330	315	269	335	269	114	56	1 984	
9 m	*Temperature*	26	27	29	30	29	28	28	28	27	27	27	26	28	4
Jakarta, Indonesia															
	Precipitation	300	300	211	147	114	97	64	43	66	112	142	203	1 798	
8 m	*Temperature*	26	26	27	27	27	27	27	27	27	27	27	26	27	1
Hong Kong															
	Precipitation	33	46	74	137	292	394	381	361	257	114	43	31	2 162	
33 m	*Temperature*	16	15	18	22	26	28	28	28	27	25	21	18	23	13
Kabul, Afghanistan															
	Precipitation	31	36	94	102	20	5	3	3	<3	15	20	10	338	
1 815 m	*Temperature*	–3	–1	6	13	18	22	25	24	20	14	7	3	12	28
Karachi, Pakistan															
	Precipitation	13	10	8	3	3	18	81	41	13	<3	3	5	196	
4 m	*Temperature*	19	20	24	28	30	31	30	29	28	28	24	20	26	12
New Delhi, India															
	Precipitation	23	18	13	8	13	74	180	172	117	10	3	10	640	
218 m	*Temperature*	14	17	23	28	33	34	31	30	29	26	20	15	25	20
Shanghai, China															
	Precipitation	48	58	84	94	94	180	147	142	130	71	51	36	1 135	
7 m	*Temperature*	4	5	9	14	20	24	28	28	23	19	12	7	16	24
Singapore															
	Precipitation	252	173	193	188	173	173	170	196	178	208	254	257	2 413	
10 m	*Temperature*	26	27	28	28	28	28	28	27	27	27	27	27	27	2
Tehran, Iran															
	Precipitation	46	38	46	36	13	3	3	3	3	8	20	31	246	
1 220 m	*Temperature*	2	5	9	16	21	26	30	29	25	18	12	6	17	28
Tokyo, Japan															
	Precipitation	48	74	107	135	147	165	142	152	234	208	97	56	1 565	
6 m	*Temperature*	3	4	7	13	17	21	25	26	23	17	11	6	14	23
Ulan Bator, Mongolia															
	Precipitation	<3	<3	3	5	10	28	76	51	23	5	5	3	208	
1 325 m	*Temperature*	–26	–21	–13	–1	6	14	16	14	8	–1	–13	–22	–3	42

AUSTRALIA, NEW ZEALAND and ANTARCTICA

		Jan.	Feb.	Mar.	Apr.	May	June	July	Aug.	Sept.	Oct.	Nov.	Dec.	Year	Annual range
Alice Springs, Australia															
	Precipitation	43	33	28	10	15	13	8	8	8	18	31	38	252	
579 m	*Temperature*	29	28	25	20	15	12	12	14	18	23	26	28	21	17
Christchurch, New Zealand															
	Precipitation	56	43	48	48	66	66	69	48	46	43	48	56	638	
10 m	*Temperature*	16	16	14	12	9	6	6	7	9	12	14	16	11	10
Darwin, Australia															
	Precipitation	386	312	254	97	15	3	<3	3	13	51	119	239	1 491	
30 m	*Temperature*	29	29	29	29	28	26	25	26	28	29	30	29	28	5
Mawson, Antarctica															
	Precipitation	11	30	20	10	44	180	4	40	3	20	0	0	362	
14 m	*Temperature*	0	–5	–10	–14	–15	–16	–18	–18	–19	–13	–5	–1	–11	18

		Jan.	Feb.	Mar.	Apr.	May	June	July	Aug.	Sept.	Oct.	Nov.	Dec.	Year	Annual Range
Melbourne, Australia															
	Precipitation	48	46	56	58	53	53	48	48	58	66	58	58	653	
35 m	*Temperature*	20	20	18	15	13	10	9	11	13	14	16	18	15	11
Perth, Australia															
	Precipitation	8	10	20	43	130	180	170	149	86	56	20	13	881	
60 m	*Temperature*	23	23	22	19	16	14	13	13	15	16	19	22	18	10
Sydney, Australia															
	Precipitation	89	102	127	135	127	117	117	76	73	71	73	73	1 181	
42 m	*Temperature*	22	22	21	18	15	13	12	13	15	18	19	21	17	10

EUROPE and U.S.S.R.

		Jan.	Feb.	Mar.	Apr.	May	June	July	Aug.	Sept.	Oct.	Nov.	Dec.	Year	Annual Range
Archangel, U.S.S.R.															
	Precipitation	31	19	25	29	42	52	62	56	63	63	47	41	530	
13 m	*Temperature*	–16	–14	–9	0	7	12	15	14	8	2	–4	–11	0	31
Athens, Greece															
	Precipitation	62	37	37	23	23	14	6	7	15	51	56	71	402	
107 m	*Temperature*	10	10	12	16	20	25	28	28	24	20	15	11	18	18
Berlin, Germany															
	Precipitation	46	40	33	42	49	65	73	69	48	49	46	43	603	
55 m	*Temperature*	–1	0	4	9	14	17	19	18	15	9	5	1	9	20
Istanbul, Turkey															
	Precipitation	109	92	72	46	38	34	34	30	58	81	103	119	816	
114 m	*Temperature*	5	6	7	11	16	20	23	23	20	16	12	8	14	18
Kazalinsk, U.S.S.R.															
	Precipitation	10	10	13	13	15	5	5	8	8	10	13	15	125	
63 m	*Temperature*	–12	–11	–3	6	18	23	25	23	16	8	–1	–7	7	37
Lisbon, Portugal															
	Precipitation	111	76	109	54	44	16	3	4	33	62	93	103	708	
77 m	*Temperature*	11	12	14	16	17	20	22	23	21	18	14	12	17	12
London, U.K.															
	Precipitation	54	40	37	37	46	45	57	59	49	57	64	48	593	
5 m	*Temperature*	4	5	7	9	12	16	18	17	15	11	8	5	11	14
Málaga, Spain															
	Precipitation	61	51	62	46	26	5	1	3	29	64	64	62	474	
33 m	*Temperature*	12	13	15	17	19	29	25	26	23	20	16	13	18	17
Moscow, U.S.S.R.															
	Precipitation	39	38	36	37	53	58	88	71	58	45	47	54	624	
156 m	*Temperature*	–13	–10	–4	6	13	16	18	17	12	6	–1	–7	4	31
Odessa, U.S.S.R.															
	Precipitation	57	62	30	21	34	34	42	37	37	13	35	71	473	
64 m	*Temperature*	–3	–1	2	9	15	20	22	22	18	12	9	1	10	25
Omsk, U.S.S.R.															
	Precipitation	15	8	8	13	31	51	51	51	28	25	18	20	318	
85 m	*Temperature*	–22	–19	–12	–1	10	16	18	16	10	1	–11	–18	–1	40
Palma de Mallorca, Spain															
	Precipitation	39	34	51	32	29	17	3	25	55	77	47	40	449	
10 m	*Temperature*	10	11	12	15	17	21	24	25	23	18	14	11	17	15
Paris, France															
	Precipitation	56	46	35	42	57	54	59	64	55	50	51	50	619	
75 m	*Temperature*	3	4	8	11	15	18	20	19	17	12	7	4	12	17
Rome, Italy															
	Precipitation	71	62	57	51	46	37	15	21	63	99	129	93	744	
17 m	*Temperature*	8	9	11	14	18	22	25	25	22	17	13	10	16	17
Shannon, Irish Republic															
	Precipitation	94	67	56	53	61	57	77	79	86	86	96	117	929	
2 m	*Temperature*	5	5	7	9	12	14	16	16	14	11	8	6	10	11
Stavanger, Norway															
	Precipitation	93	56	45	70	49	84	93	118	142	129	125	126	1 130	
85 m	*Temperature*	1	1	3	6	10	13	15	15	13	9	6	3	8	14
Stockholm, Sweden															
	Precipitation	43	30	25	31	34	45	61	76	60	48	53	48	554	
44 m	*Temperature*	–3	–3	–1	5	10	15	18	17	12	7	3	0	7	21
Verkhoyansk, U.S.S.R.															
	Precipitation	5	5	3	5	8	23	28	25	13	8	8	5	134	
100 m	*Temperature*	–50	–45	–32	–15	0	12	14	9	2	–15	–38	–48	–17	64
Warsaw, Poland															
	Precipitation	27	32	27	37	46	69	96	65	43	38	31	44	555	
110 m	*Temperature*	–3	–3	2	7	14	17	19	18	14	9	3	0	8	22

1:190 000 000

January Temperature and Ocean Currents

(Northern Hemisphere—Winter)

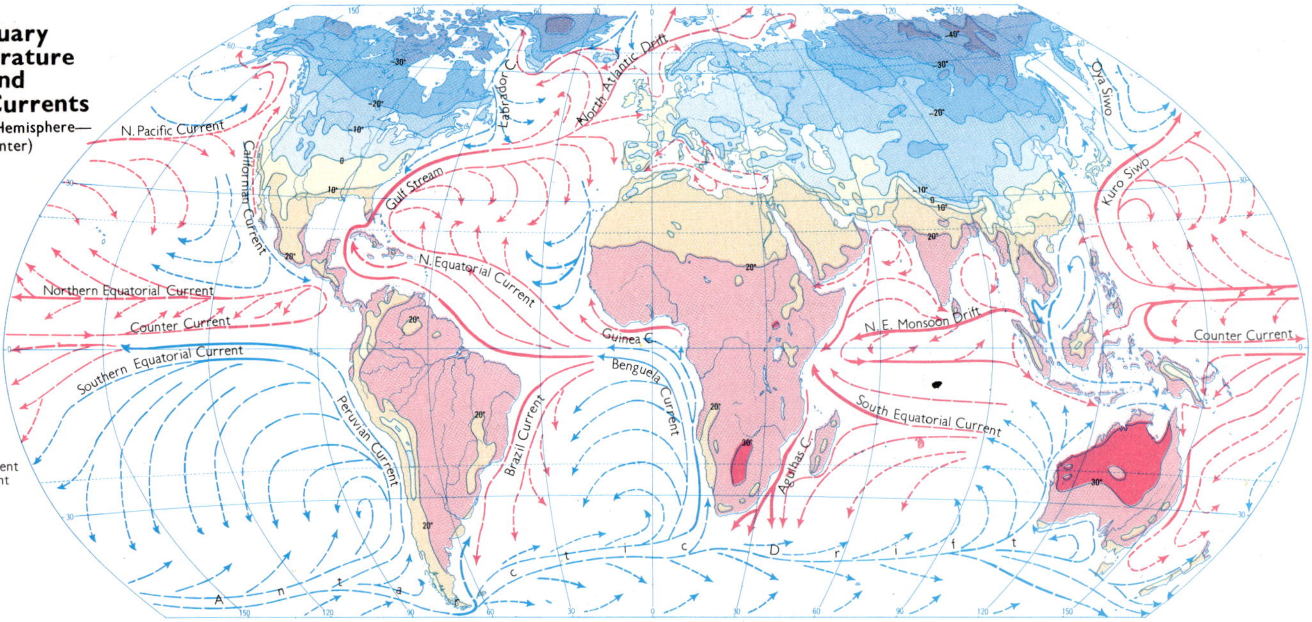

ACTUAL SURFACE TEMPERATURE

°C: 30, 20, 10, 0, –10, –20, –30, –40

Warm Current

Cold Current

July Temperature and Ocean Currents

(Northern Hemisphere—Summer)

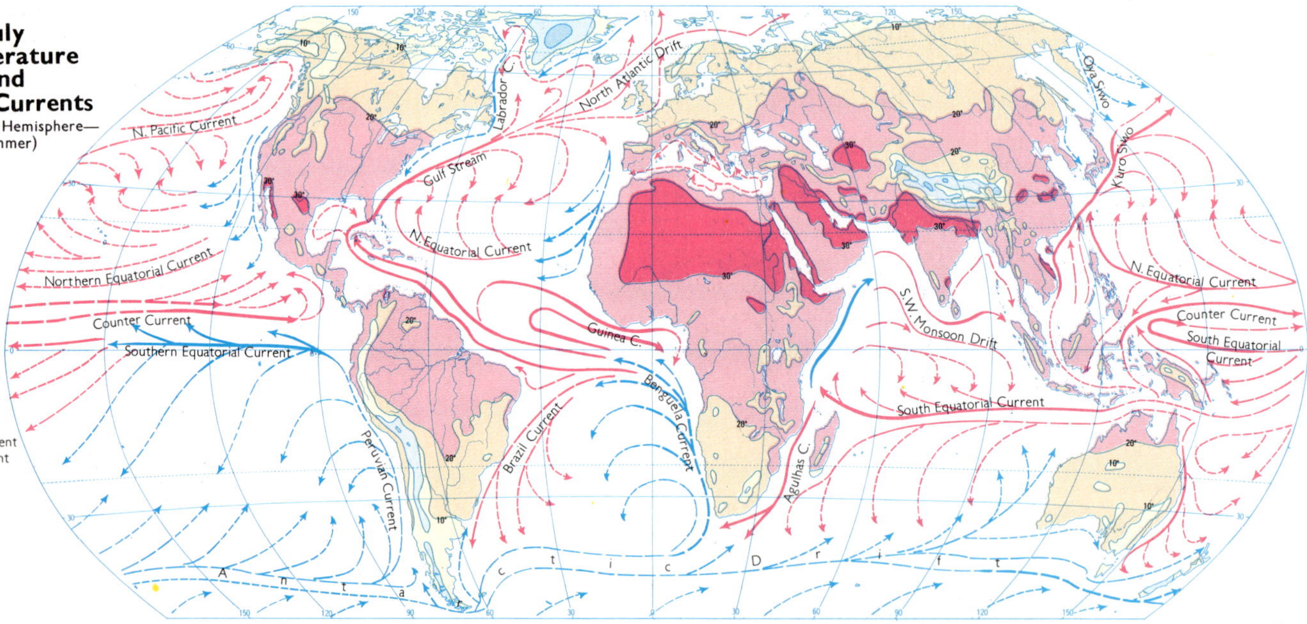

ACTUAL SURFACE TEMPERATURE

°C: 30, 20, 10, 0, –10

Warm Current

Cold Current

Annual Range of Temperature

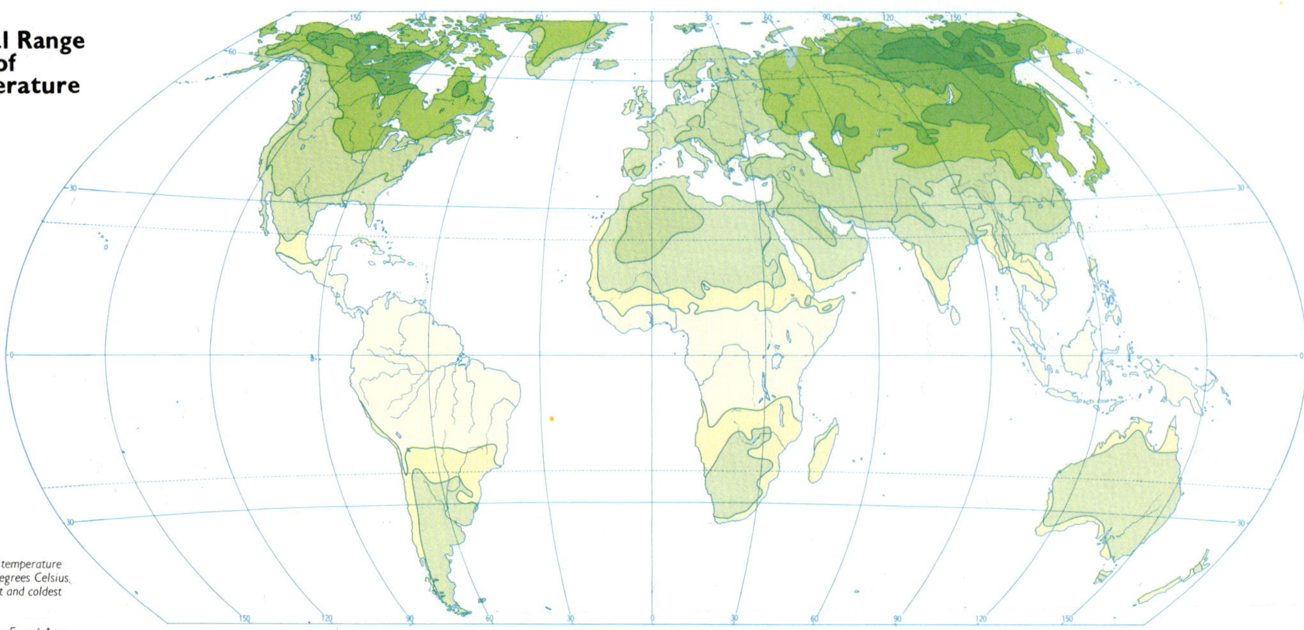

°C: 60, 50, 40, 30, 20, 10, 5, 0

The annual range of temperature is the difference in degrees Celsius, between the warmest and coldest months of the year.

Projection: *Hammer Equal Area*

January Pressure and Winds

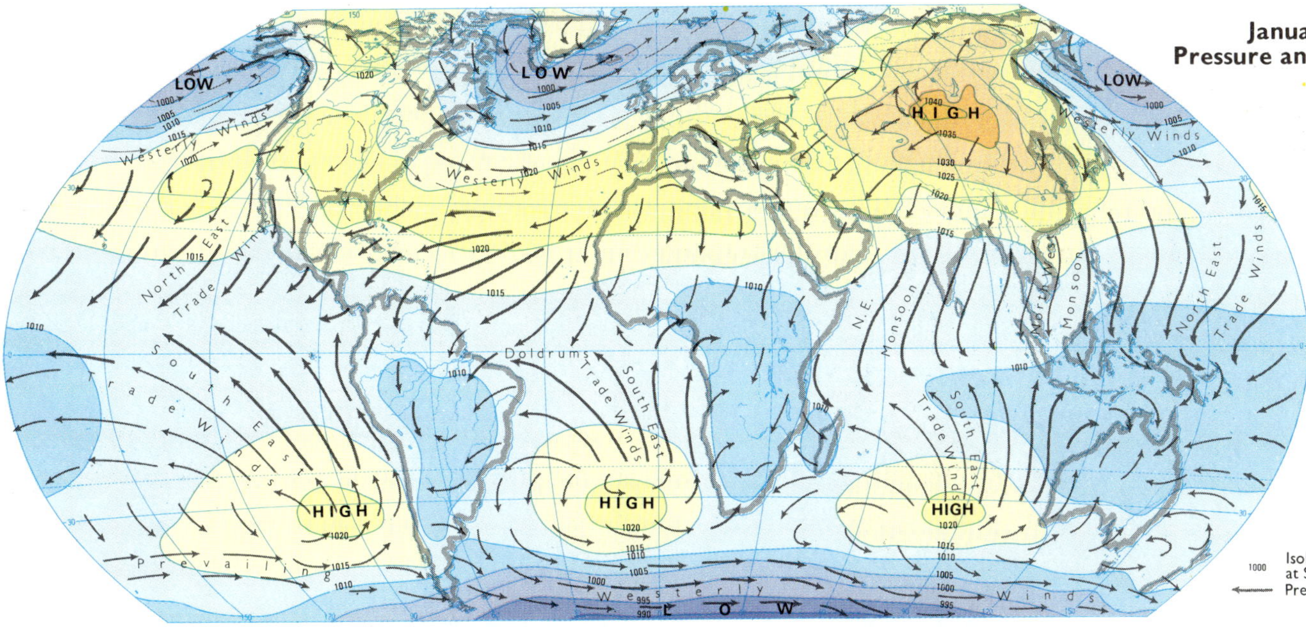

mb
1040
1035
1030
1025
1020
1015
1010
1005
1000
995
990

1000 Isobars in millibars at Sea Level
Prevailing Winds

July Pressure and Winds

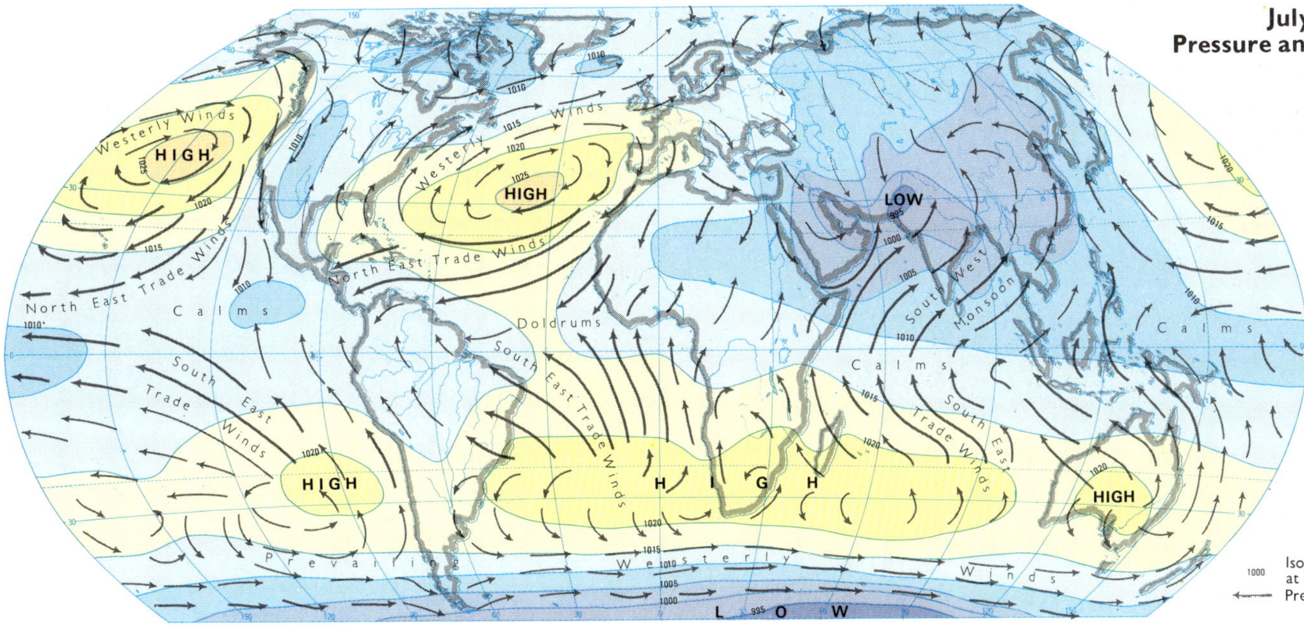

mb
1025
1020
1015
1010
1005
1000
995

1000 Isobars in millibars at Sea Level
Prevailing Winds

Annual Precipitation

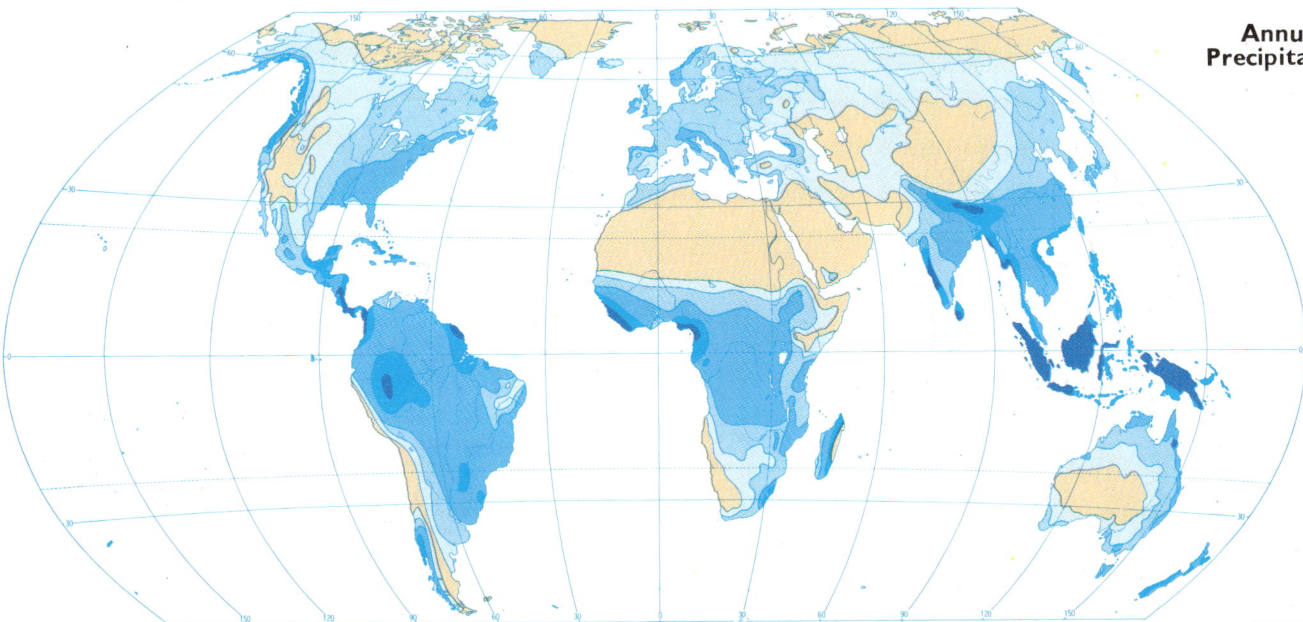

mm
3000
2000
1000
500
250

Projection: *Hammer Equal Area*

THE WORLD : Density of Population

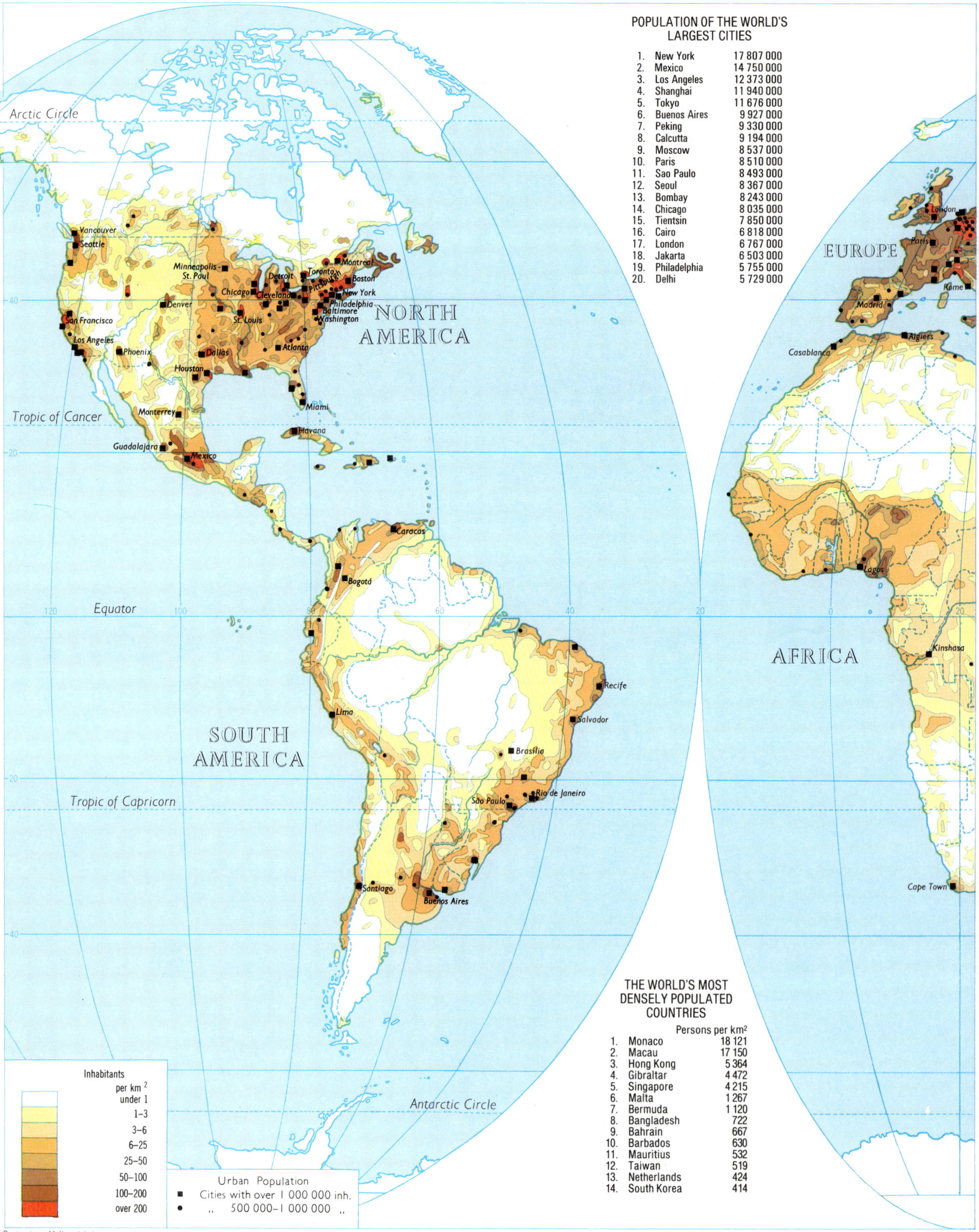

POPULATION OF THE WORLD'S LARGEST CITIES

1.	New York	17 807 000
2.	Mexico	14 750 000
3.	Los Angeles	12 373 000
4.	Shanghai	11 940 000
5.	Tokyo	11 676 000
6.	Buenos Aires	9 927 000
7.	Peking	9 330 000
8.	Calcutta	9 194 000
9.	Moscow	8 537 000
10.	Paris	8 510 000
11.	Sao Paulo	8 493 000
12.	Seoul	8 367 000
13.	Bombay	8 243 000
14.	Chicago	8 035 000
15.	Tientsin	7 850 000
16.	Cairo	6 818 000
17.	London	6 767 000
18.	Jakarta	6 503 000
19.	Philadelphia	5 755 000
20.	Delhi	5 729 000

THE WORLD'S MOST DENSELY POPULATED COUNTRIES

		Persons per km²
1.	Monaco	18 121
2.	Macau	17 150
3.	Hong Kong	5 364
4.	Gibraltar	4 472
5.	Singapore	4 215
6.	Malta	1 267
7.	Bermuda	1 120
8.	Bangladesh	722
9.	Bahrain	667
10.	Barbados	630
11.	Mauritius	532
12.	Taiwan	519
13.	Netherlands	424
14.	South Korea	414

Inhabitants per km²

- under 1
- 1–3
- 3–6
- 6–25
- 25–50
- 50–100
- 100–200
- over 200

Urban Population

- ■ Cities with over 1 000 000 inh.
- ● ,, 500 000–1 000 000 ,,

Projection: *Mollweide's Interrupted Homolographic*

THE WORLD'S MOST DENSELY POPULATED COUNTRIES

Continuation

		Persons per km²
15.	Puerto Rico	382
16.	Grenada	373
17.	San Marino	367
18.	Saint Vincent	347
19.	Belgium	329
20.	Japan	323
21.	Martinique	297
22.	Lebanon	264
23.	El Salvador	257
24.	India	251
25.	West Germany	251
26.	Sri Lanka	240
27.	Rwanda	236
28.	UK	230

Some of the lesser islands have high densities but have been omitted from this table.

For comparison the London urban area has a density of 4 270 persons per km².

POPULATION OF CITIES

The population figures used are from censuses or more recent estimates and are given in thousands for towns and cities over 200,000 (over 250,000 in Brazil and Japan and 500,000 in China, India, United States and U.S.S.R.). Where possible the population of the metropolitan area is given e.g. Greater London, Greater New York etc.

AFRICA

ALGERIA (1977)
Algiers 1 740
Oran 543
Constantine 379
Annaba 246
Tizi-Ouzou 224

ANGOLA (1982)
Luanda 700

BENIN (1982)
Cotonou 487
Porto-Novo 208

BURKINA FASO (1982)
Ouagadougou 286

CAMEROON (1983)
Douala 708
Yaoundé 485

CANARY ISLANDS (1981)
Las Palmas 360

CENTRAL AFRICAN REPUBLIC (1981)
Bangui 387

CHAD (1979)
Ndjamena 303

CONGO (1980)
Brazzaville 422

EGYPT (1976)
Cairo 6 818
Alexandria 2 318
El Giza 1 230
Shubra el Kheima 394
El Mahalla el Kubra 292
Tanta 285
Port Said 263
El Mansûra 259
Asyût 214
Zagazig 203

ETHIOPIA (1983)
Addis Ababa 1 478
Asmera 491

GABON (1983)
Libreville 350

GHANA (1984)
Accra 965
Kumasi 489

GUINEA (1980)
Conakry 763

IVORY COAST (1982)
Abidjan 1 850
Bouaké 640
Man-Danane 450
Korhogo 280

KENYA (1983)
Nairobi (1985) 1 200
Mombasa 410

LIBERIA (1984)
Monrovia 425

LIBYA (1982)
Tripoli 980
Benghazi 650
Misrātah 285

MADAGASCAR (1978)
Antananarivo 400

MALAWI (1977)
Blantyre 219

MALI (1976)
Bamako 419

MOROCCO (1981)
Casablanca 2 409
Rabat-Salé 842
Fès 562
Marrakesh 549
Meknès 487
Oujda 470
Kénitra 450
Tétouan 372
Tangier 304
Safi 256
Agadir 246
Khouribga 229
Béni-Mellal 204

MOZAMBIQUE (1970)
Maputo 384

NIGER (1977)
Niamey 225

NIGERIA (1975)
Lagos 1 477
Ibadan 847
Ogbomosho 432
Kano 399
Ilorin 282
Oshogbo 282
Abeokuta 253
Port Harcourt 242
Ilesha 224
Zaria 224
Onitsha 220
Iwo 214
Ado-Ekiti 213
Kaduna 202

SENEGAL (1979)
Dakar 799

SIERRA LEONE (1982)
Freetown 316

SOMALI REP. (1982)
Mogadishu 600

SOUTH AFRICA (1980)
Johannesburg 1 726
Cape Town 1 491
Durban 961
Pretoria 739
Port Elizabeth 585
Vanderbijlpark/ Vereeniging 448

SUDAN (1983)
Omdurman 526
Khartoum 476
Khartoum North 341
Port Sudan 207

TANZANIA (1978)
Dar-es-Salaam 757

TOGO (1980)
Lomé 283

TUNISIA (1984)
Tunis 774
Sfax 232

UGANDA (1975)
Kampala 332

ZAÏRE (1976)
Kinshasa 2 444
Kananga 704
Lubumbashi 451
Mbuji Mayi 383
Kisangani 339
Bukavu 209

ZAMBIA (1980)
Lusaka 538
Kitwe 315
Ndola 282

ZIMBABWE (1983)
Harare 681
Bulawayo 429
Chitungwiza 202

ASIA

AFGHANISTAN (1982)
Kābul 1 127

BANGLADESH (1982)
Dacca 3 459
Chittagong 1 388
Khulna 623
Narayanganj 298

BURMA (1977)
Rangoon (1983) 2 459
Mandalay 458
Kanbe (1973) 254

CAMBODIA (KAMPUCHEA) (1983)
Phnom Penh 500

CHINA (1982)
Shanghai 11 940
Peking 9 330
Tientsin 7 850
Shenyang 4 080
Wuhan 3 280
Canton 3 160
Chungking 2 690
Harbin 2 560
Chengdu 2 510
Zibo 2 264
Sian 2 220
Nanking 2 170
Taiyuan 1 790
Changchun 1 770
Dalian 1 520
Zhengzhou 1 517
Lanzhou 1 430
Jinan 1 360
Tangshan 1 351
Guiyang 1 330
Kunming 1 320
Anshan 1 240
Qiqihar 1 232
Qingdao 1 210
Hangzhou 1 201
Fushun 1 200
Fuzhou 1 142
Changsha 1 100
Jilin 1 099
Shijiazhuang 1 098
Nanchang 1 061
Baotou 1 051
Huainan 1 017
Ürümqi 944
Xuzhou 793
Suzhou (1970) 730
Wuxi (1970) 650
Hefei (1970) 630
Benxi (1970) 600
Luoyang (1970) 580
Nanning (1970) 550
Hohhot (1970) 530
Xining (1970) 500

HONG KONG (1981)
Kowloon 2 450
Hong Kong 1 184
Tsuen Wan 599

INDIA (1981)
Calcutta 9 194
Bombay 8 243
Delhi 5 729
Madras 4 289
Bangalore 2 922
Ahmadabad 2 548
Hyderabad 2 546
Pune 1 686
Kanpur 1 639
Nagpur 1 302
Jaipur 1 015
Lucknow 1 008
Coimbatore 920
Patna 919
Surat 914
Madurai 908
Indore 829
Varanasi 797
Jabalpur 757
Agra 747
Vadodara 744
Cochin 686
Dhanbad 678
Bhopal 671
Jamshedpur 670
Allahabad 650
Ulhasnagar 649
Tiruchchirappalli 610
Ludhiana 606
Srinagar 606
Vishakhapatnam 604
Amritsar 595
Gwalior 556
Calicut 546
Vijayawada 543
Meerut 537
Dharwad 527
Trivandrum 520
Salem 519
Solapur 515
Jodhpur 506
Ranchi 503

INDONESIA (1980)
Jakarta 6 503
Surabaya 2 028
Bandung 1 462
Medan 1 379
Semarang 1 026
Palembang 787
Ujung Pandang 709
Malang 512
Padang 481
Surakarta 470
Yogyakarta 399
Banjarmasin 381
Pontianak 305
Tanjung Karang 284
Balikpapan 281
Samarinda 265
Bogor 247
Jambi 230
Cirebon 224
Kediri 222
Manado 217
Ambon 209

IRAN (1976)
Tehrān 4 589
Esfahān 842
Mashhad 743
Tabrīz 715
Shirāz 448
Ahvāz 340
Bākhtarān 336
Abadan 308
Qom 247
Hamadan 230
Karaj 214

IRAQ (1970)
Baghdād 2 969
Basra 371
Mosul 293
Kirkūk 208

ISRAEL (1983)
Jerusalem 429
Tel Aviv-Jaffa 327
Haifa 226

JAPAN (1982)
Tōkyō 11 676
Yokohama 2 848
Ōsaka 2 623
Nagoya 2 093
Kyōto 1 480
Sapporo 1 465
Kobe 1 383
Fukuoka 1 121
Kitakyūshū 1 065
Kawasaki 1 055
Hiroshima 898
Sakai 809
Chiba 756
Sendai 662
Okayama 551
Kumamoto 522
Kagoshima 514
Amagasaki 510
Higashiōsaka 501
Hamamatsu 500
Funabashi 488
Shizuoka 462
Niigata 458
Sagamihara 455
Nagasaki 449
Hameji 448
Yokosuka 429
Matsuyama 413
Kanazawa 412
Matsudo 411
Kurashiki 410
Nishinoyama 410
Gifu 409
Wakayama 404
Toyonaka 397
Hachiōji 395
Kawaguchi 391
Utsunomiya 389
Ichikawa 374
Hirakata 368
Oita 367
Urawa 366
Omiya 361
Asahikawa 359
Fukuyama 353
Iwaki 352
Takatsuki 340
Suita 333
Nagano 328
Hakodate 321
Takamatsu 320
Fujisawa 313
Toyohashi 311
Nara 309
Toyama 308
Kōchi 305
Naha 302
Machida 301
Aomori 291
Akita 290
Kōriyama 290
Toyota 287
Maebashi 271
Okazaki 269
Shimonoseki 269
Miyazaki 267
Yao 266
Fukushima 265
Kawagoe 265
Yokkaichi 258
Akashi 257
Neyagawa 255
Ichinomiya 253
Sasebo 253
Tokushima 251

JORDAN (1981)
'Ammān 681
Az-Zarqā 234

KOREA, NORTH (1972)
Pyŏngyang 1 500
Hamhung 420
Chongjin 265
Kimchaek 265

KOREA, SOUTH (1980)
Seoul 8 367
Pusan 3 160
Taegu 1 607
Inchŏn 1 085
Kwangju 728
Taejon 652
Ulsan 418
Masan 387
Songnam 376
Chonju 367
Suwŏn 311

KUWAIT (1980)
Kuwait 775

LEBANON (1980)
Beirut 702

MACAU (1981)
Macau 250

MALAYSIA (1980)
Kuala Lumpur 938
Ipoh 301
Pinang 251

MONGOLIA (1980)
Ulan Bator 419

NEPAL (1981)
Katmandu 235

PAKISTAN (1981)
Karachi 5 103
Lahore 2 922
Faisalabad 1 092
Rawalpindi 806
Hyderabad 795
Multan 730
Gujranwala 597
Peshawar 555
Sialkot 296
Sargodha 294
Quetta 243
Islamabad 201

PHILIPPINES (1980)
Manila 1 630
Quezon City 1 166
Davao 610
Cebu 490
Caloocan 468
Zamboanga 344
Pasay 288
Bacolod 262
Iloilo 245
Cagayan de Oro 227

SAUDI ARABIA (1974)
Riyadh 667
Jedda 561
Mecca 367
Taif 205

SINGAPORE (1983)
Singapore 2 517

SRI LANKA (1982)
Colombo 1 412

SYRIA (1982)
Damascus 1 112
Aleppo 985
Homs 354

TAIWAN (1981)
Taipei 2 271
Kaohsiung 1 227
Taichung 607
Tainan 595
Chilung 348
Sanchung 335
Chiai 252
Hsinchu 243
Fengshan 227
Chunli 215
Yungho 214

THAILAND (1980)
Bangkok (1982) 5 468

TURKEY (1982)
İstanbul 2 949
Ankara 2 276
İzmir 1 083
Adana 864
Konya 691
Bursa 658
Gaziantep 526
Mersin 440
Kayseri 394
Diyarbakir 390
Samsun 354
Balikesir 352
Eskişehir 352
İzmit 328
Zonguldak 321
Erzurum 292
Maras 292
Antalya 290
Urfa 285
Sivas 279
Malatya 245
Denizli 211

UNITED ARAB EMIRATES (1980)
Dubai 266
Abu Dhabi 243

VIETNAM (1973)
Ho Chi Minh City (1979) 3 420
Hanoi (1979) 2 571
Haiphong (1979) 1 279
Da-Nang 492
Nha-Trang 216
Qui-Nhon 214
Hue 209

YEMEN, NORTH (1981)
Sana' 278

YEMEN, SOUTH (1981)
Aden 264

AUSTRALIA AND NEW ZEALAND

AUSTRALIA (1983)
Sydney 3 335
Melbourne 2 865
Brisbane 1 138
Adelaide 969
Perth 969
Newcastle 414
Canberra 256
Wollongong 235

NEW ZEALAND (1983)

Auckland	864
Wellington	343
Christchurch	322

EUROPE

ALBANIA (1982)

Tiranë	202

AUSTRIA (1984)

Vienna	1 531
Graz	243

BELGIUM (1983)

Brussels	989
Antwerp	491
Ghent	237
Charleroi	216
Liège	207

BULGARIA (1984)

Sofia	1 094
Plovdiv	373
Varna	295

CZECHOSLOVAKIA (1984)

Prague	1 190
Bratislava	409
Brno	383
Ostrava	325
Kosice	218

DENMARK (1984)

Copenhagen	1 366

FINLAND (1983)

Helsinki	932
Turku	257
Tampere	250

FRANCE (1982)

Paris	8 510
Lyons	1 170
Marseilles	1 080
Lille	935
Bordeaux	628
Toulouse	523
Nantes	465
Nice	449
Toulon	410
Grenoble	392
Rouen	380
Strasbourg	373
Valenciennes	337
Lens	323
St-Étienne	317
Grasse-Cannes	296
Nancy	278
Clermont-Ferrand	256
Le Havre	255
Tours	255
Rennes	234
Montpellier	221
Mulhouse	220
Orléans	220
Dijon	209
Douai	202

GERMANY, EAST (1982)

East Berlin	1 173
Leipzig	557
Dresden	521
Karl-Marx-Stadt	320
Magdeburg	288
Rostock	239
Halle	235
Erfurt	213

GERMANY, WEST (1983)

West Berlin	1 860
Hamburg	1 618
Munich	1 284
Cologne	953
Essen	635
Frankfurt	615
Dortmund	595
Düsseldorf	580
Stuttgart	571
Bremen	545
Duisburg	542
Hanover	524
Nuremberg	476
Bochum	391
Wuppertal	386
Bielefeld	308
Mannheim	300
Gelsenkirchen	295
Bonn	293
Munster	273
Wiesbaden	273
Karlsruhe	270
Mönchengladbach	258
Braunschweig	257
Kiel	248
Augsburg	247
Aachen	244
Oberhausen	226
Krefeld	222
Lübeck	216
Hagen	212

GREECE (1981)

Athens	3 027
Thessaloníki	871

HUNGARY (1984)

Budapest	2 064
Miskolc	211

IRISH REPUBLIC (1981)

Dublin	915

ITALY (1983)

Rome	2 831
Milan	1 561
Naples	1 209
Turin	1 069
Genoa	747
Palermo	712
Bologna	448
Florence	441
Catánia	380
Bari	370
Venice	341
Messina	264
Verona	262
Trieste	246
Táranto	243
Padua	231
Cágliari	225
Bréscia	204

NETHERLANDS (1984)

Rotterdam	1 025
Amsterdam	994
The Hague	672
Utrecht	501
Eindhoven	374
Arnhem	291
Heerlen-Kerkrade	266
Enschede-Hengelo	248
Tilburg	234
Nijmegen	222
Haarlem	217
Groningen	207

NORWAY (1984)

Oslo	643
Bergen	208

POLAND (1984)

Warsaw	1 649
Łodz	849
Kraków	740
Wrocław	636
Poznań	574
Gdansk	467
Szczecin	391
Katowice	363
Bydgoszcz	361
Lublin	324
Sosnowiec	254
Częstochowa	247
Białystok	245
Gdynia	243
Bytom	238
Radom	213
Gliwice	206

PORTUGAL (1981)

Lisbon	1 612
Oporto	1 315

ROMANIA (1982)

Bucharest	1 979
Braşov	334
Constanţa	307
Timişoara	302
Cluj-Napoca	301
Iasi	295
Galati	279
Craiova	253
Ploieşti	228
Brăila	225
Oradea	201

SPAIN (1981)

Madrid	3 188
Barcelona	1 755
Valencia	752
Seville	654
Zaragoza	591
Málaga	503
Bilbao	433
Valladolid	330
Palma de Mallorca	304
Hospitalet	294
Murcia	289
Córdoba	285
Granada	262
Vigo	259
Gijón	256
Alicante	251
La Coruña	232
Badalona	228

SWEDEN (1983)

Stockholm	1 420
Göteborg	699
Malmö	455

SWITZERLAND (1983)

Zürich	840
Geneva	372
Basle	365
Bern	301
Lausanne	225

U.S.S.R. (1983-84)

Moscow	8 537
Leningrad	4 827
Kiev	2 409
Tashkent	1 986
Baku	1 661
Kharkov	1 536
Minsk	1 442
Gorki	1 392
Novosibirsk	1 384
Sverdlovsk	1 286
Kuybyshev	1 250
Dnepropetrovsk	1 140
Tbilisi	1 140
Yerevan	1 114
Odessa	1 113
Omsk	1 094
Chelyabinsk	1 086
Donetsk	1 064
Perm	1 048
Ufa	1 048
Alma-Ata	1 046
Kazan	1 039
Rostov	983
Volgograd	969
Saratov	893
Riga	875
Krasnoyarsk	857
Zaporozhye	844
Voronezh	840
Lvov	728
Krivoy Rog	680
Yaroslavl	623
Karaganda	608
Kishinev	605
Krasnodar	603
Ustinov	603
Frunze	590
Vladivostok	590
Irkutsk	589
Novokuznetsk	572
Barnaul	568
Khabarovsk	568
Dushanbe	539
Vilnius	535
Tula	529
Ulyanovsk	524
Penza	522
Zhdanov	520
Samarkand	515
Orenburg	513

UNITED KINGDOM (1981)

London (1985)	6 767
Birmingham (1985)	1 007
Glasgow	762
Liverpool	510
Leeds	449
Manchester	449
Sheffield	447
Edinburgh	419
Bristol	388
Belfast	374
Coventry	314
Leicester	283
Bradford	281
Cardiff	274
Nottingham	271
Hull	268
Stoke-on-Trent	252
Wolverhampton	252
Plymouth	244
Derby	216
Southampton	204

YUGOSLAVIA (1981)

Belgrade	1 407
Zagreb	1 175
Skopje	507
Sarajevo	449
Ljubljana	305
Novi Sad	258
Split	236
Niš	231
Priština	216

NORTH AMERICA

CANADA (1983)

Toronto	3 067
Montréal	2 862
Vancouver	1 311
Ottawa	738
Edmonton	699
Calgary	634
Winnipeg	601
Québec	580
Hamilton	548
St. Catherines	304
Kitchener	294
London	287
Halifax	281
Windsor	245
Victoria	240

COSTA RICA (1984)

San José	245

CUBA (1982)

Havana	1 951
Santiago de Cuba	349
Camagüey	251

DOMINICAN REP. (1981)

Santo Domingo	1 313
Santiago	279

EL SALVADOR (1983)

San Salvador	884

GUATEMALA (1983)

Guatemala	1 300

HAITI (1982)

Port-au-Prince	888

HONDURAS (1982)

Tegucigalpa	534
San Pedro Sula	398

JAMAICA (1980)

Kingston	671

MEXICO (1979)

Mexico	14 750
Guadalajara	2 468
Netzahualcóyotl	2 331
Monterrey	2 019
Puebla	711
Ciudad Juárez	625
León	625
Tijuana	566
Acapulco	462
Torreón	407
Tampico	390
Chihuahua	386
Mexicali	349
San Luis Potosi	327
Culiacán	324
Hermosillo	319
Veracruz	307
Mérida	270
Saltillo	258
Aguascalientes	257
Morelia	251
Toluca	242
Cuernavaca	241
Reynosa	231
Durango	229
Nuevo Laredo	224
Jalapa	201

NICARAGUA (1981)

Managua	615

PANAMA (1981)

Panama	655

PUERTO RICO (1980)

San Juan	1 086
Ponce	253
Bayamón	209

UNITED STATES (1984)

New York	17 807
Los Angeles	12 373
Chicago	8 035
Philadelphia	5 755
San Francisco	5 685
Detroit	4 577
Boston	4 027
Houston	3 566
Washington	3 429
Dallas	3 348
Miami	2 799
Cleveland	2 788
St. Louis	2 398
Atlanta	2 380
Pittsburgh	2 372
Baltimore	2 245
Minneapolis-St. Paul	2 231
Seattle	2 208
San Diego	2 064
Tampa	1 811
Denver	1 791
Phoenix	1 715
Cincinnati	1 673
Milwaukee	1 568
Kansas City	1 477
Portland	1 341
New Orleans	1 319
Columbus	1 279
Sacramento	1 220
Buffalo	1 205
Indianapolis	1 195
San Antonio	1 188
Providence	1 095
Norfolk	1 026
Salt Lake City	1 025
Rochester	989
Louisville	963
Oklahoma	963
Memphis	935
Dayton	930
Birmingham	895
Nashville-Davidson	890
Greensboro	886
Albany	843
Orlando	824
Honolulu	805
Richmond	796
Jacksonville	795
Hartford	729
Scranton	727
Tulsa	726
West Palm Beach	692
Syracuse	650
Charlotte	647
Austin	645
Allentown	635
Grand Rapids	626
Toledo	611
Raleigh	609
Omaha	607
Greenville	593
Knoxville	589
Fresno	565
Baton Rouge	538
Las Vegas	536
Tucson	531
El Paso	526
Youngstown	518
Springfield	516

SOUTH AMERICA

ARGENTINA (1980)

Buenos Aires	9 927
Córdoba	982
Rosario	955
Mendoza	597
La Plata	560
San Miguel de Tucuman	497
Mar del Plata	407
San Juan	290
Santa Fé	287
Salta	260
Bahia Blanca	221
Resistencia	218

BOLIVIA (1982)

La Paz	881
Santa Cruz	377
Cochabamba	282

BRAZIL (1980)

São Paulo	8 493
Rio de Janeiro	5 091
Belo Horizonte	1 781
Salvador	1 502
Fortaleza	1 308
Recife	1 204
Brasilia	1 177
Pôrto Alegre	1 125
Nova Iguaçu	1 095
Curitiba	1 025
Belém	933
Goiânia	717
Campinas	665
Manaus	633
São Gonçalo	615
Duque de Caxias	576
Santo André	553
Guarulhos	533
Osasco	474
São Luis	449
São Bernardo do Campo	426
Natal	417
Santos	417
Maceió	399
São João de Meriti	399
Niterói	397
Teresina	378
Campos	348
Jaboatao	330
João Pessoa	330
Ribeirão Preto	318
Juiz de Fora	307
Londrina	302
Aracaju	293
Campo Grande	292
Feira de Santana	292
São José dos Campos	288
Olinda	282
Sorocaba	269
Pelotas	260
Jundiaí	259

CHILE (1983)

Santiago	4 132
Viña del Mar	299
Valparaiso	268
Talcahuano	213
Concepción	210

COLOMBIA (1980)

Bogotá	4 486
Medellin	1 812
Cali	1 232
Barranquilla	900
Bucaramanga	459
Cartagena	368
Pereira	309
Manizales	302
Cucuta	272
Ibagué	238

ECUADOR (1982)

Guayaquil	1 301
Quito	1 110

PARAGUAY (1983)

Asunción	708

PERU (1981)

Lima (1983)	5 258
Arequipa	447
Callao	441
Trujillo	355
Chiclayo	280
Chimbote	216

URUGUAY (1981)

Montevideo	1 362

VENEZUELA (1980)

Caracas	2 944
Maracaibo	901
Valencia	506
Barquisimento	489
Maracay	344
Barcelona-Puerto La Cruz	275
San Cristóbal	272
Ciudad Guayana	206

1:105 000 000

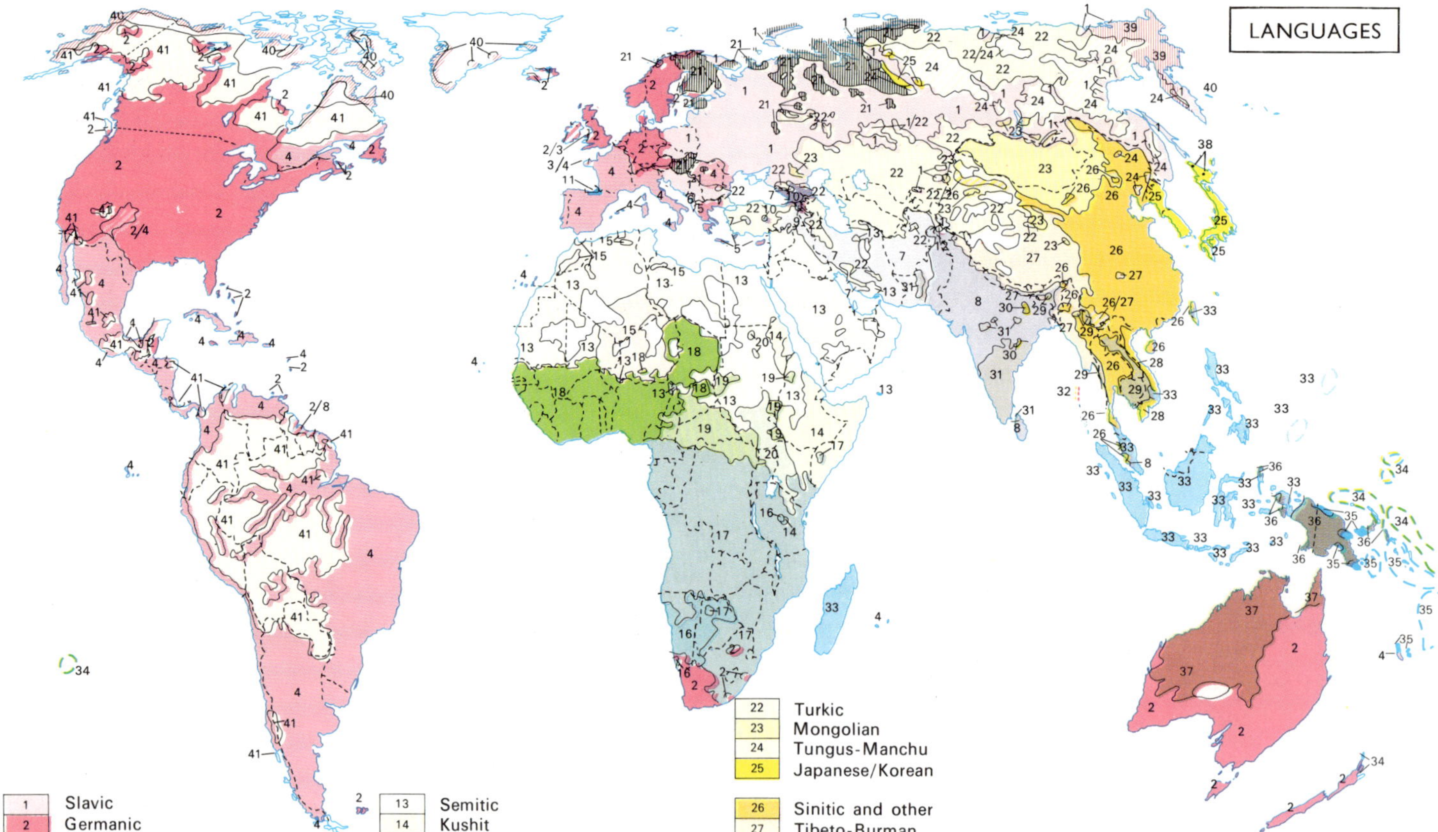

- 1 Slavic
- 2 Germanic
- 3 Celtic
- 4 Romance
- 5 Greek
- 6 Albanian
- 7 Iranian
- 8 Indo-Aryan
- 9 Armenian
- 10 Caucasian
- 11 Basque
- 12 Burushaskis
- 13 Semitic
- 14 Kushit
- 15 Berber
- 16 Khoisan
- 17 Bantu
- 18 Sudanese
- 19 E & C Sudan
- 20 Nilotic
- 21 Ural
- 22 Turkic
- 23 Mongolian
- 24 Tungus-Manchu
- 25 Japanese/Korean
- 26 Sinitic and other
- 27 Tibeto-Burman
- 28 Vietnamese
- 29 Mon-Khmer
- 30 Munda
- 31 Dravidian
- 32 Andamanese
- 33 Indonesian
- 34 Polynesian
- 35 Melanesian
- 36 Papuan
- 37 Australian Abor.
- 38 Ainu
- 39 Paleoasiatic
- 40 Eskimo-Aleut
- 41 Amerindian

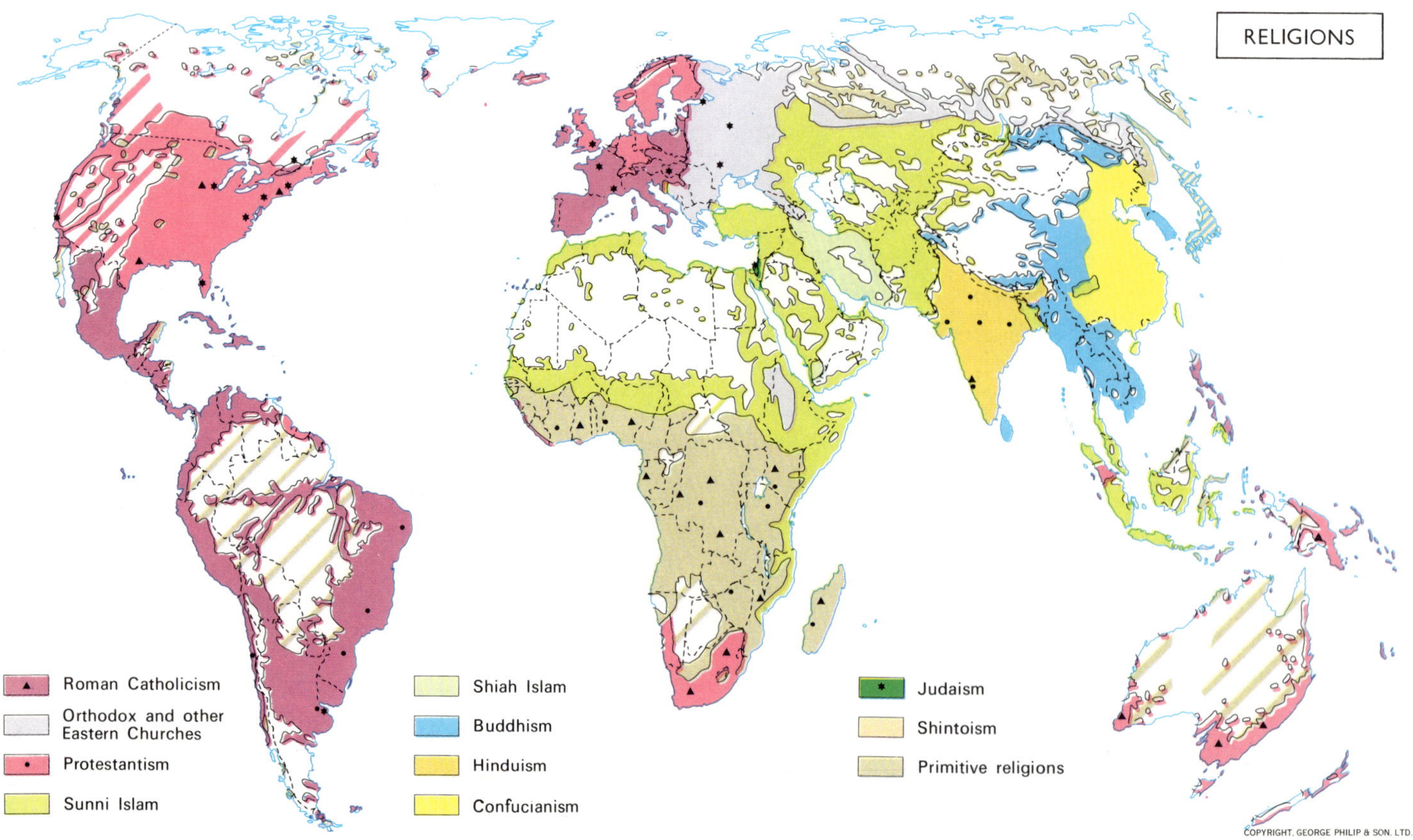

- Roman Catholicism
- Orthodox and other Eastern Churches
- Protestantism
- Sunni Islam
- Shiah Islam
- Buddhism
- Hinduism
- Confucianism
- Judaism
- Shintoism
- Primitive religions

UNITED NATIONS

The United Nations was created in 1945 to promote world peace and co-operation between nations. It is the largest international organisation in the world. It has 159 members and a budget of over two billion U.S. dollars each year. Member countries meet each year to discuss their problems and disputes in the General Assembly. Each member has one vote. The Security Council consists of 15 members who are responsible for keeping the peace between nations. The Economic and Social Council consists of 54 members who are responsible for economic, social, cultural, educational, health and related matters. The Trusteeship Council is responsible for safeguarding the interests of the inhabitants of territories which are not yet fully self-governing. The Secretariat is the chief administrative officer of the organisation. The United Nations has a number of specialised agencies which help members in many fields such as economic development (UNDP), education (UNESCO), farming (FAO) and medicine (WHO). The United Nations is based in New York.

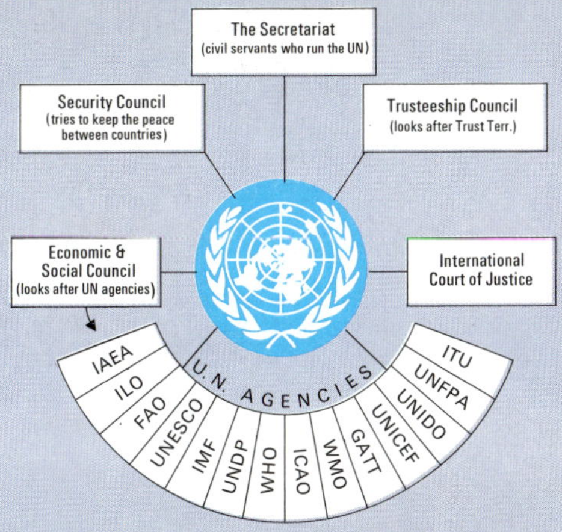

COMMONWEALTH

The Commonwealth maintains many of the ties that were formed in the days of the British Empire. The 49 members are all equal in status. There is no formal treaty or aim. The Commonwealth represents about one quarter of the world's population.

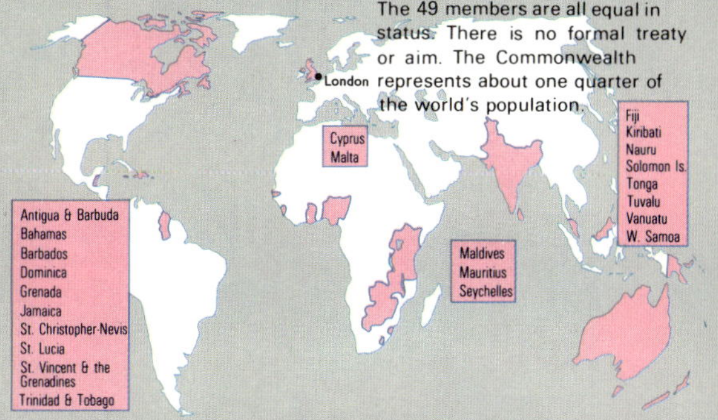

EFTA

The European Free Trade Association was founded in 1960. There are no customs duties between its members and the E.E.C. for industrial goods.

COMECON

The Council for Mutual Economic Assistance was formed to develop the trade and resources of the Soviet bloc countries.

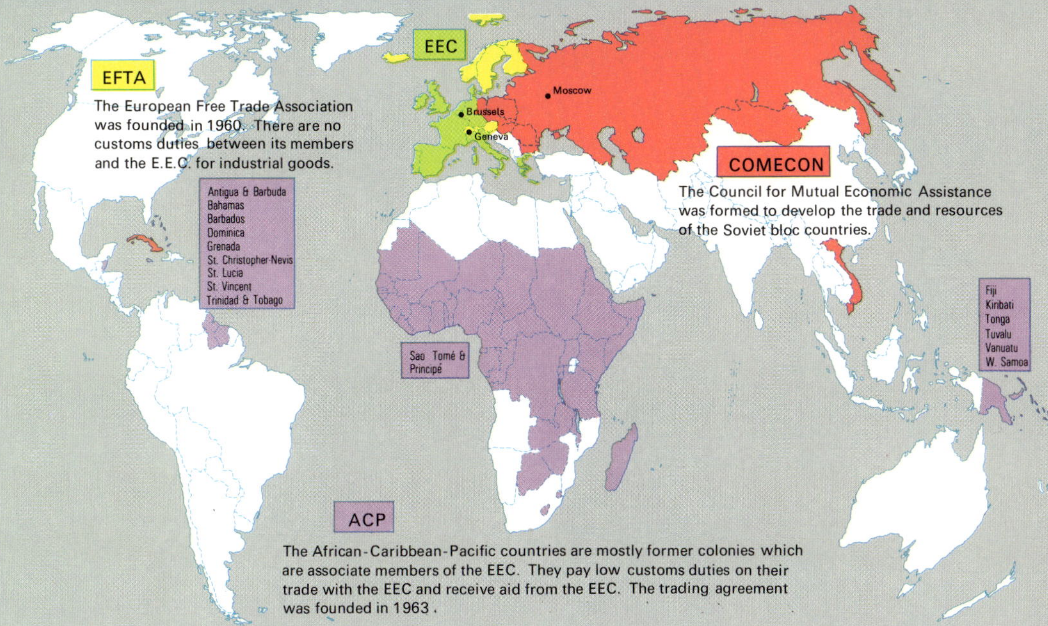

ACP

The African-Caribbean-Pacific countries are mostly former colonies which are associate members of the EEC. They pay low customs duties on their trade with the EEC and receive aid from the EEC. The trading agreement was founded in 1963.

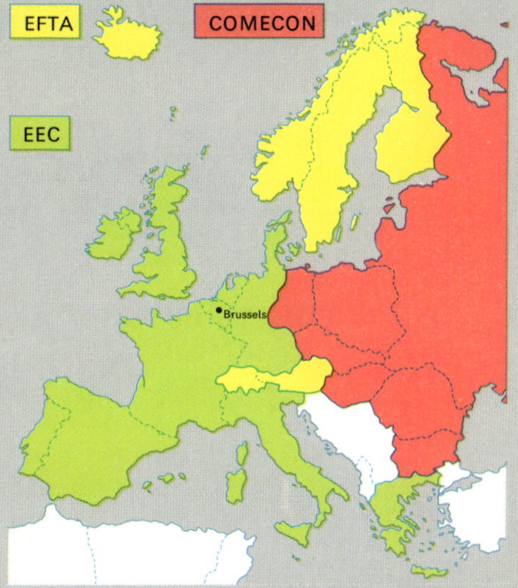

The European Economic Community or the Common Market was founded in 1957 by the Treaty of Rome. The EEC aims to integrate its members' economies, coordinate social developments and to bring about political union of the democratic countries in Europe. Its members share common agricultural and industrial policies and tariffs on external trade. The EEC has over 320 million inhabitants and is one of the wealthiest markets in the world. Some 60 nations in Africa, the Caribbean and the Pacific (ACP) are affiliated with the EEC under the Lomé Convention.

NATO

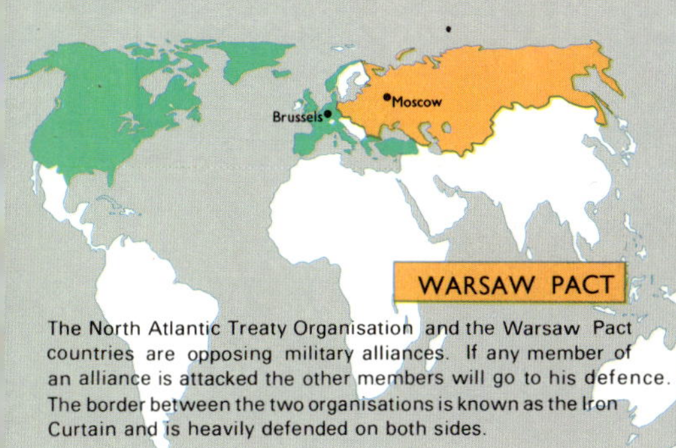

WARSAW PACT

The North Atlantic Treaty Organisation and the Warsaw Pact countries are opposing military alliances. If any member of an alliance is attacked the other members will go to his defence. The border between the two organisations is known as the Iron Curtain and is heavily defended on both sides.

OAU

The Organisation of African Unity was formed in 1963 between 30 countries. It aims to end colonialism in Africa and to defend the independence of its members. There are now 50 members, representing over 90% of the people in Africa.

ASEAN

The Association of South East Asian Nations was formed to promote political and economic co-operation among the non-communist states of the region.

OAS

The Organisation of American States encourages the social and economic growth of the developing countries of Latin America with aid from the developed countries in North America.

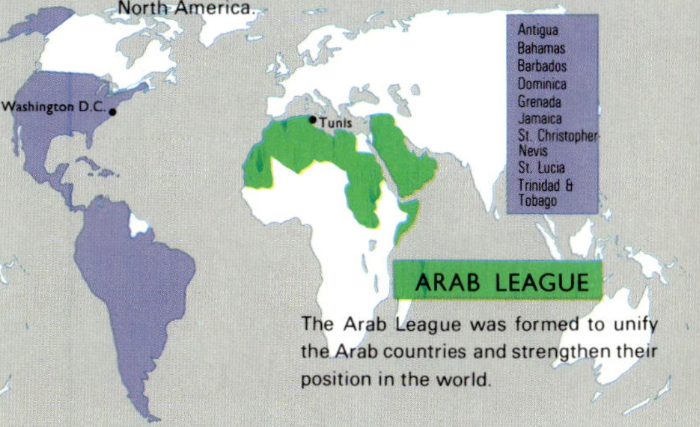

ARAB LEAGUE

The Arab League was formed to unify the Arab countries and strengthen their position in the world.

LAIA

OECD

The Organisation for Economic Co-operation and Development encourages economic growth and trade between developed and developing countries.

LAIA stands for Latin American Integration Association. It was recently formed to replace the Latin American Free Trade Association. It encourages free trade between its members.

COLOMBO PLAN

The six developed countries in the plan (Australia, Canada, Japan, New Zealand, U.K. and U.S.A.) provide aid to the developing countries in the plan.

OPEC

The Organisation of Petroleum Exporting Countries was formed in 1960. It maintains the price of oil on the world market. It controls three quarters of the world's oil supply and it is therefore very powerful.

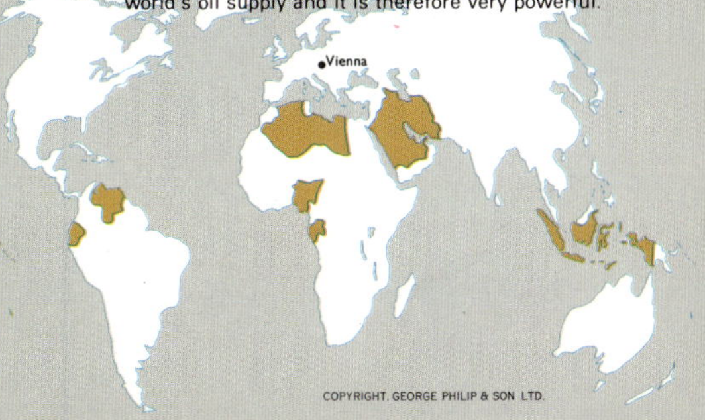

NATURAL INCREASE

The birth rates and death rates are the number of births and deaths per 1000 population each year.

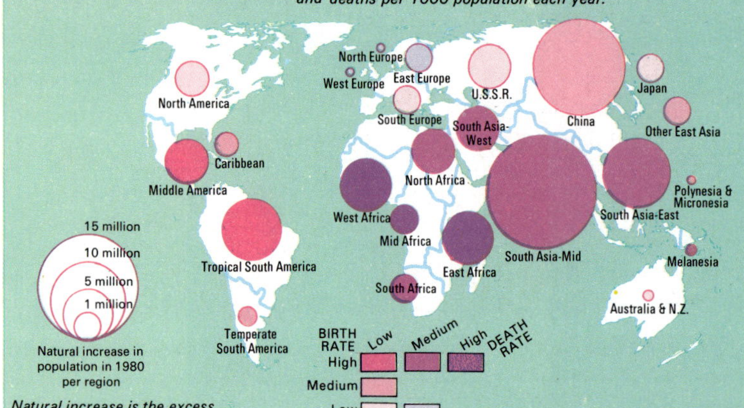

Natural increase is the excess of births over deaths.

FAMILY SIZE

Family size is the total number of children an average woman will bear in her lifetime, for each region. In 1980 the world average was 3.6 children; in 2000 it is expected to be 2.8 children.

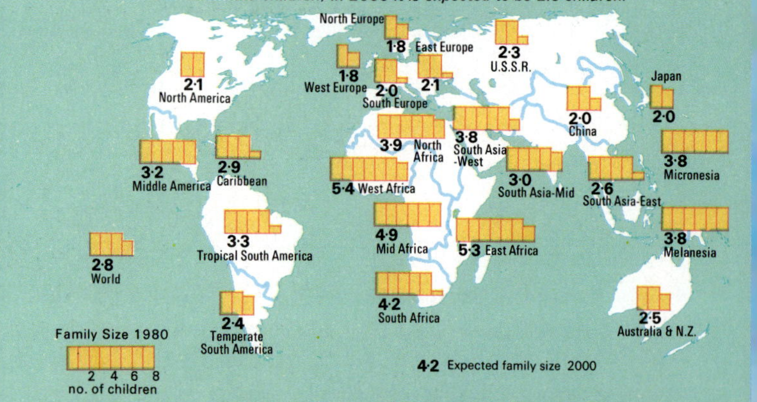

LIFE EXPECTANCY

Life expectancy is the average number of years a newly-born baby can expect to live. The world average has risen from 47 years in 1950 to 58 years in 1980, and is expected to be 64 years in 2000.

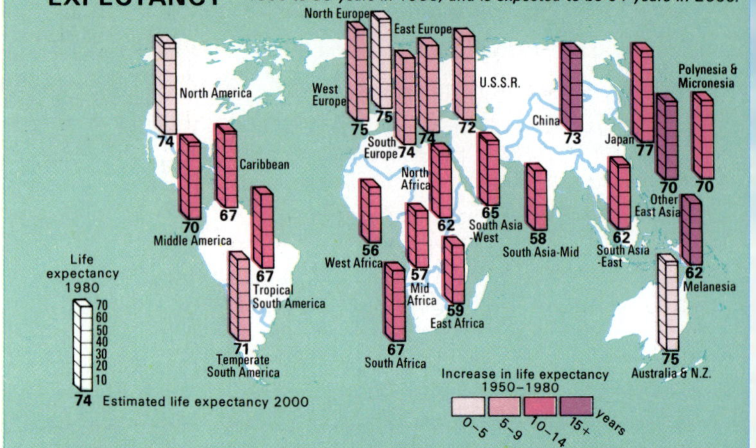

INFANT MORTALITY

The infant mortality rate for the world was 113 in 1960. It is now 81 and is expected to fall to 53 by 2000.

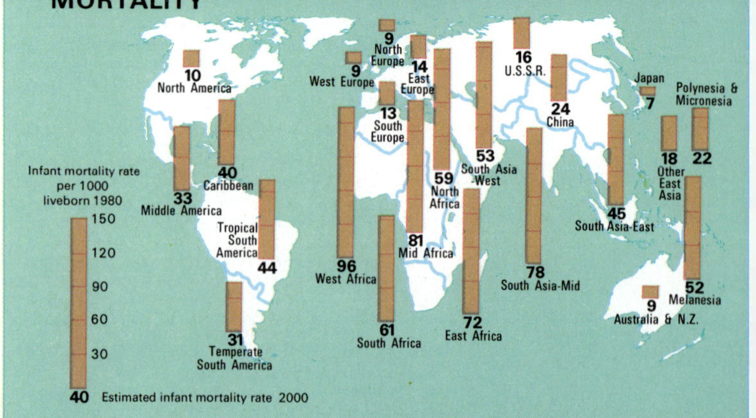

YOUNG AND OLD

Median Age is the age in years which divides the population into two equal parts, one young and the other old. The median age for the world is 23

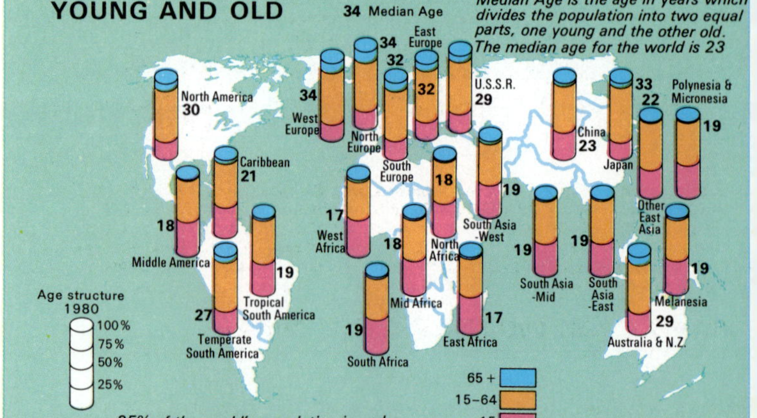

35% of the world's population is under 15 years of age whilst 6% is over 65.

AGE DISTRIBUTION PYRAMIDS

The bars represent the percentage of the population in the age group shown. The blue bars represent the males, the red bars the females. The developing countries such as India tend to have a higher proportion of young people than the developed countries such as Canada.

See page 8 for age distribution pyramid of the U.K.

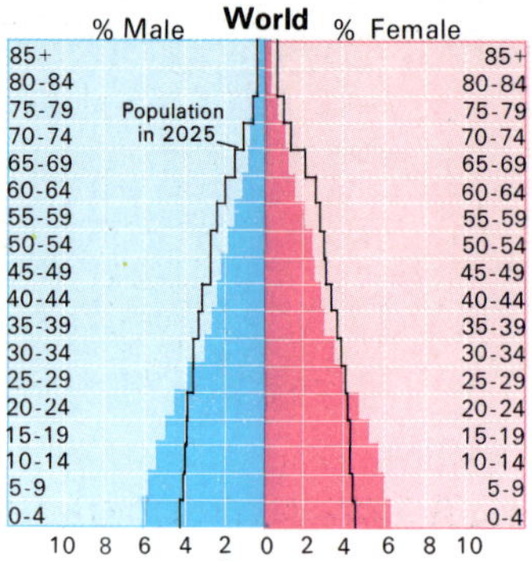

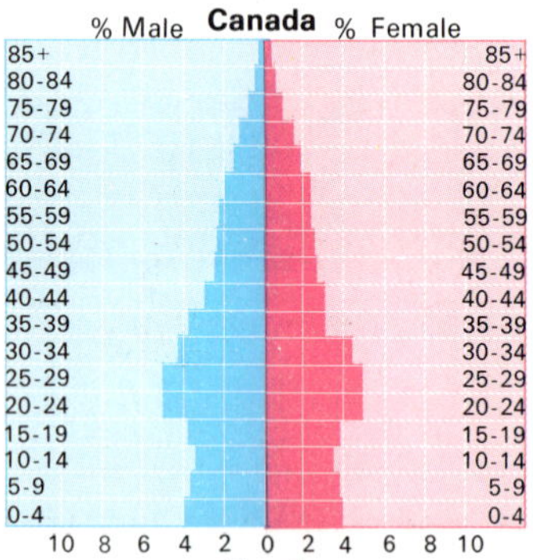

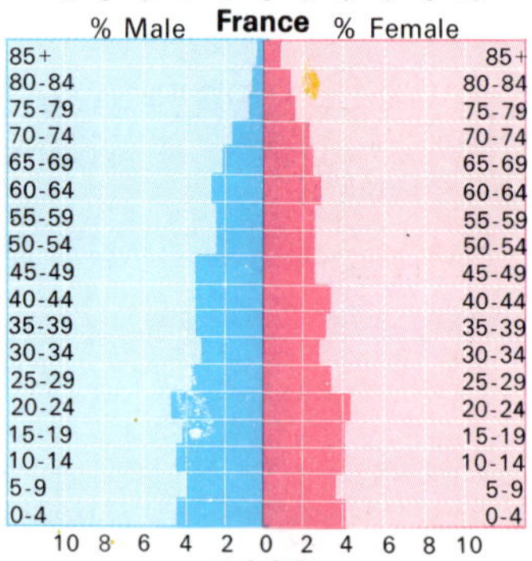

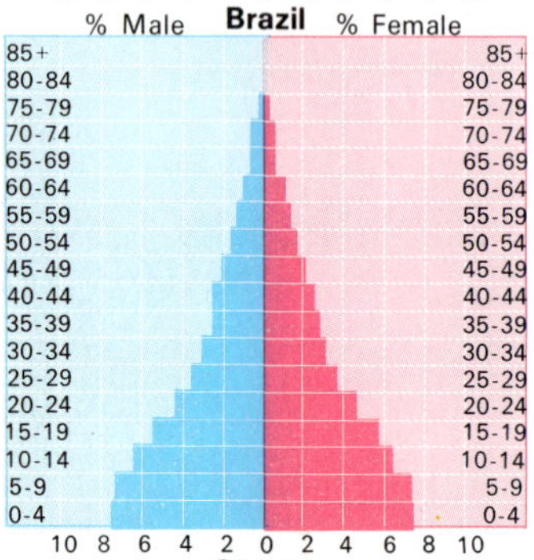

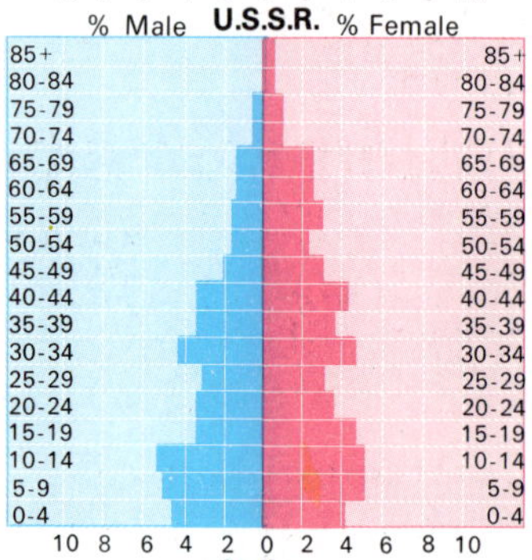

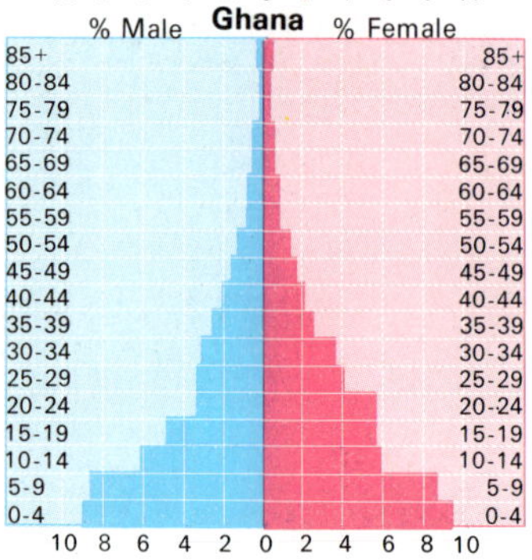

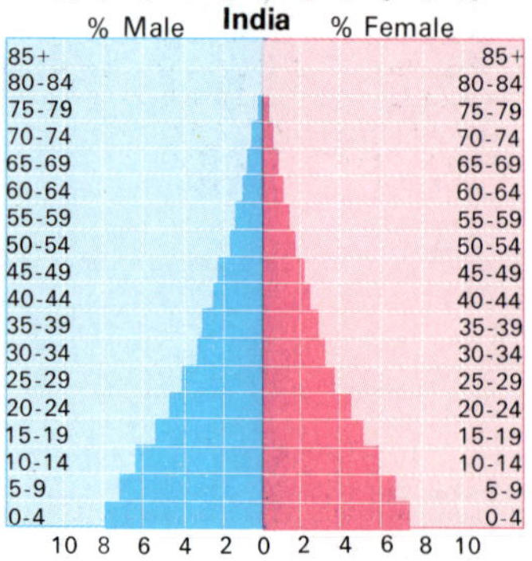

See page 125 for maps of Population Growth and Urbanisation

POPULATION BY COUNTRY

See map on pages 116-117 for greater detail.

The most populous country (China) contains a quarter of the world's population. The four most populous countries (China, India, U.S.S.R., and U.S.A.) contain half, and the first eighteen (all those countries named in larger type on the map) contain over three-quarters of the world's population. The remaining 150 countries contain only one quarter.

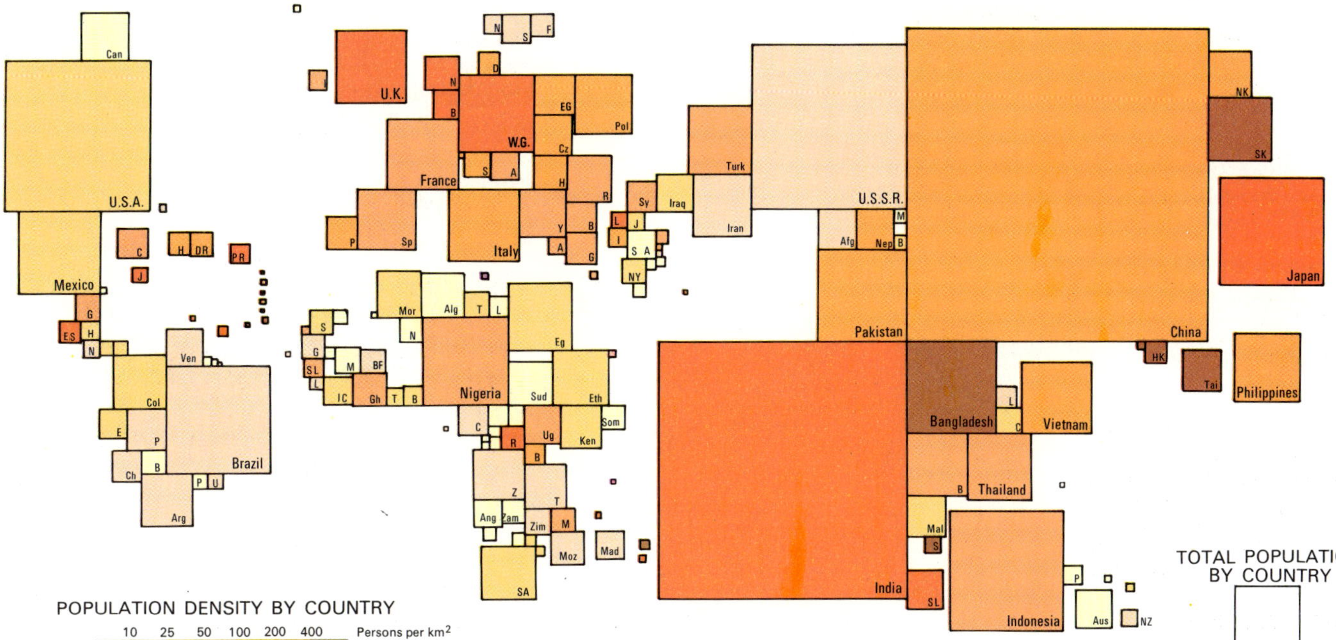

POPULATION DENSITY BY COUNTRY

10 25 50 100 200 400 Persons per km²

MIGRATIONS

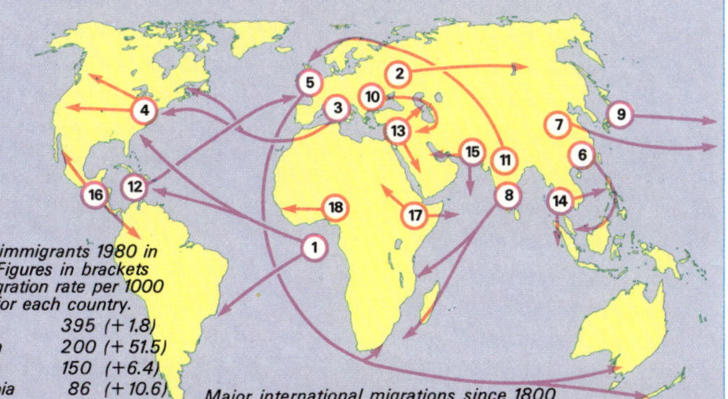

Number of immigrants 1980 in thousands. Figures in brackets show immigration rate per 1000 population for each country.

1. U.S.A. 395 (+1.8)
2. Somalia 200 (+51.5)
3. Canada 150 (+6.4)
4. S. Arabia 86 (+10.6)
5. Hong Kong 75 (+15.8)
6. Venezuela 60 (+4.2)
7. Puerto Rico 59 (+17.3)
8. Australia 50 (+3.6)
9. Ivory Coast 38 (+5.1)
10. U.A.E 30 (+48.7)

Number of emigrants 1980 in thousands. Figures in brackets show emigration rate per 1000 population for each country.

1. Ethiopia 200 (−6.6)
2. Vietnam 146 (−2.9)
3. Lebanon 80 (−29.5)
4. Cambodia 80 (−11.6)
5. Colombia 60 (−2.5)
6. Mexico 50 (−0.8)
7. Sri Lanka 43 (−3.0)
8. Philippines 40 (−0.9)
9. S. Yemen 36 (−5.4)
10. U.K. 30 (−0.5)

Major international migrations since 1800

1. Slave trade from Africa to the Americas (1500–1850)
2. Russian colonisation of Siberia (1850–1950)
3. European emigration to N. America (1850–1920)
4. Colonisation of the American West (1860–1960)
5. European emigration to Southern Africa and Oceania (1840-1960)
6. Chinese emigration to Indo-China (1860–1910)
7. Chinese emigration to the Americas (1900–1950)
8. Indian emigration to Africa (1860–1910)
9. Japanese emigration to N. America (1870–1910)
10. Jewish emigration to Israel (1949–)
11. Asian emigration to Europe (1950–1970)
12. W. Indian emigration to Europe (1950–1970)
13. Palestinian refugees to Middle East (1950–)
14. Indo-Chinese refugees to S.E. Asia, China, and North America (1970–80)
15. Afghan refugees to Pakistan and Iran (1970–)
16. Refugees in Central America (1979–)
17. Ethiopian refugees in Somalia and Sudan (1977–)
18. Immigrants evicted from Nigeria (1983)

ABORTION AND BIRTH CONTROL

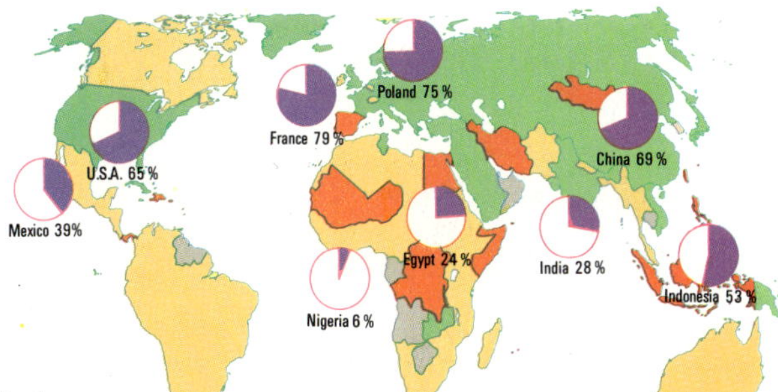

Status of Abortion
- Abortion legal
- Legal only for certain medical or juridical reasons
- Abortions illegal
- No data

Percentage of married women using contraception, for selected countries.

Legally induced abortions per 1000 live births. Total abortions in thousands are in brackets.

Bulgaria	1216 (152)	Canada	175 (66)
U.S.A.	347 (1 158)	New Zealand	133 (7)
France	207 (171)	Tunisia	77 (16)
Poland	192 (141)	India	27 (346)
Great Britain	189 (137)		

POPULATION IN 2000 A.D.

Percentage of world total is given in brackets.

World	6 119		
South Asia	2 075 (34%)	U.S.S.R.	310 (5%)
East Asia	1 475 (24%)	Europe	512 (8.5%)
Oceania	30 (0.5%)		
Africa	853 (14%)		
South America	566 (9%)		
N. America	299 (5%)		

Until comparatively recently there was little increase in the population of the world. It is thought there were about 200 million in 600 B.C., 300 million in 1000 A.D. and 500 million by 1600 A.D.. This diagram shows how the world's population has increased since then at an ever increasing rate. 90% of this increase has been in the less developed regions The world population of 1950 will have doubled by 1990 and if present trends continue it will have trebled by 2020.

POPULATION INCREASE SINCE 1650

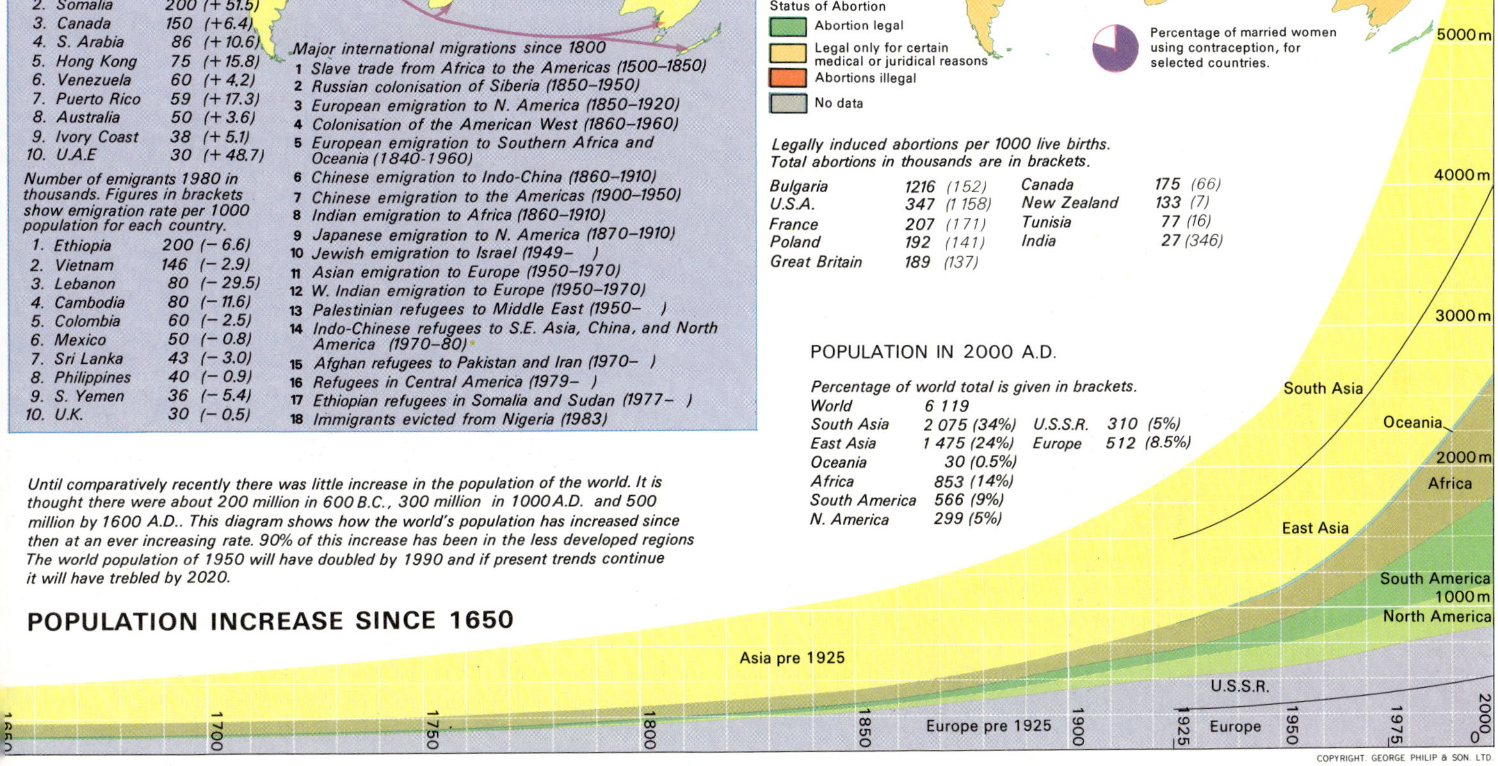

NATURAL DISASTERS

EARTHQUAKES AND VOLCANOES

- ○ Major earthquakes with dates
- ▲ Major volcanoes
- Earthquake zones (land and sea)

STORMS AND FLOODS

- ✱ Major storms and floods with dates
- Paths of winter blizzards
- Paths of tropical storms
- Areas liable to flood

PESTS

- Locust invasion areas
- Main tsetse fly areas

MAJOR FAMINES

- ◉ Sahel 1973

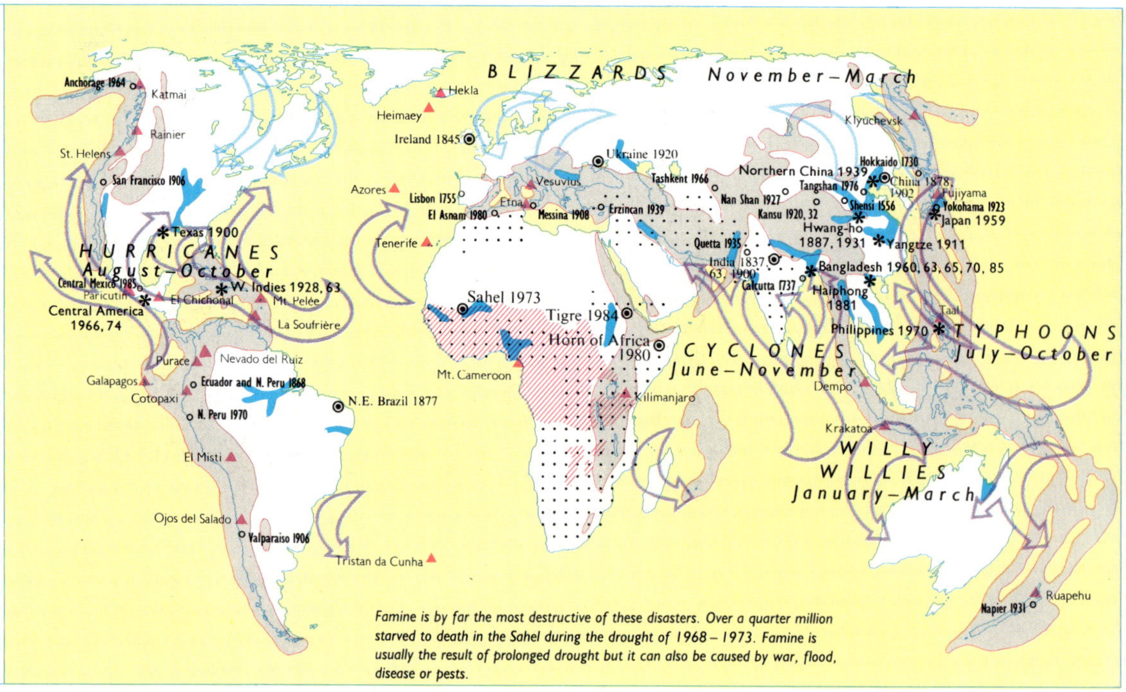

Famine is by far the most destructive of these disasters. Over a quarter million starved to death in the Sahel during the drought of 1968 – 1973. Famine is usually the result of prolonged drought but it can also be caused by war, flood, disease or pests.

Since 1945 there have been over 300 wars. Few countries in the world have been unaffected by war, strife or terrorism.

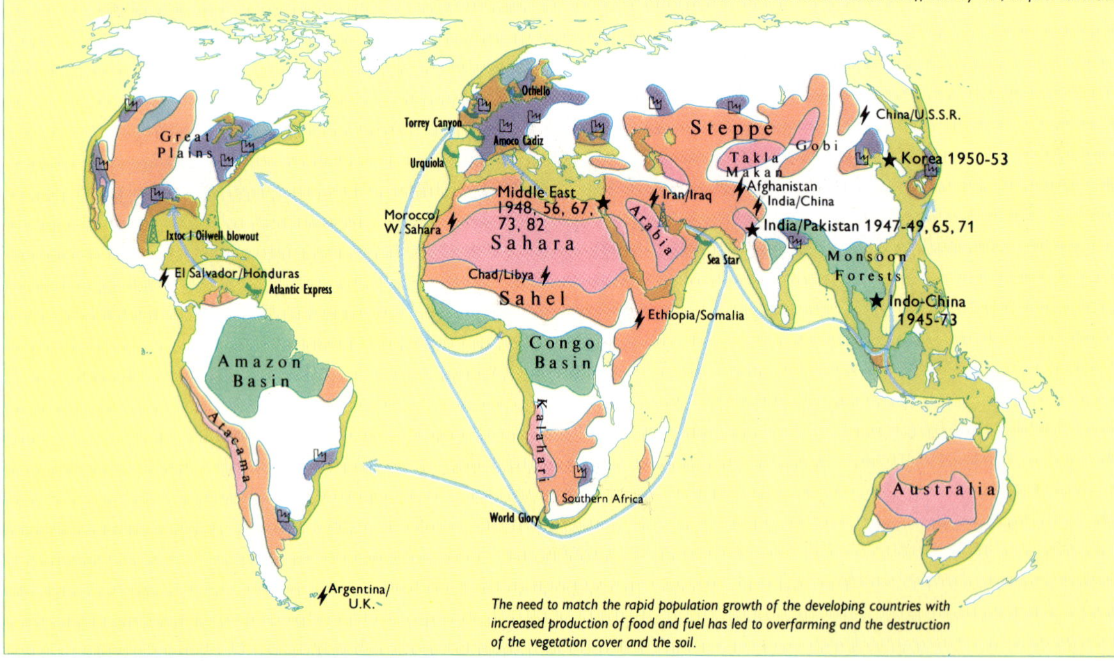

The need to match the rapid population growth of the developing countries with increased production of food and fuel has led to overfarming and the destruction of the vegetation cover and the soil.

MAN-MADE PROBLEMS

- ★ Major wars since 1945
- ϟ Other recent conflicts
- Heavily polluted sea and lakes
- Other polluted sea and lakes
- Principal oil tanker routes
- Disastrous oil spills
- Main areas of industrial pollution
- Areas affected by acid rain
- Major deserts
- Areas threatened by desertification
- Areas of rapid deforestation

Pollution tends to be a greater problem for the developed countries with their intensive industry and agriculture. Prevailing winds can carry air pollution a long way before it falls as acid rain, which is now a serious problem in Canada and Scandinavia. Traces of pollution have even been discovered in the ice of Antarctica.

MEDICAL CARE

Persons per doctor in each country

- over 25000
- 10000 – 25000
- 5000 – 10000
- 1000 – 5000
- less than 1000

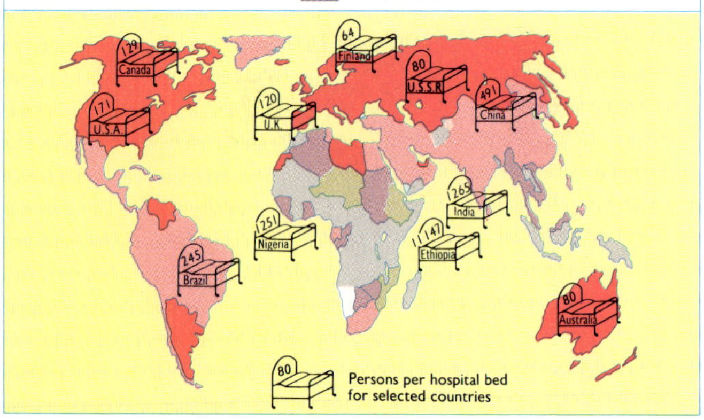

Persons per hospital bed for selected countries

NUTRITION

Calorie intake as a percentage of needs per person

- less than 80%
- 80 – 90%
- 90 – 100%
- 100 – 110%
- 110 – 120%
- over 120%

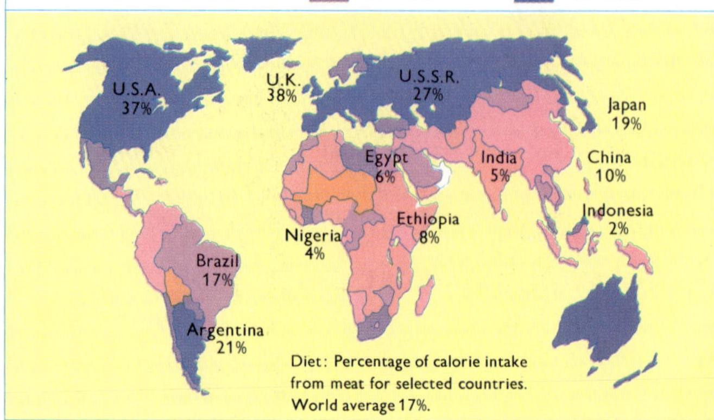

Diet: Percentage of calorie intake from meat for selected countries. World average 17%.

STANDARDS OF LIVING

THE RICH

- Countries with more than four times the world's average income
- Countries with more than twice the world's average income
- Countries with incomes just above the world's average

THE POOR

- Countries with incomes just below the world's average
- Countries with less than half of the world's average income
- Countries with less than one quarter of the world's average income
- Data not available

The world's average income is just under 2200 US$ per annum. The richest country on a per capita basis is Kuwait with an income over 200 times that of the poorest country, Mali.

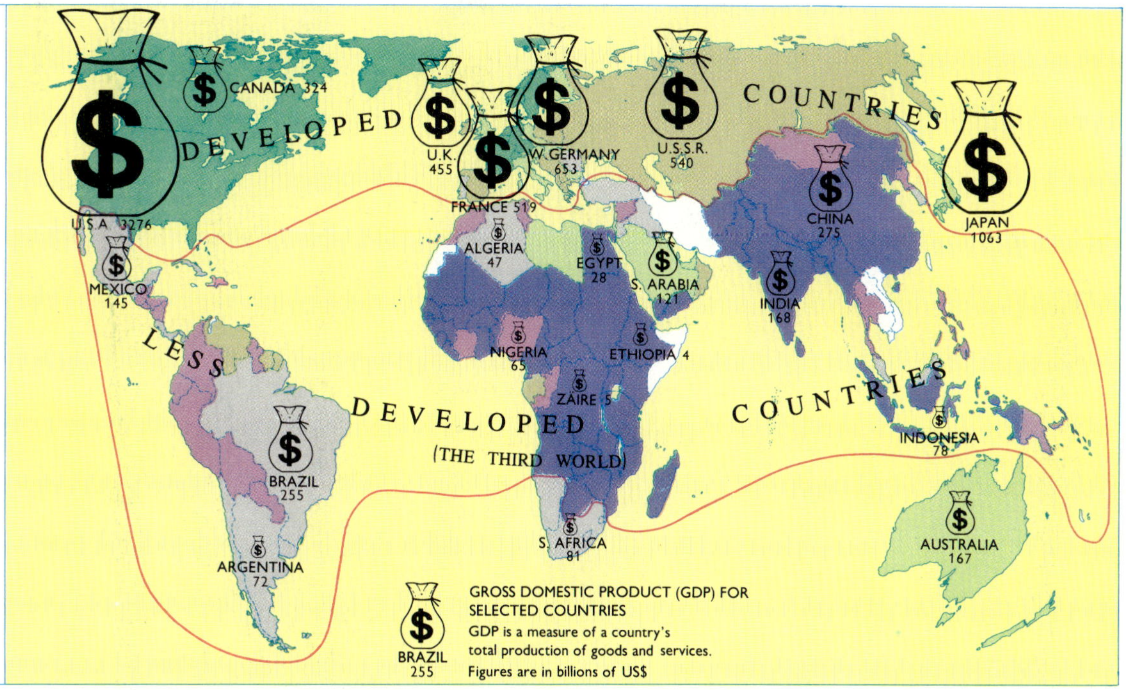

GROSS DOMESTIC PRODUCT (GDP) FOR SELECTED COUNTRIES
GDP is a measure of a country's total production of goods and services.
Figures are in billions of US$

POPULATION EXPLOSION IN THE THIRD WORLD

CURRENT RATE OF INCREASE

Annual rate of population growth in each country

- less than 1%
- 1 – 2%
- 2 – 2½%
- 2½% – 3%
- over 3%

EXPECTED RATE OF INCREASE

2034 — Date by which 1984 population of selected countries will double if present trends continue.

World = 2025

Population in 2000

Expected rate of population increase 1980 – 2000 for each continent (1mm = 2%)

Population in 1980

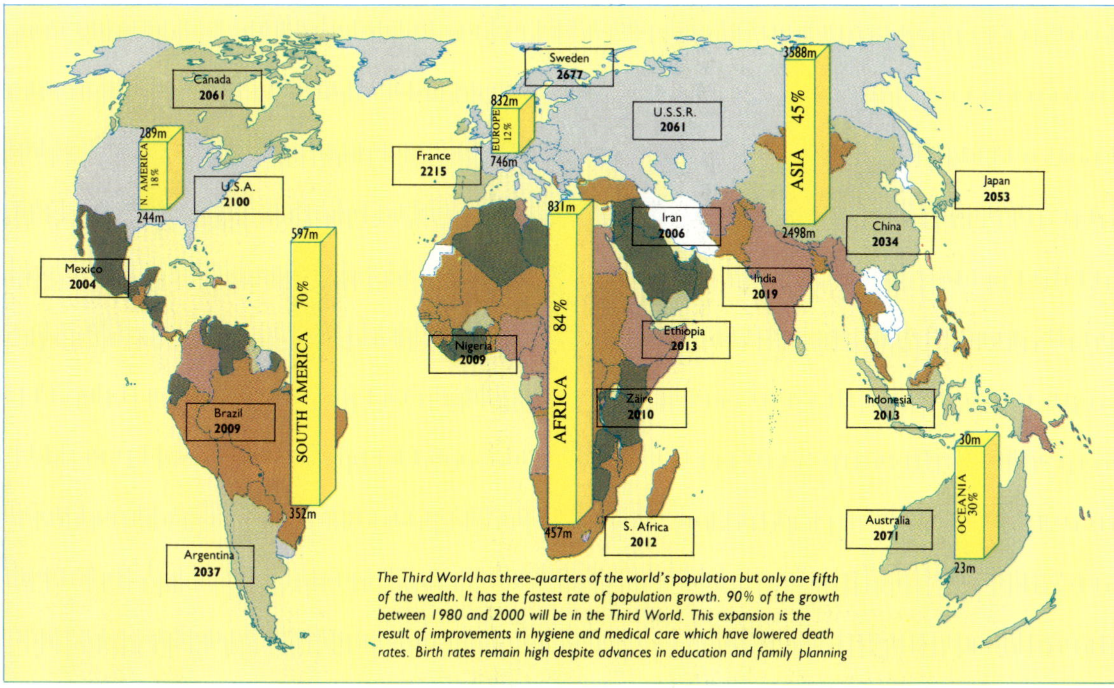

The Third World has three-quarters of the world's population but only one fifth of the wealth. It has the fastest rate of population growth. 90% of the growth between 1980 and 2000 will be in the Third World. This expansion is the result of improvements in hygiene and medical care which have lowered death rates. Birth rates remain high despite advances in education and family planning

URBANISATION

Percentage of population living in towns and cities in each country

- 75 – 100%
- 50 – 75%
- 25 – 50%
- 0 – 25%

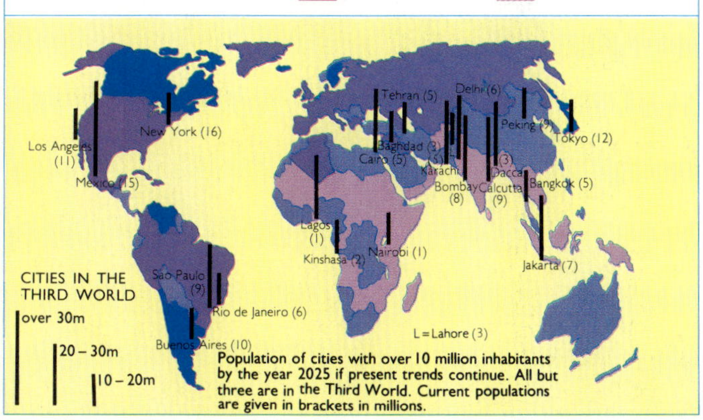

Population of cities with over 10 million inhabitants by the year 2025 if present trends continue. All but three are in the Third World. Current populations are given in brackets in millions.

ILLITERACY

Percentage of population in each country who are illiterate

- 80 – 100%
- 60 – 80%
- 40 – 60%
- 20 – 40%
- 0 – 20%

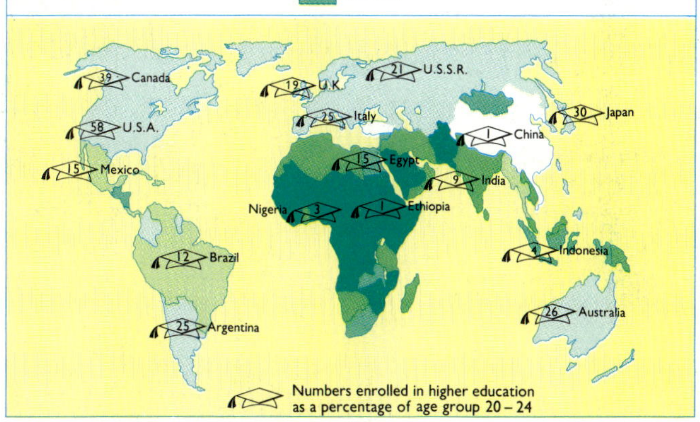

Numbers enrolled in higher education as a percentage of age group 20 – 24

ENERGY CONSUMPTION

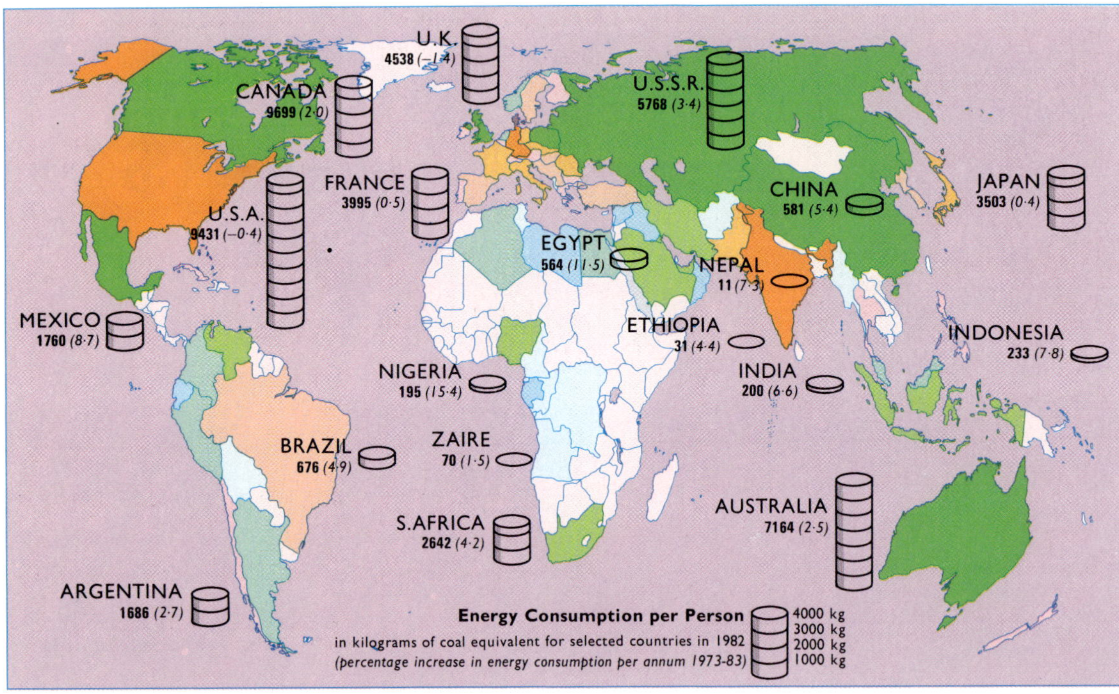

Total Energy Consumption and Production – Key to Map Colours

Figures are in million tonnes of coal equivalent for 1982

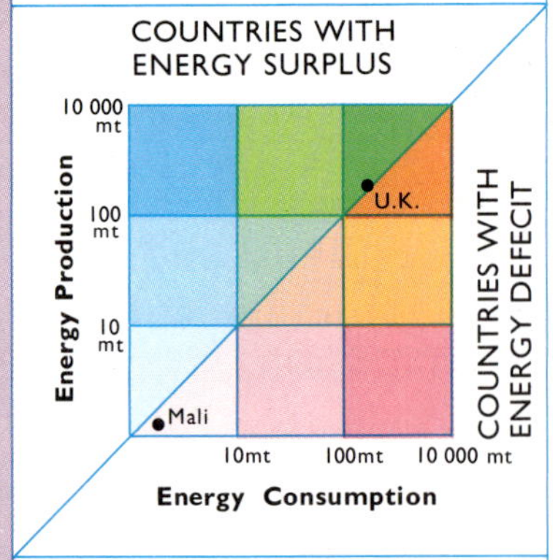

Examples :- U.K. produced 311 mt
consumed 233 mt

Mali produced 0.006 mt
consumed 0.203 mt

IMPORTANCE OF PRIMARY COMMODITIES

Primary commodities as a percentage of total exports. Primary commodities are raw materials such as minerals, fuel, food and timber.

0-25% | 25-50% | 50-75% | 75-100%

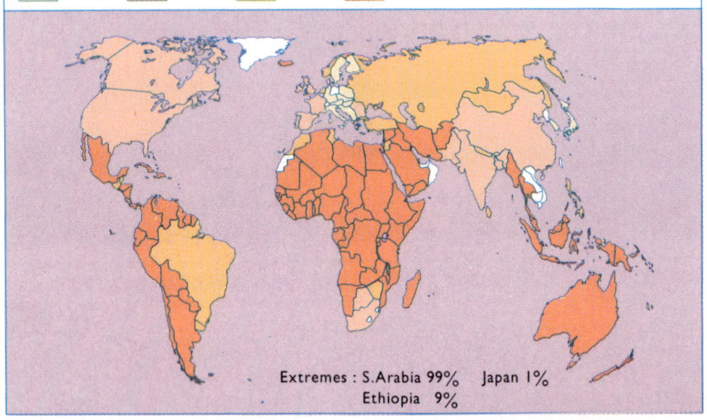

DEPENDENCE UPON AGRICULTURE

Value of agriculture as a percentage of G.D.P. (Gross Domestic Product)

0-10% | 10-20% | 20-30% | 30-40% | 40-50% | over 50%

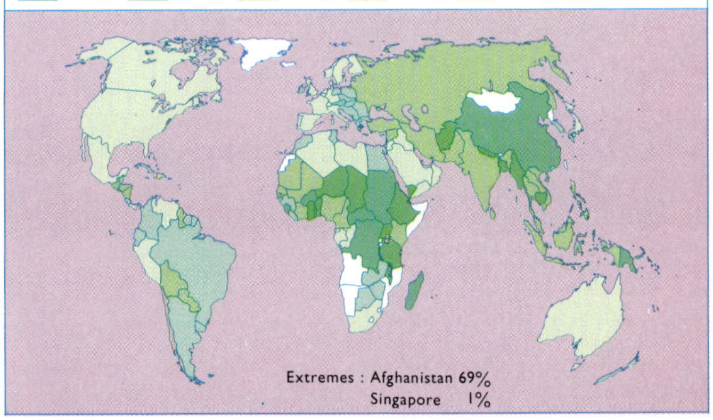

FOOD PRODUCTION

Food production per person

Percentage change from 1974-6 to 1981-3 for each country

INCREASE: over 20% | 15-20% | 10-15% | 5-10% | 0-5%

DECREASE: 0-5% | 5-10% | 10-15% | 15-20% | over 20%

TRADE IN FOOD

60.6 U.K. — Cereal imports per person for selected countries in 1983 (figures in kilograms)

Net exporters of food (value of food exports greater than food imports)

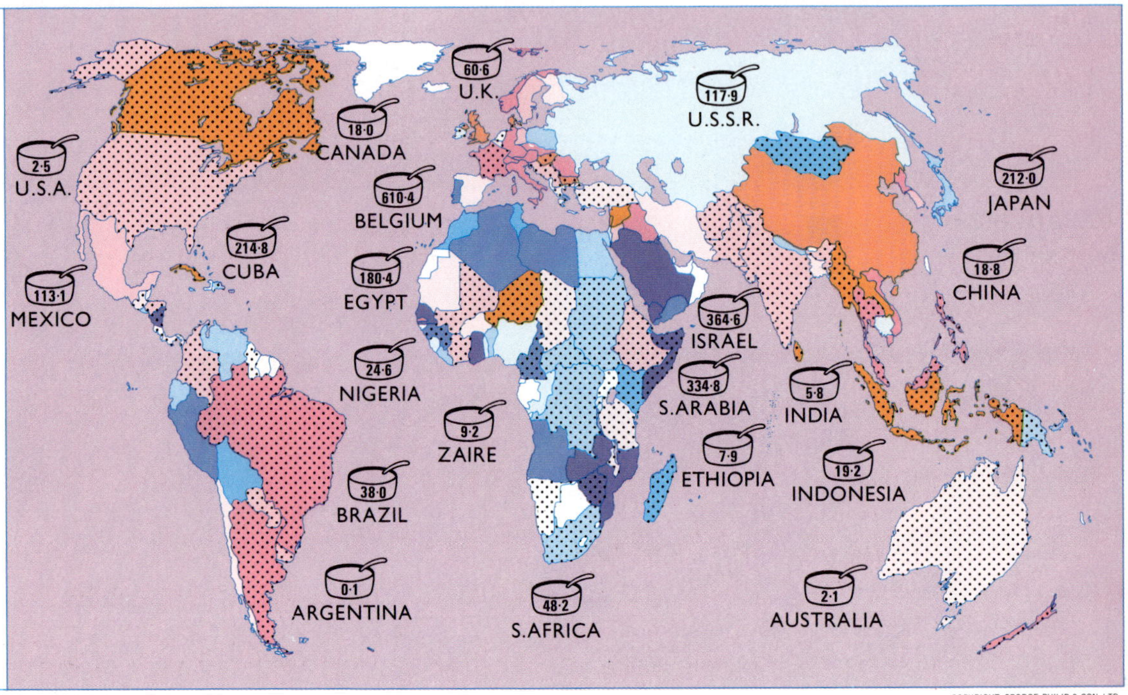

TRADE

Dependence upon Trade

Exports as a percentage of G.D.P. (Gross Domestic Product) for each country for 1982

- over 50%
- 40-50%
- 30-40%
- 20-30%
- 10-20%
- 0-10%

Value of Trade per person

Imports / Exports

Figures are in U.S. $ for selected countries in 1983

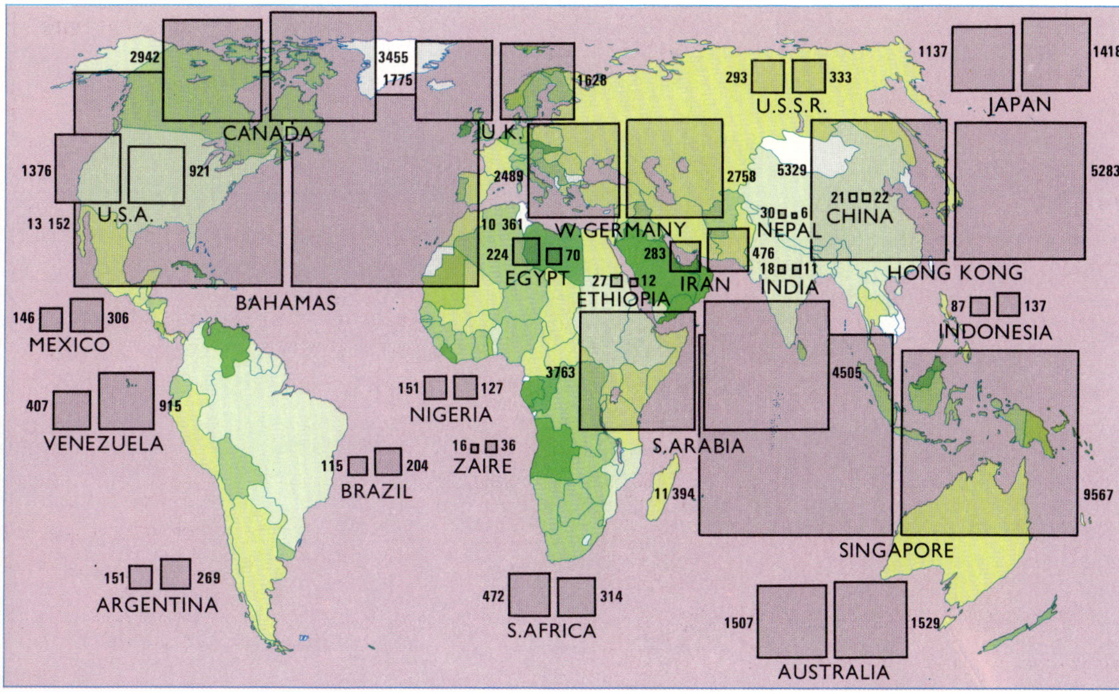

DEVELOPMENT AID

Development aid received per person in U.S. $, 1979-81 average

- 0-10$
- 10-20$
- 20-50$
- 50-100$
- over 100$

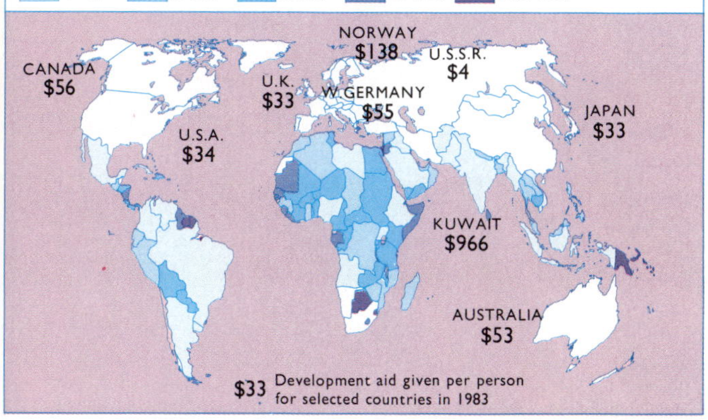

$33 Development aid given per person for selected countries in 1983

INFLATION

Annual average rate of increase 1973-83

- 0-5%
- 5-10%
- 10-15%
- 15-20%
- 20-50%
- 50-100%
- over 100%

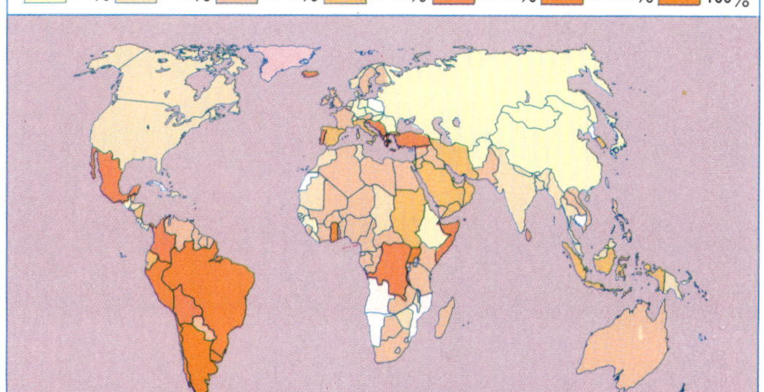

Extremes: China 1·7%
Argentina 167·8%

EMPLOYMENT

Employment by Sector in 1980
Key to Map Colours

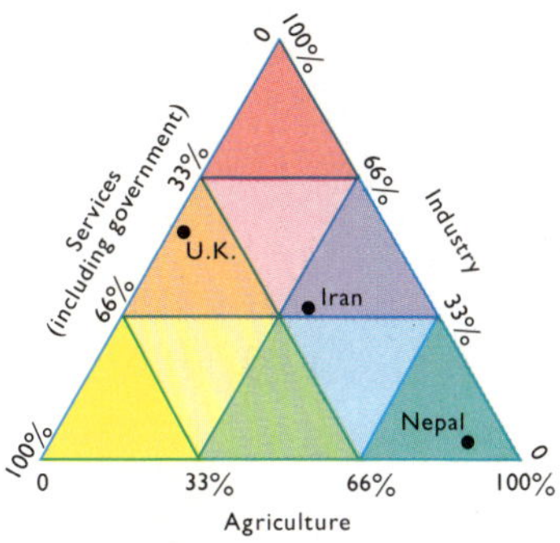

Examples:

Nepal 93% in agriculture
2% in industry
5% in services

U.K. 2% in agriculture
42% in industry
56% in services

Iran 38% in agriculture
33% in industry
29% in services

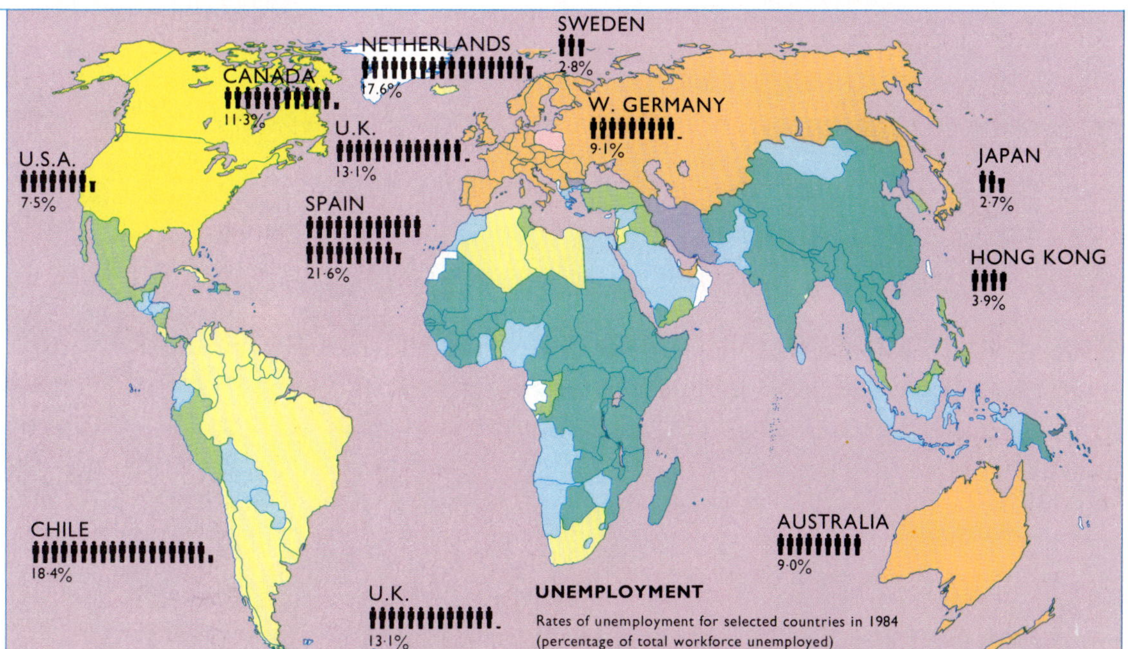

UNEMPLOYMENT

Rates of unemployment for selected countries in 1984 (percentage of total workforce unemployed)

Unemployment rates are meaningful only in developed countries where fewer people live on the land.

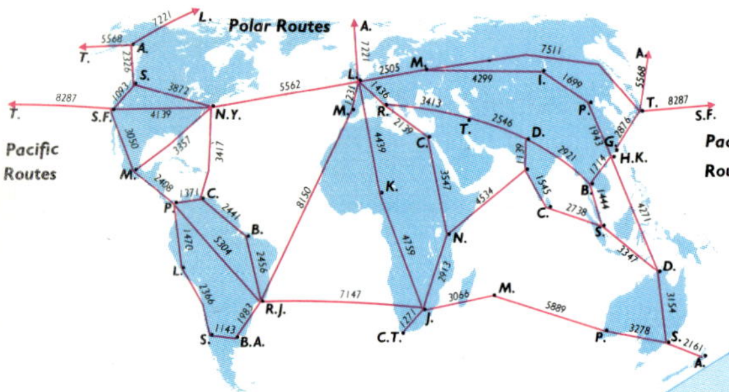

Principal Air Routes
Distances in km

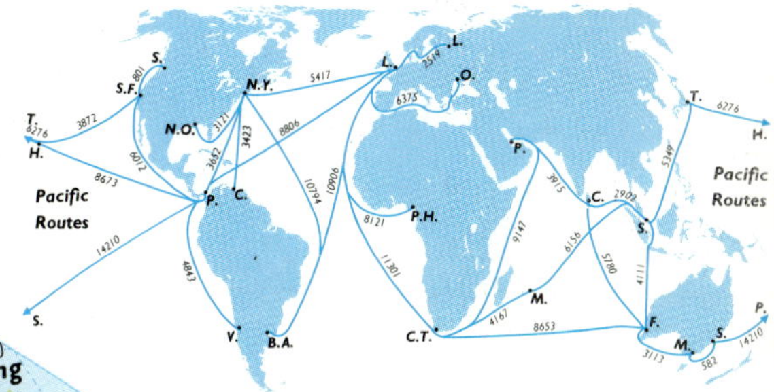

Principal Sea Routes
Distances in km

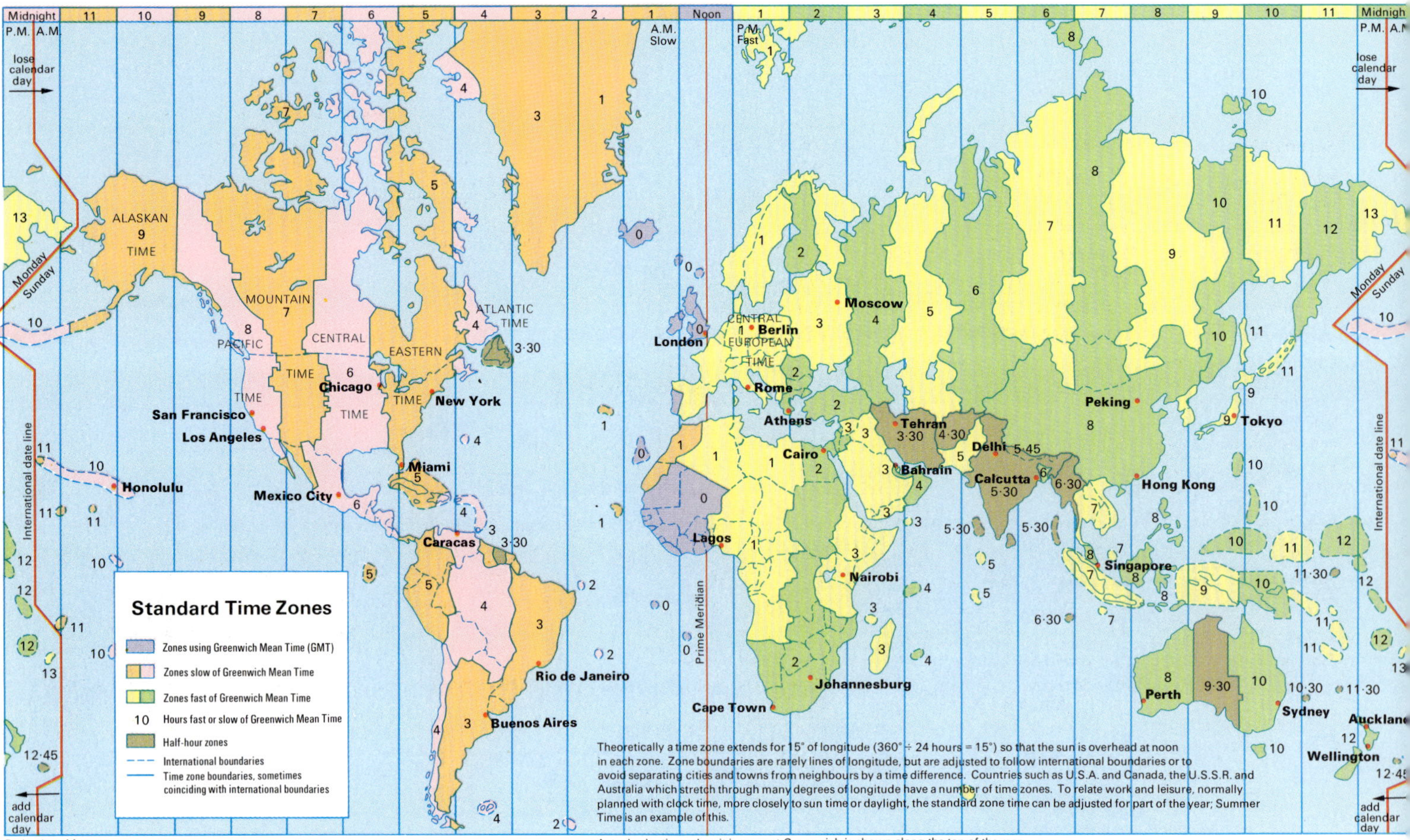

Theoretically a time zone extends for 15° of longitude (360° ÷ 24 hours = 15°) so that the sun is overhead at noon in each zone. Zone boundaries are rarely lines of longitude, but are adjusted to follow international boundaries or to avoid separating cities and towns from neighbours by a time difference. Countries such as U.S.A. and Canada, the U.S.S.R. and Australia which stretch through many degrees of longitude have a number of time zones. To relate work and leisure, normally planned with clock time, more closely to sun time or daylight, the standard zone time can be adjusted for part of the year; Summer Time is an example of this.

Projection: *Mercator*

Actual solar time when it is noon at Greenwich is shown along the top of the map

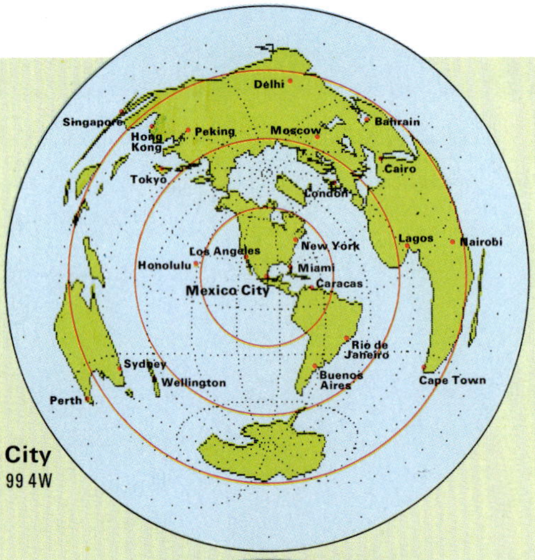

Mexico City
19 26N 99 4W

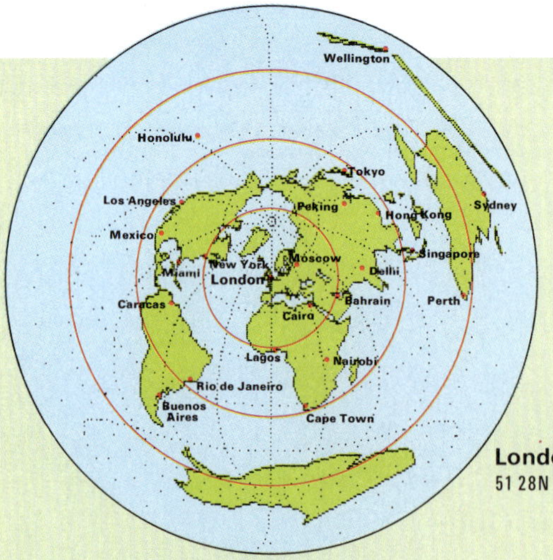

London
51 28N 0 27W

These circular maps are drawn on an Azimuthal Equidistant projection with its origin, its centre, at the city shown. The whole world is shown and so there are some strange distortions of the coastline at the edges, for example, in that of Singapore. The principal property of the projection is that all distances measured through the centre of the circle are true to scale, and so a straight line passing from the centre to any other point is a great circle and shows the shortest distance between the cities. Also that line is correct for direction/bearing and shows the great circle flight path.

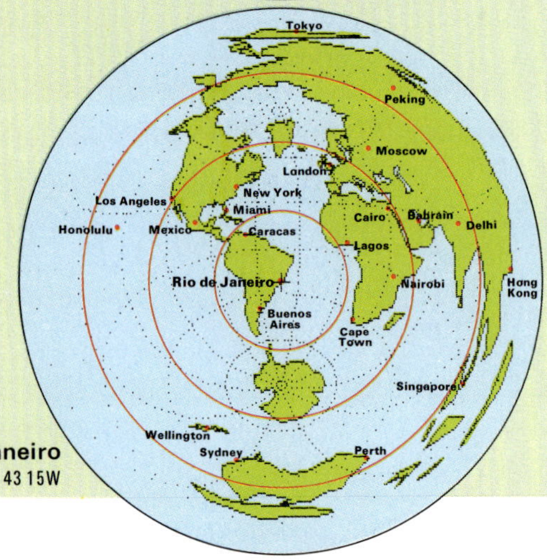

Rio de Janeiro
22 50S 43 15W

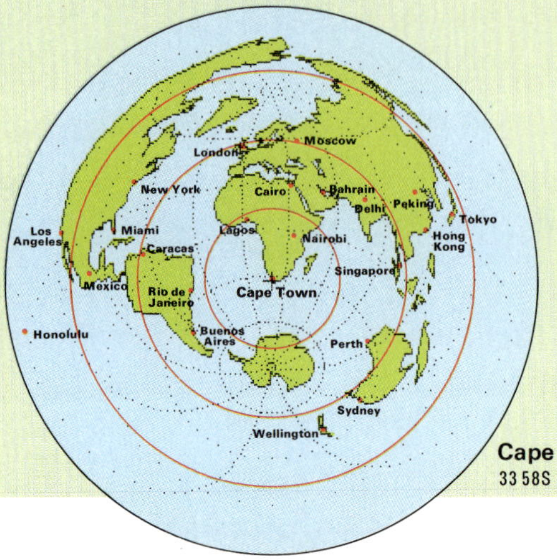

Cape Town
33 58S 18 36E

	Bahrain	Buenos Aires	Cairo	Cape Town	Caracas	Delhi	Hong Kong	Honolulu	Lagos	London	Los Angeles	Mexico	Miami	Moscow	Nairobi	New York	Peking	Perth	Rio de Janeiro	Singapore	Sydney	Tokyo
Buenos Aires	13 291																					
Cairo	1 927	11 845																				
Cape Town	7 496	6 880	7 246																			
Caracas	12 121	5 124	10 200	10 254																		
Delhi	2 618	15 784	4 400	9 278	14 186																	
Hong Kong	6 387	18 442	8 121	11 852	16 340	3 768																
Honolulu	13 882	12 158	14 195	18 555	9 671	11 984	8 911															
Lagos	5 454	7 932	3 926	4 783	7 722	8 071	11 832	16 286														
London	5 089	11 128	3 528	9 672	7 465	6 726	9 637	11 617	4 998													
Los Angeles	13 210	9 854	12 206	16 067	5 813	12 863	11 634	4 105	12 408	8 752												
Mexico	13 962	7 391	12 360	13 701	3 572	14 651	12 121	6 096	11 043	8 898	2 498											
Miami	12 182	7 113	10 441	12 334	2 190	13 495	14 430	7 806	9 045	7 102	3 759	2 050										
Moscow	3 466	13 488	2 909	10 150	9 900	4 359	7 148	11 289	6 250	2 505	9 748	10 682	9 191									
Nairobi	3 398	10 413	3 542	4 096	11 545	5 413	8 750	17 255	3 828	6 835	15 560	14 812	12 771	6 365								
New York	10 613	8 526	9 009	12 551	3 402	11 747	12 956	8 000	8 437	5 535	3 968	3 361	1 751	7 476	11 828							
Peking	6 180	19 273	7 526	12 956	14 356	3 804	1 985	8 124	11 452	8 146	10 030	12 426	12 475	5 789	9 217	10 971						
Perth	9 467	12 562	11 256	8 684	17 610	7 874	6 030	10 886	12 517	14 495	14 986	16 247	18 281	12 236	8 889	18 699	8 000					
Rio de Janeiro	11 462	1 990	9 897	6 080	4 522	14 054	17 688	13 330	6 022	9 248	10 132	7 659	6 713	11 528	8 937	7 724	17 306	13 527				
Singapore	6 319	15 860	8 246	9 650	18 332	4 148	2 581	10 789	11 149	10 867	14 099	16 593	16 951	8 437	7 446	15 330	4 489	3 909	15 729			
Sydney	12 502	11 760	14 391	10 982	15 341	10 424	7 370	8 163	15 514	17 005	12 052	12 973	15 012	14 501	12 125	16 001	8 956	3 274	13 512	6 294		
Tokyo	8 271	18 338	9 552	14 710	14 154	5 852	2 874	6 185	13 475	9 584	8 806	11 304	11 991	7 487	11 243	10 869	2 089	7 896	18 557	5 300	7 809	
Wellington	14 678	9 943	16 503	11 287	13 119	12 647	9 424	7 508	16 047	18 816	10 787	11 099	13 054	16 547	13 643	14 406	10 782	5 246	11 865	8 521	2 226	9 258

These distances are in kilometres and are the great circle distances between the cities (international airports). Great circle distances are the shortest distances between two points on the globe. They are the normal flight paths for aircraft where they are free from the restrictions of air corridors or national airspace.

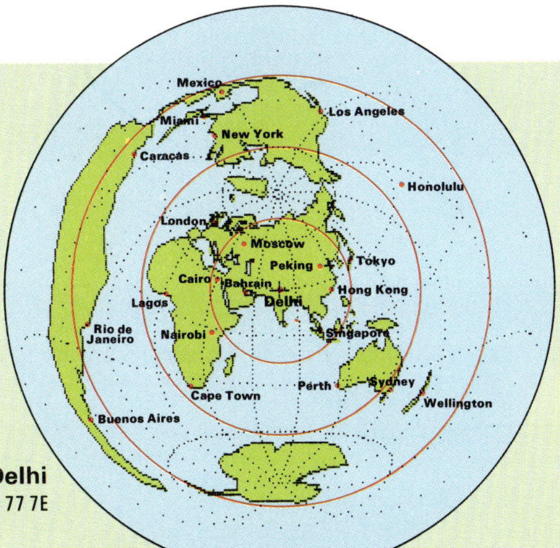

Delhi
28 34N 77 7E

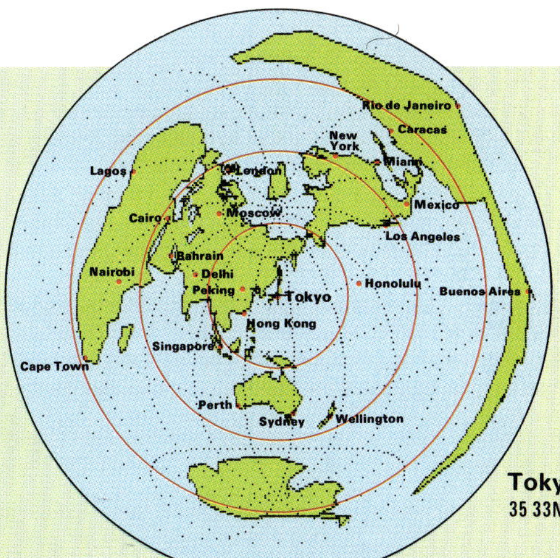

Tokyo
35 33N 139 46E

The three circles are drawn at radius 5 000, 10 000 and 15 000 km from the central city

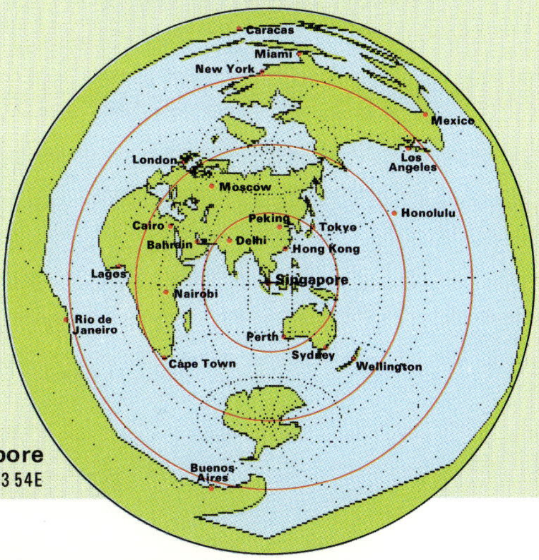

Singapore
1 21N 103 54E

- Cities shown on the distance table

The co-ordinates given are for the airport of each city

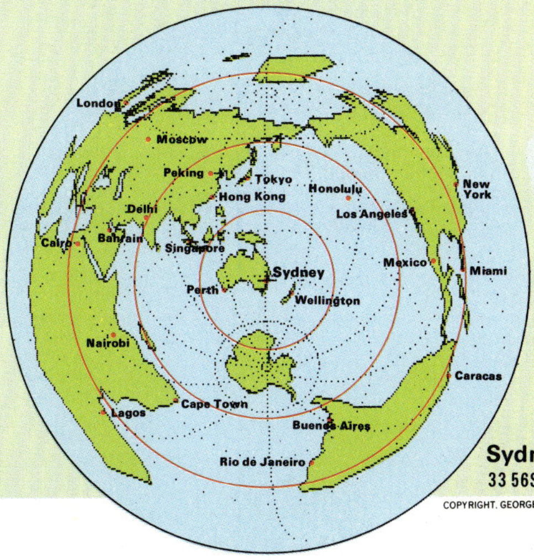

Sydney
33 56S 151 10E

INDEX

The number in bold type which follows each name in the index refers to the number of the page where that feature or place will be found.

The geographical co-ordinates which follow the place name are sometimes only approximate but are close enough for the place name to be located.

An open square □ signifies that the name refers to an administrative division of a country while a solid square ■ follows the name of a country.

Rivers have been indexed to their mouth or to their confluence.

The alphabetical order of names composed of two or more words is governed primarily by the first word and then by the second. This is an example of the rule:

West Wyalong
West Yorkshire
Westbourne
Westbury
Westbury-on-Severn
Western Australia

Names composed of a proper name (Gibraltar) and a description (Strait of) are positioned alphabetically by the proper name. All river names are followed by ⤳. If the same word occurs in the name of a town and a geographical feature, the town name is listed first followed by the name or names of the geographical features.

Names beginning with M', Mc are all indexed as if they were spelled Mac.

If the same place name occurs twice or more in the index and the places are in different countries they will be followed by the country names and the latter in alphabetical order.

Sydney, Australia
Sydney, Canada

In the index each placename is followed by its geographical co-ordinates which allow the reader to find the place on the map. These co-ordinates give the latitude and longitude of a particular place.

The latitude (or parallel) is the distance of a point north or south of the Equator measured as an angle with the centre of the earth. The Equator is latitude 0°, the North Pole is 90°N and the South Pole 90°S. On a globe the lines could be drawn as concentric circles parallel to the Equator, decreasing in diameter from the Equator until they become a point at the Poles. On the maps these lines of latitude are usually represented as lines running across the map from East to West in smooth curves. They are numbered on the sides of the map; north of the Equator the numbers increase northwards, to the south they increase southwards. The degree interval between them depends on the scale of the map. On a large scale map (for example, 1:2 000 000) the interval is one degree, but on a small scale (for example 1:50 000 000) it will be ten degrees.

Lines of longitude (or meridians) cut the latitude lines at right angles on the globe and intersect with one another at the Poles. Longitude is measured by the angle at the centre of the earth between it and the meridian of origin which runs through Greenwich (0°). It may be a measurement East or West of this line and from 0° to 180° in each direction. The longitude line of 180° runs North – South through the Pacific Ocean. On a particular map the interval between the lines of longitude is always the same as that between the lines of latitude and normally they are drawn vertically. They are numbered in the top and bottom margins and a note states East or West from Greenwich.

The unit of measurement for latitude and longitude is the degree and it is subdivided into 60 minutes. An index entry states the position of a place in degrees and minutes, a space being left between the degrees and minutes. The latitude is followed by N(orth) or S(outh) and the longitude by E(ast) or W(est).

The diagram illustrates how the reader has to estimate the required distance from the nearest line of latitude or longitude. In the diagram there is one degree, or 60 minutes between the lines and so to find the position of Calais an estimate has to be made, 57 parts of 60 north of the 50 degree latitude line and 50 parts of 60, or 50 minutes east of the one degree longitude line.

Where the map is smaller in scale it is more difficult to calculate the position of a place because there are five or ten degree intervals between the lines.

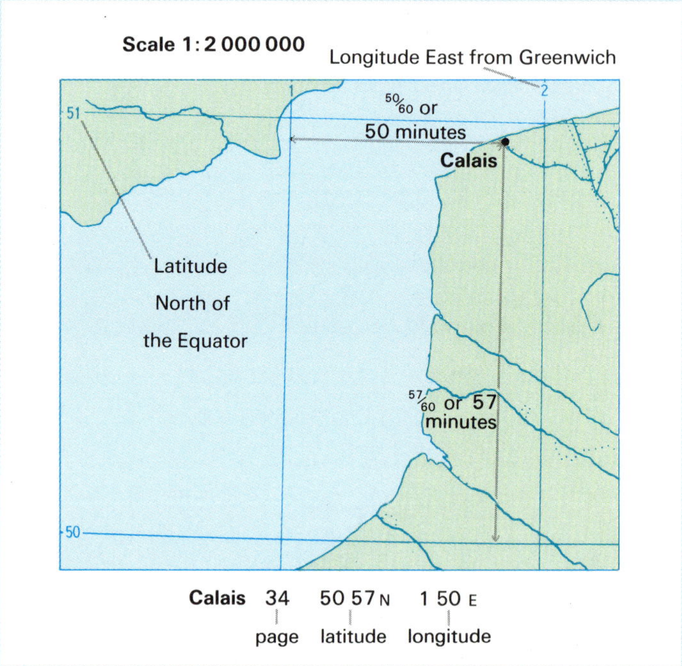

The following is a list of the principal abbreviations used in the Index.

A.S.S.R. – Autonomous Soviet Socialist Republic
Afg. – Afghanistan
Afr. – Africa
Alb. – Albania
Alg. – Algeria
Am. – America
Ant. – Antarctica
Arch. – Archipelago
Arg. – Argentina
Atl. Oc. – Atlantic Ocean
B. – Bay
B. Faso – Burkina Faso
Barb. – Barbados
Berm. – Bermuda
Bol. – Bolivia
Bots. – Botswana
Bulg. – Bulgaria
Bur. – Burma
C. – Cape (Cap, Cabo)
C.A.R. – Central African Republic
C.R. – Costa Rica
Cam. – Cameroon
Carib. – Caribbean Sea
Chan. – Channel
Col. – Colombia
Cont. – Continent
Cr. – Creek
Cur. – Curaçao
Dom. – Dominica
Dom. Rep. – Dominican Republic
E. – East
Eq. Guin. – Equatorial Guinea
Eth. – Ethiopia
Falk. – Falkland Is.
Fr. – France
Fr. G. – French Guiana
G. – Gulf (Golf, Golfo)
Ga. – Georgia
Ger. – Germany
Gr. – Great
Green. – Greenland
Gren. – Grenada
Guad. – Guadeloupe
Guat. – Guatemala
Guin. – Guinea
Guy. – Guyana
Hond. – Honduras
Hr. – Harbour
Hts. – Heights
I. – Island (Isle, Ile, Isla)
Ill. – Illinois
Ind. – Indies
Kor. – Korea
Kuw. – Kuwait
L. – Lake (Lac, Loch, Lough, Lago)
Leb. – Lebanon
Les. – Lesotho
Lib. – Liberia
Mart. – Martinique
Mass. – Massachusetts
Maurit. – Mauritania
Minn. – Minnesota
Miss. – Mississippi
Mong. – Mongolia
Mor. – Morocco
Mt. – Mountain (Mount, Mont, Monte, Monti, Montana)
N. – North
N. Cal. – New Caledonia
Nam. – Namibia
Nic. – Nicaragua
Nig. – Nigeria
Nor. – Norway
Oc. – Oceania
P.N.G. – Papua New Guinea
P.R. – Puerto Rico
Pac. Oc. – Pacific Ocean
Pan. – Panama
Par. – Paraguay
Pen. – Peninsula
Pk. – Peak
Pt. – Point (Pointe, Punta)
Ra. – Range
Rom. – Romania
S. – South
S. Oc. – Southern Ocean
Sd. – Sound
Sene. – Senegal
Si. Arab. – Saudi Arabia
Som. – Somalia
St. L. – St. Lucia
Str. – Strait
Swaz. – Swaziland
Tanz. – Tanzania
U.A.E. – United Arab Emirates
Ven. – Venezuela
W. – West
Yem. – Yemen
Zam. – Zambia
Zim. – Zimbabwe

A

Aachen, W. Ger. 36 50 47N 6 4 E
Aalborg, Den. 45 57 2N 9 54 E
Aalst, Belg. 36 50 56N 4 2 E
Aarhus, Den. 45 56 8N 10 11 E
Ābādān, Iran 56 30 22N 48 20 E
Abbey Town, U.K. 18 54 50N 3 18W
Abbots Bromley, U.K. 14 52 50N 1 52W
Abbots Langley, U.K. 15 51 43N 0 25W
Abbotsbury, U.K. 14 50 40N 2 36W
Abéché, Chad 79 13 50N 20 35 E
Aberaeron, U.K. 17 52 15N 4 16W
Aberdare, U.K. 17 51 43N 3 27W
Aberdeen, U.K. 23 57 9N 2 6W
Aberdour, U.K. 21 56 2N 3 18W
Aberdovey, U.K. 17 52 33N 4 3W
Aberfeldy, U.K. 23 56 37N 3 50W
Aberfoyle, U.K. 20 56 10N 4 23W
Abergavenny, U.K. 17 51 49N 3 1W
Abergele, U.K. 17 53 17N 3 35W
Aberlady, U.K. 21 56 0N 2 51W
Abernethy, U.K. 21 56 19N 3 18W
Aberporth, U.K. 17 52 8N 4 32W
Abersoch, U.K. 17 52 50N 4 30W
Abersychan, U.K. 17 51 44N 3 3W
Abertillery, U.K. 17 51 44N 3 9W
Aberystwyth, U.K. 17 52 25N 4 6W
Abidjan, Ivory C. 78 5 26N 3 58W
Abingdon, U.K. 14 51 40N 1 17W
Abington, U.K. 21 55 30N 3 42W
Aboyne, U.K. 23 57 4N 2 48W
Abū Dhabī, U.A.E. 57 24 28N 54 36 E
Acapulco, Mex. 94 16 51N 99 56W
Accra, Ghana 78 5 35N 0 6W
Accrington, U.K. 18 53 46N 2 22W
Achill Hd., Ire. 24 53 59N 10 15W
Achill I., Ire. 24 53 58N 10 5W
Achinsk, U.S.S.R. 49 56 20N 90 20 E
Achnasheen, U.K. 22 57 35N 5 5W
Acklins I., Baham. 95 22 30N 74 0W
Acle, U.K. 15 52 38N 1 32 E
Aconcagua, Cerro, Arg. 102 32 39S 70 0W
Acre, Isr. 57 32 55N 35 4 E
Acton Burnell, U.K. 14 52 37N 2 41W
Adamaoua Plateau, Cam. 80 7 20N 12 20 E
Adam's Bridge, Sri L. 58 9 15N 79 40 E
Adana, Turk. 47 37 0N 35 16 E
Adapazarı, Turk. 47 40 48N 30 25 E
Addis Ababa, Eth. 79 9 2N 38 42 E
Addlestone, U.K. 15 51 22N 0 30W
Adelaide, Austral. 67 34 52S 138 30 E
Adélie Land, Ant. 103 68 0S 140 0 E
Aden, S. Yem. 56 12 45N 45 0 E
Aden, G. of, Asia 56 13 0N 50 0 E
Adirondack Mts., U.S.A. 93 44 0N 74 15W
Admiralty Is., P.N.G. 64 2 0S 147 0 E
Adrar, Alg. 78 27 51N 0 11W
Adriatic Sea, Europe 40 43 0N 16 0 E
Adwick le Street, U.K. 19 53 35N 1 12W
Ægean Sea, Europe 41 37 0N 25 0 E
Afghanistan ■, Asia 57 33 0N 65 0 E
Agadès, Niger 78 16 58N 7 59 E
Agadir, Mor. 78 30 28N 9 35W
Agartala, India 59 23 50N 91 23 E
Agra, India 58 27 17N 77 58 E
Agrigento, It. 40 37 19N 13 33 E
Aguascalientes, Mex. 94 21 53N 102 12W
Ahmadabad, India 58 23 0N 72 40 E
Ahvāz, Iran 56 31 20N 48 40 E
Ahvenanmaa = Åland, Fin. 45 60 15N 20 0 E
Ailsa Craig, U.K. 20 55 15N 5 7W
Ainsdale, U.K. 18 53 37N 3 2W
Airdrie, U.K. 21 55 53N 3 57W
Aire →, U.K. 19 53 42N 0 55W
Aisgill, U.K. 18 54 23N 2 21W
Aix-en-Provence, Fr. 35 43 32N 5 27 E
Ajaccio, Fr. 35 41 55N 8 40 E
Akashi, Jap. 62 34 45N 135 0 E
Akita, Jap. 62 39 45N 140 7 E
Akranes, Ice. 44 64 19N 21 58W
Akron, U.S.A. 92 41 7N 81 31W
Aktyubinsk, U.S.S.R. 47 50 17N 57 10 E
Akure, Nig. 78 7 15N 5 5 E
Akureyri, Ice. 44 65 40N 18 6W
Al Ḥudaydah, Yem. 56 14 50N 43 0 E
Al Hūfuf, Si. Arab. 56 25 25N 49 45 E
Al Jawf, Si. Arab. 56 29 55N 39 40 E
Al Qaṭīf, Si. Arab. 56 26 35N 50 0 E
Al Qunaytirah, Syria 57 32 55N 35 45 E
Alabama □, U.S.A. 91 33 0N 87 0W
Åland, Fin. 45 60 15N 20 0 E
Alaska □, U.S.A. 88 65 0N 150 0W
Alaska, G. of, Pac. Oc. 88 58 0N 145 0W
Alaska Pen., U.S.A. 88 56 0N 160 0W
Alaska Range, U.S.A. 88 62 50N 151 0W
Alba Iulia, Rom. 43 46 8N 23 39 E
Albacete, Sp. 37 39 0N 1 50W
Albania ■, Europe 41 41 0N 20 0 E
Albany, Austral. 66 35 1S 117 58 E
Albany, Ga., U.S.A. 90 31 40N 84 10W
Albany, N.Y., U.S.A. 93 42 35N 73 47W
Albany →, Canada 89 52 17N 81 31W
Alberta □, Canada 88 54 40N 115 0W
Albrighton, U.K. 14 52 38N 2 17W
Albuquerque, U.S.A. 90 35 5N 106 47W
Albury, Austral. 70 36 3S 146 56 E
Alcalá de Henares, Sp. 37 40 28N 3 22W
Alcester, U.K. 14 52 13N 1 52W
Aldan →, U.S.S.R. 49 63 28N 129 35 E
Aldborough, U.K. 19 54 6N 1 21W
Aldbourne, U.K. 14 51 28N 1 38W
Aldbrough, U.K. 19 53 50N 0 7W
Aldeburgh, U.K. 15 52 9N 1 35 E
Alderbury, U.K. 14 51 4N 1 45W
Alderley Edge, U.K. 18 53 18N 2 15W
Alderney, U.K. 34 49 42N 2 12W
Aldershot, U.K. 15 51 15N 0 43W
Aldingham, U.K. 18 54 8N 3 3W
Aleppo, Syria 56 36 10N 37 15 E
Alessándria, It. 40 44 54N 8 37 E
Ålesund, Nor. 44 62 28N 6 12 E
Aleutian Is., Pac. Oc. 88 52 0N 175 0W
Alexander Arch., U.S.A. 88 57 0N 135 0W
Alexandria, Egypt 79 31 0N 30 0 E
Alexandria, U.K. 20 55 59N 4 40W
Alexandria, U.S.A. 90 31 20N 92 30W
Alford, Grampian, U.K. 23 57 13N 2 42W
Alford, Lincs., U.K. 19 53 16N 0 10 E
Alfreton, U.K. 19 53 6N 1 22W
Alfriston, U.K. 15 50 48N 0 10 E
Algarve, Port. 37 36 58N 8 20W
Algeciras, Sp. 37 36 9N 5 28W
Algeria ■, Africa 78 35 10N 3 11 E
Algiers, Alg. 78 36 42N 3 8 E
Alicante, Sp. 37 38 23N 0 30W
Alice Springs, Austral. 66 23 40S 133 50 E
Aligarh, India 58 27 55N 78 10 E
Alkmaar, Neth. 36 52 37N 4 45 E
Allahabad, India 59 25 25N 81 58 E
Allegheny Mts., U.S.A. 92 38 0N 80 0W
Allen →, U.K. 21 54 53N 2 13W
Allen, Bog of, Ire. 25 53 15N 7 0W
Allen, L., Ire. 24 54 12N 8 5W
Allendale, U.K. 21 54 55N 2 15W
Allenheads, U.K. 21 54 49N 2 12W
Allentown, U.S.A. 93 40 36N 75 30W
Alloa, U.K. 21 56 7N 3 49W
Allonby, U.K. 18 54 45N 3 27W
Alma Ata, U.S.S.R. 48 43 15N 76 57 E
Almelo, Neth. 36 52 22N 6 42 E
Almería, Sp. 37 36 52N 2 27W
Almond →, U.K. 21 56 27N 3 27W
Almondsbury, U.K. 14 51 33N 2 34W
Aln →, U.K. 21 55 27N 1 32W
Alness, U.K. 23 57 41N 4 15W
Alnmouth, U.K. 21 55 24N 1 37W
Alnwick, U.K. 19 55 25N 1 42W
Alphen, Neth. 36 51 29N 4 58 E
Alphington, U.K. 16 50 41N 3 32W
Alps, Europe 42 47 0N 8 0 E
Alrewas, U.K. 14 52 43N 1 44W
Alsager, U.K. 18 53 7N 2 20W
Alston, U.K. 18 54 48N 2 26W
Altai Mts., Asia 60 46 40N 92 45 E
Altarnun, U.K. 16 50 35N 4 30W
Altay, China 60 47 48N 88 10 E
Alton, U.K. 15 51 8N 0 59W
Altoona, U.S.A. 92 40 32N 78 24W
Altrincham, U.K. 18 53 25N 2 21W
Altun Shan, China 60 38 30N 88 0 E
Alva, U.K. 21 56 9N 3 49W
Alvechurch, U.K. 14 52 22N 1 58W
Alwinton, U.K. 21 55 20N 2 7W
Alyth, U.K. 23 56 38N 3 15W
Amadjuak L., Canada 89 65 0N 71 8W
Amagasaki, Jap. 62 34 42N 135 20 E
Amarillo, U.S.A. 90 35 14N 101 46W
Amazon →, S. Am. 100 0 5S 50 0W
Amazonas □, Brazil 101 4 0S 62 0W
Amble, U.K. 21 55 20N 1 36W
Ambleside, U.K. 18 54 26N 2 58W
Ambon, Indon. 63 3 35S 128 20 E
American Samoa ■, Pac. Oc. 65 14 20S 170 40W
Amersfoort, Neth. 36 52 9N 5 23 E
Amersham, U.K. 15 51 40N 0 38W
Amesbury, U.K. 14 51 10N 1 46W
Amiens, Fr. 34 49 54N 2 16 E
Amlwch, U.K. 17 53 24N 4 21W
'Ammān, Jord. 57 31 57N 35 52 E
Ammanford, U.K. 17 51 48N 4 0W
Amoy = Xiamen, China 61 24 25N 118 4 E
Ampleforth, U.K. 19 54 13N 1 8W
Ampthill, U.K. 15 52 3N 0 30W
Amravati, India 58 20 55N 77 45 E
Amritsar, India 58 31 35N 74 57 E
Amsterdam, Neth. 36 52 23N 4 54 E
Amudarya →, U.S.S.R. 48 43 40N 59 0 E
Amundsen Gulf, Canada 88 71 0N 124 0W
Amundsen Sea, Ant. 103 72 0S 115 0W
Amur →, U.S.S.R. 49 52 56N 141 10 E
An Nafūd, Si. Arab. 56 28 15N 41 0 E
An Najaf, Iraq 56 32 3N 44 15 E
An Uaimh, Ire. 24 53 39N 6 40W
Anadyr, G. of, U.S.S.R. 49 64 0N 180 0 E
Anaheim, U.S.A. 90 33 50N 118 0W
Anápolis, Brazil 101 16 15S 48 50W
Anatolia, Turk. 47 38 0N 30 0 E
Ancaster, U.K. 19 52 59N 0 32W
Ancholme →, U.K. 19 53 42N 0 32W
Anchorage, U.S.A. 88 61 10N 149 50W
Ancona, It. 40 43 37N 13 30 E
Ancrum, U.K. 21 55 31N 2 35W
Anda, China 61 46 24N 125 19 E
Andalusia, Reg., Sp. 37 37 35N 5 0W
Andaman Is., India 51 12 30N 92 30 E
Anderlecht, Belg. 36 50 50N 4 19 E
Andes, S. Am. 96 20 0S 68 0W
Andhra Pradesh □, India 58 16 0N 79 0 E
Andizhan, U.S.S.R. 48 41 10N 72 0 E
Andorra ■, Europe 35 42 30N 1 30 E
Andover, U.K. 14 51 13N 1 29W
Andreanof Is., Pac. Oc. 88 52 0N 178 0W
Andreas, U.K. 18 54 23N 4 25W
Ándria, It. 40 41 13N 16 17 E
Andropov, U.S.S.R. 46 58 5N 38 50 E
Andros I., Baham. 95 24 30N 78 0W
Angara →, U.S.S.R. 49 58 30N 97 0 E
Angarsk, U.S.S.R. 49 52 30N 104 0 E
Angers, Fr. 34 47 30N 0 35W
Anglesey, U.K. 17 53 17N 4 20W
Angmagssalik, Green. 89 65 40N 37 20W
Angmering, U.K. 15 50 48N 0 28W
Angola ■, Africa 81 12 0S 18 0 E
Angoulême, Fr. 35 45 39N 0 10 E
Anguilla, W. Ind. 94 18 14N 63 5W
Angus, Braes of, U.K. 23 56 51N 3 10W
Anhui □, China 61 32 0N 117 0 E
Anjou, Fr. 34 47 20N 0 15W
Ankara, Turk. 47 40 0N 32 54 E
Ann Arbor, U.S.A. 92 42 17N 83 45W
Annaba, Alg. 78 36 50N 7 46 E
Annalee →, Ire. 24 54 3N 7 15W
Annan, U.K. 21 55 0N 3 17W
Annan →, U.K. 21 54 58N 3 18W
Annandale, U.K. 21 55 10N 3 25W
Annecy, Fr. 35 45 55N 6 8 E
Annfield Plain, U.K. 19 54 52N 1 45W
Annobón, Atl. Oc. 73 1 25S 5 36 E
Anshan, China 61 41 5N 122 58 E
Anshun, China 60 26 18N 105 57 E
Anstey, U.K. 14 52 41N 1 14W
Anstruther, U.K. 21 56 14N 2 40W
Antalya, Turk. 47 36 52N 30 45 E
Antananarivo, Madag. 81 18 55S 47 31 E
Antarctic Pen., Ant. 103 67 0S 60 0W
Antarctica, Cont. 103 90 0S 0 0 E
Anticosti, I. d', Canada 93 49 30N 63 0W
Antigua & Barbuda ■, W. Ind. 94 17 20N 61 48W
Antofagasta, Chile 102 23 50S 70 30W
Antony, U.K. 16 50 22N 4 13W
Antrim, U.K. 24 54 43N 6 13W
Antrim □, U.K. 24 54 55N 6 20W
Antrim, Mts. of, U.K. 24 54 57N 6 8W
Antsiranana, Madag. 81 12 25S 49 20 E
Antwerp, Belg. 36 51 13N 4 25 E
Anyang, China 61 36 5N 114 21 E
Anzhero-Sudzhensk, U.S.S.R. 48 56 10N 86 0 E
Aomori, Jap. 62 40 45N 140 45 E
Apeldoorn, Neth. 36 52 13N 5 57 E
Apennines, It. 40 44 20N 10 20 E
Appalachian Mts., U.S.A. 91 38 0N 80 0W
Appleby, U.K. 18 54 35N 2 29W
Appledore, Devon, U.K. 16 51 3N 4 12W
Appledore, Kent, U.K. 15 51 2N 0 47 E
Arabia, Asia 50 25 0N 45 0 E
Arabian Desert, Egypt 79 26 0N 33 30 E
Arabian Sea, Ind. Oc. 50 16 0N 65 0 E
Aracaju, Brazil 101 10 55S 37 4W
Araçatuba, Brazil 101 21 10S 50 30W
Arad, Rom. 43 46 10N 21 20 E
Arafura Sea, E. Ind. 64 9 0S 135 0 E
Aragón □, Sp. 37 41 25N 1 0W
Araguaia →, Brazil 101 5 21S 48 41W
Arakan Yoma, Burma 59 20 0N 94 40 E
Aral Sea, U.S.S.R. 48 44 30N 60 0 E
Aralsk, U.S.S.R. 48 46 50N 61 20 E
Aran I., Ire. 24 55 0N 8 30W
Aran Is., Ire. 25 53 5N 9 42W
Arapiraca, Brazil 101 9 45S 36 39W
Ararat, Austral. 70 37 16S 143 0 E
Arbroath, U.K. 23 56 34N 2 35W
Arctic Ocean, Arctic 103 78 0N 160 0W
Arctic Red River, Canada 88 67 15N 134 0W
Ardbeg, U.K. 20 55 38N 6 6W
Ardchyle, U.K. 20 56 26N 4 24W
Ardee, Ire. 24 53 51N 6 32W
Ardennes, Belg. 36 50 0N 5 10 E
Ardentinny, U.K. 20 56 3N 4 56W
Ardgour, U.K. 22 56 45N 5 25W
Ardingly, U.K. 15 51 3N 0 3W
Ardlui, U.K. 20 56 19N 4 43W
Ardmore Pt., U.K. 20 55 40N 6 0W
Ardnamurchan, Pt. of, U.K. 22 56 44N 6 14W
Ardnave Pt., U.K. 20 55 54N 6 20W
Ardrishaig, U.K. 20 56 0N 5 27W
Ardrossan, U.K. 20 55 39N 4 50W
Ards □, U.K. 24 54 35N 5 30W
Ards Pen., U.K. 24 54 30N 5 25W
Ardvasar, U.K. 22 57 5N 5 52W
Arendal, Nor. 45 58 28N 8 46 E
Arequipa, Peru 100 16 20S 71 30W
Argentina ■, S. Am. 102 35 0S 66 0W
Argyll, U.K. 20 56 14N 5 10W
Arica, Chile 100 18 32S 70 20W
Arima, Trin. & Tob. 94 10 38N 61 17W
Arinagour, U.K. 20 56 38N 6 31W
Arisaig, U.K. 22 56 55N 5 50W
Arizona □, U.S.A. 90 34 20N 111 30W
Arkaig, L., U.K. 22 56 58N 5 10W
Arkansas □, U.S.A. 91 35 0N 92 30W
Arkansas →, U.S.A. 91 33 48N 91 4W
Arkhangelsk, U.S.S.R. 46 64 40N 41 0 E
Arkle →, U.K. 18 54 25N 1 55W
Arklow, Ire. 25 52 48N 6 10W
Arles, Fr. 35 43 41N 4 40 E
Arlon, Belg. 36 49 42N 5 49 E
Armadale, U.K. 21 55 54N 3 42W
Armagh, U.K. 24 54 22N 6 40W
Armagh □, U.K. 24 54 18N 6 37W
Armenia, Col. 100 4 35N 75 45W
Armenia □, U.S.S.R. 47 40 0N 41 0 E
Armidale, Austral. 67 30 30S 151 40 E
Arnhem, Neth. 36 51 58N 5 55 E
Arnhem Land, Austral. 66 13 10S 134 30 E
Arnold, U.K. 19 53 0N 1 8W
Arnside, U.K. 18 54 12N 2 49W
Arran, U.K. 20 55 34N 5 12W
Arras, Fr. 34 50 17N 2 46 E
Arrochar, U.K. 20 56 12N 4 45W
Arrow, L., Ire. 24 54 3N 8 20W
Arun →, U.K. 15 50 48N 0 33W
Arunachal Pradesh □, India 59 28 0N 95 0 E
Arundel, U.K. 15 50 52N 0 32W
Arusha, Tanz. 80 3 20S 36 40 E
As Salt, Jord. 57 32 2N 35 43 E
As Summān, Si. Arab. 56 25 0N 47 0 E
Asahigawa, Jap. 62 43 46N 142 22 E
Asansol, India 59 23 40N 87 1 E
Ascension I., Atl. Oc. 128 8 0S 14 15W
Ascot, U.K. 15 51 24N 0 41W
Asfordby, U.K. 15 52 45N 0 57W
Ash, Kent, U.K. 15 51 17N 1 16 E
Ash, Surrey, U.K. 15 51 14N 0 43W
Ashbourne, U.K. 19 53 2N 1 44W
Ashburton, N.Z. 71 43 53S 171 48 E
Ashburton, U.K. 16 50 31N 3 45W
Ashburton →, Austral. 66 21 40S 114 56 E
Ashby-de-la-Zouch, U.K. 14 52 45N 1 29W
Ashchurch, U.K. 14 52 0N 2 7W
Ashdown Forest, U.K. 15 51 4N 0 2 E
Ashford, Derby, U.K. 19 53 13N 1 43W
Ashford, Kent, U.K. 15 51 8N 0 53 E
Ashington, U.K. 21 55 12N 1 35W
Ashkhabad, U.S.S.R. 48 38 0N 57 50 E
Ashq'elon, Isr. 57 31 42N 34 35 E
Ashton-in-Makerfield, U.K. 18 53 29N 2 39W
Ashton-under-Lyne, U.K. 18 53 30N 2 8W
Ashurstwood, U.K. 15 51 6N 0 2 E
Ashwater, U.K. 16 50 43N 4 18W
Ashwick, U.K. 14 51 13N 2 31W
'Asīr □, Si. Arab. 56 18 40N 42 30 E
Asir, Ras, Som. 73 11 55N 51 10 E
Askrigg, U.K. 18 54 19N 2 6W
Aslackby, U.K. 19 52 53N 0 23W
Asmera, Eth. 79 15 19N 38 55 E
Aspatria, U.K. 18 54 45N 3 20W
Assam □, India 59 26 0N 93 0 E
Assen, Neth. 36 53 0N 6 35 E
Assynt, L., U.K. 22 58 25N 5 15W
Asti, It. 40 44 54N 8 11 E
Aston Clinton, U.K. 15 51 48N 0 44W
Astrakhan, U.S.S.R. 47 46 25N 48 5 E
Astwood Bank, U.K. 14 52 15N 1 55W
Asunción, Par. 102 25 10S 57 30W
Aswân, Egypt 79 24 4N 32 57 E
Atacama, Desierto de, Chile 102 24 0S 69 20W
Atbara, Sudan 79 17 42N 33 59 E
Athabasca, L., Canada 88 59 15N 109 15W
Athboy, Ire. 24 53 37N 6 55W
Athenry, Ire. 25 53 18N 8 45W
Athens, Greece 41 37 58N 23 46 E
Atherstone, U.K. 14 52 35N 1 32W
Atherton, U.K. 18 53 32N 2 30W
Athínai = Athens, Greece 41 37 58N 23 46 E
Athlone, Ire. 24 53 26N 7 57W
Atholl, Forest of, U.K. 23 56 51N 3 50W
Athy, Ire. 25 53 0N 7 0W
Atlanta, U.S.A. 91 33 50N 84 24W
Atlantic City, U.S.A. 93 39 25N 74 25W
Atlantic Ocean 128 0 0 20 0W
Atlas Mts., Mor. 72 32 30N 5 0W
Attleborough, U.K. 15 52 32N 1 1 E
Auchencairn, U.K. 21 54 51N 3 52W
Auchinleck, U.K. 20 55 28N 4 18W
Auchterarder, U.K. 21 56 18N 3 43W
Auchterderran, U.K. 21 56 8N 3 16W
Auchtermuchty, U.K. 21 56 18N 3 15W
Auchtertyre, U.K. 22 57 17N 5 35W
Auckland, N.Z. 71 36 52S 174 46 E
Audlem, U.K. 18 52 59N 2 31W
Aughnacloy, U.K. 24 54 25N 6 58W
Augsburg, W. Ger. 42 48 22N 10 54 E
Augusta, U.S.A. 90 33 29N 81 59W
Aurangabad, India 58 19 50N 75 23 E
Aurora, U.S.A. 92 41 42N 88 12W
Austin, U.S.A. 90 30 20N 97 45W
Australia ■, Oc. 66 23 0S 135 0 E
Australian Alps, Austral. 70 36 30S 148 30 E
Australian Cap. Terr. □, Austral. 70 35 30S 149 0 E
Austria ■, Europe 42 47 0N 14 0 E
Auxerre, Fr. 34 47 48N 3 32 E

Avebury, *U.K.* **14** 51 25N 1 52W
Avellino, *It.* **40** 40 54N 14 46 E
Aveton Gifford, *U.K.* **16** 50 17N 3 51W
Avich, L., *U.K.* **20** 56 17N 5 25W
Aviemore, *U.K.* **23** 57 11N 3 50W
Avignon, *Fr.* **35** 43 57N 4 50 E
Ávila, *Sp.* **37** 40 39N 4 43W
Avoca, *Ire.* **25** 52 52N 6 13W
Avon □, *U.K.* **14** 51 30N 2 40W
Avon →, *Avon, U.K.* **14** 51 30N 2 43W
Avon →, *Hants., U.K.* **14** 50 44N 1 45W
Avon →, *Warwick, U.K.* **14** 52 0N 2 9W
Avonmouth, *U.K.* **14** 51 30N 2 42W
Awe, L., *U.K.* **20** 56 15N 5 15W
Axbridge, *U.K.* **14** 51 17N 2 50W
Axe →, *U.K.* **14** 51 17N 2 52W
Axe Edge, *U.K.* **18** 53 14N 1 59W
Axholme, Isle of, *U.K.* **19** 53 30N 0 55W
Axminster, *U.K.* **16** 50 47N 3 1W
Axmouth, *U.K.* **16** 50 43N 3 2W
Ayers Rock, *Austral.* **66** 25 23S 131 5 E
Aylesbury, *U.K.* **15** 51 48N 0 49W
Aylesford, *U.K.* **15** 51 18N 0 29 E
Aylsham, *U.K.* **15** 52 48N 1 16 E
Aynho, *U.K.* **14** 51 59N 1 15W
Ayr, *U.K.* **20** 55 28N 4 37W
Ayr →, *U.K.* **20** 55 29N 4 40W
Ayr, Heads of, *U.K.* **20** 55 25N 4 43W
Ayre, Pt. of, *U.K.* **18** 54 27N 4 21W
Aysgarth, *U.K.* **18** 54 18N 2 0W
Ayton, *Borders, U.K.* **21** 55 51N 2 6W
Ayton, *N. Yorks., U.K.* **19** 54 15N 0 29W
Az Zarqā, *Jord.* **57** 32 5N 36 4 E
Azores, *Atl. Oc.* **128** 38 44N 29 0W
Azov Sea, *U.S.S.R.* **47** 46 0N 36 30 E
Azuero, Pen. de, *Pan.* **95** 7 30N 80 30W

B

Bābol, *Iran* **56** 36 40N 52 50 E
Bacabal, *Brazil* **101** 4 15S 44 45W
Bacău, *Rom.* **43** 46 35N 26 55 E
Back, *U.K.* **22** 58 17N 6 20W
Bacolod, *Phil.* **63** 10 40N 122 57 E
Bacton, *U.K.* **15** 52 50N 1 29 E
Bacup, *U.K.* **18** 53 42N 2 12W
Badajoz, *Sp.* **37** 38 50N 6 59W
Badalona, *Sp.* **37** 41 26N 2 15 E
Baffin B., *Canada* **89** 72 0N 64 0W
Baffin I., *Canada* **89** 68 0N 75 0W
Bagenalstown = Muine Bheag, *Ire.* **25** 52 42N 6 57W
Baggy Pt., *U.K.* **16** 51 11N 4 12W
Baghdād, *Iraq* **56** 33 20N 44 30 E
Bagshot, *U.K.* **15** 51 22N 0 41W
Bahamas ■, *Atl. Oc.* **95** 24 0N 75 0W
Bahawalpur, *Pak.* **58** 29 24N 71 40 E
Bahía = Salvador, *Brazil* **101** 13 0S 38 30W
Bahía Blanca, *Arg.* **102** 38 35S 62 13W
Bahrain ■, *Asia* **56** 26 0N 50 35 E
Baia Mare, *Rom.* **43** 47 40N 23 35 E
Baildon, *U.K.* **19** 53 52N 1 46W
Baile Atha Cliath = Dublin, *Ire.* **24** 53 20N 6 18W
Bain →, *U.K.* **19** 53 10N 0 15W
Bainbridge, *U.K.* **18** 54 18N 2 7W
Bakersfield, *U.S.A.* **90** 35 25N 119 0W
Bakewell, *U.K.* **19** 53 13N 1 40W
Bākhtarān, *Iran* **56** 34 23N 47 0 E
Baku, *U.S.S.R.* **47** 40 25N 49 45 E
Bala, *U.K.* **17** 52 54N 3 36W
Bala, L. = Tegid, L., *U.K.* **17** 52 53N 3 38W
Balallan, *U.K.* **22** 58 5N 6 35W
Balaton, *Hung.* **43** 46 50N 17 40 E
Balbeggie, *U.K.* **21** 56 26N 3 19W
Balboa, *Pan.* **94** 9 0N 79 30W
Balbriggan, *Ire.* **24** 53 35N 6 10W
Balderton, *U.K.* **19** 53 3N 0 46W
Baldock, *U.K.* **15** 51 59N 0 11W
Balearic Is., *Sp.* **37** 39 30N 3 0 E
Balfron, *U.K.* **20** 56 4N 4 20W
Bali □, *Indon.* **63** 8 20S 115 0 E
Balikesir, *Turk.* **47** 39 35N 27 58 E
Balikpapan, *Indon.* **63** 1 10S 116 55 E
Balkan Mts., *Bulg.* **41** 43 15N 23 0 E
Balkan Pen., *Europe* **26** 42 0N 22 0 E
Balkhash, L., *U.S.S.R.* **48** 46 0N 74 50 E
Ballachulish, *U.K.* **22** 56 40N 5 10W
Ballantrae, *U.K.* **20** 55 6N 5 0W
Ballarat, *Austral.* **70** 37 33S 143 50 E
Ballasalla, *U.K.* **18** 54 7N 4 36W
Ballater, *U.K.* **23** 57 2N 3 2W
Ballaugh, *U.K.* **18** 54 20N 4 32W
Ballina, *Mayo, Ire.* **24** 54 7N 9 10W
Ballina, *Tipp., Ire.* **25** 52 49N 8 27W
Ballinasloe, *Ire.* **25** 53 20N 8 12W
Ballinrobe, *Ire.* **24** 53 36N 9 13W
Ballinskelligs B., *Ire.* **25** 51 46N 10 11W
Balloch, *U.K.* **20** 56 0N 4 35W
Ballycastle, *U.K.* **24** 55 12N 6 15W
Ballyclare, *U.K.* **24** 54 46N 6 0W
Ballymena, *U.K.* **24** 54 53N 6 18W
Ballymena □, *U.K.* **24** 54 53N 6 18W
Ballymoney, *U.K.* **24** 55 5N 6 30W
Ballymoney □, *U.K.* **24** 55 5N 6 23W
Ballynahinch, *U.K.* **24** 54 24N 5 55W
Ballyshannon, *Ire.* **24** 54 30N 8 10W
Balmaclellan, *U.K.* **21** 55 6N 4 5W
Balmoral, *U.K.* **23** 57 3N 3 13W
Balquhidder, *U.K.* **20** 56 22N 4 22W
Balsas →, *Mex.* **94** 17 55N 102 10W
Baltic Sea, *Europe* **45** 56 0N 20 0 E
Baltimore, *Ire.* **25** 51 29N 9 22W
Baltimore, *U.S.A.* **92** 39 18N 76 37W
Baluchistan □, *Pak.* **58** 27 30N 65 0 E
Balurghat, *India* **59** 25 15N 88 44 E
Balvicar, *U.K.* **20** 56 17N 5 38W
Bamako, *Mali* **78** 12 34N 7 55W
Bamberg, *W. Ger.* **42** 49 54N 10 53 E
Bamburgh, *U.K.* **21** 55 36N 1 42W
Bamenda, *Cam.* **80** 5 57N 10 11 E
Bamford, *U.K.* **19** 53 21N 1 41W
Bampton, *Devon, U.K.* **16** 50 59N 3 29W
Bampton, *Oxon., U.K.* **14** 51 44N 1 33W
Banaras = Varanasi, *India* **59** 25 22N 83 0 E
Banbridge, *U.K.* **24** 54 21N 6 17W
Banbridge □, *U.K.* **24** 54 21N 6 16W
Banbury, *U.K.* **14** 52 4N 1 21W
Banchory, *U.K.* **23** 57 3N 2 30W
Banda Aceh, *Indon.* **63** 5 35N 95 20 E
Banda Sea, *Indon.* **63** 6 0S 130 0 E
Bandār 'Abbās, *Iran* **57** 27 15N 56 15 E
Bandar Seri Begawan, *Brunei* **63** 4 52N 115 0 E
Bandon, *Ire.* **25** 51 44N 8 45W
Bandon →, *Ire.* **25** 51 40N 8 41W
Bandundu, *Zaïre* **80** 3 15S 17 22 E
Bandung, *Indon.* **63** 6 54S 107 36 E
Banff, *U.K.* **23** 57 40N 2 32W
Bangalore, *India* **58** 12 59N 77 40 E
Bangka, Selat, *Indon.* **63** 2 30S 105 30 E
Bangkok, *Thai.* **63** 13 45N 100 35 E
Bangladesh ■, *Asia* **59** 24 0N 90 0 E
Bangor, *N. Ireland, U.K.* **24** 54 40N 5 40W
Bangor, *Wales, U.K.* **17** 53 13N 4 9W
Bangor, *U.S.A.* **93** 44 48N 68 42W
Bangui, *C.A.R.* **80** 4 23N 18 35 E
Banham, *U.K.* **15** 52 27N 1 3 E
Banjarmasin, *Indon.* **63** 3 20S 114 35 E
Banjul, *Gambia* **78** 13 28N 16 40W
Bankend, *U.K.* **21** 55 2N 3 31W
Bankfoot, *U.K.* **21** 56 30N 3 31W
Banks I., *Canada* **88** 73 15N 121 30W
Banks Pen., *N.Z.* **71** 43 45S 173 15 E
Bann →, *Down, U.K.* **24** 54 30N 6 31W
Bann →, *Londonderry, U.K.* **24** 55 10N 6 34W
Bannockburn, *U.K.* **21** 56 5N 3 55W
Bantry, *Ire.* **25** 51 40N 9 28W
Bantry, B., *Ire.* **25** 51 35N 9 50W
Banwell, *U.K.* **14** 51 19N 2 51W
Baoding, *China* **61** 38 50N 115 28 E
Baoji, *China* **60** 34 20N 107 5 E
Baotou, *China* **61** 40 32N 110 2 E
Barbados ■, *W. Ind.* **94** 13 0N 59 30W
Barcaldine, *Austral.* **67** 23 43S 145 6 E
Barcelona, *Sp.* **37** 41 21N 2 10 E
Bardney, *U.K.* **19** 53 13N 0 19W
Bardsey I., *U.K.* **17** 52 46N 4 47W
Bareilly, *India* **58** 28 22N 79 27 E
Barents Sea, *Arctic* **48** 73 0N 39 0 E
Barford, *U.K.* **14** 52 15N 1 35W
Bargoed, *U.K.* **17** 51 42N 3 22W
Barham, *U.K.* **15** 51 12N 1 10 E
Bari, *It.* **40** 41 6N 16 52 E
Bari Doab, *Pak.* **58** 30 20N 73 0 E
Barisal, *Bangla.* **59** 22 45N 90 20 E
Barisan Mts., *Indon.* **63** 3 30S 102 15 E
Barking, *U.K.* **15** 51 31N 0 10 E
Barkly Tableland, *Austral.* **67** 17 50S 136 40 E
Barlborough, *U.K.* **19** 53 17N 1 17W
Barlby, *U.K.* **19** 53 48N 1 3W
Barletta, *It.* **40** 41 20N 16 17 E
Barmby Moor, *U.K.* **19** 53 55N 0 47W
Barmoor Castle, *U.K.* **21** 55 38N 2 0W
Barmouth, *U.K.* **17** 52 44N 4 3W
Barnard Castle, *U.K.* **18** 54 33N 1 55W
Barnaul, *U.S.S.R.* **48** 53 20N 83 40 E
Barnet, *U.K.* **15** 51 37N 0 15W
Barnetby le Wold, *U.K.* **19** 53 34N 0 24W
Barnoldswick, *U.K.* **18** 53 55N 2 11W
Barnsley, *U.K.* **19** 53 33N 1 29W
Barnstaple, *U.K.* **16** 51 5N 4 3W
Barnstaple B., *U.K.* **16** 51 5N 4 25W
Baroda = Vadodara, *India* **58** 22 20N 73 10 E
Barquísimeto, *Ven.* **100** 10 4N 69 19W
Barr, *U.K.* **20** 55 13N 4 44W
Barra, *U.K.* **22** 57 0N 7 30W
Barra, Sd. of, *U.K.* **22** 57 4N 7 25W
Barra Hd., *U.K.* **22** 56 47N 7 40W
Barrancabermeja, *Col.* **100** 7 0N 73 50W
Barranquilla, *Col.* **100** 11 0N 74 50W
Barrhead, *U.K.* **20** 55 48N 4 23W
Barrhill, *U.K.* **20** 55 7N 4 46W
Barrow →, *Ire.* **25** 52 10N 6 57W
Barrow-in-Furness, *U.K.* **18** 54 8N 3 15W
Barrow upon Humber, *U.K.* **19** 53 41N 0 22W
Barrowford, *U.K.* **18** 53 51N 2 14W
Barry, *S. Glam., U.K.* **17** 51 23N 3 19W
Barry, *Tayside, U.K.* **21** 56 29N 2 45W
Barton, *U.K.* **19** 54 28N 1 38W
Barton-upon-Humber, *U.K.* **19** 53 41N 0 27W
Barvas, *U.K.* **22** 58 21N 6 31W
Barwell, *U.K.* **14** 52 35N 1 22W
Basildon, *U.K.* **15** 51 34N 0 29 E
Basingstoke, *U.K.* **14** 51 15N 1 5W
Basle, *Switz.* **42** 47 35N 7 35 E
Basra, *Iraq* **56** 30 30N 47 50 E
Bass Rock, *U.K.* **21** 56 5N 2 40W
Bass Str., *Austral.* **67** 39 15S 146 30 E
Basse-Terre, *Guad.* **94** 16 0N 61 40W
Bassein, *Burma* **59** 16 45N 94 30 E
Bassenthwaite, L., *U.K.* **18** 54 40N 3 14W
Basseterre, *Guad.* **94** 17 17N 62 43W
Bastia, *Fr.* **35** 42 40N 9 30 E
Baston, *U.K.* **15** 52 43N 0 19W
Bata, *Eq. Guin.* **80** 1 57N 9 50 E
Batangas, *Phil.* **63** 13 35N 121 10 E
Bath, *U.K.* **14** 51 22N 2 22W
Bathford, *U.K.* **14** 51 23N 2 18W
Bathgate, *U.K.* **21** 55 54N 3 38W
Bathurst, *Austral.* **70** 33 25S 149 31 E
Bathurst, *Canada* **93** 47 37N 65 43W
Batley, *U.K.* **19** 53 43N 1 38W
Batna, *Alg.* **78** 35 34N 6 15 E
Baton Rouge, *U.S.A.* **91** 30 30N 91 5W
Battle, *U.K.* **15** 50 55N 0 30 E
Batumi, *U.S.S.R.* **47** 41 30N 41 30 E
Bauru, *Brazil* **101** 22 10S 49 0W
Bavaria □, *W. Ger.* **42** 49 7N 11 30 E
Bawdsey, *U.K.* **15** 52 1N 1 27 E
Bawtry, *U.K.* **19** 53 25N 1 1W
Bayamo, *Cuba* **95** 20 20N 76 40W
Bayan Har Shan, *China* **60** 34 0N 98 0 E
Bayeux, *Fr.* **34** 49 17N 0 42W
Baykal, L., *U.S.S.R.* **49** 53 0N 108 0 E
Bayonne, *Fr.* **35** 43 30N 1 28W
Beachley, *U.K.* **14** 51 37N 2 39W
Beachy Head, *U.K.* **15** 50 44N 0 16 E
Beaconsfield, *U.K.* **15** 51 36N 0 39W
Beadnell, *U.K.* **21** 55 33N 1 38W
Beagle, Canal, *S. Am.* **102** 55 0S 68 30W
Beaminster, *U.K.* **14** 50 48N 2 44W
Bear I., *Ire.* **25** 51 38N 9 50W
Beardmore Glacier, *Ant.* **103** 84 30S 170 0 E
Bearsden, *U.K.* **20** 55 55N 4 21W
Bearsted, *U.K.* **15** 51 15N 0 35 E
Beattock, *U.K.* **21** 55 19N 3 27W
Beaufort Sea, *Arctic* **103** 72 0N 140 0W
Beaulieu, *U.K.* **14** 50 49N 1 27W
Beauly, *U.K.* **23** 57 29N 4 27W
Beauly →, *U.K.* **23** 57 26N 4 28W
Beaumaris, *U.K.* **17** 53 16N 4 7W
Beaumont, *U.S.A.* **91** 30 5N 94 8W
Beauvais, *Fr.* **34** 49 25N 2 8 E
Bebington, *U.K.* **18** 53 23N 3 1W
Beccles, *U.K.* **15** 52 27N 1 33 E
Béchar, *Alg.* **78** 31 38N 2 18W
Beckermet, *U.K.* **18** 54 26N 3 31W
Beckfoot, *U.K.* **18** 54 50N 3 25W
Beckingham, *U.K.* **19** 53 24N 0 49W
Bedale, *U.K.* **19** 54 18N 1 35W
Beddgelert, *U.K.* **17** 53 2N 4 8W
Bedford, *U.K.* **15** 52 8N 0 29W
Bedford □, *U.K.* **15** 52 4N 0 28W
Bedford Level, *U.K.* **15** 52 25N 0 5 E
Bedlington, *U.K.* **21** 55 8N 1 35W
Bedworth, *U.K.* **14** 52 28N 1 29W
Beeford, *U.K.* **19** 53 58N 0 18W
Beer, *U.K.* **16** 50 41N 3 5W
Beersheba, *Isr.* **57** 31 15N 34 48 E
Beeston, *U.K.* **19** 52 55N 1 11W
Bei'an, *China* **61** 48 10N 126 20 E
Beighton, *U.K.* **19** 53 21N 1 21W
Beijing = Peking, *China* **61** 39 55N 116 20 E
Beira, *Mozam.* **81** 19 50S 34 52 E
Beira-Baixa, *Port.* **37** 40 2N 7 30W
Beirut, *Leb.* **57** 33 53N 35 31 E
Beith, *U.K.* **20** 55 45N 4 38W
Bejaïa, Golfe de, *Alg.* **78** 36 42N 5 13 E
Belbroughton, *U.K.* **14** 52 23N 2 5W
Belcher Is., *Canada* **89** 56 15N 78 45W
Belém, *Brazil* **101** 1 20S 48 30W
Belfast, *U.K.* **24** 54 35N 5 56W
Belfast □, *U.K.* **24** 54 35N 5 56W
Belfast, L., *U.K.* **24** 54 40N 5 50W
Belford, *U.K.* **21** 55 36N 1 50W
Belfort, *Fr.* **34** 47 38N 6 50 E
Belgium ■, *Europe* **36** 50 30N 5 0 E
Belgorod, *U.S.S.R.* **47** 50 35N 36 35 E
Belgrade, *Yug.* **41** 44 50N 20 37 E
Beliton, Is., *Indon.* **63** 3 10S 107 50 E
Belize ■, *Cent. Am.* **94** 17 0N 88 30W
Belize City, *Belize* **94** 17 25N 88 0W
Bell Rock = Inchcape Rock, *U.K.* **21** 56 26N 2 24W
Bellary, *India* **58** 15 10N 76 56 E
Belle-Ile, *Fr.* **34** 47 20N 3 10W
Belle Isle, Str. of, *Canada* **89** 51 30N 56 30W
Belleville, *Canada* **92** 44 10N 77 23W
Bellingham, *U.K.* **21** 55 9N 2 16W
Belmopan, *Belize* **94** 17 18N 88 30W
Belmullet, *Ire.* **24** 54 13N 9 58W
Belo Horizonte, *Brazil* **101** 19 55S 43 56W
Beloye More, *U.S.S.R.* **46** 66 30N 38 0 E
Belper, *U.K.* **19** 53 2N 1 29W
Belsay, *U.K.* **21** 55 6N 1 53W
Belton, *Humberside, U.K.* **19** 53 33N 0 49W
Belton, *Norfolk, U.K.* **15** 52 35N 1 39 E
Belturbet, *Ire.* **24** 54 6N 7 28W
Bembridge, *U.K.* **14** 50 41N 1 4W
Ben Bheigeir, *U.K.* **20** 55 43N 6 6W
Ben Chonzie, *U.K.* **21** 56 27N 4 0W
Ben Cruachan, *U.K.* **20** 56 26N 5 8W
Ben Dearg, *U.K.* **23** 57 47N 4 58W
Ben Dorain, *U.K.* **20** 56 30N 4 42W
Ben Hope, *U.K.* **23** 58 24N 4 36W
Ben Lawers, *U.K.* **23** 56 33N 4 13W
Ben Lomond, *U.K.* **20** 56 12N 4 39W
Ben Lui, *U.K.* **20** 56 24N 4 50W
Ben Macdhui, *U.K.* **23** 57 4N 3 40W
Ben Mhor, *U.K.* **22** 57 16N 7 21W
Ben More, *Central, U.K.* **20** 56 23N 4 31W
Ben More, *Strathclyde, U.K.* **20** 56 26N 6 2W
Ben More Assynt, *U.K.* **23** 58 7N 4 51W
Ben Nevis, *U.K.* **22** 56 48N 5 0W
Ben Venue, *U.K.* **20** 56 13N 4 28W
Ben Vorlich, *U.K.* **20** 56 22N 4 15W
Ben Wyvis, *U.K.* **23** 57 40N 4 35W
Benalla, *Austral.* **70** 36 30S 146 0 E
Benares = Varanasi, *India* **59** 25 22N 83 0 E
Benbecula, *U.K.* **22** 57 26N 7 21W
Bendigo, *Austral.* **70** 36 40S 144 15 E
Beneraird, *U.K.* **20** 55 4N 4 57W
Benevento, *It.* **40** 41 7N 14 45 E
Bengal, Bay of, *Ind. Oc.* **59** 18 0N 90 0 E
Bengbu, *China* **61** 32 58N 117 20 E
Benghazi, *Libya* **79** 32 11N 20 3 E
Beni Suef, *Egypt* **79** 29 5N 31 6 E
Benin ■, *Africa* **78** 10 0N 2 0 E
Benin, Bight of, *W. Afr.* **78** 5 0N 3 0 E
Benin City, *Nig.* **78** 6 20N 5 31 E
Benington, *U.K.* **19** 52 59N 0 5 E
Bennane Hd., *U.K.* **20** 55 9N 5 2W
Benoni, *S. Afr.* **81** 26 11S 28 18 E
Benson, *U.K.* **14** 51 37N 1 6W
Bentley, *Hants., U.K.* **15** 51 12N 0 52W
Bentley, *S. Yorks., U.K.* **19** 53 33N 1 9W
Benue →, *Nig.* **78** 7 48N 6 46 E
Benxi, *China* **61** 41 20N 123 48 E
Berbera, *Som.* **73** 10 30N 45 2 E
Berbérati, *C.A.R.* **80** 4 15N 15 40 E
Bere Alston, *U.K.* **16** 50 29N 4 11W
Bere Regis, *U.K.* **14** 50 45N 2 13W
Berezniki, *U.S.S.R.* **46** 59 24N 56 46 E
Bérgamo, *It.* **40** 45 42N 9 40 E
Bergen, *Nor.* **45** 60 23N 5 20 E
Bergen-op-Zoom, *Neth.* **36** 51 30N 4 18 E
Bergerac, *Fr.* **35** 44 51N 0 30 E
Bergisch-Gladbach, *W. Ger.* **36** 50 59N 7 9 E
Berhampore, *India* **59** 24 2N 88 27 E
Berhampur, *India* **59** 19 15N 84 54 E
Bering Sea, *Pac. Oc.* **88** 58 0N 167 0 E
Bering Str., *N. Am.* **103** 66 0N 170 0W
Berkeley, *U.K.* **14** 51 41N 2 28W
Berkhamsted, *U.K.* **15** 51 45N 0 33W
Berkshire □, *U.K.* **14** 51 30N 1 20W
Berkshire Downs, *U.K.* **15** 51 30N 1 30W
Berlin, *Ger.* **42** 52 32N 13 24 E
Bermuda ■, *Atl. Oc.* **95** 32 45N 65 0W
Bern, *Switz.* **42** 46 57N 7 28 E
Berry Hd., *U.K.* **16** 50 24N 3 29W
Berwick-upon-Tweed, *U.K.* **19** 55 47N 2 0W
Berwyn Mts., *U.K.* **17** 52 54N 3 26W
Besançon, *Fr.* **34** 47 15N 6 0 E
Bethesda, *U.K.* **17** 53 11N 4 3W
Bethlehem, *Jord.* **57** 31 43N 35 12 E
Bethlehem, *U.S.A.* **93** 40 39N 75 24W
Béthune, *Fr.* **34** 50 30N 2 38 E
Betws-y-Coed, *U.K.* **17** 53 4N 3 49W
Beverley, *U.K.* **19** 53 52N 0 26W
Beverwijk, *Neth.* **36** 52 28N 4 38 E
Bewdley, *U.K.* **14** 52 23N 2 19W
Bexhill, *U.K.* **15** 50 51N 0 29 E
Bexley, *U.K.* **15** 51 26N 0 10 E
Béziers, *Fr.* **35** 43 20N 3 12 E
Bhagalpur, *India* **59** 25 10N 87 0 E
Bhatinda, *India* **58** 30 15N 74 57 E
Bhatpara, *India* **59** 22 50N 88 25 E
Bhavnagar, *India* **58** 21 45N 72 10 E
Bhimavaram, *India* **59** 16 30N 81 30 E
Bhopal, *India* **58** 23 20N 77 30 E
Bhubaneshwar, *India* **59** 20 15N 85 50 E
Bhutan ■, *Asia* **59** 27 25N 90 30 E
Białystok, *Pol.* **43** 53 10N 23 10 E
Biarritz, *Fr.* **34** 43 29N 1 33W
Bibury, *U.K.* **14** 51 46N 1 50W
Bicester, *U.K.* **14** 51 53N 1 9W
Bicton, *U.K.* **14** 52 43N 2 47W
Biddenden, *U.K.* **15** 51 7N 0 40 E
Biddulph, *U.K.* **18** 53 8N 2 11W
Bideford, *U.K.* **16** 51 1N 4 13W
Bideford Bay, *U.K.* **16** 51 5N 4 20W
Bidford on Avon, *U.K.* **14** 52 9N 1 53W
Bié Plateau, *Angola* **81** 12 0S 16 0 E
Biel, *Switz.* **42** 47 8N 7 14 E
Bielefeld, *W. Ger.* **42** 52 2N 8 31 E
Bigbury, *U.K.* **16** 50 17N 3 52W
Bigbury B., *U.K.* **16** 50 18N 3 58W
Biggar, *U.K.* **21** 55 38N 3 31W
Biggleswade, *U.K.* **15** 52 6N 0 16W
Bighorn Mts., *U.S.A.* **90** 44 30N 107 30W
Bihar □, *India* **59** 25 0N 86 0 E
Bikaner, *India* **58** 28 2N 73 18 E

Bikini Atoll, Pac. Oc. .. 64 12 0N 167 30 E
Bilbao, Sp. 37 43 16N 2 56W
Billericay, U.K. .... 15 51 38N 0 25 E
Billesdon, U.K. 15 52 38N 0 56W
Billingham, U.K. 19 54 36N 1 18W
Billinghay, U.K. 19 53 5N 0 17W
Billings, U.S.A. 90 45 43N 108 29W
Billingshurst, U.K. 15 51 2N 0 28W
Bilston, U.K. 14 52 34N 2 5W
Binbrook, U.K. 19 53 26N 0 9W
Bingham, U.K. 19 52 57N 0 55W
Binghamton, U.S.A. .. 93 42 9N 75 54W
Bingley, U.K. 18 53 51N 1 50W
Bioko, Eq. Guin. ..... 80 3 30N 8 40 E
Birch, U.K. .... 15 51 50N 0 54 E
Birchington, U.K. ..... 15 51 22N 1 18 E
Birdlip, U.K. 14 51 50N 2 7W
Birkdale, U.K. 18 53 38N 3 2W
Birkenhead, U.K. 18 53 24N 3 1W
Birmingham, U.K. 14 52 30N 1 55W
Birmingham, U.S.A. ... 91 33 31N 86 50W
Birr, Ire. 25 53 7N 7 55W
Birtley, Northumberland, U.K. 21 55 5N 2 12W
Birtley, Tyne & Wear, U.K. 21 54 53N 1 34W
Biscay, B. of, Atl. Oc. . 35 45 0N 2 0W
Bishop Auckland, U.K. 19 54 40N 1 40W
Bishop's Castle, U.K. . 14 52 29N 3 0W
Bishop's Cleeve, U.K. . 14 51 56N 2 3W
Bishop's Frome, U.K. . 14 52 8N 2 29W
Bishops Lydeard, U.K. 14 51 4N 3 12W
Bishop's Nympton, U.K. 16 50 58N 3 44W
Bishop's Stortford, U.K. 15 51 52N 0 11 E
Bishop's Waltham, U.K. 14 50 57N 1 13W
Bishopsteignton, U.K. . 16 50 32N 3 32W
Bishopstoke, U.K. 14 50 58N 1 19W
Biskra, Alg. .... 78 34 50N 5 44 E
Bismarck Arch., P.N.G. 64 2 30S 150 0 E
Bissau, Guin.-Biss. ... 78 11 45N 15 45W
Bitola, Yug. .... 41 41 5N 21 10 E
Bitton, U.K. 14 51 25N 2 27W
Biwa-Ko, Jap. .... 62 35 15N 136 10 E
Biysk, U.S.S.R. ...... 48 52 40N 85 0 E
Blaby, U.K. 14 52 34N 1 10W
Black Combe, U.K. ... 18 54 16N 3 20W
Black Esk —►, U.K. .. 21 55 14N 3 13W
Black Forest, Mts., W. Ger. .... 42 48 0N 8 0 E
Black Hd., U.K. 16 50 1N 5 6W
Black Mt. = Mynydd Du, U.K. 17 51 45N 3 45W
Black Mts., U.K. 17 51 52N 3 5W
Black Sea, Europe ... 47 43 30N 35 0 E
Black Volta —►, Africa 78 8 41N 1 33W
Blackall, Austral. ..... 67 24 25S 145 45 E
Blackburn, U.K. 18 53 44N 2 30W
Blackdown Hills, U.K. . 14 50 57N 3 15W
Blackford, U.K. 21 56 15N 3 48W
Blackmoor Gate, U.K. . 16 51 9N 3 55W
Blackmoor Vale, U.K. . 14 50 54N 2 28W
Blackpool, U.K. 18 53 48N 3 3W
Blacksod B., Ire. 24 54 6N 10 0W
Blacktown, Austral. ... 70 33 48S 150 55 E
Blackwater —►, Ire. .. 25 51 55N 7 50W
Blackwater —►, Essex, U.K. .... 15 51 44N 0 53 E
Blackwater —►, N. Ireland, U.K. 24 54 31N 6 35W
Blackwood, U.K. 21 55 40N 3 56W
Blaenau Ffestiniog, U.K. 17 53 0N 3 57W
Blaenavon, U.K. 17 51 46N 3 5W
Blagdon, U.K. 14 51 19N 2 42W
Blagoveshchensk, U.S.S.R. .... 49 50 20N 127 30 E
Blair Athol, Austral. ... 67 22 42S 147 31 E
Blair Atholl, U.K. 23 56 46N 3 50W
Blairgowrie, U.K. 23 56 36N 3 20W
Blakeney, Gloucs., U.K. 14 51 45N 2 29W
Blakeney, Norfolk, U.K. 15 52 57N 1 1 E
Blanc, Mont, Europe .. 35 45 48N 6 50 E
Blandford Forum, U.K. 14 50 52N 2 10W
Blantyre, Malawi ..... 81 15 45S 35 0 E
Blarney, Ire. 25 51 57N 8 35W
Blaydon, U.K. 19 54 56N 1 47W
Bleadon, U.K. 14 51 18N 2 57W
Blean, U.K. .... 15 51 18N 1 3 E
Bleasdale Moors, U.K. 18 53 57N 2 40W
Blenheim, N.Z. .... 71 41 38S 173 57 E
Bletchingdon, U.K. ... 14 51 51N 1 16W
Bletchley, U.K. 15 51 59N 0 44W
Blisworth, U.K. 15 52 11N 0 56W
Blockley, U.K. 14 52 1N 1 45W
Bloemfontein, S. Afr. .. 81 29 6S 26 14 E
Blofield, U.K. .... 15 52 38N 1 25 E
Blois, Fr. .... 34 47 35N 1 20 E
Bloody Foreland, Ire. . 24 55 10N 8 18W
Bloxham, U.K. 14 52 1N 1 22W
Blue Mts., Austral. ... 70 33 40S 150 0 E
Blue Mts., U.S.A. 90 45 15N 119 0W
Blue Nile —►, Sudan . 79 12 30N 34 30 E
Blue Ridge Mts., U.S.A. 91 36 30N 80 15W
Blue Stack Mts., Ire. .. 24 54 46N 8 5W
Blumenau, Brazil 102 27 0S 49 0W
Blundeston, U.K. ..... 15 52 33N 1 42 E
Blyth, Northumberland, U.K. 19 55 8N 1 32W
Blyth, Notts., U.K. 19 53 22N 1 2W
Blyth —►, U.K. 21 55 8N 1 30W
Blyth Bridge, U.K. 21 55 41N 3 22W
Blyton, U.K. 19 53 25N 0 42W
Bobo-Dioulasso, B. Faso 78 11 8N 4 13W
Bocholt, W. Ger. ..... 36 51 50N 6 35 E
Bochum, W. Ger. ..... 36 51 28N 7 12 E
Bodenham, U.K. 14 52 9N 2 41W
Bodensee, W. Ger. ... 42 47 35N 9 25 E
Bodiam, U.K. .... 15 51 1N 0 33 E
Bodinnick, U.K. 16 50 20N 4 37W
Bodmin, U.K. 16 50 28N 4 44W
Bodmin Moor, U.K. ... 16 50 33N 4 36W
Bodø, Nor. .... 44 67 17N 14 24 E
Bogan —►, Austral. ... 67 29 59S 146 17 E
Boggeragh Mts., Ire. .. 25 52 2N 8 55W
Bognor Regis, U.K. ... 15 50 47N 0 40W
Bogor, Indon. .... 63 6 36S 106 48 E
Bogota, Col. 100 4 34N 74 0W
Bohemian Forest, Czech. .... 42 49 20N 13 0 E
Boise, U.S.A. 90 43 43N 116 9W
Bolgatanga, Ghana ... 78 10 44N 0 53W
Bolivia ■, S. Am. 100 17 6S 64 0W
Bolivian Plateau, S. Am. 96 20 0S 67 30W
Bollington, U.K. 18 53 18N 2 8W
Bolney, U.K. 15 50 59N 0 11W
Bologna, It. .... 40 44 30N 11 20 E
Bolshevik, I., U.S.S.R. . 49 78 30N 102 0 E
Bolshezemelskaya Tundra, U.S.S.R. .... 46 67 0N 56 0 E
Bolsover, U.K. 19 53 14N 1 18W
Bolt Head, U.K. 16 50 13N 3 48W
Bolt Tail, U.K. 16 50 13N 3 55W
Bolton, U.K. 18 53 35N 2 26W
Bolton Abbey, U.K. ... 18 53 59N 1 53W
Bolton by Bowland, U.K. 18 53 56N 2 21W
Bolton le Sands, U.K. . 18 54 7N 2 49W
Bolungavík, Ice. 44 66 9N 23 15W
Bolzano, It. .... 40 46 30N 11 20 E
Boma, Zaïre .... 80 5 50S 13 4 E
Bombay, India .... 58 18 55N 72 50 E
Bonaparte Archipelago, Austral. .... 66 14 0S 124 30 E
Bonarbridge, U.K. 23 57 53N 4 20W
Bonchester Bridge, U.K. 21 55 23N 2 36W
Bonchurch, U.K. 14 50 36N 1 11W
Bo'ness, U.K. 21 56 0N 3 38W
Bonifacio, Str. of, Fr. . 40 41 12N 9 15 E
Bonn, W. Ger. .... 36 50 43N 7 6 E
Bonnyrigg, U.K. 21 55 52N 3 8W
Boot, U.K. 18 54 24N 3 18W
Boothia, Gulf of, Canada 89 71 0N 90 0W
Boothia Pen., Canada . 88 71 0N 94 0W
Bootle, Cumbria, U.K. . 18 54 17N 3 24W
Bootle, Merseyside, U.K. 18 53 28N 3 1W
Borås, Swed. .... 45 57 43N 12 56 E
Bordeaux, Fr. 35 44 50N 0 36W
Borders □, U.K. 21 55 35N 2 50W
Bordon, U.K. 15 51 6N 0 52W
Borehamwood, U.K. .. 15 51 40N 0 15W
Boreland, U.K. 21 55 13N 3 16W
Borgarnes, Ice. 44 64 32N 21 55W
Borneo, E. Ind. ...... 63 1 0N 115 0 E
Bornholm, Den. ...... 45 55 10N 15 0 E
Boroughbridge, U.K. .. 19 54 6N 1 23W
Borrowdale, U.K. 18 54 31N 3 10W
Borth, U.K. 17 52 29N 4 3W
Bosbury, U.K. 14 52 5N 2 27W
Boscastle, U.K. 16 50 42N 4 42W
Bosham, U.K. 15 50 50N 0 51W
Bosporus, Turk. ..... 47 41 10N 29 10 E
Boston, U.K. 19 52 59N 0 2W
Boston, U.S.A. 93 42 20N 71 0W
Botany Bay, Austral. .. 70 34 0S 151 14 E
Bothel, U.K. 18 54 43N 3 16W
Bothnia, G. of, Europe 44 63 0N 20 0 E
Botswana ■, Africa ... 81 22 0S 24 0 E
Bottesford, U.K. 19 52 57N 0 48W
Bottrop, W. Ger. ..... 36 51 34N 6 59 E
Bouaké, Ivory C. 78 7 40N 5 2W
Bouar, C.A.R. .... 80 6 0N 15 40 E
Boulogne-sur-Mer, Fr. 34 50 42N 1 36 E
Bourges, Fr. .... 34 47 9N 2 25 E
Bourgogne, Fr. ...... 34 47 0N 4 50 E
Bourke, Austral. ..... 67 30 8S 145 55 E
Bourne, U.K. 15 52 46N 0 22W
Bournemouth, U.K. ... 14 50 43N 1 53W
Bourton-on-the-Water, U.K. 14 51 53N 1 45W
Bovey Tracey, U.K. ... 16 50 36N 3 40W
Bowen, Austral. ...... 67 20 0S 148 16 E
Bowes, U.K. 18 54 31N 1 59W
Bowland, Forest of, U.K. 18 54 0N 2 30W
Bowmore, U.K. 20 55 45N 6 18W
Bowness, Solway, U.K. 18 54 57N 3 13W
Bowness, Windermere, U.K. 18 54 22N 2 56W
Box, U.K. 14 51 24N 2 16W
Box Hill, U.K. 15 51 16N 0 16W
Boxley, U.K. .... 15 51 17N 0 34 E
Boyle, Ire. 24 53 58N 8 19W
Boyne —►, Ire. 24 53 43N 6 15W
Bozeat, U.K. 15 52 14N 0 41W
Bracadale, L., U.K. ... 22 57 20N 6 30W
Bracebridge Heath, U.K. 19 53 13N 0 32W
Brackley, U.K. 14 52 3N 1 9W
Bracknell, U.K. 15 51 24N 0 45W
Braco, U.K. 21 56 16N 3 55W
Bradda Hd., U.K. 18 54 6N 4 46W
Bradford, U.K. 19 53 47N 1 45W
Bradford-on-Avon, U.K. 14 51 20N 2 15W
Brading, U.K. 14 50 41N 1 9W
Bradwell-on-Sea, U.K. 15 51 44N 0 55 E
Bradworthy, U.K. 16 50 54N 4 22W
Braemar, U.K. 23 57 2N 3 20W
Braga, Port. 37 41 35N 8 25W
Brahmaputra —►, India 59 24 2N 90 59 E
Braich-y-pwll, U.K. ... 17 52 47N 4 46W
Brăila, Rom. .... 43 45 19N 27 59 E
Brailsford, U.K. 19 52 58N 1 35W
Braintree, U.K. ...... 15 51 53N 0 34 E
Bramford, U.K. ...... 15 52 5N 1 6 E
Brampton, Canada ... 92 43 45N 79 45W
Brampton, Cambs., U.K. 15 52 19N 0 13W
Brampton, Cumbria, U.K. 18 54 56N 2 43W
Bramshott, U.K. 15 51 5N 0 47W
Brancaster, U.K. ..... 15 52 58N 0 40 E
Branco —►, Brazil 100 1 20S 61 50W
Brander, Pass of, U.K. 20 56 25N 5 10W
Brandon, Canada 88 49 50N 99 57W
Brandon, Durham, U.K. 19 54 46N 1 37W
Brandon, Suffolk, U.K. 15 52 27N 0 37 E
Brandon, Mt., Ire. 25 52 15N 10 15W
Brandon B., Ire. 25 52 17N 10 8W
Branston, U.K. 19 53 13N 0 28W
Brantford, Canada ... 92 43 10N 80 15W
Brasília, Brazil .... 101 15 47S 47 55 E
Braşov, Rom. .... 43 45 38N 25 35 E
Brasted, U.K. .... 15 51 16N 0 8 E
Bratislava, Czech. .... 43 48 10N 17 7 E
Bratsk, U.S.S.R. ..... 49 56 10N 101 30 E
Braunton, U.K. 16 51 6N 4 9W
Bray, Ire. 25 53 12N 6 6W
Bray, U.K. 15 51 30N 0 42W
Brazil ■, S. Am. 101 10 0S 50 0W
Brazilian Highlands, Brazil 101 18 0S 46 30W
Brazzaville, Congo ... 80 4 9S 15 12 E
Breadalbane, U.K. 20 56 30N 4 15W
Breage, U.K. 16 50 6N 5 17W
Breamish —►, U.K. ... 21 55 30N 1 55W
Brechin, U.K. 23 56 44N 2 40W
Breckland, U.K. ..... 15 52 30N 0 40 E
Brecon, U.K. 17 51 57N 3 23W
Brecon Beacons, U.K. 17 51 53N 3 27W
Brede, U.K. .... 15 50 56N 0 37 E
Bredon Hill, U.K. 14 52 3N 2 2W
Breiðafjörður, Ice. 44 65 15N 23 15W
Bremen, W. Ger. ..... 42 53 4N 8 47 E
Bremerhaven, W. Ger. 40 53 34N 8 35 E
Brendon Hills, U.K. ... 14 51 6N 3 25W
Brenner Pass, Alps ... 42 47 0N 11 30 E
Brent, U.K. 15 51 33N 0 18W
Brentwood, U.K. ..... 15 51 37N 0 19 E
Bréscia, It. .... 40 45 33N 10 13 E
Breslau = Wrocław, Pol. .... 43 51 5N 17 5 E
Bressay I., U.K. 22 60 10N 1 5W
Brest, Fr. 34 48 24N 4 31W
Brest, U.S.S.R. ...... 46 52 10N 23 40 E
Bretagne, Fr. 34 48 0N 3 0W
Brewood, U.K. 14 52 41N 2 10W
Brezhnev, U.S.S.R. ... 46 55 42N 52 19 E
Bride, U.K. 18 54 24N 4 23W
Bridestowe, U.K. 16 50 41N 4 7W
Bridge, U.K. .... 15 51 14N 1 8 E
Bridge of Allan, U.K. .. 21 56 9N 3 57W
Bridge of Earn, U.K. .. 21 56 20N 3 25W
Bridge of Orchy, U.K. . 20 56 29N 4 48W
Bridge of Weir, U.K. .. 20 55 51N 4 35W
Bridgend, Islay, U.K. .. 20 55 46N 6 15W
Bridgend, Mid Glam., U.K. 17 51 30N 3 35W
Bridgeport, U.S.A. 93 41 12N 73 12W
Bridgetown, Barb. 94 13 0N 59 30W
Bridgnorth, U.K. 14 52 33N 2 25W
Bridgwater, U.K. 14 51 7N 3 0W
Bridgwater B., U.K. ... 14 51 15N 3 15W
Bridlington, U.K. 19 54 6N 0 11W
Bridlington B., U.K. ... 19 54 4N 0 10W
Bridport, U.K. 14 50 43N 2 45W
Brierfield, U.K. 18 53 49N 2 15W
Brierley Hill, U.K. 14 52 29N 2 7W
Brigg, U.K. 19 53 33N 0 30W
Brighouse, U.K. 19 53 42N 1 47W
Brighstone, U.K. 15 50 38N 1 36W
Brightlingsea, U.K. ... 15 51 49N 1 1 E
Brighton, U.K. 15 50 50N 0 9W
Brightstone, U.K. 14 50 38N 1 23W
Brigstock, U.K. 15 52 27N 0 38W
Brill, U.K. 14 51 49N 1 3W
Brimfield, U.K. 14 52 18N 2 42W
Bríndisi, It. .... 41 40 39N 17 55 E
Brinklow, U.K. 14 52 25N 1 22W
Brinkworth, U.K. 14 51 33N 1 59W
Brisbane, Austral. .... 67 27 25S 153 2 E
Bristol, U.K. 14 51 26N 2 35W
Bristol Channel, U.K. . 16 51 18N 4 30W
Briston, U.K. .... 15 52 52N 1 4 E
British Columbia □, Canada 88 55 0N 125 15W
British Guiana = Guyana ■, S. Am. .. 100 5 0N 59 0W
British Isles, Europe .. 4 55 0N 4 0W
Brittany = Bretagne, Fr. 34 48 0N 3 0W
Brixham, U.K. 16 50 24N 3 31W
Brixworth, U.K. 15 52 20N 0 54W
Brize Norton, U.K. 14 51 46N 1 35W
Brno, Czech. .... 42 49 10N 16 35 E
Broad B., U.K. 22 58 14N 6 16W
Broad Chalke, U.K. ... 14 51 2N 1 54W
Broad Clyst, U.K. 16 50 46N 3 27W
Broad Haven, Ire. 24 54 20N 9 55W
Broad Law, U.K. 21 55 30N 3 22W
Broad Sd., U.K. 16 49 56N 6 19W
Broadford, U.K. 22 57 14N 5 55W
Broadhembury, U.K. .. 16 50 49N 3 16W
Broads, The, U.K. .... 15 52 45N 1 30 E
Broadstairs, U.K. ..... 15 51 21N 1 28 E
Broadway, U.K. 14 52 2N 1 51W
Broadwindsor, U.K. ... 14 50 49N 2 49W
Brockenhurst, U.K. ... 14 50 49N 1 34W
Brockton, U.S.A. 93 42 25N 79 26W
Brockworth, U.K. 14 51 51N 2 9W
Brodick, U.K. 20 55 34N 5 9W
Broken Hill, Austral. .. 70 31 58S 141 29 E
Bromborough, U.K. ... 18 53 20N 3 0W
Bromfield, U.K. 14 52 25N 2 45W
Bromham, U.K. 14 51 23N 2 3W
Bromley, U.K. .... 15 51 20N 0 5 E
Brompton, U.K. 19 54 22N 1 25W
Bromsgrove, U.K. 14 52 20N 2 3W
Bromyard, U.K. 14 52 12N 2 30W
Brooks, Canada 88 50 35N 111 55W
Brooks Ra., U.S.A. ... 88 68 40N 147 0W
Broom, L., U.K. 22 57 55N 5 15W
Broomfield, U.K. ..... 14 51 46N 0 28 E
Broomhill, U.K. 21 55 19N 1 36W
Brora, U.K. 23 58 0N 3 50W
Brora —►, U.K. 23 58 4N 3 52W
Broseley, U.K. 14 52 36N 2 30W
Brosna —►, Ire. 25 53 8N 8 0W
Brothertoft, U.K. 19 53 0N 0 5W
Brotton, U.K. 19 54 34N 0 55W
Brough, Cumbria, U.K. 18 54 32N 2 19W
Brough, Humberside, U.K. 19 53 44N 0 35W
Broughton, Borders, U.K. 21 55 37N 3 25W
Broughton, Humberside, U.K. .. 19 53 33N 0 36W
Broughton, N. Yorks., U.K. 19 54 26N 1 8W
Broughton, Northants., U.K. 15 52 22N 0 45W
Broughton-in-Furness, U.K. 18 54 17N 3 12W
Broughty Ferry, U.K. .. 21 56 29N 2 50W
Brown Willy, U.K. 16 50 35N 4 34W
Brownhills, U.K. 14 52 38N 1 57W
Broxburn, U.K. 21 55 56N 3 23W
Bruay-en-Artois, Fr. .. 34 50 29N 2 33 E
Bruce, Mt., Austral. ... 66 22 37S 118 8 E
Brue —►, U.K. 14 51 10N 2 59W
Bruges, Belg. .... 36 51 13N 3 13 E
Brunei ■, E. Ind. ..... 63 4 50N 115 0 E
Brunswick, W. Ger. ... 42 52 17N 10 28 E
Brunton, U.K. 21 55 2N 2 6W
Brussels, Belg. ...... 36 50 51N 4 21 E
Bruton, U.K. 14 51 6N 2 28W
Bryansk, U.S.S.R. .... 46 53 13N 34 25 E
Bryher I., U.K. 16 49 57N 6 21W
Brynamman, U.K. 17 51 49N 3 52W
Brynmawr, U.K. 17 51 48N 3 11W
Bucaramanga, Col. ... 100 7 0N 73 0W
Buchan, U.K. 23 57 32N 2 8W
Buchan Ness, U.K. ... 23 57 29N 1 48W
Bucharest, Rom. ..... 43 44 27N 26 10 E
Buchlyvie, U.K. 20 56 7N 4 20W
Buckden, U.K. 15 52 17N 0 16W
Buckfastleigh, U.K. ... 16 50 28N 3 47W
Buckhaven, U.K. 21 56 10N 3 2W
Buckie, U.K. 23 57 40N 2 58W
Buckingham, U.K. 15 52 0N 0 59W
Buckingham □, U.K. .. 15 51 50N 0 55W
Buckland Brewer, U.K. 16 50 56N 4 14W
Buckland Newton, U.K. 14 50 45N 2 25W
Buckley, U.K. 17 53 10N 3 5W
Budapest, Hung. ..... 43 47 29N 19 5 E
Buddon Ness, U.K. ... 21 56 29N 2 42W
Bude, U.K. 16 50 49N 4 33W
Bude Bay, U.K. 16 50 50N 4 40W
Budle B., U.K. 21 55 37N 1 45W
Budleigh Salterton, U.K. 16 50 37N 3 19W
Buenaventura, Col. ... 100 3 53N 77 4W
Buenos Aires, Arg. ... 102 34 30S 58 20W
Buffalo, U.S.A. 92 42 55N 78 50W
Bug —►, Pol. .... 43 52 31N 21 5 E
Bug —►, U.S.S.R. .... 47 46 59N 31 58 E
Buglawton, U.K. 18 53 12N 2 11W
Bugle, U.K. 16 50 23N 4 46W
Buie L., U.K. 20 56 20N 5 55W
Builth Wells, U.K. 17 52 10N 3 26W
Bujumbura, Bur. ..... 80 3 16S 29 18 E
Bukavu, Zaïre .... 80 2 20S 28 52 E
Bukhara, U.S.S.R. .... 48 39 48N 64 25 E
Bulawayo, Zimb. ..... 81 20 7S 28 32 E
Bulford, U.K. 14 51 11N 1 45W
Bulgaria ■, Europe ... 41 42 35N 25 30 E
Bulwell, U.K. 19 53 1N 1 12W
Bunbury, Austral. .... 66 33 20S 115 35 E
Buncrana, Ire. 24 55 8N 7 28W
Bundaberg, Austral. .. 67 24 54S 152 22 E
Bundoran, Ire. 24 54 24N 8 17W

Bunessan, U.K. 20 56 18N 6 15W
Bungay, U.K. 15 52 27N 1 26 E
Buntingford, U.K. 15 51 57N 0 1W
Bunwell, U.K. 15 52 30N 1 9 E
Buraydah, Si. Arab. 56 26 20N 44 8 E
Burbage, Derby, U.K. 18 53 15N 1 55W
Burbage, Leics., U.K. 14 52 31N 1 20W
Burbage, Wilts., U.K. 14 51 21N 1 40W
Burdwan, India 59 23 14N 87 39 E
Bure →, U.K. 15 52 38N 1 45 E
Burford, U.K. 14 51 48N 1 38W
Burgas, Bulg. 41 42 33N 27 29 E
Burgess Hill, U.K. 15 50 57N 0 7W
Burgh-le-Marsh, U.K. 19 53 10N 0 15 E
Burgos, Sp. 37 42 21N 3 41W
Burgundy = Bourgogne, Fr. 34 47 0N 4 50 E
Burkina Faso ■, Africa 78 12 0N 1 0W
Burley, Hants., U.K. 14 50 49N 1 41W
Burley, N. Yorks., U.K. 19 53 55N 1 46W
Burlington, U.S.A. 93 44 27N 73 14W
Burma ■, Asia 59 21 0N 96 30 E
Burnham, Essex, U.K. 15 51 37N 0 50 E
Burnham, Somerset, U.K. 14 51 14N 3 0W
Burnham Market, U.K. 15 52 57N 0 43 E
Burnie, Austral. 67 41 4S 145 56 E
Burnley, U.K. 18 53 47N 2 15W
Burnmouth, U.K. 21 55 50N 2 4W
Burntisland, U.K. 21 56 4N 3 14W
Burrelton, U.K. 21 56 30N 3 16W
Burrow Hd., U.K. 20 54 40N 4 23W
Burry Port, U.K. 17 51 41N 4 17W
Bursa, Turk. 47 40 15N 29 5 E
Burstwick, U.K. 19 53 43N 0 6W
Burton, U.K. 18 54 10N 2 43W
Burton Agnes, U.K. 19 54 4N 0 18W
Burton Bradstock, U.K. 14 50 41N 2 43W
Burton Fleming, U.K. 19 54 8N 0 20W
Burton Latimer, U.K. 15 52 23N 0 41W
Burton upon Stather, U.K. 19 53 39N 0 41W
Burton-upon-Trent, U.K. 14 52 48N 1 39W
Burundi ■, Africa 80 3 15S 30 0 E
Burwash, U.K. 15 50 59N 0 24 E
Burwell, U.K. 15 52 17N 0 20 E
Bury, U.K. 18 53 36N 2 19W
Bury St. Edmunds, U.K. 15 52 15N 0 42 E
Buryat A.S.S.R. □, U.S.S.R. 49 53 0N 110 0 E
Būshehr, Iran 56 28 20N 51 45 E
Bushey, U.K. 15 51 38N 0 20W
Bushmills, U.K. 24 55 14N 6 32W
Bute, U.K. 20 55 48N 5 2W
Bute, Kyles of, U.K. 20 55 55N 5 10W
Bute, Sd. of, U.K. 20 55 43N 5 8W
Buttermere, U.K. 18 54 32N 3 17W
Butuan, Phil. 63 8 57N 125 33 E
Buxton, U.K. 18 53 16N 1 54W
Buzău, Rom. 43 45 10N 26 50 E
Bydgoszcz, Pol. 43 53 10N 18 0 E
Byfield, U.K. 14 52 10N 1 15W
Byrd Land, Ant. 103 79 30S 125 0W
Byrrang Mts., U.S.S.R. 49 75 0N 100 0 E
Bytom, Pol. 43 50 25N 18 54 E

C

Cabimas, Ven. 100 10 23N 71 25W
Cabinda □, Angola 80 5 0S 12 30 E
Čačak, Yug. 41 43 54N 20 20 E
Cáceres, Sp. 37 39 26N 6 23W
Cachoeira do Sul, Brazil 102 30 3S 52 53W
Cader Idris, U.K. 17 52 43N 3 56W
Cádiz, Sp. 37 36 30N 6 20W
Caen, Fr. 34 49 10N 0 22W
Caenby Corner, U.K. 19 53 23N 0 32W
Caernarfon, U.K. 17 53 8N 4 17W
Caernarfon B., U.K. 17 53 4N 4 40W
Caerphilly, U.K. 17 51 34N 3 13W
Caersws, U.K. 17 52 32N 3 27W
Cagayan de Oro, Phil. 63 8 30N 124 40 E
Cágliari, It. 40 39 15N 9 6 E
Caha Mts., Ire. 25 51 45N 9 40W
Caher, Ire. 25 52 23N 7 56W
Cahersiveen, Ire. 25 51 57N 10 13W
Cahore Pt., Ire. 25 52 34N 6 11W
Caicos Is., W. Ind. 95 21 40N 71 40W
Cairn Gorm, U.K. 23 57 7N 3 40W
Cairn Table, U.K. 21 55 30N 4 0W
Cairn Toul, U.K. 23 57 3N 3 44W
Cairngorm Mts., U.K. 23 57 6N 3 42W
Cairnryan, U.K. 20 54 59N 5 0W
Cairns, Austral. 67 16 57S 145 45 E
Cairo, Egypt 79 30 1N 31 14 E
Caister-on-Sea, U.K. 15 52 38N 1 43 E
Caistor, U.K. 19 53 29N 0 20W
Caithness, Ord of, U.K. 23 58 9N 3 37W
Cajamarca, Peru 100 7 5S 78 28W
Calabar, Nig. 78 4 57N 8 20 E
Calábria □, It. 40 39 24N 16 30 E
Calais, Fr. 34 50 57N 1 50 E
Calbayog, Phil. 63 12 4N 124 38 E
Calcutta, India 59 22 36N 88 24 E
Caldbeck, U.K. 18 54 45N 3 3W
Calder →, U.K. 19 53 44N 1 21W
Calder Bridge, U.K. 18 54 27N 3 31W
Caldew →, U.K. 18 54 54N 2 59W
Caledonian Canal, U.K. 23 56 50N 5 6W
Calf of Man, U.K. 18 54 4N 4 48W
Calgary, Canada 88 51 0N 114 10W
Calgary, U.K. 20 56 34N 6 17W
Cali, Col. 100 3 25N 76 35W
Caliach Pt., U.K. 20 56 37N 6 20W
Calicut, India 58 11 15N 75 43 E
California □, U.S.A. 90 37 25N 120 0W
California, G. of, N. Am. 94 27 0N 111 0W
Callan, Ire. 25 52 33N 7 25W
Callander, U.K. 20 56 15N 4 14W
Callao, Peru 100 12 0S 77 0W
Calne, U.K. 14 51 26N 2 0W
Calshot, U.K. 14 50 49N 1 18W
Calstock, U.K. 16 50 30N 4 13W
Caltanissetta, It. 40 37 30N 14 3 E
Cam →, U.K. 15 52 21N 0 16 E
Camagüey, Cuba 95 21 20N 78 0W
Camargue, Fr. 35 43 34N 4 34 E
Cambay, G. of, India 58 20 45N 72 30 E
Camberley, U.K. 15 51 20N 0 44W
Cambo, U.K. 21 55 9N 1 57W
Cambodia ■, Asia 63 12 15N 105 0 E
Camborne, U.K. 16 50 13N 5 18W
Cambrian Mts., U.K. 17 52 25N 3 52W
Cambridge, U.K. 15 52 13N 0 8 E
Cambridge, U.S.A. 93 42 20N 71 8W
Cambridge Bay, Canada 88 69 10N 105 0W
Cambridgeshire □, U.K. 15 52 12N 0 7 E
Camden, U.K. 15 51 33N 0 10W
Camden, U.S.A. 93 39 57N 75 7W
Camel →, U.K. 16 50 28N 4 49W
Camelford, U.K. 16 50 37N 4 41W
Cameroon ■, Africa 80 6 0N 12 30 E
Campbellton, Canada 93 49 17N 54 56W
Campbelltown, Austral. 70 34 53S 138 40 E
Campbeltown, U.K. 20 55 25N 5 36W
Campeche, Mex. 94 19 50N 90 32W
Campeche, G. of, Mex. 94 19 30N 93 0W
Campina Grande, Brazil 101 7 20S 35 47W
Campinas, Brazil 102 22 50S 47 0W
Campo Grande, Brazil 101 20 25S 54 40W
Campos, Brazil 101 21 50S 41 20W
Campsie Fells, U.K. 20 56 2N 4 20W
Camrose, Canada 88 53 0N 112 50W
Can Tho, Viet. 63 10 2N 105 46 E
Canada ■, N. Am. 88 60 0N 100 0W
Canary Is., Atl. Oc. 78 29 30N 17 0W
Canaveral, C., U.S.A. 91 28 28N 80 31W
Canberra, Austral. 70 35 15S 149 8 E
Canik Mts., Turk. 47 40 30N 38 0 E
Canna, U.K. 22 57 3N 6 33W
Cannes, Fr. 35 43 32N 7 0 E
Cannington, U.K. 14 51 8N 3 4W
Cannock, U.K. 14 52 42N 2 2W
Cannock Chase, U.K. 14 52 43N 2 0W
Canonbie, U.K. 21 55 4N 2 58W
Cantabrian Mts., Sp. 37 43 0N 5 10W
Canterbury, U.K. 15 51 17N 1 5 E
Canterbury Plains, N.Z. 71 43 55S 171 22 E
Canton = Guangzhou, China 61 23 5N 113 10 E
Canton, U.S.A. 92 40 47N 81 22W
Canvey, U.K. 15 51 32N 0 35 E
Caoles, U.K. 20 56 32N 6 43W
Caolisport, Loch, U.K. 20 55 54N 5 40W
Cape Breton I., Canada 93 46 0N 60 30W
Cape Coast, Ghana 78 5 5N 1 15W
Cape Province □, S. Afr. 81 32 0S 23 0 E
Cape Town, S. Afr. 81 33 55S 18 22 E
Cape Verde Is. ■, Atl. Oc. 128 17 10N 25 20W
Cape York Peninsula, Austral. 67 12 0S 142 30 E
Capel, U.K. 15 51 8N 0 18W
Caracas, Ven. 100 10 30N 66 55W
Caratinga, Brazil 101 19 50S 42 10W
Carbost, U.K. 22 57 19N 6 21W
Cardiff, U.K. 17 51 28N 3 11W
Cardigan, U.K. 17 52 6N 4 41W
Cardigan B., U.K. 17 52 30N 4 30W
Cardington, U.K. 15 52 7N 0 23W
Carey, L., Austral. 66 29 0S 122 15 E
Caribbean Sea 95 15 0N 75 0W
Carisbrooke, U.K. 14 50 42N 1 19W
Cark, U.K. 18 54 11N 2 59W
Carleton Rode, U.K. 15 52 30N 1 6 E
Carlingford, L., Ire. 24 54 0N 6 5W
Carlisle, U.K. 18 54 54N 2 55W
Carlops, U.K. 21 55 47N 3 20W
Carlow, Ire. 25 52 50N 6 58W
Carlow □, Ire. 25 52 43N 6 50W
Carloway, U.K. 22 58 17N 6 48W
Carlton, U.K. 19 52 58N 1 6W
Carlton Colville, U.K. 15 52 27N 1 41 E
Carlton Miniott, U.K. 19 54 13N 1 22W
Carluke, U.K. 21 55 44N 3 50W
Carmarthen, U.K. 17 51 52N 4 20W
Carmarthen B., U.K. 17 51 40N 4 30W
Carnarvon, Austral. 66 24 51S 113 42 E
Carndonagh, Ire. 24 55 15N 7 16W
Carnegie, L., Austral. 66 26 5S 122 30 E
Carnforth, U.K. 18 54 8N 2 47W
Carno, U.K. 17 52 34N 3 31W
Carnoustie, U.K. 21 56 30N 2 41W
Carnsore Pt., Ire. 25 52 10N 6 20W
Carnwath, U.K. 21 55 42N 3 38W
Caroline Is., Pac. Oc. 64 8 0N 150 0 E
Carpathians, Mts., Europe 43 49 50N 21 0 E
Carpentaria, G. of, Austral. 67 14 0S 139 0 E
Carradale, U.K. 20 55 35N 5 30W
Carrauntoohill, Mt., Ire. 25 52 0N 9 49W
Carrick, U.K. 20 55 12N 4 38W
Carrick-on-Shannon, Ire. 24 53 57N 8 7W
Carrick-on-Suir, Ire. 25 52 22N 7 30W
Carrickfergus, U.K. 24 54 43N 5 50W
Carrickfergus □, U.K. 24 54 43N 5 49W
Carrickmacross, Ire. 24 54 0N 6 43W
Carron →, U.K. 22 57 30N 5 30W
Carron, L., U.K. 22 57 22N 5 35W
Carronbridge, U.K. 21 55 16N 3 46W
Carse of Gowrie, U.K. 21 56 30N 3 10W
Carsphairn, U.K. 20 55 13N 4 15W
Carstairs, U.K. 21 55 42N 3 41W
Cartagena, Col. 100 10 25N 75 33W
Cartagena, Sp. 37 37 38N 0 59W
Cartmel, U.K. 18 54 13N 2 57W
Caruaru, Brazil 101 8 15S 35 55W
Carúpano, Ven. 100 10 39N 63 15W
Casablanca, Mor. 78 33 36N 7 36W
Cascade Ra., U.S.A. 90 47 0N 121 30W
Cashel, Ire. 25 52 31N 7 53W
Casper, U.S.A. 90 42 52N 106 20W
Caspian Sea, U.S.S.R. 47 43 0N 50 0 E
Castellón □, Sp. 37 40 15N 0 5W
Castle Acre, U.K. 15 52 42N 0 42W
Castle Cary, U.K. 14 51 5N 2 32W
Castle Donington, U.K. 14 52 50N 1 20W
Castle Douglas, U.K. 21 54 57N 3 57W
Castle Eden, U.K. 19 54 45N 1 20W
Castlebar, Ire. 24 53 52N 9 17W
Castlebay, U.K. 22 56 57N 7 30W
Castleblaney, Ire. 24 54 7N 6 44W
Castleford, U.K. 19 53 43N 1 21W
Castlereagh, Ire. 24 53 47N 8 30W
Castlereagh □, U.K. 24 54 33N 5 53W
Castlereagh →, Austral. 70 30 12S 147 32 E
Castleside, U.K. 18 54 50N 1 52W
Castleton, Derby, U.K. 19 53 20N 1 47W
Castleton, N. Yorks., U.K. 19 54 27N 0 57W
Castletown, U.K. 18 54 4N 4 40W
Castletown Bearhaven, Ire. 25 51 40N 9 54W
Castries, St. Lucia 94 14 0N 60 50W
Catánia, It. 40 37 31N 15 4 E
Catanzaro, It. 40 38 54N 16 38 E
Catcleugh, U.K. 21 55 19N 2 22W
Caterham, U.K. 15 51 16N 0 4W
Caton, U.K. 18 54 5N 2 41W
Catrine, U.K. 20 55 30N 4 20W
Catsfield, U.K. 15 50 53N 0 28 E
Catterick, U.K. 19 54 23N 1 38W
Catterick Camp, U.K. 19 54 22N 1 43W
Catton, U.K. 21 54 56N 2 16W
Caucasus, U.S.S.R. 47 43 0N 44 0 E
Caulkerbush, U.K. 21 54 54N 3 40W
Cavan, Ire. 24 54 0N 7 22W
Cavan □, Ire. 24 53 58N 7 10W
Cawood, U.K. 19 53 50N 1 7W
Cawston, U.K. 15 52 47N 1 10 E
Caxias, Brazil 101 4 55S 43 20W
Caxias do Sul, Brazil 102 29 10S 51 10W
Cayenne, Fr. G. 101 5 0N 52 18W
Ceanannus Mor, Ire. 24 53 42N 6 53W
Cebu, Phil. 63 10 18N 123 54 E
Cedar Rapids, U.S.A. 90 42 0N 91 38W
Celbridge, Ire. 25 53 20N 6 33W
Celebes = Sulawesi □, Indon. 63 2 0S 120 0 E
Celebes Sea, E. Ind. 63 3 0N 123 0 E
Cemaes Bay, U.K. 17 53 24N 4 27W
Central □, U.K. 20 56 10N 4 30W
Central African Republic ■, Africa 80 7 0N 20 0 E
Central Russian Uplands, U.S.S.R. 26 54 0N 36 0 E
Central Siberian Plateau, U.S.S.R. 49 65 0N 105 0 E
Cephalonia = Kefallinía, Greece 41 38 20N 20 30 E
Ceram, Indon. 63 3 10S 129 0 E
Ceres, U.K. 21 56 18N 2 57W
Cerignola, It. 40 41 17N 15 53 E
Cerne Abbas, U.K. 14 50 49N 2 29W
Cerrig-y-drudion, U.K. 17 53 2N 3 34W
Cessnock, Austral. 70 32 50S 151 21 E
Ceuta, Mor. 78 35 52N 5 18W
Cévennes, Fr. 34 44 10N 3 50 E
Ceylon = Sri Lanka ■, Asia 58 7 30N 80 50 E
Chacewater, U.K. 16 50 15N 5 8W
Chad ■, Africa 78 15 0N 17 15 E
Chad, L., Chad 79 13 30N 14 30 E
Chagford, U.K. 16 50 40N 3 50W
Chale, U.K. 14 50 35N 1 19W
Chalfont St. Peter, U.K. 15 51 36N 0 33W
Châlons-sur-Marne, Fr. 34 48 58N 4 20 E
Chambéry, Fr. 35 45 34N 5 55 E
Champagne, Fr. 34 48 40N 4 20 E
Champlain, L., U.S.A. 93 44 30N 73 20W
Chandigarh, India 58 30 43N 76 47 E
Chandler's Ford, U.K. 14 50 59N 1 23W
Changchun, China 61 43 58N 125 19 E
Changde, China 61 29 4N 111 35 E
Changsha, China 61 28 5N 113 1 E
Changzhou, China 61 31 47N 119 58 E
Channel Is., U.K. 34 49 30N 2 40W
Chao Phraya →, Thai. 63 13 32N 100 36 E
Chapel-en-le-Frith, U.K. 18 53 19N 1 54W
Chapel St. Leonards, U.K. 19 53 13N 0 19 E
Chard, U.K. 14 50 52N 2 59W
Chardzhou, U.S.S.R. 48 39 6N 63 34 E
Charing, U.K. 15 51 12N 0 49 E
Charlbury, U.K. 14 51 52N 1 29W
Charleroi, Belg. 36 50 24N 4 27 E
Charleston, U.S.A. 91 32 47N 79 56W
Charleville = Rath Luirc, Ire. 25 52 21N 8 40W
Charleville, Austral. 67 26 24S 146 15 E
Charleville-Mézières, Fr. 34 49 44N 4 40 E
Charlotte, U.S.A. 91 35 16N 80 46W
Charlottenburg, W. Ger. 42 52 31N 13 15 E
Charlottetown, Canada 93 46 14N 63 8W
Charlton Kings, U.K. 14 51 52N 2 3W
Charlwood, U.K. 15 51 8N 0 12W
Charminster, U.K. 14 50 43N 2 28W
Charmouth, U.K. 14 50 45N 2 54W
Charnwood Forest, U.K. 14 52 43N 1 18W
Charters Towers, Austral. 67 20 5S 146 13 E
Chartham, U.K. 15 51 14N 1 1 E
Chartres, Fr. 34 48 29N 1 30 E
Châteauroux, Fr. 34 46 50N 1 40 E
Chatham, U.K. 15 51 22N 0 32 E
Chattanooga, U.S.A. 91 35 2N 85 17W
Chatteris, U.K. 15 52 27N 0 3 E
Chatton, U.K. 21 55 34N 1 55W
Cheadle, Gr. Manchester, U.K. 18 53 23N 2 14W
Cheadle, Staffs., U.K. 18 52 59N 1 59W
Cheadle Hulme, U.K. 18 53 22N 2 12W
Cheboksary, U.S.S.R. 46 56 8N 47 12 E
Cheddar, U.K. 14 51 16N 2 47W
Cheddleton, U.K. 18 53 5N 2 2W
Chelmarsh, U.K. 14 52 29N 2 25W
Chelmer →, U.K. 15 51 45N 0 42 E
Chelmsford, U.K. 15 51 44N 0 29 E
Cheltenham, U.K. 14 51 55N 2 5W
Chelyabinsk, U.S.S.R. 48 55 10N 61 24 E
Chenab →, Pak. 58 30 23N 71 2 E
Chengdu, China 60 30 38N 104 2 E
Chepstow, U.K. 17 51 38N 2 40W
Cherbourg, Fr. 34 49 39N 1 40W
Cheremkhovo, U.S.S.R. 49 53 8N 103 1 E
Cherepovets, U.S.S.R. 46 59 5N 37 55 E
Cheriton, U.K. 14 51 3N 1 9W
Cheriton Fitzpaine, U.K. 16 50 51N 3 38W
Cherkassy, U.S.S.R. 47 49 27N 32 4 E
Chernigov, U.S.S.R. 46 51 28N 31 20 E
Chernovtsy, U.S.S.R. 47 48 15N 25 52 E
Chertsey, U.K. 15 51 23N 0 30W
Cherwell →, U.K. 14 51 46N 1 18W
Chesapeake Bay, U.S.A. 92 38 0N 76 12W
Chesham, U.K. 15 51 42N 0 36W
Cheshire □, U.K. 18 53 14N 2 30W
Cheshunt, U.K. 15 51 42N 0 1W
Chesil Beach, U.K. 14 50 37N 2 33W
Chester, U.K. 18 53 12N 2 53W
Chester-le-Street, U.K. 19 54 53N 1 34W
Chesterfield, U.K. 19 53 14N 1 26W
Chesterfield Inlet, Canada 88 63 30N 90 45W
Cheviot, The, U.K. 19 55 29N 2 8W
Cheviot Hills, U.K. 19 55 20N 2 30W
Chew Magna, U.K. 14 51 21N 2 37W
Chiai, China 61 23 29N 120 25 E
Chiba, Jap. 62 35 30N 140 7 E
Chicago, U.S.A. 92 41 53N 87 40W
Chichester, U.K. 15 50 50N 0 47W
Chiclayo, Peru 100 6 42S 79 50W
Chicoutimi, Canada 93 48 28N 71 5W
Chiddingfold, U.K. 15 51 6N 0 37W
Chidley, C., Canada 89 60 23N 64 26W
Chieti, It. 40 42 22N 14 10 E
Chihli, G. of, China 61 38 30N 119 0 E
Chihuahua, Mex. 94 28 40N 106 3W
Chile ■, S. Am. 102 35 0S 72 0W
Chilham, U.K. 15 51 15N 0 59 E
Chillán, Chile 102 36 40S 72 10W
Chilpancingo, Mex. 94 17 30N 99 30W
Chiltern Hills, U.K. 15 51 44N 0 42W
Chilung, Taiwan 61 25 3N 121 45 E
Chimborazo, Ecuad. 100 1 29S 78 55W
Chimbote, Peru 100 9 0S 78 35W
Chimkent, U.S.S.R. 48 42 18N 69 36 E
China ■, Asia 60 30 0N 110 0 E
Chincha Alta, Peru 100 13 25S 76 7W
Chingola, Zam. 81 12 31S 27 53 E
Chipata, Zam. 81 13 38S 32 28 E
Chippenham, U.K. 14 51 27N 2 7W
Chipping Campden, U.K. 14 52 4N 1 48W
Chipping Norton, U.K. 14 51 56N 1 32W
Chipping Ongar, U.K. 15 51 43N 0 15 E
Chipping Sodbury, U.K. 14 51 31N 2 23W
Chirbury, U.K. 14 52 35N 3 6W
Chirnside, U.K. 21 55 47N 2 11W
Chisledon, U.K. 14 51 30N 1 44W
Chita, U.S.S.R. 49 52 0N 113 35 E
Chittagong, Bangla. 59 22 19N 91 48 E

Chollerton, *U.K.* **21** 55 4N 2 7W
Cholsey, *U.K.* **14** 51 34N 1 10W
Chongjin, *N. Kor.* **61** 41 47N 129 50 E
Chongqing = Chungking, *China* **60** 29 35N 106 25 E
Chorley, *U.K.* **18** 53 39N 2 39W
Chorrera, La, *Pan.* **94** 8 50N 79 50W
Chorzów, *Pol.* **43** 50 18N 18 57 E
Choybalsan, *Mong.* **61** 48 4N 114 30 E
Christchurch, *N.Z.* **71** 43 33S 172 47 E
Christchurch, *U.K.* **14** 50 44N 1 33W
Chudleigh, *U.K.* **16** 50 35N 3 36W
Chulmleigh, *U.K.* **16** 50 55N 3 52W
Chungking, *China* **60** 29 35N 106 25 E
Chur, *Switz.* **42** 46 52N 9 32 E
Church Stretton, *U.K.* **14** 52 32N 2 49W
Churchdown, *U.K.* **14** 51 53N 2 9W
Churchill →, *Canada* **88** 58 47N 94 12W
Ciénaga, *Col.* **100** 11 1N 74 15W
Cienfuegos, *Cuba* **95** 22 10N 80 30W
Cincinnati, *U.S.A.* **92** 39 10N 84 26W
Cinderford, *U.K.* **14** 51 49N 2 30W
Cirencester, *U.K.* **14** 51 43N 1 59W
Citlaltépetl, *Mex.* **94** 19 0N 97 20W
Ciudad Bolívar, *Ven.* **100** 8 5N 63 36W
Ciudad Guayana, *Ven.* **100** 8 0N 62 30W
Ciudad Juárez, *Mex.* **94** 31 40N 106 28W
Ciudad Madero, *Mex.* **94** 22 19N 97 50W
Ciudad Obregón, *Mex.* **94** 27 28N 109 59W
Ciudad Real, *Sp.* **37** 38 59N 3 55W
Ciudad Victoria, *Mex.* **94** 23 41N 99 9W
Clabhach, *U.K.* **20** 56 38N 6 36W
Clach Leathad, *U.K.* **20** 56 36N 7 52W
Clachan, *U.K.* **20** 55 45N 5 35W
Clackmannan, *U.K.* **21** 56 10N 3 50W
Clacton-on-Sea, *U.K.* **15** 51 47N 1 10 E
Cladich, *U.K.* **20** 56 21N 5 5W
Clara, *Ire.* **25** 53 20N 7 38W
Clare, *U.K.* **15** 52 5N 0 36 E
Clare □, *Ire.* **25** 52 20N 9 0W
Clare →, *Ire.* **24** 53 22N 9 5W
Clare I., *Ire.* **24** 53 48N 10 0W
Claremorris, *Ire.* **24** 53 45N 9 0W
Clarksville, *U.S.A.* **90** 36 32N 87 20W
Clatteringshaws L., *U.K.* **20** 55 3N 4 17W
Claverley, *U.K.* **14** 52 32N 2 19W
Clay Cross, *U.K.* **19** 53 11N 1 26W
Clay Hd., *U.K.* **18** 54 13N 4 23W
Claydon, *U.K.* **15** 52 6N 1 7 E
Clear, C., *Ire.* **25** 51 26N 9 30W
Clear I., *Ire.* **25** 51 26N 9 30W
Cleator Moor, *U.K.* **18** 54 30N 3 32W
Clee Hills, *U.K.* **14** 52 26N 2 35W
Cleethorpes, *U.K.* **19** 53 33N 0 2W
Cleeve Cloud, *U.K.* **14** 51 56N 2 0W
Clent, *U.K.* **14** 52 25N 2 6W
Cleobury Mortimer, *U.K.* **14** 52 23N 2 28W
Clermont-Ferrand, *Fr.* **34** 45 46N 3 4 E
Clevedon, *U.K.* **14** 51 26N 2 52W
Cleveland, *U.S.A.* **92** 41 28N 81 43W
Cleveland □, *U.K.* **19** 54 35N 1 8 E
Cleveland Hills, *U.K.* **19** 54 25N 1 11W
Clew B., *Ire.* **24** 53 54N 9 50W
Cley, *U.K.* **15** 52 57N 1 3 E
Clifden, *Ire.* **24** 53 30N 10 2W
Cliffe, *U.K.* **15** 51 27N 0 31 E
Clifford, *U.K.* **14** 52 6N 3 6W
Clipston, *U.K.* **15** 52 26N 0 58W
Clitheroe, *U.K.* **18** 53 52N 2 23W
Clonakilty, *Ire.* **25** 51 37N 8 53W
Clonakilty B., *Ire.* **25** 51 33N 8 50W
Cloncurry, *Austral.* **67** 20 40S 140 28 E
Clones, *Ire.* **24** 54 10N 7 13W
Clonmel, *Ire.* **25** 52 22N 7 42W
Closeburn, *U.K.* **21** 55 13N 3 45W
Cloughton, *U.K.* **19** 54 20N 0 27W
Clovelly, *U.K.* **16** 51 0N 4 25W
Clowne, *U.K.* **19** 53 18N 1 16W
Cluj-Napoca, *Rom.* **43** 46 47N 23 38 E
Clun, *U.K.* **14** 52 26N 3 2W
Clun Forest, *U.K.* **14** 52 27N 3 7W
Clunbury, *U.K.* **14** 52 25N 2 55W
Clwyd □, *U.K.* **17** 53 5N 3 20W
Clwyd →, *U.K.* **17** 53 20N 3 30W
Clyde →, *U.K.* **20** 55 56N 4 29W
Clyde, Firth of, *U.K.* **20** 55 20N 5 0W
Clydebank, *U.K.* **20** 55 54N 4 25W
Clydesdale, *U.K.* **21** 55 42N 3 50W
Coalbrookdale, *U.K.* **14** 52 38N 2 30W
Coalburn, *U.K.* **21** 55 35N 3 55W
Coalville, *U.K.* **14** 52 43N 1 21W
Coast Mts., *Canada* **88** 55 0N 129 0W
Coast Ranges, *U.S.A.* **90** 41 0N 123 0W
Coatbridge, *U.K.* **21** 55 52N 4 2W
Coatzacoalcos, *Mex.* **94** 18 7N 94 25W
Cóbh, *Ire.* **25** 51 50N 8 18W
Cobourg Pen., *Austral.* **66** 11 20S 132 15 E
Cochabamba, *Bol.* **100** 17 26S 66 10W
Cochin, *India* **58** 9 59N 76 22 E
Cockburnspath, *U.K.* **21** 55 56N 2 23W
Cockenzie, *U.K.* **21** 55 58N 2 59W
Cockerham, *U.K.* **18** 53 58N 2 49W
Cockermouth, *U.K.* **18** 54 40N 3 22W
Cockfield, *U.K.* **15** 52 8N 0 47 E
Cod, C., *U.S.A.* **93** 42 8N 70 10W
Coddenham, *U.K.* **15** 52 8N 1 8 E
Coffs Harbour, *Austral.* **67** 30 16S 153 5 E
Coggeshall, *U.K.* **15** 51 53N 0 41 E
Coimbatore, *India* **58** 11 2N 76 59 E
Coimbra, *Port.* **37** 40 15N 8 27W
Colac, *Austral.* **70** 38 21S 143 35 E
Colby, *U.K.* **18** 54 6N 4 42W
Colchester, *U.K.* **15** 51 54N 0 55 E
Cold Fell, *U.K.* **18** 54 54N 2 40W
Coldingham, *U.K.* **21** 55 53N 2 10W
Coldstream, *U.K.* **21** 55 39N 2 14W
Colebrooke, *U.K.* **16** 50 45N 3 44W
Coleford, *U.K.* **14** 51 46N 2 38W
Coleraine, *U.K.* **24** 55 8N 6 40W
Coleraine □, *U.K.* **24** 55 8N 6 40 E
Coleshill, *U.K.* **14** 52 30N 1 42W
Colima, *Mex.* **94** 19 14N 103 43W
Colinton, *U.K.* **21** 55 54N 3 17W
Coll, *U.K.* **20** 56 40N 6 35W
Collie, *Austral.* **66** 33 22S 116 8 E
Collier Law Pk., *U.K.* **18** 54 47N 1 59W
Collin, *U.K.* **21** 55 4N 3 30W
Collingbourne, *U.K.* **14** 51 16N 1 39W
Collooney, *Ire.* **24** 54 11N 8 28W
Colmar, *Fr.* **34** 48 5N 7 20 E
Colmonel, *U.K.* **20** 55 8N 4 55W
Colne, *U.K.* **18** 53 51N 2 11W
Colne →, *Essex, U.K.* **15** 51 55N 0 50 E
Colne →, *Herts., U.K.* **15** 51 36N 0 30W
Cologne, *W. Ger.* **36** 50 56N 6 58 E
Colombia ■, *S. Am.* **100** 3 45N 73 0W
Colombo, *Sri L.* **58** 6 56N 79 58 E
Colón, *Mex.* **94** 20 48N 100 3W
Colonsay, *U.K.* **20** 56 4N 6 12W
Colorado □, *U.S.A.* **90** 37 40N 106 0W
Colorado →, *Calif., U.S.A.* **90** 34 45N 114 40W
Colorado →, *Tex., U.S.A.* **90** 28 36N 95 58W
Colorado Plateau, *U.S.A.* **90** 36 40N 110 30W
Colorado Springs, *U.S.A.* **90** 38 55N 104 50W
Colstorworth, *U.K.* **15** 52 48N 0 37W
Coltishall, *U.K.* **15** 52 44N 1 21 E
Columbia, *Miss., U.S.A.* **90** 31 16N 89 50W
Columbia, *S.C., U.S.A.* **91** 34 0N 81 0W
Columbia →, *N. Am.* **90** 46 15N 124 5W
Columbus, *Ga., U.S.A.* **91** 32 30N 84 58W
Columbus, *Ohio, U.S.A.* **92** 39 57N 83 1W
Colwell, *U.K.* **21** 55 4N 2 4W
Colwich, *U.K.* **14** 52 48N 1 58W
Colwyn Bay, *U.K.* **17** 53 17N 3 44W
Colyton, *U.K.* **16** 50 44N 3 4W
Combe Martin, *U.K.* **16** 51 12N 4 2W
Comber, *U.K.* **24** 54 33N 5 45W
Comeragh Mts., *Ire.* **25** 52 17N 7 35W
Comilla, *Bangla.* **59** 23 28N 91 10 E
Comino, *Malta* **40** 36 0N 14 20 E
Communism Pk., *U.S.S.R.* **48** 38 40N 72 20 E
Como, *It.* **40** 45 48N 9 5 E
Como, L., *It.* **40** 46 5N 9 17 E
Comodoro Rivadavia, *Arg.* **102** 45 50S 67 40W
Comorin, C., *India* **58** 8 3N 77 40 E
Comoro Is. ■, *Ind. Oc.* **73** 12 10S 44 15 E
Compiègne, *Fr.* **34** 49 24N 2 50 E
Comrie, *U.K.* **21** 56 22N 4 0W
Conakry, *Guin.* **78** 9 29N 13 49W
Concepción, *Chile* **102** 36 50S 73 0W
Conchos →, *Mex.* **94** 29 32N 104 25W
Concordia, *Arg.* **102** 31 20S 58 2W
Condover, *U.K.* **14** 52 39N 2 46W
Congleton, *U.K.* **18** 53 10N 2 12W
Congo = Zaïre →, *Africa* **80** 6 4S 12 24 E
Congo ■, *Africa* **80** 1 0S 16 0 E
Congo Basin, *Africa* **72** 0 10S 24 30 E
Congresbury, *U.K.* **14** 51 20N 2 49W
Coningsby, *U.K.* **19** 53 7N 0 9W
Conisbrough, *U.K.* **19** 53 29N 1 12W
Coniston, *U.K.* **18** 54 22N 3 6W
Coniston Water, *U.K.* **18** 54 20N 3 5W
Conn, L., *Ire.* **24** 54 3N 9 15W
Connacht, *Ire.* **24** 53 23N 8 40W
Connah's Quay, *U.K.* **17** 53 13N 3 6W
Connecticut □, *U.S.A.* **93** 41 40N 72 40W
Connecticut →, *U.S.A.* **93** 41 17N 72 21W
Connel, *U.K.* **20** 56 27N 5 24W
Connel Park, *U.K.* **20** 55 22N 4 15W
Connemara, *Ire.* **24** 53 29N 9 45W
Conon →, *U.K.* **23** 57 33N 4 28W
Cononbridge, *U.K.* **23** 57 32N 4 30W
Consett, *U.K.* **18** 54 52N 1 50W
Constance, L. = Bodensee, *W. Ger.* **42** 47 35N 9 25 E
Constanța, *Rom.* **43** 44 14N 28 38 E
Constantine, *Alg.* **78** 36 25N 6 42 E
Conwy, *U.K.* **17** 53 17N 3 50W
Conwy →, *U.K.* **17** 53 18N 3 50W
Cook, Mt., *N.Z.* **71** 43 36S 170 9 E
Cook Is., *Pac. Oc.* **65** 17 0S 160 0W
Cook Strait, *N.Z.* **71** 41 15S 174 29 E
Cookham, *U.K.* **15** 51 33N 0 42W
Cookstown, *U.K.* **24** 54 40N 6 43W
Cookstown □, *U.K.* **24** 54 40N 6 43W
Coolgardie, *Austral.* **66** 30 55S 121 8 E
Cootamundra, *Austral.* **70** 34 36S 148 1 E
Cootehill, *Ire.* **24** 54 5N 7 5W
Copenhagen, *Den.* **45** 55 41N 12 34 E
Coppermine, *Canada* **88** 67 50N 115 5W
Coppermine →, *Canada* **88** 67 49N 116 4W
Copythorne, *U.K.* **14** 50 56N 1 34W
Coquet →, *U.K.* **19** 55 18N 1 45W
Coquet, I., *U.K.* **21** 55 21N 1 30W
Coral Sea, *Pac. Oc.* **64** 15 0S 150 0 E
Coral Sea Islands Terr., *Austral.* **67** 20 0S 155 0 E
Corbridge, *U.K.* **21** 54 58N 2 0W
Corby, *Lincs., U.K.* **15** 52 49N 0 31W
Corby, *Northants., U.K.* **15** 52 29N 0 41W
Córdoba, *Arg.* **102** 31 20S 64 10W
Córdoba, *Sp.* **37** 37 50N 4 50W
Cordova, *U.S.A.* **88** 60 36N 145 45W
Corfe Castle, *U.K.* **14** 50 37N 2 3W
Corfe Mullen, *U.K.* **14** 50 45N 2 0W
Corfu = Kérkira, *Greece* **41** 39 38N 19 50 E
Corinth, G. of, *Greece* **41** 38 16N 22 30 E
Cork, *Ire.* **25** 51 54N 8 30W
Cork □, *Ire.* **25** 51 50N 8 50W
Cork Harbour, *Ire.* **25** 51 46N 8 16W
Corner Brook, *Canada* **89** 48 57N 57 58W
Cornforth, *U.K.* **19** 54 42N 1 28W
Cornwall □, *U.K.* **16** 50 26N 4 40W
Cornwall, C., *U.K.* **16** 50 8N 5 42W
Coro, *Ven.* **100** 11 25N 69 41W
Coromandel Coast, *India* **58** 12 30N 81 0 E
Coronation Gulf, *Canada* **88** 68 25N 110 0W
Corpus Christi, *U.S.A.* **90** 27 50N 97 28W
Corrib, L., *Ire.* **24** 53 5N 9 10W
Corrie, *U.K.* **20** 55 39N 5 10W
Corrientes, *Arg.* **102** 27 30S 58 45W
Corringham, *U.K.* **19** 53 25N 0 42W
Corryvreckan, G. of, *U.K.* **20** 56 10N 5 44W
Corsewall Pt., *U.K.* **20** 55 0N 5 10W
Corsham, *U.K.* **14** 51 25N 2 11W
Corsica, I., *Medit. S.* **35** 42 0N 9 0 E
Corsley, *U.K.* **14** 51 12N 2 14W
Corsock, *U.K.* **21** 55 54N 3 56W
Corton, *U.K.* **15** 52 31N 1 46 E
Corumbá, *Brazil* **100** 19 0S 57 30W
Coruña, La, *Sp.* **37** 43 20N 8 25W
Corve →, *U.K.* **14** 52 22N 2 43W
Coseley, *U.K.* **14** 52 33N 2 6W
Cosenza, *It.* **40** 39 17N 16 14 E
Cosham, *U.K.* **14** 50 51N 1 3W
Costa Rica ■, *Cent. Am.* **95** 10 0N 84 0W
Costessey, *U.K.* **15** 52 40N 1 11 E
Côte d'Or, *Fr.* **34** 47 10N 4 50 E
Cotherstone, *U.K.* **18** 54 34N 1 59W
Cotonou, *Benin* **78** 6 20N 2 25 E
Cotopaxi, Vol., *Ecuad.* **100** 0 40S 78 30W
Cotswold Hills, *U.K.* **14** 51 42N 2 10W
Cottbus, *E. Ger.* **42** 51 44N 14 20 E
Cottenham, *U.K.* **15** 52 18N 0 8 E
Cottingham, *U.K.* **19** 53 47N 0 29W
Coulport, *U.K.* **20** 56 3N 4 53W
Council Bluffs, *U.S.A.* **90** 41 20N 95 50W
Coupar Angus, *U.K.* **21** 56 33N 3 17W
Coventry, *U.K.* **14** 52 25N 1 31W
Cover →, *U.K.* **18** 54 14N 1 45W
Coverack, *U.K.* **16** 50 2N 5 6W
Covington, *U.S.A.* **92** 39 5N 84 30W
Cowal, *U.K.* **20** 56 5N 5 8W
Cowan, L., *Austral.* **66** 31 45S 121 45 E
Cowbridge, *U.K.* **17** 51 28N 3 28W
Cowdenbeath, *U.K.* **21** 56 7N 3 20W
Cowes, *U.K.* **14** 50 45N 1 18W
Cowfold, *U.K.* **15** 50 58N 0 16W
Cowley, *U.K.* **14** 51 43N 1 12W
Cowpen, *U.K.* **21** 55 8N 1 34W
Cowra, *Austral.* **70** 33 49S 148 42 E
Craigavon □, *U.K.* **24** 54 30N 6 25W
Craighouse, *U.K.* **20** 55 50N 5 58W
Craignish, L., *U.K.* **20** 56 11N 5 32W
Crail, *U.K.* **21** 56 16N 2 38W
Craiova, *Rom.* **43** 44 21N 23 48 E
Cramlington, *U.K.* **21** 55 5N 1 36W
Cranborne, *U.K.* **14** 50 55N 1 55W
Cranborne Chase, *U.K.* **14** 50 56N 2 6W
Cranbrook, *Canada* **88** 49 30N 115 46W
Cranbrook, *U.K.* **15** 51 6N 0 33 E
Cranleigh, *U.K.* **15** 51 8N 0 29W
Cranshaws, *U.K.* **21** 55 51N 2 30W
Cranwell, *U.K.* **19** 53 4N 0 29W
Craven Arms, *U.K.* **14** 52 27N 2 49W
Crawford, *U.K.* **21** 55 28N 3 40W
Crawley, *U.K.* **15** 51 7N 0 10W
Credenhill, *U.K.* **14** 52 6N 2 49W
Crediton, *U.K.* **16** 50 47N 3 39W
Cree →, *U.K.* **20** 54 51N 4 24W
Creeside, *U.K.* **20** 55 4N 4 41W
Creetown, *U.K.* **20** 54 54N 4 23W
Cremona, *It.* **40** 45 8N 10 2 E
Crete, I., *Greece* **41** 35 15N 25 0 E
Creusot, Le, *Fr.* **34** 46 48N 4 24 E
Crewe, *U.K.* **18** 53 6N 2 28W
Crewkerne, *U.K.* **14** 50 53N 2 48W
Crianlarich, *U.K.* **20** 56 24N 4 37W
Criccieth, *U.K.* **17** 52 55N 4 15W
Crick, *U.K.* **14** 52 22N 1 9W
Crickhowell, *U.K.* **17** 51 52N 3 8W
Cricklade, *U.K.* **14** 51 38N 1 50W
Crieff, *U.K.* **21** 56 22N 3 50W
Criffell, *U.K.* **21** 54 56N 3 38W
Crimea, *U.S.S.R.* **47** 45 0N 34 0 E
Crinan, *U.K.* **20** 56 6N 5 34W
Crinan Canal, *U.K.* **20** 56 4N 5 30W
Croaghpatrick, *Ire.* **24** 53 46N 9 40W
Crocketford, *U.K.* **21** 55 3N 3 49W
Croglin, *U.K.* **18** 54 50N 2 37W
Cromarty, *U.K.* **23** 57 40N 4 2W
Cromarty Firth, *U.K.* **23** 57 40N 4 15W
Cromer, *U.K.* **15** 52 56N 1 18 E
Crondall, *U.K.* **15** 51 13N 0 51W
Crook, *U.K.* **19** 54 43N 1 45W
Crooklands, *U.K.* **18** 54 16N 2 43W
Crosby, *Cumbria, U.K.* **18** 54 45N 3 25W
Crosby, *Merseyside, U.K.* **18** 53 30N 3 2W
Crosby Ravensworth, *U.K.* **18** 54 34N 2 35W
Cross Fell, *U.K.* **18** 54 44N 2 29W
Crosshaven, *Ire.* **25** 51 48N 8 19W
Crosshill, *U.K.* **20** 55 19N 4 39W
Crouch →, *U.K.* **15** 51 37N 0 53 E
Crow Hd., *Ire.* **25** 51 34N 10 9W
Crow Sound, *U.K.* **16** 49 56N 6 16W
Crowborough, *U.K.* **15** 51 3N 0 9 E
Crowland, *U.K.* **15** 52 41N 0 10W
Crowle, *U.K.* **19** 53 36N 0 49W
Croyde, *U.K.* **16** 51 7N 4 13W
Croydon, *U.K.* **15** 51 18N 0 5W
Crudgington, *U.K.* **14** 52 46N 2 33W
Crummock Water L., *U.K.* **18** 54 33N 3 18W
Cruzeiro do Sul, *Brazil* **100** 7 35S 72 35W
Cuba ■, *W. Ind.* **95** 22 0N 79 0W
Cuckfield, *U.K.* **15** 51 0N 0 8W
Cúcuta, *Col.* **100** 7 54N 72 31W
Cudworth, *U.K.* **19** 53 35N 1 25W
Cuenca, *Ecuad.* **100** 2 50S 79 9W
Cuenca, *Sp.* **37** 40 5N 2 10W
Cuernavaca, *Mex.* **94** 18 55N 99 15W
Cuiabá, *Brazil* **101** 15 30S 56 0W
Cuillin Hills, *U.K.* **22** 57 14N 6 15W
Cuillin Sd., *U.K.* **22** 57 4N 6 20W
Culiacán, *Mex.* **94** 24 50N 107 23W
Cullen, *U.K.* **23** 57 45N 2 50W
Culloden Moor, *U.K.* **23** 57 29N 4 7W
Cullompton, *U.K.* **16** 50 52N 3 23W
Culm →, *U.K.* **16** 50 46N 3 31W
Culrain, *U.K.* **23** 57 55N 4 25W
Culross, *U.K.* **21** 56 4N 3 38W
Cumaná, *Ven.* **100** 10 30N 64 5W
Cumberland Plateau, *U.S.A.* **91** 36 0N 84 30W
Cumbrae Is., *U.K.* **20** 55 46N 4 54W
Cumbria □, *U.K.* **18** 54 35N 2 55W
Cumbrian Mts., *U.K.* **18** 54 30N 3 0W
Cummertrees, *U.K.* **21** 55 0N 3 20W
Cumnock, *U.K.* **20** 55 27N 4 18W
Cumnor, *U.K.* **14** 51 44N 1 20W
Cumwhinton, *U.K.* **18** 54 51N 2 49W
Cúneo, *It.* **40** 44 23N 7 31 E
Cunninghame, *U.K.* **20** 55 38N 4 35W
Cupar, *U.K.* **21** 56 20N 3 0W
Curitiba, *Brazil* **102** 25 20S 49 10W
Currie, *U.K.* **21** 55 53N 3 17W
Curry Rivel, *U.K.* **14** 51 2N 2 52W
Cuttack, *India* **59** 20 25N 85 57 E
Cuzco, *Peru* **100** 13 32S 72 0W
Cwmbran, *U.K.* **17** 51 39N 3 0W
Cyclades = Kikládhes, *Greece* **41** 37 20N 24 30 E
Cyprus ■, *Medit. S.* **47** 35 0N 33 0 E
Czechoslovakia ■, *Europe* **42** 49 0N 17 0 E
Częstochowa, *Pol.* **43** 50 49N 19 7 E

D

Da Lat, *Viet.* **63** 11 56N 108 25 E
Da Nang, *Viet.* **63** 16 4N 108 13 E
Dacca, *Bangla.* **59** 23 43N 90 26 E
Daer →, *U.K.* **21** 55 23N 3 39W
Dailly, *U.K.* **20** 55 16N 4 44W
Daingean, *Ire.* **25** 53 18N 7 15W
Dakar, *Sene.* **78** 14 34N 17 29W
Dakhla, *W. Sah.* **78** 23 50N 15 53W
Dalbeattie, *U.K.* **21** 54 55N 3 50W
Dalian, *China* **61** 38 50N 121 40 E
Dalkeith, *U.K.* **21** 55 54N 3 5W
Dallas, *U.S.A.* **91** 32 50N 96 50W
Dalmally, *U.K.* **20** 56 25N 5 0W
Dalmatia, *Yug.* **41** 43 20N 17 0 E
Dalmellington, *U.K.* **20** 55 20N 4 25W
Daloa, *Ivory C.* **78** 7 0N 6 30W
Dalry, *U.K.* **20** 55 44N 4 42W
Dalrymple, *U.K.* **20** 55 24N 4 36W
Dalton, *Cumbria, U.K.* **18** 54 9N 3 11W
Dalton, *Dumf. & Gall., U.K.* **21** 55 3N 3 22W
Dalton, *N. Yorks., U.K.* **19** 54 28N 1 32W
Dalwhinnie, *U.K.* **23** 56 56N 4 14W
Damascus, *Syria* **57** 33 30N 36 18 E
Damerham, *U.K.* **14** 50 57N 1 52W
Dampier, *Austral.* **66** 20 41S 116 42 E
Dandenong, *Austral.* **70** 38 0S 145 15 E
Dandong, *China* **61** 40 10N 124 20 E
Dannevirke, *N.Z.* **71** 40 12S 176 8 E
Danube →, *Europe* **42** 45 20N 29 40 E
Dar-es-Salaam, *Tanz.* **80** 6 50S 39 12 E
Dar'ā, *Syria* **57** 32 36N 36 7 E
Dardanelles, *Turk.* **47** 40 0N 26 0 E
Darent →, *U.K.* **15** 51 22N 0 12 E

Dargaville, *N.Z.* 71 35 57S 173 52 E
Darién, G. del, *Col.* 95 9 0N 77 0W
Darlaston, *U.K.* 14 52 35N 2 1W
Darling —►, *Austral.* 70 34 4S 141 54 E
Darling Ra., *Austral.* 66 32 30S 116 0 E
Darlington, *U.K.* 19 54 33N 1 33W
Darmstadt, *W. Ger.* 42 49 51N 8 40 E
Dart —►, *U.K.* 16 50 24N 3 36W
Dartford, *U.K.* 15 51 26N 0 15 E
Dartington, *U.K.* 16 50 26N 3 42W
Dartmoor, *U.K.* 16 50 36N 4 0W
Dartmouth, *Canada* 93 44 40N 63 30W
Dartmouth, *U.K.* 16 50 21N 3 35W
Darton, *U.K.* 19 53 36N 1 32W
Darvel, *U.K.* 20 55 37N 4 20W
Darwen, *U.K.* 18 53 42N 2 29W
Darwin, *Austral.* 66 12 25S 130 51 E
Dasht-e Kavīr, *Iran* 57 34 30N 55 0 E
Dasht-e Lūt, *Iran* 57 31 30N 58 0 E
Datong, *China* 61 40 6N 113 18 E
Dauphin, *Canada* 88 51 9N 100 5W
Dauphiné, *Fr.* 35 45 15N 5 25 E
Davao, *Phil.* 63 7 0N 125 40 E
Davenport, *U.S.A.* 92 41 30N 90 40W
Daventry, *U.K.* 14 52 16N 1 10W
David, *Pan.* 95 8 30N 82 30W
Davis Str., *N. Am.* 89 65 0N 58 0W
Dawley, *U.K.* 14 52 40N 2 29W
Dawlish, *U.K.* 16 50 34N 3 28W
Dawson, *Canada* 88 64 10N 139 30W
Dawson Creek, *Canada* 88 55 45N 120 15W
Dayton, *U.S.A.* 92 39 45N 84 10W
De Aar, *S. Afr.* 81 30 39S 24 0 E
De Grey —►, *Austral.* 66 20 12S 119 13 E
Dead Sea, *Asia* 57 31 30N 35 30 E
Deal, *U.K.* 15 51 13N 1 25 E
Dean, Forest of, *U.K.* 14 51 50N 2 35W
Dearham, *U.K.* 18 54 43N 3 28W
Dease Lake, *Canada* 88 58 25N 130 6W
Death Valley, *U.S.A.* 90 36 19N 116 52W
Deben —►, *U.K.* 15 52 4N 1 19 E
Debenham, *U.K.* 15 52 14N 1 10 E
Debrecen, *Hung.* 43 47 33N 21 42 E
Deccan, *India* 58 18 0N 79 0 E
Deddington, *U.K.* 14 51 58N 1 19W
Dee —►, *Scotland, U.K.* 23 57 4N 2 7W
Dee —►, *Wales, U.K.* 17 53 15N 3 7W
Deeping, St. Nicholas, *U.K.* 15 52 44N 0 11W
Deeping Fen, *U.K.* 15 52 45N 0 15W
Dehra Dun, *India* 58 30 20N 78 4 E
Delabole, *U.K.* 16 50 37N 4 45W
Delaware □, *U.S.A.* 93 39 0N 75 40W
Delaware —►, *U.S.A.* 93 39 20N 75 25W
Delft, *Neth.* 36 52 1N 4 22 E
Delhi, *India* 58 28 38N 77 17 E
Den Helder, *Neth.* 36 52 57N 4 45 E
Denbigh, *U.K.* 17 53 12N 3 26W
Denby Dale, *U.K.* 19 53 35N 1 40W
Deniliquin, *Austral.* 70 35 30S 144 58 E
Denizli, *Turk.* 47 37 42N 29 2 E
Denmark ■, *Europe* 45 55 30N 9 0 E
Denmark Str., *Atl. Oc.* 103 66 0N 30 0W
Denny, *U.K.* 21 56 1N 3 55W
Dent, *U.K.* 18 54 17N 2 28W
Denton, *E. Sussex, U.K.* 15 50 48N 0 5 E
Denton, *Gr. Manchester, U.K.* 18 53 26N 2 10W
Denton, *Lincs., U.K.* 19 52 52N 0 42W
Denver, *U.S.A.* 90 39 45N 105 0W
Derby, *U.K.* 19 52 55N 1 28W
Derby □, *U.K.* 19 52 55N 1 28W
Derg —►, *U.K.* 24 54 42N 7 26W
Derg, L., *Ire.* 25 53 0N 8 20W
Derry = Londonderry, *U.K.* 24 55 0N 7 20W
Derryveagh Mts., *Ire.* 24 55 0N 8 40W
Dervaig, *U.K.* 20 56 35N 6 13W
Derwent —►, *Derby, U.K.* 19 52 53N 1 17W
Derwent —►, *N. Yorks., U.K.* 19 53 45N 0 57W
Derwent —►, *Tyne & Wear, U.K.* 21 54 58N 1 40W
Derwent Water, L., *U.K.* 18 54 35N 3 9W
Des Moines, *U.S.A.* 91 41 35N 93 37W
Des Moines —►, *U.S.A.* 91 40 23N 91 25W
Desborough, *U.K.* 15 52 27N 0 50W
Desford, *U.K.* 14 52 38N 1 19W
Dessau, *E. Ger.* 42 51 49N 12 15 E
Detroit, *U.S.A.* 92 42 23N 83 5W
Deurne, *Belg.* 36 51 12N 4 24 E
Deventer, *Neth.* 36 52 15N 6 10 E
Deveron —►, *U.K.* 23 57 40N 2 31W
Devizes, *U.K.* 14 51 21N 2 0W
Devonport, *N.Z.* 71 36 49S 174 49 E
Devonport, *U.K.* 16 50 23N 4 11W
Devonshire □, *U.K.* 16 50 50N 3 40W
Dewsbury, *U.K.* 19 53 42N 1 38W
Dhanbad, *India* 59 23 50N 86 30 E
Dharwad, *India* 58 15 22N 75 15 E
Dhule, *India* 58 20 58N 74 50 E
Diamantina —►, *Austral.* 67 26 45S 139 10 E
Dibden, *U.K.* 14 50 53N 1 24W
Didcot, *U.K.* 14 51 36N 1 14W
Dieppe, *Fr.* 34 49 54N 1 4 E
Dijon, *Fr.* 34 47 20N 5 0 E
Dillingham, *U.S.A.* 88 59 5N 158 30W
Dinaric Alps, *Yug.* 40 44 0N 16 30 E
Dingle, *Ire.* 25 52 9N 10 17W
Dingle B., *Ire.* 25 52 3N 10 20W
Dingwall, *U.K.* 23 57 36N 4 26W
Diss, *U.K.* 15 52 23N 1 6 E
Distington, *U.K.* 18 54 35N 3 33W
Ditchingham, *U.K.* 15 52 28N 1 26 E
Ditchling Beacon, *U.K.* 15 50 49N 0 7W
Dittisham, *U.K.* 16 50 22N 3 36W
Ditton Priors, *U.K.* 14 52 30N 2 33W
Diyarbakir, *Turk.* 47 37 55N 40 18 E
Dizzard Pt., *U.K.* 16 50 46N 4 38W
Djibouti ■, *Africa* 56 12 0N 43 0 E
Dnepr —►, *U.S.S.R.* 46 46 30N 32 18 E
Dneprodzerzhinsk, *U.S.S.R.* 47 48 32N 34 37 E
Dnepropetrovsk, *U.S.S.R.* 47 48 30N 35 0 E
Dnestr —►, *U.S.S.R.* 47 46 18N 30 17 E
Docking, *U.K.* 15 52 55N 0 39 E
Doddington, *Cambs., U.K.* 15 52 29N 0 3 E
Doddington, *Northumberland, U.K.* 21 55 33N 2 0W
Dodecanese, *Greece* 41 36 35N 27 0 E
Dodman Pt., *U.K.* 16 50 13N 4 49W
Dodoma, *Tanz.* 80 6 8S 35 45 E
Dogger Bank, *N. Sea* 26 54 50N 2 0 E
Dolgarrog, *U.K.* 17 53 11N 3 50W
Dolgellau, *U.K.* 17 52 44N 3 53W
Dollar, *U.K.* 21 56 9N 3 41W
Dolomites, *It.* 40 46 30N 11 40 E
Dolphinton, *U.K.* 21 55 42N 3 28W
Dolton, *U.K.* 16 50 53N 4 2W
Dominica ■, *W. Ind.* 94 15 20N 61 20W
Dominican Rep. ■, *W. Ind.* 95 19 0N 70 30W
Don —►, *Humberside, U.K.* 19 53 41N 0 51W
Don —►, *Grampian, U.K.* 23 57 14N 2 5W
Don —►, *U.S.S.R.* 47 47 4N 39 18 E
Donaghadee, *U.K.* 24 54 38N 5 32W
Doncaster, *U.K.* 19 53 31N 1 9W
Dondra Head, *Sri L.* 58 5 55N 80 40 E
Donegal, *Ire.* 24 54 39N 8 8W
Donegal □, *Ire.* 24 54 53N 8 0W
Donegal B., *Ire.* 24 54 30N 8 35W
Donetsk, *U.S.S.R.* 47 48 0N 37 45 E
Dongting Hu, *China* 61 29 18N 112 45 E
Donhead, *U.K.* 14 51 1N 2 8W
Donington, *U.K.* 19 52 54N 0 12W
Donna Nook, Pt., *U.K.* 19 53 29N 0 9 E
Doon —►, *U.K.* 20 55 26N 4 41W
Doon, L., *U.K.* 20 55 15N 4 22W
Dorchester, *Dorset, U.K.* 14 50 42N 2 28W
Dorchester, *Oxon., U.K.* 14 51 38N 1 10W
Dordrecht, *Neth.* 36 51 48N 4 39 E
Dorking, *U.K.* 15 51 14N 0 20W
Dornoch, *U.K.* 23 57 52N 4 0W
Dornoch Firth, *U.K.* 23 57 52N 4 0W
Dorset □, *U.K.* 14 50 48N 2 25W
Dorstone, *U.K.* 14 52 4N 3 0W
Dortmund, *W. Ger.* 36 51 32N 7 28 E
Douai, *Fr.* 34 50 21N 3 4 E
Douala, *Cam.* 80 4 0N 9 45 E
Douglas, *I. of M., U.K.* 18 54 9N 4 29W
Douglas, *Strathclyde, U.K.* 21 55 33N 3 50W
Douglas Hd., *U.K.* 18 54 9N 4 28W
Doune, *U.K.* 21 56 12N 4 3W
Dounreay, *U.K.* 23 58 34N 3 44W
Douro —►, *Port.* 37 41 8N 8 40W
Dove —►, *N. Yorks., U.K.* 19 54 20N 0 55W
Dove —►, *Staffs., U.K.* 18 52 51N 1 36W
Dove Dale, *U.K.* 19 53 10N 1 47W
Dover, *U.K.* 15 51 7N 1 19 E
Dover, Str. of, *Europe* 34 51 0N 1 30 E
Doveridge, *U.K.* 18 52 54N 1 49 E
Dovey —►, *U.K.* 17 52 32N 4 0W
Down □, *U.K.* 24 54 20N 6 0W
Downham, *U.K.* 15 52 26N 0 15 E
Downham Market, *U.K.* 15 52 36N 0 22 E
Downpatrick, *U.K.* 24 54 20N 5 43W
Downpatrick Hd., *Ire.* 24 54 20N 9 21W
Downton, *U.K.* 14 51 0N 1 44W
Drake Passage, *S. Oc.* 103 58 0S 68 0W
Drakensberg, *S. Afr.* 81 31 0S 28 0 E
Drammen, *Nor.* 45 59 42N 10 12 E
Drava —►, *Yug.* 42 45 33N 18 55 E
Dreghorn, *U.K.* 20 55 36N 4 30W
Drenthe □, *Neth.* 36 52 52N 6 40 E
Dresden, *E. Ger.* 42 51 2N 13 45 E
Driffield, *U.K.* 19 54 0N 0 25W
Drina —►, *Yug.* 41 44 53N 19 21 E
Drogheda, *Ire.* 24 53 45N 6 20W
Droichead Nua, *Ire.* 25 53 11N 6 50W
Droitwich, *U.K.* 14 52 16N 2 10W
Dronfield, *U.K.* 19 53 18N 1 29W
Dronning Maud Land, *Ant.* 103 72 30S 12 0 E
Drumheller, *Canada* 88 51 25N 112 40W
Drumjohn, *U.K.* 20 55 14N 4 15W
Drummondville, *Canada* 93 45 55N 72 25W
Drummore, *U.K.* 20 54 41N 4 53W
Druridge B., *U.K.* 21 55 16N 1 32W
Drymen, *U.K.* 20 56 4N 4 28W
Dubai, *U.A.E.* 57 25 18N 55 20 E
Dubbo, *Austral.* 70 32 11S 148 35 E
Dubh Artach, *U.K.* 20 56 8N 6 40W
Dublin, *Ire.* 24 53 20N 6 18W
Dublin □, *Ire.* 24 53 24N 6 20W
Dublin B., *Ire.* 25 53 18N 6 5W
Dubrovnik, *Yug.* 41 42 39N 18 6 E
Duddington, *U.K.* 15 52 36N 0 32W
Duddon —►, *U.K.* 18 54 12N 3 15W
Dudley, *U.K.* 14 52 30N 2 5W
Duero —►, *Sp.* 37 41 8N 8 40W
Duffield, *U.K.* 19 52 59N 1 30W
Dufftown, *U.K.* 23 57 26N 3 9W
Duisburg, *W. Ger.* 36 51 27N 6 42 E
Dukinfield, *U.K.* 18 53 29N 2 7W
Duluth, *U.S.A.* 92 46 48N 92 10W
Dulverton, *U.K.* 14 51 2N 3 33W
Dumbarton, *U.K.* 20 55 58N 4 35W
Dumfries, *U.K.* 21 55 4N 3 37W
Dumfries & Galloway □, *U.K.* 21 55 0N 4 0W
Dun Laoghaire, *Ire.* 25 53 17N 6 9W
Dunans, *U.K.* 20 56 4N 5 9W
Dunbar, *U.K.* 21 56 0N 2 32W
Dunblane, *U.K.* 21 56 10N 3 58W
Duncansby Head, *U.K.* 23 58 39N 3 0W
Dunchurch, *U.K.* 14 52 21N 1 19W
Dundalk, *Ire.* 24 54 1N 6 25W
Dundalk Bay, *Ire.* 24 53 55N 6 15W
Dundee, *U.K.* 21 56 29N 3 0W
Dundrennan, *U.K.* 21 54 49N 3 56W
Dundrum, *U.K.* 24 54 17N 5 50W
Dundrum B., *U.K.* 24 54 12N 5 40W
Dunedin, *N.Z.* 71 45 50S 170 33 E
Dunfermline, *U.K.* 21 56 5N 3 28W
Dungannon, *U.K.* 24 54 30N 6 47W
Dungannon □, *U.K.* 24 54 30N 6 55W
Dungarvan, *Ire.* 25 52 6N 7 40W
Dungarvan Bay, *Ire.* 25 52 5N 7 35W
Dungavel, *U.K.* 21 55 37N 4 7W
Dungeness, *U.K.* 15 50 54N 0 59 E
Dunkeld, *U.K.* 23 56 34N 3 36W
Dunkerque, *Fr.* 34 51 2N 2 20 E
Dunkery Beacon, *U.K.* 14 51 15N 3 37W
Dunkirk = Dunkerque, *Fr.* 34 51 2N 2 20 E
Dúnleary = Dun Laoghaire, *Ire.* 25 53 17N 6 9W
Dunlop, *U.K.* 20 55 43N 4 32W
Dunmanus B., *Ire.* 25 51 31N 9 50W
Dunmore Hd., *Ire.* 25 52 10N 10 35W
Dunnet Hd., *U.K.* 23 58 38N 3 22W
Dunning, *U.K.* 21 56 18N 3 37W
Dunoon, *U.K.* 20 55 57N 4 56W
Duns, *U.K.* 21 55 47N 2 20W
Dunscore, *U.K.* 21 55 8N 3 48W
Dunsford, *U.K.* 16 50 41N 3 40W
Dunstable, *U.K.* 15 51 53N 0 31W
Dunster, *U.K.* 14 51 11N 3 28W
Dunston, *U.K.* 14 52 46N 2 7W
Dunvegan, *U.K.* 22 57 26N 6 35W
Durango, *Mex.* 94 24 3N 104 39W
Durban, *S. Afr.* 81 29 49S 31 1 E
Düren, *W. Ger.* 36 50 48N 6 30 E
Durg, *India* 59 21 15N 81 22 E
Durgapur, *India* 59 23 30N 87 20 E
Durham, *U.K.* 19 54 47N 1 34W
Durham, *U.S.A.* 91 36 0N 78 55W
Durham □, *U.K.* 18 54 42N 1 45W
Durlstone Hd., *U.K.* 14 50 35N 1 58W
Durness, *U.K.* 23 58 34N 4 45W
Durrësi, *Alb.* 41 41 19N 19 28 E
Durrington, *U.K.* 14 51 12N 1 47W
Dursley, *U.K.* 14 51 41N 2 21W
Dushanbe, *U.S.S.R.* 48 38 33N 68 48 E
Düsseldorf, *W. Ger.* 36 51 15N 6 46 E
Duyun, *China* 60 26 18N 107 29 E
Dvina, N. —►, *U.S.S.R.* 46 61 40N 45 30 E
Dyfed □, *U.K.* 17 52 0N 4 30W
Dymchurch, *U.K.* 15 51 2N 1 0 E
Dymock, *U.K.* 14 51 58N 2 27W
Dysart, *U.K.* 21 56 8N 3 8W
Dzerzhinsk, *U.S.S.R.* 46 56 14N 43 30 E
Dzhambul, *U.S.S.R.* 48 42 54N 71 22 E
Dzungaria, *China* 60 44 10N 88 0 E

E

Eaglesfield, *U.K.* 21 55 3N 3 12W
Eagleshan, *U.K.* 20 55 44N 4 18W
Eakring, *U.K.* 19 53 9N 0 59W
Ealing, *U.K.* 15 51 30N 0 19W
Earby, *U.K.* 18 53 55N 2 8W
Eardisland, *U.K.* 14 52 14N 2 50W
Eardisley, *U.K.* 14 52 8N 3 0W
Earith, *U.K.* 15 52 21N 0 1 E
Earl Shilton, *U.K.* 14 52 35N 1 20W
Earl Soham, *U.K.* 15 52 14N 1 15 E
Earls Barton, *U.K.* 15 52 16N 0 44W
Earl's Colne, *U.K.* 15 51 56N 0 43 E
Earlsferry, *U.K.* 21 56 11N 2 50W
Earlston, *U.K.* 21 55 39N 2 40W
Earn —►, *U.K.* 21 56 20N 3 19W
Earn, L., *U.K.* 20 56 23N 4 14W
Earsdon, *U.K.* 21 55 4N 1 30W
Easebourne, *U.K.* 15 51 0N 0 42W
Easington, *Durham, U.K.* 19 54 50N 1 24W
Easington, *Humberside, U.K.* 19 53 40N 0 7 E
Easington Colliery, *U.K.* 19 54 49N 1 19W
Easingwold, *U.K.* 19 54 8N 1 11W
East Anglian Hts., *U.K.* 15 52 10N 0 17 E
East Bergholt, *U.K.* 15 51 58N 1 2 E
East Brent, *U.K.* 14 51 14N 2 55W
East China Sea, *Asia* 61 30 5N 126 0 E
East Cowes, *U.K.* 14 50 45N 1 17W
East Dereham, *U.K.* 15 52 40N 0 57 E
East Fen, *U.K.* 19 53 4N 0 5 E
East Germany ■, *Europe* 42 52 0N 12 0 E
East Grinstead, *U.K.* 15 51 8N 0 1W
East Harling, *U.K.* 15 52 26N 0 55 E
East Ilsley, *U.K.* 14 51 33N 1 15W
East Indies, *Asia* 50 0 0 120 0 E
East Kilbride, *U.K.* 20 55 46N 4 10W
East Kirkby, *U.K.* 19 53 5N 1 15W
East Linton, *U.K.* 21 56 0N 2 40W
East London, *S. Afr.* 81 33 0S 27 55 E
East Markham, *U.K.* 19 53 15N 0 53W
East Moor, *U.K.* 19 53 15N 1 30W
East Retford, *U.K.* 19 53 19N 0 55W
East Siberian Sea, *U.S.S.R.* 49 73 0N 160 0 E
East Sussex □, *U.K.* 15 51 0N 0 20 E
East Wemyss, *U.K.* 21 56 8N 3 5W
East Wittering, *U.K.* 15 50 46N 0 53W
East Woodhay, *U.K.* 14 51 21N 1 26W
Eastbourne, *U.K.* 15 50 46N 0 18 E
Eastchurch, *U.K.* 15 51 23N 0 53 E
Easter Islands, *Pac. Oc.* 65 27 0S 109 0W
Eastern Ghats, *India* 58 14 0N 78 50 E
Eastleigh, *U.K.* 14 50 58N 1 21W
Eastnor, *U.K.* 14 52 2N 2 22W
Easton, *Avon, U.K.* 14 51 28N 2 42W
Easton, *Dorset, U.K.* 14 50 32N 2 27W
Easton, *Northants., U.K.* 15 52 37N 0 31W
Eastry, *U.K.* 15 51 15N 1 19 E
Eastwood, *U.K.* 19 53 2N 1 17W
Eaton, *U.K.* 15 52 52N 0 46W
Eaton Socon, *U.K.* 15 52 13N 0 18W
Eau Claire, *U.S.A.* 92 44 46N 91 30W
Ebberston, *U.K.* 19 54 14N 0 35W
Ebbw Vale, *U.K.* 17 51 47N 3 12W
Ebro —►, *Sp.* 37 40 43N 0 54 E
Ecclefechan, *U.K.* 21 55 3N 3 18W
Eccleshall, *U.K.* 14 52 52N 2 14W
Ech Cheliff, *Alg.* 78 36 10N 1 20 E
Echo Bay, *Canada* 88 66 5N 117 55W
Echuca, *Austral.* 70 36 10S 144 20 E
Eck, L., *U.K.* 20 56 5N 5 0W
Eckington, *U.K.* 19 53 19N 1 21W
Ecuador ■, *S. Am.* 100 2 0S 78 0W
Edam, *Neth.* 36 52 31N 5 3 E
Eday, *U.K.* 23 59 11N 2 47W
Eddrachillis B., *U.K.* 22 58 16N 5 10W
Eddystone, *U.K.* 16 50 11N 4 16W
Ede, *Neth.* 36 52 4N 5 40 E
Eden —►, *U.K.* 18 54 57N 3 2W
Edenbridge, *U.K.* 15 51 12N 0 4 E
Edenderry, *Ire.* 25 53 21N 7 3W
Edge Hill, *U.K.* 14 52 7N 1 28W
Edinburgh, *U.K.* 21 55 57N 3 12W
Edington, *U.K.* 14 51 17N 2 6W
Edmondbyers, *U.K.* 18 54 50N 1 59W
Edmonton, *Canada* 88 53 30N 113 30W
Edmundston, *Canada* 93 47 23N 68 20W
Edward, L., *Africa* 80 0 25S 29 40 E
Egersund, *Nor.* 45 58 26N 6 1 E
Egham, *U.K.* 15 51 25N 0 33W
Egmont, Mt., *N.Z.* 71 39 17S 174 5 E
Egremont, *U.K.* 18 54 28N 3 33W
Egton, *U.K.* 19 54 27N 0 45W
Egypt ■, *Africa* 79 28 0N 31 0 E
Eifel, *W. Ger.* 36 50 10N 6 45 E
Eigg, *U.K.* 22 56 54N 6 10W
Eighty Mile Beach, *Austral.* 66 19 30S 120 40 E
Eil, L., *U.K.* 22 56 50N 5 15W
Eildon, L., *Austral.* 70 37 10S 146 0 E
Eindhoven, *Neth.* 36 51 26N 5 30 E
Eire ■, *Europe* 25 53 0N 8 0W
El Aaiún, *W. Sah.* 78 27 9N 13 12W
El Asnam = Ech Cheliff, *Alg.* 78 36 10N 1 20 E
El Faiyûm, *Egypt* 79 29 19N 30 50 E
El Fâsher, *Sudan* 79 13 33N 25 26 E
El Gîza, *Egypt* 79 30 0N 31 10 E
El Jadida, *Mor.* 78 33 11N 8 17W
El Mahalla el Kubra, *Egypt* 79 31 0N 31 0 E
El Mansûra, *Egypt* 79 31 0N 31 19 E
El Minyâ, *Egypt* 79 28 7N 30 33 E
El Obeid, *Sudan* 79 13 8N 30 10 E
El Paso, *U.S.A.* 90 31 50N 106 30W
El Qâhira = Cairo, *Egypt* 79 30 1N 31 14 E
El Salvador ■, *Cent. Am.* 94 13 50N 89 0W
Elba, *It.* 40 42 48N 10 15 E
Elbasani, *Alb.* 41 41 9N 20 9 E
Elbe —►, *W. Ger.* 42 53 50N 9 0 E
Elbląg, *Pol.* 43 54 10N 19 25 E
Elburz Mts., *Iran* 56 36 0N 52 0 E
Elche, *Sp.* 37 38 15N 0 42W
Eldoret, *Kenya* 80 0 30N 35 17 E
Eleuthera, *Baham.* 95 25 0N 76 20W
Elgin, *U.K.* 23 57 39N 3 20W
Elham, *U.K.* 15 51 9N 1 7 E
Elie, *U.K.* 21 56 11N 2 50W

Elishaw, U.K. 21 55 16N 2 14W
Elizabeth, Austral. 67 34 42S 138 41 E
Elizabeth, U.S.A. 93 40 37N 74 12W
Elland, U.K. 19 53 41N 1 49W
Ellen →, U.K. 18 54 44N 3 30W
Eller Beck Bridge, U.K. 19 54 23N 0 40W
Ellesmere, U.K. 18 52 55N 2 53W
Ellesmere I., Canada 103 79 30N 80 0W
Ellesmere Port, U.K. 18 53 17N 2 55W
Ellice Is. = Tuvalu ■, Pac. Oc. 64 8 0S 178 0 E
Ellington, U.K. 21 55 14N 1 34W
Ellon, U.K. 23 57 21N 2 5W
Elmira, U.S.A. 92 42 8N 76 49W
Elmswell, U.K. 15 52 14N 0 53 E
Eluru, India 59 16 48N 81 8 E
Ely, U.K. 15 52 24N 0 16 E
Emāmrūd, Iran 56 36 30N 55 0 E
Embleton, U.K. 21 55 30N 1 38W
Emden, W. Ger. 36 53 22N 7 12 E
Emerald, Austral. 67 23 32S 148 10 E
Emmeloord, Neth. 36 52 44N 5 46 E
Emmen, Neth. 36 52 48N 6 57 E
Ems →, W. Ger. 36 52 37N 9 26 E
Enard B., U.K. 22 58 5N 5 20W
Enderbury I., Pac. Oc. 64 3 8S 171 5W
Enderby, U.K. 14 52 35N 1 15W
Enderby Land, Ant. 103 66 0S 53 0 E
Enfield, U.K. 15 51 39N 0 4W
England □, U.K. 5 53 0N 2 0W
English Channel, Europe 15 50 0N 2 0W
Ennerdale Water, U.K. 18 54 32N 3 24W
Ennis, Ire. 25 52 51N 8 59W
Enniscorthy, Ire. 25 52 30N 6 35W
Enniskillen, U.K. 24 54 20N 7 40W
Ennistimon, Ire. 25 52 56N 9 18W
Enschede, Neth. 36 52 13N 6 53 E
Ensenada, Mex. 94 31 50N 116 50W
Enstone, U.K. 14 51 55N 1 25W
Entebbe, Uganda 80 0 4N 32 28 E
Enugu, Nig. 78 6 20N 7 30 E
Epping, U.K. 15 51 42N 0 8 E
Epping Forest, U.K. 15 51 40N 0 5 E
Epsom, U.K. 15 51 19N 0 16W
Epworth, U.K. 19 53 30N 0 50W
Equatorial Guinea ■, Africa 80 2 0S 8 0 E
Erebus, Mt., Ant. 103 77 35S 167 0 E
Erfurt, E. Ger. 42 50 58N 11 2 E
Eriboll, L., U.K. 23 58 28N 4 41W
Erie, U.S.A. 92 42 10N 80 7W
Erie, L., N. Am. 92 42 15N 81 0W
Eritrea □, Eth. 79 14 0N 41 0 E
Erlangen, W. Ger. 42 49 35N 11 0 E
Erne →, U.K. 24 54 30N 8 16W
Erne, Lough, U.K. 24 54 26N 7 46W
Erode, India 58 11 24N 77 45 E
Errigal, Mt., Ire. 24 55 2N 8 8W
Erris Hd., Ire. 24 54 19N 10 0W
Errol, U.K. 21 56 24N 3 13W
Erzurum, Turk. 47 39 57N 41 15 E
Esbjerg, Den. 45 55 29N 8 29 E
Esch, Neth. 36 51 37N 5 17 E
Eschweiler, W. Ger. 36 50 49N 6 14 E
Escrick, U.K. 19 53 53N 1 3W
Eşfahān, Iran 56 33 0N 53 0 E
Esk →, Cumbria, U.K. 18 54 23N 3 21W
Esk →, Dumf. & Gall., U.K. 21 54 58N 3 4W
Esk →, N. Yorks., U.K. 19 54 27N 0 36W
Eskdale, U.K. 21 55 12N 3 4W
Eskifjörður, Ice. 44 65 3N 13 55W
Eskilstuna, Swed. 45 59 22N 16 32 E
Eskimo Pt., Canada 88 61 10N 94 15W
Eskişehir, Turk. 47 39 50N 30 35 E
Esmeraldas, Ecuad. 100 1 0N 79 40W
Esperance, Austral. 66 33 45S 121 55 E
Espinhaço, Serra do, Brazil 101 17 30S 43 30W
Essen, W. Ger. 36 51 28N 6 59 E
Essex □, U.K. 15 51 48N 0 30 E
Eston, U.K. 19 54 33N 1 6W
Estonian S.S.R. □, U.S.S.R. 46 58 30N 25 30 E
Etchingham, U.K. 15 51 0N 0 27 E
Ethiopia ■, Africa 78 8 0N 40 0 E
Ethiopian Highlands, Eth. 72 10 0N 37 0 E
Etive, L., U.K. 20 56 30N 5 12W
Etna, It. 40 37 45N 15 0 E
Eton, U.K. 15 51 29N 0 37W
Ettington, U.K. 14 52 8N 1 38W
Ettrick Forest, U.K. 21 55 30N 3 0W
Ettrick Water, U.K. 21 55 31N 2 55W
Eugene, U.S.A. 90 44 0N 123 8W
Euphrates →, Asia 56 31 0N 47 25 E
Euston, Austral. 70 34 30S 142 46 E
Euxton, U.K. 18 53 41N 2 42W
Evansville, U.S.A. 92 38 0N 87 35W
Evercreech, U.K. 14 51 8N 2 30W
Everest, Mt., Nepal 60 28 5N 86 58 E
Evesham, U.K. 14 52 6N 1 57W
Évora, Port. 37 38 33N 7 57W
Évreux, Fr. 34 49 0N 1 8 E
Évvoia, Greece 41 38 30N 24 0 E
Ewe, L., U.K. 22 57 49N 5 38W
Ewell, U.K. 15 51 20N 0 15W
Ewhurst, U.K. 15 51 9N 0 25W
Exe →, U.K. 16 50 38N 3 27W
Exeter, U.K. 16 50 43N 3 31W
Exford, U.K. 14 51 8N 3 39W
Exminster, U.K. 16 50 40N 3 29W
Exmoor, U.K. 16 51 10N 3 59W
Exmouth, Austral. 66 21 54S 114 10 E
Exmouth, U.K. 16 50 37N 3 26W
Exmouth G., Austral. 66 22 15S 114 15 E
Exton, U.K. 15 52 42N 0 38W
Eyam, U.K. 19 53 17N 1 40W
Eye, Cambs., U.K. 15 52 36N 0 11W
Eye, Suffolk, U.K. 15 52 19N 1 9 E
Eye Pen., U.K. 22 58 13N 6 10W
Eyemouth, U.K. 21 55 53N 2 5W
Eynsham, U.K. 14 51 47N 1 21W
Eyre, L., Austral. 67 29 30S 137 26 E
Eyre Cr. →, Austral. 67 26 40S 139 0 E
Eyre Pen., Austral. 66 33 30S 137 17 E

F

Fair Hd., U.K. 24 55 14N 6 10W
Fairbanks, U.S.A. 88 64 50N 147 50W
Fairfield, Austral. 70 33 53S 150 57 E
Fairford, U.K. 14 51 42N 1 48W
Fairlie, N.Z. 71 44 5S 170 49 E
Fairlie, U.K. 20 55 44N 4 52W
Fairlight, U.K. 15 50 53N 0 40 E
Faisalabad, Pak. 58 31 30N 73 5 E
Faizabad, India 59 26 45N 82 10 E
Fakenham, U.K. 15 52 50N 0 51 E
Faldingworth, U.K. 19 53 21N 0 22W
Falkenberg, Swed. 45 56 54N 12 30 E
Falkirk, U.K. 21 56 0N 3 47W
Falkland, U.K. 21 56 15N 3 13W
Falkland Is., Atl. Oc. 102 51 30S 59 0W
Fall River, U.S.A. 93 41 45N 71 5W
Falmouth, U.K. 16 50 9N 5 5W
Falmouth B., U.K. 16 50 7N 5 3W
Falstone, U.K. 21 55 10N 2 26W
Falun, Swed. 45 60 37N 15 37 E
Famagusta, Cyprus 47 35 8N 33 55 E
Fannich, L., U.K. 22 57 40N 5 0W
Fareham, U.K. 14 50 52N 1 11W
Faringdon, U.K. 14 51 39N 1 34W
Farnborough, U.K. 15 51 17N 0 46W
Farne Is., U.K. 19 55 38N 1 37W
Farnham, U.K. 15 51 13N 0 49W
Farnworth, U.K. 18 53 33N 2 24W
Faroe Is., Atl. Oc. 26 62 0N 7 0W
Farrar →, U.K. 23 57 30N 4 30W
Faslane, U.K. 20 56 3N 4 49W
Fastnet Rock, Ire. 25 51 22N 9 37W
Fauldhouse, U.K. 21 55 50N 3 44W
Faversham, U.K. 15 51 18N 0 54 E
Fawley, U.K. 14 50 49N 1 20W
Faya-Largeau, Chad 79 17 58N 19 6 E
Fayetteville, U.S.A. 91 35 0N 78 58W
Fazeley, U.K. 14 52 36N 1 42W
Fdérik, Maurit. 78 22 40N 12 45W
Feale →, Ire. 25 52 26N 9 40W
Feilding, N.Z. 71 40 13S 175 35 E
Feira de Santana, Brazil 101 12 15S 38 57W
Felixstowe, U.K. 15 51 58N 1 22 E
Felpham, U.K. 15 50 47N 0 38W
Felton, U.K. 21 55 18N 1 42W
Feltwell, U.K. 15 52 29N 0 32 E
Fenit, Ire. 25 52 17N 9 51W
Fenny Bentley, U.K. 19 53 4N 1 43W
Fenny Compton, U.K. 14 52 9N 1 20W
Fenny Stratford, U.K. 15 51 59N 0 42W
Fens, The, U.K. 15 52 45N 0 2 E
Fenwick, U.K. 20 55 38N 4 25W
Fergana, U.S.S.R. 48 40 23N 71 19 E
Fermanagh □, U.K. 24 54 21N 7 40W
Fermoy, Ire. 25 52 4N 8 18W
Fernhurst, U.K. 15 51 3N 0 43W
Ferrara, It. 40 44 50N 11 36 E
Ferryhill, U.K. 19 54 42N 1 32W
Fès, Mor. 78 34 0N 5 0W
Fetlar, U.K. 22 60 36N 0 52W
Ffestiniog, U.K. 17 52 58N 3 56W
Fianarantsoa, Madag. 81 21 26S 47 5 E
Fife □, U.K. 21 56 13N 3 2W
Fife Ness, U.K. 21 56 17N 2 35W
Fiji ■, Pac. Oc. 64 17 20S 179 0 E
Filby, U.K. 15 52 40N 1 39 E
Filey, U.K. 19 54 13N 0 18W
Filey B., U.K. 19 54 12N 0 15W
Filton, U.K. 14 51 29N 2 34W
Fincham, U.K. 15 52 38N 0 30 E
Findhorn →, U.K. 23 57 38N 3 38W
Findon, U.K. 15 50 53N 0 24W
Finedon, U.K. 15 52 20N 0 40W
Fingest, U.K. 15 51 35N 0 52W
Finisterre, C., Sp. 37 42 50N 9 19W
Finland ■, Europe 44 63 0N 27 0 E
Finland, G. of, Europe 45 60 0N 26 0 E
Finn →, Ire. 24 54 50N 7 55W
Finnart, U.K. 20 56 7N 4 48W
Finnmark fylke □, Nor. 44 69 30N 25 0 E
Finstown, U.K. 23 59 0N 3 8W
Fionnphort, U.K. 20 56 19N 6 23W
Firozabad, India 58 27 10N 78 25 E
Fishguard, U.K. 17 51 59N 4 59W
Fishtoft, U.K. 19 52 27N 0 2 E
Fitzroy →, Austral. 66 17 31S 123 35 E
Flamborough, U.K. 19 54 7N 0 7W
Flamborough Hd., U.K. 19 54 8N 0 4W
Flanders, Belg. 34 51 10N 3 15 E
Flatey, Ice. 44 65 22N 22 56W
Fleet, U.K. 15 51 16N 0 50W
Fleetwood, U.K. 18 53 55N 3 1W
Flensburg, W. Ger. 42 54 46N 9 28 E
Fletton, U.K. 15 52 34N 0 13W
Flimby, U.K. 18 54 42N 3 31W
Flinders →, Austral. 67 17 36S 140 36 E
Flinders Ranges, Austral. 67 31 30S 138 30 E
Flint, U.K. 17 53 15N 3 7W
Flint, U.S.A. 92 43 5N 83 40W
Flint →, U.S.A. 91 30 52N 84 38W
Flitwick, U.K. 15 51 59N 0 30W
Flodden, U.K. 19 55 37N 2 8W
Florence, It. 40 43 47N 11 15 E
Flores, Indon. 63 8 35S 121 0 E
Flores Sea, Indon. 63 6 30S 124 0 E
Florianópolis, Brazil 102 27 30S 48 30W
Florida □, U.S.A. 91 28 30N 82 0W
Florida, Straits of, U.S.A. 95 25 0N 80 0W
Florida Keys, U.S.A. 91 25 0N 80 40W
Florissant, U.S.A. 90 38 48N 90 20W
Flushing = Vlissingen, Neth. 36 51 26N 3 34 E
Fóggia, It. 40 41 28N 15 31 E
Folkestone, U.K. 15 51 5N 1 11 E
Fontainebleau, Fr. 34 48 24N 2 40 E
Forbach, Fr. 34 49 10N 6 52 E
Ford, U.K. 20 56 10N 5 27W
Fordham, U.K. 15 52 19N 0 23 E
Fordingbridge, U.K. 14 50 56N 1 48W
Forest Row, U.K. 15 51 6N 0 3 E
Forfar, U.K. 23 56 40N 2 53W
Formby, U.K. 18 53 34N 3 4W
Formby Pt., U.K. 18 53 33N 3 7W
Formosa = Taiwan ■, Asia 61 23 30N 121 0 E
Formosa Strait, Asia 61 24 40N 120 0 E
Forres, U.K. 23 57 37N 3 38W
Fort Augustus, U.K. 23 57 9N 4 40W
Fort Collins, U.S.A. 90 40 30N 105 4W
Fort-de-France, Mart. 94 14 36N 61 2W
Fort George, Canada 89 53 50N 79 0W
Fort Lauderdale, U.S.A. 91 26 10N 80 5W
Fort McMurray, Canada 88 56 44N 111 7W
Fort Smith, U.S.A. 90 35 25N 94 25W
Fort Wayne, U.S.A. 92 41 5N 85 10W
Fort William, U.K. 22 56 48N 5 8W
Fort Worth, U.S.A. 90 32 45N 97 25W
Fortaleza, Brazil 101 3 45S 38 35W
Forth, U.K. 21 55 45N 3 42W
Forth, Firth of, U.K. 21 56 5N 2 55W
Forth Bridge, U.K. 21 56 0N 3 24W
Fortrose, U.K. 23 57 35N 4 10W
Foshan, China 61 23 4N 113 5 E
Fothergill, U.K. 18 54 43N 3 30W
Fotheringhay, U.K. 15 52 32N 0 28W
Foulness I., U.K. 15 51 36N 0 55 E
Foulness Pt., U.K. 15 51 36N 0 59 E
Foulsham, U.K. 15 52 48N 1 1 E
Fountainhall, U.K. 21 55 45N 2 55W
Fountains Abbey, U.K. 19 54 8N 1 35W
Fovant, U.K. 14 51 4N 2 0W
Foveaux Str., N.Z. 71 46 42S 168 10 E
Fowey, U.K. 16 50 20N 4 39W
Fowey →, U.K. 16 50 20N 4 39W
Fownhope, U.K. 14 52 0N 2 37W
Foxdale, U.K. 18 54 12N 4 38W
Foxe Chan., Canada 89 65 0N 80 0W
Foyle, Lough, U.K. 24 55 6N 7 8W
Foynes, Ire. 25 52 37N 9 5W
Fraddon, U.K. 16 50 22N 4 55W
Framlingham, U.K. 15 52 14N 1 20 E
France ■, Europe 34 47 0N 3 0 E
Frankfurt am Main, W. Ger. 42 50 7N 8 40 E
Frankston, Austral. 70 38 8S 145 8 E
Frant, U.K. 15 51 5N 0 17 E
Franz Josef Land, U.S.S.R. 48 82 0N 55 0 E
Fraser →, Canada 88 49 7N 123 11W
Fraser I., Austral. 67 25 15S 153 10 E
Fraserburgh, U.K. 23 57 41N 2 0W
Fredericton, Canada 93 45 57N 66 40W
Frederikshavn, Den. 45 57 28N 10 31 E
Fredrikstad, Nor. 45 59 13N 10 57 E
Freetown, Sa. Leone 78 8 30N 13 17W
Freiburg, W. Ger. 42 48 0N 7 52 E
Fremantle, Austral. 66 32 7S 115 47 E
French Guiana ■, S. Am. 101 4 0N 53 0W
French Polynesia □, Pac. Oc. 65 20 0S 145 0 E
Freshwater, U.K. 14 50 42N 1 31W
Fresnillo, Mex. 94 23 10N 103 0W
Fresno, U.S.A. 90 36 47N 119 50W
Freuchie, U.K. 21 56 14N 3 8W
Fridaythorpe, U.K. 19 54 2N 0 40W
Friesland □, Neth. 36 53 5N 5 50 E
Frimley, U.K. 15 51 18N 0 43W
Frinton-on-Sea, U.K. 15 51 50N 1 16 E
Frisa, Loch, U.K. 20 56 34N 6 5W
Frisian Is., Europe 36 53 30N 6 0 E
Frizington, U.K. 18 54 33N 3 30W
Frobisher B., Canada 89 62 30N 66 0W
Frodsham, U.K. 18 53 17N 2 45W
Frome, U.K. 14 51 16N 2 17W
Frome →, U.K. 14 50 44N 2 5W
Frome, L., Austral. 67 30 45S 139 45 E
Frunze, U.S.S.R. 48 42 54N 74 46 E
Fuji-San, Jap. 62 35 22N 138 44 E
Fujian □, China 61 26 0N 118 0 E
Fukui, Jap. 62 36 0N 136 10 E
Fukuoka, Jap. 62 33 39N 130 21 E
Fukushima, Jap. 62 37 44N 140 28 E
Fukuyama, Jap. 62 34 35N 133 20 E
Fulwood, U.K. 18 53 47N 2 41W
Fundy, B. of, Canada 93 45 0N 66 0W
Furneaux Group, Austral. 66 40 10S 147 50 E
Furness, Pen., U.K. 18 54 12N 3 10W
Fürth, W. Ger. 42 49 29N 11 0 E
Fury and Hecla Str., Canada 89 69 56N 84 0W
Fushun, China 61 41 50N 123 56 E
Fuxin, China 61 42 5N 121 48 E
Fuzhou, China 61 26 5N 119 16 E
Fylde, U.K. 18 53 50N 2 58W
Fylingdales Moor, U.K. 19 54 22N 0 32W
Fyn, Den. 45 55 20N 10 30 E
Fyne, L., U.K. 20 56 0N 5 20W
Fyvie, U.K. 23 57 26N 2 24W

G

Gabès, Tunisia 78 33 53N 10 2 E
Gabon ■, Africa 80 0 10S 10 0 E
Gaborone, Bots. 81 24 45S 25 57 E
Gabrovo, Bulg. 41 42 52N 25 19 E
Gainesville, U.S.A. 90 29 38N 82 20W
Gainford, U.K. 19 54 34N 1 44W
Gainsborough, U.K. 19 53 23N 0 46W
Gairdner L., Austral. 66 31 30S 136 0 E
Gairloch, U.K. 22 57 42N 5 40W
Gairloch, L., U.K. 22 57 43N 5 45W
Galápagos, Pac. Oc. 65 0 0 89 0W
Galashiels, U.K. 21 55 37N 2 50W
Galaţi, Rom. 43 45 27N 28 2 E
Galgate, U.K. 18 53 59N 2 47W
Galilee, Sea of = Kinneret, Lake, Isr. 57 32 45N 35 35 E
Galle, Sri L. 58 6 5N 80 10 E
Galley Hd., Ire. 25 51 32N 8 56W
Gällivare, Swed. 44 67 9N 20 40 E
Galloway, U.K. 20 55 0N 4 25W
Galloway, Mull of, U.K. 20 54 38N 4 50W
Galmpton, U.K. 16 50 23N 3 32W
Galston, U.K. 20 55 36N 4 22W
Galty Mts., Ire. 25 52 22N 8 10W
Galtymore, Ire. 25 52 22N 8 12W
Galveston, U.S.A. 91 29 15N 94 48W
Galway, Ire. 25 53 16N 9 4W
Galway □, Ire. 24 53 16N 9 3W
Galway B., Ire. 25 53 10N 9 20W
Gambia ■, W. Afr. 78 13 25N 16 0W
Gamboa, Pan. 94 9 8N 79 42W
Gamlingay, U.K. 15 52 9N 0 11W
Gan Jiang →, China 61 29 15N 116 0 E
Ganga →, India 59 23 20N 90 30 E
Ganganagar, India 58 29 56N 73 56 E
Ganges = Ganga →, India 59 23 20N 90 30 E
Gansu □, China 60 36 0N 104 0 E
Gao, Mali 78 16 15N 0 5W
Gap, Fr. 34 44 33N 6 5 E
Garboldisham, U.K. 15 52 24N 0 57 E
Garda, L. di, It. 40 45 40N 10 40 E
Gare, L., U.K. 20 56 1N 4 50W
Garelochhead, U.K. 20 56 7N 4 50W
Garforth, U.K. 19 53 48N 1 22W
Gargrave, U.K. 18 53 58N 2 7W
Garlieston, U.K. 20 54 47N 4 22W
Garonne →, Fr. 35 45 2N 0 36W
Garoua, Cam. 80 9 19N 13 21 E
Garry →, U.K. 23 56 47N 3 47W
Garsdale Head, U.K. 18 54 19N 2 19W
Garstang, U.K. 18 53 53N 2 47W
Garston, U.K. 18 53 21N 2 55W
Garvald, U.K. 21 55 55N 2 39W
Garvellachs, Is., U.K. 20 56 14N 5 48W
Gary, U.S.A. 92 41 35N 87 20W
Garzê, China 60 31 39N 99 58 E
Gascony, Fr. 35 43 45N 0 20 E
Gascoyne →, Austral. 66 24 52S 113 37 E
Gaspé, Pén. de, Canada 93 48 45N 65 40W
Gatehouse of Fleet, U.K. 20 54 53N 4 10W
Gateshead, U.K. 19 54 57N 1 37W
Gatley, U.K. 18 53 25N 2 15W
Gatun, Pan. 94 9 16N 79 55W
Gatun, L., Pan. 94 9 7N 79 56W
Gävle, Swed. 45 60 40N 17 9 E
Gawthwaite, U.K. 18 54 16N 3 6W
Gaya, India 59 24 47N 85 4 E
Gayton, U.K. 15 52 45N 0 35 E
Gaywood, U.K. 15 52 46N 0 26 E
Gaza, Egypt 57 31 30N 34 28 E
Gaziantep, Turk. 47 37 6N 37 23 E
Gdańsk, Pol. 43 54 22N 18 40 E
Gdańsk Bay, Pol. 43 54 30N 19 20 E
Gdynia, Pol. 43 54 35N 18 33 E
Gedney, U.K. 15 52 47N 0 5 E
Geelong, Austral. 70 38 10S 144 22 E
Gejiu, China 60 23 20N 103 10 E
Gelderland □, Neth. 36 52 5N 6 10 E

Gelsenkirchen, W. Ger. 36 51 30N 7 5 E
Geneva, Switz. 42 46 12N 6 9 E
Geneva, L., Switz. 42 46 26N 6 30 E
Genk, Belg. 36 50 58N 5 32 E
Gennargentu, Mti. del, It. 40 40 0N 9 10 E
Genoa, It. 40 44 24N 8 56 E
Geographe Chan., Austral. 66 24 30S 113 0 E
George, S. Afr. 81 33 58S 22 29 E
George Town, Malay. 63 5 25N 100 15 E
Georgetown, Guy. 100 6 50N 58 12W
Georgia □, U.S.A. 91 32 0N 82 0W
Georgia □, U.S.S.R. 47 42 0N 43 0 E
Georgian B., Canada 92 45 15N 81 0W
Gera, E. Ger. 42 50 53N 12 11 E
Geraldton, Austral. 66 28 48S 114 32 E
Germiston, S. Afr. 81 26 15S 28 10 E
Gerona, Sp. 37 41 58N 2 46 E
Gerrans B., U.K. 16 50 12N 4 57W
Gerrards Cross, U.K. 15 51 35N 0 32W
Ghaghara →, India 59 25 45N 84 40 E
Ghana ■, W. Afr. 78 6 0N 1 0W
Ghaziabad, India 58 28 42N 77 26 E
Ghent, Belg. 36 51 2N 3 42 E
Giant's Causeway, U.K. 24 55 15N 6 30W
Gibraltar, Europe 37 36 7N 5 22W
Gibraltar, Str. of, Medit. S. 37 35 55N 5 40W
Gibraltar Pt., U.K. 19 53 6N 0 20 E
Gibson Desert, Austral. 66 24 0S 126 0 E
Gifford, U.K. 21 55 54N 2 45W
Gifu, Jap. 62 35 30N 136 45 E
Giggleswick, U.K. 18 54 5N 2 19W
Gigha, U.K. 20 55 42N 5 45W
Gijón, Sp. 37 43 32N 5 42W
Gilbert Is. = Kiribati ■, Pac. Oc. 65 1 0N 176 0 E
Gillingham, Dorset, U.K. 14 51 2N 2 15W
Gillingham, Kent, U.K. 15 51 23N 0 34 E
Gilsland, U.K. 18 55 0N 2 34W
Girdle Ness, U.K. 23 57 9N 2 2W
Gironde →, Fr. 35 45 32N 1 7W
Girvan, U.K. 20 55 15N 4 50W
Girvan →, U.K. 20 55 18N 4 51W
Gisborne, N.Z. 71 38 39S 178 5 E
Gisburn, U.K. 18 53 56N 2 16W
Gizhiga, U.S.S.R. 49 62 3N 160 30 E
Gizhiga, G., U.S.S.R. 49 61 0N 158 0 E
Gladstone, Austral. 67 25 57S 114 17 E
Glanton, U.K. 21 55 25N 1 54W
Glasgow, U.K. 20 55 52N 4 14W
Glastonbury, U.K. 14 51 9N 2 42W
Glemsford, U.K. 15 52 6N 0 41 E
Glen →, U.K. 15 52 50N 0 7W
Glen Affric, U.K. 22 57 15N 5 0W
Glen Almond, U.K. 21 56 28N 3 50W
Glen Coe, U.K. 19 56 40N 5 0W
Glen Etive, U.K. 20 56 37N 5 0W
Glen Garry, U.K. 22 57 3N 5 7W
Glen Helen, U.K. 18 54 14N 4 35W
Glen Mor, U.K. 23 57 12N 4 37 E
Glen Moriston, U.K. 22 57 10N 4 58W
Glen Orchy, U.K. 20 56 27N 4 52W
Glen Spean, U.K. 23 56 53N 4 40W
Glenbarr, U.K. 20 55 34N 5 40W
Glendale, U.S.A. 90 34 7N 118 18W
Gleneagles, U.K. 21 56 16N 3 44W
Glengarriff, Ire. 25 51 45N 9 33W
Glenkens, The, U.K. 20 55 10N 4 15W
Glenluce, U.K. 20 54 53N 4 50W
Glenmaye, U.K. 18 54 11N 4 42W
Glenorchy, Austral. 67 31 55S 139 46 E
Glenrothes, U.K. 20 56 12N 3 11W
Glenties, Ire. 24 54 48N 8 18W
Glentrool Village, U.K. 20 55 5N 4 30W
Gliwice, Pol. 43 50 22N 18 41 E
Glossop, U.K. 18 53 27N 1 56W
Gloucester, U.K. 14 51 52N 2 15W
Gloucestershire □, U.K. 14 51 44N 2 10W
Gnosall, U.K. 14 52 48N 2 15W
Goa □, India 58 15 33N 73 59 E
Goat Fell, U.K. 20 55 37N 5 11W
Gobi, Asia 60 44 0N 111 0 E
Godalming, U.K. 15 51 12N 0 37W
Godavari →, India 58 16 25N 82 18 E
Godmanchester, U.K. 15 52 19N 0 11W
Godshill, U.K. 14 50 38N 1 13W
Godstone, U.K. 15 51 15N 0 3W
Goiânia, Brazil 101 16 43S 49 20W
Goil, L., U.K. 20 56 8N 4 52W
Gold Coast, Austral. 67 28 0S 153 25 E
Golden Vale, Ire. 25 52 33N 8 17W
Golspie, U.K. 23 57 58N 3 58W
Gomel, U.S.S.R. 46 52 28N 31 0 E
Gometra I., U.K. 20 56 30N 6 18W
Gómez Palacio, Mex. 94 25 40N 104 0W
Gonder, Eth. 79 12 39N 37 30 E
Good Hope, C. of, S. Afr. 81 34 24S 18 30 E
Goodrich, U.K. 14 51 52N 2 38W
Goodwood, U.K. 15 50 53N 0 44W
Goole, U.K. 19 53 42N 0 52W
Goondiwindi, Austral. 67 28 30S 150 21 E
Gorakhpur, India 59 26 47N 83 23 E
Gordon, U.K. 21 55 41N 2 32W
Gorebridge, U.K. 21 55 51N 3 2W
Gorey, Ire. 25 52 41N 6 18W
Goring, Oxon., U.K. 14 51 31N 1 8W
Goring, W. Sussex, U.K. 15 50 49N 0 26W
Gorki, U.S.S.R. 46 56 20N 44 0 E
Gorleston, U.K. 15 52 35N 1 44 E
Görlitz, E. Ger. 42 51 10N 14 59 E
Gort, Ire. 25 53 4N 8 50W
Gorzów Wielkopolski, Pol. 42 52 43N 15 15 E
Gosberton, U.K. 19 52 52N 0 10W
Gosford, Austral. 70 33 23S 151 18 E
Gosforth, U.K. 18 54 24N 3 27W
Gosport, U.K. 14 50 48N 1 8W
Göteborg, Swed. 45 57 43N 11 59 E
Gotha, E. Ger. 42 50 56N 10 42 E
Gotland, Swed. 45 57 30N 18 33 E
Gouda, Neth. 36 52 1N 4 42 E
Goudhurst, U.K. 15 51 7N 0 28 E
Gouin, Rés., Canada 93 48 35N 74 40W
Goulburn, Austral. 70 34 44S 149 44 E
Gourock, U.K. 20 55 58N 4 49W
Governador Valadares, Brazil 101 18 15S 41 57W
Gower, The, U.K. 17 51 35N 4 10W
Gowna, L., Ire. 24 53 52N 7 35W
Gowrie, Carse of, U.K. 21 56 30N 3 10W
Goya, Arg. 102 29 10S 59 10W
Gozo, Malta 40 36 0N 14 13 E
Grafham Water, U.K. 15 52 18N 0 17W
Grafton, Austral. 67 29 38S 152 58 E
Graham Bell, I., U.S.S.R. 48 80 5N 70 0 E
Graham Land, Ant. 103 65 0S 64 0W
Grainthorpe, U.K. 19 53 27N 0 5 E
Grampian □, U.K. 23 57 0N 3 0W
Grampian Mts., U.K. 23 56 50N 4 0W
Gran Canaria, Can. Is. 78 27 55N 15 35W
Gran Chaco, S. Am. 96 25 0S 61 0W
Granada, Sp. 37 37 10N 3 35W
Granard, Ire. 24 53 47N 7 30W
Grand Bahama, Baham. 95 26 40N 78 30W
Grand Canyon National Park, U.S.A. 90 36 15N 112 20W
Grand Cayman, W. Ind. 95 19 20N 81 20W
Grand Rapids, U.S.A. 92 42 57N 86 40W
Grande de Santiago →, Mex. 94 21 36N 105 26W
Grande Prairie, Canada 88 55 10N 118 50W
Grange-over-Sands, U.K. 18 54 12N 2 55W
Grangemouth, U.K. 21 56 1N 3 43W
Grangetown, U.K. 19 54 36N 1 7W
Grantham, U.K. 19 52 55N 0 39W
Grantown-on-Spey, U.K. 23 57 19N 3 36W
Grantshouse, U.K. 21 55 53N 2 17W
Grasmere, U.K. 18 54 28N 3 2W
Grassington, U.K. 18 54 5N 2 0W
Gravesend, U.K. 15 51 25N 0 22 E
Grayrigg, U.K. 18 54 22N 2 40W
Grays, U.K. 15 51 28N 0 23 E
Graz, Austria 42 47 4N 15 27 E
Great Abaco I., Baham. 95 26 25N 77 10W
Great Australian Bight, Austral. 66 33 30S 130 0 E
Great Ayton, U.K. 19 54 29N 1 8W
Great Baddow, U.K. 15 51 43N 0 31 E
Great Barrier Reef, Austral. 67 18 0S 146 50 E
Great Basin, U.S.A. 90 40 0N 116 30W
Great Bear L., Canada 88 65 30N 120 0W
Great Bentley, U.K. 15 51 51N 1 5 E
Great Blasket I., Ire. 25 52 5N 10 30W
Great Britain, Europe 5 54 0N 2 15W
Great Chesterford, U.K. 15 52 4N 0 11 E
Great Clifton, U.K. 18 54 39N 3 29W
Great Divide, The, Austral. 70 35 0S 149 17 E
Great Dividing Ra., Austral. 67 23 0S 146 0 E
Great Dunmow, U.K. 15 51 52N 0 22 E
Great Falls, U.S.A. 90 47 27N 111 12W
Great Harwood, U.K. 18 53 43N 2 30W
Great Inagua I., Baham. 95 21 0N 73 20W
Great Indian Desert = Thar Desert, India 58 28 0N 72 0 E
Great Malvern, U.K. 14 52 7N 2 19W
Great Massingham, U.K. 15 52 47N 0 41 E
Great Missenden, U.K. 15 51 42N 0 42W
Great Orme's Head, U.K. 17 53 20N 3 52W
Great Ouse →, U.K. 15 52 47N 0 22 E
Great Plains, N. Am. 82 47 0N 105 0W
Great Salt Lake, U.S.A. 90 41 0N 112 30W
Great Sandy Desert, Austral. 66 21 0S 124 0 E
Great Shefford, U.K. 14 51 29N 1 27W
Great Shelford, U.K. 15 52 9N 0 9 E
Great Shunner Fell, U.K. 18 54 22N 2 16W
Great Slave L., Canada 88 61 23N 115 38W
Great Stour = Stour →, U.K. 15 51 15N 1 20 E
Great Torrington, U.K. 16 50 57N 4 9W
Great Victoria Desert, Austral. 66 29 30S 126 30 E
Great Waltham, U.K. 15 51 47N 0 29 E
Great Whernside, U.K. 18 54 9N 1 59W
Great Wyrley, U.K. 14 52 40N 2 1W
Great Yarmouth, U.K. 15 52 40N 1 45 E
Great Yeldham, U.K. 15 52 1N 0 33 E
Greater Antilles, W. Ind. 95 17 40N 74 0W
Greater London □, U.K. 15 51 30N 0 5W
Greater Manchester □, U.K. 18 53 30N 2 15W
Greater Sunda Is., Indon. 63 7 0S 112 0 E
Greatham, U.K. 19 54 38N 1 14W
Greece ■, Europe 41 40 0N 23 0 E
Greeley, U.S.A. 90 40 30N 104 40W
Green B., U.S.A. 92 45 0N 87 30W
Green Bay, U.S.A. 92 44 30N 88 0W
Green Hammerton, U.K. 19 54 2N 1 17W
Green Lowther, U.K. 21 55 22N 3 44W
Greenhead, U.K. 21 54 58N 2 31W
Greenland ■, N. Am. 89 66 0N 45 0W
Greenland Sea, Arctic 103 73 0N 10 0W
Greenlaw, U.K. 21 55 42N 2 28W
Greenock, U.K. 20 55 57N 4 46W
Greenodd, U.K. 18 54 14N 3 3W
Greenore, Ire. 24 54 2N 6 8W
Greenore Pt., Ire. 25 52 15N 6 20W
Greensboro, U.S.A. 91 36 7N 79 46W
Greenwich, U.K. 15 51 28N 0 0 E
Grenada ■, W. Ind. 94 12 10N 61 40W
Grenoble, Fr. 35 45 12N 5 42 E
Greta →, U.K. 18 54 9N 2 36W
Gretna, U.K. 21 54 59N 3 4W
Gretna Green, U.K. 21 55 0N 3 3W
Gretton, U.K. 15 52 33N 0 40W
Grey Range, Austral. 67 27 0S 143 30 E
Greymouth, N.Z. 71 42 29S 171 13 E
Greystoke, U.K. 18 54 39N 2 52W
Gribbin Head, U.K. 16 50 18N 4 41W
Griffith, Austral. 70 34 18S 146 2 E
Grimsby, U.K. 19 53 35N 0 5W
Gris-Nez, C., Fr. 34 50 52N 1 35 E
Grizebeck, U.K. 18 54 16N 3 10W
Grodno, U.S.S.R. 46 53 42N 23 52 E
Groningen, Neth. 36 53 15N 6 35 E
Groote Eylandt, Austral. 67 14 0S 136 40 E
Groznyy, U.S.S.R. 47 43 20N 45 45 E
Gruinard B., U.K. 22 57 56N 5 35W
Guadalajara, Mex. 94 20 40N 103 20W
Guadalajara, Sp. 37 40 37N 3 12W
Guadalete →, Sp. 37 36 35N 6 13W
Guadeloupe ■, W. Ind. 94 16 20N 61 40W
Guadiana →, Port. 37 37 14N 7 22W
Guadix, Sp. 37 37 18N 3 11W
Gualeguay, Arg. 102 33 10S 59 14W
Guam, Pac. Oc. 64 13 27N 144 45 E
Guangdong □, China 61 23 0N 113 0 E
Guangxi Zhuangzu Zizhiqu □, China 61 24 0N 109 0 E
Guangzhou, China 61 23 5N 113 10 E
Guantánamo, Cuba 95 20 10N 75 14W
Guaporé →, Brazil 100 11 55S 65 4W
Guard Bridge, U.K. 21 56 21N 2 52W
Guardafui, C. = Asir, Ras, Som. 73 11 55N 51 10 E
Guatemala, Guat. 94 14 40N 90 22W
Guatemala ■, Cent. Am. 94 15 40N 90 30W
Guaviare →, Col. 100 4 3N 67 44W
Guayaquil, Ecuad. 100 2 15S 79 52W
Guaymas, Mex. 94 27 59N 110 54W
Guelph, Canada 92 43 35N 80 20W
Guernsey, U.K. 34 49 30N 2 35W
Guestling Green, U.K. 15 50 53N 0 40 E
Guildford, U.K. 15 51 14N 0 34W
Guilin, China 61 25 18N 110 15 E
Guinea ■, W. Afr. 78 10 20N 10 0W
Guinea, Gulf of, Atl. Oc. 72 3 0N 2 30 E
Guinea-Bissau ■, Africa 78 12 0N 15 0W
Guisborough, U.K. 19 54 32N 1 2W
Guiyang, China 60 26 32N 106 40 E
Guizhou □, China 60 27 0N 107 0 E
Gujarat □, India 58 23 20N 71 0 E
Gujranwala, Pak. 58 32 10N 74 12 E
Gujrat, Pak. 58 32 40N 74 2 E
Gulbarga, India 58 17 20N 76 50 E
Gulf, The, Asia 56 27 0N 50 0 E
Gullane, U.K. 21 56 2N 2 50W
Guntur, India 59 16 23N 80 30 E
Gurnard's Head, U.K. 16 50 12N 5 37W
Guyana ■, S. Am. 100 5 0N 59 0W
Gwalchmai, U.K. 17 53 16N 4 23W
Gwalior, India 58 26 12N 78 10 E
Gweebarra B., Ire. 24 54 52N 8 21W
Gweedore, Ire. 24 55 4N 8 15W
Gweek, U.K. 16 50 6N 5 12W
Gwennap, U.K. 16 50 12N 5 9W
Gwent □, U.K. 17 51 45N 2 55W
Gweru, Zimb. 81 19 28S 29 45 E
Gwynedd □, U.K. 17 53 0N 4 0W
Gympie, Austral. 67 26 11S 152 38 E
Györ, Hung. 43 47 41N 17 40 E

H

Haarlem, Neth. 36 52 23N 4 39 E
Hachinohe, Jap. 62 40 30N 141 29 E
Hackney, U.K. 15 51 33N 0 2W
Hackthorpe, U.K. 18 54 37N 2 42W
Haddenham, U.K. 15 51 46N 0 56W
Haddington, U.K. 21 55 57N 2 48W
Hadleigh, U.K. 15 52 3N 0 58 E
Hadley, U.K. 14 52 42N 2 28W
Hadlow, U.K. 15 51 12N 0 20 E
Hadrians Wall, U.K. 19 55 0N 2 30W
Haeju, N. Kor. 61 38 3N 125 45 E
Hafnarfjörður, Ice. 44 64 4N 21 57W
Hagen, W. Ger. 36 51 21N 7 29 E
Hags Hd., Ire. 25 52 57N 9 30W
Haifa, Isr. 57 32 46N 35 0 E
Haikou, China 61 20 1N 110 16 E
Ḥā'il, Si. Arab. 56 27 28N 41 45 E
Hailar, China 61 49 12N 119 37 E
Hailsham, U.K. 15 50 52N 0 17 E
Hainan, China 61 19 0N 109 30 E
Hainton, U.K. 19 53 21N 0 13W
Haiphong, Viet. 60 20 47N 106 41 E
Haiti ■, W. Ind. 95 19 0N 72 30W
Hakodate, Jap. 62 41 45N 140 44 E
Halberton, U.K. 16 50 55N 3 24W
Hale, U.K. 18 53 24N 2 21W
Halesowen, U.K. 14 52 27N 2 5W
Halesworth, U.K. 15 52 21N 1 30 E
Halifax, Canada 93 44 38N 63 35W
Halifax, U.K. 18 53 43N 1 51W
Halifax B., Austral. 67 18 50S 147 0 E
Halkirk, U.K. 23 58 30N 3 30W
Halle, Ger. 42 51 29N 12 0 E
Hallow, U.K. 14 52 14N 2 15W
Hallworthy, U.K. 16 50 38N 4 34W
Halmahera, Indon. 63 0 40N 128 0 E
Halmstad, Swed. 45 56 41N 12 52 E
Halstead, U.K. 15 51 59N 0 39 E
Haltwhistle, U.K. 21 54 58N 2 27W
Hamadān, Iran 56 34 52N 48 32 E
Hamāh, Syria 56 35 5N 36 40 E
Hamamatsu, Jap. 62 34 45N 137 45 E
Hambledon, U.K. 14 50 56N 1 6W
Hambleton Hills, U.K. 19 54 17N 1 12W
Hamburg, W. Ger. 42 53 32N 9 59 E
Hämeenlinna, Fin. 45 61 0N 24 28 E
Hamersley Ra., Austral. 66 22 0S 117 45 E
Hamilton, Berm. 95 32 15N 64 45W
Hamilton, Canada 92 43 15N 79 50W
Hamilton, N.Z. 71 37 47S 175 19 E
Hamilton, U.K. 21 55 47N 4 2W
Hamm, W. Ger. 36 51 40N 7 49 E
Hammerfest, Nor. 44 70 39N 23 41 E
Hammersmith, U.K. 15 51 30N 0 15W
Hammond, U.S.A. 92 41 40N 87 30W
Hampshire □, U.K. 14 51 3N 1 20W
Hampshire Downs, U.K. 14 51 10N 1 10W
Hampton in Arden, U.K. 14 52 26N 1 42W
Hangzhou, China 61 30 18N 120 11 E
Hanko, Fin. 45 59 59N 22 57 E
Hanningfield Water, U.K. 15 51 40N 0 30 E
Hanoi, Viet. 60 21 5N 105 55 E
Hanover, W. Ger. 42 52 23N 9 43 E
Haora, India 59 22 37N 88 20 E
Happy Valley, Canada 89 53 15N 60 20W
Harare, Zimb. 81 17 43S 31 2 E
Harbin, China 61 45 46N 126 51 E
Hardangerfjorden, Nor. 45 60 15N 6 0 E
Harewood, U.K. 19 53 54N 1 30W
Haringey, U.K. 15 51 35N 0 7W
Harlech, U.K. 17 52 52N 4 7W
Harleston, U.K. 15 52 25N 1 18 E
Harlingen, Neth. 36 53 11N 5 25 E
Harlow, U.K. 15 51 47N 0 9 E
Harpenden, U.K. 15 51 48N 0 20W
Harrietsham, U.K. 15 51 15N 0 41 E
Harrington, U.K. 18 54 37N 3 55W
Harris, U.K. 22 57 50N 6 55W
Harris, Sd. of, U.K. 22 57 44N 7 6W
Harrisburg, U.S.A. 93 40 18N 76 52W
Harrogate, U.K. 19 53 59N 1 32W
Harrow, U.K. 15 51 35N 0 15W
Hartest, U.K. 15 52 7N 0 41 E
Hartford, U.S.A. 93 41 47N 72 41W
Harthill, U.K. 21 55 52N 3 45W
Hartland, U.K. 16 50 59N 4 29W
Hartland Pt., U.K. 16 51 2N 4 32W
Hartlebury, U.K. 14 52 20N 2 13W
Hartlepool, U.K. 19 54 42N 1 11W
Hartley, U.K. 21 55 5N 1 27W
Hartpury, U.K. 14 51 55N 2 18W
Harwell, U.K. 14 51 40N 1 17W
Harwich, U.K. 15 51 56N 1 18 E
Harz, Europe 26 51 40N 10 40 E
Hasa, Si. Arab. 56 26 0N 49 0 E
Haslemere, U.K. 15 51 5N 0 41W
Haslingden, U.K. 18 53 43N 2 20W
Hasselt, Belg. 36 50 56N 5 21 E
Hastings, N.Z. 71 39 39S 176 52 E
Hastings, U.K. 15 50 51N 0 36 E
Hatfield, U.K. 15 51 46N 0 11W
Hatfield Broad Oak, U.K. 15 51 48N 0 16 E
Hatherleigh, U.K. 16 50 49N 4 4W
Hathersage, U.K. 19 53 20N 1 39W
Hatteras, C., U.S.A. 91 35 10N 75 30W
Haugh of Urr, U.K. 21 55 0N 3 51W
Haughley, U.K. 15 52 13N 0 59 E
Hauraki Gulf, N.Z. 71 36 35S 175 5 E
Hauxley, U.K. 21 55 21N 1 35W
Havana, Cuba 95 23 8N 82 22W
Havant, U.K. 15 50 51N 0 59W
Haverfordwest, U.K. 17 51 48N 4 59W
Haverhill, U.K. 15 52 6N 0 27 E
Haverigg, U.K. 18 54 12N 3 16W
Havering, U.K. 15 51 33N 0 20 E
Havre, Le, Fr. 34 49 30N 0 5 E
Hawaiian Is., Pac. Oc. 90 20 30N 156 0W
Hawera, N.Z. 71 39 35S 174 19 E
Hawes, U.K. 18 54 18N 2 12W
Haweswater, U.K. 18 54 32N 2 48W
Hawick, U.K. 21 55 25N 2 48W
Hawkchurch, U.K. 16 50 47N 2 56W

Hawke B., N.Z. 71 39 25S 177 20 E
Hawkesbury Upton, U.K. 14 51 34N 2 19W
Hawkhurst, U.K. 15 51 2N 0 31 E
Hawkshead, U.K. 18 54 23N 3 0W
Haworth, U.K. 18 53 50N 1 57W
Hawsker, U.K. 19 54 27N 0 34W
Haxby, U.K. 19 54 1N 1 4W
Hay-on-Wye, U.K. 17 52 4N 3 9W
Hay River, Canada 88 60 51N 115 44W
Hayburn Wyke, U.K. 19 54 22N 0 28W
Haydon Bridge, U.K. 21 54 58N 2 15W
Hayle, U.K. 16 50 12N 5 25W
Hayton, U.K. 18 54 55N 2 45W
Hayward's Heath, U.K. 15 51 0N 0 5W
Heacham, U.K. 15 52 55N 0 30 E
Headcorn, U.K. 15 51 10N 0 39 E
Heanor, U.K. 19 53 1N 1 20W
Heathfield, U.K. 15 50 58N 0 18 E
Hebburn, U.K. 21 54 59N 1 30W
Hebden Bridge, U.K. 18 53 45N 2 0W
Hebei □, China 61 39 0N 116 0 E
Hebrides, U.K. 22 57 30N 7 0W
Hechuan, China 60 30 2N 106 12 E
Heckington, U.K. 19 52 59N 0 17W
Hedmark fylke □, Nor. 44 61 17N 11 40 E
Hednesford, U.K. 14 52 43N 2 0W
Hedon, U.K. 19 53 44N 0 11W
Heerlen, Neth. 36 50 55N 6 0 E
Hefei, China 61 31 52N 117 18 E
Hegang, China 61 47 20N 130 19 E
Heidelberg, W. Ger. 42 49 23N 8 41 E
Heilbronn, W. Ger. 42 49 8N 9 13 E
Heilongjiang □, China 61 48 0N 126 0 E
Hekla, Ice. 44 63 56N 19 35W
Helensburgh, U.K. 20 56 0N 4 44W
Heligoland, W. Ger. 42 54 10N 7 51 E
Hellifield, U.K. 18 54 0N 2 13W
Helmond, Neth. 36 51 29N 5 41 E
Helmsdale, U.K. 23 58 7N 3 40W
Helmsley, U.K. 19 54 15N 1 2W
Helperby, U.K. 19 54 8N 1 20W
Helsby, U.K. 18 53 16N 2 47W
Helsingborg, Swed. 45 56 3N 12 42 E
Helsingør, Den. 45 56 2N 12 35 E
Helsinki, Fin. 45 60 15N 25 3 E
Helston, U.K. 16 50 7N 5 17W
Helvellyn, U.K. 18 54 31N 3 1W
Hemel Hempstead, U.K. 15 51 45N 0 28W
Hempton, U.K. 15 52 50N 0 49 E
Hemsworth, U.K. 19 53 37N 1 21W
Hemyock, U.K. 16 50 50N 3 15W
Henan □, China 61 34 0N 114 0 E
Henfield, U.K. 15 50 56N 0 17W
Hengelo, Neth. 36 52 16N 6 48 E
Hengyang, China 61 26 51N 112 30 E
Henley-in-Arden, U.K. 14 52 18N 1 47W
Henley-on-Thames, U.K. 15 51 32N 0 53W
Henlow, U.K. 15 52 2N 0 18W
Henstridge, U.K. 14 50 59N 2 24W
Henzada, Burma 59 17 38N 95 26 E
Herāt, Afg. 57 34 20N 62 7 E
Hereford, U.K. 14 52 4N 2 42W
Hereford and Worcester □, U.K. 14 52 10N 2 30W
Hermosillo, Mex. 94 29 4N 110 58W
Herne, W. Ger. 36 51 33N 7 12 E
Herne Bay, U.K. 15 51 22N 1 8 E
Herning, Den. 45 56 8N 8 58 E
Herstmonceux, U.K. 15 50 53N 0 21 E
Hertford, U.K. 15 51 47N 0 4W
Hertford □, U.K. 15 51 51N 0 5W
's-Hertogenbosch, Neth. 36 51 42N 5 17 E
Hesse □, W. Ger. 42 50 40N 9 20 E
Hessle, U.K. 19 53 44N 0 28 E
Hethersett, U.K. 15 52 35N 1 10 E
Hetton-le-Hole, U.K. 21 54 49N 1 26W
Hexham, U.K. 19 54 58N 2 7W
Heybridge, U.K. 15 51 44N 0 42 E
Heysham, U.K. 18 54 5N 2 53W
Heytesbury, U.K. 14 51 11N 2 7W
Heywood, U.K. 18 53 36N 2 13W
High Atlas, Mor. 72 32 30N 5 0W
High Bentham, U.K. 18 54 8N 2 31W
High Borrow Bridge, U.K. 18 54 26N 2 43W
High Ercall, U.K. 14 52 46N 2 37W
High Hesket, U.K. 18 54 47N 2 49W
High Pike, U.K. 18 54 43N 3 4W
High Willhays, U.K. 16 50 41N 3 59W
High Wycombe, U.K. 15 51 37N 0 45W
Higham Ferrers, U.K. 15 52 18N 0 36W
Highbridge, U.K. 14 51 13N 2 59W
Highclere, U.K. 14 51 20N 1 22W
Highland □, U.K. 22 57 30N 5 0W
Highley, U.K. 14 52 25N 2 23W
Hightae, U.K. 21 55 5N 3 27W
Highworth, U.K. 14 51 38N 1 42W
Hilgay, U.K. 15 52 34N 0 23 E
Hillingdon, U.K. 15 51 33N 0 29W
Hillsborough, U.K. 24 54 28N 6 6W
Hilo, U.S.A. 90 19 44N 155 5W
Hilpsford Pt., U.K. 18 54 4N 3 12W
Hilversum, Neth. 36 52 14N 5 10 E
Himachal Pradesh □, India 58 31 30N 77 0 E
Himalaya, Mts., Asia 60 29 0N 84 0 E
Himeji, Jap. 62 34 50N 134 40 E
Hinckley, U.K. 14 52 33N 1 21W
Hinderwell, U.K. 19 54 32N 0 45W
Hindhead, U.K. 15 51 6N 0 42W
Hindley, U.K. 18 53 32N 2 35W
Hindu Kush, Asia 57 36 0N 71 0 E
Hingham, U.K. 15 52 35N 0 59 E
Hinkley Pt., U.K. 14 50 59N 3 32W
Hinstock, U.K. 14 52 50N 2 28W
Hiroshima, Jap. 62 34 24N 132 30 E
Hispaniola, W. Ind. 95 19 0N 71 0W
Histon, U.K. 15 52 15N 0 6 E
Hitchin, U.K. 15 51 57N 0 16W
Ho Chi Minh City, Viet. 63 10 58N 106 40 E
Hobart, Austral. 66 42 50S 147 21 E
Hodder →, U.K. 18 53 57N 2 27W
Hoddesdon, U.K. 15 51 45N 0 1W
Hodge →, U.K. 19 54 14N 0 55W
Hoff, U.K. 18 54 34N 2 31W
Hoggar, Mts., Alg. 78 23 0N 6 30 E
Hog's Back, U.K. 15 51 13N 0 40W
Hohhot, China 61 40 52N 111 40 E
Hokitika, N.Z. 71 42 42S 171 0 E
Hokkaidō □, Jap. 62 43 30N 143 0 E
Holbeach, U.K. 15 52 48N 0 1 E
Holbeach Marsh, U.K. 15 52 52N 0 5 E
Holderness, U.K. 19 53 45N 0 5W
Holguín, Cuba 95 20 50N 76 20W
Holkham, U.K. 15 52 57N 0 48 E
Holland Fen, U.K. 19 53 0N 0 8W
Holland-on-Sea, U.K. 15 51 48N 1 12 E
Holme, Humberside, U.K. 19 53 50N 0 48W
Holme, N. Yorks., U.K. 18 53 34N 1 50W
Holmes Chapel, U.K. 18 53 13N 2 21W
Holmfirth, U.K. 19 53 34N 1 48W
Holmwood, U.K. 15 51 12N 0 19W
Holsworthy, U.K. 16 50 48N 4 21W
Holt, U.K. 15 52 55N 1 4 E
Holy I., England, U.K. 19 55 42N 1 48W
Holy I., Scotland, U.K. 20 55 31N 5 4W
Holy I., Wales, U.K. 17 53 17N 4 37W
Holyhead, U.K. 17 53 18N 4 38W
Holywell, U.K. 17 53 16N 3 14W
Holywood, U.K. 24 54 38N 5 50W
Homs, Syria 56 34 40N 36 45 E
Honduras ■, Cent. Am. 94 14 40N 86 30W
Honduras, G. de, Cent. Am. 94 16 50N 87 0W
Hong →, Viet. 60 20 17N 106 34 E
Hong Kong ■, Asia 61 22 11N 114 14 E
Honington, U.K. 19 52 58N 0 35W
Honiton, U.K. 16 50 48N 3 11W
Honolulu, U.S.A. 90 21 19N 157 52W
Honshū, Jap. 62 36 0N 138 0 E
Hoo, U.K. 15 51 25N 0 33 E
Hook, U.K. 15 51 17N 0 55W
Hook Hd., Ire. 25 52 8N 6 57W
Hoorn, Neth. 36 52 38N 5 4 E
Horden, U.K. 19 54 45N 1 17W
Horley, U.K. 15 51 10N 0 10W
Horn, C., Chile 102 55 50S 67 30W
Horn Head, Ire. 24 55 13N 8 0W
Horncastle, U.K. 19 53 13N 0 8W
Horndean, U.K. 15 50 50N 0 59W
Horningsham, U.K. 14 51 11N 2 16W
Hornsby, Austral. 70 33 42S 151 2 E
Hornsea, U.K. 19 53 55N 0 10W
Horsens, Den. 45 55 52N 9 51 E
Horsforth, U.K. 19 53 50N 1 39W
Horsham, Austral. 70 36 44S 142 13 E
Horsham, U.K. 15 51 4N 0 20W
Horsham St. Faith, U.K. 15 52 41N 1 15 E
Horsted Keynes, U.K. 15 51 2N 0 1W
Horton-in-Ribblesdale, U.K. 18 54 9N 2 19W
Horwich, U.K. 18 53 37N 2 33W
Hospitalet de Llobregat, Sp. 37 41 21N 2 6 E
Hotan, China 60 37 25N 79 55 E
Houghton-le-Spring, U.K. 19 54 51N 1 28W
Houghton Regis, U.K. 15 51 54N 0 32W
Hounslow, U.K. 15 51 29N 0 20W
Houston, U.S.A. 91 29 50N 95 20W
Hovd, Mong. 60 48 2N 91 37 E
Hove, U.K. 15 50 50N 0 10W
Hoveton, U.K. 15 52 45N 1 23 E
Hovingham, U.K. 19 54 10N 0 59W
Hövsgöl Nuur, Mong. 60 51 0N 100 30 E
Howden, U.K. 19 53 45N 0 52W
Howth Hd., Ire. 24 53 21N 6 0W
Hoxne, U.K. 15 52 22N 1 11 E
Hoy I., U.K. 23 58 50N 3 15W
Hoylake, U.K. 18 53 24N 3 11W
Hrádec Králové, Czech. 42 50 15N 15 50 E
Hron →, Czech. 43 47 49N 18 45 E
Huainan, China 61 32 39N 117 2 E
Huambo, Angola 81 12 42S 15 54 E
Huancayo, Peru 100 12 5S 75 12W
Huang He →, China 60 37 55N 118 50 E
Huangshi, China 61 30 10N 115 3 E
Huánuco, Peru 100 9 55S 76 15W
Hubei □, China 61 31 0N 112 0 E
Hucknall, U.K. 19 53 3N 1 12W
Huddersfield, U.K. 19 53 38N 1 49W
Hudson →, U.S.A. 93 40 42N 74 2W
Hudson Bay, Canada 89 52 51N 102 23W
Hudson Str., Canada 89 62 0N 70 0W
Hue, Viet. 63 16 30N 107 35 E
Huelva, Sp. 37 37 18N 6 57W
Huesca, Sp. 37 42 8N 0 25W
Hugh Town, U.K. 16 49 55N 6 19W
Hughenden, Austral. 67 20 52S 144 10 E
Hughes, U.S.A. 88 66 0N 154 20W
Hull, Canada 93 45 25N 75 44W
Hull = Kingston-upon-Hull, U.K. 19 53 45N 0 20W
Hull →, U.K. 19 53 43N 0 25W
Hullavington, U.K. 14 51 31N 2 9W
Hulme End, U.K. 18 53 8N 1 51W
Humber →, U.K. 19 53 40N 0 10W
Humber, Mouth of the, U.K. 19 53 32N 0 8 E
Humberside □, U.K. 19 53 50N 0 30W
Humboldt →, U.S.A. 90 40 2N 118 31W
Hume, L., Austral. 70 36 0S 147 0 E
Humshaugh, U.K. 21 55 3N 2 8W
Húnaflói, Ice. 44 65 50N 20 50W
Hunan □, China 61 27 30N 111 30 E
Hungary ■, Europe 43 47 20N 19 20 E
Hungary, Plain of, Europe 26 47 0N 20 0 E
Hungerford, U.K. 14 51 25N 1 30W
Hŭngnam, N. Kor. 61 39 49N 127 45 E
Hunmanby, U.K. 19 54 12N 0 19W
Hunstanton, U.K. 15 52 57N 0 30 E
Hunter →, Austral. 70 32 52S 151 46 E
Hunterston, U.K. 20 55 43N 4 55W
Huntingdon, U.K. 15 52 20N 0 11W
Huntington, U.S.A. 92 38 20N 82 30W
Huntly, U.K. 23 57 27N 2 48W
Huntsville, U.S.A. 91 34 45N 86 35W
Hurlford, U.K. 20 55 35N 4 29W
Huron, L., N. Am. 92 45 0N 83 0W
Hursley, U.K. 14 51 1N 1 23W
Hurstbourne Tarrant, U.K. 14 51 17N 1 27W
Hurstpierpoint, U.K. 15 50 56N 0 11W
Húsavík, Ice. 44 66 3N 17 21W
Husband's Bosworth, U.K. 14 52 27N 1 3W
Huyton, U.K. 18 53 25N 2 52W
Hyde, U.K. 18 53 26N 2 6W
Hyderabad, India 58 17 22N 78 29 E
Hyderabad, Pak. 58 25 23N 68 24 E
Hynish, U.K. 20 56 27N 6 54W
Hynish B., U.K. 20 56 29N 6 40W
Hythe, U.K. 15 51 4N 1 5 E

I

Iaşi, Rom. 43 47 10N 27 40 E
Ibadan, Nig. 78 7 22N 3 58 E
Ibagué, Col. 100 4 20N 75 20W
Iberian Peninsula, Europe 26 40 0N 5 0W
Ibiza, Sp. 37 38 54N 1 26 E
Ibstock, U.K. 14 52 42N 1 23W
Icá, Peru 100 14 0S 75 48W
Iceland ■, Atl. Oc. 44 65 0N 19 0W
Ichinomiya, Jap. 62 35 18N 136 48 E
Idaho □, U.S.A. 90 44 10N 114 0W
Idar-Oberstein, W. Ger. 36 49 43N 7 19 E
Idle →, U.K. 19 53 27N 0 49W
Idmiston, U.K. 14 51 8N 1 43W
Idsworth, U.K. 15 50 56N 0 56W
Igarka, U.S.S.R. 49 67 30N 86 33 E
Iglésias, It. 40 39 19N 8 27 E
Iguaçu Falls, Brazil 102 25 41S 54 26W
IJsselmeer, Neth. 36 52 45N 5 20 E
Ilchester, U.K. 14 51 0N 2 41W
Île-de-France, Fr. 34 49 0N 2 20 E
Ilfracombe, U.K. 16 51 13N 4 8W
Ilhéus, Brazil 101 14 49S 39 2W
Ilkeston, U.K. 19 52 59N 1 19W
Ilkley, U.K. 18 53 56N 1 49W
Illinois □, U.S.A. 91 40 15N 89 30W
Ilminster, U.K. 14 50 55N 2 56W
Iloilo, Phil. 63 10 45N 122 33 E
Immingham, U.K. 19 53 37N 0 12W
Imphal, India 59 24 48N 93 56 E
Inari, Fin. 44 68 54N 27 5 E
Ince, U.K. 18 53 32N 2 38W
Inchcape Rock, U.K. 21 56 26N 2 24W
Inchkeith, I., U.K. 21 56 2N 3 8W
Inchon, S. Kor. 61 37 27N 126 40 E
Inchture, U.K. 21 56 26N 3 8W
Indaal, L., U.K. 20 55 44N 6 20W
India ■, Asia 58 20 0N 78 0 E
Indian Ocean 129 5 0S 75 0 E
Indiana □, U.S.A. 92 40 0N 86 0W
Indianapolis, U.S.A. 92 39 42N 86 10W
Indonesia ■, Asia 63 5 0S 115 0 E
Indore, India 58 22 42N 75 53 E
Indus →, Pak. 58 24 20N 67 47 E
Ingatestone, U.K. 15 51 40N 0 23W
Ingleborough, U.K. 18 54 11N 2 23W
Ingleton, U.K. 18 54 9N 2 29W
Ingoldmells, Pt., U.K. 19 53 11N 0 21 E
Inishbofin, Ire. 24 53 35N 10 12W
Inishmore, Ire. 25 53 8N 9 45W
Inishowen, Ire. 24 55 14N 7 15W
Inkberrow, U.K. 14 52 13N 1 59W
Inkpen Beacon, U.K. 14 51 22N 1 28W
Inn →, Austria 40 48 35N 13 28 E
Innellan, U.K. 20 55 54N 4 58W
Inner Hebrides, U.K. 22 57 0N 6 30W
Inner Mongolia □, China 61 42 0N 112 0 E
Inner Sound, U.K. 22 57 30N 5 55W
Innerleithen, U.K. 21 55 37N 3 4W
Innsbruck, Austria 42 47 16N 11 23 E
Inny →, Ire. 25 53 30N 7 50W
Interlaken, Switz. 42 46 41N 7 50 E
Inuvik, Canada 88 68 16N 133 40W
Inveraray, U.K. 20 56 13N 5 5W
Inverbervie, U.K. 23 56 50N 2 17W
Invercargill, N.Z. 71 46 24S 168 24 E
Inverell, Austral. 67 29 45S 151 8 E
Invergarry, U.K. 23 57 5N 4 48W
Invergordon, U.K. 23 57 41N 4 10W
Invergowrie, U.K. 21 56 29N 3 5W
Inverkeithing, U.K. 21 56 2N 3 24W
Invermoriston, U.K. 23 57 13N 4 38W
Inverness, U.K. 23 57 29N 4 12W
Inverurie, U.K. 23 57 15N 2 21W
Iona, U.K. 20 56 20N 6 25W
Ionian Is., Greece 41 38 40N 20 0 E
Ionian Sea, Greece 41 37 30N 17 30 E
Iowa □, U.S.A. 91 42 18N 93 30W
Iowa City, U.S.A. 90 41 40N 91 35W
Ipoh, Malay. 63 4 35N 101 5 E
Ipswich, U.K. 15 52 4N 1 9 E
Iquique, Chile 100 20 19S 70 5W
Iquitos, Peru 100 3 45S 73 10W
Iráklion, Greece 41 35 20N 25 12 E
Iran ■, Asia 57 33 0N 53 0 E
Irapuato, Mex. 94 20 40N 101 30W
Iraq ■, Asia 56 33 0N 44 0 E
Irchester, U.K. 15 52 17N 0 40W
Ireland ■, Europe 24 53 0N 8 0W
Ireland's Eye, Ire. 24 53 25N 6 4W
Irian Jaya □, Indon. 64 4 0S 137 0 E
Iringa, Tanz. 80 7 48S 35 43 E
Irish Republic ■, Europe 25 53 0N 8 0W
Irish Sea, Europe 18 54 0N 5 0W
Irkutsk, U.S.S.R. 49 52 18N 104 20 E
Irlam, U.K. 18 53 26N 2 27W
Ironbridge, U.K. 14 52 38N 2 29W
Irrawaddy →, Burma 59 15 50N 95 6 E
Irt →, U.K. 18 54 24N 3 25W
Irthing →, U.K. 21 54 55N 2 55W
Irthlingborough, U.K. 15 52 20N 0 37W
Irtysh →, U.S.S.R. 48 61 4N 68 52 E
Irvine, U.K. 20 55 37N 4 40W
Irvine →, U.K. 20 55 35N 4 40W
Irvinestown, U.K. 24 54 28N 7 38W
Isabela, Phil. 63 10 12N 122 59 E
Ísafjörður, Ice. 44 66 5N 23 9W
Ishim →, U.S.S.R. 48 57 45N 71 10 E
İskenderun, Turk. 47 36 32N 36 10 E
Isla →, U.K. 23 56 32N 3 20W
Islamabad, Pak. 58 33 40N 73 10 E
Islay, U.K. 20 55 46N 6 10W
Islay Sound, U.K. 20 55 45N 6 5W
Isle of Whithorn, U.K. 20 54 42N 4 22W
Isle of Wight □, U.K. 14 50 40N 1 20W
Isleham, U.K. 15 52 21N 0 24 E
Islip, U.K. 14 51 49N 1 12W
Ismâ'ilîya, Egypt 79 30 37N 32 18 E
Israel ■, Asia 57 32 0N 34 50 E
İstanbul, Turk. 47 41 0N 29 0 E
Itabuna, Brazil 101 14 48S 39 16W
Italy ■, Europe 40 42 0N 13 0 E
Itchen →, U.K. 14 50 57N 1 20W
Ivanovo, U.S.S.R. 46 52 7N 25 29 E
Ivinghoe, U.K. 15 51 50N 0 38W
Ivory Coast ■, Africa 78 7 30N 5 0W
Ivugivik, Canada 89 62 24N 77 55W
Ivybridge, U.K. 16 50 24N 3 56W
Iwaki, Jap. 62 37 3N 140 55 E
Ixworth, U.K. 15 52 18N 0 50 E
Izhevsk = Ustinov, U.S.S.R. 46 56 51N 53 14 E
İzmir, Turk. 47 38 25N 27 8 E

J

Jabalpur, India 58 23 9N 79 58 E
Jackson, U.S.A. 91 32 20N 90 10W
Jacksonville, U.S.A. 91 30 15N 81 38W
Jaén, Sp. 37 37 44N 3 43W
Jaffna, Sri L. 58 9 45N 80 2 E
Jaipur, India 58 27 0N 75 50 E
Jakarta, Indon. 63 6 9S 106 49 E
Jamaica ■, W. Ind. 94 18 10N 77 30W
Jambi, Indon. 63 1 38S 103 30 E
James B., Canada 89 51 30N 80 0W
Jammu, India 58 32 43N 74 54 E
Jammu & Kashmir □, India 58 34 25N 77 0 E
Jamnagar, India 58 22 30N 70 6 E
Jamshedpur, India 59 22 44N 86 12 E
Japan ■, Asia 62 36 0N 136 0 E
Japan, Sea of, Asia 62 40 0N 135 0 E
Japurá →, Brazil 100 3 8S 64 46W
Jarrow, U.K. 21 54 58N 1 28W
Java, I., Indon. 63 7 0S 110 0 E
Java Sea, E. Ind. 63 4 35S 107 15 E
Jedburgh, U.K. 21 55 28N 2 33W
Jedda, Si. Arab. 56 21 29N 39 10 E
Jena, E. Ger. 42 50 56N 11 33 E
Jequié, Brazil 101 13 51S 40 5W
Jerez de la Frontera, Sp. 37 36 41N 6 7W
Jericho, Jord. 57 31 52N 35 27 E
Jersey, I., U.K. 34 49 13N 2 7W

Jersey City, U.S.A. 93 40 41N 74 8W
Jerusalem, Asia 57 31 47N 35 10 E
Jervaulx, U.K. 19 54 19N 1 41W
Jervis Bay, Austral. 70 35 8S 150 43 E
Jhansi, India 58 25 30N 78 36 E
Jhelum →, Pak. 58 31 20N 72 10 E
Jiamusi, China 61 46 40N 130 26 E
Ji'an, China 61 27 6N 114 59 E
Jiangsu □, China 61 33 0N 120 0 E
Jiangxi □, China 61 27 30N 116 0 E
Jilin, China 61 43 44N 126 30 E
Jilin □, China 61 44 0N 124 0 E
Jima, Eth. 79 7 40N 36 47 E
Jinan, China 61 36 38N 117 1 E
Jinja, Uganda 80 0 25N 33 12 E
Jinzhou, China 61 41 5N 121 3 E
Jixi, China 61 45 20N 130 50 E
João Pessoa, Brazil 101 7 10S 34 52W
Johannesburg, S. Afr. 81 26 10S 28 2 E
John o' Groats, U.K. 23 58 39N 3 3W
Johnstone, U.K. 20 55 50N 4 31W
Johnstown, U.S.A. 92 40 19N 78 53W
Johor Baharu, Malay. 63 1 28N 103 46 E
Jönköping, Swed. 45 57 45N 14 10 E
Jonquière, Canada 93 48 27N 71 14W
Jordan ■, Asia 57 31 0N 36 0 E
Jordan →, Asia 57 31 48N 35 32 E
Jos, Nig. 78 9 53N 8 51 E
Joseph Bonaparte G., Austral. 66 14 35S 128 50 E
Jotunheimen, Nor. 44 61 35N 8 25 E
Juan de Fuca Str., Canada 90 48 15N 124 0W
Juàzeiro do Norte, Brazil 101 7 10S 39 18W
Juiz de Fora, Brazil 101 21 43S 43 19W
Juliaca, Peru 100 15 25S 70 10W
Julianehåb, Green. 89 60 43N 46 0W
Jullundur, India 58 31 20N 75 40 E
Jundiaí, Brazil 102 24 30S 47 0W
Juneau, U.S.A. 88 58 20N 134 20W
Jura, U.K. 20 56 0N 5 50W
Jura, Mts., Europe 42 46 40N 6 5 E
Jura, Paps of, U.K. 20 55 55N 6 0W
Jura, Sd. of, U.K. 20 55 57N 5 45W
Jurby Hd., U.K. 18 54 23N 4 31W
Juruá →, Brazil 100 2 37S 65 44W
Jutland = Jylland, Den. 45 56 25N 9 30 E
Jylland, Den. 45 56 25N 9 30 E
Jyväskylä, Fin. 44 62 14N 25 50 E

K

Kābul, Afg. 57 34 28N 69 11 E
Kabwe, Zam. 81 14 30S 28 29 E
Kaduna, Nig. 78 10 30N 7 21 E
Kaesŏng, N. Kor. 61 37 58N 126 35 E
Kagoshima, Jap. 62 31 35N 130 33 E
Kaifeng, China 61 34 49N 114 30 E
Kaiserslautern, W. Ger. 36 49 30N 7 43 E
Kaitaia, N.Z. 71 35 8S 173 17 E
Kajaani, Fin. 44 64 17N 27 46 E
Kakinada, India 59 16 57N 82 11 E
Kalahari, Africa 81 24 0S 21 30 E
Kalamazoo, U.S.A. 92 42 20N 85 35W
Kalemie, Zaïre 80 5 55S 29 9 E
Kalgoorlie-Boulder, Austral. 66 30 40S 121 22 E
Kalimantan, Indon. 63 0 0 114 0 E
Kalinin, U.S.S.R. 46 56 55N 35 55 E
Kaliningrad, U.S.S.R. 46 54 42N 20 32 E
Kaluga, U.S.S.R. 46 54 35N 36 10 E
Kamchatka Pen., U.S.S.R. 49 57 0N 160 0 E
Kamensk Uralskiy, U.S.S.R. 48 56 25N 62 2 E
Kames, U.K. 20 55 53N 5 15W
Kamina, Zaïre 80 8 45S 25 0 E
Kamloops, Canada 88 50 40N 120 20W
Kampala, Uganda 80 0 20N 32 30 E
Kampuchea = Cambodia ■, Asia 63 12 15N 105 0 E
Kananga, Zaïre 80 5 55S 22 18 E
Kanazawa, Jap. 62 36 30N 136 38 E
Kanchenjunga, Nepal 59 27 50N 88 10 E
Kandy, Sri L. 58 7 18N 80 43 E
Kangaroo I., Austral. 67 35 45S 137 0 E
Kanin, Pen., U.S.S.R. 46 68 0N 45 0 E
Kankan, Guin. 78 10 23N 9 15W
Kano, Nig. 78 12 2N 8 30 E
Kanpur, India 58 26 28N 80 20 E
Kansas □, U.S.A. 90 38 40N 98 0W
Kansas City, Kans., U.S.A. 91 39 0N 94 40W
Kansas City, Mo., U.S.A. 91 39 0N 94 30W
Kansk, U.S.S.R. 49 56 20N 95 37 E
Kanturk, Ire. 25 52 10N 8 55W
Kaohsiung, Taiwan 61 22 35N 120 16 E
Kaolack, Sene. 78 14 5N 16 8W
Kara Bogaz Gol, Zaliv, U.S.S.R. 47 41 0N 53 30 E
Kara Kalpak A.S.S.R. □, U.S.S.R. 48 43 0N 60 0 E
Kara Kum, U.S.S.R. 48 39 30N 60 0 E
Kara Sea, U.S.S.R. 48 75 0N 70 0 E
Karachi, Pak. 58 24 53N 67 0 E
Karaganda, U.S.S.R. 48 49 50N 73 10 E
Karakoram Ra., Asia 58 35 30N 77 0 E
Karbalā, Iraq 56 32 36N 44 3 E
Karl-Marx-Stadt, E. Ger. 42 50 50N 12 55 E
Karlskrona, Swed. 45 56 10N 15 35 E
Karlsruhe, W. Ger. 42 49 3N 8 23 E
Karlstad, Swed. 45 59 23N 13 30 E
Karratha, Austral. 66 20 53S 116 40 E
Karsakpay, U.S.S.R. 48 47 55N 66 40 E
Karshi, U.S.S.R. 48 38 53N 65 48 E
Kāshān, Iran 56 34 5N 51 30 E
Kashi, China 60 39 30N 76 2 E
Kassala, Sudan 79 16 0N 36 0 E
Kassel, W. Ger. 42 51 19N 9 32 E
Katmandu, Nepal 59 27 45N 85 20 E
Katoomba, Austral. 70 33 41S 150 19 E
Katowice, Pol. 43 50 17N 19 5 E
Katrine, L., U.K. 20 56 15N 4 30W
Katsina, Nig. 78 13 0N 7 32 E
Kattegatt, Den. 45 57 0N 11 20 E
Kauai, U.S.A. 90 22 0N 159 30W
Kaunas, U.S.S.R. 46 54 54N 23 54 E
Kavála, Greece 41 40 57N 24 28 E
Kawagoe, Jap. 62 35 55N 139 29 E
Kawasaki, Jap. 62 35 35N 139 42 E
Kawthoolei □, Burma 59 18 0N 97 30 E
Kayes, Mali 78 14 25N 11 30W
Kayseri, Turk. 47 38 45N 35 30 E
Kazakhstan □, U.S.S.R. 48 50 0N 70 0 E
Kazan, U.S.S.R. 46 55 48N 49 3 E
Kea, U.K. 16 50 13N 5 4W
Keady, U.K. 24 54 15N 6 42W
Keal, Loch na, U.K. 20 56 30N 6 5W
Kecskemét, Hung. 43 46 57N 19 42 E
Kediri, Indon. 63 7 51S 112 1 E
Keelby, U.K. 19 53 34N 0 15W
Keele, U.K. 18 53 0N 2 17W
Keeper Hill, Ire. 25 52 46N 8 17W
Keewatin, Canada 88 49 46N 94 34W
Kefallinía, Greece 41 38 20N 20 30 E
Keflavík, Ice. 44 64 2N 22 35W
Kegworth, U.K. 14 52 50N 1 17W
Keighley, U.K. 18 53 52N 1 54W
Keith, U.K. 23 57 33N 2 58W
Keld, U.K. 18 54 24N 2 11W
Kellerberrin, Austral. 66 31 36S 117 38 E
Kells = Ceanannus Mor, Ire. 24 53 42N 6 53W
Kells, Rhinns of, U.K. 20 55 9N 4 22W
Kelowna, Canada 88 49 50N 119 25W
Kelsale, U.K. 15 52 15N 1 30 E
Kelsall, U.K. 18 53 14N 2 44W
Kelso, U.K. 21 55 36N 2 27W
Kelvedon, U.K. 15 51 50N 0 43 E
Kemble, U.K. 14 51 40N 2 1W
Kemerovo, U.S.S.R. 48 55 20N 86 5 E
Kemi, Fin. 44 65 44N 24 34 E
Kempsey, U.K. 14 52 8N 2 11W
Kempston, U.K. 15 52 7N 0 30W
Ken, L., U.K. 21 55 0N 4 8W
Kendal, U.K. 18 54 19N 2 44W
Kenilworth, U.K. 14 52 22N 1 35W
Kenitra, Mor. 78 34 15N 6 40W
Kenmare, Ire. 25 51 52N 9 35W
Kenmare →, Ire. 25 51 40N 10 0W
Kennet →, U.K. 14 51 24N 0 58W
Kenninghall, U.K. 15 52 26N 1 0 E
Kenora, Canada 88 49 47N 94 29W
Kent □, U.K. 15 51 12N 0 40 E
Kentisbeare, U.K. 16 50 51N 3 18W
Kenton, U.K. 16 50 37N 3 28W
Kentucky □, U.S.A. 91 37 20N 85 0W
Kenya ■, Africa 80 1 0N 38 0 E
Kerala □, India 58 11 0N 76 15 E
Kerch, U.S.S.R. 47 45 20N 36 20 E
Kérkira, Greece 41 39 38N 19 50 E
Kermān, Iran 57 30 15N 57 1 E
Kerrera I., U.K. 20 56 24N 5 32W
Kerry □, Ire. 25 52 7N 9 35W
Kerry Hd., Ire. 25 52 26N 9 56W
Kessingland, U.K. 15 52 25N 1 41 E
Keswick, U.K. 18 54 35N 3 9W
Ketchikan, U.S.A. 88 55 25N 131 40W
Kettering, U.K. 15 52 24N 0 44W
Kettle Ness, U.K. 19 54 32N 0 41W
Kettlewell, U.K. 18 54 8N 2 2W
Keweenaw Pen., U.S.A. 92 47 30N 88 0W
Kexby, U.K. 19 53 21N 0 41W
Key West, U.S.A. 91 24 33N 82 0W
Keyingham, U.K. 19 53 42N 0 7W
Keymer, U.K. 15 50 55N 0 5W
Keynsham, U.K. 14 51 25N 2 30W
Keyworth, U.K. 14 52 52N 1 8W
Khabarovsk, U.S.S.R. 49 48 30N 135 5 E
Khaniá, Greece 41 35 30N 24 4 E
Kharagpur, India 59 22 20N 87 25 E
Kharkov, U.S.S.R. 47 49 58N 36 20 E
Khartoum, Sudan 79 15 31N 32 35 E
Khaskovo, Bulg. 41 41 56N 25 30 E
Kherson, U.S.S.R. 47 46 35N 32 35 E
Khíos, I., Greece 41 38 20N 26 0 E
Khorrāmshahr, Iran 56 30 29N 48 15 E
Khouribga, Mor. 78 32 58N 6 57W
Khulna, Bangla. 59 22 45N 89 34 E
Khulna □, Bangla. 59 22 25N 89 35 E
Khurasan, Iran 57 34 0N 57 0 E
Kibworth Beauchamp, U.K. 15 52 33N 0 59W
Kicking Horse Pass, Canada 88 51 28N 116 16W
Kidderminster, U.K. 14 52 24N 2 13W
Kidlington, U.K. 14 51 49N 1 18W
Kidsgrove, U.K. 18 53 6N 2 15W
Kidstones, U.K. 18 54 15N 2 2W
Kidwelly, U.K. 17 51 44N 4 20W
Kiel, W. Ger. 42 54 16N 10 8 E
Kielce, Pol. 43 50 52N 20 42 E
Kielder, U.K. 21 55 14N 2 35W
Kiev, U.S.S.R. 47 50 30N 30 28 E
Kigali, Rwanda 80 1 59S 30 4 E
Kigoma-Ujiji, Tanz. 80 4 55S 29 36 E
Kikládhes, Greece 41 37 20N 24 30 E
Kikwit, Zaïre 80 5 5S 18 45 E
Kilbirnie, U.K. 20 55 46N 4 42W
Kilbrannan Sd., U.K. 20 55 40N 5 23W
Kilcreggan, U.K. 20 55 59N 4 50W
Kildare, Ire. 25 53 10N 6 50W
Kildare □, Ire. 25 53 10N 6 50W
Kildonan, U.K. 23 58 10N 3 50W
Kilfinan, U.K. 20 55 57N 5 19W
Kilham, U.K. 19 54 4N 0 22W
Kilimanjaro, Tanz. 80 3 7S 37 20 E
Kilkee, Ire. 25 52 41N 9 40W
Kilkeel, U.K. 24 54 4N 6 0W
Kilkenny, Ire. 25 52 40N 7 17W
Kilkenny □, Ire. 25 52 35N 7 15W
Kilkhampton, U.K. 16 50 53N 4 30W
Kilkieran B., Ire. 25 53 18N 9 45W
Killala, Ire. 24 54 13N 9 12W
Killala B., Ire. 24 54 20N 9 12W
Killaloe, Ire. 25 52 48N 8 28W
Killarney, Ire. 25 52 2N 9 30W
Killarney, Lakes of, Ire. 25 52 0N 9 30W
Killary Harbour, Ire. 24 53 38N 9 52W
Killchianaig, U.K. 20 56 2N 5 48W
Killean, U.K. 20 55 38N 5 40W
Killiecrankie, Pass of, U.K. 23 56 44N 3 46W
Killin, U.K. 20 56 28N 4 20W
Killinghall, U.K. 19 54 1N 1 33W
Killybegs, Ire. 24 54 38N 8 26W
Kilmacolm, U.K. 20 55 54N 4 39W
Kilmarnock, U.K. 20 55 36N 4 30W
Kilmartin, U.K. 20 56 8N 5 29W
Kilmaurs, U.K. 20 55 37N 4 33W
Kilmelford, U.K. 20 56 16N 5 30W
Kilninver, U.K. 20 56 20N 5 30W
Kilrenny, U.K. 21 56 15N 2 40W
Kilrush, Ire. 25 52 39N 9 30W
Kilsby, U.K. 14 52 20N 1 11W
Kilsyth, U.K. 21 55 58N 4 3W
Kilwinning, U.K. 20 55 40N 4 41W
Kimberley, Austral. 66 16 20S 127 0 E
Kimberley, S. Afr. 81 28 43S 24 46 E
Kimbolton, U.K. 15 52 17N 0 23W
Kincardine, U.K. 21 56 4N 3 43W
Kindu, Zaïre 80 2 55S 25 50 E
Kineton, U.K. 14 52 10N 1 30W
King Frederick VI Coast, Green. 89 63 0N 43 0W
King Sd., Austral. 66 16 50S 123 20 E
Kingarth, U.K. 20 55 45N 5 2W
Kinghorn, U.K. 21 56 4N 3 10W
King's Lynn, U.K. 15 52 45N 0 25 E
King's Sutton, U.K. 14 52 1N 1 16W
King's Worthy, U.K. 14 51 6N 1 18W
Kingsbarns, U.K. 21 56 18N 2 40W
Kingsbridge, U.K. 16 50 17N 3 46W
Kingsbury, U.K. 14 52 33N 1 41W
Kingscourt, Ire. 24 53 55N 6 48W
Kingskerswell, U.K. 16 50 30N 3 34W
Kingsland, U.K. 14 52 15N 2 49W
Kingsteignton, U.K. 16 50 32N 3 35W
Kingston, Canada 92 44 14N 76 30W
Kingston, Jam. 94 18 0N 76 50W
Kingston, U.K. 14 51 18N 1 40W
Kingston-upon-Hull, U.K. 19 53 45N 0 20W
Kingston-upon-Thames, U.K. 15 51 23N 0 20W
Kingstown, St. Vinc. 94 13 10N 61 10W
Kingswear, U.K. 16 50 21N 3 33W
Kingswood, U.K. 14 51 26N 2 31W
Kington, U.K. 14 52 12N 3 2W
Kingussie, U.K. 23 57 5N 4 2W
Kinlochewe, U.K. 22 57 37N 5 20W
Kinlochleven, U.K. 22 56 42N 4 59W
Kinnairds Hd., U.K. 23 57 40N 2 0W
Kinneret, Lake, Isr. 57 32 45N 35 35 E
Kinross, U.K. 21 56 13N 3 25W
Kinsale, Ire. 25 51 42N 8 31W
Kinsale, Old Hd. of, Ire. 25 51 37N 8 32W
Kinshasa, Zaïre 80 4 20S 15 15 E
Kintyre, U.K. 20 55 30N 5 35W
Kintyre, Mull of, U.K. 20 55 17N 5 55W
Kippen, U.K. 20 56 8N 4 12W
Kippure, Ire. 25 53 11N 6 23W
Kirensk, U.S.S.R. 49 57 50N 107 55 E
Kirgizia □, U.S.S.R. 48 42 0N 75 0 E
Kirgiziya Steppe, U.S.S.R. 47 50 0N 55 0 E
Kiribati ■, Pac. Oc. 65 1 0N 176 0 E
Kirk Michael, U.K. 18 54 17N 4 35W
Kirkbean, U.K. 21 54 56N 3 35W
Kirkbride, U.K. 18 54 54N 3 13W
Kirkburton, U.K. 19 53 36N 1 42W
Kirkby, U.K. 18 53 29N 2 54W
Kirkby-in-Ashfield, U.K. 19 53 6N 1 15W
Kirkby Lonsdale, U.K. 18 54 13N 2 36W
Kirkby Malzeard, U.K. 19 54 10N 1 38W
Kirkby Moorside, U.K. 19 54 16N 0 56W
Kirkby Stephen, U.K. 18 54 27N 2 23W
Kirkby Thore, U.K. 18 54 38N 2 34W
Kirkcaldy, U.K. 21 56 7N 3 10W
Kirkcolm, U.K. 20 54 59N 5 4W
Kirkconnel, U.K. 21 55 23N 4 0W
Kirkcowan, U.K. 20 54 53N 4 38W
Kirkcudbright, U.K. 21 54 50N 4 3W
Kirkcudbright B., U.K. 21 54 46N 4 0W
Kirkham, U.K. 18 53 47N 2 52W
Kirkinner, U.K. 20 54 49N 4 28W
Kirkintilloch, U.K. 21 55 57N 4 10W
Kirkland Lake, Canada 92 48 9N 80 2W
Kirkliston, U.K. 21 55 55N 3 27W
Kirkoswald, U.K. 18 54 46N 2 41W
Kirkoswold, U.K. 20 55 19N 4 48W
Kirkstone P., U.K. 18 54 29N 2 55W
Kirkūk, Iraq 56 35 30N 44 21 E
Kirkwall, U.K. 23 58 59N 2 59W
Kirkwhelpington, U.K. 21 55 9N 2 0W
Kirov, U.S.S.R. 46 58 35N 49 40 E
Kirovabad, U.S.S.R. 47 40 45N 46 20 E
Kirovograd, U.S.S.R. 47 48 35N 32 20 E
Kirovsk, U.S.S.R. 46 48 35N 38 30 E
Kirriemuir, U.K. 23 56 41N 3 0W
Kirtling, U.K. 15 52 11N 0 27 E
Kirtlington, U.K. 14 51 54N 1 9W
Kirton, U.K. 19 52 56N 0 3W
Kirton-in-Lindsey, U.K. 19 53 29N 0 35W
Kiruna, Swed. 44 67 52N 20 15 E
Kisangani, Zaïre 80 0 35N 25 15 E
Kishinev, U.S.S.R. 47 47 0N 28 50 E
Kismayu, Som. 73 0 22S 42 32 E
Kisumu, Kenya 80 0 3S 34 45 E
Kitakyūshū, Jap. 62 33 50N 130 50 E
Kitchener, Canada 92 43 27N 80 29W
Kíthira, Greece 41 36 9N 23 0 E
Kitikmeot □, Canada 88 70 0N 110 0W
Kitimat, Canada 88 54 3N 128 38W
Kitwe, Zam. 81 12 54S 28 13 E
Klagenfurt, Austria 42 46 38N 14 20 E
Klerksdorp, S. Afr. 81 26 51S 26 38 E
Klondike, Canada 88 64 0N 139 26W
Knapdale, U.K. 20 55 55N 5 30W
Knaresborough, U.K. 19 54 1N 1 29W
Knebworth, U.K. 15 51 52N 0 11W
Knighton, U.K. 17 52 21N 3 2W
Knockmealdown Mts., Ire. 25 52 16N 8 0W
Knossos, Greece 41 35 16N 25 10 E
Knott End, U.K. 18 53 55N 3 0W
Knottingley, U.K. 19 53 42N 1 15W
Knowle, U.K. 14 52 23N 1 43W
Knoxville, U.S.A. 91 35 58N 83 57W
Knutsford, U.K. 18 53 18N 2 22W
Kōbe, Jap. 62 34 45N 135 10 E
København = Copenhagen, Den. 45 55 41N 12 34 E
Koblenz, W. Ger. 36 50 21N 7 36 E
Kodiak I., U.S.A. 88 57 30N 152 45W
Koforidua, Ghana 78 6 3N 0 17W
Kokand, U.S.S.R. 48 40 30N 70 57 E
Kokchetav, U.S.S.R. 48 53 20N 69 25 E
Kokkola, Fin. 44 63 50N 23 8 E
Kola Pen., U.S.S.R. 46 67 30N 38 0 E
Kolding, Den. 45 55 30N 9 29 E
Kolguyev, I., U.S.S.R. 46 69 20N 48 30 E
Kolomna, U.S.S.R. 46 55 8N 38 45 E
Kolwezi, Zaïre 80 10 40S 25 25 E
Kolyma →, U.S.S.R. 49 69 30N 161 0 E
Kolyma Ra., U.S.S.R. 49 63 0N 157 0 E
Komandorskiye, Is., U.S.S.R. 49 55 0N 167 0 E
Komsomolets I., U.S.S.R. 49 80 30N 95 0 E
Komsomolsk, U.S.S.R. 49 50 30N 137 0 E
Konya, Turk. 47 37 52N 32 35 E
Kópavogur, Ice. 44 64 6N 21 55W
Korce, Alb. 41 40 37N 20 50 E
Korea, North ■, Asia 61 40 0N 127 0 E
Korea, South ■, Asia 61 36 0N 128 0 E
Korea Strait, Asia 61 34 0N 129 30 E
Kōriyama, Jap. 62 37 24N 140 23 E
Korla, China 60 41 45N 86 4 E
Kortrijk, Belg. 36 50 50N 3 17 E
Koryak Range, U.S.S.R. 49 61 0N 171 0 E
Kos, Greece 41 36 50N 27 15 E
Košice, Czech. 43 48 42N 21 15 E
Kôstî, Sudan 79 13 8N 32 43 E
Kostroma, U.S.S.R. 46 57 50N 40 58 E
Kota, India 58 25 14N 75 49 E
Kota Baharu, Malay. 63 6 7N 102 14 E
Kota Kinabalu, Malay. 63 6 0N 116 4 E
Kotka, Fin. 45 60 28N 26 58 E
Kra, Isthmus of, Thai. 63 10 15N 99 30 E
Kragujevac, Yug. 41 44 2N 20 56 E
Krakatau, Indon. 63 6 10S 105 20 E
Kraków, Pol. 43 50 4N 19 57 E
Krasnodar, U.S.S.R. 47 45 5N 39 0 E
Krasnoturinsk, U.S.S.R. 46 59 46N 60 12 E
Krasnovodsk, U.S.S.R. 48 40 0N 52 52 E
Krasnoyarsk, U.S.S.R. 49 56 8N 93 0 E
Krefeld, W. Ger. 36 51 20N 6 32 E
Kremenchug, U.S.S.R. 47 49 5N 33 25 E
Krishna →, India 59 15 57N 80 59 E
Kristiansand, Nor. 45 58 9N 8 1 E
Kristianstad, Swed. 45 56 2N 14 9 E
Kristiansund, Nor. 44 63 7N 7 45 E
Krivoy Rog, U.S.S.R. 47 47 51N 33 20 E
Kroonstad, S. Afr. 81 27 43S 27 19 E
Krung Thep = Bangkok, Thai. 63 13 45N 100 35 E
Kruševac, Yug. 41 43 35N 21 28 E
Kuala Lumpur, Malay. 63 3 9N 101 41 E

Kuala Trengganu, *Malay.* **63** 5 20N 103 8 E
Kuangchou = Guangzhou, *China* **61** 23 5N 113 10 E
Kuantan, *Malay.* **63** 3 49N 103 20 E
Kucing, *Malay.* **63** 1 33N 110 25 E
Kueiyang = Guiyang, *China* **60** 26 32N 106 40 E
Kumanovo, *Yug.* **41** 42 9N 21 42 E
Kumasi, *Ghana* **78** 6 41N 1 38W
Kunlun Shan, *Asia* **60** 36 0N 86 30 E
Kunming, *China* **60** 25 1N 102 41 E
Kuopio, *Fin.* **44** 62 53N 27 35 E
Kura →, *U.S.S.R.* **47** 39 50N 49 20 E
Kurashiki, *Jap.* **62** 34 40N 133 50 E
Kure, *Jap.* **62** 34 14N 132 32 E
Kurgan, *U.S.S.R.* **48** 55 26N 65 18 E
Kuria Maria Is., *Ind. Oc.* **57** 17 30N 55 58 E
Kuril Is., *U.S.S.R.* **49** 45 0N 150 0 E
Kurnool, *India* **58** 15 45N 78 0 E
Kurri Kurri, *Austral.* **70** 32 50S 151 28 E
Kursk, *U.S.S.R.* **46** 51 42N 36 11 E
Kurume, *Jap.* **62** 33 15N 130 30 E
Kushiro, *Jap.* **62** 43 0N 144 25 E
Kustanay, *U.S.S.R.* **48** 53 10N 63 35 E
Kütahya, *Turk.* **47** 39 30N 30 2 E
Kutaisi, *U.S.S.R.* **47** 42 19N 42 40 E
Kutch, Gulf of, *India* **58** 22 50N 69 15 E
Kutch, Rann of, *India* **58** 24 0N 70 0 E
Kuwait, *Kuw.* **56** 29 30N 47 30 E
Kuwait ■, *Asia* **56** 29 30N 47 30 E
Kuybyshev, *U.S.S.R.* **46** 53 8N 50 6 E
Kwangju, *S. Kor.* **61** 35 9N 126 54 E
Kyle, *U.K.* **20** 55 32N 4 25W
Kyle of Lochalsh, *U.K.* **22** 57 17N 5 43W
Kyōto, *Jap.* **62** 35 0N 135 45 E
Kyūshū, *Jap.* **62** 33 0N 131 0 E
Kzyl-Orda, *U.S.S.R.* **48** 44 48N 65 28 E

L

Labe = Elbe →, *Ger.* **42** 53 50N 9 0 E
Labé, *Guin.* **78** 11 24N 12 16W
Labrador, Coast of □, *Canada* **89** 53 20N 61 0W
Labrador City, *Canada* **89** 52 57N 66 55W
Laccadive Is. = Lakshadweep Is., *Ind. Oc.* **51** 10 0N 72 30 E
Laceby, *U.K.* **19** 53 32N 0 10W
Lachlan →, *Austral.* **70** 34 22S 143 55 E
Lacock, *U.K.* **14** 51 24N 2 8W
Ladock, *U.K.* **16** 50 19N 4 58W
Ladoga, L., *U.S.S.R.* **46** 61 15N 30 30 E
Ladybank, *U.K.* **21** 56 16N 3 8W
Lafayette, *U.S.A.* **90** 30 18N 92 0W
Lagan →, *U.K.* **24** 54 35N 5 55W
Lagg, *U.K.* **20** 55 51N 5 50W
Laggan B., *U.K.* **20** 55 40N 6 20W
Lagos, *Nig.* **78** 6 25N 3 27 E
Lagos, *Port.* **37** 37 5N 8 41W
Lahore, *Pak.* **58** 31 32N 74 22 E
Lahti, *Fin.* **45** 60 58N 25 40 E
Lairg, *U.K.* **23** 58 1N 4 24W
Lake Charles, *U.S.A.* **90** 30 15N 93 10W
Lake District, *U.K.* **18** 54 30N 3 10W
Lakenheath, *U.K.* **15** 52 25N 0 30 E
Lakewood, *U.S.A.* **92** 41 28N 81 50W
Lakshadweep Is., *Ind. Oc.* **51** 10 0N 72 30 E
Lambay I., *Ire.* **24** 53 30N 6 0W
Lamberhurst, *U.K.* **15** 51 5N 0 21 E
Lambeth, *U.K.* **15** 51 27N 0 7W
Lambley, *U.K.* **21** 54 56N 2 30W
Lambourn, *U.K.* **14** 51 31N 1 31W
Lamlash, *U.K.* **20** 55 32N 5 8W
Lammermuir, *U.K.* **21** 55 50N 2 25W
Lammermuir Hills, *U.K.* **21** 55 50N 2 40W
Lampeter, *U.K.* **17** 52 6N 4 6W
Lanark, *U.K.* **21** 55 40N 3 48W
Lancashire □, *U.K.* **18** 53 40N 2 30W
Lancaster, *U.K.* **18** 54 3N 2 48W
Lancaster Sd., *Canada* **89** 74 13N 84 0W
Lanchester, *U.K.* **19** 54 50N 1 44W
Lancing, *U.K.* **15** 50 49N 0 19W
Landkey, *U.K.* **16** 51 2N 4 0W
Land's End, *U.K.* **16** 50 4N 5 43W
Langholm, *U.K.* **21** 55 9N 2 59W
Langness, *U.K.* **18** 54 3N 4 37W
Langport, *U.K.* **14** 51 2N 2 51W
Langstrothdale Chase, *U.K.* **18** 54 14N 2 13W
Langtoft, *U.K.* **15** 52 42N 0 19W
Langtree, *U.K.* **16** 50 55N 4 11W
Lansing, *U.S.A.* **92** 42 47N 84 40W
Lanzhou, *China* **60** 36 1N 103 52 E
Laoag, *Phil.* **63** 18 7N 120 34 E
Laois □, *Ire.* **25** 53 0N 7 20W
Laos ■, *Asia* **63** 17 45N 105 0 E
Lapford, *U.K.* **16** 50 52N 3 49W
Lapland, *Europe* **44** 68 7N 24 0 E
Laptev Sea, *U.S.S.R.* **49** 76 0N 125 0 E
Larbert, *U.K.* **21** 56 2N 3 50W
Laredo, *U.S.A.* **90** 27 34N 99 29W
Largs, *U.K.* **20** 55 48N 4 51W
Lárisa, *Greece* **41** 39 49N 22 28 E
Larkhall, *U.K.* **21** 55 44N 4 0W
Larne, *U.K.* **24** 54 52N 5 50W
Las Palmas, *Can. Is.* **78** 28 7N 15 26W
Las Vegas, *U.S.A.* **90** 36 10N 115 5W
Laskill, *U.K.* **19** 54 19N 1 6W
Lasswade, *U.K.* **21** 55 53N 3 8W
Latakia, *Syria* **56** 35 30N 35 45 E
Latina, *It.* **40** 41 26N 12 53 E
Latvia □, *U.S.S.R.* **46** 56 50N 24 0 E
Lauder, *U.K.* **21** 55 43N 2 45W
Lauderdale, *U.K.* **21** 55 43N 2 44W
Launceston, *Austral.* **67** 41 24S 147 8 E
Launceston, *U.K.* **16** 50 38N 4 21W
Laune →, *Ire.* **25** 52 5N 9 40W
Laurencekirk, *U.K.* **23** 56 50N 2 30W
Laurentian Plateau, *Canada* **82** 52 0N 70 0W
Laurieston, *U.K.* **21** 54 57N 4 2W
Lausanne, *Switz.* **42** 46 32N 6 38 E
Laval, *Fr.* **34** 48 4N 0 48W
Lavendon, *U.K.* **15** 52 11N 0 39W
Lavenham, *U.K.* **15** 52 7N 0 48 E
Lawers, *U.K.* **21** 56 31N 4 9W
Lawrence, *U.S.A.* **93** 42 40N 71 9W
Laxey, *U.K.* **18** 54 15N 4 23W
Laxfield, *U.K.* **15** 52 18N 1 23 E
Laxford, L., *U.K.* **22** 58 25N 5 10W
Lazonby, *U.K.* **18** 54 45N 2 42W
Lea, *U.K.* **19** 53 22N 0 45W
Lea →, *U.K.* **15** 51 30N 0 10W
Leadenham, *U.K.* **19** 53 5N 0 33W
Leadhills, *U.K.* **21** 55 25N 3 47W
Leamington, *U.K.* **14** 52 18N 1 32W
Leatherhead, *U.K.* **15** 51 18N 0 20W
Lebanon ■, *Asia* **56** 34 0N 36 0 E
Lecce, *It.* **41** 40 20N 18 10 E
Lechlade, *U.K.* **14** 51 42N 1 40W
Ledbury, *U.K.* **14** 52 3N 2 25W
Leduc, *Canada* **88** 53 15N 113 30W
Lee, *U.K.* **14** 50 47N 1 11W
Lee →, *Ire.* **25** 51 50N 8 30W
Leeds, *U.K.* **19** 53 48N 1 34W
Leek, *U.K.* **18** 53 7N 2 2W
Leer, *W. Ger.* **36** 53 13N 7 29 E
Leeton, *Austral.* **70** 34 33S 146 23 E
Leeuwarden, *Neth.* **36** 53 15N 5 48 E
Leeuwin, C., *Austral.* **66** 34 20S 115 9 E
Leghorn, *It.* **40** 43 32N 10 18 E
Legnica, *Pol.* **42** 51 12N 16 10 E
Leicester, *U.K.* **14** 52 39N 1 9W
Leicester □, *U.K.* **14** 52 40N 1 10W
Leiden, *Neth.* **36** 52 9N 4 30 E
Leigh, *Gr. Manchester, U.K.* **18** 53 29N 2 31W
Leigh, *Hereford & Worcs., U.K.* **14** 52 10N 2 21W
Leighton Buzzard, *U.K.* **15** 51 55N 0 39W
Leinster □, *Ire.* **25** 53 0N 7 10W
Leinster, Mt., *Ire.* **25** 52 38N 6 47W
Leintwardine, *U.K.* **14** 52 22N 2 51W
Leipzig, *E. Ger.* **42** 51 20N 12 23 E
Leiston, *U.K.* **15** 52 13N 1 35 E
Leith, *U.K.* **21** 55 59N 3 10W
Leith Hill, *U.K.* **15** 51 10N 0 23W
Leitholm, *U.K.* **21** 55 42N 2 16W
Leitrim, *Ire.* **24** 54 0N 8 5W
Leitrim □, *Ire.* **24** 54 8N 8 0W
Lek →, *Neth.* **36** 51 54N 4 35 E
Lelant, *U.K.* **16** 50 11N 5 26W
Lelystad, *Neth.* **36** 52 30N 5 25 E
Lena →, *U.S.S.R.* **49** 72 52N 126 40 E
Lendalfoot, *U.K.* **20** 55 12N 4 55W
Lenham, *U.K.* **15** 51 14N 0 44 E
Leninakan, *U.S.S.R.* **47** 40 47N 43 50 E
Leningrad, *U.S.S.R.* **46** 59 55N 30 20 E
Leninsk-Kuznetskiy, *U.S.S.R.* **48** 54 44N 86 10 E
Lennox Hills, *U.K.* **20** 56 3N 4 12W
Lennoxtown, *U.K.* **20** 55 58N 4 14W
Lens, *Fr.* **34** 50 26N 2 50 E
Leominster, *U.K.* **14** 52 15N 2 43W
León, *Mex.* **94** 21 7N 101 40W
León, *Sp.* **37** 42 38N 5 34W
Lérida, *Sp.* **37** 41 37N 0 39 E
Lerwick, *U.K.* **22** 60 10N 1 10W
Lesbos, I. = Lésvos, *Greece* **41** 39 10N 26 20 E
Lesbury, *U.K.* **21** 55 25N 1 37W
Leskovac, *Yug.* **41** 43 0N 21 58 E
Leslie, *U.K.* **21** 56 12N 3 12W
Lesmahagow, *U.K.* **21** 55 38N 3 55W
Lesotho ■, *Africa* **81** 29 40S 28 0 E
Lésvos, *Greece* **41** 39 10N 26 20 E
Leswalt, *U.K.* **20** 54 56N 5 6W
Letchworth, *U.K.* **15** 51 58N 0 13W
Lethbridge, *Canada* **88** 49 45N 112 45W
Letterkenny, *Ire.* **24** 54 57N 7 42W
Leuchars, *U.K.* **21** 56 23N 2 53W
Leven, *Fife, U.K.* **21** 56 12N 3 0W
Leven, *Humberside, U.K.* **19** 53 54N 0 18W
Leven →, *U.K.* **19** 54 27N 1 15W
Leven, L., *U.K.* **21** 56 12N 3 22W
Leverburgh, *U.K.* **22** 57 46N 7 0W
Leverkusen, *W. Ger.* **36** 51 2N 6 59 E
Lewes, *U.K.* **15** 50 53N 0 2 E
Lewis, *U.K.* **22** 58 10N 6 40W
Lewis, Butt of, *U.K.* **22** 58 30N 6 12W
Lewisham, *U.K.* **15** 51 27N 0 1W
Lexington, *U.S.A.* **92** 38 6N 84 30W
Leyburn, *U.K.* **19** 54 19N 1 50W
Leyland, *U.K.* **18** 53 41N 2 42W
Leysdown on Sea, *U.K.* **15** 51 23N 0 57 E
Lhasa, *China* **60** 29 50N 91 3 E
Liaodong, Gulf of, *China* **61** 40 20N 121 10 E
Liaoning □, *China* **61** 41 40N 122 30 E
Liaoyang, *China* **61** 41 15N 123 10 E
Liaoyüan, *China* **61** 42 55N 125 10 E
Liberia ■, *W. Afr.* **78** 6 30N 9 30W
Libreville, *Gabon* **80** 0 25N 9 26 E
Libya ■, *N. Afr.* **79** 27 0N 17 0 E
Libyan Desert, *Africa* **79** 25 0N 25 0 E
Lichfield, *U.K.* **14** 52 40N 1 50W
Lichinga, *Mozam.* **81** 13 13S 35 11 E
Liechtenstein ■, *Europe* **42** 47 8N 9 35 E
Liège, *Belg.* **36** 50 38N 5 35 E
Liepaja, *U.S.S.R.* **46** 56 30N 21 0 E
Liffey →, *Ire.* **25** 53 21N 6 20W
Lifford, *Ire.* **24** 54 50N 7 30W
Ligurian Sea, *It.* **40** 43 20N 9 0 E
Likasi, *Zaïre* **80** 10 55S 26 48 E
Lille, *Fr.* **34** 50 38N 3 3 E
Lille Bælt, *Den.* **45** 55 20N 9 45 E
Lillehammer, *Nor.* **45** 61 8N 10 30 E
Lilleshall, *U.K.* **14** 52 45N 2 22W
Lilongwe, *Malawi* **81** 14 0S 33 48 E
Lima, *Peru* **100** 12 0S 77 0W
Limassol, *Cyprus* **47** 34 42N 33 1 E
Limavady, *U.K.* **24** 55 3N 6 58W
Limavady □, *U.K.* **24** 55 0N 6 55W
Limburg □, *Neth.* **36** 51 20N 5 55 E
Limerick, *Ire.* **25** 52 40N 8 38W
Limerick □, *Ire.* **25** 52 30N 8 50W
Límnos, *Greece* **41** 39 50N 25 5 E
Limoges, *Fr.* **35** 45 50N 1 15 E
Limpopo →, *Mozam.* **81** 25 15S 33 30 E
Limpsfield, *U.K.* **15** 51 15N 0 1 E
Linares, *Sp.* **37** 38 10N 3 40W
Lincluden, *U.K.* **21** 55 5N 3 40W
Lincoln, *U.K.* **19** 53 14N 0 32W
Lincoln, *U.S.A.* **90** 40 50N 96 42W
Lincoln □, *U.K.* **19** 53 14N 0 32W
Lincoln Wolds, *U.K.* **19** 53 20N 0 5W
Lindale, *U.K.* **18** 54 14N 2 54W
Lingfield, *U.K.* **15** 51 11N 0 1W
Linkinhorne, *U.K.* **16** 50 31N 4 22W
Linköping, *Swed.* **45** 58 28N 15 36 E
Linlithgow, *U.K.* **21** 55 58N 3 38W
Linnhe, L., *U.K.* **20** 56 36N 5 25W
Linslade, *U.K.* **15** 51 55N 0 40W
Linton, *U.K.* **15** 52 6N 0 19 E
Linxia, *China* **60** 35 36N 103 10 E
Linz, *Austria* **42** 48 18N 14 18 E
Lion, G. du, *Fr.* **35** 43 0N 4 0 E
Lípari, Is., *It.* **40** 38 30N 14 50 E
Lipetsk, *U.S.S.R.* **46** 52 37N 39 35 E
Lisbon, *Port.* **37** 38 42N 9 10W
Lisburn, *U.K.* **24** 54 30N 6 9W
Liscannor, B., *Ire.* **25** 52 57N 9 24W
Liskeard, *U.K.* **16** 50 27N 4 29W
Lismore, *Austral.* **67** 28 44S 153 21 E
Lismore, *Ire.* **25** 52 8N 7 58W
Lismore I., *U.K.* **20** 56 30N 5 30W
Liss, *U.K.* **15** 51 3N 0 53W
Listowel, *Ire.* **25** 52 27N 9 30W
Litcham, *U.K.* **15** 52 43N 0 49 E
Litherland, *U.K.* **18** 53 29N 3 0W
Lithgow, *Austral.* **70** 33 25S 150 8 E
Lithuania □, *U.S.S.R.* **46** 55 30N 24 0 E
Little Minch, *U.K.* **22** 57 35N 6 45W
Little Ouse →, *U.K.* **15** 52 25N 0 50 E
Little Rock, *U.S.A.* **91** 34 41N 92 10W
Little Walsingham, *U.K.* **15** 52 53N 0 51 E
Littleborough, *U.K.* **18** 53 38N 2 8W
Littlehampton, *U.K.* **15** 50 48N 0 32W
Littleport, *U.K.* **15** 52 27N 0 18 E
Littlestone-on-Sea, *U.K.* **15** 50 59N 0 59 E
Liuzhou, *China* **61** 24 22N 109 22 E
Liverpool, *Austral.* **70** 33 54S 150 58 E
Liverpool, *U.K.* **18** 53 25N 3 0W
Liverpool Plains, *Austral.* **70** 31 15S 150 15 E
Livingston, *U.K.* **21** 55 52N 3 33W
Livingstone, *Zam.* **81** 17 46S 25 52 E
Lizard, *U.K.* **16** 49 58N 5 10W
Lizard Pt., *U.K.* **16** 49 57N 5 11W
Ljubljana, *Yug.* **40** 46 4N 14 33 E
Llandeilo, *U.K.* **17** 51 53N 4 0W
Llandovery, *U.K.* **17** 51 59N 3 49W
Llandrindod Wells, *U.K.* **17** 52 15N 3 23W
Llandudno, *U.K.* **17** 53 19N 3 51W
Llanelli, *U.K.* **17** 51 41N 4 11W
Llanerchymedd, *U.K.* **17** 53 20N 4 22W
Llanfair Caereinion, *U.K.* **17** 52 39N 3 20W
Llanfair Talhaiarn, *U.K.* **17** 53 13N 3 37W
Llanfairfechan, *U.K.* **17** 53 15N 3 58W
Llangefni, *U.K.* **17** 53 15N 4 20W
Llangollen, *U.K.* **17** 52 58N 3 10W
Llanidloes, *U.K.* **17** 52 28N 3 31W
Llanllyfni, *U.K.* **17** 53 2N 4 18W
Llanos, *S. Am.* **100** 5 0N 71 35W
Llanrhystyd, *U.K.* **17** 52 19N 4 9W
Llantrisant, *U.K.* **17** 51 33N 3 22W
Llantwit-Major, *U.K.* **17** 51 24N 3 29W
Llanwrtyd Wells, *U.K.* **17** 52 6N 3 39W
Llanyblodwel, *U.K.* **14** 52 47N 3 8W
Llanymynech, *U.K.* **14** 52 48N 3 6W
Lleyn Peninsula, *U.K.* **17** 52 55N 4 35W
Loanhead, *U.K.* **21** 55 53N 3 10W
Lobito, *Angola* **81** 12 18S 13 35 E
Lochaber, *U.K.* **22** 56 55N 5 0W
Lochans, *U.K.* **20** 54 52N 5 1W
Lochboisdale, *U.K.* **22** 57 10N 7 20W
Lochbuie, *U.K.* **20** 56 21N 5 52W
Lochcarron, *U.K.* **22** 57 25N 5 30W
Lochdonhead, *U.K.* **20** 56 27N 5 40W
Lochearnhead, *U.K.* **20** 56 24N 4 19W
Lochgelly, *U.K.* **21** 56 7N 3 18W
Lochgilphead, *U.K.* **20** 56 2N 5 37W
Lochgoilhead, *U.K.* **20** 56 10N 4 54W
Lochinver, *U.K.* **22** 58 9N 5 15W
Lochmaben, *U.K.* **21** 55 8N 3 27W
Lochmaddy, *U.K.* **22** 57 36N 7 10W
Lochnagar, *U.K.* **23** 56 57N 3 14W
Lochranza, *U.K.* **20** 55 42N 5 18W
Lochwinnoch, *U.K.* **20** 55 47N 4 39W
Lochy →, *U.K.* **22** 56 52N 5 3W
Lockerbie, *U.K.* **21** 55 7N 3 21W
Lod, *Isr.* **57** 31 57N 34 54 E
Loddon, *U.K.* **15** 52 32N 1 29 E
Łódź, *Pol.* **43** 51 45N 19 27 E
Lofoten, *Nor.* **44** 68 30N 15 0 E
Loftus, *U.K.* **19** 54 33N 0 52W
Logan, Mt., *Canada* **88** 60 31N 140 22W
Logroño, *Sp.* **37** 42 28N 2 27W
Loire →, *Fr.* **34** 47 16N 2 10W
Lolland, *Den.* **45** 54 45N 11 30 E
Lombardy □, *It.* **40** 45 35N 9 45 E
Lomé, *Togo* **78** 6 9N 1 20 E
Lomond, L., *U.K.* **20** 56 8N 4 38W
Łomza, *Pol.* **43** 53 10N 22 2 E
London, *Canada* **92** 42 59N 81 15W
London, *U.K.* **15** 51 30N 0 5W
London, Greater □, *U.K.* **15** 51 30N 0 5W
Londonderry, *U.K.* **24** 55 0N 7 20W
Londonderry □, *U.K.* **24** 55 0N 7 20W
Londrina, *Brazil* **102** 23 18S 51 10W
Long, L., *U.K.* **20** 56 4N 4 50W
Long Beach, *U.S.A.* **90** 33 46N 118 12W
Long Bennington, *U.K.* **19** 52 59N 0 45W
Long Clawson, *U.K.* **15** 52 51N 0 56W
Long Crendon, *U.K.* **15** 51 47N 1 0W
Long Eaton, *U.K.* **19** 52 54N 1 16W
Long I., *Baham.* **95** 23 20N 75 10W
Long I., *U.S.A.* **93** 40 50N 73 20W
Long Itchington, *U.K.* **14** 52 16N 1 24W
Long Melford, *U.K.* **15** 52 5N 0 44 E
Long Mynd, *U.K.* **14** 52 35N 2 50W
Long Preston, *U.K.* **18** 54 0N 2 16W
Long Sutton, *U.K.* **15** 52 47N 0 9 E
Longford, *Ire.* **24** 53 43N 7 50W
Longford, *U.K.* **14** 51 53N 2 14W
Longford □, *Ire.* **24** 53 42N 7 45W
Longforgan, *U.K.* **21** 56 28N 3 8W
Longframlington, *U.K.* **21** 55 18N 1 47W
Longhorsley, *U.K.* **21** 55 15N 1 46W
Longhoughton, *U.K.* **21** 55 26N 1 36W
Longridge, *U.K.* **18** 53 50N 2 37W
Longton, *U.K.* **18** 53 43N 2 48W
Longtown, *Cumbria, U.K.* **18** 55 1N 2 59W
Longtown, *Hereford & Worcs., U.K.* **14** 51 58N 2 59W
Löningen, *W. Ger.* **36** 52 43N 7 44 E
Looe, *U.K.* **16** 50 24N 4 25W
Loop Hd., *Ire.* **25** 52 34N 9 55W
Lop Nor, *China* **60** 40 20N 90 10 E
Lorca, *Sp.* **37** 37 41N 1 42W
Lorient, *Fr.* **34** 47 45N 3 23W
Lorn, *U.K.* **20** 56 26N 5 10W
Lorn, Firth of, *U.K.* **20** 56 20N 5 40W
Los Angeles, *Chile* **102** 37 28S 72 23W
Los Angeles, *U.S.A.* **90** 34 0N 118 10W
Los Mochis, *Mex.* **94** 25 45N 108 57W
Lossiemouth, *U.K.* **23** 57 43N 3 17W
Lostwithiel, *U.K.* **16** 50 24N 4 41W
Lothian □, *U.K.* **21** 55 50N 3 0W
Loughborough, *U.K.* **14** 52 46N 1 11W
Loughrea, *Ire.* **25** 53 11N 8 33W
Loughros More B., *Ire.* **24** 54 48N 8 30W
Louisiana □, *U.S.A.* **91** 30 50N 92 0W
Louisville, *U.S.A.* **92** 38 15N 85 45W
Lourdes, *Fr.* **35** 43 6N 0 3W
Louth, *Ire.* **24** 53 47N 6 33W
Louth, *U.K.* **19** 53 23N 0 0 E
Louth □, *Ire.* **24** 53 55N 6 30W
Louvière, La, *Belg.* **36** 50 27N 4 10 E
Lowell, *U.S.A.* **93** 42 38N 71 19W
Lower Beeding, *U.K.* **15** 51 2N 0 15W
Lower California, *Mex.* **94** 31 10N 115 12W
Lower Hutt, *N.Z.* **71** 41 10S 174 55 E
Lower Tunguska →, *U.S.S.R.* **49** 64 20N 93 0 E
Lowes Water L., *U.K.* **18** 54 35N 3 23W
Lowestoft, *U.K.* **15** 52 29N 1 44 E
Lowick, *U.K.* **21** 55 38N 1 57W
Lowther Hills, *U.K.* **21** 55 20N 3 40W
Luanda, *Angola* **80** 8 50S 13 15 E
Luanshya, *Zam.* **81** 13 3S 28 28 E
Lubbock, *U.S.A.* **90** 33 40N 101 53W
Lübeck, *W. Ger.* **42** 53 52N 10 41 E
Lublin, *Pol.* **43** 51 12N 22 38 E
Lubumbashi, *Zaïre* **81** 11 40S 27 28 E
Luce Bay, *U.K.* **20** 54 45N 4 48W
Lucknow, *India* **59** 26 50N 81 0 E
Lüda = Dalian, *China* **61** 38 50N 121 40 E
Ludgershall, *U.K.* **14** 51 15N 1 38W
Ludgvan, *U.K.* **16** 50 9N 5 30W
Ludhiana, *India* **58** 30 57N 75 56 E
Ludlow, *U.K.* **14** 52 23N 2 42W
Ludwigshafen, *W. Ger.* **42** 49 27N 8 27 E

Lugano, *Switz.* .... **42** 46 0N 8 57 E
Lugnaquilla, *Ire.* **25** 52 58N 6 28W
Lugo, *Sp.* **37** 43 2N 7 35W
Lugwardine, *U.K.* **14** 52 4N 2 38W
Luing I., *U.K.* **20** 56 15N 5 40W
Luleå, *Swed.* .... **44** 65 35N 22 10 E
Lundy, *U.K.* **16** 51 10N 4 41W
Lune →, *U.K.* **18** 54 0N 2 51W
Lünen, *W. Ger.* ...... **36** 51 36N 7 31 E
Luoyang, *China* ...... **61** 34 40N 112 26 E
Lurgan, *U.K.* **24** 54 28N 6 20W
Lusaka, *Zam.* .... **81** 15 28S 28 16 E
Luss, *U.K.* **20** 56 6N 4 40W
Luton, *U.K.* **15** 51 53N 0 24W
Lutterworth, *U.K.* **14** 52 28N 1 12W
Luxembourg, *Lux.* ..... **36** 49 37N 6 9 E
Luxembourg ■, *Europe* **36** 50 0N 6 0 E
Luzern, *Switz.* .... **42** 47 3N 8 18 E
Luzhou, *China* .... **60** 28 52N 105 20 E
Luzon, *Phil.* .... **63** 16 0N 121 0 E
Lvov, *U.S.S.R.* .... **47** 49 50N 24 0 E
Lyakhov Is., *U.S.S.R.* . **49** 73 40N 141 0 E
Lybster, *U.K.* **23** 58 18N 3 16W
Lydd, *U.K.* .... **15** 50 57N 0 56 E
Lydford, *U.K.* **16** 50 38N 4 7W
Lydham, *U.K.* **14** 52 31N 2 59W
Lyell Range, *N.Z.* ..... **71** 41 38S 172 20 E
Lyme Bay, *U.K.* **16** 50 36N 2 55W
Lyme Regis, *U.K.* **16** 50 44N 2 57W
Lyminge, *U.K.* .... **15** 51 7N 1 6 E
Lymington, *U.K.* **14** 50 46N 1 32W
Lymm, *U.K.* **18** 53 23N 2 30W
Lympne, *U.K.* .... **15** 51 4N 1 2 E
Lynchburg, *U.S.A.* **92** 37 23N 79 10W
Lyndhurst, *U.K.* **14** 50 53N 1 33W
Lyneham, *U.K.* **14** 51 30N 1 57W
Lynemouth, *U.K.* **21** 55 15N 1 29W
Lynmouth, *U.K.* **16** 51 14N 3 50W
Lynn Lake, *Canada* ... **88** 56 51N 101 3W
Lynton, *U.K.* **16** 51 14N 3 50W
Lyons, *Fr.* .... **35** 45 46N 4 50 E
Lytchett Minster, *U.K.* . **14** 50 44N 2 3W
Lytham St. Anne's, *U.K.* **18** 53 45N 2 58W
Lythe, *U.K.* **19** 54 30N 0 40W

M

Ma'ān, *Jord.* .... **56** 30 12N 35 44 E
Maarianhamina, *Fin.* .. **45** 60 5N 19 55 E
Maastricht, *Neth.* .... **36** 50 50N 5 40 E
Mablethorpe, *U.K.* .... **19** 53 21N 0 14 E
Macapá, *Brazil* **101** 0 5N 51 4W
Macau ■, *Asia* ...... **61** 22 16N 113 35 E
Macclesfield, *U.K.* **18** 53 16N 2 9W
McClure Str., *Canada* . **103** 75 0N 119 0W
Macdonnell Ranges,
Austral. .... **66** 23 40S 133 0 E
Macduff, *U.K.* **23** 57 40N 2 30W
Macedonia □, *Greece* **41** 40 39N 22 0 E
Macedonia □, *Yug.* ... **41** 41 53N 21 40 E
Maceió, *Brazil* **101** 9 40S 35 41W
Macgillycuddy's Reeks,
Ire. **25** 52 2N 9 45W
Machakos, *Kenya* .... **80** 1 30S 37 15 E
Machala, *Ecuad.* **100** 3 20S 79 57W
Machars, The, *U.K.* ... **20** 54 46N 4 30W
Machrihanish, *U.K.* ... **20** 55 25N 5 42W
Machynlleth, *U.K.* **17** 52 36N 3 51W
Macintyre →, *Austral.* **67** 28 37S 150 47 E
Mackay, *Austral.* ..... **67** 21 8S 149 11 E
Mackay, L., *Austral.* .. **66** 22 30S 129 0 E
McKeesport, *U.S.A.* .. **92** 40 21N 79 50W
Mackenzie →, *Austral.* **67** 23 38S 149 46 E
Mackenzie →, *Canada* **88** 69 10N 134 20W
Mackenzie Mts.,
Canada **88** 64 0N 130 0W
McKinley, Mt., *U.S.A.* . **88** 63 2N 151 0W
M'Clintock Chan.,
Canada **88** 72 0N 102 0W
Macon, *U.S.A.* **90** 32 50N 83 37W
Macquarie →, *Austral.* **70** 30 5S 147 30 E
Macquarie Harbour,
Austral. .... **67** 42 15S 145 23 E
Macquarie Is., *S. Oc.* . **64** 54 36S 158 55 E
Macroom, *Ire.* **25** 51 54N 8 57W
Madadeni, *S. Afr.* .... **81** 27 43S 30 3 E
Madagascar ■, *Africa* **81** 20 0S 47 0 E
Madeira, *Atl. Oc.* **78** 32 50N 17 0W
Madeira →, *Brazil* ... **100** 3 22S 58 45W
Madeley, *Salop, U.K.* . **14** 52 38N 2 28W
Madeley, *Staffs., U.K.* . **18** 52 59N 2 20W
Madhya Pradesh □,
India .... **59** 21 50N 81 0 E
Madīnat ash Sha'b,
S. Yem. .... **56** 12 50N 45 0 E
Madison, *U.S.A.* **92** 43 5N 89 25W
Madiun, *Indon.* ...... **63** 7 38S 111 32 E
Madley, *U.K.* **14** 52 3N 2 51W
Madras, *India* .... **58** 13 8N 80 19 E
Madre, L., *U.S.A.* **91** 26 0N 97 40W
Madre, Sierra, *Mex.* .. **94** 16 0N 93 0W
Madrid, *Sp.* **37** 40 25N 3 45W
Madurai, *India* .... **58** 9 55N 78 10 E
Maesteg, *U.K.* **17** 51 36N 3 40W
Magadan, *U.S.S.R.* ... **49** 59 38N 150 50 E
Magdalena →, *Col.* .. **100** 11 6N 74 51W
Magdeburg, *E. Ger.* .. **42** 52 8N 11 36 E
Magee, I., *U.K.* **24** 54 48N 5 44W
Magelang, *Indon.* .... **63** 7 29S 110 13 E
Magellan's Str., *Chile* . **102** 52 30S 75 0W
Maggiore, L., *It.* ..... **40** 46 0N 8 35 E
Magherafelt, *U.K.* **24** 54 44N 6 37W
Maghull, *U.K.* **18** 53 31N 2 56W
Magnitogorsk, *U.S.S.R.* **46** 53 27N 59 4 E
Mahajanga, *Madag.* .. **81** 17 0S 47 0 E
Maiden Bradley, *U.K.* . **14** 51 9N 2 18W
Maiden Newton, *U.K.* . **14** 50 46N 2 35W
Maidenhead, *U.K.* **15** 51 31N 0 42W
Maidstone, *U.K.* ..... **15** 51 16N 0 31 E
Maiduguri, *Nig.* ...... **79** 12 0N 13 20 E
Main →, *U.K.* **24** 54 49N 6 20W
Maine □, *U.S.A.* **93** 45 20N 69 0W
Maine →, *Ire.* **25** 52 10N 9 40W
Mainland, *Orkney, U.K.* **23** 59 0N 3 10W
Mainland, *Shetland,*
U.K. **22** 60 15N 1 22W
Mainz, *W. Ger.* ...... **36** 50 0N 8 17 E
Maitland, *Austral.* .... **70** 32 33S 151 36 E
Majorca, I. = Mallorca,
Sp. .... **37** 39 30N 3 0 E
Makasar, Str. of, *Indon.* **63** 1 0S 118 20 E
Maker, *U.K.* **16** 50 20N 4 10W
Makeyevka, *U.S.S.R.* . **47** 48 0N 38 0 E
Makhachkala, *U.S.S.R.* **47** 43 0N 47 30 E
Makran Coast Range,
Pak. .... **58** 25 40N 64 0 E
Mal B., *Ire.* **25** 52 50N 9 30W
Malabar Coast, *India* . **58** 11 0N 75 0 E
Malacca, Str. of, *Indon.* **63** 3 0N 101 0 E
Málaga, *Sp.* **37** 36 43N 4 23W
Malang, *Indon.* ...... **63** 7 59S 112 45 E
Malanje, *Angola* ..... **80** 9 36S 16 17 E
Mälaren, *Swed.* ...... **45** 59 30N 17 10 E
Malatya, *Turk.* .... **47** 38 25N 38 20 E
Malawi ■, *Africa* ..... **81** 13 0S 34 0 E
Malay Pen., *Asia* .... **63** 7 25N 100 0 E
Malaysia ■, *Asia* .... **63** 5 0N 110 0 E
Maldives ■, *Ind. Oc.* . **129** 7 0N 73 0 E
Maldon, *U.K.* .... **15** 51 43N 0 41 E
Malham Tarn, *U.K.* ... **18** 54 6N 2 11W
Mali ■, *Africa* **78** 15 0N 2 0W
Mallaig, *U.K.* **22** 57 0N 5 50W
Mallorca, *Sp.* .... **37** 39 30N 3 0 E
Mallow, *Ire.* **25** 52 8N 8 40W
Malmédy, *Belg.* ...... **36** 50 25N 6 2 E
Malmesbury, *U.K.* **14** 51 35N 2 5W
Malmö, *Swed.* .... **45** 55 36N 12 59 E
Malpas, *U.K.* **18** 53 3N 2 47W
Malta ■, *Europe* ..... **40** 35 50N 14 30 E
Maltby, *U.K.* **19** 53 25N 1 12W
Malton, *U.K.* **19** 54 9N 0 48W
Malvern, *U.K.* **14** 52 7N 2 19W
Malvern Hills, *U.K.* ... **14** 52 0N 2 19W
Malvern Wells, *U.K.* .. **14** 52 4N 2 19W
Malvinas, Is. = Falkland
Is., *Atl. Oc.* **102** 51 30S 59 0W
Man, I. of, *U.K.* **18** 54 15N 4 30W
Manaar, Gulf of, *Asia* . **58** 8 30N 79 0 E
Manacles, The, *U.K.* .. **16** 50 3N 5 5W
Manado, *Indon.* ...... **63** 1 29N 124 51 E
Managua, *Nic.* **94** 12 6N 86 20W
Manaus, *Brazil* **100** 3 0S 60 0W
Manby, *U.K.* .... **19** 53 22N 0 6 E
Manchester, *U.K.* **18** 53 30N 2 15W
Manchester, *U.S.A.* ... **93** 42 58N 71 29W
Manchuria, *China* .... **61** 42 0N 125 0 E
Mandalay, *Burma* .... **59** 22 0N 96 4 E
Manea, *U.K.* .... **15** 52 29N 0 10 E
Mangalore, *India* .... **58** 12 55N 74 47 E
Mangotsfield, *U.K.* ... **14** 51 29N 2 29W
Manila, *Phil.* .... **63** 14 40N 121 3 E
Manitoba □, *Canada* . **88** 55 30N 97 0W
Manizales, *Col.* **100** 5 5N 75 32W
Manly, *Austral.* ...... **70** 33 48S 151 17 E
Mannheim, *W. Ger.* ... **42** 49 28N 8 29 E
Manningtree, *U.K.* .... **15** 51 56N 1 3 E
Mans, Le, *Fr.* .... **34** 48 0N 0 10 E
Mansfield, *U.K.* **19** 53 8N 1 12W
Mansfield, *U.S.A.* **92** 40 45N 82 30W
Mansfield Woodhouse,
U.K. **19** 53 11N 1 11W
Mantes-la-Jolie, *Fr.* ... **34** 49 0N 1 41 E
Manton, *U.K.* **15** 52 37N 0 41W
Mantua, *It.* .... **40** 45 20N 10 42 E
Manukau, *N.Z.* .... **71** 37 1S 174 55 E
Manzhouli, *China* .... **61** 49 35N 117 25 E
Maoming, *China* ..... **61** 21 50N 110 54 E
Maputo, *Mozam.* ..... **81** 25 58S 32 32 E
Mar del Plata, *Arg.* ... **102** 38 0S 57 30W
Maracaibo, *Ven.* **100** 10 40N 71 37W
Maracaibo, L., *Ven.* ... **100** 9 40N 71 30W
Maracay, *Ven.* **100** 10 15N 67 28W
Marajó, I. de, *Brazil* .. **101** 1 0S 49 30W
Maranhão = São Luís,
Brazil **101** 2 39S 44 15W
Marañón →, *Peru* ... **100** 4 30S 73 35W
Marazion, *U.K.* **16** 50 8N 5 29W
March, *U.K.* .... **15** 52 33N 0 5 E
Marden, *U.K.* **14** 52 7N 2 42W
Maree L., *U.K.* **22** 57 40N 5 30W
Mareeba, *Austral.* .... **67** 16 59S 145 28 E
Mareham le Fen, *U.K.* . **19** 53 7N 0 3W
Marfleet, *U.K.* **19** 53 45N 0 15W
Margarita I., *Ven.* **100** 11 0N 64 0W
Margate, *U.K.* .... **15** 51 23N 1 24 E
Maribor, *Yug.* .... **40** 46 36N 15 40 E
Maricourt, *Canada* ... **89** 56 34N 70 49W
Marie-Galante, *W. Ind.* **94** 15 56N 61 16W
Marília, *Brazil* **101** 22 13S 50 0W
Maringá, *Brazil* **102** 23 26S 52 2W
Mark, *U.K.* **20** 55 2N 5 1W
Market Bosworth, *U.K.* **14** 52 37N 1 24W
Market Deeping, *U.K.* . **15** 52 40N 0 20W
Market Drayton, *U.K.* . **18** 52 55N 2 30W
Market Harborough,
U.K. **15** 52 29N 0 55W
Market Lavington, *U.K.* **14** 51 17N 1 59W
Market Rasen, *U.K.* ... **19** 53 24N 0 20W
Market Weighton, *U.K.* **19** 53 52N 0 40W
Markfield, *U.K.* **14** 52 42N 1 18W
Markinch, *U.K.* **21** 56 12N 3 9W
Marks Tey, *U.K.* ...... **15** 51 53N 0 48 E
Marlborough, *U.K.* **14** 51 26N 1 44W
Marlborough □, *N.Z.* .. **71** 41 45S 173 33 E
Marlborough Downs,
U.K. **14** 51 25N 1 55W
Marlow, *U.K.* **15** 51 34N 0 47W
Marmara, Sea of, *Turk.* **47** 40 45N 28 15 E
Marne →, *Fr.* .... **34** 48 48N 2 24 E
Marnhull, *U.K.* **14** 50 58N 2 20W
Maroua, *Cam.* .... **80** 10 40N 14 20 E
Marple, *U.K.* **18** 53 23N 2 5W
Marquesas Is., *Pac. Oc.* **65** 9 30S 140 0W
Marrakech, *Mor.* **78** 31 9N 8 0W
Marseilles, *Fr.* .... **35** 43 18N 5 23 E
Marshall Is., *Pac. Oc.* . **64** 9 0N 171 0 E
Marshfield, *U.K.* **14** 51 27N 2 18W
Marske by the Sea,
U.K. **19** 54 35N 1 0W
Marston Moor, *U.K.* .. **19** 53 58N 1 17W
Martaban, G. of, *Burma* **59** 16 5N 96 30 E
Martham, *U.K.* .... **15** 52 42N 1 38 E
Martinique, *W. Ind.* ... **94** 14 40N 61 0W
Martley, *U.K.* **14** 52 14N 2 22W
Martock, *U.K.* **14** 50 58N 2 47W
Mary Kathleen, *Austral.* **67** 20 44S 139 48 E
Maryborough, *Austral.* **67** 37 0S 143 44 E
Maryland □, *U.S.A.* ... **93** 39 10N 76 40W
Maryport, *U.K.* **18** 54 43N 3 30W
Marytavy, *U.K.* **16** 50 34N 4 6W
Masan, *S. Kor.* ...... **61** 35 11N 128 32 E
Maseru, *Les.* .... **81** 29 18S 27 30 E
Masham, *U.K.* **19** 54 15N 1 40W
Mashhad, *Iran* .... **57** 36 20N 59 35 E
Mask, L., *Ire.* **24** 53 36N 9 24W
Massachusetts □,
U.S.A. **93** 42 25N 72 0W
Massif Central, *Fr.* ... **35** 45 30N 3 0 E
Masterton, *N.Z.* ...... **71** 40 56S 175 39 E
Masvingo, *Zimb.* ..... **81** 20 8S 30 49 E
Matadi, *Zaïre* .... **80** 5 52S 13 31 E
Matamoros, *Mex.* **94** 25 33N 103 15W
Matera, *It.* .... **40** 40 40N 16 37 E
Matlock, *U.K.* **19** 53 8N 1 32W
Mato Grosso □, *Brazil* **101** 14 0S 55 0W
Matsue, *Jap.* .... **62** 35 25N 133 10 E
Matsuyama, *Jap.* ..... **62** 33 45N 132 45 E
Matterhorn, *Switz.* .... **42** 45 58N 7 39 E
Maturín, *Ven.* **100** 9 45N 63 11W
Maubeuge, *Fr.* .... **34** 50 17N 3 57 E
Mauchline, *U.K.* **20** 55 31N 4 23W
Maughold, *U.K.* **18** 54 18N 4 17W
Maughold Hd., *U.K.* .. **18** 54 18N 4 17W
Maui, *U.S.A.* .... **90** 20 45N 156 20 E
Mauna Loa, *U.S.A.* ... **90** 21 8N 157 10W
Mauritania ■, *Africa* .. **78** 20 50N 10 0W
Mauritius ■, *Ind. Oc.* . **129** 20 0S 57 0 E
Mawgan, *U.K.* **16** 50 4N 5 10W
Mawlaik, *Burma* ..... **59** 23 40N 94 26 E
Maxwellheugh, *U.K.* .. **21** 55 35N 2 23W
May, I. of, *U.K.* **21** 56 11N 2 32W
May Pen, *Jam.* **94** 17 58N 77 15W
Maybole, *U.K.* **20** 55 21N 4 41W
Mayfield, *Derby, U.K.* . **19** 53 1N 1 47W
Mayfield, *E. Sussex,*
U.K. .... **15** 51 1N 0 17 E
Maynooth, *Ire.* **24** 53 22N 6 38W
Mayo □, *Ire.* **24** 53 47N 9 7W
Mazar-e Sharif, *Afg.* .. **57** 36 41N 67 0 E
Mazatlán, *Mex.* **94** 23 13N 106 25W
Mbabane, *Swaz.* ..... **81** 26 18S 31 6 E
Mbandaka, *Zaïre* ..... **80** 0 1N 18 18 E
Mbanza Ngungu, *Zaïre* **80** 5 12S 14 53 E
Mbeya, *Tanz.* .... **80** 8 54S 33 29 E
Mbini □, *Eq. Guin.* ... **80** 1 30N 10 0 E
Mbuji-Mayi, *Zaïre* .... **80** 6 9S 23 40 E
Mdantsane, *S. Afr.* ... **81** 32 56S 27 46 E
Mealsgate, *U.K.* **18** 54 46N 3 14W
Measham, *U.K.* **14** 52 43N 1 30W
Meath □, *Ire.* **24** 53 32N 6 40W
Mecca, *Si. Arab.* ..... **56** 21 30N 39 54 E
Mechelen, *Belg.* ..... **36** 50 58N 5 41 E
Medan, *Indon.* .... **63** 3 40N 98 38 E
Medellín, *Col.* **100** 6 15N 75 35W
Medicine Hat, *Canada* **88** 50 0N 110 45W
Medina, *Si. Arab.* .... **56** 24 35N 39 52 E
Mediterranean Sea,
Europe .... **38** 35 0N 15 0 E
Medley, *Canada* **88** 54 25N 110 16W
Medstead, *U.K.* **14** 51 7N 1 4W
Medway →, *U.K.* .... **15** 51 28N 0 45 E
Meekatharra, *Austral.* . **66** 26 32S 118 29 E
Meerut, *India* .... **58** 29 1N 77 42 E
Mei Xian, *China* ...... **61** 24 16N 116 6 E
Meknès, *Mor.* **78** 33 57N 5 33W
Mekong →, *Asia* .... **63** 9 30N 106 15 E
Melanesia, *Pac. Oc.* .. **64** 4 0S 155 0 E
Melbourn, *U.K.* ...... **15** 52 5N 0 1 E
Melbourne, *Austral.* ... **70** 37 50S 145 0 E
Melbourne, *U.K.* **14** 52 50N 1 25W
Melfort, Loch, *U.K.* ... **20** 56 13N 5 33W
Melitopol, *U.S.S.R.* ... **47** 46 50N 35 22 E
Melksham, *U.K.* **14** 51 22N 2 9W
Melmerby, *U.K.* **18** 54 44N 2 35W
Melrose, *U.K.* **21** 53 35N 2 44W
Melsonby, *U.K.* **19** 54 28N 1 41W
Melton, *U.K.* .... **15** 52 51N 1 1 E
Melton Constable, *U.K.* **15** 52 52N 1 1 E
Melton Mowbray, *U.K.* **15** 52 46N 0 52W
Melvich, *U.K.* **23** 58 33N 3 55W
Melville I., *Austral.* .... **66** 11 30S 131 0 E
Melville Pen., *Canada* . **89** 68 0N 84 0W
Memphis, *U.S.A.* **91** 35 7N 90 0W
Menai Bridge, *U.K.* ... **17** 53 14N 4 11W
Menai Strait, *U.K.* **17** 53 14N 4 10W
Menan = Chao
Phraya →, *Thai.* ... **63** 13 32N 100 36 E
Mendip Hills, *U.K.* **14** 51 17N 2 40W
Mendlesham, *U.K.* .... **15** 52 15N 1 4 E
Mendoza, *Arg.* **102** 32 50S 68 52W
Menindee, *Austral.* ... **70** 32 20S 142 25 E
Menorca, *Sp.* .... **37** 40 0N 4 0 E
Mere, *U.K.* **14** 51 5N 2 16W
Mérida, *Mex.* **94** 20 58N 89 37W
Mérida, *Ven.* **100** 8 24N 71 8W
Meriden, *U.K.* **14** 52 27N 1 36W
Merrick, *U.K.* **20** 55 8N 4 30W
Merse, *U.K.* **21** 55 40N 2 30W
Mersea I., *U.K.* ...... **15** 51 48N 0 55 E
Mersey →, *U.K.* **18** 53 20N 2 56W
Merseyside □, *U.K.* ... **18** 53 25N 2 55W
Mersin, *Turk.* .... **47** 36 51N 34 36 E
Merthyr Tydfil, *U.K.* ... **17** 51 45N 3 23W
Merton, *U.K.* **15** 51 25N 0 13W
Meru, *Tanz.* .... **80** 3 15S 36 46 E
Mesa, *U.S.A.* **90** 33 20N 111 56W
Mesopotamia, *Asia* ... **56** 33 30N 44 0 E
Messina, *It.* .... **40** 38 10N 15 32 E
Messina, Str. of, *It.* ... **40** 38 5N 15 35 E
Metheringham, *U.K.* .. **19** 53 9N 0 22W
Methil, *U.K.* **21** 56 10N 3 1W
Methven, *U.K.* **21** 56 25N 3 35W
Methwold, *U.K.* ...... **15** 52 30N 0 33 E
Metz, *Fr.* .... **34** 49 8N 6 10 E
Meuse →, *Europe* ... **34** 50 45N 5 41 E
Mevagissey, *U.K.* **16** 50 16N 4 48W
Mevagissey Bay, *U.K.* . **16** 50 15N 4 40W
Mexborough, *U.K.* **19** 53 29N 1 18W
Mexicali, *Mex.* **94** 32 40N 115 29W
México, *Mex.* **94** 19 20N 99 10W
Mexico ■, *Cent. Am.* . **94** 20 0N 100 0W
Mexico, G. of,
Cent. Am. **94** 25 0N 90 0W
Miami, *U.S.A.* **91** 25 45N 80 15W
Micheldever, *U.K.* **14** 51 7N 1 17W
Michigan □, *U.S.A.* ... **92** 44 40N 85 40W
Michigan, L., *U.S.A.* .. **92** 44 0N 87 0W
Mickle Fell, *U.K.* **18** 54 38N 2 16W
Mickleover, *U.K.* **19** 52 55N 1 32W
Mickleton, *Durham,*
U.K. **18** 54 36N 2 3W
Mickleton, *Oxon., U.K.* **14** 52 5N 1 45W
Micronesia, *Pac. Oc.* . **64** 11 0N 160 0 E
Mid Calder, *U.K.* **21** 55 53N 3 23W
Mid Glamorgan □, *U.K.* **17** 51 40N 3 25W
Middle Zoy, *U.K.* **14** 51 5N 2 54W
Middleham, *U.K.* **19** 54 17N 1 49W
Middlemarsh, *U.K.* ... **14** 50 51N 2 29W
Middlesbrough, *U.K.* .. **19** 54 35N 1 14W
Middleton,
Gr. Manchester, U.K. **18** 53 33N 2 12W
Middleton, *Norfolk, U.K.* **15** 52 43N 0 29 E
Middleton Cheney, *U.K.* **14** 52 4N 1 17W
Middleton-in-Teesdale,
U.K. **18** 54 38N 2 5W
Middleton on the
Wolds, *U.K.* **19** 53 56N 0 35W
Middlewich, *U.K.* **18** 53 12N 2 28W
Midhurst, *U.K.* **15** 50 59N 0 44W
Midland, *U.S.A.* **90** 32 0N 102 3W
Midleton, *Ire.* **25** 51 52N 8 12W
Midsomer Norton, *U.K.* **14** 51 17N 2 29W
Midway Is., *Pac. Oc.* .. **64** 28 13N 177 22W
Mieres, *Sp.* **37** 43 18N 5 48W
Mikkeli, *Fin.* .... **44** 61 43N 27 15 E
Milan, *It.* .... **40** 45 28N 9 10 E
Milborne Port, *U.K.* ... **14** 50 58N 2 28W
Mildenhall, *U.K.* ..... **15** 52 20N 0 30 E
Mildura, *Austral.* ..... **70** 34 13S 142 9 E
Milford Haven, *U.K.* ... **17** 51 43N 5 2W
Milford Haven, B., *U.K.* **17** 51 40N 5 10W
Milford on Sea, *U.K.* .. **14** 50 44N 1 36W
Milk →, *U.S.A.* **90** 48 5N 106 15W
Millbrook, *U.K.* **16** 50 19N 4 12W
Milleur Pt., *U.K.* **20** 55 2N 5 5W
Millom, *U.K.* **18** 54 13N 3 16W
Millport, *U.K.* **20** 55 45N 4 55W
Milltown Malbay, *Ire.* . **25** 52 51N 9 25W
Milnathort, *U.K.* **21** 56 14N 3 25W
Milngavie, *U.K.* **20** 55 57N 4 20W
Milnthorpe, *U.K.* **18** 54 14N 2 47W
Milton, *Dumf. & Gall.,*
U.K. **20** 55 18N 4 50W
Milton, *Hants., U.K.* ... **14** 50 45N 1 40W
Milton, *Highland, U.K.* . **23** 57 18N 4 32W
Milton Abbot, *U.K.* ... **16** 50 35N 4 16W
Milton Keynes, *U.K.* .. **15** 52 3N 0 42W

Milverton, *U.K.* **14** 51 2N 3 15W
Milwaukee, *U.S.A.* **92** 43 9N 87 58W
Minas Gerais □, *Brazil* **101** 18 50S 46 0W
Minatitlán, *Mex.* **94** 17 59N 94 31W
Minchinghampton, *U.K.* **14** 51 42N 2 10W
Mindanao, *Phil.* ...... **63** 8 0N 125 0 E
Mindoro, *Phil.* .... **63** 13 0N 121 0 E
Minehead, *U.K.* **14** 51 12N 3 29W
Minneapolis, *U.S.A.* ... **91** 44 58N 93 20W
Minnesota □, *U.S.A.* .. **91** 46 40N 94 0W
Minnigaff, *U.K.* **20** 54 58N 4 30W
Minorca = Menorca, *Sp.* .... **37** 40 0N 4 0 E
Minsk, *U.S.S.R.* ...... **46** 53 52N 27 30 E
Minster, *U.K.* .... **15** 51 20N 1 20 E
Minster-on-Sea, *U.K.* . **15** 51 25N 0 50 E
Minsterley, *U.K.* **14** 52 38N 2 56W
Mirfield, *U.K.* **19** 53 37N 1 54W
Mirzapur, *India* ...... **59** 25 10N 82 34 E
Miskolc, *Hung.* ...... **43** 48 7N 20 50 E
Misrātah, *Libya* ...... **79** 32 24N 15 3 E
Mississippi □, *U.S.A.* . **91** 33 0N 90 0W
Mississippi →, *U.S.A.* **91** 29 0N 89 15W
Mississippi, Delta of the, *U.S.A.* **91** 29 15N 90 30W
Missouri □, *U.S.A.* ... **91** 38 25N 92 30W
Missouri →, *U.S.A.* .. **91** 38 50N 90 8W
Misterton, *Notts., U.K.* **19** 53 27N 0 49W
Misterton, *Somerset, U.K.* **14** 50 51N 2 46W
Mitcheldean, *U.K.* **14** 51 51N 2 29W
Mitchell →, *Austral.* . **67** 15 12S 141 35 E
Mitchelstown, *Ire.* **25** 52 16N 8 18W
Mittelland Kanal, *W. Ger.* .... **36** 52 23N 7 45 E
Mitumba, Mts., *Zaïre* . **80** 6 0S 29 0 E
Miyazaki, *Jap.* .... **62** 31 56N 131 30 E
Mizen Hd., *Cork, Ire.* .. **25** 51 27N 9 50W
Mizen Hd., *Wicklow, Ire.* **25** 52 52N 6 4W
Mizoram □, *India* .... **59** 23 30N 92 40 E
Mmabatho, *S. Afr.* .... **81** 25 49S 25 30 E
Mo i Rana, *Nor.* ...... **44** 66 15N 14 7 E
Mobile, *U.S.A.* **91** 30 41N 88 3W
Mobutu Sese Seko, L., *Africa* .... **80** 1 30N 31 0 E
Moçâmedes = Namibe, *Angola* .... **81** 15 7S 12 11 E
Modbury, *U.K.* **16** 50 21N 3 53W
Módena, *It.* .... **40** 44 39N 10 55 E
Moe, *Austral.* .... **70** 38 12S 146 19 E
Moffat, *U.K.* **21** 55 20N 3 27W
Mogadishu, *Som.* ..... **73** 2 2N 45 25 E
Mogilev, *U.S.S.R.* .... **46** 53 55N 30 18 E
Moidart, L., *U.K.* **22** 56 47N 5 40W
Mojave Desert, *U.S.A.* **90** 35 0N 116 30W
Mold, *U.K.* **17** 53 10N 3 10W
Moldavia □, *U.S.S.R.* . **47** 47 0N 28 0 E
Mole →, *U.K.* **15** 51 13N 0 15W
Mollendo, *Peru* **100** 17 0S 72 0W
Mölndal, *Swed.* ...... **45** 57 40N 12 3 E
Molokai, *U.S.A.* **90** 21 8N 157 0W
Moluccas, *Indon.* .... **63** 1 0S 127 0 E
Mombasa, *Kenya* ..... **80** 4 2S 39 43 E
Mona Passage, *W. Ind.* **95** 18 0N 67 40W
Monach Is., *U.K.* **22** 57 32N 7 40W
Monaco ■, *Europe* ... **35** 43 46N 7 23 E
Monadhliath Mts., *U.K.* **23** 57 10N 4 4W
Monaghan, *Ire.* **24** 54 15N 6 58W
Monaghan □, *Ire.* **24** 54 10N 7 0W
Monastir = Bitola, *Yug.* **41** 41 5N 21 10 E
Monclova, *Mex.* **94** 26 50N 101 30W
Moncton, *Canada* **93** 46 7N 64 51W
Moneymore, *U.K.* **24** 54 42N 6 40W
Monghyr, *India* ...... **59** 25 23N 86 30 E
Mongolia ■, *Asia* .... **60** 47 0N 103 0 E
Mongu, *Zam.* .... **81** 15 16S 23 12 E
Moniaive, *U.K.* **21** 55 11N 3 55W
Monifieth, *U.K.* **21** 56 30N 2 48W
Monkton, *U.K.* **20** 55 30N 4 37W
Monmouth, *U.K.* **17** 51 48N 2 43W
Monnow →, *U.K.* **14** 51 54N 2 48W
Monroe, *U.S.A.* **90** 32 32N 92 4W
Monrovia, *Lib.* **78** 6 18N 10 47W
Mons, *Belg.* .... **36** 50 27N 3 58 E
Montana □, *U.S.A.* ... **90** 47 0N 110 0W
Montbéliard, *Fr.* ...... **34** 47 31N 6 48 E
Montceau-les-Mines, *Fr.* .... **34** 46 40N 4 23 E
Monte-Carlo, *Monaco* . **35** 43 46N 7 23 E
Montego Bay, *Jam.* .. **94** 18 30N 78 0W
Montería, *Col.* **100** 8 46N 75 53W
Monterrey, *Mex.* **94** 25 40N 100 30W
Montes Claros, *Brazil* . **101** 16 30S 43 50W
Montevideo, *Urug.* ... **102** 34 50S 56 11W
Montgomery, *U.K.* **17** 52 34N 3 9W
Montgomery, *U.S.A.* .. **91** 32 20N 86 20W
Montluçon, *Fr.* .... **35** 46 22N 2 36 E
Montpelier, *U.S.A.* **93** 44 15N 72 38W
Montpellier, *Fr.* ...... **35** 43 37N 3 52 E
Montréal, *Canada* **93** 45 31N 73 34W
Montrose, *U.K.* **23** 56 43N 2 28W
Montserrat, *W. Ind.* ... **94** 16 40N 62 10W
Moonie →, *Austral.* .. **67** 29 19S 148 43 E
Moorfoot Hills, *U.K.* .. **21** 55 44N 3 8W
Moose Jaw, *Canada* .. **88** 50 24N 105 30W
Moosehead L., *U.S.A.* . **93** 45 34N 69 40W
Mopti, *Mali* **78** 14 30N 4 0W
Moradabad, *India* .... **58** 28 50N 78 50 E
Morar L., *U.K.* **22** 56 57N 5 40W
Moray Firth, *U.K.* **23** 57 50N 3 30W
Morebattle, *U.K.* **21** 55 30N 2 20W
Morecambe, *U.K.* **18** 54 5N 2 52W
Morecambe B., *U.K.* .. **18** 54 7N 3 0W
Morelia, *Mex.* **94** 19 42N 101 7W
Morena, Sierra, *Sp.* ... **37** 38 20N 4 0W
Moreton-in-Marsh, *U.K.* **14** 51 59N 1 42W
Moretonhampstead, *U.K.* **16** 50 39N 3 45W
Morley, *U.K.* **19** 53 45N 1 36W
Morocco ■, *N. Afr.* ... **78** 32 0N 5 50W
Morogoro, *Tanz.* ..... **80** 6 50S 37 40 E
Morpeth, *U.K.* **19** 55 11N 1 41W
Morte Bay, *U.K.* **16** 51 10N 4 13W
Morte Pt., *U.K.* **16** 51 13N 4 14W
Mortehoe, *U.K.* **16** 51 21N 4 12W
Mortimer's Cross, *U.K.* **14** 52 17N 2 50W
Morton Fen, *U.K.* **15** 52 45N 0 23W
Morvern, *U.K.* **22** 56 38N 5 44W
Morwell, *Austral.* ..... **70** 38 10S 146 22 E
Morwenstow, *U.K.* **16** 50 53N 4 32W
Moscow, *U.S.S.R.* .... **46** 55 45N 37 35 E
Moselle →, *Europe* .. **34** 50 22N 7 36 E
Moshi, *Tanz.* .... **80** 3 22S 37 18 E
Mossley, *U.K.* **18** 53 31N 2 1W
Mossoró, *Brazil* **101** 5 10S 37 15W
Mostaganem, *Alg.* .... **78** 35 54N 0 5 E
Mostar, *Yug.* .... **41** 43 22N 17 50 E
Mosul, *Iraq* .... **56** 36 15N 43 5 E
Motcombe, *U.K.* **14** 51 1N 2 12W
Motherwell, *U.K.* **21** 55 48N 4 0W
Mottisfont, *U.K.* **14** 51 22N 1 32W
Moulmein, *Burma* .... **59** 16 30N 97 40 E
Moulton, *U.K.* **15** 52 17N 0 51W
Mount Barker, *Austral.* **66** 34 38S 117 40 E
Mount Gambier, *Austral.* .... **70** 37 50S 140 46 E
Mount Isa, *Austral.* ... **67** 20 42S 139 26 E
Mount Lofty Ra., *Austral.* .... **67** 34 35S 139 5 E
Mountain Ash, *U.K.* ... **17** 51 42N 3 22W
Mountmellick, *Ire.* **25** 53 7N 7 20W
Mounts Bay, *U.K.* **16** 50 3N 5 27W
Mountsorrel, *U.K.* **14** 52 43N 1 9W
Mourne →, *U.K.* **24** 54 45N 7 39W
Mourne Mts., *U.K.* ... **24** 54 10N 6 0W
Mouscron, *Belg.* ..... **36** 50 45N 3 12 E
Moville, *Ire.* **24** 55 11N 7 3W
Moy →, *Ire.* **24** 54 5N 8 50W
Moyle □, *U.K.* **24** 55 10N 6 15W
Mozambique ■, *Africa* **81** 19 0S 35 0 E
Mozambique Chan., *Africa* .... **81** 20 0S 39 0 E
Mu Us Shamo, *China* . **61** 39 0N 109 0 E
Mubarraz, *Si. Arab.* .. **56** 25 29N 49 40 E
Much Dewchurch, *U.K.* **14** 51 58N 2 45W
Much Marcle, *U.K.* ... **14** 51 59N 2 27W
Much Wenlock, *U.K.* .. **14** 52 36N 2 34W
Muck, *U.K.* **22** 56 50N 6 15W
Mudanjiang, *China* ... **61** 44 38N 129 30 E
Mudgee, *Austral.* ..... **70** 32 32S 149 31 E
Mufulira, *Zam.* .... **81** 12 32S 28 15 E
Muine Bheag, *Ire.* **25** 52 42N 6 57W
Muir of Ord, *U.K.* **23** 57 30N 4 35W
Muirdrum, *U.K.* **21** 56 31N 2 40W
Muirhead, *U.K.* **21** 55 54N 4 5W
Muirkirk, *U.K.* **21** 55 31N 4 6W
Mülheim, *W. Ger.* .... **36** 51 26N 6 53 E
Mulhouse, *Fr.* .... **34** 47 40N 7 20 E
Mull, *U.K.* **20** 56 27N 6 0W
Mull, Ross of, *U.K.* ... **20** 56 20N 6 15W
Mull, Sound of, *U.K.* .. **20** 56 30N 5 50W
Mullet Pen., *Ire.* **24** 54 10N 10 2W
Mullingar, *Ire.* **24** 53 31N 7 20W
Mullion, *U.K.* **16** 50 1N 5 15W
Multan, *Pak.* .... **58** 30 15N 71 36 E
Mumbles Hd., *U.K.* ... **17** 51 33N 4 0W
Munchen-Gladbach, *W. Ger.* .... **36** 51 12N 6 23 E
Mundesley, *U.K.* ..... **15** 52 53N 1 24 E
Munich, *W. Ger.* ..... **42** 48 8N 11 33 E
Münster, *W. Ger.* ..... **36** 51 58N 7 37 E
Munster □, *Ire.* **25** 52 20N 8 40W
Murchison →, *Austral.* **66** 27 45S 114 0 E
Murcia, *Sp.* **37** 38 20N 1 10W
Mureş →, *Rom.* ..... **43** 46 15N 20 13 E
Murmansk, *U.S.S.R.* .. **46** 68 57N 33 10 E
Murray →, *S. Austral., Austral.* .... **70** 35 20S 139 22 E
Murray →, *W. Austral., Austral.* .... **67** 32 33S 115 45 E
Murrumbidgee →, *Austral.* .... **70** 34 43S 143 12 E
Murton, *U.K.* **19** 54 51N 1 22W
Murwillumbah, *Austral.* **67** 28 18S 153 27 E
Muscat, *Oman* .... **57** 23 40N 58 38 E
Musgrave Ras., *Austral.* **66** 26 0S 132 0 E
Musselburgh, *U.K.* ... **21** 55 57N 3 3W
Muswellbrook, *Austral.* **70** 32 16S 150 56 E
Mutare, *Zimb.* .... **81** 18 58S 32 38 E
Muthill, *U.K.* **21** 56 20N 3 50W
Muzaffarpur, *India* .... **59** 26 7N 85 23 E
Mwanza, *Tanz.* ...... **80** 2 30S 32 58 E
Mweelrea, *Ire.* **24** 53 37N 9 48W
My Tho, *Viet.* .... **63** 10 29N 106 23 E
Myddle, *U.K.* **14** 52 49N 2 47W
Myitkyina, *Burma* .... **59** 25 24N 97 26 E
Mymensingh, *Bangla.* . **59** 24 45N 90 24 E
Mynydd Du, *U.K.* **17** 51 45N 3 45W
Mynydd Prescelly, *U.K.* **17** 51 57N 4 48W
Mysore, *India* .... **58** 12 17N 76 41 E

N

Naas, *Ire.* **25** 53 12N 6 40W
Nābulus, *Jord.* .... **57** 32 14N 35 15 E
Nafferton, *U.K.* **19** 54 1N 0 24W
Nagaland □, *India* .... **59** 26 0N 94 30 E
Nagano, *Jap.* .... **62** 36 40N 138 10 E
Nagaoka, *Jap.* .... **62** 37 27N 138 51 E
Nagasaki, *Jap.* .... **62** 32 47N 129 50 E
Nagoya, *Jap.* .... **62** 35 10N 136 50 E
Nagpur, *India* .... **58** 21 8N 79 10 E
Naha, *Jap.* .... **62** 26 13N 127 42 E
Nailsea, *U.K.* **14** 51 25N 2 44W
Nailsworth, *U.K.* **14** 51 41N 2 12W
Nairn, *U.K.* **23** 57 35N 3 54W
Nairobi, *Kenya* .... **80** 1 17S 36 48 E
Nakuru, *Kenya* .... **80** 0 15S 36 4 E
Nalchik, *U.S.S.R.* ..... **47** 43 30N 43 33 E
Nam Co, *China* ...... **60** 30 30N 90 45 E
Namangan, *U.S.S.R.* .. **48** 41 0N 71 40 E
Namib Desert, *Nam.* .. **81** 22 30S 15 0 E
Namibe, *Angola* ...... **81** 15 7S 12 11 E
Namibia ■, *Africa* .... **81** 22 0S 18 9 E
Nampula, *Mozam.* .... **81** 15 6N 39 15 E
Namur, *Belg.* .... **36** 50 27N 4 52 E
Nan Shan, *China* ..... **60** 38 30N 99 0 E
Nanaimo, *Canada* **88** 49 10N 124 0W
Nanchang, *China* .... **61** 28 42N 115 55 E
Nanchong, *China* .... **60** 30 43N 106 2 E
Nancy, *Fr.* .... **34** 48 42N 6 12 E
Nanda Devi, *India* .... **58** 30 23N 79 59 E
Nanjing = Nanking, *China* .... **61** 32 2N 118 47 E
Nanking, *China* ...... **61** 32 2N 118 47 E
Nanning, *China* ...... **60** 22 48N 108 20 E
Nanping, *China* ...... **61** 26 38N 118 10 E
Nantes, *Fr.* **34** 47 12N 1 33W
Nantong, *China* ...... **61** 32 1N 120 52 E
Nantucket Sd., *U.S.A.* . **93** 41 30N 70 15W
Nantwich, *U.K.* **18** 53 5N 2 31W
Napier, *N.Z.* .... **71** 39 30S 176 56 E
Naples, *It.* .... **40** 40 50N 14 17 E
Nappa, *U.K.* **18** 53 58N 2 14W
Nara, *Jap.* .... **62** 34 40N 135 49 E
Narayanganj, *Bangla.* . **59** 23 40N 90 33 E
Narberth, *U.K.* **17** 51 48N 4 45W
Narborough, *U.K.* **14** 52 34N 1 12W
Nare Head, *U.K.* **16** 50 12N 4 55W
Narmada →, *India* ... **58** 21 38N 72 36 E
Narrandera, *Austral.* .. **70** 34 42S 146 31 E
Narrogin, *Austral.* .... **66** 32 58S 117 14 E
Narromine, *Austral.* ... **70** 32 12S 148 12 E
Narvik, *Nor.* .... **44** 68 28N 17 26 E
Naseby, *U.K.* **15** 52 24N 0 59W
Nashua, *U.S.A.* **93** 42 50N 71 25W
Nashville, *U.S.A.* **91** 36 12N 86 46W
Nasik, *India* .... **58** 19 58N 73 50 E
Nassau, *Baham.* **95** 25 0N 77 20W
Nasser, L., *Egypt* .... **79** 23 0N 32 30 E
Nässjö, *Swed.* .... **45** 57 39N 14 42 E
Natal, *Brazil* **81** 5 47S 35 13W
Natal □, *S. Afr.* ...... **101** 28 30S 30 30 E
Nauru ■, *Pac. Oc.* ... **64** 1 0S 166 0 E
Navan = An Uaimh, *Ire.* **24** 53 39N 6 40W
Navenby, *U.K.* **19** 53 7N 0 32W
Naver →, *U.K.* **23** 58 34N 4 15W
Náxos, *Greece* ...... **41** 37 8N 25 25 E
Nazareth, *Isr.* .... **57** 32 42N 35 17 E
Naze, The, *U.K.* ...... **15** 51 53N 1 19 E
Ndjamena, *Chad* ..... **79** 12 10N 14 59 E
Ndola, *Zam.* .... **81** 13 0S 28 34 E
Neagh, L., *U.K.* **24** 54 35N 6 25W
Neath, *U.K.* **17** 51 39N 3 49W
Nebraska □, *U.S.A.* .. **90** 41 30N 100 0W
Needham Market, *U.K.* **15** 52 9N 1 2 E
Needles, The, *U.K.* ... **14** 50 39N 1 35W
Negro →, *Arg.* **102** 41 2S 62 47W
Negro →, *Brazil* **100** 3 0S 60 0W
Negros, *Phil.* .... **63** 9 30N 122 40 E
Neijiang, *China* ...... **60** 29 35N 104 55 E
Neilston, *U.K.* **20** 55 47N 4 27W
Neiva, *Col.* **100** 2 56N 75 18W
Nellore, *India* .... **58** 14 27N 79 59 E
Nelson, *N.Z.* .... **71** 41 18S 173 16 E
Nelson, *U.K.* **18** 53 50N 2 14W
Nelson →, *Canada* ... **88** 54 33N 98 2W
Nelspruit, *S. Afr.* ..... **81** 25 29S 30 59 E
Nenagh, *Ire.* **25** 52 52N 8 11W
Nene →, *U.K.* .... **15** 52 38N 0 13 E
Nepal ■, *Asia* .... **59** 28 0N 84 30 E
Nephin, *Ire.* **24** 54 1N 9 21W
Ness, Loch, *U.K.* **23** 57 15N 4 30W
Neston, *U.K.* **18** 53 17N 3 3W
Netanya, *Isr.* .... **57** 32 20N 34 51 E
Nether Stowey, *U.K.* .. **14** 51 0N 3 10W
Netherbury, *U.K.* **14** 50 46N 2 45W
Netherlands ■, *Europe* **36** 52 0N 5 30 E
Netley, *U.K.* **14** 50 53N 1 21W
Netley Marsh, *U.K.* ... **14** 50 55N 1 32W
Nettlebed, *U.K.* **15** 51 34N 0 54W
Nettleham, *U.K.* **19** 53 15N 0 28W
Neuchâtel, *Switz.* ..... **42** 47 0N 6 55 E
Neukirchen, *W. Ger.* .. **36** 54 52N 8 44 E
Neuss, *W. Ger.* ...... **36** 51 12N 6 39 E
Neustadt, *W. Ger.* .... **36** 49 21N 8 10 E
Neuwied, *W. Ger.* .... **36** 50 26N 7 29 E
Nevada □, *U.S.A.* **90** 39 20N 117 0W
Nevada, Sierra, *Sp.* ... **37** 37 3N 3 15W
Nevada, Sierra, *U.S.A.* **90** 39 0N 120 30W
Nevers, *Fr.* .... **34** 47 0N 3 9 E
New Abbey, *U.K.* **21** 54 59N 3 38W
New Alresford, *U.K.* .. **14** 51 6N 1 10W
New Amsterdam, *Guy.* **101** 6 15N 57 36W
New Bedford, *U.S.A.* .. **93** 41 40N 70 52W
New Brighton, *N.Z.* ... **71** 43 29S 172 43 E
New Brighton, *U.K.* ... **18** 53 27N 3 2W
New Brunswick □, *Canada* **93** 46 50N 66 30W
New Caledonia, *Pac. Oc.* .... **64** 21 0S 165 0 E
New Castile, *Sp.* **37** 39 45N 3 20W
New Cumnock, *U.K.* .. **20** 55 24N 4 13W
New Forest, *U.K.* **14** 50 53N 1 40W
New Galloway, *U.K.* .. **21** 55 4N 4 10W
New Guinea, *Pac. Oc.* **64** 4 0S 136 0 E
New Hampshire □, *U.S.A.* **93** 43 40N 71 40W
New Haven, *U.S.A.* ... **93** 41 20N 72 54W
New Hebrides = Vanuatu ■, *Pac. Oc.* **64** 15 0S 168 0 E
New Holland, *U.K.* **19** 53 42N 0 22W
New Jersey □, *U.S.A.* . **93** 40 30N 74 10W
New London, *U.S.A.* .. **93** 41 23N 72 8W
New Luce, *U.K.* **20** 54 57N 4 50W
New Mexico □, *U.S.A.* **90** 34 30N 106 0W
New Mills, *U.K.* **18** 53 22N 2 0W
New Orleans, *U.S.A.* .. **91** 30 0N 90 5W
New Plymouth, *N.Z.* .. **71** 39 4S 174 5 E
New Quay, *U.K.* **17** 52 13N 4 21W
New Radnor, *U.K.* **17** 52 15N 3 10W
New Romney, *U.K.* ... **15** 50 59N 0 57 E
New Ross, *Ire.* **25** 52 24N 6 58W
New Rossington, *U.K.* **19** 53 30N 1 4W
New Siberian Is., *U.S.S.R.* .... **49** 75 0N 142 0 E
New South Wales □, *Austral.* .... **70** 33 0S 146 0 E
New York □, *U.S.A.* .. **93** 42 40N 76 0W
New York City, *U.S.A.* . **93** 40 45N 74 0W
New Zealand ■, *Pac. Oc.* .... **71** 40 0S 176 0 E
Newark, *U.S.A.* **93** 40 41N 74 12W
Newark-on-Trent, *U.K.* **19** 53 6N 0 48W
Newbiggin-by-the-Sea, *U.K.* **21** 55 12N 1 31W
Newbigging, *U.K.* **21** 55 42N 3 33W
Newburgh, *U.K.* **21** 56 21N 3 15W
Newburn, *U.K.* **21** 54 57N 1 45W
Newbury, *U.K.* **14** 51 24N 1 19W
Newby Bridge, *U.K.* .. **18** 54 16N 2 59W
Newcastle, *Austral.* ... **70** 33 0S 151 46 E
Newcastle, *U.K.* **24** 54 13N 5 54W
Newcastle Emlyn, *U.K.* **17** 52 2N 4 29W
Newcastle-under-Lyme, *U.K.* **18** 53 2N 2 15W
Newcastle-upon-Tyne, *U.K.* **19** 54 59N 1 37W
Newcastleton, *U.K.* ... **21** 55 10N 2 50W
Newent, *U.K.* **14** 51 56N 2 24W
Newfoundland □, *Canada* **89** 53 0N 58 0W
Newham, *U.K.* .... **15** 51 31N 0 2 E
Newhaven, *U.K.* ...... **15** 50 47N 0 4 E
Newington, *Kent, U.K.* **15** 51 5N 1 8 E
Newington, *Kent, U.K.* **15** 51 21N 0 40 E
Newlyn, *U.K.* **16** 50 6N 5 33W
Newlyn East, *U.K.* **16** 50 22N 5 3W
Newman, *Austral.* .... **66** 23 18S 119 45 E
Newmarket, *Ire.* **25** 52 13N 9 0W
Newmarket, *Lewis, U.K.* **22** 58 14N 6 24W
Newmarket, *Suffolk, U.K.* .... **15** 52 15N 0 23 E
Newmilns, *U.K.* **20** 55 36N 4 20W
Newnham, *U.K.* **14** 51 48N 2 27W
Newport, *Dyfed, U.K.* . **17** 52 1N 4 53W
Newport, *Essex, U.K.* . **15** 51 58N 0 13 E
Newport, *Gwent, U.K.* . **17** 51 35N 3 0W
Newport, *I. of W., U.K.* **14** 50 42N 1 18W
Newport, *Salop, U.K.* . **14** 52 47N 2 22W
Newport News, *U.S.A.* **91** 37 2N 76 30W
Newport on Tay, *U.K.* . **21** 56 27N 2 56W
Newport Pagnell, *U.K.* **15** 52 5N 0 42W
Newquay, *U.K.* **16** 50 24N 5 6W
Newry, *U.K.* **24** 54 10N 6 20W
Newry & Mourne □, *U.K.* **24** 54 10N 6 15W
Newton Abbot, *U.K.* .. **16** 50 32N 3 37W
Newton Arlosh, *U.K.* .. **18** 54 53N 3 15W
Newton-Aycliffe, *U.K.* . **19** 54 36N 1 33W
Newton Ferrers, *U.K.* . **16** 50 19N 4 3W
Newton le Willows, *U.K.* **18** 53 28N 2 40W
Newton St. Cyres, *U.K.* **16** 50 46N 3 35W
Newton Stewart, *U.K.* . **20** 54 57N 4 30W
Newtongrange, *U.K.* .. **21** 55 52N 3 4W
Newtonmore, *U.K.* ... **23** 57 4N 4 7W
Newtown, *Scotland, U.K.* **21** 55 34N 2 38W
Newtown, *Wales, U.K.* **17** 52 31N 3 19W
Newtownabbey, *Ire.* .. **24** 54 40N 5 55W
Newtownabbey □, *U.K.* **24** 54 45N 6 0W
Newtownards, *U.K.* ... **24** 54 37N 5 40W
Nha Trang, *Viet.* ..... **63** 12 16N 109 10 E
Niagara Falls, *Canada* **92** 43 7N 79 5W
Niagara Falls, *U.S.A.* .. **92** 43 5N 79 0W
Niamey, *Niger* .... **78** 13 27N 2 6 E
Nicaragua ■, *Cent. Am.* **94** 11 40N 85 30W
Nicaragua, L., *Nic.* ... **94** 12 0N 85 30W
Nice, *Fr.* .... **35** 43 42N 7 14 E
Nicobar Is., *Ind. Oc.* .. **51** 9 0N 93 0 E
Nicosia, *Cyprus* ...... **47** 35 10N 33 25 E
Nicoya, Pen. de, *C.R.* . **94** 9 45N 85 40W

Nidd →, U.K. 19 54 1N 1 32W
Nidderdale, U.K. 19 54 5N 1 46W
Niger ■, W. Afr. 78 13 30N 10 0 E
Niger →, W. Afr. 78 5 33N 6 33 E
Nigeria ■, W. Afr. 78 8 30N 8 0 E
Niigata, Jap. 62 37 58N 139 0 E
Niihau, U.S.A. 90 21 55N 160 10W
Nijmegen, Neth. 36 51 50N 5 52 E
Nikolayev, U.S.S.R. 47 46 58N 32 0 E
Nikolayevsk, U.S.S.R. 49 50 0N 45 35 E
Nile →, Africa 79 30 10N 31 6 E
Nîmes, Fr. 35 43 50N 4 23 E
Ninety Mile Beach, The, Austral. 70 38 15S 147 24 E
Ninfield, U.K. 15 50 53N 0 26 E
Ningbo, China 61 29 51N 121 28 E
Ningxia Huizu Zizhiqu □, China 60 38 0N 106 0 E
Niort, Fr. 35 46 19N 0 29W
Nipigon, L., Canada 92 49 50N 88 30W
Niš, Yug. 41 43 19N 21 58 E
Niterói, Brazil 101 22 52S 43 0W
Nith →, U.K. 21 55 20N 3 5W
Nithsdale, U.K. 21 55 14N 3 50W
Niton, U.K. 14 50 35N 1 14W
Nizhniy Tagil, U.S.S.R. 46 57 55N 59 57 E
Nkongsamba, Cam. 80 4 55N 9 55 E
Nobeoka, Jap. 62 32 36N 131 41 E
Nogales, Mex. 94 31 20N 110 56W
Nordelph, U.K. 15 52 34N 0 18 E
Nordhorn, W. Ger. 36 52 27N 7 4 E
Nordvik, U.S.S.R. 49 74 2N 111 32 E
Nore →, Ire. 25 52 40N 7 20W
Norfolk, U.S.A. 91 36 40N 76 15W
Norfolk □, U.K. 15 52 39N 1 0 E
Norfolk Broads, U.K. 15 52 30N 1 15 E
Norfolk I., Pac. Oc. 64 28 58S 168 3 E
Norham, U.K. 21 55 44N 2 9W
Norilsk, U.S.S.R. 49 69 20N 88 6 E
Norman, U.S.A. 90 35 12N 97 30W
Normandy, Fr. 34 48 45N 0 10 E
Normanton, U.K. 19 53 41N 1 26W
Norrbotten □, Swed. 44 66 30N 22 30 E
Norrköping, Swed. 45 58 37N 16 11 E
Norrland □, Swed. 44 66 50N 18 0 E
Norseman, Austral. 66 32 8S 121 43 E
North Battleford, Canada 88 52 50N 108 17W
North Bay, Canada 92 46 20N 79 30W
North Berwick, U.K. 21 56 4N 2 44W
North Cape, Nor. 44 71 15N 25 40 E
North Carolina □, U.S.A. 91 35 30N 80 0W
North Cerney, U.K. 14 51 45N 1 58W
North Channel, U.K. 20 55 0N 5 30W
North Collingham, U.K. 19 53 8N 0 46W
North Dakota □, U.S.A. 90 47 30N 100 0W
North Dorset Downs, U.K. 14 50 50N 2 30W
North Down □, U.K. 24 54 40N 5 45W
North Downs, U.K. 15 51 17N 0 30 E
North Esk →, U.K. 23 56 44N 2 25W
North European Plain 26 55 0N 20 0 E
North Foreland, U.K. 15 51 22N 1 28 E
North Hill, U.K. 16 50 33N 4 26W
North Hykeham, U.K. 19 53 10N 0 35W
North I., N.Z. 71 38 0S 175 0 E
North Minch, U.K. 22 58 5N 5 55W
North Molton, U.K. 16 51 3N 3 48W
North Petherton, U.K. 14 51 6N 3 1W
North Pole, Arctic 103 90 0N 0 0 E
North Queensferry, U.K. 21 56 1N 3 22W
North Rhine Westphalia □, W. Ger. 42 51 55N 7 0 E
North Ronaldsay, U.K. 23 59 20N 2 30W
North Sea, Europe 26 56 0N 4 0 E
North Somercotes, U.K. 19 53 28N 0 9 E
North Sunderland, U.K. 21 55 35N 1 40W
North Tawton, U.K. 16 50 48N 3 55W
North Thoresby, U.K. 19 53 27N 0 3W
North Tidworth, U.K. 14 51 14N 1 40W
North Tyne →, U.K. 19 54 59N 2 7W
North Uist, U.K. 22 57 40N 7 15W
North Walsham, U.K. 15 52 49N 1 22 E
North West Highlands, U.K. 22 57 35N 5 2W
North West Territories □, Canada 89 67 0N 110 0W
North York Moors, U.K. 19 54 25N 0 50W
North Yorkshire □, U.K. 19 54 15N 1 25W
Northallerton, U.K. 19 54 20N 1 26W
Northam, Austral. 66 31 35S 116 42 E
Northam, U.K. 16 51 2N 4 13W
Northampton, U.K. 15 52 14N 0 54W
Northampton □, U.K. 15 52 16N 0 55W
Northern Ireland □, U.K. 24 54 45N 7 0W
Northern Marianas, Pac. Oc. 64 17 0N 145 0 E
Northern Territory □, Austral. 66 16 0S 133 0 E
Northfleet, U.K. 15 51 26N 0 20 E
Northiam, U.K. 15 50 59N 0 39 E
Northland □, N.Z. 71 35 30S 173 30 E
Northleach, U.K. 14 51 49N 1 50W
Northrepps, U.K. 15 52 53N 1 20 E
Northumberland □, U.K. 19 55 12N 2 0W
Northumberland Str., Canada 93 46 20N 64 0W
Northwich, U.K. 18 53 16N 2 30W
Northwold, U.K. 15 52 33N 0 37 E
Norton, N. Yorks., U.K. 19 54 9N 0 48W
Norton, Suffolk, U.K. 15 52 15N 0 52 E
Norton Fitzwarren, U.K. 14 51 1N 3 10W
Norway ■, Europe 44 63 0N 11 0 E
Norwegian Sea, Atl. Oc. 44 66 0N 1 0 E
Norwich, U.K. 15 52 38N 1 17 E
Noss Hd., U.K. 23 58 29N 3 4W
Nottingham, U.K. 19 52 57N 1 10W
Nottingham □, U.K. 19 53 10N 1 0W
Nouâdhibou, Maurit. 78 20 54N 17 0W
Nouakchott, Maurit. 78 18 9N 15 58W
Nouméa, N. Cal. 64 22 17S 166 30 E
Nova Scotia □, Canada 93 45 10N 63 0W
Novara, It. 40 45 27N 8 36 E
Novaya Zemlya, U.S.S.R. 48 75 0N 56 0 E
Novi Sad, Yug. 41 45 18N 19 52 E
Novocherkassk, U.S.S.R. 47 47 27N 40 5 E
Novokuznetsk, U.S.S.R. 48 53 45N 87 10 E
Novomoskovsk, U.S.S.R. 46 54 5N 38 15 E
Novorossiysk, U.S.S.R. 47 44 43N 37 46 E
Novoshakhtinsk, U.S.S.R. 47 47 46N 39 58 E
Novosibirsk, U.S.S.R. 48 55 0N 83 5 E
Nubian Desert, Sudan 79 21 30N 33 30 E
Nuevo Laredo, Mex. 94 27 30N 99 30W
Nullarbor Plain, Austral. 66 30 45S 129 0 E
Nuneaton, U.K. 14 52 32N 1 29W
Nunney, U.K. 14 51 13N 2 20W
Nuremburg, W. Ger. 42 49 26N 11 5 E
Nyasa, L., Africa 81 12 30S 34 30 E
Nyíregyháza, Hung. 43 47 58N 21 47 E
Nykøbing, Den. 45 56 48N 8 51 E

O

Oa, Mull of, U.K. 20 55 35N 6 20W
Oa, The, Pen., U.K. 20 55 36N 6 17W
Oadby, U.K. 14 52 37N 1 7W
Oahe L., U.S.A. 90 45 30N 100 25W
Oahu, U.S.A. 90 21 30N 158 0W
Oakengates, U.K. 14 52 42N 2 29W
Oakham, U.K. 15 52 40N 0 43W
Oakland, U.S.A. 90 37 50N 122 18W
Oakleigh, Austral. 70 37 54S 145 6 E
Oamaru, N.Z. 71 45 5S 170 59 E
Oaxaca, Mex. 94 17 2N 96 40W
Ob →, U.S.S.R. 48 66 45N 69 30 E
Ob, G. of, U.S.S.R. 48 70 0N 73 0 E
Oban, U.K. 20 56 25N 5 30W
Oberhausen, W. Ger. 36 51 28N 6 50 E
Ochil Hills, U.K. 21 56 14N 3 40W
Ochiltree, U.K. 20 55 26N 4 23W
October Revolution I., U.S.S.R. 49 79 30N 97 0 E
Odense, Den. 45 55 22N 10 23 E
Odessa, U.S.A. 90 31 51N 102 23W
Odessa, U.S.S.R. 47 46 30N 30 45 E
Odiham, U.K. 15 51 16N 0 56W
Odra →, Pol. 42 53 33N 14 38 E
Offaly □, Ire. 25 53 15N 7 30W
Offenbach, W. Ger. 42 50 6N 8 46 E
Ogbomosho, Nig. 78 8 1N 4 11 E
Ogden, U.S.A. 90 41 13N 112 1W
Ohio □, U.S.A. 92 40 20N 14 10 E
Ohio →, U.S.A. 92 38 0N 86 0W
Ōita, Jap. 62 33 14N 131 36 E
Okavango Swamps, Bots. 81 18 45S 22 45 E
Okayama, Jap. 62 34 40N 133 54 E
Okazaki, Jap. 62 34 57N 137 10 E
Okehampton, U.K. 16 50 44N 4 1W
Okhotsk, U.S.S.R. 49 59 20N 143 10 E
Okhotsk, Sea of, Asia 49 55 0N 145 0 E
Oklahoma □, U.S.A. 90 35 20N 97 30W
Oklahoma City, U.S.A. 91 35 25N 97 30W
Ólafsfjörður, Ice. 44 66 4N 18 39W
Öland, Swed. 45 56 45N 16 38 E
Old Basing, U.K. 14 51 16N 1 3W
Old Castile, Sp. 37 41 55N 4 0W
Old Castle, Ire. 24 53 46N 7 10W
Old Kilpatrick, U.K. 20 55 56N 4 34W
Old Leake, U.K. 19 53 2N 0 6 E
Oldbury, Gloucs., U.K. 14 51 38N 2 30W
Oldbury, W. Midlands, U.K. 14 52 30N 2 0W
Oldenburg, W. Ger. 36 53 10N 8 10 E
Oldham, U.K. 18 53 33N 2 8W
Oldmeldrum, U.K. 23 57 20N 2 19W
Olekminsk, U.S.S.R. 49 60 25N 120 30 E
Olinda, Brazil 101 8 1S 34 51W
Ollerton, U.K. 19 53 12N 1 1W
Olney, U.K. 15 52 9N 0 42W
Olomouc, Czech. 42 49 38N 17 12 E
Olsztyn, Pol. 43 53 48N 20 29 E
Olympia, Greece 41 37 39N 21 39 E
Olympus, Mt., Greece 41 40 6N 22 23 E
Omagh, U.K. 24 54 36N 7 20W
Omagh □, U.K. 24 54 35N 7 15W
Omaha, U.S.A. 91 41 15N 96 0W
Oman ■, Si. Arab. 57 23 0N 58 0 E
Oman, G. of, Asia 57 24 30N 58 30 E
Ombersley, U.K. 14 52 17N 2 12W
Omdurmân, Sudan 79 15 40N 32 28 E
Ōmiya, Jap. 62 35 54N 139 38 E
Omsk, U.S.S.R. 48 55 0N 73 12 E
Ōmuta, Jap. 62 33 0N 130 26 E
Onchan, U.K. 18 54 11N 4 27W
Onega →, U.S.S.R. 46 63 58N 37 55 E
Onega, G. of, U.S.S.R. 46 64 30N 37 0 E
Onega, L., U.S.S.R. 46 62 0N 35 30 E
Onehunga, N.Z. 71 36 55S 174 48 E
Onny →, U.K. 14 52 30N 2 50W
Ontario □, Canada 88 52 0N 88 10W
Ontario, L., N. Am. 92 43 40N 78 0W
Opole, Pol. 43 50 42N 17 58 E
Oporto, Port. 37 41 8N 8 40W
Oradea, Rom. 43 47 2N 21 58 E
Oran, Alg. 78 35 45N 0 39W
Orange, Austral. 70 33 15S 149 7 E
Orange →, S. Afr. 81 28 41S 16 28 E
Orange Free State □, S. Afr. 81 28 30S 27 0 E
Ord, Mt., Austral. 66 17 20S 125 34 E
Ordos = Mu Us Shamo, China 61 39 0N 109 0 E
Ordzhonikidze, U.S.S.R. 47 43 0N 44 35 E
Örebro, Swed. 45 59 20N 15 18 E
Oregon □, U.S.A. 90 44 0N 121 0W
Orekhovo-Zuyevo, U.S.S.R. 46 55 50N 38 55 E
Orel, U.S.S.R. 46 52 57N 36 3 E
Orenburg, U.S.S.R. 46 51 45N 55 6 E
Orense, Sp. 37 42 19N 7 55W
Orford, U.K. 15 52 6N 1 31 E
Orford Ness, U.K. 15 52 6N 1 31 E
Orinoco →, Ven. 100 9 15N 61 30W
Orissa □, India 59 20 0N 84 0 E
Oristano, It. 40 39 54N 8 35 E
Orizaba, Mex. 94 18 51N 97 6W
Orkney □, U.K. 23 59 0N 3 0W
Orkney Is., U.K. 23 59 0N 3 0W
Orlando, U.S.A. 91 28 30N 81 25W
Orléans, Fr. 34 47 54N 1 52 E
Ormesby St. Margaret, U.K. 15 52 39N 1 42 E
Ormskirk, U.K. 18 53 35N 2 53W
Örnsköldsvik, Swed. 44 63 17N 18 40 E
Oronsay, Pass of, U.K. 20 56 0N 6 10W
Oronsay I., U.K. 20 56 0N 6 14W
Orsk, U.S.S.R. 46 51 12N 58 34 E
Orton Tebay, U.K. 18 54 28N 2 35W
Oruro, Bol. 100 18 0S 67 9W
Orwell →, U.K. 15 52 2N 1 12 E
Ōsaka, Jap. 62 34 40N 135 30 E
Osh, U.S.S.R. 48 40 37N 72 49 E
Oshawa, Canada 92 43 50N 78 50W
Oshogbo, Nig. 78 7 48N 4 37 E
Osijek, Yug. 41 45 34N 18 41 E
Osizweni, S. Afr. 81 27 49S 30 7 E
Oslo, Nor. 45 59 55N 10 45 E
Oslo Fjord, Nor. 45 58 30N 10 0 E
Osmotherley, U.K. 19 54 22N 1 18W
Osnabrück, W. Ger. 36 52 16N 8 2 E
Osorno, Chile 102 40 25S 73 0W
Ossett, U.K. 19 53 40N 1 35W
Ostend, Belg. 36 51 15N 2 50 E
Östersund, Swed. 44 63 10N 14 38 E
Ostrava, Czech. 43 49 51N 18 18 E
Osumi, Is., Jap. 62 30 30N 130 45 E
Oswaldtwistle, U.K. 18 53 44N 2 27W
Oswestry, U.K. 14 52 52N 3 3W
Otago □, N.Z. 71 44 45S 169 10 E
Otaru, Jap. 62 43 10N 141 0 E
Otley, U.K. 19 53 54N 1 41W
Otranto, Str. of, It. 41 40 15N 18 40 E
Ōtsu, Jap. 62 35 0N 135 50 E
Ottawa, Canada 93 45 27N 75 42W
Ottawa →, Canada 93 45 27N 74 8W
Otter →, U.K. 16 50 47N 3 12W
Otter Ferry, U.K. 20 56 1N 5 20W
Otterburn, U.K. 21 55 14N 2 12W
Ottery St. Mary, U.K. 16 50 45N 3 16W
Ouagadougou, B. Faso 78 12 25N 1 30W
Oujda, Mor. 78 34 41N 1 55W
Oulton, U.K. 15 52 29N 1 40 E
Oulton Broad, U.K. 15 52 28N 1 43 E
Oulu, Fin. 44 65 1N 25 29 E
Oulu, L., Fin. 44 64 25N 27 0 E
Oundle, U.K. 15 52 28N 0 28W
Ouse →, E. Sussex, U.K. 15 50 43N 0 3 E
Ouse →, N. Yorks., U.K. 19 54 3N 0 7 E
Outer Hebrides, U.K. 22 57 30N 7 40W
Outwell, U.K. 15 52 36N 0 14 E
Over Wallop, U.K. 14 51 9N 1 35W
Overstand, U.K. 15 52 55N 1 20W
Overton, U.K. 14 51 14N 1 16W
Oviedo, Sp. 37 43 25N 5 50W
Owston Ferry, U.K. 19 53 28N 0 47W
Ox Mts., Ire. 24 54 6N 9 0W
Oxford, U.K. 14 51 45N 1 15W
Oxford □, U.K. 14 51 45N 1 15W
Oykel →, U.K. 23 57 55N 4 26W
Ozark Plateau, U.S.A. 91 37 20N 91 40W

P

Paarl, S. Afr. 81 33 45S 18 56 E
Pacaraima, Sierra, Ven. 100 4 0N 62 30W
Pachuca, Mex. 94 20 10N 98 40W
Pacific Ocean 64 10 0N 140 0W
Padang, Indon. 63 1 0S 100 20 E
Paddock Wood, U.K. 15 51 13N 0 24 E
Padiham, U.K. 18 53 48N 2 20W
Padstow, U.K. 14 50 33N 4 57W
Padstow Bay, U.K. 16 50 35N 4 58W
Padua, It. 40 45 24N 11 52 E
Pagalu = Annobón, Atl. Oc. 73 1 25S 5 36 E
Paignton, U.K. 16 50 26N 3 33W
Painswick, U.K. 14 51 47N 2 11W
Paisley, U.K. 20 55 51N 4 27W
Pakistan ■, Asia 58 30 0N 70 0 E
Palawan, Phil. 63 9 30N 118 30 E
Palembang, Indon. 63 3 0S 104 50 E
Palencia, Sp. 37 42 1N 4 34W
Palermo, It. 40 38 8N 13 20 E
Palgrave, U.K. 15 52 22N 1 7 E
Palk Strait, Asia 58 10 0N 79 45 E
Palma de Mallorca, Sp. 37 39 35N 2 39 E
Palmer →, Austral. 66 24 46S 133 25 E
Palmerston North, N.Z. 71 40 21S 175 39 E
Palmira, Col. 100 3 32N 76 16W
Pamirs, U.S.S.R. 48 37 40N 73 0 E
Pamlico Sd., U.S.A. 91 35 20N 76 0W
Pampas, Arg. 96 35 0S 63 0W
Pamplona, Sp. 37 42 48N 1 38W
Panamá, Pan. 94 9 0N 79 25W
Panama ■, Cent. Am. 95 8 48N 79 55W
Panamá, G. de, Pan. 95 8 4N 79 20W
Panama Canal, Pan. 94 9 10N 79 37W
Panay, Phil. 63 11 10N 122 30 E
Pančevo, Yug. 41 44 52N 20 41 E
Pangbourne, U.K. 14 51 28N 1 5W
Pantelleria, It. 40 36 52N 12 0 E
Papua New Guinea ■, Oc. 64 8 0S 145 0 E
Pará □, Brazil 101 3 20S 52 0W
Paraguay ■, S. Am. 102 23 0S 57 0W
Paraguay →, Par. 102 27 18S 58 38W
Paramaribo, Surinam 101 5 50N 55 10W
Paraná, Arg. 102 31 45S 60 30W
Paraná →, Arg. 102 33 43S 59 15W
Parecis, Serra dos, Brazil 100 13 0S 60 0W
Parepare, Indon. 63 4 0S 119 40 E
Paris, Fr. 34 48 50N 2 20 E
Parkes, Austral. 70 33 9S 148 11 E
Parma, It. 40 44 50N 10 20 E
Parnaíba →, Brazil 101 3 0S 41 50W
Parracombe, U.K. 16 51 11N 3 55W
Parramatta, Austral. 70 33 48S 151 1 E
Parrett →, U.K. 14 51 7N 2 58W
Partney, U.K. 19 53 12N 0 7 E
Parton, U.K. 18 54 34N 3 35W
Passage West, Ire. 25 51 52N 8 20W
Pasto, Col. 100 1 13N 77 17W
Patagonia, Arg. 102 45 0S 69 0W
Patcham, U.K. 15 50 52N 0 9W
Pateley Bridge, U.K. 19 54 5N 1 45W
Paterson, U.S.A. 93 40 55N 74 10W
Patna, India 59 25 35N 85 12 E
Patna, U.K. 20 55 21N 4 30W
Pátrai, Greece 41 38 14N 21 47 E
Patrick, U.K. 18 54 13N 4 41W
Patrington, U.K. 19 53 41N 0 1W
Patterdale, U.K. 18 54 33N 2 55W
Pau, Fr. 35 43 19N 0 25W
Paull, U.K. 19 53 42N 0 12W
Pavia, It. 40 45 10N 9 10 E
Pavlodar, U.S.S.R. 48 52 33N 77 0 E
Pawtucket, U.S.A. 93 41 51N 71 22W
Paz, La, Bol. 100 16 20S 68 10W
Pazardzhik, Bulg. 41 42 12N 24 20 E
Peace →, Canada 88 59 0N 111 25W
Peacehaven, U.K. 15 50 47N 0 1 E
Peak, The, U.K. 18 53 24N 1 53W
Peasenhall, U.K. 15 52 17N 1 24 E
Pechora →, U.S.S.R. 46 68 13N 54 15 E
Pécs, Hung. 43 46 5N 18 15 E
Peebles, U.K. 21 55 40N 3 12W
Peel, U.K. 18 54 14N 4 40W
Peel Fell, U.K. 21 55 17N 2 35W
Pegasus Bay, N.Z. 71 43 20S 173 10 E
Pegswood, U.K. 21 55 12N 1 38W
Pegu, Burma 59 17 20N 96 29 E
Pegu Yoma, Burma 59 19 0N 96 0 E
Pegwell Bay, U.K. 15 51 18N 1 22 E
Pekanbaru, Indon. 63 0 30N 101 15 E
Peking, China 61 39 55N 116 20 E
Peloponnese □, Greece 41 37 10N 22 0 E
Pelotas, Brazil 102 31 42S 52 23W
Pelvoux, Massif de, Fr. 35 44 52N 6 20 E
Pematangsiantar, Indon. 63 2 57N 99 5 E
Pemba, Tanz. 80 5 0S 39 45 E
Pembridge, U.K. 14 52 13N 2 54W
Pembroke, U.K. 17 51 41N 4 57W
Pembury, U.K. 15 51 8N 0 20 E
Pen-y-Ghent, U.K. 18 54 10N 2 15W
Pen-y-groes, U.K. 17 53 3N 4 18W
Penang = Pinang, Malay. 63 5 25N 100 15 E
Penarth, U.K. 17 51 26N 3 11W
Pendeen, U.K. 16 50 11N 5 39W
Pendle Hill, U.K. 18 53 53N 2 18W
Penicuik, U.K. 21 55 50N 3 14W
Peninsular Malaysia □, Malay. 63 4 0N 102 0 E
Penistone, U.K. 19 53 31N 1 38W
Penkridge, U.K. 14 52 44N 2 8W
Pennines, U.K. 18 54 50N 2 20W
Pennsylvania □, U.S.A. 92 40 50N 78 0W
Penpont, U.K. 21 55 14N 3 49W

Penrith, Austral. 70 33 43S 150 38 E
Penrith, U.K. 18 54 40N 2 45W
Penryn, U.K. 16 50 10N 5 7W
Pensacola, U.S.A. 90 30 30N 87 10W
Penshurst, U.K. 15 51 10N 0 12 E
Pentire Pt., U.K. 16 50 35N 4 57W
Pentland Firth, U.K. 23 58 43N 3 10W
Pentland Hills, U.K. 21 55 48N 3 25W
Penwortham, U.K. 18 53 45N 2 44W
Penza, U.S.S.R. 46 53 15N 45 5 E
Penzance, U.K. 16 50 7N 5 32W
Peoria, U.S.A. 92 40 40N 89 40W
Pereira, Col. 100 4 49N 75 43W
Perm, U.S.S.R. 46 58 0N 57 10 E
Perouse Str., La, Jap. 64 45 40N 142 0 E
Perpignan, Fr. 35 42 42N 2 53 E
Perranporth, U.K. 16 50 21N 5 9W
Perranzabuloe, U.K. 16 50 18N 5 7W
Pershore, U.K. 14 52 7N 2 4W
Persian Gulf = Gulf, The, Asia 56 27 0N 50 0 E
Perth, Austral. 66 31 57S 115 52 E
Perth, U.K. 21 56 24N 3 27W
Peru ■, S. Am. 100 8 0S 75 0W
Perúgia, It. 40 43 6N 12 24 E
Pescara, It. 40 42 28N 14 13 E
Peshawar, Pak. 58 34 2N 71 37 E
Peterborough, Canada 92 44 20N 78 20W
Peterborough, U.K. 15 52 35N 0 14W
Peterchurch, U.K. 14 52 3N 2 57W
Peterhead, U.K. 23 57 30N 1 49W
Peterlee, U.K. 19 54 45N 1 18W
Petersfield, U.K. 15 51 0N 0 56W
Petropavlovsk, U.S.S.R. 48 54 53N 69 13 E
Petropavlovsk-Kamchatskiy, U.S.S.R. 49 53 3N 158 43 E
Petrópolis, Brazil 101 22 33S 43 9W
Petrozavodsk, U.S.S.R. 46 61 41N 34 20 E
Petworth, U.K. 15 50 59N 0 37W
Pevensey, U.K. 15 50 49N 0 20 E
Pevensey Levels, U.K. 15 50 50N 0 20 E
Pewsey, U.K. 14 51 20N 1 46W
Pewsey, Vale of, U.K. 14 51 20N 1 46W
Pforzheim, W. Ger. 42 48 53N 8 43 E
Philadelphia, U.S.A. 93 40 0N 75 10W
Philippines ■, Asia 63 12 0N 123 0 E
Phnom Penh, Cambod. 63 11 33N 104 55 E
Phoenix, U.S.A. 90 33 30N 112 10W
Phoenix Is., Pac. Oc. 65 3 30S 172 0W
Piacenza, It. 40 45 2N 9 42 E
Piatra Neamţ, Rom. 43 46 56N 26 21 E
Picardie, Fr. 34 49 50N 3 0 E
Picardy = Picardie, Fr. 34 49 50N 3 0 E
Pickering, U.K. 19 54 15N 0 46W
Pickering, Vale of, U.K. 19 54 0N 0 45W
Pidley, U.K. 15 52 33N 0 4W
Piedmont □, It. 40 45 0N 7 30 E
Piedras Negras, Mex. 94 28 42N 100 31W
Pierowall, U.K. 23 59 20N 3 0W
Pietermaritzburg, S. Afr. 81 29 35S 30 25 E
Pilbara, Austral. 66 21 15S 118 16 E
Pilcomayo →, Par. 102 25 21S 57 42W
Pilling, U.K. 18 53 55N 2 54W
Pilton, U.K. 14 51 0N 2 35W
Pinang, Malay. 63 5 25N 100 15 E
Pinchbeck, U.K. 15 52 48N 0 9W
Pindus Mts., Greece 41 40 0N 21 0 E
Pine Bluff, U.S.A. 90 34 10N 92 0W
Pingxiang, China 60 22 6N 106 46 E
Pinhoe, U.K. 16 50 44N 3 29W
Pinjarra, Austral. 66 32 37S 115 52 E
Pinwherry, U.K. 20 55 9N 4 50W
Piotrków Trybunalski, Pol. 43 51 23N 19 43 E
Piracicaba, Brazil 102 22 45S 47 40W
Piraiévs, Greece 41 37 57N 23 42 E
Pirbright, U.K. 15 51 17N 0 40W
Pirmasens, W. Ger. 36 49 12N 7 30 E
Pisa, It. 40 43 43N 10 23 E
Pistóia, It. 40 43 57N 10 53 E
Pitcairn I., Pac. Oc. 65 25 5S 130 5W
Piteşti, Rom. 43 44 52N 24 54 E
Pitlochry, U.K. 23 56 43N 3 43W
Pittenweem, U.K. 21 56 13N 2 43W
Pittsburgh, U.S.A. 92 40 25N 79 55W
Pittsfield, U.S.A. 93 42 28N 73 17W
Piura, Peru 100 5 15S 80 38W
Pladda, I., U.K. 20 55 25N 5 7W
Plata, La, Arg. 102 35 0S 57 55W
Plata, Río de la, S. Am. 102 34 45S 57 30W
Plauen, E. Ger. 42 50 29N 12 9 E
Plenty, Bay of, N.Z. 71 37 45S 177 0 E
Pleven, Bulg. 41 43 26N 24 37 E
Płock, Pol. 43 52 32N 19 40 E
Ploieşti, Rom. 43 44 57N 26 5 E
Plovdiv, Bulg. 41 42 8N 24 44 E
Plymouth, U.K. 16 50 23N 4 9W
Plymouth Sd., U.K. 16 50 20N 4 10W
Plympton, U.K. 16 50 24N 4 2W
Plymstock, U.K. 16 50 22N 4 6W
Plynlimon = Pumlumon Fawr, U.K. 17 52 29N 3 47W
Plzen, Czech. 42 49 45N 13 22 E
Po →, It. 40 44 57N 12 4 E
Pocklington, U.K. 19 53 56N 0 48W
Podolsk, U.S.S.R. 46 55 25N 37 30 E
Pointe-à-Pitre, Guad. 94 16 10N 61 30W
Pointe Noire, Congo 80 4 48S 11 53 E
Poitiers, Fr. 34 46 35N 0 20 E
Poland ■, Europe 43 52 0N 20 0 E
Polden Hills, U.K. 14 51 7N 2 50W
Polegate, U.K. 15 50 49N 0 15 E
Polesworth, U.K. 14 52 37N 1 37W
Polperro, U.K. 16 50 19N 4 31W
Polruan, U.K. 16 50 17N 4 36W
Poltava, U.S.S.R. 47 49 35N 34 35 E
Polynesia, Pac. Oc. 64 10 0S 162 0W
Ponce, P.R. 95 18 1N 66 37W
Pondicherry, India 58 11 59N 79 50 E
Ponta Grossa, Brazil 102 25 7S 50 10W
Pontardawe, U.K. 17 51 43N 3 51W
Pontardulais, U.K. 17 51 42N 4 3W
Pontchartrain, L., U.S.A. 90 30 12N 90 0W
Pontefract, U.K. 19 53 42N 1 19W
Ponteland, U.K. 21 55 7N 1 45W
Pontevedra, Sp. 37 42 26N 8 40W
Pontianak, Indon. 63 0 3S 109 15 E
Pontrilas, U.K. 14 51 56N 2 53W
Pontypool, U.K. 17 51 42N 3 1W
Pontypridd, U.K. 17 51 36N 3 21W
Poole, U.K. 14 50 42N 1 58W
Poole Harbour, U.K. 14 50 41N 2 0W
Pooley Bridge, U.K. 18 54 37N 2 49W
Poona = Pune, India 58 18 29N 73 57 E
Poopó, L., Bol. 100 18 30S 67 35W
Popayán, Col. 100 2 27N 76 36W
Popocatépetl, Volcán, Mex. 94 19 2N 98 38W
Pori, Fin. 45 61 29N 21 48 E
Porirua, N.Z. 71 41 8S 174 52 E
Porlock, U.K. 14 51 13N 3 36W
Porlock B., U.K. 14 51 14N 3 37W
Porlock Hill, U.K. 14 51 12N 3 40W
Porsangen Fjord, Nor. 44 70 45N 25 0 E
Port Antonio, Jam. 94 18 10N 76 30W
Port Arthur, U.S.A. 90 30 0N 94 0W
Port Askaig, U.K. 20 55 51N 6 8W
Port-au-Prince, Haiti 95 18 40N 72 20W
Port Augusta, Austral. 67 32 30S 137 50 E
Port Bannatyne, U.K. 20 55 51N 5 4W
Port Carlisle, U.K. 18 54 56N 3 12W
Port-Cartier, Canada 89 50 2N 66 50W
Port Charlotte, U.K. 20 55 44N 6 22W
Port Elizabeth, S. Afr. 81 33 58S 25 40 E
Port Ellen, U.K. 20 55 38N 6 10W
Port Erin, U.K. 18 54 5N 4 45W
Port-Gentil, Gabon 80 0 40S 8 50 E
Port Glasgow, U.K. 20 55 57N 4 40W
Port Harcourt, Nig. 78 4 40N 7 10 E
Port Hedland, Austral. 66 20 25S 118 35 E
Port Isaac, U.K. 16 50 35N 4 50W
Port Isaac B., U.K. 16 50 36N 4 50W
Port Laoise, Ire. 25 53 2N 7 20W
Port Logan, U.K. 20 54 42N 4 57W
Port Macquarie, Austral. 67 31 25S 152 25 E
Port Moresby, P.N.G. 64 9 24S 147 8 E
Port of Spain, Trin. & Tob. 94 10 40N 61 31W
Port Phillip B., Austral. 70 38 10S 144 50 E
Port Pirie, Austral. 67 33 10S 138 1 E
Port Said, Egypt 79 31 16N 32 18 E
Port St. Mary, U.K. 18 54 5N 4 45W
Port Sudan, Sudan 79 19 32N 37 9 E
Port Sunlight, U.K. 18 53 22N 3 0W
Port Talbot, U.K. 17 51 35N 3 48W
Port William, U.K. 20 54 46N 4 35W
Portadown, U.K. 24 54 27N 6 26W
Portaferry, U.K. 24 54 23N 5 32W
Portage La Prairie, Canada 88 49 58N 98 18W
Portarlington, Ire. 25 53 10N 7 10W
Porthcawl, U.K. 17 51 28N 3 42W
Porthleven, U.K. 16 50 5N 5 19W
Porthmadog, U.K. 17 52 55N 4 13W
Portishead, U.K. 14 51 29N 2 46W
Portland, Austral. 70 38 20S 141 35 E
Portland, Maine, U.S.A. 93 43 40N 70 15W
Portland, Oreg., U.S.A. 90 45 35N 122 40W
Portland, Bill of, U.K. 14 50 31N 2 27W
Portland, I. of, U.K. 14 50 32N 2 25W
Portnacroish, U.K. 20 56 34N 5 24W
Portnahaven, U.K. 20 55 40N 6 30W
Pôrto Alegre, Brazil 102 30 5S 51 10W
Porto Novo, Benin 78 6 23N 2 42 E
Pôrto Velho, Brazil 100 8 46S 63 54W
Porton, U.K. 14 51 8N 1 42W
Portovíejo, Ecuad. 100 1 7S 80 28W
Portpatrick, U.K. 20 54 50N 5 7W
Portree, U.K. 22 57 25N 6 11W
Portrush, U.K. 24 55 13N 6 40W
Portslade, U.K. 15 50 50N 0 11W
Portsmouth, U.K. 14 50 48N 1 6W
Portsmouth, U.S.A. 93 43 5N 70 45W
Portsoy, U.K. 23 57 41N 2 41W
Portstewart, U.K. 24 55 12N 6 43W
Portugal ■, Europe 37 40 0N 7 0W
Portumna, Ire. 25 53 5N 8 12W
Posadas, Arg. 102 27 30S 55 50W
Postbridge, U.K. 16 50 36N 3 54W
Potchefstroom, S. Afr. 81 26 41S 27 7 E
Potenza, It. 40 40 40N 15 50 E
Potomac →, U.S.A. 92 38 0N 76 23W
Potosí, Bol. 100 19 38S 65 50W
Potsdam, E. Ger. 42 52 23N 13 4 E
Potter Heigham, U.K. 15 52 44N 1 33 E
Potterne, U.K. 14 51 19N 2 0W
Potters Bar, U.K. 15 51 42N 0 11W
Potterspury, U.K. 15 52 5N 0 52W
Poulaphouca Res., Ire. 25 53 8N 6 30W
Poulton le Fylde, U.K. 18 53 51N 2 59W
Poundstock, U.K. 16 50 44N 4 34W
Powell, L., U.S.A. 90 37 25N 110 45W
Powick, U.K. 14 52 9N 2 15W
Powys □, U.K. 17 52 20N 3 20W
Poyang Hu, China 61 29 10N 116 10 E
Poznań, Pol. 42 52 25N 16 55 E
Prague, Czech. 42 50 5N 14 22 E
Prato, It. 40 43 53N 11 5 E
Prawle Pt., U.K. 16 50 13N 3 41W
Prees, U.K. 18 52 54N 2 40W
Preesall, U.K. 18 53 55N 2 58W
Prescot, U.K. 18 53 27N 2 49W
Preshute, U.K. 14 51 24N 1 45W
Presidente Prudente, Brazil 101 22 5S 51 25W
Presque Isle, U.S.A. 93 46 40N 68 0W
Prestatyn, U.K. 17 53 20N 3 24W
Prestbury, U.K. 14 51 54N 2 2W
Presteigne, U.K. 17 52 17N 3 0W
Preston, Borders, U.K. 21 55 48N 2 18W
Preston, Dorset, U.K. 14 50 38N 2 26W
Preston, Lancs., U.K. 18 53 46N 2 42W
Prestonpans, U.K. 21 55 58N 3 0W
Prestwich, U.K. 18 53 32N 2 18W
Prestwick, U.K. 20 55 30N 4 38W
Pretoria, S. Afr. 81 25 44S 28 12 E
Prince Albert, Canada 88 53 15N 105 50W
Prince Edward I. □, Canada 93 46 20N 63 20W
Prince George, Canada 88 53 55N 122 50W
Prince of Wales I., Canada 88 73 0N 99 0W
Prince Rupert, Canada 88 54 20N 130 20W
Princes Risborough, U.K. 15 51 43N 0 50W
Princess Charlotte B., Austral. 67 14 25S 144 0 E
Princetown, U.K. 16 50 33N 4 0W
Pripyat Marshes, U.S.S.R. 46 52 0N 28 10 E
Priština, Yug. 41 42 40N 21 13 E
Prizren, Yug. 41 42 13N 20 45 E
Probus, U.K. 16 50 17N 4 55W
Prokopyevsk, U.S.S.R. 48 54 0N 86 45 E
Prome, Burma 59 18 49N 95 13 E
Provence, Fr. 35 43 40N 5 46 E
Providence, U.S.A. 93 41 50N 71 28W
Prudhoe, U.K. 21 54 57N 1 52W
Prudhoe Bay, U.S.A. 88 70 20N 148 20W
Prut →, Rom. 41 46 3N 28 10 E
Przemyśl, Pol. 43 49 50N 22 45 E
Puddletown, U.K. 14 50 45N 2 21W
Pudsey, U.K. 19 53 47N 1 40W
Puebla, Mex. 94 19 3N 98 12W
Pueblo, U.S.A. 90 38 20N 104 40W
Puerto La Cruz, Ven. 100 10 13N 64 38W
Puerto Montt, Chile 102 41 28S 73 0W
Puerto Rico ■, W. Ind. 95 18 15N 66 45W
Pula, It. 40 39 0N 9 0 E
Pulborough, U.K. 15 50 58N 0 30W
Pulham Market, U.K. 15 52 25N 1 15 E
Pulham St. Mary, U.K. 15 52 25N 1 14 E
Pumlumon Fawr, U.K. 17 52 29N 3 47W
Pune, India 58 18 29N 73 57 E
Punjab □, India 58 31 0N 76 0 E
Punjab □, Pak. 58 30 0N 72 0 E
Punta Arenas, Chile 102 53 10S 71 0W
Punto Fijo, Ven. 100 11 50N 70 13W
Purbeck, Isle of, U.K. 14 50 40N 2 5W
Purfleet, U.K. 15 51 29N 0 15 E
Purley, U.K. 14 51 29N 1 4W
Purnia, India 59 25 45N 87 31 E
Purus →, Brazil 100 3 42S 61 28W
Pusan, S. Kor. 61 35 5N 129 0 E
Puy-de-Dôme, Fr. 35 45 46N 2 57 E
Pwllheli, U.K. 17 52 54N 4 26W
Pyŏngyang, N. Kor. 61 39 0N 125 30 E
Pyrenees, Europe 35 42 45N 0 18 E

Q

Qandahār, Afg. 57 31 32N 65 30 E
Qatar ■, Asia 56 25 30N 51 15 E
Qattâra Depression, Egypt 79 29 30N 27 30 E
Qazvin, Iran 56 36 15N 50 0 E
Qena, Egypt 79 26 10N 32 43 E
Qingdao, China 61 36 5N 120 20 E
Qinghai □, China 60 36 0N 98 0 E
Qinghai Hu, China 60 36 40N 100 10 E
Qingjiang, China 61 33 30N 119 2 E
Qiqihar, China 61 47 26N 124 0 E
Qom, Iran 56 34 40N 51 0 E
Quadring, U.K. 19 52 53N 0 9W
Quainton, U.K. 15 51 51N 0 53W
Quantock Hills, U.K. 14 51 8N 3 10W
Queanbeyan, Austral. 70 35 17S 149 14 E
Québec, Canada 93 46 52N 71 13W
Québec □, Canada 89 50 0N 70 0W
Queen Charlotte Is., Canada 88 53 20N 132 10W
Queen Elizabeth Is., Canada 103 76 0N 95 0W
Queen Maud G., Canada 88 68 15N 102 30W
Queenborough, U.K. 15 51 24N 0 46 E
Queensbury, U.K. 18 53 46N 1 50W
Queensferry, U.K. 21 56 0N 3 25W
Queensland □, Austral. 67 22 0S 142 0 E
Queenstown, N.Z. 71 45 1S 168 40 E
Queenstown, S. Afr. 81 31 52S 26 52 E
Querétaro, Mex. 94 20 36N 100 23W
Quetta, Pak. 58 30 15N 66 55 E
Quezon City, Phil. 63 14 38N 121 0 E
Qui Nhon, Viet. 63 13 40N 109 13 E
Quimper, Fr. 34 48 0N 4 9W
Quito, Ecuad. 100 0 15S 78 35W
Quorndon, U.K. 14 52 45N 1 10W

R

Raasay, U.K. 22 57 25N 6 4W
Raasay, Sd. of, U.K. 22 57 30N 6 8W
Rabat, Malta 40 35 53N 14 25 E
Rabat, Mor. 78 34 2N 6 48W
Rackheath, U.K. 15 52 41N 1 22 E
Radcliffe, Gr. Manchester, U.K. 18 53 35N 2 19W
Radcliffe, Notts., U.K. 19 52 57N 1 3W
Radley, U.K. 14 51 42N 1 14W
Radnor Forest, U.K. 17 52 17N 3 10W
Radom, Pol. 43 51 23N 21 12 E
Radstock, U.K. 14 51 17N 2 25W
Ragusa, It. 40 36 56N 14 42 E
Rainham, U.K. 15 51 22N 0 36 E
Rainworth, U.K. 19 53 8N 1 6W
Raipur, India 59 21 17N 81 45 E
Rajahmundry, India 59 17 1N 81 48 E
Rajasthan □, India 58 26 45N 73 30 E
Rajkot, India 58 22 15N 70 56 E
Raleigh, U.S.A. 91 35 47N 78 39W
Rame Head, U.K. 16 50 19N 4 14W
Rampside, U.K. 18 54 6N 3 10W
Rampur, India 58 28 50N 79 5 E
Ramree Kyun, Burma 59 19 0N 94 0 E
Ramsbottom, U.K. 18 53 36N 2 20W
Ramsbury, U.K. 14 51 26N 1 37W
Ramsey, Cambs., U.K. 15 52 27N 0 6W
Ramsey, Essex, U.K. 15 51 55N 1 12 E
Ramsey, I. of M., U.K. 18 54 20N 4 21W
Ramsey Bay, U.K. 18 54 23N 4 20W
Ramsgate, U.K. 15 51 20N 1 25 E
Rancagua, Chile 102 34 10S 70 50W
Ranchi, India 59 23 19N 85 27 E
Rangoon, Burma 59 16 45N 96 20 E
Rannoch, L., U.K. 23 56 41N 4 20W
Rannoch Moor, U.K. 20 56 38N 4 48W
Rasht, Iran 56 37 20N 49 40 E
Rath Luirc, Ire. 25 52 21N 8 40W
Rathdrum, Ire. 25 52 57N 6 13W
Rathfriland, U.K. 24 54 12N 6 12W
Rathkeale, Ire. 25 52 32N 8 57W
Rathlin I., U.K. 24 55 18N 6 14W
Rathlin O'Birne I., Ire. 24 54 40N 8 50W
Rattray Hd., U.K. 23 57 38N 1 50W
Raukumara Ra., N.Z. 71 38 5S 177 55 E
Raunds, U.K. 15 52 20N 0 32W
Raurkela, India 59 22 14N 84 50 E
Ravenglass, U.K. 18 54 21N 3 25W
Ravenna, It. 40 44 28N 12 15 E
Ravenstonedale, U.K. 18 54 26N 2 26W
Rawalpindi, Pak. 58 33 38N 73 8 E
Rawmarsh, U.K. 19 53 27N 1 20W
Rawtenstall, U.K. 18 53 42N 2 18W
Rayleigh, U.K. 15 51 36N 0 38 E
Reading, U.K. 15 51 27N 0 57W
Reading, U.S.A. 93 40 20N 75 53W
Recife, Brazil 101 8 0S 35 0W
Reculver, U.K. 15 51 22N 1 12 E
Red → = Hong Viet. 60 20 17N 106 34 E
Red →, U.S.A. 91 31 0N 91 40W
Red Deer, Canada 88 52 20N 113 50W
Red Dial, U.K. 18 54 48N 3 9W
Red Sea, Asia 56 25 0N 36 0 E
Redbridge, U.K. 15 51 35N 0 7 E
Redcar, U.K. 19 54 37N 1 4W
Redditch, U.K. 14 52 18N 1 57W
Rede →, U.K. 21 55 8N 2 12W
Redesmouth, U.K. 21 55 7N 2 12W
Redhill, U.K. 15 51 14N 0 10W
Redlynch, U.K. 14 50 59N 1 42W
Redmile, U.K. 19 52 54N 0 48W
Redmire, U.K. 19 54 19N 1 55W
Redruth, U.K. 16 50 14N 5 14W
Ree, L., Ire. 24 53 35N 8 0W
Reedham, U.K. 15 52 34N 1 33 E
Reepham, U.K. 15 52 46N 1 6 E
Reeth, U.K. 18 54 23N 1 56W
Regensburg, W. Ger. 42 49 1N 12 7 E
Réggio di Calábria, It. 40 38 7N 15 38 E
Réggio nell' Emilia, It. 40 44 42N 10 38 E
Regina, Canada 88 50 27N 104 35W
Reigate, U.K. 15 51 14N 0 11W
Reims, Fr. 34 49 15N 4 1 E
Reindeer L., Canada 88 57 15N 102 15W
Remscheid, W. Ger. 36 51 11N 7 12 E
Renfrew, U.K. 20 55 52N 4 24W
Renmark, Austral. 67 34 11S 140 43 E
Rennes, Fr. 34 48 7N 1 41W
Reno, U.S.A. 90 39 30N 119 50W
Repton, U.K. 14 52 50N 1 32W
Resistencia, Arg. 102 27 30S 59 0W
Reston, U.K. 21 55 51N 2 11W
Réthímnon, Greece 41 35 18N 24 30 E
Reykjavík, Ice. 44 64 10N 21 57 E
Reynosa, Mex. 94 26 5N 98 18W

Rhayader, U.K. 17 52 19N 3 30W
Rheidol →, U.K. 17 52 25N 4 5W
Rhein →, W. Ger. 36 51 52N 6 20 E
Rheine, W. Ger. 36 52 17N 7 25 E
Rhine = Rhein →, W. Ger. 36 51 52N 6 20 E
Rhineland-Palatinate □, W. Ger. 42 50 0N 7 0 E
Rhins, The, U.K. 20 54 52N 5 3W
Rhode Island □, U.S.A. 93 41 38N 71 37W
Rhodes = Ródhos, Greece 41 36 15N 28 10 E
Rhodesia = Zimbabwe ■, Africa 81 20 0S 30 0 E
Rhodope Mts., Bulg. 41 41 40N 24 20 E
Rhondda, U.K. 17 51 39N 3 30W
Rhône →, Fr. 35 43 28N 4 42 E
Rhosllanerchrugog, U.K. 17 53 3N 3 4W
Rhossili, U.K. 17 51 34N 4 18W
Rhum, U.K. 22 57 0N 6 20W
Rhyl, U.K. 17 53 19N 3 29W
Rhymney, U.K. 17 51 32N 3 7W
Ribble →, U.K. 18 54 13N 2 20W
Ribeirão Prêto, Brazil 101 21 10S 47 50W
Riccall, U.K. 19 53 50N 1 4W
Riccarton, N.Z. 71 43 32S 172 37 E
Riccarton Junc., U.K. 21 55 16N 2 43W
Richmond, N. Yorks., U.K. 19 54 24N 1 43W
Richmond, Surrey, U.K. 15 51 28N 0 18W
Richmond, U.S.A. 92 37 33N 77 27W
Rickmansworth, U.K. 15 51 38N 0 28W
Ridsdale, U.K. 21 55 9N 2 8W
Rievaulx, U.K. 19 54 16N 1 7W
Riga, U.S.S.R. 46 56 53N 24 8 E
Riga, G. of, U.S.S.R. 46 57 40N 23 45 E
Rijeka, Yug. 40 45 20N 14 21 E
Rijswijk, Neth. 36 52 4N 4 22 E
Rillington, U.K. 19 54 10N 0 41W
Rímini, It. 40 44 3N 12 33 E
Rîmnicu Vîlcea, Rom. 43 45 9N 24 21 E
Rimouski, Canada 93 48 27N 68 30W
Rineanna, Ire. 25 52 42N 85 7W
Ringford, U.K. 21 54 55N 4 3W
Ringmer, U.K. 15 50 53N 0 5 E
Ringwood, U.K. 14 50 50N 1 48W
Rio Branco, Brazil 100 9 58S 67 49W
Río Cuarto, Arg. 102 33 10S 64 25W
Rio de Janeiro, Brazil 101 23 0S 43 12W
Río Gallegos, Arg. 102 51 35S 69 15W
Rio Grande, Brazil 102 32 0S 52 20W
Rio Grande →, U.S.A. 90 25 57N 97 9W
Rio Grande do Norte □, Brazil 94 5 40S 36 0W
Río Muni = Mbini □, Eq. Guin. 80 1 30N 10 0 E
Ríobamba, Ecuad. 100 1 50S 78 45W
Ripley, Derby, U.K. 19 53 3N 1 24W
Ripley, N. Yorks., U.K. 19 54 3N 1 34W
Ripon, U.K. 19 54 8N 1 31W
Risca, U.K. 17 51 36N 3 6W
Rishton, U.K. 18 53 46N 2 26W
Riverside, U.S.A. 90 34 0N 117 22W
Riyadh, Si. Arab. 56 24 41N 46 42 E
Roade, U.K. 15 52 10N 0 53W
Roadhead, U.K. 18 55 4N 2 44W
Roag, L., U.K. 22 58 10N 6 55W
Roanne, Fr. 35 46 3N 4 4 E
Roanoke, U.S.A. 92 37 19N 79 55W
Robe →, Ire. 24 53 38N 9 10W
Roberton, U.K. 21 55 24N 2 53W
Robin Hood's Bay, U.K. 19 54 26N 0 31W
Rocester, U.K. 18 52 56N 1 50W
Rochdale, U.K. 18 53 36N 2 10W
Roche, U.K. 16 50 24N 4 50W
Rochelle, La, Fr. 35 46 10N 1 9W
Rochester, Kent, U.K. 15 51 22N 0 30 E
Rochester, Northumberland, U.K. 21 55 16N 2 16W
Rochester, Minn., U.S.A. 90 44 1N 92 28W
Rochester, N.Y., U.S.A. 92 43 10N 77 40W
Rochford, U.K. 15 51 36N 0 42 E
Rockall, Atl. Oc. 26 57 37N 13 42W
Rockcliffe, U.K. 18 54 58N 3 0W
Rockford, U.S.A. 92 42 20N 89 0W
Rockhampton, Austral. 67 23 22S 150 32 E
Rockingham, U.K. 15 52 32N 0 43W
Rockingham Forest, U.K. 15 52 28N 0 42W
Rocky Mts., N. Am. 90 55 0N 121 0W
Ródhos, Greece 41 36 15N 28 10 E
Roding →, U.K. 15 51 31N 0 7 E
Roe →, U.K. 24 55 10N 6 59W
Roeselare, Belg. 36 50 57N 3 7 E
Rogaland fylke □, Nor. 45 59 12N 6 20 E
Rogans Seat, U.K. 18 54 25N 2 10W
Rogate, U.K. 15 51 0N 0 51W
Roma, Austral. 67 26 32S 148 49 E
Roma = Rome, It. 40 41 54N 12 30 E
Romania ■, Europe 43 46 0N 25 0 E
Rome, It. 40 41 54N 12 30 E
Romney Marsh, U.K. 15 51 0N 1 0 E
Romsey, U.K. 14 51 0N 1 29W
Rona, U.K. 22 57 33N 6 0W
Ronse, Belg. 36 50 45N 3 35 E
Roosendaal, Neth. 36 51 32N 4 29 E
Roper →, Austral. 67 14 43S 135 27 E
Ropsley, U.K. 19 52 53N 0 31W
Roraima, Mt., Ven. 101 5 10N 60 40W
Rosario, Arg. 102 33 0S 60 40W
Roscommon, Ire. 24 53 38N 8 11W
Roscommon □, Ire. 24 53 40N 8 15W
Roscrea, Ire. 25 52 58N 7 50W
Roseau, Dom. 94 15 20N 61 24W
Rosedale Abbey, U.K. 19 54 22N 0 51W
Roskilde, Den. 45 55 38N 12 3 E
Rosneath, U.K. 20 56 1N 4 49W
Ross Ice Shelf, Ant. 103 80 0S 180 0 E
Ross on Wye, U.K. 14 51 55N 2 34W
Ross Sea, Ant. 103 74 0S 178 0 E
Rossall Pt., U.K. 18 53 55N 3 2W
Rossan Pt., Ire. 24 54 42N 8 47W
Rosslare, Ire. 25 52 17N 6 23W
Rostock, E. Ger. 42 54 4N 12 9 E
Rostov, U.S.S.R. 47 47 15N 39 45 E
Rosyth, U.K. 21 56 2N 3 26W
Rothbury, U.K. 21 55 19N 1 55W
Rothbury Forest, U.K. 21 55 19N 1 50W
Rother →, U.K. 15 50 59N 0 40 E
Rotherham, U.K. 19 53 26N 1 21W
Rothes, U.K. 23 57 31N 3 12W
Rothesay, U.K. 20 55 50N 5 3W
Rothwell, Northants., U.K. 15 52 25N 0 48W
Rothwell, W. Yorks., U.K. 19 53 46N 1 29W
Rotorua, N.Z. 71 38 9S 176 16 E
Rotorua, L., N.Z. 71 38 5S 176 18 E
Rotterdam, Neth. 36 51 55N 4 30 E
Rottingdean, U.K. 15 50 48N 0 3W
Roubaix, Fr. 34 50 40N 3 10 E
Rouen, Fr. 34 49 27N 1 4 E
Rousay, U.K. 23 59 10N 3 2W
Rowanburn, U.K. 21 55 5N 2 54W
Rowrah, U.K. 18 54 34N 3 26W
Roxburgh, U.K. 21 55 34N 2 30W
Roxby, U.K. 19 53 38N 0 37W
Royston, U.K. 15 52 3N 0 1W
Royton, U.K. 18 53 34N 2 7W
Ruahine Ra., N.Z. 71 39 55S 176 2 E
Rub' al Khali, Si. Arab. 56 18 0N 48 0 E
Rubery, U.K. 14 52 24N 1 59W
Rubh a' Mhail, U.K. 20 55 55N 6 10W
Rubha Hunish, U.K. 22 57 42N 6 20W
Rudgwick, U.K. 15 51 7N 0 54W
Rudston, U.K. 19 54 6N 0 19W
Rufford, U.K. 18 53 37N 2 50W
Rugby, U.K. 14 52 23N 1 16W
Rugeley, U.K. 14 52 47N 1 56W
Rum Jungle, Austral. 66 13 0S 130 59 E
Runcorn, U.K. 18 53 20N 2 44W
Ruse, Bulg. 41 43 48N 25 59 E
Rushden, U.K. 15 52 17N 0 37W
Ruskington, U.K. 19 53 5N 0 23W
Russian S.F.S.R. □, U.S.S.R. 46 62 0N 105 0 E
Rutherglen, U.K. 20 55 50N 4 11W
Ruthin, U.K. 17 53 7N 3 20W
Ruthwell, U.K. 21 55 0N 3 24W
Rwanda ■, Africa 80 2 0S 30 0 E
Ryan, L., U.K. 20 55 0N 5 2W
Ryazan, U.S.S.R. 46 54 40N 39 40 E
Rybinsk = Andropov, U.S.S.R. 46 58 5N 38 50 E
Rybinsk Res., U.S.S.R. 46 58 30N 38 0 E
Rydal, U.K. 18 54 28N 2 59W
Ryde, U.K. 14 50 44N 1 9W
Rye, U.K. 15 50 57N 0 46 E
Rye →, U.K. 19 54 12N 0 53W
Rye Bay, U.K. 15 50 50N 0 50 E
Ryhope, U.K. 21 54 52N 1 22W
Ryton, Tyne & Wear, U.K. 21 54 58N 1 44W
Ryton, Warwick, U.K. 14 52 23N 1 25W
Ryūkyū Is., Jap. 62 26 0N 128 0 E
Rzeszów, Pol. 43 50 5N 21 58 E

S

Saarbrücken, W. Ger. 36 49 15N 6 58 E
Saaremaa, U.S.S.R. 46 58 30N 22 30 E
Saarland □, W. Ger. 36 49 15N 7 0 E
Saba, W. Ind. 94 17 42N 63 26W
Sabadell, Sp. 37 41 28N 2 7 E
Sabah □, Malay. 63 6 0N 117 0 E
Sabhah, Libya 79 27 9N 14 29 E
Sacramento, U.S.A. 90 38 33N 121 30 E
Sacriston, U.K. 19 54 49N 1 38W
Saddell, U.K. 20 55 31N 5 30W
Saffron Walden, U.K. 15 52 2N 0 15 E
Safi, Mor. 78 32 18N 9 20W
Sagar, India 58 14 14N 75 6 E
Saginaw, U.S.A. 92 43 26N 83 55W
Saginaw B., U.S.A. 92 43 50N 83 40W
Sahara, Africa 78 23 0N 5 0 E
Saharan Atlas, Alg. 78 34 9N 3 29 E
Saharanpur, India 58 29 58N 77 33 E
Saigon = Ho Chi Minh City, Viet. 63 10 58N 106 40 E
St. Abb's, U.K. 21 55 54N 2 7W
St. Abb's Head, U.K. 21 55 55N 2 10W
St. Agnes, U.K. 16 50 18N 5 13W
St. Agnes Hd., U.K. 16 50 19N 5 14W
St. Agnes I., U.K. 16 49 53N 6 20W
St. Albans, U.K. 15 51 44N 0 19W
St. Alban's Head, U.K. 14 50 34N 2 3W
St. Andrews, U.K. 21 56 20N 2 48W
St. Ann's, U.K. 21 55 14N 3 28W
St. Asaph, U.K. 17 53 15N 3 27W
St. Austell, U.K. 16 50 20N 4 48W
St. Bees, U.K. 18 54 29N 3 36W
St. Bee's Hd., U.K. 18 54 30N 3 38 E
St. Blazey, U.K. 16 50 22N 4 48W
St. Boniface, Canada 88 49 53N 97 5W
St. Boswells, U.K. 21 55 34N 2 39W
St. Briavels, U.K. 14 51 44N 2 39W
St. Brides B., U.K. 17 51 48N 5 15W
St.-Brieuc, Fr. 34 48 30N 2 46W
St. Budeaux, U.K. 16 50 23N 4 10W
St. Buryan, U.K. 16 50 4N 5 34W
St. Catharines, Canada 92 43 10N 79 15W
St. Catherine's Pt., U.K. 14 50 34N 1 18W
St. Christopher-Nevis ■, W. Ind. 94 17 20N 62 40W
St. Clair, L., Canada 92 42 30N 82 45W
St.-Claude, Fr. 35 46 22N 5 52 E
St. Clears, U.K. 17 51 48N 4 30W
St. Columb Major, U.K. 16 50 26N 4 56W
St. David's, U.K. 17 51 54N 5 16W
St. David's Head, U.K. 17 51 55N 5 16W
St. Dennis, U.K. 16 50 23N 4 53W
St. Dominick, U.K. 16 50 28N 4 15W
St. Elias Mts., Canada 88 60 33N 139 28W
St. Endellion, U.K. 16 50 33N 4 49W
St. Enoder, U.K. 16 50 22N 4 57W
St. Erth, U.K. 16 50 10N 5 26W
St.-Étienne, Fr. 35 45 27N 4 22 E
St. Fillans, U.K. 21 56 25N 4 7W
St. Gallen, Switz. 42 47 25N 9 20 E
St. George's, Gren. 94 12 5N 61 43W
St. George's Channel, U.K. 25 52 0N 6 0W
St. Germans, U.K. 16 50 24N 4 19W
St. Helena, Atl. Oc. 128 15 55S 5 44W
St. Helena B., S. Afr. 81 32 40S 18 10 E
St. Helens, I. of W., U.K. 14 50 42N 1 6W
St. Helens, Merseyside, U.K. 18 53 28N 2 44W
St. Helier, U.K. 34 49 11N 2 6W
St-Hyacinthe, Canada 93 45 40N 72 58W
St. Issey, U.K. 16 50 30N 4 55W
St. Ives, Cambs., U.K. 15 52 20N 0 5W
St. Ives, Cornwall, U.K. 16 50 13N 5 29W
St. Ives Bay, U.K. 16 50 15N 5 27W
St-Jean, L., Canada 93 48 40N 72 0W
St-Jérôme, Canada 93 45 47N 74 0W
St. John, Canada 93 45 20N 66 8W
St. John's, Antigua 94 17 6N 61 51W
St. John's, Canada 89 47 35N 52 40W
St. John's, U.K. 18 54 13N 4 38W
St. Johns Chapel, U.K. 18 54 43N 2 10W
St. Joseph, U.S.A. 90 39 46N 94 50W
St. Just, U.K. 16 50 7N 5 41W
St. Keverne, U.K. 16 50 3N 5 5W
St. Kew, U.K. 16 50 34N 4 48W
St. Lawrence →, Canada 93 49 30N 66 0W
St. Lawrence, Gulf of, Canada 89 48 25N 62 0W
St. Leonards, U.K. 15 50 51N 0 34 E
St. Levan, U.K. 16 50 3N 5 36W
St.-Lô, Fr. 34 49 7N 1 5W
St-Louis, Sene. 78 16 8N 16 27W
St. Louis, U.S.A. 92 38 40N 90 12W
St. Lucia ■, W. Ind. 94 14 0N 60 50W
St. Maarten, W. Ind. 94 18 0N 63 5W
St. Mabyn, U.K. 16 50 30N 4 45W
St.-Malo, Fr. 34 48 39N 2 1W
St. Margaret's-at-Cliffe, U.K. 15 51 10N 1 23 E
St. Margaret's Hope, U.K. 23 58 49N 2 58W
St-Martin, I., W. Ind. 94 18 0N 63 0W
St. Martin's I., U.K. 16 49 58N 6 16W
St. Mary Bourne, U.K. 14 51 16N 1 24W
St. Mary's, U.K. 16 49 55N 6 17W
St. Mary's Sd., U.K. 16 49 53N 6 19W
St. Mawes, U.K. 16 50 10N 5 1W
St. Merryn, U.K. 16 50 31N 4 58W
St. Michael's Mt., U.K. 16 50 7N 5 30W
St. Minver, U.K. 16 50 34N 4 52W
St. Monance, U.K. 21 56 13N 2 46W
St.-Nazaire, Fr. 34 47 17N 2 12W
St. Neots, U.K. 15 52 14N 0 16W
St-Niklaas, Belg. 36 51 10N 4 8 E
St. Osyth, U.K. 15 51 47N 1 4 E
St. Paul, U.S.A. 91 44 54N 93 5W
St. Peter Port, U.K. 34 49 27N 2 31W
St. Petersburg, U.S.A. 91 27 45N 82 40W
St.-Pierre et Miquelon □, N. Am. 89 46 55N 56 10W
St.-Quentin, Fr. 34 49 50N 3 16 E
St. Stephen, U.K. 16 50 20N 4 52W
St. Teath, U.K. 16 50 34N 4 45W
St.-Tropez, Fr. 35 43 17N 6 38 E
St. Tudy, U.K. 16 50 33N 4 45W
St. Vincent and the Grenadines ■, W. Ind. 94 13 0N 61 10W
Saintfield, U.K. 24 54 28N 5 50W
Sakai, Jap. 62 34 30N 135 30 E
Sakhalin, U.S.S.R. 49 51 0N 143 0 E
Salado →, Arg. 102 31 40S 60 41W
Salamanca, Sp. 37 40 58N 5 39W
Salcombe, U.K. 16 50 14N 3 47W
Salcombe Regis, U.K. 16 50 41N 3 11W
Sale, Austral. 70 38 6S 147 6 E
Sale, U.K. 18 53 26N 2 19W
Salem, India 58 11 40N 78 11 E
Salen, U.K. 20 56 31N 5 57W
Salerno, It. 40 40 40N 14 44 E
Salford, U.K. 18 53 30N 2 17W
Salford Priors, U.K. 14 52 10N 1 52W
Salisbury = Harare, Zimb. 81 17 43S 31 2 E
Salisbury, U.K. 14 51 4N 1 48W
Salisbury Plain, U.K. 14 51 13N 1 50W
Salonica = Thessaloníki, Greece 41 40 38N 22 58 E
Salop = Shropshire □, U.K. 14 52 36N 2 45W
Salt Lake City, U.S.A. 90 40 45N 111 58W
Salta, Arg. 102 24 57S 65 25W
Saltash, U.K. 16 50 25N 4 13W
Saltburn by the Sea, U.K. 19 54 35N 0 58W
Saltcoats, U.K. 20 55 38N 4 47W
Saltee Is., Ire. 25 52 7N 6 37W
Saltergate, U.K. 19 54 20N 0 40W
Saltfleet, U.K. 19 53 25N 0 11 E
Saltfleetby, U.K. 19 53 23N 0 10 E
Saltillo, Mex. 94 25 25N 101 0W
Salto, Urug. 102 31 27S 57 50W
Saltwood, U.K. 15 51 4N 1 5 E
Salvador, Brazil 101 13 0S 38 30W
Salween →, Burma 59 16 31N 97 37 E
Salzburg, Austria 42 47 48N 13 2 E
Salzgitter, W. Ger. 42 52 13N 10 22 E
Samarinda, Indon. 63 0 30S 117 9 E
Samarkand, U.S.S.R. 48 39 40N 66 55 E
Sámos, Greece 41 37 45N 26 50 E
Sampford Courtenay, U.K. 16 50 47N 3 58W
Samsun, Turk. 47 41 15N 36 22 E
San Angelo, U.S.A. 90 31 30N 100 30W
San Antonio, U.S.A. 90 29 30N 98 30W
San Bernardino, U.S.A. 90 34 7N 117 18W
San Carlos, Phil. 63 15 55N 120 20 E
San Cristóbal, Ven. 100 16 50N 92 40W
San Diego, U.S.A. 90 32 43N 117 10W
San Fernando, Mex. 94 30 0N 115 10W
San Francisco, U.S.A. 90 37 47N 122 30W
San Jorge, G., Arg. 102 46 0S 66 0W
San José, C.R. 95 10 0N 84 2W
San Jose, U.S.A. 90 37 20N 121 53W
San Juan, Arg. 102 31 30S 68 30W
San Juan, P.R. 95 18 28N 66 8W
San Luis Potosí, Mex. 94 22 9N 100 59W
San Marino ■, Europe 40 43 56N 12 25 E
San Matías, G., Arg. 102 41 30S 64 0W
San Miguel de Tucumán, Arg. 102 26 50S 65 20W
San Pedro Sula, Hond. 94 15 30N 88 0W
San Salvador, El Salv. 94 13 40N 89 10W
San Salvador de Jujuy, Arg. 102 24 10S 64 48W
San Sebastián, Sp. 37 43 17N 1 58W
Sana', Yem. 56 15 27N 44 12 E
Sanda I., U.K. 20 55 17N 5 35W
Sanday, U.K. 23 59 15N 2 30W
Sandbach, U.K. 18 53 9N 2 23W
Sandbank, U.K. 20 55 58N 4 57W
Sandgate, U.K. 15 51 5N 1 9 E
Sandhead, U.K. 20 54 48N 4 58W
Sandhurst, U.K. 15 51 21N 0 48W
Sandness, U.K. 22 60 18N 1 38W
Sandown, U.K. 14 50 39N 1 9W
Sandringham, U.K. 15 52 50N 0 30 E
Sandwich, U.K. 15 51 16N 1 21 E
Sandy, U.K. 15 52 8N 0 18W
Sangli, India 58 16 55N 74 33 E
Sanquhar, U.K. 21 55 21N 3 56W
Santa Ana, Mex. 94 30 33N 111 7W
Santa Ana, U.S.A. 90 33 48N 117 55W
Santa Clara, Cuba 95 22 20N 80 0W
Santa Cruz, Bol. 100 17 43S 63 10W
Santa Cruz de Tenerife, Can. Is. 78 28 28N 16 15W
Santa Fe, Arg. 102 31 35S 60 41W
Santa Fe, U.S.A. 90 35 40N 106 0W
Santa Maria, Brazil 102 29 40S 53 48W
Santa Marta, Col. 100 11 15N 74 13W
Santander, Sp. 37 43 27N 3 51W
Santarém, Brazil 101 2 25S 54 42W
Santarém, Port. 37 39 12N 8 42W
Santiago, Chile 102 33 24S 70 40W
Santiago de Compostela, Sp. 37 42 52N 8 37W
Santiago de Cuba, Cuba 95 20 0N 75 49W
Santiago de los Cabelleros, Dom. Rep. 95 19 30N 70 40W
Santo André, Brazil 102 23 39S 46 29W
Santo Domingo, Dom. Rep. 95 18 30N 64 54W
Santos, Brazil 102 24 0S 46 20W
São Francisco →, Brazil 101 10 30S 36 24W
São José do Rio Prêto, Brazil 101 20 50S 49 20W
São Luís, Brazil 101 2 39S 44 15W
São Paulo, Brazil 102 23 32S 46 37W
São Roque, C. de, Brazil 101 5 30S 35 16W
São Tomé & Principe ■, Africa 73 0 12N 6 39 E
Saône →, Fr. 34 45 44N 4 50 E
Sapporo, Jap. 62 43 0N 141 21 E

Sarajevo, *Yug.* **41** 43 52N 18 26 E
Saransk, *U.S.S.R.* **46** 54 10N 45 10 E
Saratov, *U.S.S.R.* **46** 51 30N 46 2 E
Sarawak □, *Malay.* **63** 2 0N 113 0 E
Sardinia, I., *It.* **40** 40 0N 9 0 E
Sargodha, *Pak.* **58** 32 10N 72 40 E
Sarh, *Chad* **79** 9 5N 18 23 E
Sarnia, *Canada* **92** 42 58N 82 23W
Sasebo, *Jap.* **62** 33 10N 129 43 E
Saskatchewan □, *Canada* **88** 54 40N 106 0W
Saskatchewan →, *Canada* **88** 53 37N 100 40W
Saskatoon, *Canada* **88** 52 10N 106 38W
Sássari, *It.* **40** 40 44N 8 33 E
Satpura Ra., *India* **58** 21 25N 76 10 E
Satu Mare, *Rom.* **43** 47 46N 22 55 E
Sauðarkrókur, *Ice.* **44** 65 45N 19 40W
Saudi Arabia ■, *Asia* **56** 26 0N 44 0 E
Sault Ste. Marie, *Canada* **92** 46 30N 84 20W
Saundersfoot, *U.K.* **17** 51 43N 4 42W
Sava →, *Yug.* **41** 44 50N 20 26 E
Savanna la Mar, *Jam.* **94** 18 10N 78 10W
Savannah, *U.S.A.* **91** 32 4N 81 4W
Savona, *It.* **40** 44 19N 8 29 E
Savonlinna, *Fin.* **44** 61 52N 28 53 E
Sawbridgeworth, *U.K.* **15** 51 49N 0 10 E
Sawel, Mt., *U.K.* **24** 54 48N 7 5W
Sawston, *U.K.* **15** 52 7N 0 11 E
Sawtry, *U.K.* **15** 52 26N 0 17W
Saxilby, *U.K.* **19** 53 16N 0 40W
Saxlingham Nethergate, *U.K.* **15** 52 33N 1 16 E
Saxmundham, *U.K.* **15** 52 13N 1 29 E
Saydā, *Leb.* **57** 33 35N 35 25 E
Scafell Pikes, *U.K.* **18** 54 26N 3 14W
Scalasaig, *U.K.* **20** 56 4N 6 10W
Scalby, *U.K.* **19** 54 18N 0 26W
Scalby Ness, *U.K.* **19** 54 18N 0 25W
Scalloway, *U.K.* **22** 60 9N 1 16W
Scalpay, *U.K.* **22** 57 51N 6 40W
Scamblesby, *U.K.* **19** 53 17N 0 5W
Scandinavia, *Europe* **44** 64 0N 12 0 E
Scapa Flow, *U.K.* **23** 58 52N 3 6W
Scarba, I., *U.K.* **20** 56 10N 5 42W
Scarborough, *U.K.* **19** 54 17N 0 24W
Scarinish, *U.K.* **20** 56 30N 6 48W
Scarning, *U.K.* **15** 52 40N 0 53W
Schefferville, *Canada* **89** 54 48N 66 50W
Schenectady, *U.S.A.* **93** 42 50N 73 58W
Schiedam, *Neth.* **36** 51 55N 4 25 E
Schleswig-Holstein □, *W. Ger.* **42** 54 10N 9 40 E
Schwerin, *E. Ger.* **42** 53 37N 11 22 E
Scilly, Isles of, *U.K.* **16** 49 55N 6 15W
Scole, *U.K.* **15** 52 22N 1 10 E
Scone, *U.K.* **21** 56 25N 3 26W
Scopwick, *U.K.* **19** 53 6N 0 24W
Scotland □, *U.K.* **20** 57 0N 4 0W
Scranton, *U.S.A.* **93** 41 22N 75 41W
Scremerston, *U.K.* **21** 55 44N 1 59W
Scridain, L., *U.K.* **20** 56 23N 6 7W
Scunthorpe, *U.K.* **19** 53 35N 0 38W
Seaford, *U.K.* **15** 50 46N 0 8 E
Seaham, *U.K.* **21** 54 51N 1 20W
Seahouses, *U.K.* **21** 55 35N 1 39W
Seamer, *U.K.* **19** 54 14N 0 27W
Seascale, *U.K.* **18** 54 24N 3 29W
Seaton, *Cumbria, U.K.* **18** 54 40N 3 31W
Seaton, *Devon, U.K.* **16** 50 42N 3 3W
Seaton Delaval, *U.K.* **21** 55 1N 1 33W
Seattle, *U.S.A.* **90** 47 41N 122 15W
Sedbergh, *U.K.* **18** 54 20N 2 31W
Sedgefield, *U.K.* **19** 54 40N 1 27W
Seend, *U.K.* **14** 51 20N 2 2W
Segovia, *Sp.* **37** 40 57N 4 10W
Seil, I., *U.K.* **20** 56 17N 5 37W
Seine →, *Fr.* **34** 49 26N 0 26 E
Sekondi-Takoradi, *Ghana* **78** 4 58N 1 45W
Selborne, *U.K.* **15** 51 5N 0 55W
Selby, *U.K.* **19** 53 47N 1 5W
Selkirk, *U.K.* **21** 55 33N 2 50W
Selsey, *U.K.* **15** 50 44N 0 47W
Selsey Bill, *U.K.* **15** 50 44N 0 47W
Selvas, *Brazil* **100** 6 30S 67 0W
Selwyn Ra., *Austral.* **67** 21 10S 140 0 E
Semarang, *Indon.* **63** 7 0S 110 26 E
Semipalatinsk, *U.S.S.R.* **48** 50 30N 80 10 E
Sendai, *Jap.* **62** 38 15N 140 53 E
Senegal ■, *W. Afr.* **78** 14 30N 14 30W
Senegal →, *W. Afr.* **78** 15 48N 16 32W
Sennen, *U.K.* **16** 50 4N 5 42W
Seoul, *S. Kor.* **61** 37 31N 126 58 E
Seph →, *U.K.* **19** 54 17N 1 9W
Sequoia Nat. Park, *U.S.A.* **90** 36 30N 118 30W
Serbia □, *Yug.* **41** 43 30N 21 0 E
Seremban, *Malay.* **63** 2 43N 101 53 E
Serena, La, *Chile* **102** 29 55S 71 10W
Serpukhov, *U.S.S.R.* **46** 54 55N 37 28 E
Sétif, *Alg.* **78** 36 9N 5 26 E
Settat, *Mor.* **78** 33 0N 7 40W
Settle, *U.K.* **18** 54 5N 2 18W
Setúbal, *Port.* **37** 38 30N 8 58W
Sevastopol, *U.S.S.R.* **47** 44 35N 33 30 E
Seven →, *U.K.* **19** 54 11N 0 51W
Sevenoaks, *U.K.* **15** 51 16N 0 11 E
Severn →, *U.K.* **14** 51 35N 2 38W
Severn Beach, *U.K.* **14** 51 34N 2 39W
Severn Stoke, *U.K.* **14** 52 5N 2 13W
Severnaya Zemlya, *U.S.S.R.* **49** 79 0N 100 0 E
Seville, *Sp.* **37** 37 23N 6 0W
Seward Pen., *U.S.A.* **88** 65 0N 164 0W
Seychelles ■, *Ind. Oc.* **129** 5 0S 56 0 E
Seyðisfjörður, *Ice.* **44** 65 16N 14 0W
Sfax, *Tunisia* **79** 34 49N 10 48 E
Shaanxi □, *China* **61** 35 0N 109 0 E
Shache, *China* **60** 38 20N 77 10 E
Shaftesbury, *U.K.* **14** 51 0N 2 12W
Shahjahanpur, *India* **58** 27 54N 79 57 E
Shakhty, *U.S.S.R.* **47** 47 40N 40 16 E
Shaldon, *U.K.* **16** 50 32N 3 31W
Shan □, *Burma* **59** 21 30N 98 30 E
Shandong □, *China* **61** 36 0N 118 0 E
Shanghai, *China* **61** 31 15N 121 26 E
Shangrao, *China* **61** 28 25N 117 59 E
Shanklin, *U.K.* **14** 50 39N 1 9W
Shannon →, *Ire.* **25** 52 35N 9 30W
Shantou, *China* **61** 23 18N 116 40 E
Shanxi □, *China* **61** 37 0N 112 0 E
Shaoguan, *China* **61** 24 48N 113 35 E
Shaoyang, *China* **61** 27 14N 111 25 E
Shap, *U.K.* **18** 54 32N 2 40W
Shapinsay, *U.K.* **23** 59 2N 2 50W
Shark B., *Austral.* **66** 11 20S 130 30 E
Sharpness, *U.K.* **14** 51 43N 2 28W
Shawbury, *U.K.* **14** 52 48N 2 40W
Shawinigan, *Canada* **93** 46 35N 72 50W
Shebbear, *U.K.* **16** 50 52N 4 12W
Sheelin, Lough, *Ire.* **24** 53 48N 7 20W
Sheep Haven, *Ire.* **24** 55 12N 7 55W
Sheerness, *U.K.* **15** 51 26N 0 47 E
Sheffield, *U.K.* **19** 53 23N 1 28W
Shefford, *U.K.* **15** 52 2N 0 20W
Shelekhov G., *U.S.S.R.* **49** 59 30N 157 0 E
Shellharbour, *Austral.* **70** 34 31S 150 51 E
Shelling Rocks, *Ire.* **25** 51 45N 10 35W
Shenfield, *U.K.* **15** 51 39N 0 21 E
Shenyang, *China* **61** 41 50N 123 25 E
Shepparton, *Austral.* **70** 36 23S 145 26 E
Sheppey, I. of, *U.K.* **15** 51 23N 0 50 E
Shepshed, *U.K.* **14** 52 47N 1 18W
Shepton Mallet, *U.K.* **14** 51 11N 2 31W
Sherborne, *U.K.* **14** 50 56N 2 31W
Sherborne St. John, *U.K.* **14** 51 18N 1 7W
Sherbrooke, *Canada* **93** 45 28N 71 57W
Sherburn, *N. Yorks., U.K.* **19** 54 12N 0 32W
Sherburn, *N. Yorks., U.K.* **19** 53 47N 1 15W
Shere, *U.K.* **15** 51 13N 0 28W
Sherfield English, *U.K.* **14** 51 1N 1 35W
Sheriff Hutton, *U.K.* **19** 54 5N 1 0W
Sheriff Muir, *U.K.* **21** 56 12N 3 53W
Sheringham, *U.K.* **15** 52 56N 1 11 E
Sherston, *U.K.* **14** 51 35N 2 13W
Sherwood Forest, *U.K.* **19** 53 5N 1 5W
Shetland □, *U.K.* **22** 60 30N 1 30W
Shetland Is., *U.K.* **22** 60 30N 1 30W
Shiel, L., *U.K.* **22** 56 48N 5 32W
Shieldaig, *U.K.* **22** 57 31N 5 39W
Shifnal, *U.K.* **14** 52 40N 2 23W
Shijiazhuang, *China* **61** 38 2N 114 28 E
Shikoku, *Jap.* **62** 33 30N 133 30 E
Shilbottle, *U.K.* **21** 55 23N 1 42W
Shildon, *U.K.* **19** 54 37N 1 39W
Shiliguri, *India* **59** 26 45N 88 25 E
Shillelagh, *Ire.* **25** 52 46N 6 32W
Shillingstone, *U.K.* **14** 50 54N 2 15W
Shillong, *India* **59** 25 35N 91 53 E
Shimonoseki, *Jap.* **62** 33 58N 131 0 E
Shin, L., *U.K.* **23** 58 7N 4 30W
Shipbourne, *U.K.* **15** 51 13N 0 19 E
Shipdham, *U.K.* **15** 52 38N 0 53 E
Shipley, *U.K.* **19** 53 50N 1 47W
Shipston-on-Stour, *U.K.* **14** 52 4N 1 38W
Shipton-under-Wychwood, *U.K.* **14** 51 51N 1 35W
Shīrāz, *Iran* **56** 29 42N 52 30 E
Shirebrook, *U.K.* **19** 53 13N 1 11W
Shizuoka, *Jap.* **62** 35 0N 138 24 E
Shkoder, *Alb.* **41** 42 6N 19 20 E
Shoeburyness, *U.K.* **15** 51 31N 0 49 E
Shoreham-by-Sea, *U.K.* **15** 50 50N 0 17W
Shotts, *U.K.* **21** 55 49N 3 47W
Shreveport, *U.S.A.* **91** 32 30N 93 50W
Shrewsbury, *U.K.* **14** 52 42N 2 45W
Shrewton, *U.K.* **14** 51 11N 1 55W
Shrivenham, *U.K.* **14** 51 36N 1 39W
Shropshire □, *U.K.* **14** 52 36N 2 45W
Shuangyashan, *China* **61** 46 28N 131 5 E
Siam = Thailand ■, *Asia* **63** 16 0N 102 0 E
Sian, *China* **61** 34 2N 109 0 E
Siberia, *U.S.S.R.* **50** 60 0N 100 0 E
Sibiu, *Rom.* **43** 45 45N 24 9 E
Sible Hedingham, *U.K.* **15** 51 58N 0 37 E
Sibsey, *U.K.* **19** 53 3N 0 1 E
Sichuan □, *China* **60** 31 0N 104 0 E
Sicily, *It.* **40** 37 30N 14 30 E
Sidbury, *U.K.* **16** 50 43N 3 12W
Sidlaw Hills, *U.K.* **21** 56 32N 3 10W
Sidlesham, *U.K.* **15** 50 46N 0 46W
Sidmouth, *U.K.* **16** 50 40N 3 13W
Sidon = Saydā, *Leb.* **57** 33 35N 35 25 E
Siegen, *W. Ger.* **36** 50 52N 8 2 E
Siena, *It.* **40** 43 20N 11 20 E
Sierra Leone ■, *W. Afr.* **78** 9 0N 12 0W
Sighty Crag, *U.K.* **21** 55 8N 2 37W
Siglufjörður, *Ice.* **44** 66 12N 18 55W
Sikhote Alin Ra., *U.S.S.R.* **49** 46 0N 136 0 E
Sikkim □, *India* **59** 27 50N 88 30 E
Silloth, *U.K.* **18** 54 53N 3 25W
Silsden, *U.K.* **18** 53 55N 1 55W
Silverstone, *U.K.* **14** 52 5N 1 3W
Silverton, *U.K.* **16** 50 49N 3 29W
Simferopol, *U.S.S.R.* **47** 44 55N 34 3 E
Simonsbath, *U.K.* **14** 51 8N 3 45W
Simonside, *U.K.* **21** 55 17N 2 0W
Simpson Desert, *Austral.* **67** 25 0S 137 0 E
Sinai Peninsula, *Egypt* **79** 29 30N 34 0 E
Sind Sagar Doab, *Pak.* **58** 32 0N 71 30 E
Singapore ■, *Asia* **63** 1 17N 103 51 E
Singleton, *U.K.* **15** 50 55N 0 45W
Sioux Falls, *U.S.A.* **91** 43 35N 96 40W
Siping, *China* **61** 33 25N 114 10 E
Siracusa, *It.* **40** 37 4N 15 17 E
Sittingbourne, *U.K.* **15** 51 20N 0 43 E
Sittwe, *Bur.* **59** 20 18N 92 45 E
Sivas, *Turk.* **47** 39 43N 36 58 E
Siwalik Range, *Nepal* **59** 28 0N 83 0 E
Sizewell, *U.K.* **15** 52 13N 1 38 E
Sjælland, *Den.* **45** 55 30N 11 30 E
Skagerrak, *Den.* **45** 57 30N 9 0 E
Skagway, *U.S.A.* **88** 59 23N 135 20W
Skegness, *U.K.* **19** 53 9N 0 20 E
Skellefteå, *Swed.* **44** 64 45N 20 58 E
Skellingthorpe, *U.K.* **19** 53 14N 0 37W
Skelmersdale, *U.K.* **18** 53 34N 2 49W
Skelmorlie, *U.K.* **20** 55 52N 4 53W
Skelton, *Cleveland, U.K.* **19** 54 33N 0 59W
Skelton, *Cumbria, U.K.* **18** 54 42N 2 50W
Skerries, The, *U.K.* **17** 53 27N 4 40W
Skibbereen, *Ire.* **25** 51 33N 9 16W
Skiddaw, *U.K.* **18** 54 39N 3 9W
Skien, *Nor.* **45** 59 12N 9 35 E
Skikda, *Alg.* **78** 36 50N 6 58 E
Skipness, *U.K.* **20** 55 46N 5 20W
Skipsea, *U.K.* **19** 53 58N 0 13W
Skipton, *U.K.* **18** 53 57N 2 1W
Skopje, *Yug.* **41** 42 1N 21 32 E
Skull, *Ire.* **25** 51 32N 9 40W
Skye, *U.K.* **22** 57 15N 6 10W
Slaidburn, *U.K.* **18** 53 57N 2 28W
Slaley, *U.K.* **21** 54 55N 2 4W
Slaney →, *Ire.* **25** 52 52N 6 45W
Sleaford, *U.K.* **19** 53 0N 0 22W
Sleat, Sd. of, *U.K.* **22** 57 5N 5 47W
Sledmere, *U.K.* **19** 54 4N 0 35W
Sleights, *U.K.* **19** 54 27N 0 40W
Slieve Aughty, *Ire.* **25** 53 4N 8 30W
Slieve Bloom, *Ire.* **25** 53 4N 7 40W
Slieve Donard, *U.K.* **24** 54 10N 5 57W
Slieve Gullion, *U.K.* **24** 54 8N 6 26W
Slieve Mish, *Ire.* **25** 52 12N 9 50W
Slievenamon, *Ire.* **25** 52 25N 7 37W
Sligo, *Ire.* **24** 54 17N 8 28W
Sligo □, *Ire.* **24** 54 10N 8 35W
Sligo B., *Ire.* **24** 54 20N 8 40W
Sliven, *Bulg.* **41** 42 42N 26 19 E
Slough, *U.K.* **15** 51 30N 0 35W
Slovenská Socialisticka Republika □, *Czech.* **43** 48 30N 20 0 E
Slyne Hd., *Ire.* **24** 53 25N 10 10W
Smederevo, *Yug.* **41** 44 40N 20 57 E
Smethwick, *U.K.* **14** 52 29N 1 58W
Smithfield, *U.K.* **18** 54 59N 2 51W
Smolensk, *U.S.S.R.* **46** 54 45N 32 0 E
Snaefell, *U.K.* **18** 54 18N 4 26W
Snainton, *U.K.* **19** 54 14N 0 33W
Snaith, *U.K.* **19** 53 42N 1 1W
Snake →, *U.S.A.* **90** 46 12N 119 2W
Snape, *U.K.* **15** 52 11N 1 29 E
Snettisham, *U.K.* **15** 52 52N 0 30 E
Snizort, L., *U.K.* **22** 57 33N 6 28W
Snowdon, *U.K.* **17** 53 4N 4 8W
Snowy Mts., *Austral.* **70** 36 30S 148 20 E
Sobral, *Brazil* **101** 3 50S 40 20W
Sochi, *U.S.S.R.* **47** 43 35N 39 40 E
Society Is., *Pac. Oc.* **65** 17 0S 151 0W
Socotra, *Ind. Oc.* **57** 12 30N 54 0 E
Söderhamn, *Swed.* **45** 61 18N 17 10 E
Sofia, *Bulg.* **41** 42 45N 23 20 E
Sogn og Fjordane fylke □, *Nor.* **44** 61 40N 6 0 E
Sognefjorden, *Nor.* **45** 61 10N 5 50 E
Sohâg, *Egypt* **79** 26 33N 31 43 E
Soham, *U.K.* **15** 52 20N 0 20 E
Sokoto, *Nig.* **78** 13 2N 5 16 E
Solapur, *India* **58** 17 43N 75 56 E
Solent, The, *U.K.* **14** 50 45N 1 25W
Solihull, *U.K.* **14** 52 26N 1 47W
Solimões → = Amazon →, *S. Am.* **100** 0 5S 50 0W
Solingen, *W. Ger.* **36** 51 10N 7 4 E
Solomon Is. ■, *Oc.* **64** 6 0S 155 0 E
Solway Firth, *U.K.* **18** 54 45N 3 38W
Somali Rep. ■, *E. Afr.* **73** 7 0N 47 0 E
Somerby, *U.K.* **15** 52 42N 0 49W
Somerset □, *U.K.* **14** 51 9N 3 0W
Somersham, *U.K.* **15** 52 24N 0 0 E
Somerton, *U.K.* **14** 51 3N 2 45W
Sompting, *U.K.* **15** 50 51N 0 20W
Søndre Strømfjord, *Green.* **89** 66 59N 50 40W
Sonning, *U.K.* **15** 51 28N 0 53W
Sorbie, *U.K.* **20** 54 46N 4 26W
Soria, *Sp.* **37** 41 43N 2 32W
Sorisdale, *U.K.* **20** 56 40N 6 28W
Sorn, *U.K.* **20** 55 31N 4 18W
Sorocaba, *Brazil* **102** 23 31S 47 27W
Sosnowiec, *Pol.* **43** 50 20N 19 10 E
Sousse, *Tunisia* **79** 35 50N 10 38 E
South Africa, Rep. of ■, *Africa* **81** 32 0S 17 0 E
South Australia □, *Austral.* **66** 32 0S 139 0 E
South Barrule, *U.K.* **18** 54 9N 4 36W
South Bend, *U.S.A.* **92** 41 38N 86 20W
South Benfleet, *U.K.* **15** 51 33N 0 34 E
South Brent, *U.K.* **16** 50 26N 3 50W
South Carolina □, *U.S.A.* **91** 33 45N 81 0W
South Cave, *U.K.* **19** 53 46N 0 37W
South China Sea, *Asia* **63** 10 0N 113 0 E
South Dakota □, *U.S.A.* **90** 45 0N 100 0W
South Dorset Downs, *U.K.* **14** 50 40N 2 26W
South Downs, *U.K.* **15** 50 53N 0 10W
South Elkington, *U.K.* **19** 53 22N 0 5W
South Esk →, *U.K.* **23** 56 44N 3 3W
South Foreland, *U.K.* **15** 51 7N 1 23 E
South Georgia, *Atl. Oc.* **102** 54 30S 37 0W
South Glamorgan □, *U.K.* **17** 51 30N 3 20W
South Hayling, *U.K.* **15** 50 47N 0 56W
South I., *N.Z.* **71** 44 0S 170 0 E
South Korea ■, *Asia* **61** 36 0N 128 0 E
South Molton, *U.K.* **16** 51 1N 3 50W
South Orkney Is., *Ant.* **103** 63 0S 45 0W
South Petherton, *U.K.* **14** 50 57N 2 49W
South Petherwin, *U.K.* **16** 50 35N 4 22W
South Platte →, *U.S.A.* **90** 41 7N 100 42W
South Pole, *Ant.* **103** 90 0S 0 0 E
South Ronaldsay, *U.K.* **23** 58 46N 2 58W
South Sandwich Is., *Ant.* **103** 57 0S 27 0W
South Shetland Is., *Ant.* **103** 62 0S 59 0W
South Shields, *U.K.* **19** 54 59N 1 26W
South Tawton, *U.K.* **16** 50 44N 3 55W
South Tyne →, *U.K.* **19** 54 46N 2 25W
South Uist, *U.K.* **22** 57 20N 7 15W
South West Africa = Namibia ■, *Africa* **81** 22 0S 18 9 E
South Woodham Ferrers, *U.K.* **15** 51 40N 0 37 E
South Yemen ■, *Asia* **56** 15 0N 48 0 E
South Yorkshire □, *U.K.* **19** 53 30N 1 20W
Southam, *U.K.* **14** 52 16N 1 24W
Southampton, *U.K.* **14** 50 54N 1 23W
Southampton I., *Canada* **89** 64 30N 84 0W
Southampton Water, *U.K.* **14** 50 52N 1 21W
Southborough, *U.K.* **15** 51 10N 0 15 E
Southend, *U.K.* **20** 55 18N 5 38W
Southend-on-Sea, *U.K.* **15** 51 32N 0 42 E
Southern Alps, *N.Z.* **71** 43 41S 170 11 E
Southern Ocean **103** 62 0S 60 0 E
Southern Uplands, *U.K.* **21** 55 30N 3 3W
Southery, *U.K.* **15** 52 32N 0 23 E
Southland □, *N.Z.* **71** 45 51S 168 13 E
Southminster, *U.K.* **15** 51 40N 0 51 E
Southport, *U.K.* **18** 53 38N 3 1W
Southwark, *U.K.* **15** 51 29N 0 5W
Southwell, *U.K.* **19** 53 4N 0 57W
Southwick, *U.K.* **15** 50 50N 0 14W
Southwold, *U.K.* **15** 52 19N 1 41 E
Sovetskaya Gavan, *U.S.S.R.* **49** 48 50N 140 0 E
Soviet Union ■ = Union of Soviet Socialist Republics ■, *Eurasia* **48** 60 0N 100 0 E
Sowerby, *U.K.* **19** 54 13N 1 19W
Soweto, *S. Afr.* **81** 26 14S 27 54 E
Spain ■, *Europe* **37** 40 0N 5 0W
Spalding, *U.K.* **15** 52 47N 0 9W
Spanish Town, *Jam.* **94** 18 0N 76 57W
Sparkford, *U.K.* **14** 51 2N 2 33W
Spean Bridge, *U.K.* **22** 56 53N 4 55W
Speke, *U.K.* **18** 53 21N 2 51W
Spelve, L., *U.K.* **20** 56 22N 5 45W
Spencer G., *Austral.* **67** 34 0S 137 20 E
Spennymoor, *U.K.* **19** 54 43N 1 35W
Sperrin Mts., *U.K.* **24** 54 50N 7 0W
Spey →, *U.K.* **23** 57 26N 3 25W
Spézia, La, *It.* **40** 44 8N 9 50 E
Spilsby, *U.K.* **19** 53 10N 0 6 E
Spithead, *U.K.* **15** 50 43N 1 5W
Spitzbergen = Svalbard, *Arctic* **103** 78 0N 17 0 E
Split, *Yug.* **40** 43 31N 16 26 E
Spofforth, *U.K.* **19** 53 57N 1 28W
Spokane, *U.S.A.* **90** 47 45N 117 25W
Springfield, *Ill., U.S.A.* **92** 39 48N 89 40W
Springfield, *Mass., U.S.A.* **93** 42 8N 72 37W
Springfield, *Mo., U.S.A.* **91** 37 15N 93 20W
Springfield, *Ohio, U.S.A.* **92** 39 58N 83 48W
Sproatley, *U.K.* **19** 53 46N 0 9W
Spurn Hd., *U.K.* **19** 53 34N 0 8 E
Sredinnyy Ra., *U.S.S.R.* **49** 57 0N 160 0 E
Srednekolymsk, *U.S.S.R.* **49** 67 27N 153 40 E
Sri Lanka ■, *Asia* **58** 7 30N 80 50 E
Srinagar, *India* **58** 34 5N 74 50 E

Staffa, *U.K.* **20** 56 26N 6 21W
Stafford, *U.K.* **14** 52 49N 2 9W
Stafford □, *U.K.* **14** 52 53N 2 10W
Staindrop, *U.K.* **19** 54 35N 1 49W
Staines, *U.K.* **15** 51 26N 0 30W
Stainforth, *U.K.* **19** 53 37N 0 59W
Stainmore For., *U.K.* **18** 54 29N 2 5W
Stainton, *U.K.* **19** 53 17N 0 23W
Staithes, *U.K.* **19** 54 33N 0 47W
Stalbridge, *U.K.* **14** 50 57N 2 22W
Stalham, *U.K.* **15** 52 46N 1 31 E
Stalingrad = Volgograd, *U.S.S.R.* **47** 48 40N 44 25 E
Stallingborough, *U.K.* **19** 53 36N 0 11W
Stalybridge, *U.K.* **18** 53 29N 2 4W
Stamford, *U.K.* **15** 52 39N 0 29W
Stamford, *U.S.A.* **93** 41 5N 73 30W
Stamford Bridge, *U.K.* **19** 53 59N 0 53W
Stamfordham, *U.K.* **21** 55 3N 1 53W
Standish, *U.K.* **18** 53 35N 2 39W
Standon, *U.K.* **15** 51 53N 0 2 E
Stanford on Teme, *U.K.* **14** 52 17N 2 26W
Stanhope, *U.K.* **18** 54 45N 2 0W
Stanley, *Falk.* **102** 51 40S 59 51W
Stanley, *Durham, U.K.* **19** 54 53N 1 42W
Stanley, *Tayside, U.K.* **21** 56 29N 3 28W
Stannington, *U.K.* **21** 55 7N 1 41W
Stanovoy Ra., *U.S.S.R.* **49** 55 0N 130 0 E
Stansted Mountfitchet, *U.K.* **15** 51 54N 0 13 E
Stanwix, *U.K.* **18** 54 54N 2 56W
Stapleford, *U.K.* **19** 52 56N 1 16W
Staplehurst, *U.K.* **15** 51 9N 0 35 E
Stara Zagora, *Bulg.* **41** 42 26N 25 39 E
Start Bay, *U.K.* **16** 50 15N 3 35W
Start Pt., *U.K.* **16** 50 13N 3 38W
Staunton, *U.K.* **14** 51 58N 2 19W
Stavanger, *Nor.* **45** 58 57N 5 40 E
Staveley, *Cumbria, U.K.* **18** 54 24N 2 49W
Staveley, *Derby, U.K.* **19** 53 16N 1 20W
Stavropol, *U.S.S.R.* **47** 45 5N 42 0 E
Stenhousemuir, *U.K.* **21** 56 2N 3 46W
Sterlitamak, *U.S.S.R.* **46** 53 40N 56 0 E
Stevenage, *U.K.* **15** 51 54N 0 11W
Stevenston, *U.K.* **20** 55 38N 4 46W
Stewart I., *N.Z.* **71** 46 58S 167 54 E
Stewarton, *U.K.* **20** 55 40N 4 30W
Steyning, *U.K.* **15** 50 54N 0 19W
Stillington, *U.K.* **19** 54 7N 1 5W
Stinchar →, *U.K.* **20** 55 10N 4 50W
Stiperstones Mt., *U.K.* **14** 52 36N 2 57W
Stirling, *U.K.* **21** 56 7N 3 57W
Stobo, *U.K.* **21** 55 38N 3 18W
Stockbridge, *U.K.* **14** 51 7N 1 30W
Stockholm, *Swed.* **45** 59 20N 18 3 E
Stockport, *U.K.* **18** 53 25N 2 11W
Stocksbridge, *U.K.* **19** 53 30N 1 36W
Stockton, *U.S.A.* **90** 38 0N 121 20W
Stockton-on-Tees, *U.K.* **19** 54 34N 1 20W
Stoke, *U.K.* **15** 51 26N 0 41 E
Stoke Ferry, *U.K.* **15** 52 34N 0 31 E
Stoke Fleming, *U.K.* **16** 50 19N 3 36W
Stoke Mandeville, *U.K.* **15** 51 46N 0 47W
Stoke-on-Trent, *U.K.* **18** 53 1N 2 11W
Stoke Prior, *U.K.* **14** 52 18N 2 5W
Stokenham, *U.K.* **16** 50 15N 3 40W
Stokesley, *U.K.* **19** 54 27N 1 12W
Stone, *Bucks., U.K.* **15** 51 48N 0 52W
Stone, *Staffs., U.K.* **18** 52 55N 2 10W
Stonehaven, *U.K.* **23** 56 58N 2 11W
Stonehouse, *Gloucs., U.K.* **14** 51 45N 2 18W
Stonehouse, *Strathclyde, U.K.* **21** 55 42N 4 0W
Stonham Aspall, *U.K.* **15** 52 11N 1 7 E
Stony Stratford, *U.K.* **15** 52 4N 0 51W
Storm B., *Austral.* **67** 43 10S 147 30 E
Stornoway, *U.K.* **22** 58 12N 6 23W
Stort →, *U.K.* **15** 51 50N 0 7 E
Stotfold, *U.K.* **15** 52 2N 0 13W
Stour →, *Dorset, U.K.* **14** 50 48N 2 7W
Stour →, *Hereford & Worcs., U.K.* **14** 52 25N 2 13W
Stour →, *Kent, U.K.* **15** 51 15N 1 20 E
Stour →, *Suffolk, U.K.* **15** 51 55N 1 5 E
Stourbridge, *U.K.* **14** 52 28N 2 8W
Stourport, *U.K.* **14** 52 21N 2 18W
Stow, *U.K.* **21** 55 41N 2 50W
Stow Bardolph, *U.K.* **15** 52 38N 0 24 E
Stow-on-the-Wold, *U.K.* **14** 51 55N 1 42W
Stowmarket, *U.K.* **15** 52 11N 1 0 E
Strabane, *U.K.* **24** 54 50N 7 28W
Strabane □, *U.K.* **24** 54 45N 7 25W
Strachur, *U.K.* **20** 56 10N 5 5W
Stradbroke, *U.K.* **15** 52 19N 1 16 E
Stralsund, *E. Ger.* **42** 54 17N 13 5 E
Strangford, L., *U.K.* **24** 54 30N 5 37W
Stranraer, *U.K.* **20** 54 54N 5 0W
Strasbourg, *Fr.* **34** 48 35N 7 42 E
Stratford-on-Avon, *U.K.* **14** 52 12N 1 42W
Stratford St. Mary, *U.K.* **15** 51 58N 0 59 E
Strath Earn, *U.K.* **21** 56 20N 3 50W
Strath Spey, *U.K.* **23** 57 15N 3 40W
Strathaven, *U.K.* **21** 55 40N 4 4W
Strathclyde □, *U.K.* **20** 56 0N 4 50W
Strathmore, *U.K.* **23** 56 40N 3 4W
Strathpeffer, *U.K.* **23** 57 35N 4 32W
Strathy Pt., *U.K.* **23** 58 35N 4 0W
Strathyre, *U.K.* **20** 56 14N 4 20W
Stratmiglo, *U.K.* **21** 56 16N 3 15W
Stratton, *Cornwall, U.K.* **16** 50 49N 4 31W
Stratton, *Wilts., U.K.* **14** 51 41N 1 45W
Stratton St. Margaret, *U.K.* **14** 51 35N 1 45W
Streatley, *U.K.* **14** 51 31N 1 9W
Street, *U.K.* **14** 51 7N 2 43W
Strensall, *U.K.* **19** 54 3N 1 2W
Stretford, *U.K.* **18** 53 27N 2 19W
Stretton, *U.K.* **18** 53 21N 2 34W
Strichen, *U.K.* **23** 57 35N 2 5W
Striven, L., *U.K.* **20** 55 58N 5 9W
Stromeferry, *U.K.* **22** 57 20N 5 33W
Stromness, *U.K.* **23** 58 58N 3 18W
Stronachlachar, *U.K.* **20** 56 15N 4 35W
Strone, *U.K.* **20** 55 59N 4 54W
Stronsay, *U.K.* **23** 59 8N 2 38W
Stroud, *U.K.* **14** 51 44N 2 12W
Studland, *U.K.* **14** 50 39N 1 58W
Studley, *U.K.* **14** 52 16N 1 54W
Sturminster Marshall, *U.K.* **14** 50 48N 2 4W
Sturminster Newton, *U.K.* **14** 50 56N 2 18W
Sturt Cr. →, *Austral.* **66** 20 8S 127 24 E
Sturton, *U.K.* **19** 53 22N 0 39W
Stuttgart, *W. Ger.* **42** 48 46N 9 10 E
Subotica, *Yug.* **41** 46 6N 19 49 E
Suck →, *Ire.* **25** 53 17N 8 18W
Sucre, *Bol.* **100** 19 0S 65 15W
Sudan ■, *Africa* **78** 15 0N 30 0 E
Sudbury, *Canada* **92** 46 30N 81 0W
Sudbury, *Derby, U.K.* **19** 52 53N 1 43W
Sudbury, *Suffolk, U.K.* **15** 52 2N 0 44 E
Suez, *Egypt* **79** 29 58N 32 31 E
Suffolk □, *U.K.* **15** 52 16N 1 0 E
Suir →, *Ire.* **25** 52 15N 7 10W
Sukkur, *Pak.* **58** 27 42N 68 54 E
Sulawesi □, *Indon.* **63** 2 0S 120 0 E
Sulby, *U.K.* **18** 54 18N 4 29W
Sullom Voe, *U.K.* **22** 60 30N 1 20W
Sulu Sea, *E. Ind.* **63** 8 0N 120 0 E
Sumatra □, *Indon.* **63** 0 40N 100 20 E
Sumbawa, *Indon.* **63** 8 26S 117 30 E
Sumburgh Hd., *U.K.* **22** 59 52N 1 17W
Summer Is., *U.K.* **22** 58 0N 5 27W
Sumy, *U.S.S.R.* **47** 50 57N 34 50 E
Sunart, L., *U.K.* **22** 56 42N 5 43W
Sunda Str., *Indon.* **63** 6 20S 105 30 E
Sundarbans, The, *Asia* **59** 22 0N 89 0 E
Sunderland, *U.K.* **19** 54 54N 1 22W
Sundsvall, *Swed.* **44** 62 23N 17 17 E
Sunk Island, *U.K.* **19** 53 38N 0 7W
Sunninghill, *U.K.* **15** 51 25N 0 40W
Sunshine, *Austral.* **70** 37 48S 144 52 E
Superior, L., *N. Am.* **92** 47 40N 87 0W
Sūr, *Leb.* **57** 33 19N 35 16 E
Surabaya, *Indon.* **63** 7 17S 112 45 E
Surakarta, *Indon.* **63** 7 35S 110 48 E
Surat, *India* **58** 21 12N 72 55 E
Surgut, *U.S.S.R.* **48** 61 14N 73 20 E
Surinam ■, *S. Am.* **101** 4 0N 56 0W
Surrey □, *U.K.* **15** 51 16N 0 30W
Surtsey, *Ice.* **44** 63 20N 20 30W
Sutlej →, *Pak.* **58** 29 23N 71 3 E
Sutterton, *U.K.* **19** 52 54N 0 8W
Sutton, *U.K.* **15** 51 22N 0 13W
Sutton Bridge, *U.K.* **15** 52 46N 0 12 E
Sutton Coldfield, *U.K.* **14** 52 33N 1 50W
Sutton Courtenay, *U.K.* **14** 51 39N 1 16W
Sutton-in-Ashfield, *U.K.* **19** 53 7N 1 20W
Sutton-on-Sea, *U.K.* **19** 53 18N 0 18 E
Sutton Scotney, *U.K.* **14** 51 9N 1 20W
Suva, *Fiji* **64** 18 6S 178 30 E
Suzhou, *China* **61** 31 19N 120 38 E
Svalbard, *Arctic* **103** 78 0N 17 0 E
Svendborg, *Den.* **45** 55 4N 10 35 E
Sverdlovsk, *U.S.S.R.* **46** 56 50N 60 30 E
Sverdrup Is., *Canada* **103** 79 0N 97 0W
Swadlincote, *U.K.* **14** 52 47N 1 34W
Swaffham, *U.K.* **15** 52 38N 0 42 E
Swale →, *U.K.* **19** 54 5N 1 20W
Swan Hill, *Austral.* **70** 35 20S 143 33 E
Swanage, *U.K.* **14** 50 36N 1 59W
Swansea, *U.K.* **17** 51 37N 3 57W
Swaziland ■, *Africa* **81** 26 30S 31 30 E
Sweden ■, *Europe* **44** 57 0N 15 0 E
Swift Current, *Canada* **88** 50 20N 107 45W
Swilly, L., *Ire.* **24** 55 12N 7 35W
Swindon, *U.K.* **15** 51 33N 1 47W
Swineshead, *U.K.* **19** 52 56N 0 11W
Swinton, *Borders, U.K.* **21** 55 43N 2 14W
Swinton, *Gr. Manchester, U.K.* **18** 53 31N 2 21W
Swinton, *S. Yorks., U.K.* **19** 53 28N 1 20W
Switzerland ■, *Europe* **42** 46 30N 8 0 E
Swords, *Ire.* **24** 53 27N 6 15W
Sydney, *Austral.* **70** 33 53S 151 10 E
Sydney, *Canada* **93** 46 7N 60 7W
Syktyvkar, *U.S.S.R.* **46** 61 45N 50 40 E
Symington, *U.K.* **21** 55 35N 3 36W
Symonds Yat, *U.K.* **14** 51 50N 2 38W
Syracuse, *U.S.A.* **93** 43 4N 76 11W
Syrdarya →, *U.S.S.R.* **48** 46 3N 61 0 E
Syria ■, *Asia* **56** 35 0N 38 0 E
Syrian Desert, *Asia* **56** 31 0N 40 0 E
Syston, *U.K.* **14** 52 42N 1 5W
Syzran, *U.S.S.R.* **46** 53 12N 48 30 E
Szczecin, *Pol.* **42** 53 27N 14 27 E
Szeged, *Hung.* **43** 46 16N 20 10 E
Székesfehérvár, *Hung.* **43** 47 15N 18 25 E

T

Tabora, *Tanz.* **80** 5 2S 32 50 E
Tabrīz, *Iran* **56** 38 7N 46 20 E
Tabūk, *Si. Arab.* **56** 28 23N 36 36 E
Tacna, *Peru* **100** 18 0S 70 20W
Tacoma, *U.S.A.* **90** 47 15N 122 30W
Tacuarembó, *Urug.* **102** 31 45S 56 0W
Tadcaster, *U.K.* **19** 53 53N 1 16W
Tadley, *U.K.* **14** 51 21N 1 8W
Tadzhikistan □, *U.S.S.R.* **48** 35 30N 70 0 E
Taegu, *S. Kor.* **61** 35 50N 128 37 E
Taejŏn, *S. Kor.* **61** 36 20N 127 28 E
Taganrog, *U.S.S.R.* **47** 47 12N 38 50 E
Tagus = Tajo →, *Sp.* **37** 38 40N 9 24W
Tahiti, *Pac. Oc.* **65** 17 37S 149 27W
Taichung, *Taiwan* **61** 24 10N 120 35 E
Taimyr Pen., *U.S.S.R.* **49** 75 0N 100 0 E
Tain, *U.K.* **23** 57 49N 4 4W
Tainan, *Taiwan* **61** 23 17N 120 18 E
Taipei, *Taiwan* **61** 25 2N 121 30 E
Taiwan ■, *Asia* **61** 23 30N 121 0 E
Taiyuan, *China* **61** 37 52N 112 33 E
Ta'izz, *Yem.* **56** 13 35N 44 2 E
Tajo →, *Sp.* **37** 38 40N 9 24W
Tak, *Thai.* **59** 16 52N 99 8 E
Takamatsu, *Jap.* **62** 34 20N 134 5 E
Takaoka, *Jap.* **62** 36 47N 137 0 E
Takapuna, *N.Z.* **71** 36 47S 174 47 E
Takasaki, *Jap.* **62** 36 20N 139 0 E
Takeley, *U.K.* **15** 51 52N 0 16 E
Takla Makan, *China* **60** 39 0N 83 0 E
Talca, *Chile* **102** 35 28S 71 40W
Talcahuano, *Chile* **102** 36 40S 73 10W
Talgarth, *U.K.* **17** 51 59N 3 15W
Tallahassee, *U.S.A.* **91** 30 25N 84 15W
Tallinn, *U.S.S.R.* **46** 59 22N 24 48 E
Tamar →, *U.K.* **16** 50 33N 4 15W
Tambov, *U.S.S.R.* **46** 52 45N 41 28 E
Tame →, *U.K.* **14** 52 43N 1 45W
Tamerton Foliot, *U.K.* **16** 50 25N 4 10W
Tamil Nadu □, *India* **58** 11 0N 77 0 E
Tampa, *U.S.A.* **91** 27 57N 82 38W
Tampere, *Fin.* **44** 61 30N 23 50 E
Tampico, *Mex.* **94** 22 20N 97 50W
Tamworth, *Austral.* **67** 31 7S 150 58 E
Tamworth, *U.K.* **14** 52 38N 1 41W
Tana, L., *Eth.* **79** 13 5N 37 30 E
Tanami Desert, *Austral.* **66** 18 50S 132 0 E
Tandragee, *U.K.* **24** 54 22N 6 23W
Tanga, *Tanz.* **80** 5 5S 39 2 E
Tanganyika, L., *E. Afr.* **80** 6 40S 30 0 E
Tangier, *Mor.* **78** 35 50N 5 49W
Tangshan, *China* **61** 39 38N 118 10 E
Tanworth, *U.K.* **14** 52 20N 1 50W
Tanzania ■, *E. Afr.* **80** 6 40S 34 0 E
Tapajós →, *Brazil* **101** 2 24S 54 41W
Tarābulus, *Leb.* **56** 34 31N 35 50 E
Tarābulus, *Libya* **79** 32 49N 13 7 E
Taranaki □, *N.Z.* **71** 39 5S 174 51 E
Táranto, *It.* **40** 40 30N 17 11 E
Táranto, G. di, *It.* **40** 40 0N 17 15 E
Tarbat Ness, *U.K.* **23** 57 52N 3 48W
Tarbert, *Strathclyde, U.K.* **20** 55 55N 5 25W
Tarbert, *W. Isles, U.K.* **22** 57 54N 6 49W
Tarbes, *Fr.* **35** 43 15N 0 3 E
Tarbet, *U.K.* **20** 56 13N 4 44W
Tarbolton, *U.K.* **20** 55 30N 4 30W
Taree, *Austral.* **70** 31 50S 152 30 E
Tarija, *Bol.* **100** 21 30S 64 40W
Tarim Basin, *China* **60** 40 0N 84 0 E
Tarleton, *U.K.* **18** 53 41N 2 50W
Tarnów, *Pol.* **43** 50 3N 21 0 E
Tarporley, *U.K.* **18** 53 10N 2 42W
Tarragona, *Sp.* **37** 41 5N 1 17 E
Tarrasa, *Sp.* **37** 41 34N 2 1 E
Tashkent, *U.S.S.R.* **48** 41 20N 69 10 E
Tasman B., *N.Z.* **71** 40 59S 173 25 E
Tasman Sea, *Pac. Oc.* **71** 36 0S 160 0 E
Tasmania □, *Austral.* **67** 42 0S 146 30 E
Tatar A.S.S.R. □, *U.S.S.R.* **46** 55 30N 51 30 E
Tattenhall, *U.K.* **18** 53 7N 2 47W
Taunton, *U.K.* **14** 51 1N 3 7W
Taupo, *N.Z.* **71** 38 41S 176 7 E
Taupo, L., *N.Z.* **71** 38 46S 175 55 E
Tauranga, *N.Z.* **71** 37 42S 176 11 E
Taurus Mts., *Turk.* **47** 37 0N 35 0 E
Tavistock, *U.K.* **16** 50 33N 4 9W
Tavoy, *Burma* **59** 14 2N 98 12 E
Taw →, *U.K.* **16** 17 37S 177 55 E
Tay →, *U.K.* **21** 56 37N 3 38W
Tay, Firth of, *U.K.* **21** 56 25N 3 8W
Tay, L., *U.K.* **21** 56 30N 4 10W
Tay Bridge, *U.K.* **21** 56 28N 3 0W
Taynuilt, *U.K.* **20** 56 25N 5 15W
Tayport, *U.K.* **21** 56 27N 2 52W
Tayside □, *U.K.* **21** 56 25N 3 30W
Tbilisi, *U.S.S.R.* **47** 41 43N 44 50 E
Te Anau, L., *N.Z.* **71** 45 15S 167 45 E
Te Aroha, *N.Z.* **71** 37 32S 175 44 E
Tebay, *U.K.* **18** 54 25N 2 35W
Tees →, *U.K.* **19** 54 36N 1 25W
Teesdale, *U.K.* **18** 54 37N 2 10W
Teesside, *U.K.* **19** 54 37N 1 13W
Tegid, L., *U.K.* **17** 52 53N 3 38W
Tegucigalpa, *Hond.* **94** 14 5N 87 14W
Tehrān, *Iran* **56** 35 44N 51 30 E
Tehuantepec, Gulf of, *Mex.* **94** 15 50N 95 0W
Tehuantepec, Isthmus of, *Mex.* **94** 17 0N 94 30W
Teifi →, *U.K.* **17** 52 4N 4 14W
Teign →, *U.K.* **16** 50 41N 3 42W
Teignmouth, *U.K.* **16** 50 33N 3 30W
Tejo →, *Port.* **37** 38 40N 9 24W
Tel Aviv-Jaffa, *Isr.* **57** 32 4N 34 48 E
Telemark fylke □, *Nor.* **45** 59 25N 8 30 E
Telford, *U.K.* **14** 52 42N 2 31W
Teluk Betung, *Indon.* **63** 5 20S 105 10 E
Tema, *Ghana* **78** 5 41N 0 0 E
Teme →, *U.K.* **14** 52 23N 2 15W
Temirtau, *U.S.S.R.* **48** 50 5N 72 56 E
Temora, *Austral.* **70** 34 30S 147 30 E
Temple Combe, *U.K.* **14** 51 0N 2 25W
Temple Ewell, *U.K.* **15** 51 9N 1 15 E
Temple Sowerby, *U.K.* **18** 54 38N 2 33W
Templemore, *Ire.* **25** 52 48N 7 50W
Tenbury, *U.K.* **14** 52 18N 2 35W
Tenby, *U.K.* **17** 51 40N 4 42W
Tenerife, *Can. Is.* **78** 28 15N 16 35W
Tennessee □, *U.S.A.* **91** 36 0N 86 30W
Tennessee →, *U.S.A.* **91** 37 4N 88 34W
Tenterden, *U.K.* **15** 51 4N 0 42 E
Teófilo Otoni, *Brazil* **101** 17 50S 41 30W
Tepic, *Mex.* **94** 21 30N 104 54W
Téramo, *It.* **40** 42 40N 13 40 E
Teresina, *Brazil* **101** 5 9S 42 45W
Terni, *It.* **40** 42 34N 12 38 E
Terre Haute, *U.S.A.* **92** 39 28N 87 24W
Teruel, *Sp.* **37** 40 22N 1 8W
Test →, *U.K.* **14** 51 7N 1 30W
Tetbury, *U.K.* **14** 51 37N 2 9W
Tetlin, *U.S.A.* **88** 63 14N 142 50W
Tetney, *U.K.* **19** 53 30N 0 1W
Tétouan, *Mor.* **78** 35 35N 5 21W
Tetovo, *Yug.* **41** 42 1N 21 2 E
Tettenhall, *U.K.* **14** 52 35N 2 7W
Teviot →, *U.K.* **21** 55 21N 2 51W
Teviotdale, *U.K.* **21** 55 25N 2 50W
Teviothead, *U.K.* **21** 55 19N 2 55W
Tewkesbury, *U.K.* **14** 51 59N 2 8W
Texas □, *U.S.A.* **90** 31 40N 98 30W
Texel, *Neth.* **36** 53 5N 4 50 E
Teynham, *U.K.* **15** 51 19N 0 50 E
Thailand ■, *Asia* **63** 16 0N 102 0 E
Thailand, G. of, *Asia* **63** 11 30N 101 0 E
Thal Desert, *Pak.* **58** 31 10N 71 30 E
Thame, *U.K.* **15** 51 44N 0 58W
Thame →, *U.K.* **15** 51 35N 1 8W
Thames →, *U.K.* **15** 51 30N 0 35 E
Thanet, I. of, *U.K.* **15** 51 21N 1 20 E
Thar Desert, *India* **58** 28 0N 72 0 E
Thatcham, *U.K.* **14** 51 24N 1 17W
Thaxted, *U.K.* **15** 51 57N 0 20 E
The Entrance, *Austral.* **70** 33 21S 151 30 E
The Grenadines, Is., *W. Ind.* **94** 12 40N 61 20W
The Hague, *Neth.* **36** 52 7N 4 17 E
The Pas, *Canada* **88** 53 45N 101 15W
Theale, *U.K.* **14** 51 26N 1 5W
Thessaloníki, *Greece* **41** 40 38N 22 58 E
Thessaloniki, Gulf of, *Greece* **41** 40 15N 22 45 E
Thessaly □, *Greece* **41** 39 30N 22 0 E
Thetford, *U.K.* **15** 52 25N 0 44 E
Thies, *Sene.* **78** 14 50N 16 51W
Thimphu, *Bhutan* **59** 27 31N 89 45 E
Thionville, *Fr.* **34** 49 20N 6 10 E
Thirlmere, L., *U.K.* **18** 54 32N 3 4W
Thirsk, *U.K.* **19** 54 15N 1 20W
Thirston, *U.K.* **21** 55 20N 1 34W
Thisted, *Den.* **45** 56 58N 8 40 E
Thompson →, *Canada* **88** 50 15N 121 24W
Thornaby on Tees, *U.K.* **19** 54 36N 1 19W
Thornbury, *U.K.* **14** 51 36N 2 31W
Thorndon, *U.K.* **15** 52 16N 1 8 E
Thorne, *U.K.* **19** 53 36N 0 56W
Thorney, *U.K.* **15** 52 37N 0 8W
Thornham, *U.K.* **15** 52 59N 0 35 E
Thornhill, *U.K.* **21** 55 15N 3 46W
Thornthwaite, *U.K.* **18** 54 36N 3 13W
Thornton, *U.K.* **18** 53 52N 3 1W
Thornton Dale, *U.K.* **19** 54 14N 0 41W
Thorpe, *U.K.* **15** 52 38N 1 20 E
Thorpe le Soken, *U.K.* **15** 51 50N 1 11 E
Thrace □, *Greece* **41** 41 9N 25 30 E
Thrapston, *U.K.* **15** 52 24N 0 32W
Threlkeld, *U.K.* **18** 54 37N 3 2W
Threshfield, *U.K.* **18** 54 5N 2 2W
Thule, *Green.* **103** 77 40N 69 0W
Thunder Bay, *Canada* **92** 48 20N 89 15W
Thurlby, *U.K.* **15** 52 45N 0 21W
Thurles, *Ire.* **25** 52 40N 7 53W
Thurmaston, *U.K.* **14** 52 40N 1 8W
Thursby, *U.K.* **18** 54 40N 3 3W
Thurso, *U.K.* **23** 58 34N 3 31W
Tian Shan, *China* **60** 43 0N 84 0 E
Tianshui, *China* **60** 34 32N 105 40 E
Tiber →, *It.* **40** 41 44N 12 14 E
Tiberias, *Isr.* **57** 32 47N 35 32 E
Tibesti, *Chad* **79** 21 0N 17 30 E
Ticehurst, *U.K.* **15** 51 2N 0 23 E
Tickhill, *U.K.* **19** 53 25N 1 8W
Tideswell, *U.K.* **19** 53 17N 1 46W
Tientsin, *China* **61** 39 10N 117 15 E
Tierra del Fuego □, *Arg.* **102** 54 0S 67 45W
Tighnabruaich, *U.K.* **20** 55 55N 5 13W
Tigris →, *Iraq* **56** 37 0N 42 30 E

Tijuana, Mex. 94 32 30N 117 10W
Tiksi, U.S.S.R. 49 71 40N 128 45 E
Tilburg, Neth. 36 51 31N 5 6 E
Tilbury, U.K. 15 51 27N 0 24 E
Till →, U.K. 19 55 35N 2 3W
Tillicoultry, U.K. 21 56 9N 3 44W
Tilmanstone, U.K. 15 51 13N 1 18 E
Tilt →, U.K. 23 56 50N 3 50W
Timaru, N.Z. 71 44 23S 171 14 E
Timbuktu = Tombouctou, Mali 78 16 50N 3 0W
Timişoara, Rom. 43 45 43N 21 15 E
Timmins, Canada 92 48 28N 81 25W
Timor, Indon. 63 9 0S 125 0 E
Timor Sea, E. Ind. 66 10 0S 127 0 E
Tingewick, U.K. 14 51 59N 1 4W
Tintagel, U.K. 16 50 40N 4 45W
Tintagel Hd., U.K. 16 50 40N 4 46W
Tipperary, Ire. 25 52 28N 8 10W
Tipperary □, Ire. 25 52 37N 7 55W
Tipton, U.K. 14 52 32N 2 4W
Tiptree, U.K. 15 51 48N 0 46 E
Tiranë, Alb. 41 41 18N 19 49 E
Tiree, U.K. 20 56 31N 6 55W
Tiree, Passage of, U.K. 20 56 30N 6 30W
Tîrgu Mureş, Rom. 43 46 31N 24 38 E
Tiruchchirappalli, India 58 10 45N 78 45 E
Tisbury, U.K. 14 51 4N 2 4W
Tisza →, Hung. 43 46 8N 20 2 E
Titchfield, U.K. 14 50 51N 1 13W
Titicaca, L., Peru 100 15 30S 69 30W
Titograd, Yug. 41 42 30N 19 19 E
Tiverton, U.K. 16 50 54N 3 30W
Tizi-Ouzou, Alg. 78 36 42N 4 3 E
Toamasina, Madag. 81 18 10S 49 25 E
Tobago, W. Ind. 94 11 10N 60 30W
Tobermory, U.K. 20 56 37N 6 4W
Tobol →, U.S.S.R. 48 58 10N 68 12 E
Tocantins →, Brazil 101 1 45S 49 10W
Toddington, U.K. 15 51 57N 0 31W
Todmorden, U.K. 18 53 43N 2 7W
Togliatti, U.S.S.R. 46 53 32N 49 24 E
Togo ■, W. Afr. 78 6 15N 1 35 E
Tokelau Is., Pac. Oc. 64 9 0S 171 45W
Tōkyō, Jap. 62 35 45N 139 45 E
Tolageak, U.S.A. 88 70 2N 162 50W
Tolbukhin, Bulg. 41 43 37N 27 49 E
Toledo, Sp. 37 39 50N 4 2W
Toledo, U.S.A. 92 41 37N 83 33W
Toliara, Madag. 81 23 21S 43 40 E
Tollesbury, U.K. 15 51 46N 0 51 E
Toluca, Mex. 94 19 20N 99 40W
Tom Price, Austral. 66 22 40S 117 48 E
Tombouctou, Mali 78 16 50N 3 0W
Tomnavoulin, U.K. 23 57 19N 3 18W
Tomsk, U.S.S.R. 48 56 30N 85 5 E
Tonbridge, U.K. 15 51 12N 0 18 E
Tone →, U.K. 16 50 59N 3 15W
Tong, U.K. 14 52 39N 2 18W
Tonga ■, Pac. Oc. 64 19 50S 174 30W
Tonga Trench, Pac. Oc. 64 18 0S 175 0W
Tongue, U.K. 23 58 29N 4 25W
Tonkin, G. of, Asia 60 20 0N 108 0 E
Toowoomba, Austral. 67 27 32S 151 56 E
Topeka, U.S.A. 91 39 3N 95 40W
Topsham, U.K. 16 50 40N 3 27W
Tor Bay, U.K. 16 50 26N 3 31W
Torbay, U.K. 16 50 26N 3 31W
Torne älv →, Swed. 44 65 50N 24 12 E
Toronto, Canada 92 43 39N 79 20W
Torpoint, U.K. 16 50 23N 4 12W
Torquay, U.K. 16 50 27N 3 31W
Torran Rocks, U.K. 20 56 14N 6 24W
Torrens, L., Austral. 67 31 0S 137 50 E
Torreón, Mex. 94 25 33N 103 26W
Torridge →, U.K. 16 50 51N 4 10W
Torridon, L., U.K. 22 57 35N 5 50W
Torthorwald, U.K. 21 55 7N 3 30W
Tortosa, Sp. 37 40 49N 0 31 E
Toruń, Pol. 43 53 0N 18 39 E
Torver, U.K. 18 54 20N 3 7W
Tory I., Ire. 24 55 17N 8 12W
Totland, U.K. 14 50 41N 1 32W
Totley, U.K. 19 53 18N 1 32W
Totnes, U.K. 16 50 26N 3 41W
Totton, U.K. 14 50 55N 1 29W
Toulon, Fr. 35 43 10N 5 55 E
Toulouse, Fr. 35 43 37N 1 27 E
Tournai, Belg. 36 50 35N 3 25 E
Tours, Fr. 34 47 22N 0 40 E
Towcester, U.K. 15 52 7N 0 56W
Town Yetholm, U.K. 21 55 33N 2 19W
Townsville, Austral. 67 19 15S 146 45 E
Toyama, Jap. 62 36 40N 137 15 E
Toyohashi, Jap. 62 34 45N 137 25 E
Trabzon, Turk. 47 41 0N 39 45 E
Trail, Canada 88 49 5N 117 40W
Tralee, Ire. 25 52 16N 9 42W
Tralee B., Ire. 25 52 17N 9 55W
Tramore, Ire. 25 52 10N 7 10W
Tranent, U.K. 21 55 57N 2 58W
Transcaucasia, U.S.S.R. 47 42 0N 44 0 E
Transvaal □, S. Afr. 81 25 0S 29 0 E
Transylvanian Alps, Rom. 43 45 30N 25 0 E
Trápani, It. 40 38 1N 12 30 E
Traralgon, Austral. 70 38 12S 146 34 E
Trawsfynydd, U.K. 17 52 54N 3 55W
Tredegar, U.K. 17 51 47N 3 16W
Tregaron, U.K. 17 52 14N 3 56W
Trent →, U.K. 19 53 33N 0 44W
Trentham, U.K. 18 52 59N 2 12W
Trentino-Alto Adige □, It. 40 46 30N 11 0 E
Trento, It. 40 46 5N 11 8 E
Trenton, U.S.A. 93 40 15N 74 41W
Tresco I., U.K. 16 49 57N 6 20W
Treshnish Is., U.K. 20 56 30N 6 25W
Trevose Hd., U.K. 16 50 33N 5 3W
Trier, W. Ger. 36 49 45N 6 37 E
Trieste, It. 40 45 39N 13 45 E
Trim, Ire. 24 53 34N 6 48W
Trimdon, U.K. 19 54 43N 1 23W
Trimley, U.K. 15 51 59N 1 19 E
Trincomalee, Sri L. 58 8 38N 81 15 E
Trinidad, W. Ind. 94 10 30N 61 15W
Trinidad & Tobago ■, W. Ind. 94 10 30N 61 20W
Tripoli = Tarābulus, Leb. 56 34 31N 35 50 E
Tripoli = Tarābulus, Libya 79 32 49N 13 7 E
Tristan da Cunha, Atl. Oc. 128 37 6S 12 20W
Trivandrum, India 58 8 41N 77 0 E
Trois-Rivières, Canada 93 46 25N 72 34W
Trollhättan, Swed. 45 58 17N 12 20 E
Troms fylke □, Nor. 44 68 56N 19 0 E
Tromsø, Nor. 44 69 40N 18 56 E
Trondheim, Nor. 44 63 36N 10 25 E
Troon, U.K. 20 55 33N 4 40W
Trossachs, The, U.K. 20 56 14N 4 24W
Trostan, U.K. 24 55 4N 6 10W
Trotternish, U.K. 22 57 32N 6 15W
Trowbridge, U.K. 14 51 18N 2 12W
Troy, U.S.A. 93 42 45N 73 39W
Troyes, Fr. 34 48 19N 4 3 E
Trujillo, Peru 100 8 6S 79 0W
Truk, Pac. Oc. 64 7 25N 151 46 E
Trull, U.K. 14 50 58N 3 8W
Trumpington, U.K. 15 52 11N 0 6 E
Truro, U.K. 16 50 17N 5 2W
Tselinograd, U.S.S.R. 48 51 10N 71 30 E
Tsimlyansk Res., U.S.S.R. 47 48 0N 43 0 E
Tsu, Jap. 62 34 45N 136 25 E
Tsugaru Str., Jap. 62 41 30N 140 30 E
Tuam, Ire. 24 53 30N 8 50W
Tuamotu Arch., Pac. Oc. 65 17 0S 144 0W
Tuath, Loch, U.K. 20 56 30N 6 15W
Tubuai Is., Pac. Oc. 65 25 0S 150 0W
Tucson, U.S.A. 90 32 14N 110 59W
Tula, U.S.S.R. 46 54 13N 37 38 E
Tulcán, Ecuad. 100 0 48N 77 43W
Tulla, L., U.K. 20 56 33N 4 47W
Tullamore, Ire. 25 53 17N 7 30W
Tullow, Ire. 25 52 48N 6 45W
Tulsa, U.S.A. 91 36 10N 96 0W
Tulua, Col. 100 4 6N 76 11W
Tumaco, Col. 100 1 50N 78 45W
Tummel, L., U.K. 23 56 43N 3 55W
Tunbridge Wells, U.K. 15 51 7N 0 16 E
Tuncurry, Austral. 70 32 17S 152 29 E
Tunis, Tunisia 78 36 50N 10 11 E
Tunisia ■, Africa 78 33 30N 9 10 E
Tunja, Col. 100 5 33N 73 25W
Tunstall, U.K. 15 52 7N 1 28 E
Tura, India 59 25 30N 90 16 E
Turfan Depression, China 50 42 40N 89 25 E
Turin, It. 40 45 4N 7 40 E
Turkana, L., Kenya 80 3 30N 36 5 E
Turkey ■, Eurasia 47 39 0N 36 0 E
Turkmenistan □, U.S.S.R. 48 39 0N 59 0 E
Turks Is., W. Ind. 95 21 20N 71 20W
Turku, Fin. 45 60 30N 22 19 E
Turnberry, U.K. 20 55 19N 4 50W
Turnu-Severin, Rom. 43 44 39N 22 41 E
Turriff, U.K. 23 57 32N 2 28W
Tuskar Rock, Ire. 25 52 12N 6 10W
Tutbury, U.K. 14 52 52N 1 41W
Tuticorin, India 58 8 50N 78 12 E
Tuvalu ■, Pac. Oc. 64 8 0S 178 0 E
Tuxford, U.K. 19 53 14N 0 52W
Tuxtla Gutiérrez, Mex. 94 16 50N 93 10W
Tuz Gölü, Turk. 47 38 45N 33 30 E
Tuzla, Yug. 41 44 34N 18 41 E
Twatt, U.K. 23 59 6N 3 15W
Tweed →, U.K. 21 55 42N 2 10W
Tweedmouth, U.K. 21 55 46N 2 1W
Tweedshawe, U.K. 21 55 26N 3 29W
Twenty, U.K. 15 52 43N 0 20W
Twyford, Berks., U.K. 15 51 29N 0 51W
Twyford, Hants., U.K. 14 51 1N 1 19W
Tychy, Pol. 43 50 9N 18 59 E
Tydd St. Mary, U.K. 15 52 45N 0 9 E
Tyldesley, U.K. 18 53 31N 2 29W
Tyler, U.S.A. 90 32 18N 95 18W
Tyndrum, U.K. 20 56 26N 4 41W
Tyne →, Tyne & Wear, U.K. 19 54 58N 1 28W
Tyne →, Lothian, U.K. 21 55 58N 2 45W
Tyne & Wear □, U.K. 19 54 55N 1 35W
Tynemouth, U.K. 19 55 1N 1 27W
Tyre = Sūr, Leb. 57 33 19N 35 16 E
Tyrol □, Austria 42 47 3N 10 43 E
Tyrrhenian Sea, Europe 40 40 0N 12 30 E
Tyumen, U.S.S.R. 48 57 11N 65 29 E
Tywardreath, U.K. 16 50 21N 4 40W
Tywi →, U.K. 17 51 48N 4 20W
Tywyn, U.K. 17 52 36N 4 5W

U

Ube, Jap. 62 33 56N 131 15 E
Uberaba, Brazil 101 19 50S 47 55W
Uberlândia, Brazil 101 19 0S 48 20W
Ucayali →, Peru 100 4 30S 73 30W
Uckfield, U.K. 15 50 58N 0 6 E
Udaipur, India 58 24 36N 73 44 E
Uddevalla, Swed. 45 58 21N 11 55 E
Uddingston, U.K. 21 55 50N 4 3W
Údine, It. 40 46 5N 13 10 E
Ufa, U.S.S.R. 46 54 45N 55 55 E
Uffculme, U.K. 16 50 54N 3 19W
Ufford, U.K. 15 52 6N 1 22 E
Uganda ■, E. Afr. 80 2 0N 32 0 E
Ugborough, U.K. 16 50 22N 3 53W
Uig, U.K. 22 57 35N 6 20W
Uitenhage, S. Afr. 81 33 40S 25 28 E
Ujung Pandang, Indon. 63 5 10S 119 20 E
Ukraine □, U.S.S.R. 47 49 0N 32 0 E
Ulan Bator, Mong. 60 47 55N 106 53 E
Ulan Ude, U.S.S.R. 49 51 45N 107 40 E
Ulceby Cross, U.K. 19 53 14N 0 6 E
Ulhasnagar, India 58 19 15N 73 10 E
Ullapool, U.K. 22 57 54N 5 10W
Ullswater, U.K. 18 54 35N 2 52W
Ulm, W. Ger. 42 48 23N 10 0 E
Ulster □, U.K. 24 54 35N 6 30W
Ulva, I., U.K. 20 56 30N 6 12W
Ulverston, U.K. 18 54 13N 3 7W
Ulyanovsk, U.S.S.R. 46 54 20N 48 25 E
Ulyasutay, Mong. 60 47 56N 97 28 E
Umbria □, It. 40 42 53N 12 30 E
Umeå, Swed. 44 63 45N 20 20 E
Umtata, S. Afr. 81 31 36S 28 49 E
Ungava B., Canada 89 59 30N 67 30W
Ungava Pen., Canada 89 60 0N 74 0W
Union of Soviet Socialist Republics ■, Eurasia 48 60 0N 100 0 E
United Arab Emirates ■, Asia 57 23 50N 54 0 E
United Kingdom ■, Europe 5 55 0N 3 0W
United States of America ■, N. Am. 90 37 0N 96 0W
United States Trust Terr. of the Pacific Is. □, Pac. Oc. 64 10 0N 160 0 E
Unst, U.K. 22 60 50N 0 55W
Upavon, U.K. 14 51 17N 1 49W
Upington, S. Afr. 81 28 25S 21 15 E
Upper Heyford, U.K. 14 51 54N 1 16W
Upper L. Erne, U.K. 24 54 14N 7 22W
Upper Volta ■ = Burkina Faso ■, Africa 78 12 0N 1 0W
Uppingham, U.K. 15 52 36N 0 43W
Uppsala, Swed. 45 59 53N 17 38 E
Upton, U.K. 18 53 14N 2 52W
Upton-upon-Severn, U.K. 14 52 4N 2 12W
Upwey, U.K. 14 50 40N 2 29W
Ural Mts., U.S.S.R. 46 60 0N 59 0 E
Uralsk, U.S.S.R. 46 51 20N 51 20 E
Uranium City, Canada 88 59 34N 108 37W
Ure →, U.K. 19 54 20N 1 25W
Urgench, U.S.S.R. 48 41 40N 60 41 E
Urmia, L., Iran 56 37 50N 45 30 E
Urmston, U.K. 18 53 28N 2 22W
Uruguay ■, S. Am. 102 32 30S 56 30W
Uruguay →, S. Am. 102 34 12S 58 18W
Ürümqi, China 60 43 45N 87 45 E
Usk →, U.K. 17 51 37N 2 56W
Üsküdar, Turk. 47 41 0N 29 5 E
Usselby, U.K. 19 53 25N 0 21W
Ust-Kamenogorsk, U.S.S.R. 48 50 0N 82 36 E
Ust Urt Plateau, U.S.S.R. 48 44 0N 55 0 E
Ustinov, U.S.S.R. 46 56 51N 53 14 E
Utah □, U.S.A. 90 39 30N 111 30W
Utica, U.S.A. 93 43 5N 75 18W
Utrecht, Neth. 36 52 5N 5 8 E
Utsunomiya, Jap. 62 36 30N 139 50 E
Uttar Pradesh □, India 58 27 0N 80 0 E
Uttoxeter, U.K. 18 52 53N 1 50W
Uzbekistan □, U.S.S.R. 48 41 30N 65 0 E

V

Vaasa, Fin. 44 63 6N 21 38 E
Vadodara, India 58 22 20N 73 10 E
Vadsø, Nor. 44 70 3N 29 50 E
Val d'Or, Canada 92 48 7N 77 47W
Valdez, U.S.A. 88 61 14N 146 17W
Valdivia, Chile 102 39 50S 73 14W
Valence, Fr. 35 44 57N 4 54 E
Valencia, Sp. 37 39 27N 0 23W
Valencia, Ven. 100 10 11N 68 0W
Valenciennes, Fr. 34 50 20N 3 34 E
Valentia Hr., Ire. 25 51 56N 10 17W
Valentia I., Ire. 25 51 54N 10 22W
Valladolid, Sp. 37 41 38N 4 43W
Valledupar, Col. 100 10 29N 73 15W
Valletta, Malta 40 35 54N 14 30 E
Valley, U.K. 17 53 17N 4 31W
Valparaíso, Chile 102 33 2S 71 40W
Van, L., Turk. 47 38 30N 43 0 E
Van Diemen G., Austral. 66 11 45S 132 0 E
Vancouver, Canada 88 49 15N 123 10W
Vancouver I., Canada 88 49 50N 126 0W
Vänern, Swed. 45 58 47N 13 30 E
Vanua Levu, Fiji 64 16 33S 179 15 E
Vanuatu ■, Pac. Oc. 64 15 0S 168 0 E
Varanasi, India 59 25 22N 83 0 E
Varangar Fjord, Nor. 44 70 3N 29 25 E
Vardar →, Yug. 41 40 35N 22 50 E
Värmlands län □, Swed. 45 60 0N 13 20 E
Varna, Bulg. 41 43 13N 27 56 E
Västerås, Swed. 45 59 37N 16 38 E
Västmanlands län □, Swed. 45 59 45N 16 20 E
Vatnajökull, Ice. 44 64 30N 16 48W
Vättern, Swed. 45 58 25N 14 30 E
Växjö, Swed. 45 56 52N 14 50 E
Vendée □, Fr. 34 46 50N 1 35W
Venezuela ■, S. Am. 100 8 0N 65 0W
Venice, It. 40 45 27N 12 20 E
Venlo, Neth. 36 51 22N 6 11 E
Ventnor, U.K. 14 50 35N 1 12W
Veracruz, Mex. 94 19 10N 96 10W
Vercelli, It. 40 45 19N 8 25 E
Vereeniging, S. Afr. 81 26 38S 27 57 E
Verkhoyansk, U.S.S.R. 49 67 35N 133 25 E
Verkhoyansk Ra., U.S.S.R. 49 66 0N 129 0 E
Vermont □, U.S.A. 93 43 40N 72 50W
Verona, It. 40 45 27N 11 0 E
Versailles, Fr. 34 48 48N 2 8 E
Verviers, Belg. 36 50 37N 5 52 E
Verwood, U.K. 14 50 53N 1 53W
Veryan, U.K. 16 50 13N 4 56W
Veryan Bay, U.K. 16 50 12N 4 51W
Vestmannaeyjar, Ice. 44 63 27N 20 15W
Vesuvius, Mt., It. 40 40 50N 14 22 E
Viborg, Den. 45 56 27N 9 23 E
Vickerstown, U.K. 18 54 8N 3 17W
Victoria, Canada 88 48 30N 123 25W
Victoria □, Austral. 70 37 0S 144 0 E
Victoria →, Austral. 66 15 10S 129 40 E
Victoria, L., Austral. 70 33 57S 141 15 E
Victoria, L., E. Afr. 80 1 0S 33 0 E
Victoria Falls, Zimb. 81 17 58S 25 52 E
Victoria I., Canada 88 71 0N 111 0W
Victoria Ld., Ant. 103 75 0S 160 0 E
Vienna, Austria 42 48 12N 16 22 E
Vientiane, Laos 51 17 58N 102 36 E
Vietnam ■, Asia 63 19 0N 106 0 E
Vigo, Sp. 37 42 12N 8 41W
Vijayawada, India 59 16 31N 80 39 E
Villahermosa, Mex. 94 17 59N 92 55W
Villefranche-sur-Saône, Fr. 35 45 59N 4 43 E
Vilnius, U.S.S.R. 46 54 38N 25 19 E
Vilyuysk, U.S.S.R. 49 63 40N 121 35 E
Viña del Mar, Chile 102 33 0S 71 30W
Vineland, U.S.A. 93 39 30N 75 0W
Vinnitsa, U.S.S.R. 47 49 15N 28 30 E
Virgin Is., W. Ind. 95 18 40N 64 30W
Virginia □, U.S.A. 91 37 45N 78 0W
Viscount Melville Sd., Canada 88 74 10N 108 0W
Vishakhapatnam, India 59 17 45N 83 20 E
Vistula = Wisła →, Pol. 43 54 22N 18 55 E
Vitebsk, U.S.S.R. 46 55 10N 30 15 E
Viterbo, It. 40 42 25N 12 8 E
Viti Levu, Fiji 64 17 30S 177 30 E
Vitim →, U.S.S.R. 49 59 26N 112 34 E
Vitória, Brazil 101 20 20S 40 22W
Vitoria, Sp. 37 42 50N 2 41W
Vitória da Conquista, Brazil 101 14 51S 40 51W
Vlaardingen, Neth. 36 51 55N 4 21 E
Vladimir, U.S.S.R. 46 56 15N 40 30 E
Vladivostok, U.S.S.R. 49 43 10N 131 53 E
Vlissingen, Neth. 36 51 26N 3 34 E
Vlóré, Alb. 41 40 32N 19 28 E
Voil, L., U.K. 20 56 20N 4 25W
Volga →, U.S.S.R. 46 48 30N 46 0 E
Volga Hts., U.S.S.R. 47 51 0N 46 0 E
Volgograd, U.S.S.R. 47 48 40N 44 25 E
Vologda, U.S.S.R. 46 59 10N 40 0 E
Vólos, Greece 41 39 24N 22 59 E
Volta, L., Ghana 78 7 30N 0 15 E
Volta Redonda, Brazil 101 22 31S 44 5W
Volzhskiy, U.S.S.R. 47 48 56N 44 46 E
Voorburg, Neth. 36 52 5N 4 24 E
Vorkuta, U.S.S.R. 46 67 48N 64 20 E
Voronezh, U.S.S.R. 46 51 40N 39 10 E
Voroshilovgrad, U.S.S.R. 47 48 38N 39 15 E
Vosges, Fr. 34 48 20N 7 10 E
Vryburg, S. Afr. 81 26 55S 24 45 E
Vyrnwy, L., U.K. 17 52 48N 3 30W

W

Waal →, Neth. 36 51 59N 4 30 E
Wabash →, U.S.A. 92 37 46N 88 2W
Waco, U.S.A. 91 31 33N 97 5W
Wâd Medanî, Sudan 79 14 28N 33 30 E
Waddenzee, Neth. 36 53 6N 5 10 E
Waddesdon, U.K. 15 51 50N 0 54W

Waddingham, *U.K.* **19** 53 28N 0 31W
Waddington, *U.K.* **19** 53 10N 0 31W
Waddington, Mt., *Canada* **88** 51 23N 125 15W
Wadebridge, *U.K.* **16** 50 31N 4 51W
Wadhurst, *U.K.* **15** 51 3N 0 21 E
Wagga Wagga, *Austral.* **70** 35 7S 147 24 E
Wagin, *Austral.* **66** 33 17S 117 25 E
Wainfleet All Saints, *U.K.* **19** 53 7N 0 16 E
Waipara, *N.Z.* **71** 43 3S 172 46 E
Waitaki →, *N.Z.* **71** 44 56S 171 7 E
Wakatipu, L., *N.Z.* **71** 45 5S 168 33 E
Wakayama, *Jap.* **62** 34 15N 135 15 E
Wakefield, *U.K.* **19** 53 41N 1 31W
Walberswick, *U.K.* **15** 52 18N 1 39 E
Wałbrzych, *Pol.* **42** 50 45N 16 18 E
Walbury Hill, *U.K.* **14** 51 22N 1 28W
Waldron, *U.K.* **15** 50 56N 0 13 E
Wales □, *U.K.* **17** 52 30N 3 30W
Walgett, *Austral.* **67** 30 0S 148 5 E
Wallachia, *Rom.* **43** 44 35N 25 0 E
Wallasey, *U.K.* **18** 53 26N 3 2W
Wallingford, *U.K.* **14** 51 40N 1 15W
Wallis & Futuna, *Pac. Oc.* **64** 13 18S 176 10W
Wallsend, *U.K.* **19** 54 59N 1 30W
Walmer, *U.K.* **15** 51 12N 1 23 E
Walney, Isle of, *U.K.* **18** 54 5N 3 15W
Walpole, *U.K.* **15** 52 44N 0 13 E
Walsall, *U.K.* **14** 52 36N 1 59W
Walsoken, *U.K.* **15** 52 41N 0 12 E
Waltham, *U.K.* **19** 53 32N 0 6W
Waltham Abbey, *U.K.* **15** 51 40N 0 1 E
Waltham Forest, *U.K.* **15** 51 37N 0 2 E
Waltham on the Wolds, *U.K.* **15** 52 49N 0 48W
Walton-on-the-Naze, *U.K.* **15** 51 52N 1 17 E
Walvis Bay, *S. Afr.* **81** 23 0S 14 28 E
Wanborough, *U.K.* **14** 51 33N 1 40W
Wandsworth, *U.K.* **15** 51 28N 0 15W
Wanganui, *N.Z.* **71** 39 56S 175 3 E
Wangaratta, *Austral.* **70** 36 21S 146 19 E
Wansbeck, *U.K.* **21** 55 12N 1 28W
Wantage, *U.K.* **14** 51 35N 1 25W
Warboys, *U.K.* **15** 52 25N 0 5W
Warburton →, *Austral.* **67** 28 4S 137 28 E
Wardington, *U.K.* **14** 52 8N 1 17W
Wardle, *U.K.* **18** 53 7N 2 35W
Ward's Stone, *U.K.* **18** 54 2N 2 39W
Ware, *U.K.* **15** 51 48N 0 2W
Wareham, *U.K.* **14** 50 41N 2 8W
Wark, *U.K.* **21** 55 5N 2 14W
Warkworth, *U.K.* **21** 55 22N 1 38W
Warley, *U.K.* **14** 52 30N 2 0W
Warminster, *U.K.* **14** 51 12N 2 11W
Warracknabeal, *Austral.* **70** 36 9S 142 26 E
Warrego →, *Austral.* **67** 30 24S 145 21 E
Warrenpoint, *U.K.* **24** 54 7N 6 15W
Warrington, *U.K.* **18** 53 25N 2 38W
Warrnambool, *Austral.* **70** 38 25S 142 30 E
Warsaw, *Pol.* **43** 52 13N 21 0 E
Warsop, *U.K.* **19** 53 13N 1 9W
Warta →, *Pol.* **43** 52 35N 14 39 E
Warthe = Warta →, *Pol.* **43** 52 35N 14 39 E
Warwick, *Austral.* **67** 28 10S 152 1 E
Warwick, *U.K.* **14** 52 17N 1 36W
Warwick □, *U.K.* **14** 52 20N 1 30W
Wasatch Ra., *U.S.A.* **90** 40 30N 111 15W
Wash, The, *U.K.* **19** 52 58N 0 20 E
Washford, *U.K.* **14** 51 9N 3 22W
Washington, *U.K.* **21** 54 55N 1 30W
Washington, *U.S.A.* **92** 38 52N 77 0W
Washington □, *U.S.A.* **90** 47 45N 120 30W
Wast Water, L., *U.K.* **18** 54 26N 3 18W
Watchet, *U.K.* **14** 51 10N 3 20W
Waterbeach, *U.K.* **15** 52 16N 0 11 E
Waterbury, *U.S.A.* **93** 41 32N 73 0W
Waterford, *Ire.* **25** 52 16N 7 8W
Waterford □, *Ire.* **25** 52 10N 7 40W
Waterford Harb., *Ire.* **25** 52 10N 6 58W
Watergate Bay, *U.K.* **16** 50 26N 5 4W
Waterloo, *U.K.* **18** 53 29N 3 2W
Watford, *U.K.* **15** 51 38N 0 23W
Wath, *U.K.* **19** 53 29N 1 20W
Watlington, *Norfolk, U.K.* **15** 52 40N 0 24 E
Watlington, *Oxon., U.K.* **15** 51 38N 1 0W
Watton, *U.K.* **15** 52 35N 0 50 E
Waveney →, *U.K.* **15** 52 24N 1 20 E
Waver →, *U.K.* **18** 54 50N 3 15W
Weald, The, *U.K.* **15** 51 7N 0 9 E
Wear →, *U.K.* **19** 54 55N 1 22W
Weardale, *U.K.* **18** 54 44N 2 5W
Wearhead, *U.K.* **18** 54 45N 2 14W
Weaver →, *U.K.* **18** 53 17N 2 35W
Weaverham, *U.K.* **18** 53 15N 2 30W
Weddell Sea, *Ant.* **103** 72 30S 40 0W
Wedmore, *U.K.* **14** 51 14N 2 50W
Wednesbury, *U.K.* **14** 52 33N 2 1W
Wednesfield, *U.K.* **14** 52 36N 2 3W
Weedon Bec, *U.K.* **14** 52 14N 1 6W
Weifang, *China* **61** 36 47N 119 10 E
Weldon, *U.K.* **21** 55 16N 1 46W
Welford, *Berks., U.K.* **14** 51 28N 1 24W
Welford, *Northants., U.K.* **14** 52 26N 1 5W
Welkom, *S. Afr.* **81** 28 0S 26 50 E
Welland →, *U.K.* **15** 52 43N 0 10W
Wellesley Is., *Austral.* **67** 16 42S 139 30 E
Wellingborough, *U.K.* **15** 52 18N 0 41W
Wellington, *Austral.* **70** 32 35S 148 59 E
Wellington, *N.Z.* **71** 41 19S 174 46 E
Wellington, *Salop, U.K.* **14** 52 42N 2 31W
Wellington, *Somerset, U.K.* **14** 50 58N 3 13W
Wellow, *U.K.* **14** 51 20N 2 22W
Wells, *Norfolk, U.K.* **15** 52 57N 0 51 E
Wells, *Somerset, U.K.* **14** 51 12N 2 39W
Welney, *U.K.* **15** 52 31N 0 15 E
Wels, *Austria* **42** 48 9N 14 1 E
Welshpool, *U.K.* **17** 52 40N 3 9W
Welton, *U.K.* **19** 53 19N 0 29W
Welwyn Garden City, *U.K.* **15** 51 49N 0 11W
Wem, *U.K.* **14** 52 52N 2 45W
Wembury, *U.K.* **16** 50 19N 4 6W
Wemyss Bay, *U.K.* **20** 55 52N 4 54W
Wendover, *U.K.* **15** 51 46N 0 45W
Wenhaston, *U.K.* **15** 52 17N 1 35 E
Wenlock Edge, *U.K.* **14** 52 30N 2 43W
Wensleydale, *U.K.* **18** 54 18N 2 0W
Wensum →, *U.K.* **15** 52 35N 1 20 E
Wenzhou, *China* **61** 28 0N 120 38 E
Weobley, *U.K.* **14** 52 9N 2 52W
Werribee, *Austral.* **70** 37 54S 144 40 E
Werrington, *U.K.* **16** 50 40N 4 22W
Weser →, *W. Ger.* **42** 53 33N 8 30 E
West Auckland, *U.K.* **19** 54 38N 1 42W
West Bengal □, *India* **59** 23 0N 88 0 E
West Bridgford, *U.K.* **19** 52 56N 1 8W
West Bromwich, *U.K.* **14** 52 32N 2 1W
West Calder, *U.K.* **21** 55 51N 3 34W
West Coker, *U.K.* **14** 50 55N 2 40W
West Fen, *U.K.* **19** 53 5N 0 5W
West Germany ■, *Europe* **42** 52 0N 9 0 E
West Glamorgan □, *U.K.* **17** 51 40N 3 55W
West Grinstead, *U.K.* **15** 50 58N 0 19W
West Haddon, *U.K.* **14** 52 21N 1 5W
West Kilbride, *U.K.* **20** 55 41N 4 50W
West Kirby, *U.K.* **18** 53 22N 3 11W
West Linton, *U.K.* **21** 55 45N 3 24W
West Lulworth, *U.K.* **14** 50 37N 2 14W
West Malling, *U.K.* **15** 51 16N 0 25 E
West Meon, *U.K.* **14** 51 2N 1 3W
West Mersea, *U.K.* **15** 51 46N 0 55 E
West Midlands □, *U.K.* **14** 52 30N 1 55W
West Moors, *U.K.* **14** 50 49N 1 50W
West Parley, *U.K.* **14** 50 46N 1 52W
West Rasen, *U.K.* **19** 53 23N 0 23W
West Schelde →, *Neth.* **36** 51 23N 3 50 E
West Siberian Plain, *U.S.S.R.* **48** 62 0N 75 0 E
West Sussex □, *U.K.* **15** 50 55N 0 30W
West Tarbert, L., *U.K.* **20** 55 58N 5 30W
West Virginia □, *U.S.A.* **92** 39 0N 81 0W
West Wyalong, *Austral.* **70** 33 56S 147 10 E
West Yorkshire □, *U.K.* **19** 53 45N 1 40W
Westbourne, *U.K.* **15** 50 53N 0 55W
Westbury, *Salop, U.K.* **14** 52 40N 2 57W
Westbury, *Wilts., U.K.* **14** 51 16N 2 11W
Westbury-on-Severn, *U.K.* **14** 51 49N 2 24W
Westerham, *U.K.* **15** 51 16N 0 5 E
Western Australia □, *Austral.* **66** 25 0S 118 0 E
Western Ghats, *India* **58** 14 0N 75 0 E
Western Isles □, *U.K.* **22** 57 30N 7 10W
Western Sahara ■, *Africa* **78** 25 0N 13 0W
Western Samoa ■, *Pac. Oc.* **64** 14 0S 172 0W
Westfield, *U.K.* **15** 50 53N 0 30 E
Westhoughton, *U.K.* **18** 53 34N 2 30W
Westland Bight, *N.Z.* **71** 42 55S 170 5 E
Westmeath □, *Ire.* **24** 53 30N 7 30W
Weston, *U.K.* **14** 52 51N 2 2W
Weston-super-Mare, *U.K.* **14** 51 20N 2 59W
Westport, *Ire.* **24** 53 44N 9 31W
Westport, *N.Z.* **71** 41 46S 171 37 E
Westray, *U.K.* **23** 59 18N 3 0W
Westruther, *U.K.* **21** 55 45N 2 34W
Westward Ho!, *U.K.* **16** 51 2N 4 16W
Wetherby, *U.K.* **19** 53 56N 1 23W
Wetwang, *U.K.* **19** 54 2N 0 35W
Wexford, *Ire.* **25** 52 20N 6 28W
Wexford □, *Ire.* **25** 52 20N 6 25W
Wexford Harb., *Ire.* **25** 52 20N 6 25W
Wey →, *U.K.* **15** 51 19N 0 29W
Weybourne, *U.K.* **15** 52 57N 1 9 E
Weybridge, *U.K.* **15** 51 22N 0 28W
Weymouth, *U.K.* **14** 50 36N 2 28W
Whakatane, *N.Z.* **71** 37 57S 177 1 E
Whaley Bridge, *U.K.* **18** 53 20N 2 0W
Whalley, *U.K.* **18** 53 49N 2 25W
Whalsay, *U.K.* **22** 60 22N 1 0W
Whalton, *U.K.* **21** 55 7N 1 46W
Whangarei, *N.Z.* **71** 35 43S 174 21 E
Whaplode, *U.K.* **15** 52 42N 0 3W
Wharfe →, *U.K.* **19** 53 55N 1 30W
Wharfedale, *U.K.* **18** 54 7N 2 4W
Whauphill, *U.K.* **20** 54 48N 4 31W
Wheatley Hill, *U.K.* **19** 54 45N 1 23W
Whernside, *U.K.* **18** 54 14N 2 24W
Whichham, *U.K.* **18** 54 14N 3 22W
Whimple, *U.K.* **16** 50 46N 3 21W
Whipsnade, *U.K.* **15** 51 51N 0 32W
Whissendine, *U.K.* **15** 52 43N 0 46W
Whiston, *U.K.* **18** 53 25N 2 45W
Whitburn, *U.K.* **21** 55 52N 3 41W
Whitby, *U.K.* **19** 54 29N 0 37W
Whitchurch, *Devon, U.K.* **16** 50 31N 4 7W
Whitchurch, *Hants., U.K.* **14** 51 14N 1 20W
Whitchurch, *Hereford & Worcs., U.K.* **14** 51 51N 2 41W
Whitchurch, *Salop, U.K.* **18** 52 58N 2 42W
White Esk →, *U.K.* **21** 55 14N 3 11W
White Horse Hill, *U.K.* **14** 51 35N 1 35W
White Nile →, *Sudan* **79** 15 38N 32 31 E
White Russia □, *U.S.S.R.* **46** 53 30N 27 0 E
White Sea, *U.S.S.R.* **46** 66 30N 38 0 E
Whiteadder Water →, *U.K.* **21** 55 47N 2 20W
Whitehaven, *U.K.* **18** 54 33N 3 35W
Whitehead, *U.K.* **24** 54 45N 5 42W
Whitehorse, *Canada* **88** 60 43N 135 3W
Whitehorse, Vale of, *U.K.* **14** 51 37N 1 30W
Whitekirk, *U.K.* **21** 56 2N 2 36W
Whitesand B., *U.K.* **16** 50 18N 4 20W
Whithorn, *U.K.* **20** 54 44N 4 25W
Whitley Bay, *U.K.* **21** 55 4N 1 28W
Whitney, Mt., *U.S.A.* **90** 36 35N 118 14W
Whitstable, *U.K.* **15** 51 21N 1 2 E
Whittington, *Derby, U.K.* **19** 53 17N 1 26W
Whittington, *Salop, U.K.* **14** 52 53N 3 0W
Whittlesey, *U.K.* **15** 52 34N 0 8W
Whittlesford, *U.K.* **15** 52 6N 0 9 E
Whitton, *U.K.* **19** 53 42N 0 39W
Whitwell, *Derby, U.K.* **19** 53 16N 1 11W
Whitwell, *I. of W., U.K.* **14** 50 35N 1 19W
Whitwick, *U.K.* **14** 52 45N 1 23W
Whitworth, *U.K.* **18** 53 40N 2 11W
Whixley, *U.K.* **19** 54 2N 1 19W
Whyalla, *Austral.* **67** 33 2S 137 30 E
Wichita, *U.S.A.* **91** 37 40N 97 20W
Wichita Falls, *U.S.A.* **90** 33 57N 98 30W
Wick, *U.K.* **23** 58 26N 3 5W
Wickford, *U.K.* **15** 51 37N 0 31 E
Wickham, *U.K.* **14** 50 54N 1 11W
Wickham Market, *U.K.* **15** 52 9N 1 21 E
Wicklow, *Ire.* **25** 53 0N 6 2W
Wicklow □, *Ire.* **25** 52 59N 6 25W
Wicklow Mts., *Ire.* **25** 53 0N 6 30W
Wickwar, *U.K.* **14** 51 35N 2 23W
Widdrington, *U.K.* **21** 55 15N 1 35W
Widecombe, *U.K.* **16** 50 34N 3 48W
Widemouth, *U.K.* **16** 50 45N 4 34W
Widnes, *U.K.* **18** 53 22N 2 44W
Wiesbaden, *W. Ger.* **36** 50 7N 8 17 E
Wigan, *U.K.* **18** 53 33N 2 38W
Wight, I. of, *U.K.* **14** 50 40N 1 20W
Wigmore, *U.K.* **14** 52 19N 2 51W
Wigston, *U.K.* **14** 52 35N 1 6W
Wigton, *U.K.* **18** 54 50N 3 9W
Wigtown, *U.K.* **20** 54 52N 4 27W
Wigtown B., *U.K.* **20** 54 46N 4 15W
Wilhelm II Land, *Ant.* **103** 68 0S 90 0 E
Wilhelmshaven, *W. Ger.* **42** 53 30N 8 9 E
Wilkes Barre, *U.S.A.* **93** 41 15N 75 52W
Wilkes Land, *Ant.* **103** 69 0S 120 0 E
Willemstad, *Cur.* **94** 12 5N 69 0W
Willenhall, *U.K.* **14** 52 36N 2 3W
Willesborough, *U.K.* **15** 51 8N 0 55 E
Williamstown, *Austral.* **70** 37 51S 144 52 E
Willingdon, *U.K.* **15** 50 47N 0 17 E
Williton, *U.K.* **14** 51 9N 3 20W
Willoughby, *U.K.* **19** 53 14N 0 12 E
Wilmington, *U.K.* **16** 50 46N 3 8W
Wilmington, *U.S.A.* **93** 39 45N 75 32W
Wilmslow, *U.K.* **18** 53 19N 2 14W
Wilnecote, *U.K.* **14** 52 36N 1 40W
Wilsons Promontory, *Austral.* **70** 38 55S 146 25 E
Wilton, *U.K.* **14** 51 5N 1 52W
Wiltshire □, *U.K.* **14** 51 20N 2 0W
Wimblington, *U.K.* **15** 52 31N 0 5 E
Wimborne Minster, *U.K.* **14** 50 48N 2 0W
Wimmera →, *Austral.* **70** 36 8S 141 56 E
Wincanton, *U.K.* **14** 51 3N 2 24W
Winchelsea, *U.K.* **15** 50 55N 0 43 E
Winchester, *U.K.* **14** 51 4N 1 19W
Windermere, *U.K.* **18** 54 24N 2 56W
Windermere, L., *U.K.* **18** 54 20N 2 57W
Windhoek, *Nam.* **81** 22 35S 17 4 E
Windrush →, *U.K.* **14** 51 48N 1 35W
Windsor, *Canada* **92** 42 18N 83 0W
Windsor, *U.K.* **15** 51 28N 0 36W
Windward Passage, *W. Ind.* **95** 20 0N 74 0W
Windygates, *U.K.* **21** 56 12N 3 1W
Wing, *U.K.* **15** 51 54N 0 41W
Wingham, *Austral.* **70** 31 48S 152 22 E
Wingham, *U.K.* **15** 51 16N 1 12 E
Winkleigh, *U.K.* **16** 50 49N 3 57W
Winnipeg, *Canada* **88** 49 54N 97 9W
Winnipeg, L., *Canada* **88** 52 0N 97 0W
Winsford, *U.K.* **18** 53 12N 2 31W
Winslow, *U.K.* **15** 51 57N 0 52W
Winster, *U.K.* **19** 53 9N 1 42W
Winston-Salem, *U.S.A.* **91** 36 7N 80 15W
Winterborne Abbas, *U.K.* **14** 50 43N 2 30W
Winterthur, *Switz.* **42** 47 30N 8 44 E
Winterton, *Humberside, U.K.* **19** 53 39N 0 37W
Winterton, *Norfolk, U.K.* **15** 52 43N 1 43 E
Wirksworth, *U.K.* **19** 53 5N 1 34W
Wirral, *U.K.* **18** 53 25N 3 0W
Wisbech, *U.K.* **15** 52 39N 0 10 E
Wisborough Green, *U.K.* **15** 51 2N 0 30W
Wisconsin □, *U.S.A.* **92** 44 30N 90 0W
Wishaw, *U.K.* **21** 55 46N 3 55W
Wiske →, *U.K.* **19** 54 26N 1 27W
Wisła →, *Pol.* **43** 54 22N 18 55 E
Witbank, *S. Afr.* **81** 25 51S 29 14 E
Witham, *U.K.* **15** 51 48N 0 39 E
Witham →, *U.K.* **19** 53 3N 0 8W
Withern, *U.K.* **19** 53 19N 0 9 E
Withernsea, *U.K.* **19** 53 43N 0 2 E
Witley, *U.K.* **15** 51 9N 0 39W
Witney, *U.K.* **14** 51 47N 1 29W
Witten, *W. Ger.* **36** 51 26N 7 19 E
Wittersham, *U.K.* **15** 51 1N 0 42 E
Wiveliscombe, *U.K.* **14** 51 2N 3 20W
Wivenhoe, *U.K.* **15** 51 51N 0 59 E
Włocławek, *Pol.* **43** 52 40N 19 3 E
Woburn, *U.K.* **15** 51 59N 0 37W
Woburn Sands, *U.K.* **15** 52 1N 0 38W
Wodonga, *Austral.* **70** 36 5S 146 50 E
Woking, *U.K.* **15** 51 18N 0 33W
Wokingham, *U.K.* **15** 51 25N 0 50W
Wolf Rock, *U.K.* **16** 49 56N 5 50W
Wolfsburg, *W. Ger.* **42** 52 27N 10 49 E
Wollongong, *Austral.* **70** 34 25S 150 54 E
Wolsingham, *U.K.* **18** 54 44N 1 52W
Wolverhampton, *U.K.* **14** 52 35N 2 6W
Wolverton, *U.K.* **15** 52 3N 0 48W
Wolviston, *U.K.* **19** 54 39N 1 25W
Wombwell, *U.K.* **19** 53 31N 1 23W
Wŏnsan, *N. Kor.* **61** 39 11N 127 27 E
Wonston, *U.K.* **14** 51 9N 1 18W
Woodbridge, *U.K.* **15** 52 6N 1 19 E
Woodbury, *U.K.* **16** 50 40N 3 24W
Woodhall Spa, *U.K.* **19** 53 10N 0 12W
Woodhouse, *U.K.* **19** 53 23N 1 21W
Woodley, *U.K.* **15** 51 26N 0 54W
Woods, L. of the, *Canada* **88** 49 15N 94 45W
Woodstock, *U.K.* **14** 51 51N 1 20W
Wookey, *U.K.* **14** 51 13N 2 41W
Wookey Hole, *U.K.* **14** 51 13N 2 41W
Wool, *U.K.* **14** 50 41N 2 13W
Woolacombe, *U.K.* **16** 51 10N 4 12W
Wooler, *U.K.* **21** 55 33N 2 0W
Wootton Bassett, *U.K.* **14** 51 32N 1 55W
Wootton Wawen, *U.K.* **14** 52 16N 1 47W
Worcester, *S. Afr.* **81** 33 39S 19 27 E
Worcester, *U.K.* **14** 52 12N 2 12W
Worcester, *U.S.A.* **93** 42 14N 71 49W
Worfield, *U.K.* **14** 52 34N 2 22W
Workington, *U.K.* **18** 54 39N 3 34W
Worksop, *U.K.* **19** 53 19N 1 9W
Wormit, *U.K.* **21** 56 26N 2 59W
Worms, *W. Ger.* **42** 49 37N 8 21 E
Worplesdon, *U.K.* **15** 51 16N 0 36W
Wortham, *U.K.* **15** 52 22N 1 3 E
Worthing, *U.K.* **15** 50 49N 0 21W
Wotton-under-Edge, *U.K.* **14** 51 37N 2 20W
Woy Woy, *Austral.* **70** 33 30S 151 19 E
Wragby, *U.K.* **19** 53 17N 0 18W
Wrangel I., *U.S.S.R.* **49** 71 0N 180 0 E
Wrangle, *U.K.* **19** 53 3N 0 9 E
Wrath, C., *U.K.* **22** 58 38N 5 0W
Wrekin, The, *U.K.* **14** 52 41N 2 35W
Wrentham, *U.K.* **15** 52 24N 1 39 E
Wrexham, *U.K.* **17** 53 5N 3 0W
Writtle, *U.K.* **15** 51 44N 0 27 E
Wrocław, *Pol.* **43** 51 5N 17 5 E
Wrotham, *U.K.* **15** 51 18N 0 20 E
Wroughton, *U.K.* **14** 51 31N 1 47W
Wroxham, *U.K.* **15** 52 42N 1 23 E
Wuhan, *China* **61** 30 31N 114 18 E
Wuhu, *China* **61** 31 22N 118 21 E
Wuppertal, *W. Ger.* **36** 51 15N 7 8 E
Würzburg, *W. Ger.* **42** 49 46N 9 55 E
Wutongqiao, *China* **60** 29 22N 103 50 E
Wuxi, *China* **61** 31 30N 120 30 E
Wuzhou, *China* **61** 23 30N 111 18 E
Wye, *U.K.* **15** 51 11N 0 56 E
Wye →, *U.K.* **14** 51 36N 2 40W
Wylye →, *U.K.* **14** 51 8N 1 53W
Wymondham, *Leics., U.K.* **15** 52 45N 0 42W
Wymondham, *Norfolk, U.K.* **15** 52 34N 1 7 E
Wyndham, *Austral.* **66** 15 33S 128 3 E
Wyoming □, *U.S.A.* **90** 42 48N 109 0W
Wyre →, *U.K.* **18** 53 52N 2 57W
Wyre Forest, *U.K.* **14** 52 24N 2 24W

X

Xiaguan, *China* **60** 25 32N 100 16 E
Xiamen, *China* **61** 24 25N 118 4 E
Xiangfan, *China* **61** 32 2N 112 8 E
Xiangtan, *China* **61** 27 51N 112 54 E
Xiangyang, *China* **61** 32 1N 112 8 E
Xingu →, *Brazil* **101** 1 30S 51 53W
Xining, *China* **60** 36 34N 101 40 E
Xinjiang Uygur Zizhiqu □, *China* **60** 42 0N 86 0 E
Xuzhou, *China* **61** 34 18N 117 10 E

Y

Yablonovy Ra., *U.S.S.R.* **49** 53 0N 114 0 E
Yakut A.S.S.R. □, *U.S.S.R.* **49** 62 0N 130 0 E
Yakutsk, *U.S.S.R.* **49** 62 5N 129 50 E
Yamagata, *Jap.* **62** 38 15N 140 15 E
Yamal, Peninsula, *U.S.S.R.* **48** 71 0N 70 0 E
Yambol, *Bulg.* **41** 42 30N 26 36 E
Yamuna →, *India* **59** 25 30N 81 53 E
Yana →, *U.S.S.R.* **49** 71 30N 136 0 E
Yangtze Kiang →, *China* **60** 31 40N 122 0 E
Yanji, *China* **61** 42 59N 129 30 E
Yantai, *China* **61** 37 34N 121 22 E
Yaoundé, *Cam.* **80** 3 50N 11 35 E
Yarcombe, *U.K.* **16** 50 51N 3 6W
Yare →, *U.K.* **15** 52 36N 1 28 E
Yarm, *U.K.* **19** 54 31N 1 21W
Yarmouth, *U.K.* **14** 50 42N 1 29W
Yaroslavl, *U.S.S.R.* **46** 57 35N 39 55 E
Yarrow, *U.K.* **21** 55 32N 3 0W
Yate, *U.K.* **14** 51 32N 2 26W
Yatsushiro, *Jap.* **62** 32 30N 130 40 E
Yatton, *U.K.* **14** 51 23N 2 50W
Yaxley, *U.K.* **15** 52 31N 0 14W
Yazd, *Iran* **56** 31 55N 54 27 E
Yealmpton, *U.K.* **16** 50 21N 4 0W
Yell, *U.K.* **22** 60 35N 1 5W
Yell Sd., *U.K.* **22** 60 33N 1 15W
Yellow Sea, *China* **61** 35 0N 123 0 E
Yellowknife, *Canada* **88** 62 27N 114 29W
Yellowstone →, *U.S.A.* **90** 47 58N 103 59W
Yellowstone National Park, *U.S.A.* **90** 44 35N 110 0W
Yemen ■, *Si. Arab.* **56** 15 0N 44 0 E
Yenisey →, *U.S.S.R.* **48** 71 50N 82 40 E
Yeo →, *U.K.* **14** 51 10N 3 0W
Yeovil, *U.K.* **14** 50 57N 2 38W
Yerevan, *U.S.S.R.* **47** 40 10N 44 31 E
Yes Tor, *U.K.* **16** 50 41N 3 59W
Yibin, *China* **60** 28 45N 104 32 E
Yichang, *China* **61** 30 40N 111 20 E
Yichuan, *China* **60** 36 2N 110 10 E
Yining, *China* **60** 43 58N 81 10 E
Yogyakarta, *Indon.* **63** 7 49S 110 22 E
Yokkaichi, *Jap.* **62** 35 0N 136 38 E
Yokohama, *Jap.* **62** 35 27N 139 28 E
Yokosuka, *Jap.* **62** 35 20N 139 40 E
Yonkers, *U.S.A.* **93** 40 57N 73 51W
York, *U.K.* **19** 53 58N 1 7W
York, *U.S.A.* **92** 39 57N 76 43W
York, Vale of, *U.K.* **19** 54 15N 1 25W
Yorkshire Wolds, *U.K.* **19** 54 0N 0 30W
Yosemite National Park, *U.S.A.* **90** 38 0N 119 30W
Yoshkar Ola, *U.S.S.R.* **46** 56 38N 47 55 E
Youghal, *Ire.* **25** 51 58N 7 51W
Youghal B., *Ire.* **25** 51 55N 7 50W
Youlgreave, *U.K.* **19** 53 12N 1 50W
Youngstown, *U.S.A.* **92** 41 7N 80 41W
Yoxall, *U.K.* **14** 52 45N 1 49W
Yoxford, *U.K.* **15** 52 16N 1 30 E
Ypres, *Belg.* **36** 50 51N 2 53 E
Ystalyfera, *U.K.* **17** 51 46N 3 48W
Ythan →, *U.K.* **23** 57 26N 2 12W
Yuan Jiang →, *China* **61** 28 55N 111 50 E
Yucatán, Península de, *Mex.* **94** 19 30N 89 0W
Yucatan Str., *Carib.* **94** 22 0N 86 30W
Yugoslavia ■, *Europe* **41** 44 0N 20 0 E
Yukon →, *N. Am.* **88** 65 30N 150 0W
Yukon Territory □, *Canada* **88** 63 0N 135 0W
Yunnan □, *China* **60** 25 0N 102 30 E
Yuzhno-Sakhalinsk, *U.S.S.R.* **49** 46 58N 142 45 E

Z

Zaandam, *Neth.* **36** 52 26N 4 49 E
Zabrze, *Pol.* **43** 50 18N 18 50 E
Zagorsk, *U.S.S.R.* **46** 56 20N 38 10 E
Zagreb, *Yug.* **40** 45 50N 16 0 E
Zagros Mts., *Iran* **56** 33 45N 47 0 E
Zahlah, *Leb.* **57** 33 52N 35 50 E
Zaïre ■, *Africa* **80** 3 0S 23 0 E
Zaïre →, *Africa* **80** 6 4S 12 24 E
Zákinthos, *Greece* **41** 37 47N 20 57 E
Zambezi →, *Africa* **81** 18 55S 36 4 E
Zambia ■, *Africa* **81** 15 0S 28 0 E
Zamboanga, *Phil.* **63** 6 59N 122 3 E
Zamora, *Sp.* **37** 41 30N 5 45W
Zante = Zákinthos, *Greece* **41** 37 47N 20 57 E
Zanzibar, *Tanz.* **80** 6 12S 39 12 E
Zaporozhye, *U.S.S.R.* **47** 47 50N 35 10 E
Zaragoza, *Sp.* **37** 41 39N 0 53W
Zaria, *Nig.* **78** 11 0N 7 40 E
Zeebrugge, *Belg.* **36** 51 19N 3 12 E
Zeist, *Neth.* **36** 52 5N 5 15 E
Zhangjiakou, *China* **61** 40 48N 114 55 E
Zhangzhou, *China* **61** 24 30N 117 35 E
Zhanjiang, *China* **61** 21 15N 110 20 E
Zhdanov, *U.S.S.R.* **47** 47 5N 37 31 E
Zhejiang □, *China* **61** 29 0N 120 0 E
Zhengzhou, *China* **61** 34 45N 113 34 E
Zhitomir, *U.S.S.R.* **47** 50 20N 28 40 E
Zibo, *China* **61** 36 47N 118 3 E
Zielona Góra □, *Pol.* **42** 51 57N 15 30 E
Zigong, *China* **60** 29 15N 104 48 E
Ziguinchor, *Sene.* **78** 12 35N 16 20W
Žilina, *Czech.* **43** 49 12N 18 42 E
Zimbabwe ■, *Africa* **81** 20 0S 30 0 E
Zion Nat. Park, *U.S.A.* **90** 37 25N 112 50W
Zlatoust, *U.S.S.R.* **46** 55 10N 59 40 E
Zonguldak, *Turk.* **47** 41 28N 31 50 E
Zrenjanin, *Yug.* **41** 45 22N 20 23 E
Zug, *Switz.* **42** 47 10N 8 31 E

MAP PROJECTIONS

MAP PROJECTIONS

A map projection is the systematic depiction on a plane surface of the imaginary lines of latitude or longitude from a globe of the earth. This network of lines is called the graticule and forms the framework upon which an accurate depiction of the earth is made. The map graticule, which is the basis of any map, is constructed sometimes by graphical means, but often by using mathematical formulae to give the intersections of the graticule plotted as x and y co-ordinates. The choice between projections is based upon which properties the cartographer wishes the map to possess, the map scale and also the extent of the area to be mapped. Since the globe is three dimensional, it is not possible to depict its surface on a two dimensional plane without distortion. Preservation of one of the basic properties listed below can only be secured at the expense of the others and the choice of projection is often a compromise solution.

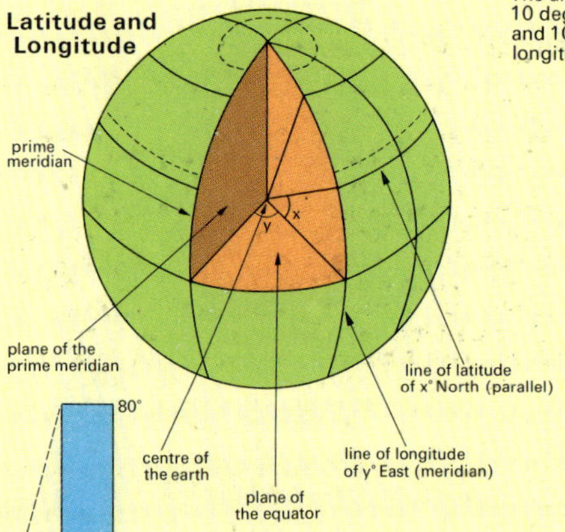

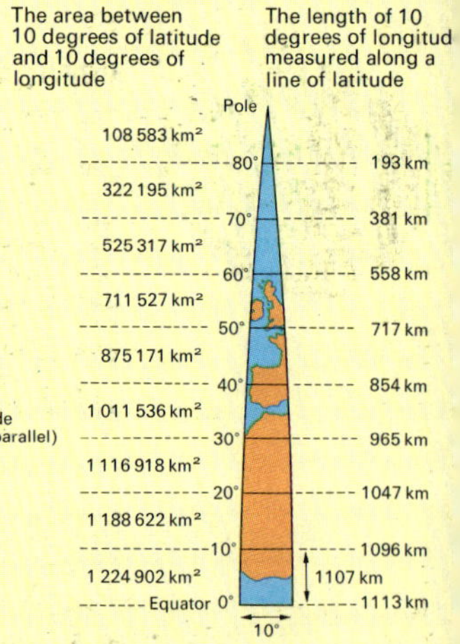

Correct Area

In these projections the areas from the globe are to scale on the map. For example, if you look at the diagram at the top right, areas of 10° x 10° are shown from the equator to the poles. The proportion of this area at the extremities are approximately 11:1. An equal area projection will retain that proportion in its portrayal of those areas. This is particularly useful in the mapping of densities and distributions. Projections with this property are termed **Equal Area, Equivalent or Homolographic.**

Correct Distance

In these projections the scale is correct along the meridians, or in the case of the Azimuthal Equidistant scale is true along any line drawn from the centre of the projection. They are called **Equidistant**.

Correct Shape

This property can only be true within small areas as it is achieved only by having a uniform scale distortion along both x and y axes of the projection. The projections are called **Conformal** or **Orthomorphic.**

In order to minimise the distortions at the edges of some projections, central portions of them are often selected for atlas maps. Below are listed some of the major types of projection.

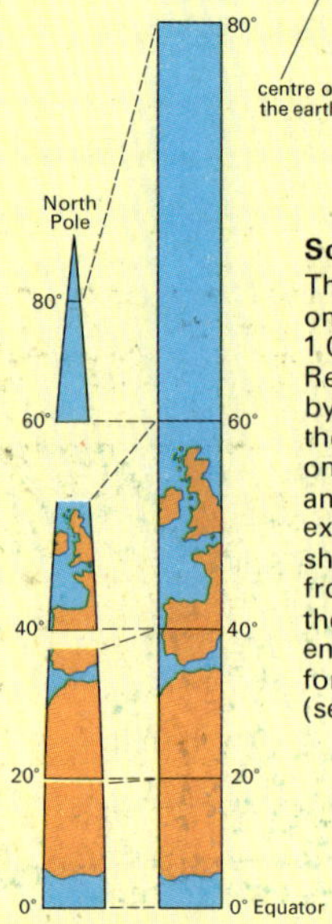

Scale Measurement

The **Representative Fraction** 1:1 000 000 means that 1 unit on the map represents 1 million on the earth. So 1 cm = 1 000 000 cm or 10 km. In SI units (the metric system) the Representative Fraction can be converted to the scale of 1 cm by moving the decimal point through five places, usually deleting the last five zeros thus :- 1: 20 000 000 – 1cm = 200 km. Scale on map projections can only be correct along specific meridians and parallels or from one or two specific points. To take an extreme example of scale distortion, the diagram on the left shows how a portion of the earth's surface, when unwrapped from around a globe (**a gore**) compares with the same area at the same equatorial scale but on Mercator's Projection. The enlargement of scale away from the equator is considerable and for this reason a variable scale for each line of latitude is given (see below).

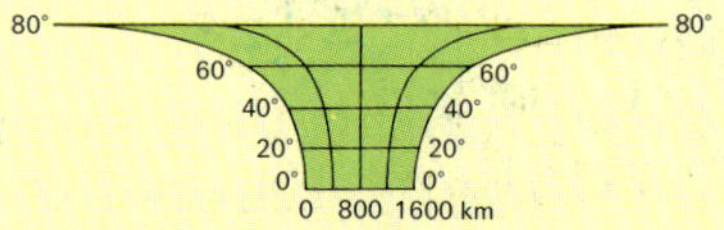

AZIMUTHAL OR ZENITHAL PROJECTIONS

These are constructed by the projection of part of the graticule from the globe onto a plane tangential to any single point on it. This plane may be tangential to the equator (**equatorial case**), the poles (**polar case**) or any other point (**oblique case**). Any straight line drawn from the point at which the plane touches the globe is the shortest distance from that point and is known as a **great circle**. In its **Gnomonic** construction *any* straight line on the map is a great circle, but there is great exaggeration towards the edges and this reduces its general uses. There are five different ways of transferring the graticule onto the plane and these are shown on the right. The central diagram below shows how the graticules vary, using the polar case as the example.

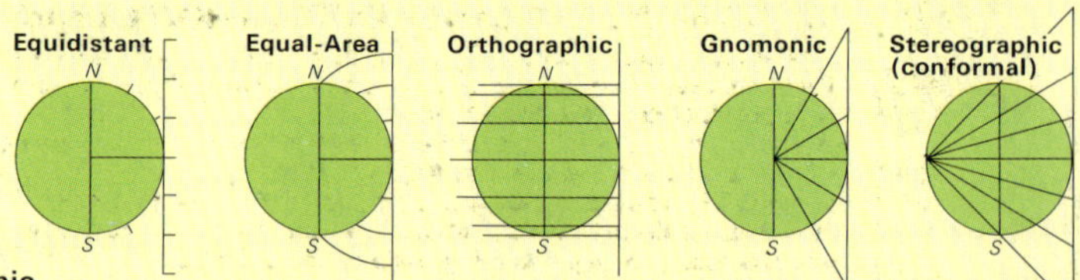

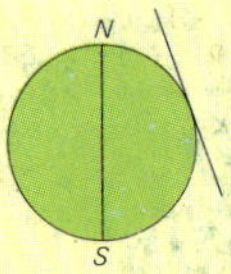

Oblique Case

The plane touches the globe at any point between the equator and poles. The oblique orthographic uses the distortion in azimuthal projections away from the centre to give a graphic depiction of the earth as seen from any desired point in space. It can also be used in both Polar and Equatorial cases. It is used not only for the earth but also for the moon and planets.

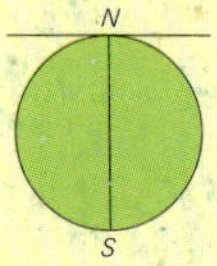

Polar Case

The polar case is the simplest to construct and the diagram below shows the differing effects of all five methods of construction comparing their coverage, distortion etc., using North America as the example.

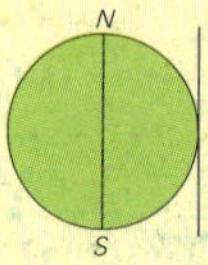

Equatorial Case

The example shown here is Lambert's Equivalent Azimuthal. It is the only projection which is both equal area and where bearing is true from the centre.

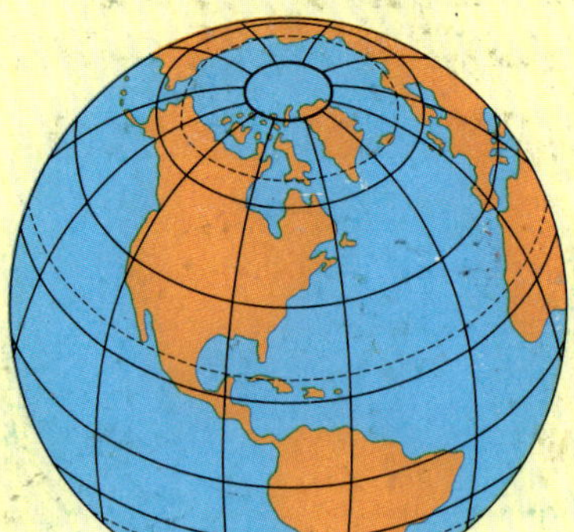

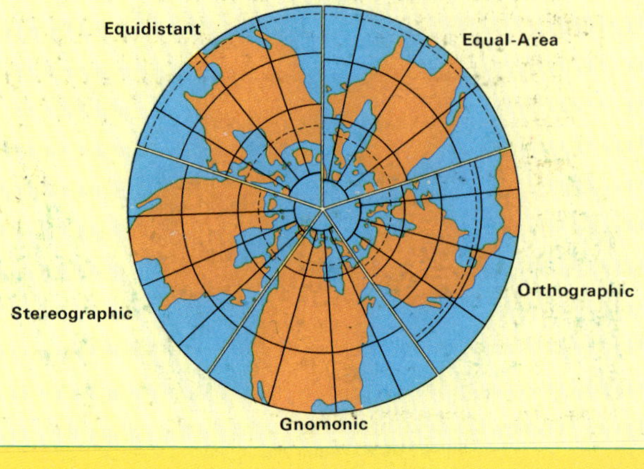

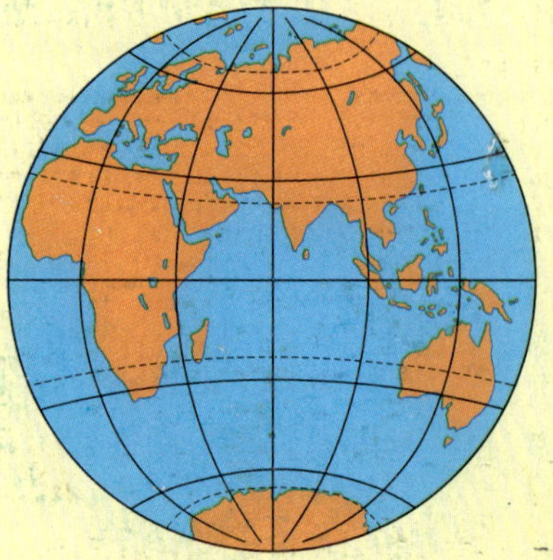